HANDBOOK OF INTERNATIONAL HUMAN RESOURCE MANAGEMENT

HANDBOOK OF INTERNATIONAL HUMAN RESOURCE MANAGEMENT

Integrating People, Process, and Context

Edited by

PAUL R. SPARROW

A John Wiley and Sons, Ltd., Publication

This edition first published 2009
© 2009 John Wiley & Sons, Ltd

Registered office
John Wiley & Sons Ltd, The Atrium, Southern Gate, Chichester, West Sussex, PO19 8SQ, United Kingdom

For details of our global editorial offices, for customer services and for information about how to apply for permission to reuse the copyright material in this book please see our website at www.wiley.com.

ISBN 978-1-4051-6740-6 (H/B)

A catalogue record for this book is available from the British Library.

Library of Congress Cataloging-in-Publication Data

Handbook of international human resource management : integrating people, process, and context / edited by Paul R. Sparrow.
p. cm. – (Blackwell handbooks in management)
Includes bibliographical references and index.
ISBN 978-1-4051-6740-6 (H/B)
1. International business enterprises–Personnel management.   2. Personnel management.   I. Sparrow, Paul.
HF5549.5.E45H357 2009
658.3–dc22   2009013325

Set in 10/12pt Baskerville by Aptara Inc., New Delhi, India
Printed in Great Britain by CPI Antony Rowe, Chippenham, Wiltshire

Contents

List of Figures

List of Tables

Notes on the Contributors

NANCY ADLER
Nancy Adler is Professor of Organizational Behavior at McGill University, Canada. She has a BA, MBA and PhD all at the University of California, Los Angeles. She has held leadership positions in the Academy of International Business, the Society for Intercultural Education, Training and Research (SIETAR), and the Academy of Management. She has taught executives in the People's Republic of China, at INSEAD, France, and at Bocconi University, Italy, and has held the Citicorp Visiting Doctoral Professorship at the University of Hong Kong. Her research interests cover: strategic international human resources management, expatriation, global women leaders, international negotiating, and international organization development.

RUTH AGUILERA
Ruth V. Aguilera is an Associate Professor in the Department of Business Administration at the College of Business and in the Institute of Labor and Industrial Relations and Center for Professional Responsibility of Business, and Society Fellow at the University of Illinois at Urbana-Champaign. She received a Graduate Diploma in Business Analysis from the University of Lancaster (1990), a Licenciatura in Economics (1992) from the University of Barcelona, and MA (1996) and PhD (1999) degrees in Sociology from Harvard University. Her research interests are in: corporate governance, organizational theory, and historical comparative methods.

SOON ANG
Soon Ang is the Goh Tjoei Kok Chair Professor in International Management and IT at the Nanyang Business School, Nanyang Technological University, Singapore. She holds concurrent appointments as director of the Human Resource Round Table Singapore (HARRT-Singapore); executive director for the Center for Leadership and Cultural Intelligence (CLCI), and academic adviser to the Singapore's Ministry of Defense SAFTI Leadership Development Center. She received her PhD

in management from the University of Minnesota. Her research interests are in: global leadership, outsourcing, and cultural intelligence.

DAVID ASHTON
David Ashton is Professor (Emeritus) at The Centre for Labour Market Studies at the University of Leicester, UK. His research interests cover: the theory of skill formation, the impact of globalization on national VET systems, the comparative analysis of skill formation systems, workplace learning, high performance work organizations, and the skill strategies of multinational and transnational corporations.

WILHELM BARNER-RASMUSSEN
Wilhelm Barner-Rasmussen holds the Hanken Foundation assistant professorship in management and organization. His previous work experience includes several acting professorships in management and organization at Hanken, and the academic directorship of Hanken & IFL Corporate Development, Hanken's executive education alliance with the Stockholm School of Economics. His current academic interests focus on knowledge transfer in multinationals, specifically issues related to language, communication, organizational identity, and location of headquarters units.

INGMAR BJÖRKMAN
Ingmar Björkman is Professor of Management and Organization and Head of the Department of Management and Organization at Hanken. He is affiliated with the INSEAD Euro-Asia and Comparative Research Center. He has held visiting professor positions at Hong Kong University, ESSEC, and INSEAD. His research interests focus on international human resource management, knowledge creation and transfer in multinational corporations, and integration of international mergers and acquisitions.

TANYA BONDAROUK
Tanya Bondarouk is Assistant Professor of Human Resource Management at the University of Twente, the Netherlands. Her PhD was in the field of Information Technology Implementation. Her research interests concern electronic HRM and Human Resource Information Systems in both private and public sectors. She has conducted research projects with the Dutch Ministry of Internal Affairs, KPN (Dutch Telecom Company), Dow Chemical, Ford, IBM, ABN AMRO bank, Shell, and Unit4Agresso.

CHRIS BREWSTER
Chris Brewster is Professor of International Human Resource Management at Reading University, UK. He has substantial experience as a practitioner and gained his doctorate from the LSE before becoming an academic. He researches in the field of international and comparative HRM; and has published over twenty books and more than a hundred articles. In 2002 he was given the Georges Petipas award by the practitioner body, the World Federation of Personnel Managers Associations. In 2006 Chris was awarded an Honorary Doctorate by the University of Vaasa, Finland.

PHIL BROWN

Phil Brown, is Professor of Management at Cardiff University's School of Social Sciences. He is the Research Convenor for Work, Employability and the Labour Market (WELM) network. His research interests cover: the knowledge Economy; global labour markets; opportunity, inequality and social stratification; skill formation and workforce development; the future of work; and graduate employability.

PAWAN BUDHWAR

Pawan Budhwar is Professor of International HRM and Head of Group at Aston Business School. He has a BA (Economics and Geography), University College, Rohtak, India; MBA (Personnel Management and Marketing), MD University, Rohtak, India; MA (Industrial Sociology), MD University, Rohtak, India; MPhil (Industrial Sociology), MD University, Rohtak, India; and PhD (Cross-National Comparative HRM), Manchester Business School. His current research interests are: transfer of HRM policies and practices from headquarters of multinational companies to Indian subsidiaries, Expatriation, HRM and firm's performance, and work processes in Indian call centers.

FANG LEE COOKE

Fang Lee Cooke is Professor of HRM and Chinese Studies at Manchester Business School. Prior to coming to the UK, she had four years lecturing experience in Sun Yat-sen (Zhongshan) University and five years working experience in the energy industry with Sino-British engineering project teams in Guangdong Province, China. Her research interests cover three main strands within an overarching theme of organizational and societal change and impact on the nature of work, employment relations and human resource management (HRM): the role of employee involvement in technological and business innovations; employment relations and labor market restructuring, effectiveness of employment legislation, gender and HRM in China; and comparative and international studies.

HELEN DE CIERI

Helen De Cieri (MA, PhD) is a Professor of Management and the Director of the Australian Center for Research in Employment and Work (ACREW) in the Department of Management. From 1996 to 2002, Helen was the Editor of the *Asia Pacific Journal of Human Resources*. She is a departmental editor (*Strategic Human Resources and Industrial Relations*) for the *Journal of International Business Studies* and currently serves on several editorial boards, including the *Academy of Management Journal*, and *Human Resource Management*. Her research interests are in: strategic human resource management (HRM); global HRM; HRM in multinational networks.

TONY EDWARDS

Tony Edwards is Reader in Comparative HRM at King's College, London. His doctorate examined the ways in which multinationals identify innovative practices in their international operations and subsequently diffuse these across the firm. His current research focuses on the management of labor in multinational companies. He has investigated the influence of the US business system on employment relations in American MNCs and the management of human resources during and after international mergers and acquisitions.

MATS EHRNROOTH
Mats Ehrnrooth is a Researcher and Doctoral Student, affiliated with the Department of Management and Organization, Swedish School of Economics, Finland.

MARILYN FENWICK
Marilyn Fenwick (PhD, University of Melbourne), is Honorary Senior Research Fellow with the Department of Management, Monash University, and Director of the HRM research consultancy, Global Mobility Management. She researches, consults and publishes in the areas of global mobility and project team management, and international HR performance management and development.

MIKE HARVEY
Michael Harvey was appointed Professor of International Business at Bond University in 2006. He also holds the position of Distinguished Chair of Global Business at the University of Mississippi. He has a BBA (Southern Methodist University), an MBA (Southern Methodist University) and a PhD (University of Arizona).

ANNE-WIL HARZING
Anne-Wil Harzing is Professor in International Management at the University of Melbourne, Australia. She has a BA in Economics and Linguistics, Hogeschool Enschede, Netherlands, MA in Business Administration and International Management from Maastricht University, Netherlands and PhD in International Management, University of Bradford, United Kingdom. Her research interests are in: HQ-subsidiary relations; international HRM; cross-cultural management; and the role of language in international business.

SUSAN HETRICK
Dr Susan Hetrick is joint Managing Director of People Academy. She works with Company Boards and senior teams to deliver innovative people solutions to challenging strategic business issues. A former Board level HR Director, she has extensive practitioner experience working with global companies in the financial services, telecoms, FMCG and business advisory sectors. Susan has a doctorate in Organizational Behaviour and Human Resource Management from City Business School, and is a visiting fellow at Glasgow University and the Helsinki School of Economics.

MARIA KRAIMER
Maria Kraimer is an Associate Professor at the Henry B. Tippie College of Business, University of Iowa, US. She was previously Associate Professor and Reader, University of Melbourne, Australia. She has a BS, MBA and PhD from the University of Illinois at Chicago. Her research covers issues related to employee empowerment, career development, and expatriate assignments

HUGH LAUDER
Hugh Lauder is Professor of Education and Political Economy at the Department of Education, University of Bath, UK. He is Head of the Policy and Management Research Group. His research interests cover: political economy of skill formation; educational policy; and the political economy of education. He is working on a research program that examines the tensions between the role of education as an

engine for economic competitiveness and national wealth creation that results in the production of inequalities between nations, institutions and social groups.

PAUL E.M. LIGTHART

Paul E.M. Ligthart is an assistant professor in strategy at the Radboud University Nijmegen in the Netherlands. His main research interests are corporate strategy with respect to competition and cooperation in business networks, strategic HRM, and innovation strategies. He has national and international publications and a number of book chapters. As a consultant, he has participated in a number of business network studies and policy evaluation studies for private and public organizations.

FABRICE LUMINEAU

Fabrice Lumineau is a researcher at IMD. He received his PhD in strategic management from HEC Paris in 2008. His main research interests focus on interorganizational relationships, opportunism, and contractual design.

KRISTIINA MÄKELÄ

Kristiina Mäkelä is a Post Doctoral researcher at the Department of Management and Organization at Hanken. She earned her PhD at Helsinki School of Economics. Her research interests cover: international business, knowledge and competence issues in multinational corporations, interpersonal-level knowledge sharing, innovation. She is currently working on a Tekes-funded project on Cross-Border Competence Management at Hanken and an international research project on the commercialization of innovations at London Business School.

MARGARET-ANN MCLEAN

Margaret-Ann McLean (BA, Graduate Diploma in Educational Psychology and Careers Education) is an International Staffing Specialist with World Vision International, currently based in Singapore. She has 17 years work experience in the human resources field, working in the public and not-for-profit sectors and is a registered psychologist in Australia.

GRAEME MARTIN

Graeme Martin is Professor of HRM at the Business School, University of Glasgow, UK and Director of Centre for Reputation Management through People (CRMP). He also teaches and holds visiting appointments in Sweden, the USA, Italy, Columbia, and Australia. His research interests cover: strategic HR and leadership; organizational reputation management; branding and human resources; information and communications technologies; managing people; and human capital.

WOLFGANG MAYRHOFER

Wolfgang Mayrhofer is a Professor of Business Administration and holds a chair for Management and Organizational Behavior at Wirtschaftsuniversität Wien, Austria. Previously, he held teaching and research positions at the University of Paderborn and the Dresden University of Technology, both in Germany. His research interests focus on international comparative research in human resource management and leadership, careers, and systems theory.

BERTRAND MOINGEON

Bertrand Moingeon is Professor of Strategic Management and Deputy Dean at HEC Paris. He is in charge of Executive Education and Academic Development. He holds a postgraduate diploma in Strategy and Management (HEC Doctoral Program), a PhD in Sociology, and a postdoctoral diploma in Management. He was a Visiting Research Scholar at the Harvard Business School. His research interests cover: the management of change, strategic management, corporate identity, and organizational learning.

KOK-YEE NG

Kok-Yee Ng is Associate Professor of Human Resource Management at Nanyang Technological University, Singapore. She is the Director of Research for the Center for Leadership and Cultural Intelligence at the Nanyang Business School. She received her PhD in Organizational Behavior from Michigan State University. Her primary research interests are in cross-cultural/international organizational behavior, focusing on cultural intelligence, leadership, and teams. She has conducted workshops on cultural intelligence for Hamilton Sundstrand, MTV Asia, and Tata Consulting Services. She is currently co-leading a team of research investigators on a multi-year leadership project for the Singapore Armed Forces.

MILORAD NOVICEVIC

Milorad M. Novicevic (PhD University of Oklahoma) is an Associate Professor of Management at the University of Mississippi. He has published more than 90 articles in various journals including the *Leadership Quarterly*; *Human Resource Management*; *European Management Journal*; *Journal of World Business*; *Business Horizons*; *Organizational Dynamics*; *Business Ethics: A European Review*, *Research in Personnel and Human Resources Management*; *International Journal of Human Resource Management*; *Human Resource Management Review*, and *Journal of Vocational Behavior*.

STEPHEN NYAMBEGERA

Stephen Nyambegera is Professor of Management and Dean Faculty of Social Science at Daystar University, Nairobi, Kenya. He was previously a Senior Lecturer at Daystar University. He received a BA and then MBA in India and his PhD from the University of Sheffield. His research has specialized on Human Resource Management and Organizational Psychology, HRM in developing countries *vis-à-vis* developed countries, and the role of ethnicity in management.

ALEXANDRE PERRIN

Alexandre Perrin is Assistant Professor in Strategic Management at Audencia Nantes School of Management. His Doctorate was in Management Science at University of Nice Sophia Antipolis. He has a Master in research, University of Nice Sophia Antipolis and Specialized in Knowledge Management and Business Intelligence while at the European School of Management. His research interests cover: knowledge management; organizational learning; communities of practice; and collaborative tools.

SEBASTIAN REICHE

Sebastian Reiche is Assistant Professor in the Managing People in Organizations department at IESE. He earned his PhD from the University of Melbourne, Australia, where he also taught in the fields of Human Resource Management and Cross-Cultural Management. His research focuses on how organizations access, maintain, and leverage knowledge resources, primarily from a multinational and cross-cultural perspective.

ASTRID REICHEL

Astrid Reichel works as an Assistant Professor at the Department of Management, WU Wirtschaftsuniversitaet Wien, Austria. Previously, she held teaching and research positions at the University of Vienna and the University of Natural Resources and Life Sciences, Vienna. She received her Master and Doctoral degrees in Business Administration from the University of Vienna. Her research focuses on international and comparative human resource management, the human resource management-performance-link and career management.

HUUB RÜEL

Huub Rüel is Assistant Professor of International Management at the Nikos Capacity Group at the University of Twente, the Netherlands. Previously he has worked at Kuwait–Maastricht Business School (KMBS), Kuwait and the University of Utrecht. He has a Bachelor, Human Resource Management (Saxion University of Applied Science), Master of Science, Psychology (Netherlands Open University), PhD, Business Administration/Human Resource Management (Twente University).

SONJA SACKMANN

Sonja Sackmann is Professor, Institut for Human Resources and Organization Research at the University Bw Munich, and a Managing Partner at MZSG, Management Zentrum, St Gallen. Her research interests cover organizational culture (assessment and development), organizational development, intercultural management, team development, and management–executive development. She is on the advisory board of MUWIT, Kongress für Weiterbildung und Personalentwicklung and has served on the Editorial Boards of *Organization*, *Journal of East European Management Studies* and *Journal of Management Inquiry*.

PAUL SPARROW

Paul Sparrow is Professor of International HRM and Director of the Centre for Performance-led HR at Lancaster University Management School. He has a BSc (Hons) Psychology from Manchester University, and MSc Applied Psychology and PhD from Astin University. He is a former editor of the *Journal of Occupational and Organizational Psychology* and is currently an Editorial Board Member of the: *British Journal of Management*; *European Management Review*; *Career Development International*; *International Journal of Cross-Cultural Management*; and *Cross-Cultural Management: An International Journal*. His research focuses on the impact of globalization on international HRM, changes in the employment relationship, and the nature of strategic competence.

Vesa Suutari

Vesa Suutari acts as a Professor of International Management and as a Vice Dean of the Faculty of Business Studies at the University of Vaasa, Finland. His recent research interests are on international human resource management and cross-cultural management. He has published various international journal articles and book chapters on issues such as European management cultures, expatriate management, self-initiated expatriation, global leadership, global careers, diversity management, and international knowledge transfers.

Abhijeet Vadera

Abhijeet Vadera is a Doctoral Student at the Department of Business Administration, University of Illinois at Urbana Champaign. He has a PGD, Management from The Indian School of Business (ISB) and a BE, Civil Engineering from the University of Bombay. His teaching and research interests cover positive (creativity) and negative (white collar crime/corruption) deviance in and of organizations, organizational identity and identification.

Karina van de Voorde

Karina van de Voorde is a doctoral candidate in Human Resource Studies in the School of Social and Behavioural Sciences at Tilburg University. Her research interests include strategic HRM, organizational climate, employee well-being, and research methods.

Lynn Van Dyne

Lynn Van Dyne is Professor of Management at the Eli Broad Graduate School of Management, Michigan State University. She conducts research, teaches and provides consulting services on a variety of topics in Organizational Behavior and Management - with a special emphasis on international management and organizational behaviour. She is currently Associate Editor for *Organizational Behavior and Human Decision Processes*, has served as Consulting Editor of *Journal of Organizational Behavior* and on the Editorial Boards of: *Academy of Management Journal*; *Academy of Management Review*; *Academy of Management Executive*; *Academy of Management Perspectives*; *Human Relations*; and *Journal of Organizational Behavior*.

Catherine Welch

Catherine Welch is a senior lecturer in international business at the University of Sydney. Her research interests lie in the internationalization of firms, including international project operations, and the use of qualitative methods. Her research has appeared in journals such as *Management International Review, International Business Review* and *Journal of Business Ethics*.

Denice Welch

Denice Welch is a Professor at Melbourne Business School. She has published in various international journals including *Journal of Management Studies, Management International Review, International Business Review* and the *International Journal of Human Resource Management*. Denice co-authored three editions of the leading global textbook in International Human Resource Management.

PAT WRIGHT

Patrick M. Wright is William J. Conaty GE Professor of Strategic Human Resources and Director of the Center for Advanced Human Resource Studies in the School of Industrial and Labor Relations, Cornell University, USA. He holds a BA in psychology from Wheaton College, and an MBA and a PhD in Organizational Behavior/Human Resource Management from Michigan State University. He teaches, conducts research, and consults in the area of strategic human resource management (SHRM), particularly focusing on how firms use people as a source of competitive advantage. He has published widely in leading international journals and worked with a number of the world's leading firms in their efforts to align HR with business strategy.

About the Editor

Paul Sparrow is one of the UK's leading authorities on international HR and its management. His research focuses on the impact of globalization on international HRM, changes in the employment relationship, and the nature of strategic competence. In 2008 he was voted among the Top 25 Most Influential HR Thinkers by *Human Resources Magazine.* An organizational psychologist by training, he is the author of a number of books within the territory of HRM. He has a wide range of international links and combines his extensive writing career with an academic involvement in executive education and consulting. He has deep experience in the commercial world having worked as a consultant in his earlier career with PA Consulting. Paul joined Lancaster in November 2006 to take up the Chair and Director's post in the Centre for Performance-Led HR.

Part I

METHOD AND RESEARCH LENSES

1

Integrating People, Process, and Context Issues in the Field of IHRM

PAUL SPARROW

DEFINING THE TERRITORY FOR INTERNATIONAL HRM

Schuler, Sparrow and Budhwar (2009) have recently explained and positioned the different views that have existed about the nature of International Human Resource Management (IHRM). From the mid-1980s to the turn of the 1990s the field was considered to be in its 'infancy' (Laurent, 1986). In bringing a degree of structure through the introduction of a new journal – the *International Journal of Human Resource Management* – Poole (1990: 1) saw IHRM as "...the worldwide management of people in the multinational enterprise". However, since these early beginnings, there has been both an evolution of territory covered by the field and more critical discussion of whether this evolution has been toward an expanded field, or represents a process of fragmentation.

The critical argument runs as follows: the field has since become fragmented, the majority of theories have been created outside the field of IHRM, and this has created an experimentation and abstractness in thinking that merely confuses the identity of a field (Peltonen, 2006; De Cieri *et al.*, 2007; Hippler, 2008). For example, De Cieri *et al.* (2007) question the calls for greater integration of theory and research emphasis within the field. They argue that globalization – when seen in terms of the worldwide flow of capital, knowledge and other resources necessary to interconnect international product markets – is associated with concomitant processes involved in the growth in scope and scale of competition (Harzing, 2002), and that this is increasing the requirement of IHRM academics to understand the (many) ways in which multinational corporations (MNCs) operate effectively. Drawing principally upon previous reviews by Schuler, Budhwar and Florkowski (2002) and Scullion and Paauwe (2004), De Cieri *et al.* (2007) go on to analyze recent research and practice in the field of IHRM and question its theoretical progress. They argue that rather than integration, imitation is becoming more important – as greater attention is given to the politics of globalization and local context – and rather than attempt to integrate ideas and claim more encompassing approaches we should draw reference from theory in existing practices and disciplines that help to explain the complex problems (and often dysfunctional impacts) faced when trying to manage across national boundaries.

In contrast (though to be fair, these authors share some of the sentiment of a critical perspective) the evolutionary view of the field (Stahl and Björkman, 2006; Sparrow and Braun, 2008a, b) considers that IHRM has moved not through a haphazard and opportunistic expansion, but through a sequential development of thinking that has captured the successively evolving cultural, geographical and in-stitutional challenges faced by the MNC, and that while IHRM indeed now covers a large and complex territory, it has come to represent an accepted set of doctrine about the nature of the subject. This observation that there is a logical pattern to the 'issues-driven' concerns that the field of IHRM has to face, absorb, interpret then reanalyze through international lenses has driven the selection of contributions to this volume, with a number of contemporary issues – reverse knowledge flows, skill supply strategies, employer branding, e-enablement, outsourcing, global networks – now needing to find voice within the literature.

In tracking the evolution of definitions, Scullion (1995, 2005) observes that while there has been little consensus, definitions have broadly concentrated on exam-ining the HR issues, problems, strategies, policies and practices that firms pursue in relation to the internationalization of their business. Drawing upon Schuler, Budhwar and Florkowski's (2002) view, Scullion (2005: 5) observes that IHRM has encompassed the need to understand "... how MNCs manage their geographically dispersed workforce in order to leverage their HR resources for both local and global competitive advantage".

As a subject matter Briscoe and Schuler (2004: 1) note that IHRM therefore has to be "... about human resource management in an international environ-ment... problems created in an MNC performing business in more than one coun-try, rather than those posed by working for a foreign firm at home or by employing foreign employees in the local firm". Peltonen (2006: 523) draws attention to the need to understand both the design of, and effects of, solutions to these problems: IHRM is "... a branch of management studies that investigates the design of and effects of organizational human resource practices in cross-cultural contexts". By similarly concentrating on a problem solution approach to IHRM – i.e., by focusing on the issues created as a consequence of internationalization in the conduct of business operations – Dickmann et al. (2008: 7) see IHRM as necessarily entailing exploration of "... how MNCs manage the competing demands of ensuring that the organization has an international coherence in and cost-effective approach to the way it manages its people in all the countries it covers, while also ensuring that it can be responsive to the differences in assumptions about what works from one lo-cation to another". Two other contributions can be seen to adopt a similar perspec-tive. Dowling, Festing and Engle (2008: 293) bound IHRM as "... the implications that the process of internationalization has for the activities and policies of HRM" while Sparrow and Braun (2008a: 96) define it as "... the ways in which the HRM function contributes to the process of globalization within multinational firms".

TERRITORIAL EXPANSION WITHIN THE IHRM FIELD

Given an increasingly complex set of contextual factors, as the IHRM field has expanded, and the problems of internationalization have become more deeply embedded within organizations, the field has also expanded to include '...all issues related to the management of people in an international context... [including] human resource issues facing MNCs in different parts of their organizations... [and] comparative analyses of HRM in different countries' (Stahl and Björkman, 2006: 1). Reflecting this broader territory, for Brewster, Sparrow, and Vernon (2007: 5) the field is best understood as a combination of three separate territories or literatures: 'the subject matter of IHRM is covered under three headings: cross-cultural management; comparative human resource management; and international human resource management'.

There is little new in trying to carve out the different branches of the field. Werner (2002) carried out an analysis of the research that has been published in the field of international management. He concentrated his analysis on research that has looked at the management of firms in a multinational context by analyzing systematically research published in the top US journals, i.e., the discourse that is important within the US (and increasingly non-US) academic promotion system. It should be noted that the list of journals relevant to the US career system excludes many relevant journals for the field of cross-cultural management such as *International Journal of HRM*, *International Journal of Cross Cultural Management* and *Applied Psychology: An International Review*. His analysis provided us with a clear picture of the field as it was traditionally defined. Early international management research could broadly be divided into three categories:

1. Studies that look at the management of firms in a multinational context, i.e., the international aspects of management that do not exist in domestic firms, such as the internationalization process, entry mode decisions, foreign subsidiary management and expatriate management.
2. Comparisons of management practices across different cultures (cross-cultural studies) and nations (cross-national comparisons).
3. Studies that look at management in specific (single) countries within the domain of international management (in order to overcome the bias of early work that had a North American perspective).

Werner (2002) contended that the field, as defined by 271 articles, could be broken down into 12 domains:

◆ *Global business environment:* threats and opportunities of global economy, global markets, political and regulatory environments and international risk.
◆ *Internationalization:* descriptions and measurement of internationalization as a process, its antecedents and consequences.
◆ *Entry mode decisions:* predictors of entry mode choices, equity ownership levels and consequences of entry mode decisions.

- *Foreign direct investment (FDI):* timing, motivation, location and firm and host country consequences of FDI.
- *International exchange:* international exchange, determinants of exporting, export intermediaries and consequences of exporting.
- *International joint ventures (IJVs):* partner selection, partner relations and consequences of IJVs.
- *Strategic alliances and networks:* alliance relationships, networks and outcomes of strategic alliances.
- *Transfer of knowledge:* antecedents of knowledge transfer, processes and consequences of transfer.
- *Multinational enterprises (MNEs)/multinational corporations (MNCs):* multinational enterprise strategies and policies, models of MNEs.
- *Subsidiary-HQ relations:* subsidiary role, strategies and typologies, subsidiary control and performance.
- *Subsidiary and multinational team management:* sudsidiary HRM practices, subsidiary behaviors, multinational negotiations and multinational team management.
- *Expatriate management:* expatriate management, issues for expatriates, expatriate and repatriate reactions.

Reflecting the direction of the broader field of international management, early research in the subset field of International Human Resource Management (IHRM) also focused on the role of multinational corporations (MNCs). Finding and nurturing the people able to implement international strategy was seen as critical for such firms and considerable attention was given to the management of expatriates. IHRM was considered to have the same main dimensions as HRM in a national context but to operate on a larger scale, with more complex strategic considerations, more complex coordination and control demands, and some additional HR functions considered necessary to accommodate the need for greater operating unit diversity, more external stakeholder influence, higher levels of risk exposure, and more personal insight into employees' lives and family situation (Dowling *et al.*, 1998). Research therefore focused on understanding those HR functions that had to change when firms became international. It began to identify important contingencies that influenced the HR function as it became more internationalized, such as the country in which the MNC operated, the size and life cycle stage of the firm, and the type of employee (parent company national, home country national and third country national). IHRM, then, focuses on how different organizations manage their people across national borders.

In the Comparative HRM (CHRM) field (generally but not exclusively of more interest to European researchers, but a different field in its own right) research traditionally incorporated a country comparison perspective, asking the following questions: How is HRM structured in individual countries? What strategies are discussed? What is actually put into practice? What are the main differences and similarities between countries and to what extent are HR policies influenced by national factors such as culture, government policy, educational systems? The bulk of work in the CHRM field has then concentrated on the culture-bound versus the culture-specific thesis; consideration of which HRM practices are more or less culture sensitive; and an empirical examination of patterns of convergence or divergence in HRM practices across national borders. Returning to Werner's (2002) outline of international management research, the CHRM field has covered his second and third categories, i.e., comparisons of management practices across different cultures and nations and studies that look at management in specific (single) countries. It concentrates (still) on how people are managed differently in different countries by analyzing practices within firms of different national origin in the same country or comparing practices between different nations or regions.

MORE CRITICAL VOICES

More critical comments about the most appropriate territory to cover and levels of analysis to adopt are inevitable, given this expansion. As attention turns from the mechanisms of policy and practice needed to specifically manage international cadres of people and internationalizing organizations, toward the need to understand any one policy and practice in its broader international context, the reality is that almost any academics (or academic field with which they identify) may feel that they have something to say about the phenomena (this observation could be applied to any core area of functional practice and policy, such as IT, marketing, or finance).

Reflecting on calls for more critical analysis of the field (De Cieri *et al.*, 2007), we have to ask: To what extent do attempts at theoretical integration answer legitimate needs (a one-last heave approach aimed at linking some of the most viable theories prevalent in the field), or from a post-modernist perspective, a misguided attempt at all-encompassing explanation that seek stable truths in a topic best understood through more modest and temporary sets of assumptions and reflections on complex and unpredictable change processes? Or, can it be argued that recent calls for more critical examination of the field, and discussion of issues such as the impact of power, domination or ideology on core IHRM topics such as expatriation and HQ-subsidiary relationships in MNCs (see, for example, Peltonen, 2006) merely reflect the natural inclinations and hobbies of researchers trained in broader disciplines (such as sociology), and as such should only be of passing interest and note to researchers operating at a different level of analysis? The counter argument to a critical view, of course, is to point out that a critical view is generally only of interest once every five years or so (it serves to remind researchers of some broader truths and acts as a health check), but once said, it has little more of importance in terms of illumination for what in the main are more immediate issues-based problems being researched by IHRM academics. In other words, critical views merely reflect a natural acknowledgment that we are examining organizational issues that are of high complexity, in an environment of changing context, and with questionable assumptions about the existence of rules of the past that can be generalized to future actions, and therefore concerns that there are too many predictable and contingent solutions that can help organizations to explain how best they can solve IHRM problems.

A Reassertion of Institutional Perspectives

Recently considerable attention has been given to the impact of institutions on international business (see, for example, Henisz and Swaminathan, 2008; Peng *et al.*, 2008). The argument is that international business is embedded in a system of transactions between parties that reside in different nations and that this requires an understanding of the institutional characteristics that alter the costs in engaging in business activity in one nation compared to another. All aspects of MNC behavior – choices about location, how they organize local subsidiaries, choices made about technology, capital and labor, and choices made about investments and strategies, are subject to institutional variation. We have to understand the 'rich constellation of interdependent structures and systems within a country, across dyadic pairs of countries, and at the level of the international state system' (Henisz and Swaminathan, 2008: 539), how senior managers respond to such institutional variation (and whether this determines success or failure), and the performance implications of any specific policy or practice in both home and other-country environments. The messages for IHRM research seem to be self-evident from this specification for broader international management research.

Reflecting this need to incorporate institutional levels of analysis, some recent IHRM volumes have taken a more contextual approach, placing organizational action within broader institutional frameworks. So, for example, Edwards and Rees (2007: 22) see IHRM as requiring an understanding of "complex relationship between globalization, national systems and companies" which provides us with "four distinct 'levels of analysis' for interpreting and understanding HRM strategies and practices [the globalization effect, the regional effect, the national effect, and the organization effect]".

The key questions for academics is to decide when such expansion and evolution of definition represents legitimate development of a core concept, or at what point it merely signals the 'muscling in' to a territory of academic discourse from other, essentially separate, disciplines, who now feel empowered to say something? Is a more inclusive discourse beneficial and enriching, should it be a sign of weakness and incoherence?

One way of thinking about this is to consider the underlying theories that have come to dominate thinking. Given this evolution of definition, not surprisingly there are perhaps 20 theories that have featured in the core literature (Sparrow and Braun, 2008a). These include, in broad sequence over time: life cycle models of internationalization; organization design and information processing perspectives; theories of socialization and lateral coordination; contingency models of integration and differentiation; resource dependency theories of power and control of resources; the resource-base of the firm and capability development; knowledge management and organizational learning theories; relational and social capital theory; and the recent re-emergence of attention to institutional theory. As the challenges of internationalization have become more complex, there has been a "transfusion" of ideas across these theories (Sparrow and Braun, 2008a: 96) as researchers have attempted to better understand organizational behavior. The task of producing a grand theory that brings together the diverse perspectives inherent in these theories is therefore neither feasible nor desirable – by their nature they each shed light on the many different processes and phenomena that come to the fore as HRM is managed in an international context. However, if one links these theories to the sorts of organizational problems they help to solve – and I argue here that there has been a clear logic to the successive problems that the internationalization of people management have revealed over time – then the value each theory brings to the analysis of these problems becomes clear.

To summarize, the broad evolution has been to encompass (previously separate) fields of comparative and cross-cultural management into the originally more pre-scribed field of international HRM. This broader, more encompassing field could also be described these days as CIHRM (comparative and international human re-source management).

Firm-Level Globalization Processes

Coming from the perspective that IHRM must focus on the ways in which the HRM function contributes to the process of globalization within multinational firms, Brewster *et al.* (2005) use data from a multi-method study of globalization of HRM processes at firm level to advance a model of factors involved in this process. Based on a survey of 64 MNCs, a survey of 732 HR professionals and seven longitudinal case studies, they use principal components analysis to identify five organizational drivers of IHRM: efficiency orientation, global service provision, information ex-change, pursuit of core business processes, and localization of decision making. They separate out three enabling factors, called HR affordability, a central HR phil-osophy, and HR knowledge transfer. Cluster analysis is then used to show the pres-ence of different combinations or 'recipes' of these factors across the organizations. They advance the argument that the added value of IHRM functions lies in their ability to balance coordination and local sensitivity and that a global HRM strategy can be seen in many firms, whereby they are managing HRM processes through the application of global rulesets, but that far from any universalistic strategies, we see complex combinations of optimization and standardization strategies applied to these global HR rulesets. They argue that attention also needs to be given to a range of processes that lead to renewed global coordination of HRM, such as e-enablement, employer branding, and skill supply strategies. The implications of such developments for structures, strategies, and processes need to be understood.

For De Cieri *et al.* (2007: 284) the term 'global' rather than 'international' used by these researchers reflects the view that IHRM has become "...a key aspect of MNE strategic planning and implementation" and part of a bigger set of questions aimed at understanding "...what determines the international success and failure of firms". Big theory, they argue, does not assist us in answering such questions.

This observation is clearly supported by a range of other studies that have re-cently addressed these factors. Pudelko and Harzing (2007) remind us that, at the country level, the debate has always been about convergence or divergence of HR practice while at the organizational level it has been about standardization ver-sus localization of practice, with standardization (at least theoretically) either being based on a country-of-origin effect or a dominance effect (whereby superior performance may elevate any country into a dominance effect based on assumed best practice). Their study of survey data from 849 HR managers in nine groups of companies headquartered in, and with matched subsidiaries in, the US, Japan, and Germany, found that sudsidiaries in the three different countries acted differently. US multinationals were localizing practices to a degree in Japanese sudsidiaries, and significantly in Germany. Motivations for localization also differed: Japanese sudsidiaries in the US localized for dominance reasons but localized in Germany for local institutional reasons. The subsidiary's strategic role has much importance.

Much is understood, for example, about how MNC headquarters export and diffuse HR policies and practices out to subsidiaries, but less has been written about reverse diffusion processes, whereby advances in sudsidiaries influence other parts of the MNC operation. Bouquet and Birkinshaw (2008) note that the attention of executives at corporate headquarters is scarce and ask how do subsidiaries gain attention? Their survey of 283 subsidiaries suggested that the answer depends on weight (the structural position that a subsidiary occupies within the corporate system) and voice (the strategies used to gain attention), the success of the latter depending on geographic distance and its type of competence (with manufacturing, R&D, strategic support services or centres of excellence with knowledge that can be leveraged into other markets gaining most attention).

Dickmann and Müller-Camen (2006) argue that we have several typologies of MNCs based on strategies and structures – these serve some purpose in demonstrating the complex processes at play – but most of these HRM-based typologies are either theoretical, or are only loosely based on empirical evidence. A universalistic perspective over-emphazises commonalities in strategy and technology, while a concentration on institutional factors and business systems risks seeking self-confirmatory evidence of key national characteristics. They argue for a process perspective (focusing on broad processes such as innovation or lateral coordination) as a way of understanding patterns of IHRM. They use a two-dimensional matrix of standardization/uniformity versus knowledge networking to categorize IHRM. Six case studies, based on large German MNCs operating in Germany, the UK, and Spain, are used to operationalize this taxonomy of IHRM strategies and policies. Ninety-eight interviews are used to differentiate four levels of evidence across each dimension of the matrix. They argue that the combination of high knowledge networking, but low levels of standardization, is an under-researched type of IHRM strategy.

Similarly, Farndale and Paauwe (2007) call for a deeper examination of how multinationals balance the dualities between producing similarities or maintaining differences in global HR practices, and how both sets of practices respond to either competitive or institutional pressures. Summarizing a range of theories applied to HRM (such as neo-institutional theory, the resource-based view of the firm, strategic balance theory, human agency, and strategic choice) they argue for a more contextual understanding of the competing drivers for change in HRM. The collaborative research project across four universities produced interviews with 214 people in 17 countries from 14 case study organizations. Talent management, job postings and expatriate management were the most common globally coordinated practices, with continued country differentiation in terms of, for example, employee rela-tions, graduate resourcing and so forth. Organizational heritage (actions initiated for internal cultural and historical reasons) were also evident, as was the idiosyn-cratic impact of dominant global HR coalitions (senior management actors). At the global level external competitive pressures (and imitation behavior such as bench-marking) drove practice, while at the national level institutional pressures were still prevalent. The unsurprising conclusion of the research was: "... given the multitude of contextual factors and strategic choice opportunities, it is not surprising that the HR practices across these high-performing firms were found to be both similar in some respects and vary in others at the global and the national level" (Farndale and Paauwe, 2007: 371).

OUTLINING THE RESEARCH AGENDA

This volume is divided into four parts. Part I contains a number of chapters that help to establish important research lenses that may be brought to the field of Interna-tional HRM. These include the need to understand and develop theories that cross multiple levels of analysis, the lessons not just from international management but also from a comparative management perspective, and the changing assumptions about the role of national culture in modern workplace settings. Parts II, III, and IV then cover three different levels of analysis and the interplay between them: Individ-ual (People), Firm-level (Process), and Societal (Context). Each of these levels of analysis needs to be applied over time to what is a dynamic field. The key groups of people central to international organizations, the processes being used at firm-level to help to globalize HRM and the contextual factors and societal pressures have all developed and changed in recent years.

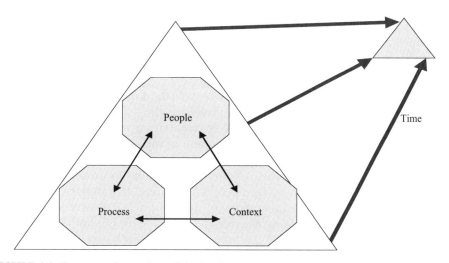

FIGURE 1.1 Conceptual overview of the book structure.

Reconsidering Method: Questioning Our Research Lenses

In an attempt to guide cross-cultural and MNC research in each different area of HR practice, and to help researchers to generate *a priori* hypotheses, Aycan (2005) uses a systematic review of the literature in six areas: human resource planning and career management, job analysis and design, recruitment and selection, performance appraisal, compensation and reward management, and training and development. She argues that in order to improve theoretical analysis and move from a 'how practices differ' to a 'why they differ' perspective, we need to explain the cultural and institutional contingencies for HRM practices. Her analysis identifies 10 different theoretical perspectives, and different models of culture-fit are used to present definitions of 14 cultural constructs. Complexity is the order of the day. Four directional propositions are derived from the cultures literatures concerning recruitment and selection alone, along with 15 institutional contingencies that are linked to a further four propositions about recruitment and selection. The same process is adopted for the other areas of HR practice, resulting in 35 propositions in total.

Even when culture has been assessed in some direct way, or where cross-country differences are used as a proxy for culture, there are a range of difficult methodological issues that have to be addressed (Sparrow, 2006a), such as:

- theoretical equivalence of measurement (with an overabundence of instruments producing inconsistent and incomparable results);
- ecological fallacy (whereby national level data is used to predict individual level behavior, which leads to incorrect estimations of the real effects of the contextual variables);
- contextual determination (where cross-national differences may be assumed without having data for other countries as well because other contextual variables – for example, wealth or institutional effects – might explain the positioning of individuals on the scale in question); and
- structural equivalence of meaning (where a construct has a different meaning at the individual level than was the case at the national level).

Wright and van de Voorde (Chapter 2) look at the topic of IHRM using ideas, concepts, and models that emerge from multilevel theory and research. They examine the concept of variance and look at research on mean differences in the use of HR practices across countries, the amount of variance explained by country, and the extent to which culture moderates the relationship between HR practices and outcomes; they also argue that differences have more to do with institutional contexts than with culture *per se*. We need better differentiation between cultural, institutional, and structural explanations of differences in HR practice, and outcomes from these practices. From the existing culture–HRM literature, it remains unclear *how* employees in different cultures perceive and subsequently react to HR practices. The fact that culture has impacts at the country, company, work unit, and individual level requires multilevel research models. They distinguish between cross-level (how higher-level factors impact individual level factors) and multilevel models (patterns of relationships replicated at all levels of analysis). They also address the different aggregation models that may be used in IHRM research. Drawing upon Gerhart and Fang's (2005) recent analysis, these concepts are used to criticize many of the assumptions often drawn from Hofstede's work on culture and argue that if such critical methodological lenses were applied to much of the IHRM literature, it would be reasonable to assume that many reported significant mean differences across countries may not translate into considerable amounts of variance explained by countries. Moreover, variance in levels of practice is not evidence that they are inappropriate or ineffective across different countries.

Mayrhofer and Reichel (Chapter 3) briefly trace the different traditions within IHRM and comparative HRM (CHRM) research, noting that a surprising number of IHRM research texts, including the otherwise inclusive work of Stahl and Björkman (2006), tend not to address comparative research issues. They look back to see what has been achieved over the past decades within the comparative field, but also look ahead to identify crucial issues. They develop a structuring device to capture the content issues in comparative research, such as level of analysis, core themes, and theoretical foundations and the practical organization of comparative HRM research. They consider what research needs to look at (the levels of analysis issue), why comparisons should be conducted (contrasting phenomenon and theory-driven approaches), the importance of thematic research themes (such as HR practices, HR configurations or the HRM–performance link) and raise questions about the embeddedness of comparisions in time (the question of when to compare). Through this device and an analysis of published abstracts, they identify aspects of comparative HRM that have largely been ignored. Their analysis shows that there is a clear focus at the organizational level of analysis, with both the individual and country level following. Virtually no contributions can be found at the level of groups, networks of organizations or supranational units. This is one reason why some of the contributions in this volume have been chosen for their focus on non-traditional international work forms. Finally, they review four major constraints facing comparative research, including: conceptual issues around areas of interest, theory and data; comparative research methodology; the mechanics of the research process; and the politics of creating a scientific discourse within the academic community.

In the final contribution to Part I, Sackmann (Chapter 4) outlines changes in the contextual factors that have shaped our conceptions of culture, and how our assumptions about culture, have, in turn, influenced research methodologies and research questions. She describes three different conceptualizations of culture with their contextual influences, underlying assumptions, and methodological consequences and explores their impact on the field of IHRM research. Three streams of research are examined: cross-national comparisons, studies of intercultural interactions, and the multiple culture perspective. The specific context that drove the emergence of each stream of research, their respective theories, assumptions and frameworks, and of the research foci and methods preferred in each perspective are examined. The key contributors and the major contributions to knowledge gleaned from each research stream are highlighted. She argues that the first approach has had an overly-dominant impact on the field of IHRM. A national focus may still be relevant for certain issues such as HRM policies and HRM practices as influenced by a nation's jurisdiction, though even legislation and national frameworks allow for variation at the practice level between organizations located in the same nation. Researchers studying issues of culture relevant to an increasingly multicultural world and capable of capturing the emerging cultural realities of current and future work life and organizations needs to go beyond this perspective. She argues that the intercultural interaction perspective, which has demonstrated the importance of contextual analysis and process-orientation in cultural research, reveals insights about the emergence and negotiation of culture, and should be used to shed light on processes of implementing, adopting, using, and recontextualizing HRM systems and instruments in different locations of an international or global firm. However, to capture the new multicultural work realities we also need a conceptualization of culture that considers it as a collective, socially-constructed phenomenon. Organizations, and the individuals who work within them, may be home to and carriers of several cultures. Individuals may identify with and hold simultaneous membership in several cultural groups. Research in the IHRM field needs to recognize and acknowledge the implications of a changing business context, new forms of organizational design, and management through an increasingly multicultural workforce.

Managing Key People and Staff Groups in International Organizations

Attention also has to be given to a series of important generic issues that may be applied to key people and staff groups in international organizations. There has been a wealth of research into expatriates as a population and the experience of the international assignment. However, as organizations continue to globalize, they are drawing upon an ever-wider range of people placed into international roles. De Cieri *et al.* (2007) note that IHRM research is beginning to move away from its traditional focus on multinational enterprises (multinational or transnational enterprises for whom the central integration of their substantial and actively managed investments in foreign countries into the core of the organization is a strategic imperative) into other organizational forms (such as global startups, strategic networks, and cross-border alliances), that while not displaying formal IHRM structures, nonetheless highlight the complexities, sophistication, and challenges associated with international management.

We need to develop our understanding about relatively under-researched groups of people. The latter include: atypical forms of employee such as short-term assignees and self-initiated movers; inpatriates; international project operations; and women in international management. Two generic issues are also considered at the individual level of analysis. These include the role of cultural intelligence and the implications for organizations in designing systems to build this; and the role of political capital for expatriates and international teams.

Sackmann (2003) has drawn attention to the need to better understand the skills needed to work, navigate and manage in this multicultural environment. This challenge is taken up by Ng, Van Dyne, and Ang (Chapter 5). In a 2006 special issue of *Group and Organization Management* on "Old constructs, new frontiers" cross-cultural researchers discussed the construct of cultural intelligence with various writers arguing how their frameworks describe different ways in which the meta-cognitions and learning strategies of international employees operate. Ng, Van Dyne, and Ang point out that selecting executives who can function effectively in international joint ventures and multinational enterprises has constituted a central theme in much contemporary IHRM research and practice. However, the changing nature of international work, reviewed later by Suutari and Brewster (Chapter 7), means that selection issues become important now for a much broader population than just expatriates, and the task and work demands are more complex. Yet selection decisions for staffing international assignments continue to be based on informal and low-utility selection strategies and criteria. They argue that research evidence, however, shows that previous international experiences do not necessarily translate into learning and effectiveness about international working – previous overseas experience appears to explain less than 1 per cent of the variance in interaction adjustment. The reason is that the experience-effectiveness relationship is moderated by an individual-level capability, called cultural intelligence. This they define as a set of cross-cultural capabilities that describe a person's capacity to function effectively in culturally diverse settings (Earley and Ang, 2003). They draw attention to a set of learning capabilities that maximize the developmental benefits of international assignments and advance a model to show why previous work on international experience and adjustment has only a weak relationship with effectiveness and argue the conceptual and applied benefits of using cultural intelligence as a selection tool to identify those with international executive potential.

For Harvey and Novicevic (Chapter 6) the issue is not just one of human capital (skills and competencies), but also of capital. They examine the role that different forms of people-related capital play in assisting international employees in their roles. In their work they have noted that global leaders have to possess a complex amalgamation of technical, functional, cultural, social, and political competencies to navigate successfully the intricacies of changing cross-border responsibilities. They make a distinction between social capital and political capital, and use political influence theory to understand the importance of the capital that global leaders accumulated during global assignments. Social capital leads to trust. Political capital leads to legitimacy. Human capital leads to competencies. Cultural capital leads to social inclusion and acceptance. Social capital is typically reflected in the standing the manager has in the organization and his or her concomitant ability to use that standing to influence others. It is used to help to build on and meld the many cultural norms that exist in a foreign subsidiary. However, global leaders also have to accumulate political capital – including reputational capital (i.e., being known in the network for getting things done) and representative capital (the capacity to effectively build constituent support and acquire legitimacy by using traditional forms of power) – thereby being in a position to remove obstacles to cooperation. They explore the research agenda around these key forms of capital.

For Suutari and Brewster (Chapter 7) another major weakness in our understanding about key groups of individuals has been too much focus on expatriates. We know much about the management of expatriates, yet little is known about the challenge of engaging the wider range of international employees inside organizations today. In reality, other types of international assignees are starting to become more common than traditional expatriates. These different groups involve:

- short-term assignees such as project assignees, development assignees and commuters;
- people who select a more permanent global career involving various international jobs across difference companies and contexts, due to the internationalization of business and careers.

An extensive proportion of people working abroad are not following the traditional expatriate route to leave for an international assignment as an internal transfer within an MNC, but instead look for international job possibilities on their own from external job markets. These people can be referred to as self-initiated assignees.

Suutari and Brewster review the research and literature concerning these untypical forms of international assignees – noting that none of the forms of assignment characterized in the literature as 'atypical' or 'different' is really new, but they are all more prevalent and under-researched. They summarize the literature on some key forms of international working – migration, global careerists, self-initiated international experiences, international commuters, short-term assignees, frequent flyers, and virtual internationalists – and then examine the implications that these atypical forms of international working have for various HRM processes within organizations. They draw attention to a compendium of reasons for using each form, such as managerial control, skill transfer, management development, international cadre, costs, and family reasons, and highlight pressing research needs in the areas of recruitment, performance management, and compensation. Ultimately, the challenge is one of understanding diversity.

In addition to the issue of greater diversity in forms of international working, many multinationals also have growing business opportunities in developing and emerging economies. This, however, creates the challenge of accessing, applying, and leveraging local knowledge to offset a lack of experience in more culturally and institutionally distant environments. Reiche, Kraimer, and Harzing (Chapter 8) note that most international assignment research has taken a unidirectional approach, focusing on staff and knowledge transfers from the corporate headquarters to foreign subsidiaries. Inpatriation is the transfer of foreign nationals from the subsidiary into a multinational's HQ. Inpatriates can have profound knowledge of a subsidiary context but also an ability to engage in cross-unit brokerage. They review literature on knowledge transfer through international assignments, examine the different roles of inpatriate assignments, and explore the processes and determinants that facilitate knowledge sharing. Both expatriation and inpatriation involve the establishment of cross-unit linkages and the conduct of boundary-spanning activities, but expatriation tends to have higher status, a lower requirement for rapid acculturation, and more asymmetric information power. Reiche, Kraimer and Harzing focus on individual-level processes that influence how knowledge is transferred in organizations, and draw attention to a range of important social processes that have to be in place before inpatriation can lead to any cross-unit knowledge sharing. This depends on social processes such as the ability to exert social influence and build social networks. They take a social capital perspective, arguing its benefits for boundary-spanning, solidarity, adjustment, and information sharing roles. They draw attention to the importance of acculturation attitudes and political skills, and discuss the role played by HRM practices in building this social capital.

Welch, Welch and Fenwick (Chapter 9) point to another set of important individuals about whom little is known. They build an argument that the bulk of IHRM research tends to assume that firms internationalize only through foreign direct investment (FDI). They draw attention to the importance of a range of operating modes (such as exporting, foreign direct investment, equity joint ventures, international alliances in their various forms, licensing and franchising, management contracts, outsourcing, "offshoring" and contract manufacturing) in international management. The HR challenges associated with each operation mode have not been extensively studied. Moreover, of these operating modes, one of the most underresearched yet highly practiced is international project operations. The nature of international project work raises HR issues that are different to those encountered in more traditional work settings. They argue for a more contextualized approach to IHRM research and theory building, one that accounts for contextual differences in the firm's internationalization process. To understand the nature of such issues, they focus on a special group of international assignees, independent consultants, who are an integral part of the delivery of international development projects by supplier firms. They use a life cycle stage model of international projects and a qualitative study of this work group to look at motivations, performance, career outcomes, and the general HRM agenda. This context is more akin to a 'body shop' resourcing model. Many international project firms share a common characteristic of being heavily dependent on attracting sufficient numbers of skilled external contractors in often highly competitive circumstances. The role of power and reputation in international working therefore comes to the fore, along with issues of work continuity, loyalty, compensation, and on-site support.

While on the issue of power, many researchers have argued that globalization is empowering for some, yet disempowering and impoverishing for others, particularly unskilled employees in developing countries, but also to women (De Cieri, Chapter 10). Yet women represent about 19 per cent of the international assignee community, and research also suggests that women are more highly represented among self-initiated expatriates than in the corporate expatriate sector. Picking up the issue of diversity in international working touched upon earlier by Suutari and Brewster (Chapter 7), De Cieri, in a final contribution at the individual level of analysis, focuses on the gender issues involved, and the debate as to whether HRM policies and practices utilized in MNCs provide equal benefits to men and women. She outlines a variety of forms of participation by women in international management (board membership, traditional international assignments, and frequent flyer or global project team members), reviews different explanations for women's under-representation in international management (social, cultural, structural and systematic discrimination against women, biases in organizational decision making and structures, and individual or person-centered factors) and discusses the implications for policy makers, employers, individuals, and researchers. De Cieri argues that while IHRM research has begun to examine the flexible forms of international assignments, there has been little attention to gender issues relevant to these forms of employment. Given the comments made earlier about the frequent need to introduce novel theory to explain international phenomena, De Cieri draws upon identity theory and gender stereotyping, token theory, and selection systems to explain many of the issues faced in the international management of women, and highlights the growing awareness of the problems associated with under-utilization of this particular human capital pool.

MANAGING GLOBALIZATION PROCESSES AT THE LEVEL OF THE FIRM

In addition to the above topics generally explored at the individual level of analysis, research in the field of IHRM also needs to shed light on the initiatives being pursued at the firm level, and the processes involved as organizations attempt to globalize their HRM functions. Global HRM is not simply about understanding and covering these staff around the world. It also concerns managing international HRM activities, increasingly through the application of global rule-sets. However, such application of course takes place within the bounds of institutional influences. A range of recent work has drawn upon institutional and country-of-origin perspectives to examine these processes (Colling and Clark, 2006; Ferner *et al.*, 2005).

Ferner *et al.* (2005) examine the internationalization of diversity policies in US MNCs using both a comparative institutionalist and a power/interests perspective. They draw upon data from 118 respondents in six companies to develop six case studies highlighting differing conceptualizations of diversity in the US and the UK. They then draw upon theories that help to explain subsidiary embeddedness, strategic role, stickiness of tacit knowledge transfer, institutional distance, political charters of subsidiaries, sources of power, and creative and resistive hybridization strategies. Ferner *et al.* (2005) argue that the use of local power resources enables UK actors to resist internationalization of focus, and helps to create compromise accommodations. These arguments are related to work on the transfer of HR practices across national business systems and highlight the role of control systems as an organizational capability in attempts to transmit standardized policies.

Colling and Clark (2006) use the inflow of US foreign direct investment into the UK electricity industry to test the country-of-origin effect in MNCs. They adopt an institutionalist approach using documentary analysis and interviews with union officials to examine three questions in relation to pay systems and union recognition: in what circumstances are sector effects communicated transnationally; what consequences are there for the management of employment; and how are cross-national employment trends influenced by national business systems? Attention is also given to sector-level developments in governance in both countries and the way these help to shape organizational strategy. They discuss the research issues associated with study across levels of analysis, such as moving from national to transnational sector effects. They identify a range of first-order effects (push and pull factors, alongside strategic and opportunistic behavior), second-order effects (organizational forms and changes in management style) and third-order effects (the ramifications for employment relations).

We need to address the learning and knowledge management issues involved in these processes. Edwards (Chapter 11) draws attention to the interlocking nature of institutions in areas such as corporate governance, training and employment regulation, and how these have given rise to distinctive 'national business systems' (Whitley, 1999). He also notes the different 'knowledge structures' that characterize national systems, and how these can constrain the ability of individuals to learn from those in other parts of the firm. MNCs are linked into multiple national systems, and the cross-national diversity in business practice they face provides both opportunities and constraints to organizational learning. They can observe practices in operation in one part of the organization and attempt to transfer them to other parts. He distinguishes between 'forward diffusion' where the direction of diffusion flows with the hierarchy of the firm, and 'reverse diffusion' where practices that originate in the foreign subsidiaries are transferred to the rest of the company, including the domestic operations. Reverse diffusion processes are important to study, because they play a role in the hybridization of national business systems, but can also change the expectations of people inside organizations concerning the legitimacy of groups at a range of levels to influence the policy formation process. Drawing upon evidence from three linked projects, he reviews theories of management orientation and information processing to explain the likelihood of reverse transfers, and outlines the challenges faced from national institutional differences (the institutional 'props' necessary for the operation of a practice, or the institutional or cultural 'constraints' to transfer) and the different types of dominance effects. Consideration is also given to the organizational politics processes involved, including incentives (such as status and resource claims at individual or unit level) and constraints (including various forms of resistance).

Sticking to the theme of international transfer of practice, Björkman, Barner-Rasmussen, Ehrnrooth, and Mäkelä (Chapter 12) note that with regard to the question about whether subsidiary HRM practices should resemble those of local firms (localization) or those of the foreign parent organization (standardization), only the latter entails a transfer of practices within the MNC. They discuss the strategic value of planned transfers of practices, but also the reasons why they do not always work out in the way intended by the headquarters. They focus on the transfer of performance management systems as a lead practice that is often globalized as MNCs strive for a degree of global standardization across subsidiary units embedded in very different national cultures and institutional contexts. Drawing upon the work of Kostova (Kostova, 1999; Kostova and Roth, 2002) on practice transfer, and Martin and Beaumont's (2001) process model of strategic HRM change in MNCs, they develop a model of MNC-internal factors that influence the transfer of HRM practices from headquarters to foreign units. Four different adoption patterns, referred to as ideal types, or archetypes, of foreign subsidiary adoption, are identified on the basis of different combinations of high versus low levels of implementation and internalization (true believers, ritualists, non-conformists, and dissidents). They then discuss how human, social, and organizational capital explains the outcomes and different adoption patterns. In particular, they tease out three different types of social capital (structural, relational, and cognitive) that become important, and two different forms of organizational capital, in an attempt to inspire researchers to conduct further conceptual and empirical research on this topic.

The literature on knowledge management underlines the fact that fragmented initiatives often coexist in those organizations that implement knowledge management tools or processes. Moingeon, Lumineau, and Perrin (Chapter 13) argue that while attention has been given to the role of networks and the use of social network analysis as a way of understanding the operation of such networks (Harvey and Novicevic, Chapter 6; and Sparrow, Brewster, and Ligthart, Chapter 18) international HR professionals are also faced with the need to promote more innovative ways of working that often transcends the boundaries of their firms as well as nations. They look at communities of practice (CoPs) – specifically an interorganizational community of practice (ICP) – as an important mechanism through which collective knowledge can be created, held and transferred internationally. For many international organizations virtual forms of working have risen in importance. How can the study of unstructured, spontaneous, self-managing, and emergent groups - and the social interactions that surround learning within and outside them – inform the IHRM field? They draw attention to the alignment of new practices and the promotion of lateral processes and organizational forms that might assist in the management of such forms of international working. They lay out appropriate theory using the mechanism of a learning mix model (covering four elements: strategic, technological, organizational, and a learning identity) and adopt a 'netnography,' form of analysis – an analysis of archival data, interviews of community volunteers, and direct observations of meetings organized by the community – to examine how portfolios of practice emerge, how information sharing tools are used, the governance of the community, and the creation of shared identities.

The study of virtual communities also brings to the fore the role of technology as an enabler of more global forms of management. Bondarouk and Rüel (Chapter 14) examine the web-enabled transformation of HR in international companies. E-enablement, or web technology, has given a boost to the options for international companies in standardizing and harmonizing their HR policies and practices in all corners of the company right around the world. It is argued that international companies, in this way, could become truly global companies. As part of this, HR policy making should be centralized, while the execution of HR practices should be in the hands of employees and managers, assisted in this by (frequently outsourced) Shared Service Centers. Bondarouk and Rüel conceptualize and explore the IT-enabled transformation of HR in an international community, but again using theoretical frames quite novel to the IHRM fields. They draw upon insights out of sociology – specifically the theory of structuration – in order to understand what happened during IT-enabled HR transformation. They introduce the notion of 'HRM frames', where the HR transformation in organizations (whether IT-enabled or not) influences employees' behaviors at the same time as it is influenced by human actions, to analyze the underlying assumptions, values, and interpretations that employees have about the IT-enabled HRM transformation in organizations. They argue that such an analysis is central to understanding the role of IT-enabled change in both HR processes and the HR function itself. Where a technology is used where the interpretations of key groups of people is involved (HR professionals, line managers, and employees), these interpretaions (and adoption patterns) will differ significantly. They draw attention to the difficulties and conflicts around e-enabled HR transformations and the necessary role changes, competency modifications, restructuring, and globalization of the HR function.

Martin and Hetrick (Chapter 15) examine employer branding as an international coordination strategy within IHRM. There has been much debate in the HR profession about the management of employer brands internationally and it is an important challenge for many large international organizations. Martin and Hetrick note that, often seen in the context of global 'talent wars', IHRM researchers can see a trend among international and multinational organizations to use employer branding as an important tool for creating a sense of 'corporateness' among often decentralized MNCs, and as a key means of differentiating themselves in overseas labor markets. Yet we still know little about the linkages between HR and marketing in the brand management process, despite increasing awareness that the HR function is now becoming involved in this work on an international scale. Martin and Hetrick argue this is surprising, given that it is being adopted as a means of reconciling a key tension faced by international organizations – balancing the needs for corporate integration, control, and legitimacy on the one hand with local differentiation, autonomy and initiative on the other. They develop a simplified model of the branding process, theorizing key variables (such as corporate and organizational identity), reviewing the evidence as to whether it works in an international context, and illustrate some of the problems faced, drawing upon ongoing research inside a large financial services MNC. Despite many supposed attractions to the practice, they highlight the challenges of facing unreceptive contexts for change (where MNC subsidiaries in different countries hold markedly different and somewhat negative views of corporate headquarters' leadership, HR, and people management policies). Company image and positioning is difficult to manage internationally, because cultural brands rely on corporate stories being seen as locally authentic and charismatically appealing to employees in settings that may be marked by large cultural and institutional distances between headquarters and subsidiaries. They reveal the challenges faced in attempting to disentangle national and organizational culture effects.

Reflecting the attention given to talent management processes on a global scale, Ashton, Brown, and Lauder (Chapter 16) argue that there is a weakness in both the IHRM and talent management literature. In the context of globalization, it does not focus on the issue of skill. Yet, we are witnessing a major transformation in the process of skill formation, with it being 'freed' from the constraints of national vocational education and training (VET) and industrial relations systems, as MNCs (better called transnational corporations – TNCs) are now operating *outside* the

boundaries of national systems. They outline the changes taking place in the production of skill in relation to economic globalization and explain why this process is
central to organizational competitiveness. They review work from the national systems perspective as well as that associated with globalization processes within IHRM.
The latter, they argue, points to some of the new skills associated with the emergence of globally oriented MNCs, the skills required to manage knowledge through
Centers of Excellence, to negotiate and manage alliances with other companies and
institutions as well as the skills to manage talent at a global level. However, this literature remains too focused on the agenda of the IHR professionals. They ask why
transnationals approach the process of skill creation and use in different ways, and
how the wider institutional and market conditions within which they operate shape
their responses. They argue that as the processes related to the creation and use
of skills have changed fundamentally, we must reconceptualize the notion of skill,
moving beyond just a human capital approach. They analyze the capacity for TNCs
to develop a portfolio of skill strategies and lay out the nature of consequence of
these strategies.

Another transformational force is that of offshoring and outsourcing. Globalization through offshoring skilled employment from developed countries such as the
US and the UK to emerging markets such as India and China has become a major
topic of debate. It adds the additional complexity to IHRM analysis because it
requires an understanding of the implications that multisourced HR functions have
for global HR strategy. Cooke and Budhwar (Chapter 17) contrast outsourcing and
offshoring strategies. They review global trends – such as push factors driven by
organizations' needs to acquire outsourcing services, as well as pull factors coming
from international HR outsourcing provider firms keen to expand their services in
different business areas and geographical locations – and then the motives behind
each strategy. The motives are seen through the lens of core-periphery models, the
transaction cost economic model, Ulrich's HR operating model, and environmental
uncertainty models. They position HR offshoring as part of the firm's internationalization plan. A range of different modes are identified within this, such as captive
offshoring, outsourcing directly to HR service providers operating in offshore
countries, outsourcing to an HR outsourcing service provider onshore who then
offshores some of the processes to other countries for strategic and operational
reasons, or co-sourcing. They find that the primary motives of HR outsourcing
are to gain access to external expertise and cost efficiency – transformational HR
outsourcing has not yet taken root – and that HR outsourcing is more likely to be
adopted by MNCs rather than by local firms, especially in such emerging markets
as China and India. Building on the arguments that each different internationalization strategy adopted by an MNC has different implications for the role of the
HR function (Bartlett and Ghoshal, 1989; Farndale and Paauwe, 2005), Cooke and
Budhwar consider the implications for global HR structures and strategy and
highlight the implications of this for the role of in-house HR teams in the decision-
making process of HR offshoring/outsourcing, the management of outsourcing
relationships and the skills needed by HR professionals. Particular attention is
drawn to the need to manage organizational and societal cultural differences within
this. They focus on the phenomenon of HR offshored outsourcing, particularly to

India and China, arguing that this is an area that is least covered in the existing literature, and yet lies at the heart of many HR function strategies. The combined complexity of international HRM and HR outsourcing necessitates such analysis.

In the context of many of the firm-level change processes discussed, Sparrow, Brewster, and Ligthart (Chapter 18) argue that there are then four academic debates shaping much current IHRM research: the nature of IHRM structures and strategies and the ensuing IHRM research agenda; the changing technological context and the impact of developments in shared services, e-enablement, outsourcing, and offshoring; the role of line managers and business partners in the effective conduct of IHRM; and the role of knowledge management, networking, and social capital processes. They outline some of the key issues in each of these four areas, and then explore networking and social capital processes through the use of social network analysis in a case study organization. IHRM academics need to help global HR functions to position themselves inside the rest of the organization so that they can best achieve the needs of their (many and diverse) stakeholders, and realize the intentions behind business partner roles in global context. The combination of developments in technology, process streamlining, and sourcing are also moving the focus of the IHRM function away from managing a global set of managers toward becoming a function that can operate a series of value-adding HR processes within the business internationally. Yet these developments are impossible to disentangle from parallel debates about specialization, core capability, and the technological enablement of service delivery (cross-culturally). Given the evidence that the role of line managers varies in a significant and consistent manner across countries, IHRM researchers also have to understand how best to build upon the role of line managers in the conduct of IHRM and how to best achieve the HR business partner role. Although five main forms of global knowledge management, or integration mechanisms, have featured in the literature (Sparrow, 2006b) – organizational design and the specific issue of centers of excellence; managing systems and technology-driven approaches to global knowledge management systems; capitalizing on expatriate advice networks; coordinating international management teams; and developing communities of practice or global expertise networks – very little is known about the role of networks in enabling many of these knowledge management mechanisms. They use social network analysis to point to some of these linkages, arguing that the value of social network analysis to the field of IHRM lies in its ability to look at both micro- and macro-level linkages between individual actions and institutional outcomes, and vice versa. They draw upon six network features: social capital; structural holes; density of connections; level of centralization; reachability; and the level of reciprocity. Their analysis shows the complexity of network actors involved in practice in the delivery of IHRM and that a very high proportion of these actors are in line management roles.

ORGANIZATIONAL ACTION IN CONTEXT

As the previous section shows, there are a wide range of firm-level processes associated with internationalization that require us to import both new and old

frameworks and models from outside the field to understand the trajectories that
are being followed, and their likely end states.

As the challenge of integrating even traditional theories within IHRM proves too
difficult (for De Cieri *et al.*, 2007, such integration is also undesirable), the IHRM
field has also begun to give more attention to understanding not only micro-level
variables that help us to understand cross-national transfer of HRM practices, but
also the way in which macro-level issues are of concern to the organization. This
is why attention is given in this volume to some macro themes – such as the role
of not-for-profit (Fenwick and McLean, Chapter 19), ethics (Vadera and Aguilera,
Chapter 20), ethnicity (Nyambegera, Chapter 21), and finally altruistic leadership
(Adler, Chapter 22) in IHRM. These are, in essence, some of the bottom-up processes of globalization that, at certain points in time, can derail even the most carefully considered firm-level strategy. Global phenomena such as the credit crunch
of 2008 remind us that there are deeper societal waves and sentiments that, at the
end of the day, can influence organizational action. Hopefully, the inclusion of the
topics noted above helps to address the call by Guillén (2001), cited by De Cieri
et al. (2007), to help researchers move across levels of analysis and link IHRM research topics to issues that cross world systems to nation states, industries, sectors,
communities, organizations, and groups.

Fenwick and McLean (Chapter 19) argue that globalization has affected the environments of international non-governmental organizations (INGOs) through the
growth and proliferation of supraterritorial social relations, global corporations,
global civil society, and global regimes; and the internationalization of major financial markets, technical, manufacturing, and service sectors. INGOs are values-based
organizations – but there are parallels from their management to the strengthening
calls for increased corporate social responsibility among multinationals. Increased
levels of competition between INGOs for resources and markets means that we need
to understand how trust and legitimacy are engendered – a challenge faced by many
more traditional multinationals. They argue that to understand trust and legitimacy we have to look at the underlying processes of greater accountability and efficiency, increased formalization and professionalization. An important future IHRM
research agenda is to understand not just the advantages, but also some of the disadvantages of relying on values-based coordination. Their analysis is relevant to those
researching any other international workgroups or organizational forms that are
(potentially) values-based. They use a case study of one of the most visible types of
social purpose international NGO – intermediate private aid and development organizations – to illustrate how academic understanding of international NGOs has
some broader resonance with the challenges faced by many IHRM researchers, and
conclusions are drawn about the implications for future IHRM research.

Vadera and Aguilera (Chapter 20) provide a systematic comparative analysis of
corporate ethics by looking at the usage of different corporate ethics concepts in
three countries, the US, the UK, and India. Organizations across the globe are implementing ethics programs – but with mixed results – given the complexity for
multinational enterprises operating in several different economies simultaneously.
They argue that integration of ethics programs has to be examined along with institutional, industry- and country-level, and organizational forces that affect their

success. Only then can we garner a holistic view of the role of IHRM in the formulation and implementation of ethics programs in multinational enterprises. They consider how the formulation, content, communication of, and effectiveness of ethics programs varies across a range of multilevel forces such as cultures, country-level, and institutional factors. The need to integrate and align a range of IHRM policies and practices with an ethics ethos is signaled.

The challenge of dealing with multicultural assumptions in international organizations is ever present. However, we often consider diversity from too narrow a frame – talking about the more comfortable issues of national cultures. In practice, we are really talking about individual identities – and these are rooted within many aspects of the social environment within which multinationals have to manage. Nyambegera (Chapter 21) points out that the IHRM literature says very little about the importance of ethnicity, or indeed on developing approaches to ethnicity that fit IHRM policies and practices. As societies globalize and become more plural, MNCs have to come to terms with phenomena such as intracultural diversity and growing intercultural communalities. Many have assumed that ethnicity as an element of culture would gradually disappear as an organizational form, but the available literature suggests that ethnic groups are becoming even stronger. Written before events in Kenya were to bring ethnicity back to center stage, Nyambegera prophetically notes that the field of IHRM has slowly been "educated", and in turn tries to educate others, about the workings of culture, but that we now need to unravel what is implied by ethnicity and how people's thinking about it influences their behavior inside international organizations. This task is undertaken in the contribution.

Adler (Chapter 22) concludes the volume by noting that shaping history is the bottom-line challenge of global leadership – creating a twenty-first century in which organizations enhance, rather than diminish, civilization. She reminds us that many economic and societal trends appear to be heading in the wrong direction, and questions how we can remarry idealism with contemporary global realities. Much of this depends upon the style of global leadership that is pursued within organizations, and the ability of such leadership to provide unifying images and strategies. She examines the contribution that women as leaders (of countries, or organizations) has made to changing ethos, but concludes that what is needed ultimately is not more diversity in representation within MNCs. People world wide may want what all women symbolize – but what only some women leaders in fact exhibit – so ultimately it is the provision of a form of leadership in the world that will foster global society's survival and prosperity that will determine the future trajectory of much IHRM.

CONCLUSION

To summarize from the review of issues in each of the four main sections that have captured the latest content of IHRM research, this chapter has argued that the field of IHRM finds itself having to understand and unravel four key issues: the research lenses that are best suited to analyzing the phenomena of internationalization faced by MNCs and other global organizations; the management issues associated with both key blocks of individuals, and the key HR processes as applied to these individuals; the processes that operate primarily at the level of the firm, which are either driving or constraining a rebalancing between global and local HR practice (a leading-edge practice-led lens has been used to identify what these processes may be); and finally, but very importantly, some of the bottom-up consequences of globalization that can still serve to influence corporate policy. Only with some complete, multilevel, and time-sensitive frames of reference will we be able to manage our research, and our organizations, intelligently into the future.

<h2 style="text-align:center">REFERENCES</h2>

Aycan, Z. (2005). The interplay between cultural and institutional/structural contingencies in human resource practices. *International Journal of Human Resource Management*, 16 (7), 1038–1119.

Bartlett, C., and Ghoshal, S. (1989). *Managing Across Borders: The Transnational Solution* (1st edn). Boston, MA: Harvard Business School Press.

Bouquet, C., and Birkinshaw, J. (2008). Weight versus voice: How foreign subsidiaries gain attention from corporate headquarters. *Academy of Management Journal*, 51 (3), 577–601.

Brewster, C., Sparrow, P.R., and Vernon, G (2007). *International Human Resource Management*. London: Chartered Institute of Personnel and Development.

Brewster, C., Sparrow, P.R., and Harris, H. (2005). Towards a new model of globalising HRM. *International Journal of Human Resource Management*, 16 (6), 949–970.

Briscoe, D., and Schuler, R.S. (2004). *International Human Resource Management* (2nd edn). New York and London: Routledge.

Colling, T., and Clark, I. (2006). What happened when the Americans took over Britain's electricity industry? Exploring trans-national sector effects on employment relations. *International Journal of HRM*, 17 (9), 1625–1644.

De Cieri, H., Wolfram Cox, J., and Fenwick, M. (2007). A review of international human resource management: Integration, interrogation, imitation. *International Journal of Management Reviews*, 9 (4), 281–302.

Dickmann, M., and Müller-Camen, M. (2006). A typology of international human resource management strategies and processes. *International Journal of HRM*, 17 (4), 580–601.

Dickmann, M., Brewster, C., and Sparrow, P.R. (eds) (2008). *International Human Resource Management: A European Perspective*. London: Routledge.

Dowling, P.J., Welch, D.E., and Schuler, R.S. (1998). *International Human Resource Management*. Cincinnati, OH: South-Western.

Dowling, P.J., Engle Sr, A.D., and Festing, M. (2008). *International Dimensions of Human Resource Management*.

Earley, P.C., and Ang, S. (2003). *Cultural Intelligence: Individual Interactions Across Cultures*. Palo Alto: Stanford University Press.

Edwards, T., and Rees, C. (2007). *International Human Resource Management: Globalisation, National Systems and Multinational Companies*. London: Financial Times/Prentice Hall.

Farndale, E., and Paauwe, J. (2005). *The role of corporate HR functions in MNCs: The interplay between corporate, regional/national and plant level*. International Programs Visiting Fellow Working Papers. US: Cornell University.

Farndale, E., and Paauwe, J. (2007). Uncovering competitive and institutional drivers of HRM practices in multinational corporations. *Human Resource Management Journal*, 17 (4), 355–375.

Ferner, A., Almond, P., and Colling, T. (2005). Institutional theory and the cross-national transfer of employment policy: The case of 'workforce diversity' in US multinationals. *Journal of International Business Studies*, 36 (3), 304–321.

Gerhart, B., and Fang, M. (2005). National culture and human resource management: Assumptions and evidence. *International Journal of Human Resource Management*, 16 (6), 971–986.

Guillén, M. (2001). Is globalisation civilising, destructive or feeble? A critique of five key debates in the social sciences literature. *Annual Review of Sociology*, 27, 235–260.

Harzing, A.-W. (2002). Acquisitions versus Greenfield investments: International strategy and management of entry modes. *Strategic Management Journal*, 23, 211–227.

Henisz, W., and Swaminathan, A. (2008). Introduction: Institutions and international business. *Journal of International Business*, 39, 537–539.

Hippler, T. (2008). Book review of handbook of research in international human resource management. *Journal of International Management*, 14, 89–92.

Kostova, T. (1999). Transnational transfer of strategic organizational practices: A contextual perspective. *Academy of Management Review*, 24 (2), 308–324.

Kostova, T., and Roth, K. (2002). Adoption of an organizational practice by subsidiaries of multinational corporations: Institutional and relational effects. *Academy of Management Journal*, 45 (1), 215–233.

Laurent, A. (1986). The cross-cultural puzzle of international human resource management. *Human Resource Management*, 25 (1), 91–102.

Martin, G., and Beaumont, P.B. (2001). Transforming multinational enterprises: Towards a process model of strategic human resource management change. *International Journal of Human Resource Management*, 12 (8), 1234–1250.

Peltonen, T. (2006). Critical theoretical perspectives on international human resource management. In G.K. Stahl and I. Björkman (eds), *Handbook of Research in International Human Resource Management*. Cheltenham: Edward Elgar, pp. 523–535.

Peng, M.W., Wang, D.Y.L., and Jiang, Y. (2008). An institution-based view of international business strategy: A focus on emerging economies. *Journal of International Business*, 39, 920–936.

Poole, M. (1990). Editorial: Human resource management in an international perspective. *International Journal of Human Resource Management*, 1 (1), 1–15.

Pudelko, M., and Harzing, A.-W. (2007). Country-of-origin, localization, or dominance effect? An empirical investigation of HRM practices in foreign subsidiaries. *Human Resource Management*, 46 (4), 535–559.

Sackmann, S.A. (2003). Cultural complexity as a challenge in the management of global companies. In Bertelsmann Foundation (ed.), *Corporate Cultures in Global Interaction. Liz Mohn – A Cultural Forum Vol. III*. Gütersloh, Germany: Bertelsmann, pp. 58–81.

Schuler, R.S., Budhwar, P.S., and Florkowski, G.W. (2002). International human resource management: Review and critique. *International Journal of Management Reviews*, 4 (1), 41–70.

Schuler R.S., Sparrow, P.R., and Budhwar, P.S. (2009). Preface. In P.S. Budhwar, R.S. Schuler and P.R. Sparrow (eds), *Major Works in International Human Resource Management*. London: Sage.

Scullion, H. (1995). *International human resource management*. In J. Storey (ed.), *Human Resource Management: A Critical Text*. London: Routledge.

Scullion, H. (2005). International HRM: An introduction. In H. Scullion and M Linehan (eds), *International Human Resource Management: A Critical Text*. Basingstoke: Palgrave Macmillan, pp. 3–21.

Scullion, H., and Paauwe, J. (2004). International human resource management: Recent developments in theory and empirical research. In A.-W. Harzing and J. Van Ruysseveldt (eds), *International Human Resource Management* (2nd edn), London: Sage, pp. 65–88.

Sparrow, P.R. (2006a). International management: Key challenges for industrial and organizational psychology. In G. Hodginson and J.K. Ford (eds), *International Review of Industrial and Organizational Psychology*, Vol 21. London: John Wiley & Sons, pp. 189–266.

Sparrow, P.R. (2006b). Knowledge management in Global organizations. In G. Stahl and I. Björkman (eds), *Handbook of Research into International HRM*. London: Edward Elgar, pp. 113–138.

Sparrow, P.R., and Braun, W. (2008a). HR strategy theory in international context. In M. Harris (ed.), *The Handbook of Research in International Human Resource Management*. Mahwah, NJ: Lawrence Erlbaum, pp. 77–106.

Sparrow, P.R., and Braun, W. (2008b). HR sourcing and shoring: Strategies, drivers, success factors and implications for HR. In M. Dickmann, C. Brewster and P.R. Sparrow (eds), *International Human Resource Management: A European Perspective*. London: Routledge, pp. 39–66.

Stahl, G.K., and Bjorkman, I. (eds) (2006). *Handbook of Research in International Human Resource Management*. Cheltenham: Edward Elgar Publishing.

Werner, S. (2002). Recent developments in international management research: A review of 20 top management journals. *Journal of Management*, 28 (3), 277–305.

Whitley, R. (1999). *Divergent Capitalisms: The Social Structuring and Change of Business Systems*. Oxford: Oxford University Press.

2

Multilevel Issues in IHRM: Mean Differences, Explained Variance, and Moderated Relationships

PATRICK WRIGHT AND KARINA VAN DE VOORDE

INTRODUCTION

Assume the following case.[1] A large multinational organization decides to implement a pay for performance system, complete with forced distribution rankings and large merit pay increase differences across performance categories as part of its effort to build a 'performance-based culture'. Resident cross-cultural experts warn against such an approach because they argue that in collectivist cultures such as China, individualistic-based HR practices such as this simply will not work, and in fact may actually result in lower, rather than higher performance. Such warning shows great consistency with what Hofstede wrote when he stated:

> In the management literature there are numerous unquestioning extrapolations of organizational solutions beyond the border of the country in which they were developed. This is especially true for the exportation of management theories from the United States to the rest of the world, for which the non-US importers are at least as responsible as the US exporters... However the empirical basis for American management theories is American organizations; and we should not assume without proof that they apply elsewhere.
>
> —(Hofstede, 1980a, b: 373)

Such admonitions have been repeated over the years to the point that multinational firms should be paralyzed with fear of exporting their HRM systems, and incurring

[1] Support for this chapter was provided by the Center for Advanced Human Resource Studies (CAHRS) in the School of ILR at Cornell University. All opinions and mistakes are the responsibility of the authors, however, and not of CAHRS.

significant costs by developing customized HR systems for every different country or locale. Similarly, cross-cultural researchers have made a living out of studying the varieties of HR systems and approaches that exist across different countries and regions.

While neither denying that differences in HR systems exist, nor that some of the variety of practices is due to real differences across countries, we will attempt to dissect the issue of International HRM using ideas, concepts, and models emerging from multilevel theory and research. We posit that three ideas are critical to this line of research:

1. Mean differences in the use of HR practices across countries.
2. The amount of variance in HR practices that is explained by countries.
3. The extent to which countries (or specifically culture) moderate the relationships between HR practices and outcomes.

Our conclusion is that these differences may not be as large as we think they are, and may in fact be due less to differences in culture and more to differences in institutional contexts.

THE CONCEPT OF VARIANCE

The concept of variation, or variance, is central to all scientific endeavors. The scientific research process first assumes that variance exists in one or more variables, and second aims at understanding and/or explaining this variation (Kerlinger, 1973). For instance, Nunnaly and Bernstein (1994) stated that 'One might say that scientific issues are posed only to the extent that they vary with respect to particular attributes...The purpose of a scientific theory is to explain as much variation of interrelated variables as possible' (p. 116). In the context of strategic International HRM research, we first assume that variation or variance in HR practices exists across different cultural or country contexts. This is an assumption based in empirical data, most significantly that provided by Brewster and his colleagues (1999a, b, 2003, 2005) and consequently is neither innovative nor profound. However, this first issue deals with the extent to which mean differences in the use of practices are observed across countries.

Second, even when mean differences are observed, it is important to understand the extent to which the total variance in HR practices is explained by country or culture. With large sample sizes, even small differences in means may have statistically significant results, yet little of the variance in practices is explained by country.

Finally, the fact that different countries tend to use practices to a different extent may not necessarily mean that those practices are not best practices. The most important question deals with the extent to which the relationship between practices and some important outcomes (e.g., turnover, climate, or firm performance) differ across countries.

The purpose of this chapter is to use recent developments in multilevel research to examine the concepts of mean differences, explained variance, and moderation within the International HRM (IHRM) literature. To begin this analysis, we briefly review some of the major findings with regard to IHRM practices.

RESEARCH ON VARIANCE IN HR PRACTICES ACROSS COUNTRIES

It is not our intention to review the extensive literature on IHRM, but we refer to some work for illustrative purposes. In line with our ideas we will discuss studies showing variance in HR practices across countries, studies showing covariance between culture and HR practices, and studies showing interaction effects of culture, additionally the studies are situated at different levels of analysis.

The Cranet project addresses the issue of national differences in HR policies and practices across countries. The latest survey data from 2004 continue to indicate that variance in HR practices such as recruitment and selection methods, pay systems, and communication exists across different country contexts (Brewster *et al.*, 2007). Mayrhofer and Brewster (2005) concluded using Cranet data from a period of 15 years that there are still significant differences between European countries in the usage of HR practices. In the beginning of the 1990s European countries converged; however, between the mid-1990s and the end of the 1990s the heterogeneity of HR practices in Europe increased again.

Jackson (2002) addresses the question of whether the way value is attached to people manifesting and represented in HR policies and practices in organizations differs across countries. Results of an explorative study in seven countries indicate that cultural factors (like individualism vs collectivism), the level of industrial development of a country, and the nature of cultural interactions influence management perceptions of the value of people in organizations.

Based on studies described above, we can conclude that HRM practices, and possibly their impact, vary across countries. However, the majority of studies in the IHRM literature attribute the observed country differences ex post to cultural factors, but they do not make any distinction between cultural, institutional or structural explanations *a priori* (Aycan, 2005; Tayeb, 1994; Clark *et al.*, 1999). In the next section we will discuss some studies showing covariance between national culture and HR practices.

Papalexandris and Panayotopoulou (2004) investigated the relationship between nine dimensions of societal culture as revealed by the GLOBE study and HR practices gathered through the Cranet research project in 19 European countries. They found that the HR practice internal communication was most strongly related to societal culture (for example, ingroup collectivism is negatively related to all methods of upward and downward communication), and reward management practices were least related to societal culture. Looking at the results of a study comparing HR compensation practices in 24 countries, three datasets suggest that national culture provides an important explanation for variance in the utilization of different compensation practices in different countries (Schuler and Rogovsky, 1998). Newman and Nollen (1996) also investigated interactions between HR practices and cultures. In a study among European and Asian work units of one multinational company they concluded that business performance is better when management practices are congruent with national culture. For example, in collectivist cultures performance was higher in work units with less individual employee emphasis, whereas in individualist cultures performance was higher in work units where management emphasized employee contribution. The above three studies relied on nation as a proxy for measuring culture, without directly measuring national culture. More critical perspectives on the use of national culture as a proxy explanatory of IHRM, the methodological debates being encountered by industrial and organizational psychologists and HRM researchers as they pursue this kind of research, and the existing evidence base have been reviewed by Sparrow (2006a, b).

The discipline of IHRM research examines HR from a managerial perspective. Budhwar and Sparrow (2002) examined the influence of national culture on managerial thinking regarding the strategic management of human resources amongst a sample of 48 Indian and British HR specialists in the manufacturing sector. They concluded that although managerial thinking with regard to the importance of integrating HRM into business and corporate strategy and the devolution of HRM to line managers rather than to HR specialists is converging, there is still strong divergence in managerial thinking about HRM practices. Aycan *et al.* (2000) also investigated managerial beliefs and assumptions. In their model the sociocultural context (paternalism, power distance, fatalism, and loyalty toward community) influences HRM practices via managerial assumptions about the nature of their employees. Support for their model was found using managers in 10 countries. For example, in high power distance and paternalistic cultural contexts, managers assumed employee reactivity and this assumption resulted in lower job enrichment and empowerment.

The literature on relationships between culture and HRM practices in different countries and the literature on relationships between managerial perceptions in different cultures has investigated the effect of HR practices; however, what remains unclear is *how* employees in different cultures perceive and subsequently react to HR practices. Robert *et al.* (2000) investigated whether culture moderates the relationship between perceived management practices and individual level outcomes using single firm employee data from the United States, Mexico, Poland, and India. Empowerment was negatively associated with satisfaction in India, but positively associated in the other three samples from different countries. Continuous improvement was positively associated in all four samples.

The studies described above are situated at different levels of analysis (country, company, work unit, individual) suggesting that culture influences HR practices and outcomes at each of these different levels of analysis. Therefore, in the next section we will explain the impact of culture on HRM by using multilevel theories and research.

While multilevel theorizing has existed for decades, over the past 20 years an increased emphasis on multilevel examinations of phenomena has been observed in the organizational literature. We first examine two types of multilevel theories, and then examine some of the accepted concepts for aggregating measures of constructs from one level to represent constructs at another level.

MULTILEVEL THEORY AND CONCEPTS: CROSS-LEVEL VS MULTILEVEL MODELS

First, multilevel theories largely consist of cross-level and multilevel theories. Cross-level theories describe 'the relationship between independent and dependent variables at different levels' (Rousseau, 1985: 20). The most common use of cross-level models describes how higher level (e.g., group or organizational) factors impact lower level (individual) factors. Cross-level theories can differ in the nature of the predictions for these higher-to-lower level propositions. First, some cross-level theories propose homogeneity such that both the higher level characteristic and lower level characteristic are homogeneous within groups. Second, some cross-level theories suggest heterogeneity among the lower level phenomena such that there will be variance in reacting to a homogeneous higher level factor (Klein *et al.*, 1994).

Within the context of Hofstede's cultural propositions, while variance across individuals within countries is acknowledged, these differences seemed to be ignored. He states 'relatively small shifts of group means (i.e., country differences) ... nevertheless, may have considerable consequences for group behaviour and institutions' (1980: 72). In a cross-level sense, the proposition seems to be that within a country, the vast majority of people will, based on their cultural values, have similar reactions to particular HR practices.

Second, multilevel models 'specify patterns of relationships replicated across levels of analysis' (Rousseau, 1985: 22). In such models the relationships between independent and dependent variables generalizes across organizational entities. Again, in the contexts of IHRM research, such propositions would suggest that at the individual level, people with certain cultural values will react similarly to particular HRM practices, and that at the country level, the effectiveness of those practices will be dependent upon the mean level of cultural values of people within the country.

MODELS FOR AGGREGATION

Next we turn to examine how multilevel researchers have approached the process for making the case both theoretically and empirically for aggregating lower level measures to construct higher level measures of constructs.

Composition models

Chan (1998) presented a comprehensive overview of the various composition models that can be posited for multilevel phenomena, as well as their implications for measurement. First, an additive model consists of summing and/or averaging lower level scores into a unit level variable, regardless of the within-unit variance. This is predominantly what has been used in the vast majority of cross-cultural research as well as research examining differences in HRM practices across countries. With regard to HRM practices, this is not a problem because the focus is simply on examining whether practices are used differentially across countries without necessarily explaining the underlying causes of those differences. However, with regard to studies examining differences in cultural values, an additive model may be less appropriate.

Second, a direct consensus model averages lower level scores, but requires consensus or agreement on the within-unit scores. A consensus model assumes conceptually (and thus, must be demonstrated empirically) not just that there are mean differences across groups, but that there is little within-group variance in the construct. This seems much more applicable to research on country differences in culture, particularly when the goal is, as Hofstede does, to apply the aggregated score to the larger unit, and consequently assume no variance within the unit. We should note that this is not an explicit assumption within Hofstede's work, but is rather an implicit assumption based on the implications of his work. In fact, some studies that allegedly examine the impact of culture use country as a proxy for culture, attributing the scores found by Hofstede (1980a, b, 1990) on the cultural dimension to the individuals from a given country.

Third, a referent shift model is like a direct consensus model in that (a) it uses an aggregation of the lower level scores, (b) requires consensus or agreement on the within unit scores, but, instead of individuals responding as to their own psychological state, they are responding as to their perceptions of an unit (e.g. 'members of this department focus on customers'). Such a referent shift model has not been applicable to research on HRM practices across countries, but might be applicable to studying cultural differences across countries.

Fourth, a dispersion model focuses on the variance within the unit rather than the consensus within the unit (e.g. diversity). This is implicitly recognized within the cross cultural research stream which often pays lip service to the fact that cultures are not monolithic, yet continues to assume that variance within the culture is unimportant. For instance, Adler (2002a, b: 18–19) states 'Diversity exists both within and among cultures; however, within a single culture certain behaviors are favoured and others repressed. . .'.

Finally, a process model proposes similar relationships among composition variables at one level that are also present at other levels.

APPLYING MULTILEVEL CONCEPTS TO IHRM

The major problems with such research comparing HR practices across countries can be explained by looking at some of Hofstede's work with regard to country differences in culture. Gerhart and Fang (2005) provided an outstanding critique of Hofstede's (1980a, b, 1990) work on cultural differences across countries, and these issues are directly applicable to studies of HR practices. As noted before, the main issues revolve around mean differences, explained variance, and moderation.

Mean differences in HRM practices

Not unlike much of the research comparing the use of HRM practices across countries, Hofstede's (1980a, b, 1990) studies on country differences in culture were based on large samples of individuals reporting their values along the dimensions identified by Hofstede. His analyses consisted primarily of conducting significance tests for mean differences across countries, and then extrapolating from these mean differences to draw conclusions about the importance of culture. His 1980 study reported ANOVA results on eight items from his national culture scale, all of which revealed significant F-statistics. He concluded that 'we see that the country effect is highly significant (beyond the 0.001 level) in all eight cases' (1980: 71). From the significant F-statistics he justified aggregating responses within countries to form his measure of national culture.

Consistent with an additive model of composition, summing based on mean differences seems reasonably appropriate. If the only purpose in aggregating is to provide a score for each country, then additive models serve that purpose. It allows researchers to determine if, on average, countries differ in their approaches to HRM. For instance, Mayrhofer and Brewster (2005) discuss how the mean differences across European countries have converged and diverged over time. This is valuable information for those examining IHRM issues.

However, such a model says nothing about relationships with other variables (a process model) which seem to be the most important implication of Hofstede's work. Again, following on the work of Hofstede, many authors have extrapolated from mean differences in cultures (like Schuler and Rogovsky, 1998; Newman and Nollen, 1996) to conclude that certain HR practices might be more or less effective. However, if much variation in culture exists within a country, then such implications may be entirely unwarranted. As Gerhart and Fang noted (2005), for such an implication to be true, management discretion has to be substantially constrained and organizations must be forced to hire at random from the population (such that the sample hired will exhibit a mean culture score reasonably similar to the country score). If both these assumptions are not met, then a firm could hire individualistic employees within a collectivist culture, and still effectively use HR practices more consistent with individualism.

In addition, extrapolating the mean differences approach to IHRM, even when authors find mean differences in HR practices, could be due to a number of factors unrelated to country or culture. If different types of organizations are surveyed (e.g., small firms in one country and large firms in another country), or firms from different industries (more capital intensive firms in one country and less capital intensive firms in another country) the mean differences may be interesting, but due to factors other than country or culture.

Explained variance

While mean differences in culture or use of HR practices may be interesting, it may be overstated in terms of its importance. This stems from the fact that the F-statistics are highly influenced by sample size, and consequently, small mean differences can be significant with large samples (Gerhart and Fang, 2005). To assess adequately the importance of country as a predictor of culture measures or HR practices, a better measure would be the amount of variance explained by country. So, the important question is how much variance is explained by country? Usually the answer to this question is not reported in much of the culture research, nor in the HR practice research.

Gerhart and Fang (2005) specifically examined the culture research to assess the amount of variance in culture measures that are explained by country. With regard to Hofstede's original (1980a, b) work, they recalculated ICC (1, 1) values for each country using the ANOVA results reported by Hofstede. ICC (1, 1) serves as an index of variance explained and showed that across the eight items cited by Hofstede, country explained only between 1% and 12% of the variance, with a median of 2% and a mean of 4%.

They then went on to examine similar research results reported by Oyserman *et al.* (2002), England and Harpaz (1990), and Ruiz-Quintanilla and England (1996). From the reported statistics in each of these studies they were able to calculate the amount of variance explained by country and reported that these studies found this across the three studies to be 1.5–4.4%, 2.8%, and 3.8%, respectively.

Such an analysis has not been performed with regard to much of the IHRM literature, but it seems reasonable to assume that even when studies report significant mean differences across countries, that may not translate into considerable amounts of variance explained by countries.

It must be noted that explained variance moves us from an additive model to more of a consensus model. For a country to explain significant amounts of variance requires that there is much less variance within a country than across countries. Multilevel researchers often use ICC (1, 1) as a measure of the consensus (Shrout and Fleiss, 1979), which justifies aggregating lower level scores to a higher level construct. Again, much of the cultural literature seems to implicitly assume reasonably high levels of homogeneity, at least with regard to the implications that these researchers draw.

For example, in one of the most influential IHRM books, Dowling *et al.* (2008) state

> It is now generally recognized that culturally insensitive attitudes and behaviours stemming from ignorance of misguided beliefs ('my way is best' or 'what works at home will work here') not only are inappropriate but often cause business failure ... Activities such as hiring, promoting, rewarding and dismissal will be determined by the practices of the host country and are often based on a value system peculiar to that country's culture.
>
> The analyses by Gerhart and Fang (2005) suggest such implications are seriously flawed.

Moderation

Finally, even if country explains large amounts of the variance in HRM practices (or culture), such results may not imply that certain HRM practices are *inappropriate* or *ineffective* across different countries. Returning to the quote by Dowling and colleagues, note that the implication is that the inappropriate use of practices will result in 'business failure', i.e., pointing to an *outcome* of the practices. Previous models of composition have simply examined the differences between countries or variance explained by each country, but have not specifically addressed the relationship between either culture or practices on organizational outcomes.

What is implicit in the arguments underlying the mean differences or explained variance approaches is that the differential presence of practices *implies* differential outcomes for any practice use. In essence, this suggests that the country (or culture) moderates the relationship between HR practices and outcomes such as turnover or financial performance.

Wright and Nishii (2008) developed a cross-level model describing the relationship between HR practices and firm performance. While not all aspects of the model are relevant here, a few aspects can help to illustrate the moderating role of culture in the HR practices and performance relationship. In particular, they distinguish between intended HR practices actual HR practices, perceived HR practices, and employee reactions.

The intended HR practices represent the formal policies of the organization regarding the HR practices that should be implemented for a given job. These policies are often dictated by the HR department, and are assumed to be uniform for all holders of a given post. For instance, a firm may have a policy that among all engineers, the highest performers should receive a 9% merit increase, the average performers a 5% increase, and the low performers a 2% increase. The actual practices represent the true HR practices as they are implemented by the supervisor, manager, or other individual tasked with delivering those practices for that job. Again, for instance, a given manager of a group of engineers may decide to give merit increases of 6%, 5% and 4% to all the high-, average- and low-performing engineers in his department. The perceived practices consist of how employees perceive the practices that they and their immediate co-workers have experienced. Workers in the group discussed above may perceive that there is no pay for performance, or that any differences in pay are attributable to something other than performance. Finally, employee reactions to the practices refer to how individual employees respond affectively and behaviorally to the practices with which they perceive they are being managed.

The first linkage between intended practices and actual practices concerns implementation. Cultural orientations might influence the way managers implement new HR practices, since managers base their implementation partly on societal cultural assumptions (see studies by Budhwar and Sparrow, 2002; Aycan *et al.*, 2000). The linkage between the actual and the perceived HR practices represents the communication challenge. Individual employees perceive and interpret the HR and other organizational practices in their organization. Moreover, people's cultural backgrounds influence the way they collect, process, store, and use information from their environment (Shaw, 1990). Once people have processed the information, they will form some internal strategy for how they will react, and again cultural differences can play a moderating role (see study by Robert *et al.*, 2000).

In much of the OB literature these types of cultural interactions are tested by assigning a country-level score to individuals (an additive model) at the individual level of analysis (Tsui *et al.*, 2007); however, to the extent that individuals within a country can differ on cultural orientations, such an attribution may be inappropriate. In addition, according to a dispersion model, particularly this variance in cultural orientations within an organization in a certain country might have consequences as well.

CONCLUSION

This chapter has argued that existing research and theory in IHRM literature has overstated the role of national culture in the use of HR practices across countries, and the extent to which culture moderates the relationship between HR practices and outcomes. It has suggested a multilevel framework for examining these issues as a means of increasing our understanding of the phenomena we seek to explain. Such an analysis suggests two important future directions for IHRM research.

First, distinguishing among the concepts of mean differences, explained variance, and moderation as well as the implications of each concept will help to clarify the implications of any given study. Mean differences tell us whether or not average HRM practices differ across countries or organizational contexts, but does not necessarily tell us either the causes or consequences of those differences. Explained variance across countries tells us how much knowing the country can help us to predict the HRM system that might be in place, but again, does not tell us the causes or consequences of those differences. However, studies that examine multivariate correlates of those practices (e.g., not just country, but organizational, cultural, industry, institutional, etc.) can help us to understand the causes and consequences as well as the relative importance of each. Finally, studies on moderation (e.g., Robert *et al.*, 2000) can better help us to unwind the consequences of differences in HRM practices. It is only these latter studies that can truly inform practitioners regarding the potential effectiveness or appropriateness of different practices in different countries or cultures.

Second, there is a need to develop multilevel theories of IHRM. We can integrate Hofstede's ideas of the role of national culture in international management within a cross-level model describing the relationship between HR and performance (as suggested by Wright and Nishii, 2008).

Third, there is a need to conduct multilevel research to assess empirically the role of culture at national, organizational, and individual level simultaneously. As Gerhart and Fang (2005) noted, organizational differences may explain more variance than country differences in culture. Certainly, individual differences may explain more variance in reactions to HRM practice than organizational or country differences. Multilevel empirical research may help us to understand how firms across countries can select individuals that will be attracted to the firm's global HRM system, rather than simply trying to create customized HRM systems within each country.

REFERENCES

Adler, N.J. (2002a). Global managers: No longer men alone. *International Journal of Human Resource Management*, 13, 743–760.

Adler, N.J. (2002b). *International Dimensions of Organizational Behavior* (4th edn). Cincinnati, OH: South-Western.

Aycan, Z. (2005). The interplay between cultural and institutional/structural contingencies in human resource practices. *International Journal of Human Resource Management*, 16 (7), 1038–1119.

Aycan, Z., Kanungo, R.N., Mendonca, M., Yu, K., Deller, J., Stahl, G., and Khursid, A. (2000). Impact of culture on human resource management practices: A ten country comparison. *Applied Psychology: An international Review*, 49 (1), 192–220.

Brewster, C. (1999a). Different paradigms in strategic HRM: Questions raised by comparative research. In P. Wright, L. Dyer, J. Boudreau and G. Milkovich (eds), *Research in Personnel and HRM*. Supplement 4. Greenwich, CT: JAI Press.

Brewster, C. (1999b). Strategic human resource management: The value of different paradigms. *Management International Review*, 39 (3), 45–64.

Brewster, C. (2003). Human resource management in Europe. In S. Warner (ed.), *The International Encyclopaedia of Business and Management in Europe*, Third edition. London: Thomson Learning.

Brewster, C., and Suutari, V. (2005). Global HRM: Aspects of a research agenda. *Personnel Review*, 34 (1), 5–21.

Brewster, C., Sparrow, P.R., and Vernon, G (2007). *International Human Resource Management*. London: Chartered Institute of Personnel and Development.

Budhwar, P.S., and Sparrow, P.R. (2002). Strategic HRM through the cultural looking glass: Mapping the cognition of British and Indian managers. *Organization Studies*, 23 (4), 599–638.

Chan, D. (1998). Functional relations among constructs in the same content domain at different levels of analysis: A typology of composition models. *Journal of Applied Psychology*, 2, 234–246.

Clark, T., Gospel, H., and Montgomery, J. (1999). Running on the Spot? A review of twenty years of research on the management of human resources in comparative and international perspective. *International Journal of Human Resource Management*, 10 (3), 520–544.

Dowling, P.J., Festing, M. and Engle, A.D. (2008). *International Human Resource Management*, Fifth edition. London: Thomson Learning.

England, G.W., and Harpaz, I. (1990). How working is defined: National contexts and demographic and organizational role influences. *Journal of Organizational Behavior*, 11, 253–266.

Gerhart, B., and Fang, M. (2005). National culture and human resource management: Assumptions and evidence. *International Journal of Human Resource Management*, 16 (6), 971–986.

Hofstede, G (1980a). *Culture's Consequences: International Differences in Work-Related Values*. Beverly Hills, CA: Sage.

Hofstede, G. (1980b). Motivation, leadership and organization: Do American theories apply abroad? *Organizational Dynamics*, Summer, 42–63.

Hofstede, G., Neuijen B., Ohayv, D.D., and Sanders, G. (1990). Measuring organizational cultures: A qualitative and quantitative study across twenty cases. *Administrative Science Quarterly*, 35, 286–316.

Jackson, T. (2002). The management of people across cultures: Valuing people differently. *Human Resource Management*, 41 (4), 455–475.

Kerlinger, F.N. (1973). *Foundations of Behavioral Research* (2nd edn). London: Holt, Rinehart & Winston.

Klein, K.J., Dansereau, F., and Hall, R.J. (1994). Levels issues in theory development, data collection and analysis. *Academy of Management Review*, 19 (2), 195–229.

Mayrhofer, W., and Brewster, C. (2005). European human resource management: Researching developments over time. *Management Revue*, 16 (1), 36–62.

Newman, K.L., and Nollen, S.D. (1996). Culture and congruence: The fit between management practices and national culture. *Journal of International Business Studies*, 27 (4), 753–779.

Nunnaly, J.C., and Bernstein, I.H. (1994). *Psychometric Theory* (3rd edn). New York, NY: McGraw-Hill.

Oyserman D., Coon, H.M., and Kemmelmeier, M. (2002). Rethinking individualism and collectivism: Evaluation of theoretical assumptions and meta-analyses. *Psychological Bulletin*, 128, 3–72.

Papalexandris, N., and Panayotopoulou, L. (2004). Exploring the mutual interaction of societal culture and human resource management practices: Evidence from 19 countries. *Employee Relations*, 26 (5), 495–509.

Robert, C., Probst, T.M., Martocchio, J.J., Drasgow, F., and Lawler, J.J. (2000). Empowerment and continuous improvement in the United States, Mexico, Poland, and India: Predicting fit on the basis of the dimensions of power distance and individualism. *Journal of Applied Psychology*, 85 (5), 643–658.

Rousseau, D.M. (1985). Issues of level in organizational research: Multi-level and cross- level perspectives. *Research in Organizational Behavior*, 7, 1–37.

Ruiz-Quintanilla, S.A., and England G.W. (1996). How working is defined: Structure and stability. *Journal of Organizational Behavior*, 17, 515–40.

Schuler, R.S., and Rogovsky, N. (1998). Understanding compensation practice variations across firms: The impact of national culture. *Journal of International Business Studies*, 29 (1), 159–77.

Shaw, J.B. (1990). A cognitive categorization model for the study of intercultural management. *Academy of Management Review*, 15 (4), 626–645.

Shrout, P.E., and Fleiss, J.L. (1979). Intraclass correlations: Uses in assessing rater reliability. *Psychological Bulletin*, 86, 420–8.

Sparrow, P.R (2006a). International management: Key challenges for industrial and organizational psychology. In G. Hodginson and J.K. Ford (eds), *International Review of Industrial and Organizational Psychology*, Vol 21. London: John Wiley & Sons, pp. 189–266.

Sparrow, P.R. (2006b). Knowledge management in Global organizations. In G. Stahl and I. Björkman (eds), *Handbook of Research into International HRM*. London: Edward Elgar, pp. 113–138.

Tayeb, M. (1994). Organizations and national culture: Methodology considered. *Organization Studies*, 15 (3), 429–446.

Tsui, A.S., Nifadkar, S.S., and Yi Ou, A. (2007). Cross-national, cross-cultural organizational behavior research: Advances, gaps, and recommendations. *Journal of Management*, 33, 246–478.

Wright, P.M., and Nishii, L. (2008). Strategic HRM and organizational behavior: Integrating multiple levels of analysis. In D. Guest, J. Paauwe and P. Wright (eds), *Human Resource Management and Performance: Progress and Prospects*, Blackwell Publishing.

3

Comparative Analysis of HR

Wolfgang Mayrhofer and Astrid Reichel

Introduction

Comparative human resource management (CHRM) is closely connected with international HRM (IHRM) and its development. The 1980s and early 1990s represented the infant stages of IHRM research with the first signs of an emerging field of its own. For example, in 1987, the first IHRM conference was held in Singapore and the subsequent biannual gatherings have meanwhile established themselves as the primary worldwide forum for IHRM researchers. Likewise, the *International Journal of Human Resource Management* released its first volume in 1990 and has since become the leading outlet for IHRM research. In these early days, the general view about the major tasks for IHRM research arguably is best summarized by Laurent: "...The challenge faced by the infant field of international human resource management is to solve a multidimensional puzzle located at the crossroad of national and organizational culture" (Laurent, 1986: 101). There was major consensus that IHRM consisted of three broad streams as formulated by Dowling (1999):

1. Looking at individuals, especially expatriates, from a cross-cultural management perspective to better understand what happens when people leave their home country to work abroad. Research focusing on different elements of the expatriate cycle is typical for this area (e.g., Hays, 1974; Harvey, 1982; Lawton, 1984; Mendenhall, Dunbar, and Oddou, 1987).
2. Comparative HRM, looking at HRM in different countries. It describes and compares various elements of HRM in the light of national, cultural, and regional differences (e.g., Brewster and Tyson, 1991; Begin, 1992; Hegewisch and Brewster, 1993; Boxall, 1995).
3. Various aspects of HRM in companies operating across national borders. Specifically, HR-related problems of multinational companies (MNCs) are addressed (e.g., Heenan, 1975; Desatnick and Benneth, 1978; Tung, 1984; Doz and Prahalad, 1986; Lorange, 1986; Milliman and Glinow, 1990).

Handbook of International Human Resource Management. Edited by Paul R. Sparrow
© 2009 John Wiley & Sons, Ltd

Developments at the macro-level such as increasing economic interdependencies across national borders, globalization, and the rise in importance of MNCs have propelled the maturing of IHRM and its establishment as a segment of HRM in its own right. This is reflected, for example, in the growing number of participants in the IHRM conferences compared to its beginnings; the rising number of conference contributions in various divisions during the annual conference of the Academy of Management as possibly the leading worldwide forum of management researchers; the development of a book series dedicated to global HRM by a leading international publisher (see, for example, Sparrow *et al.*, 2004, as part of the global HRM series edited by Schuler, Jackson, Sparrow, and Poole); or the growth in number of issues of the *International Journal of Human Resource Management.*

Within IHRM, the different streams of research have gained momentum too, and developed their own universe. They expanded into distinct scientific discourses with separate streams of literature, for example handbooks, sometimes with little cross-referencing. Within these streams, specific workshops and communities of researchers deal with a wide variety of themes. Currently, there is some effort to redefine the scope and content of IHRM and a dispute prevails about the 'real' content of IHRM and the relative importance of the various streams within IHRM. Recent major works on IHRM emphasize different aspects, thus explicitly or implicitly (re) defining the field and the place of CHRM within it. For Stahl and Björkman (2006), comparative HRM is not a major perspective. Their handbook puts the emphasis on other aspects of IHRM such as various types of organizations, a wide variety of theoretical angles and the identification of core themes. In a similar vein, other major works see little or no significant role for CHRM. They put the emphasis on various types of organizations and contextualization (e.g., Schuler and Tarique, 2007, emphasizing MNEs and SMEs; Briscoe and Schuler, 2004, focusing on HR in MNCs and the importance of international context) or concentrate on working internationally and related core tasks (e.g., Dickmann *et al.*, 2008; Scullion and Linehan, 2005; Dowling *et al.*, 2008). Other contributions take an explicitly comparative angle and see CHRM as integral or core element of IHRM (e.g., Brewster *et al.*, 2007; Harzing and van Ruysseveldt, 2004; the global HRM series edited by Schuler, Jackson, Sparrow, and Poole).

Both the maturation of IHRM and the developments within CHRM lead the latter to a crossroads, triggering the need for some reflection – a task undertaken in this chapter. On the one hand, it is time to take stock, i.e., to look back to see what has been achieved over the past decades; on the other hand, looking ahead, we need to identify crucial issues to further develop the field as various future roads are now open.

A STRUCTURING TOOL FOR COMPARATIVE ANALYSIS OF HR

This chapter provides a brief look into the past and points towards major issues that have to be addressed in order to further develop the field. Using the comparative research cube (coreQB) as a structuring device, the chapter addresses major conditions for positive future development of the field. This includes content issues such as level of analysis, core themes and theoretical foundations as well as methodological and procedural requirement touching upon specifics of objective and interpretative approaches and respective methods in a comparative setting, and the practical organization of CHRM research. In addition, some suggestions concerning the positioning of IHRM in general and CHRM in particular within the overall array of scientific disciplines are made.

Comparative HR analyses implicitly or explicitly have to address at least four issues.

1. What the research looks at. This leads to the issue of the level and the units of analysis.
2. Why the comparison is conducted and how the results are explained. Behind this lies different types of reasoning in choosing the perspective of comparison, the concrete level and unit of analysis, and explaining results.
3. Thematic research topics, i.e., identifying core themes of the analysis.
4. Time, i.e., when to compare.

These issues are addressed in turn and combined into a structuring tool for comparative analysis of HR called coreQB (comparative research cube).

Level of analysis

Addressing the level of analysis implicitly relies on an actor-related view of CHRM research. Individual as well as collective actors of various kinds as well as the respective structures and processes are seen as central for HRM and its analysis. In order to group these actors, the degree of social complexity constitutes a useful main differentiation criterion. On the one hand, these actors are characterized by low social complexity. The emerging social relationships within these actors are either non-existent, as in the case of individuals, or have comparatively little complexity, e.g., in face-to-face groups. On the other hand, collective actors, such as countries or supranational units, show high social complexity. The internal environment of these collective actors is constituted by a complex fabric of social relationships.

Management research in general and comparative management research in particular can address various units of analysis located at different levels of social complexity. Figure 3.1 outlines the resulting continuum of possible levels of analysis and illustrates it with some concrete examples.

It demonstrates the broad variety of possible levels and related units of analysis, many of them spanning across different kinds of boundaries. The concrete choice chosen by researchers, as usual, is determined by the various factors influencing the 'context of discovery'. They include financial incentives by sponsoring agencies, economic or political relevance, personal interest of the researcher, assumed importance in the scientific discourse, or contribution to a political, ideological or personal agenda.

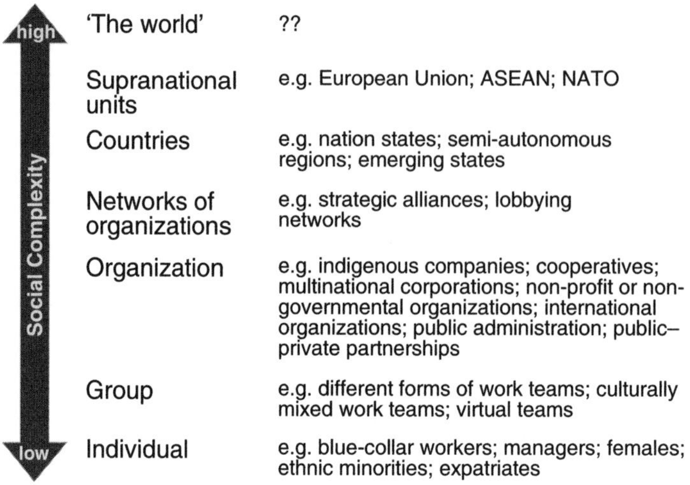

FIGURE 3.1 Levels and units of analysis in comparative HRM research.

Type of reasoning

Deciding on the level of analysis does not automatically imply a specific type of reasoning used in comparative HR research. For example, a country-comparative study of indigenous Belgian companies still leaves open the question of the comparative benchmark, i.e.:

◆ Which other companies will they be compared with, for example indigenous or MNC subsidiaries?
◆ What countries are involved; for example, the Netherlands, France, southern Sicily, Poland?

Implicit in the reasoning is the issue of why units of analysis are compared, what is looked at, and how results are to be explained. When this kind of grounding as a differentiation criterion is applied, two basic approaches for choosing criteria for comparison exist:

1. *Phenomenon-driven approaches.* These rely on criteria that are 'there', taken for granted, visible, and self-evident. There is no or only little grounding in good theory. The choice of the 'obvious' or 'natural' as well as ad-hoc or ex-post explanations dominate. Most country comparative studies can serve as an example for that approach. Comparing specific HR issues, such as knowledge transfer between full-time employed and volunteers in non-profit organizations across EU countries, in itself, does not automatically demand an explanation about the major focus of comparison, i.e., EU countries. The basic element of analysis and comparison – the country – is 'there', is taken for granted, visible and is self-evident.

Type of reasoning

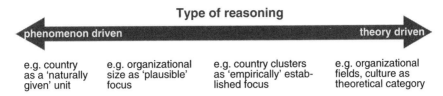

FIGURE 3.2 Type of reasoning in comparative HRM research.

2. *Theory-driven approaches.* The criteria for comparison are not 'there', but are gained from the specific theoretical perspective used for the analysis. There is explicit and firm grounding in good theory, a theoretically guided choice about the level of analysis and theory-based explanations of the findings. An example is the use of organizational fields as outlined by neo-institutionalist theories as the criterion for comparison. There are of course different views about what constitutes organizational fields and how they can empirically be analyzed (see, for example, Djelic and Quack, 2003). Hence, organizational fields do not exist *per se*, but have to be constructed in line with the chosen theoretical framework. Doing comparative HRM research along this line requires sound theoretical grounding as *conditio sine qua non* (a condition without which it could not be).

These two basic approaches form the endpoints of a continuum of different mixtures to be found in existing research of phenomenon and theory-driven reasoning (see Figure 3.2).

To be sure, the same standard of comparison may be the result of two very different types of reasoning. For example, using country as a standard of comparison can be the result of a more phenomenon driven argument building on the self-evidence of countries; or it can be the result of thorough theoretical reasoning, for example, along the lines of the national business systems approach emphasizing the importance of nation states for the specific configuration of institutional arrangements (Whitley, 1999).

Core themes

Based on the chosen unit(s) of analysis and the type of reasoning, comparative HR analysis then typically covers four major clusters of themes which are largely parallel with what we can find within HRM research in general. These themes are differentiated according to content–context dimensions, with HR content (such as typical HR practices) on the one end of the continuum and the external context of HR on the other end.

First, different HR practices are in the focus. Usually, they revolve around the core functions of HRM, i.e., resourcing, appraisal and development, rewarding, and communication. HR practices refer to those actions and instruments within the organizations that deal with HR tasks at an operative level.

Core themes

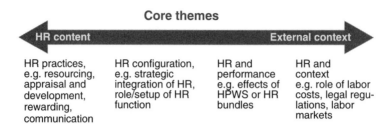

HR content			External context
HR practices, e.g. resourcing, appraisal and development, rewarding, communication	HR configuration, e.g. strategic integration of HR, role/setup of HR function	HR and performance e.g. effects of HPWS or HR bundles	HR and context e.g. role of labor costs, legal regulations, labor markets

FIGURE 3.3 Core themes in comparative HRM research.

Second, HR configuration addresses the structural setup of HR within the organization, its role in various organizational processes such as strategic decision making, or the role distribution between line management and HR specialists in conducting HR tasks.

Third, the link between HRM and performance is a core theme cluster with two facets. On the one hand, it addresses HR outcomes. In this respect, performance is 'intra-HR', i.e., tied to the result of HR processes. Examples include the quality of training measures or motivational effects of performance related pay. On the other hand, the link between HR measures as well as outcomes and organizational performance is addressed. Here the consequences of HR for various aspects of the internal organizational context such as overall organizational performance are addressed. Examples include effects of money spent on training and development on the financial performance of the organization or the effect of different career paths on the organizational ability to recruit rare talent.

Fourth, the external context and its effects for HRM are a major theme. This takes into account effects of different national or cultural contexts as well as the role that sector, industry or developments such as globalization play. Figure 3.3 presents the four core themes.

Embeddedness in time – a crucial dimension of CHRM

Like all other research, comparative analysis of HR is embedded in time. Time is a core dimension of research in social sciences but is often neglected or only implicitly acknowledged. In CHRM research it is absolutely crucial, since the comparative focus provokes time related questions. How was it in the past? How will it be in the future?

In addition, comparative research often has built-in time lags. The process of data gathering as well as data analysis frequently is time consuming as it most often involves different countries, large groups of geographically dispersed researchers and cultural as well as practical barriers of communicating with each other.

In terms of conceptual inclusion of time into the research design, there are two basic options:

On the one hand, cross-sectional 'snapshot' studies look at the chosen level and unit of analysis at a specific point or short period in time. For example, comparing the integration of HRM into the corporate strategy, devolvement of HRM to line managers and the perceived influence of national culture on HRM in a cross-national comparative context, i.e., the UK and India (Budhwar and Sparrow, 2002) provides researchers with a snapshot about the situation. However, crucial questions about how it has been in the past, how things develop over time and relative to each other have to remain unanswered.

On the other hand, longitudinal studies, sometimes even using a panel design, provide such insight. They follow the units of analysis over an extended period of time and can detect changes and trends within and between them. For example, Cranet, a network of researchers interested, among other things, in comparative HR analysis, has followed the developments of HR in European countries since 1990 and was able to take up the issues of convergence or divergence of HRM in Europe (Brewster *et al.*, 2004).

coreQB – comparative research cube

Figure 3.4 brings together the dimensions outlined above and opens up and structures a space within which comparative HR analysis can be located.

The comparative research cube is a diagnostic tool for past research efforts by locating emphases and neglected areas of CHRM as well as a compass for future research efforts. It is highly flexible as you can zoom in and out on specific segments of the dimensions and can be adapted to specific usages. As a tool for diagnosing deficits of research, it can be used to sort and systematize existing research efforts

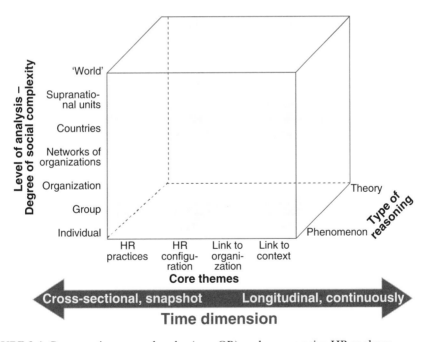

FIGURE 3.4 Comparative research cube (coreQB) and comparative HR analyses.

and results. It visualizes where there is a greater and less emphasis in research and where blind spots and uncharted territories exist. In a similar way, the research cube can also be used to support cumulative research demanding long-term efforts with future steps drawing on previous work and continuing, intensifying and enlarging it. Locating existing bodies of research in the research cube and outlining future efforts that follow the dictum of cumulative research allows a systematic research agenda to be built that is aware of major dimensions of CHRM research. The research cube can also be used as an instrument for detecting new research topics. It can be read as a three-dimensional version of a morphological table, i.e., a creativity tool helping researchers to creatively detect topics worth researching. For example, if one is interested in HR performance and its link to organizational performance, one can use the research cube by moving up and down the social complexity axis asking oneself what topics come up if one looks at performance issues at a higher complexity level, e.g., the EU, or at a lower level, e.g., virtual work teams. In addition, one can use the third dimension, type of reasoning, to 'play' with different criteria for comparison. In such a way, one systematically can screen the 'space of opportunities' to gain new and promising starting points for future research.

ANALYSIS OF PAST CHRM RESEARCH

Looking back at the work done in CHRM, this section uses the coreQB not only to identify major areas of work but also to identify aspects that have largely been ignored. Putting aside book publications and working papers, the analysis concentrates on articles published in journals that are listed in a major academic electronic database of the field, *EBSCO Business Source Premier*. This database provides full text access to more than 2,300 journals, including more than 1,100 peer-reviewed business publications.

An extensive research in all peer-reviewed articles published in the years from 1990 to 2005 was conducted, using a broad range of search terms. Each combination presented in the matrix in Table 3.1 was searched for in 'author-supplied keywords' as well as in 'abstract or author-supplied abstract'. In addition, the following two further criteria were used.

TABLE 3.1 Search terms for comparative HR research.

	HRM	*human resourc**	*personnel manage**
comparative	30 articles	21 new articles	0 new articles
cross cultural	1 new article	7 new articles	0 new articles
country compar*	0 new articles	1 new article	0 new articles
culture* compare*	0 new articles	0 new articles	0 new articles
intercultur*	0 new articles	3 new articles	0 new articles
cross nation*	3 new articles	3 new articles	0 new articles

First, articles had to be comparative in a geographical or cultural sense. Contrasts between units of analysis, e.g., organizations, in two or more different countries, are as well considered as comparisons between groups of countries formed by criteria such as geographical distance, cultural similarity, economic output, political power, historical bonds, etc. In contrast, the analysis did not include articles comparing different types of companies (e.g., public versus private) or regions of one country (e.g., states of the USA). Contributions that concentrate on HRM in multinational companies and are typically concerned with the transfer of practices and policies from home-country facilities to the host countries or with the management of expatriates were only included if they analyze two or more home and/or host countries.

Second, there was a focus on core areas of HRM, i.e., issues of organizing and configuring HR within the firm and major HR practices. The former includes, for example, the strategic role of HRM, HRM department characteristics and the assignment of HRM responsibilities among the HRM department and line managers. The latter basically comprises four typical sets of activities (see, for example, Losey *et al.*, 2005; Bach, 2005), i.e., employee resourcing (especially recruiting and selection), development (human capital investment), rewarding (non-monetary and monetary incentives), and communication (internal communication flow).

Using the keyword combinations and the additional two criteria, author-supplied abstracts were reviewed. If it was clear from the abstract that one or both of the two criteria were not met, the article was documented as a search finding, the reason for exclusion was noted and the article was not examined further. From those articles where the abstract suggested the two criteria to be fulfilled, the full version was examined in order to gain complete information on the four dimensions of the coreQB. Table 3.1 displays the number of articles found when applying this procedure.

Out of a total of 168 articles from 65 different peer-reviewed journals, 69 of them from 27 different journals (see Appendix 3.1 for the list of journals) fulfilled our two criteria. The vast majority (27) of these articles, identified as international comparative, were published in the *International Journal of Human Resource Management*, followed by *Human Resource Management* with seven, and *International Studies of Management and Organization* with four. The articles included fall into two broad categories:

1. Empirical studies examining differences and similarities in HRM in a comparative way.
2. Conceptual papers concerned with problems and opportunities that comparative research faces, and mostly present frameworks for comparative research in HRM.

Out of the 69 articles identified, 23 are conceptual, 7 are literature reviews and 39 are empirical. For those 39 empirical papers all dimensions of the research cube can be determined.

Table 3.2 sums up the results of the categorization of all empirical articles regarding the dimensions of coreQB.

TABLE 3.2 Categories of coreQB – results for empirical articles.

Dimension	Categories	Results
Units of Analysis	Supranational unit	0
	Country	10
	Networks of Organizations	0
	Organization	19
	Group	0
	Individual	10
Type of Reasoning	Phenomenon driven	37
	Theory driven	2
Core Theme	Comparison of one or more sets of HR practices and/or HR configuration (strategy, devolvement)	24
	Link to some kind of output like satisfaction, performance, commitment	8
	Other topics	7
Embeddedness in Time	Cross-sectional, snapshot	36
	Longitudinal, continuous	3

The analysis shows that there is a clear focus at the organizational level of analysis with the greatest single number of contributions looking at organizations. Both the individual and the country level follow. Virtually no contributions can be found at the level of groups, networks of organizations and supranational units.

In order to be categorized as theory driven, the choice of units of analysis has to be determined by *ex ante* theoretically defined criteria. Choosing the countries first and assuming differences in dependent variables due to different cultures or market forces, etc., still leaves the choice as phenomenon driven. The convenience of a phenomenon-driven approach is possibly one reason for the results obtained. Only two of the 39 empirical papers followed theoretical criteria when choosing their units of analysis. One used a model of the distribution of foreign direct investments among highly industrialized countries for choosing the countries to analyze. The other one compared a representative country for a modernist political system with one operating in a neo-traditional polity.

It is not surprising that when applying our selection criteria for comparative and HRM we find them as topics in the articles selected, but it is interesting that the vast majority of empirical papers (24 of 39) appears to define the comparison of a set of practices (from a different or the same group) as their core topic. 'How does recruiting/development/compensation or devolvement differ between companies in various countries' are very typical core questions. Only eight papers link HRM to some kind of outcome variable such as performance, satisfaction or commitment. Seven articles cover various other topics – e.g., myths behind HRM in different countries.

Most often, the empirical articles are cross-sectional and snapshot. Only three of the 39 empirical articles are longitudinal studies explicitly taking account of the embeddedness in time. The 30 non-empirical papers include seven literature reviews, four of them offering broad overviews on the subject of IHRM and all of them dating back 7 to 15 years; the other three overviews deal with very specific topics such as competency management in US and France. The remaining 23 papers propose different conceptual frameworks for research on international comparative HRM. Ten of them – the largest group – design rather broad frameworks integrating potential influencing factors on various levels, mostly with an emphasis on national contexts; seven articles restrict their models to specific geographic areas (e.g., Asia, German-speaking countries) or the comparison of specific regions (e.g., Eastern vs Western); four create frameworks with a rather specific perspective (e.g., systems perspective); and two are concerned with general problems and challenges of international comparative HRM. None of the conceptual articles explicitly includes the time dimension.

In spite of some limitations, such as the concentration on journal articles (i.e., disregarding books and edited volumes or the sometimes misleading keywords), a clear picture emerges. Over the past one and a half decades, CHRM has put a strong emphasis on organizations, followed by country and individuals. However, little is done at the group, network and supranational level. Most of CHRM research is almost exclusively phenomenon driven and there is very little solid theoretical foundation that is consistently used. In terms of core themes, there is an emphasis on HR practices and configurations and less focus on various outcome measures at the HR and organizational level. However, the work linked to various outcome variables has grown in recent times. The empirical studies are almost exclusively snapshot/cross-sectional and only very rarely longitudinal studies.

Looking through the articles included in this analysis, two further aspects beyond the dimensions in the coreQB emerge as side notes:

1. CHRM seems to be an ambiguous label. Many CHRM contributions are not explicitly labeled as such by the authors, but are 'hidden' beneath other keywords. This leads to a surprisingly small number of publications. This raises the question of why this is the case and whether researchers in this field, as well as the field itself, would not be better off in the long run if they promoted their core area of expertise more actively.
2. Contributions to CHRM are concentrated in very few journals. Out of 69 articles from 27 journals, 55% come from three journals, namely *IJHRM* (39%), *HRM* (US 10%) and *ISMO* (6%). Given the considerable rejection rates in these papers, this might encourage the founding of a new journal focusing exclusively on IHRM.

FUTURE DEVELOPMENT OF COMPARATIVE HRM RESEARCH

In this final section, based on developments in the broader societal and economic context, past literature in CHRM and current trends in the academic HR debate, we review four constraints that we believe presently limit the pace and scope of future development of comparative HR analysis:

1. Conceptual issues revolving around potential areas of interest, available theory and data as well as the object of research itself.
2. Research methodology in a comparative setting.
3. Specifics of the research process.
4. The political game of how to become an identifiable discourse within the scientific community.

Conceptual constraints

At the conceptual level, issues that have to be dealt with relate to the questions of what to look at, which theories and data to use, and how to clarify the object, i.e., CHRM.

The first issue concerns the need to concentrate on fruitful research themes. Traditionally, CHRM has been fascinated with looking at similarities and differences. When taking a national perspective and analyzing how HR issues are dealt with elsewhere, much of comparative HR analysis originally was of descriptive nature recording parallels and differences. However, the fascination of 'here we are different, here alike' slowly, but surely is fading – at least for those world regions such as Europe or North America where a substantial literature has emerged and is available in the global scientific discourse. While merely descriptive analyses showing commonalities and differences still have some value, they become increasingly limited in the well-researched regions of the world. To be sure, this is not the case for those regions of the world such as sub-Saharan Africa or parts of Asia where either little is known or where the locally available knowledge is not fed into the global scientific discourse. This can happen for a number of reasons such as lack of language skills that prohibit participation in the global scientific discourse, lack of monetary resources to conduct proper research or meet with fellow researchers, or political constraints when conducting research. The identification of fruitful research themes beyond the mere description of similarities and varieties is supported by the availability of reference points. Two such points can be identified:

1. Future research themes can come from the scientific discourse itself. Based on what has been done up to now, promising themes are identified. This supports the rigor component of research and increases the potential for cumulative work.
2. Themes can emerge from practical problems in the world of work. Such an approach emphasizes the relevance component. Potentially, it has greater societal effects. In addition, it allows access to specific types of grant money linked to specific themes deemed important by policy makers, practitioner foundations or science managers.

Both alternatives are not mutually exclusive, but mark different points of departure. For example, looking at the scientific discourse on European CHRM, the coreQB reveals a lack of research at the group, network of organizations and supranational level and comparatively little work based on good theory and longitudinal data.

Examples of starting points for future research based on this diagnosis of the scientific discourse include:

♦ an analysis of basic national HR indicators and their development over time in different parts of the EU/non-EU, for example, old EU-15, new EU-10+2 countries and future access countries;
♦ the use of institutional theories to define organizational fields and the application of these fields as measures for comparison, for example, between MNCs and indigenous companies; or
♦ setting up a longitudinal cohort study with an organizational panel and/or using existing panel data.

Employing practical problems as the point of departure and again looking at European CHRM, a number of core themes are widely debated among political and economical decision makers within the EU, for example European integration, economic performance at the national and organizational level, becoming a knowledge society or sustainability. For European CHRM, this could lead to future research such as:

♦ HR developmental routes of newer compared to older EU-member states;
♦ consequences of different patterns of opening up national labor markets for HR and organizational performance;
♦ comparing different institutional environments and their effects for HR practices to increase interdepartmental knowledge flow; or
♦ effects of different national regulations about environmental balance sheets on HR recruitment and compensation practices.

The second issue is the need to introduce more and better-elaborated theory. This is a general call in organization research and arguably is never wrong. However, in the case of CHRM this call seems to be especially justified. While it is part of the efforts for a better theoretical foundation of HRM overall, the specific comparative angle in CHRM requires adequate theoretical perspectives. Most of them explicitly take into account the time perspective and a developmental perspective, i.e., how current differences between units of analysis – most often countries – will develop in the future. Against this backdrop, three groups of theories can be differentiated:

1. *A focus on differences.* The theoretical arguments run along the broad line of pointing at crucial differences at the macro-level that lead to distinct differences at the level of organizations or individual behavior. Examples include arguments pointing toward varieties of capitalism (Hall and Soskice, 2001), national business systems (Whitley, 1999) or culture theories (Schwartz, 2004; House *et al.*, 2004).
2. *Convergence of global logics of capitalism.* This ultimately leads to similar approaches at the organizational level. Rational choice models (for their

applicability in HR see, e.g., Matiaske, 2004) are a major example for this type of argument.

3. *The world polity approach* (Meyer *et al.*, 1997). According to world polity theory, there is a worldwide replacement of traditional particularistic schemes through *universal* standards associated with modernity. Global myths such as rationality or equality exist that exert considerable influence on all kinds of actors, be it individual or collective, economic or political. However, these global myths do not lead to uniformity. On the contrary, due to specific local conditions there is a great variety of differences in how these global myths are actually realized.

The third issue is the need to make better use of existing datasets. Much of current CHRM research is small scale, rather ad hoc, heavily restrained in terms of resources, and limited to a comparatively small number of units of analysis, typically countries. This is no surprise since setting up one's own database is difficult if it goes beyond 'convenience samples'. One of these problems is a lack of local contacts in different countries that are interested and have the capacity and resources for data gathering and analysis.

However, a rarely used alternative to creating one's own pool of data is the exploitation of publicly available databases offering comparative data. While this is not possible for all research questions, there are a number of such sources providing raw data that can be used for a number of research purposes in CHRM. An important caveat is in place, however. When using existing databases, one has to adapt the research questions and operationalizations to the database, and not vice versa. Often, this imposes a severe restriction and is also perceived negatively in some publication outlets.

Looking at work in HRM in general and CHRM in particular, it seems that HRM research has great difficulties in agreeing on its 'object'. While there is some consensus on core functions of HRM such as recruitment and selection, training and development or compensation, there are a great variety of views on what HRM 'actually' is (see, for example, the different basic approaches pointed out by Legge, 2005). In addition, scanning through the research literature reveals that what is researched when HRM is the focus of interest varies widely. There is no established canon that researchers refer to when investigating various aspects of HRM. There are four reasons for this:

1. HRM is still a very young branch within the scientific disciplines. Compared to classical disciplines such as economics or psychology, business administration in general and HRM in particular have a relatively recent history. Hence, it is still regarded as a virtue to come up with a view on what HRM, IHRM or CHRM really are.
2. Business practice has a large influence on HRM and there is a need to connect to the language and thinking of practitioners. Hence, being up to date and fashionable is highly valued. For example, the current discussion about human capital management is partly due to rhetoric used in practitioner circles about personnel being the most valuable asset.

3. Being a young branch sometimes leads to clear leaps in the understanding of the field. For example, while it was quite controversial at one time whether the change from personnel to human resource management constituted more than a change in names, in hindsight it marks such a leap.

4. Perhaps most importantly, what HRM 'really' is inevitably varies across time and space. Even if one agrees on some basic functions of HRM, the concrete context matters a lot. For example, it is easy to see that HRM clearly has to be different in circumstances of the 1950s vs today; a labor surplus vs a labor shortage; a dictatorship vs a democracy; a centrally planned economy vs a free market economy; or an individualistic vs a collectivist culture.

This creates major problems for CHRM research. If there is, at best, moderate agreement about core aspects of HRM that should be researched, if there is little – if any – agreement about how to operationalize HRM and, worst of all, if HRM is a moving target constantly changing its shape due to the sometimes rapid development of our understanding and the differences due to various contexts, then crucial questions emerge:

- How can we compare what might be decisively different in national contexts in a snapshot/cross-sectional analysis?
- How do we cope with progress in our understanding of HRM in longitudinal research where the research 'object' changes due to different practices and concepts?
- What does this mean for cumulative research which requires a certain amount of joint understanding and established views?

While there are currently few answers to these questions, they constitute crucial aspects for the future development of the field.

Methodological constraints

Comparative HRM also is affected by three major methodological constraints typical for research conducted across national and/or cultural boundaries:

1. The use of theoretical frameworks across national and cultural boundaries is well debated (e.g., Hofstede, 1983a, b; Adler and Graham, 1989; Doktor *et al.*, 1991). Currently, this debate seems more or less closed. While some difficulties are acknowledged, the emerging tacit assumption behind much of the current work is: 'Let's assume it sufficiently works somehow.'

2. There is the problem of making sense of the local environment in a comparative setting which affects the design of the studies as well as the interpretation of the results. There has been considerable criticism of a 'safari research' (Peterson, 2001) type of approach in comparative research. Here researchers analyze countries or cultures about which they have little first-hand knowledge and very limited contact with local experts. In CHRM analysis, there has been a very positive move towards culturally mixed research teams or even large-scale

global research networks. Examples include the European Management Development Partnership (EMD) in the area of training and development (e.g.,
Mabey and Gooderham, 2005), and Cranet following the developments in
national HRM policies and practices around the globe (e.g., Brewster *et al.*,
2004).

3. The use of established analytical methods across national and cultural
   boundaries is a longstanding issue. In the objective paradigm with its focus on questionnaire-based data gathering, this is widely debated and 'quasi-
   solutions' are offered. Several translation–retranslation techniques supporting
   a preferably identical meaning of the questions provide a cornerstone within
   these approaches. There is less discussion in the interpretative paradigm,
   though, especially methods linked to the analysis of texts heavily depend on
   sufficient insight into the respective language.

The last issue should not be understated. In culturally mixed teams doing interpretative analysis a number of tricky issues evolve which cannot easily be solved and
where little established advice is available. We use the example of a current country and culture comparative project to illustrates the subtle interpretation issues
that arise. The 5C-project (cross-cultural contemporary careers collaboration) focuses on views of career concepts, career success, and career transitions of business
school graduates, nurses, and blue-collar workers from two different age cohorts in
11 countries selected according to Schwartz's framework of cultural values (Austria,
China, Costa Rica, Israel, Japan, Malaysia, Mexico, South Africa, USA, Spain, Serbia,
and Montenegro). Data gathering has been conducted through semistructured
face-to-face interviews in the local language with an average length of 45 minutes.
Overall, this lead to 195 fully transcribed interviews in seven languages. Using a vari-
ant of qualitative content analysis (Mayring, 2003), an open-coding process following the suggested paraphrasing ⇒ generalization ⇒ categorization procedure was
applied to the available texts. This resulted in core categories that denote crucial
dimensions of the analyzed concepts. This approach leads to a number of problems
typical for interpretative analysis in a comparative setting.

Such a comparative research process raises questions of when to change from
the local language to the *lingua franca* of the research group, i.e., English. The
team made a decision that at the level of generalizations and core categories
English language should be used. This resulted in enhanced comparability because
everybody can access core results from all countries and an increasing robustness
of the results because of concentration on main effects that 'survive' the translation. However, there is a price to pay for such a procedure. On the one hand, all
the 'classical' translation problems emerge. For example, if German interviewees
mention '*die Wirtschaft*' as a major influencing factor for emerging careers, an adequate translation is difficult. Of course, a number of words for '*Wirtschaft*' such
as economy, industry, commerce, or business world are available. However, in German language this also can be a reference to abstract, collective actors ('*Das ist
gut für die Wirtschaft*') or even have mythical–religious undertones ('*Wirtschaftswun-
der*'), both of which are much harder to get across the language barrier
satisfactorily.

At a very practical level, the citation of original interview passages in publications is a problem, too, since the global reach of many national languages is limited and many readers do not understand what is cited; however, a translation into English often reduces or even completely erases the specific flavor of the quotation. On the other hand, beyond classical translation problems a number of difficulties arise in the specific comparative research setting. There are potential losses of richness due to a different number and degree of language changes. In the project there can be no change from the original language, for example when US members of the team look at South African core categories; one language change, for example when Austrian researchers look at US core categories; or two language changes, for example when Malaysian members look at Spanish core categories formulated in English. In turn, this leads to losses of nuances, difficulties in consulting the original interview texts which sometimes is practically impossible for non-native speakers, for example in Japanese interviews, or a lack of density when discussing texts in culturally mixed interpretation groups or struggling for coding categories and interpretations.

Again, there are no easy solutions for such issues. Most certainly, suggestions how to handle these problems properly cannot come solely from within the IHRM or CHRM literatures. Rather, this provides a fruitful task for the discourses specializing on various methodologies within the interpretative paradigm.

Procedural constraints

At the level of organizing the research process in a CHRM setting, and with research team members coming from different countries and cultures, three major issues arise:

1. Problems in forming culturally mixed teams.
2. Continuous management of longstanding research teams across national and cultural boundaries.
3. Working together with 'strangers'.

First, with regard to the problem of forming culturally mixed research teams, there currently exists a lot of verbal and considerable material support for cross-border work from policy makers and grant agencies. For example, some initiatives within the EU framework such as the COST program within the 7th framework specifically support cross-border collaboration of researchers. In addition, the background of junior researchers changes significantly. Often, they have substantial experience in working in culturally mixed teams from the student level on. In addition, a number of high-ranking academic associations such as the European Group for Organization Studies (EGOS) or the Academy of Management regularly offer workshops supporting the collaboration of young academics from different countries.

Second, not only the formation, but also the continuous management of longstanding research teams across national and cultural boundaries is a potential problem. There is comparatively little experience available due to fragility of such teams. A number of typical problems arise during the life-course of such teams.

Longstanding teams often are quite diverse in terms of time spent in the academic system and preferences for scientific work. Hence, team members often have very different resources available which leads to greatly varying contributions. In turn, this raises questions of relative fairness and sharing of the work load. Beyond that, they often have different objectives for their academic work, e.g., heavily practitioner vs clearly science oriented. This regularly leads to sometimes fruitful, sometimes dysfunctional tensions within the research team when it comes to crucial crossroads about the future course of work. Over time, roles of key researchers change, too. Besides a certain amount of fluctuation, with some individuals dropping out and others joining the team, there is also a change in the role staying in the research team due to factors such as seniority, priorities, personal life circumstances or acceptance within the team. Within the academic environment where notions of equality are frequent and skepticism toward formal relations prevail, keeping a longstanding research team workable across national and cultural borders is not easy, given the dynamic of the internal roles.

Third, the need of working together with 'strangers' due to external incentive structures is a relatively recent phenomenon. As mentioned above, external incentive structures, such as EU framework programs, strongly support the formation of international teams and ongoing international collaboration. In order to gain access to such funds, teams are often partly formed around criteria that go beyond technical knowledge and established personal relationships, e.g., an emphasis on geographical location beyond expertise due to explicit or assumed criteria of grant agencies. As a result, there can be very little, if any, knowledge in advance of the prospective team members.

This leads to a number of potential pitfalls such as different explicit or implicit interest and agendas when joining the research projects, e.g., in terms of the degree of scientific interest, interest in building networks or learning from others without being able and/or willing to adequately give in return. Beyond the immediate effects on the research team itself, this also leads to an increasing commercialization and functionalization of research. When grant money becomes the major or sole driver for establishing an international research team, it is more than likely that the interest and the capacity for comparative work will fade once the money is gone. Hence, what one expects to see is the increasing emergence of 'business-like' research networks driven less by interest in the topic and joint views about how to tackle problems but by the interest in getting financed.

Political constraints

Finally, like every other scientific discourse, IHRM in general and CHRM in particular is embedded in a broader context. Among others, this context consists of the various scientific disciplines struggling not only to uncover more of the truth, but also competing for monetary and non-monetary resources enabling future research as well as the attention of fellow researchers in neighboring disciplines and the general public. In the current global context with its many voices, this requires substantial visibility, which seems to call for a consistent and attractive brand. To turn CHRM into such a brand, at least three steps are likely to be essential:

1. Developing a shared understanding of IHRM as the umbrella and backdrop for comparative research.
2. Establishing the label and consistent use of the term comparative research.
3. Increasing the visibility of IHRM and CHRM in top journals.

First, it is important to develop a shared understanding of IHRM as the umbrella under which IHRM researchers rally and that provides the backdrop against which comparative HR analyses are conducted. Of course, IHRM also covers other aspects beyond CHRM. As a concept and as a label, however, it can serve the purpose of common ground. This includes a moratorium on creative interpretations about what IHRM and CHRM 'really' is all about and what components it includes. At least for the time being, exploiting what already exists in terms of frameworks and definitions seems to be a good approach to create the basis for cumulative research efforts.

Second, the mere fact of flagging comparative studies as such is a step forward. As the brief literature review about CHRM has demonstrated, many significant contributions in the field – whether deliberate or not – fail to use CHRM as a label signifying their work. In building a recognizable brand, an established label and the consistent use of it is crucial.

Third, in the long run CHRM as a field in its own right can only survive if it becomes attractive for good – and, ideally, good young – researchers. A major step toward that is an increase in the visibility of IHRM and CHRM in top journals. This signals that the topic is substantial enough to get published in top journals, which again is a prerequisite for getting excellent people interested.

CONCLUSION

To conclude, much of what has been said about constraints for the future development of CHRM sounds strangely familiar:

◆ see to it that your theoretical basis is sound; carefully choose what you deal with in your research;
◆ make your life as easy as possible by building on the work of others and using available data;
◆ be as clear as possible about what you are actually looking at;
◆ get the methodology right and make sure you can work together with others of similar interest;
◆ make yourself heard in the concert – or is it the cacophony? – of academic voices.

All of this is not new, but has guided scientific research and development of disciplines and fields for a long time – CHRM is nevertheless well advised to stick to these lessons, too, if it wants a fruitful future development. This would seem particularly important at this point in time, given the increasing influence of comparative and institutional explanations within many areas of IHRM that were previously examined on a more contingent basis.

APPENDIX 3.1

Academy of Management Journal
Academy of Management Review
Applied Psychology: An International Review
ASEAN Economic Bulletin
Asia Pacific Business Review
Competitiveness Review
Cross Cultural Management
Employee Relations
Human Resource Development International
Human Resource Development Quarterly
Human Resource Management
Industrial Relations
Information & Software Technology
International Business Review
International Executive
International Journal of Human Resource Management
International Journal of Manpower
International Journal of Research in Marketing
International Journal of Training & Development
International Studies of Management & Organization
Journal of European Industrial Training
Journal of International Business Studies
Journal of Management Development
Journal of World Business
Organization Science
Organization Studies
Public Personnel Management

REFERENCES

Adler, N.J., and Graham, J.L. (1989). Cross-cultural interaction: The international comparison fallacy. *Journal of International Business Studies*, 20 (3), 515–537.

Bach, S. (2005). *Managing Human Resources: Personnel Management in Transition*. Oxford: Blackwell.

Begin, J.P. (1992). Comparative human resource management (HRM): A systems perspective. *International Journal of Human Resource Management*, 3, 379–408.

Boxall, P. (1995). Building the theory of comparative HRM. *Human Resource Management Journal*, 5 (5), 5–17.

Brewster, C., and Tyson, S. (eds) (1991). *International Comparisons in Human Resource Management*. London: Pitman.

Brewster, C., Mayrhofer, W., and Morley, M. (eds) (2004). *Human Resource Management in Europe. Evidence of Convergence?* Oxford: Elsevier/Butterworth-Heinemann.

Brewster, C., Sparrow, P.R., and Vernon, G (2007). *International Human Resource Management*. London: Chartered Institute of Personnel and Development.

Briscoe, D., and Schuler, R.S. (2004). *International Human Resource Management* (2nd edn). New York and London: Routledge.

Budhwar, P.S., and Sparrow, P.R (2002). Strategic HRM through the cultural looking glass: Mapping the cognition of British and Indian managers. *Organization Studies*, 23 (4), 599–638.

Desatnick, R.L., and Benneth, M.L. (1978). *Human Resources Management in the Multinational Company*. New York: Nichols.

Dickmann, M., Brewster, C., and Sparrow, P.R. (eds) (2008). *International Human Resource Management: A European Perspective*. London: Routledge.

Djelic, M.-L., and Quack, S. (eds) (2003). *Globalization and Institutions. Redefining the Rules of the Economic Game*. Cheltenham: Edward Elgar.

Doktor, R., Tung, R.L., and Glinow, M.A.v. (1991). Incorporating international dimensions in management theory building. *Academy of Management Review*, 16 (2), 259–261.

Dowling, P.J. (1999). Completing the puzzle: Issues in the development of the field of international human resource management. *Management International Review*, 39 (4), 27–43.

Dowling, P.J., Festing, M., and Engle, A.D. (2008). *International Human Resource Management*, Fifth edition. London: Thomson Learning.

Doz, Y.L., and Prahalad, C. (1986). Controlled variety: A challenge for human resource management in the MNC. *Human Resource Management*, 25 (1), 55–71.

Hall, P., and Soskice, D. (eds) (2001). *Varieties of Capitalism: The Institutional Foundations of Comparative Advantage*. Oxford: Oxford University Press.

Harvey, M. (1982). The other side of foreign assignments: Dealing with the repatriation dilemma. *Columbia Journal of World Business*, Spring, 53–59.

Harzing, A.-W., and van Ruysseveldt, J. (2004). *International Human Resource Management*. London: Sage.

Hays, R.D. (1974). Expatriate selection: Insuring success and avoiding failure. *Journal of International Business Studies*, 5, 25–37.

Heenan, D.A. (1975). *Multinational Management of Human Resources: A System Approach*. Austin, Texas: University of Texas.

Hegewisch, A., and Brewster, C. (eds). (1993). *European Developments in Human Resouurce Management*. London: Kogan Page.

Hofstede, G. (1983a). National cultures in four dimensions. *International Studies of Management and Organization*, 13 (2), 46–74.

Hofstede, G. (1983b). The cultural relativity of organizational practices and theories. *Journal of International Business Studies*, 14 (3), 75–89.

House, R.J., Hanges, P., Javidan, M., Dorfman, P, and Gupta, V. (2004). *Culture, Leadership and Organization: A GLOBE Study of 62 Societies*. Thousand Oaks, CA: Sage.

Laurent, A. (1986). The Cross-cultural puzzle of international human resource management. *Human Resource Management*, 25 (1), 91–102.

Lawton, M. (1984). Designing appropriate expatriate compensation systems. *Benefits International*, 13 (10), 1–7.

Legge, K. (2005). *Human Resource Management. Rhetorics and Realities*. Basingstoke: Palgrave Macmillan.

Lorange, P. (1986). Human resource management in multinational cooperative ventures. *Human Resource Management*, 23 (1), 133–148.

Losey, M., Meisinger, S., and Ulrich, D. (eds). (2005). *The Future of Human Resource Management*. Hoboken, NJ.: John Wiley & Sons.

Mabey, C., and Gooderham, P. (2005). The impact of management development on the organizational performance of European firms. *European Management Review*, 2 (2), 131–142.

Matiaske, W. (2004). Pourquoi pas? Rational choice as a basic theory of HRM. *Management Revue*, 15 (2), 249–263.

Mayring, P. (2003). Einführung in die qualitative Sozialforschung (Introduction to qualitative social research), Fifth edition. Weinheim: Beltz-UTB.

Mendenhall, M.E., Dunbar, E., and Oddou, G.R. (1987). Expatriate selection, training and career pathing: A review and critique. *Human Resource Management*, 26 (3), 331–345.

Meyer, J.W., Boli, J., Thomas, G.M., and Ramirez, F.O. (1997). World society and the nation-state. *The American Journal of Sociology*, 103 (1), 144–181.

Milliman, J.F., and Glinow, M.A.v. (1990). A life cycle approach to strategic international human resource management in MNCs. *Personnel and Human Resource Management* (Sup. 2), 21–35.

Peterson, M.F. (2001). International collaboration in organizational behavior research. *Journal of Organizational Behavior*, 22 (1), 59–81.

Schuler, R.S., and Tarique, I. (2007). International human resource management: A North American perspective, a thematic update and suggestions for future research. *International Journal of Human Resource Management*, 18 (5), 717–734.

Schwartz, S.H. (2004). Mapping and interpreting cultural differences around the world. In H. Vinken, J. Soeters, and P. Ester (eds), *Comparing Cultures, Dimensions of Culture in a Comparative Perspective*. Leiden: Brill, pp. 43–73.

Scullion, H., and Linehan, M. (2005). *International Human Resource Management*. London: Palgrave Macmillan.

Sparrow, P.R., Brewster, C., and Harris, H. (2004). *Globalizing Human Resource Management*. London: Routledge.

Stahl, G.K., and Bjorkman, I. (eds) (2006). *Handbook of Research in International Human Resource Management*. Cheltenham: Edward Elgar Publishing.

Tung, R.L. (1984). Strategic management of human resources in the multinational enterprise. *Human Resource Management*, 23 (2), 129–143.

Whitley, R. (1999). *Divergent Capitalisms: The Social Structuring and Change of Business Systems*. Oxford: Oxford University Press.

4

Contextual Influences on Cultural Research: Shifting Assumptions for New Workplace Realities

Sonja Sackmann

Introduction

The context of business has changed over the years due to technological, political, economic, and sociocultural developments. These changes have not only implications for the design of organizations and their management and, consequently, human resource management (HRM) but also for the kind of questions that need to be explored in research. In addition, these contextual factors have shaped conceptions of culture and assumptions about culture that have, in turn, influenced research methodologies and research questions. This chapter outlines theses changes, describes three different conceptualizations of culture with their contextual influences, underlying assumptions and methodological consequences, and explores their impact on the field of international HRM (IHRM) research. Future avenues for IHRM research are addressed, methodological issues outlined, and challenges discussed that researchers may face.

With rising internationalization and globalization of firms, culture is increasingly recognized as a phenomenon that has an impact on business and work realities of modern organizations. Neither practitioners nor researchers can therefore ignore addressing culture, especially when they examine HRM issues in the context of internationally or globally acting firms. In their extensive review of the field labeled IHRM, several authors criticize the fact that culture has been either ignored in IHRM research or insufficiently considered (e.g., Clark *et al.*, 1999, 2000; Keating and Thompson, 2004; Kiessling and Harvey, 2005; Schuler *et al.*, 2002). Of the 20,287 reviewed studies, 41% could not or did not offer an explanation for their results and those that did, assumed either cultural (22%), institutional factors

(19%) or a combination of both (Clark *et al.*, 2000; Kiessling and Harvey, 2005: 25). One of the reasons why culture is still frequently treated as a residual variable in IHRM research is seen in the difficulty of defining and operationalizing it. This is most likely why the Hofstede dimensions and scales of national culture are readily used in those IHRM studies that include "culture" *ex ante*. More recent work shows, however, that culture cannot necessarily be equated with nation and that it may be more complex and dynamic than the four or five dimensions that Hofstede (2003) suggests.

The frequent use of the term culture, its ubiquitous nature and the selective reference to the same publications suggest intuitively a common understanding of the concept of culture covering or blurring differences in meaning that exist in the literature. More than a century of research in the area of anthropology from which the concept was borrowed has not resulted in an agreed definition. A similar diversity can be found in the management literature (e.g., Sackmann, 1991). Since researchers and practitioners are also a "product" of the culture(s) into which they have been socialized, conceptualizations of culture and the methods of choice for researching it tend to be influenced by the dominant logic or paradigm of the respective fields. When employing the concept in research or practice it is, therefore, important to explicate the implied meanings of the concept and related assumptions and be aware of the implications that these may have for research.

Recent reviews of international cross-cultural management research (Boyacigiller *et al.*, 2004; Sackmann and Phillips, 2004; Sackmann *et al.*, 1997) have identified and described three streams of research that are guided by different assumptions, conceptions of culture and methods of researching it:

1. cross-national comparison,
2. intercultural interaction, and,
3. multiple cultures perspective.

The authors argue that the dominant logic and paradigm in researching culture has been guided by cross-national comparisons (CNC). This logic and paradigm has spilled over to research in the field of IHRM where most of the research is also conducted from and influenced by the CNC perspective (e.g., Clark *et al.*, 1999; Keating and Thompson, 2004; Kiessling and Harvey, 2005; Schuler *et al.*, 2002; Stahl and Bjorkman, 2006). The CNC stream of research is based on the assumption that culture is considered a correlate of, and basically equivalent to, nation.

The developments in the spheres of technology, communications, society, politics, and economics during the past decade (e.g., Castells, 2000, 2003, 2005) have impacted the ways in which:

- organizations are designed and function (e.g., Doz *et al.*, 2001; Mowshowitz, 2002),
- people relate to these organizations and to each other (e.g., Shimoni and Bergmann, 2006) and
- people deal with this newly emerging "flat" organizational reality (e.g., Friedman, 2005).

Given these contextual changes, Boyacigiller *et al.* (2004) and Sackmann and colleagues (1997, 2004) have argued that the assumption of culture equals nation may no longer be adequate either for research that attempts to identify culture or for managerial practice. The authors propose that the perspective of multiple cultures may be more appropriate to capture these contextual changes. The same applies to research in the field of IHRM.

In this chapter, I will first outline the current and emerging business realities that firms face today and are likely to face in the future. Then I describe the three different conceptualizations for culture and how different contexts have influenced these different logics including their underlying assumptions, views, and definitions. These, in turn, have shaped and will continue to shape the kind of research questions considered relevant in the field of IHRM research and, hence, have produced and will continue to produce different kinds of knowledge in the field. Additional avenues for research are explored on the basis of these three different conceptualizations of culture and challenges that will need to be addressed in future IHRM research.

CURRENT BUSINESS REALITIES AND THEIR IMPLICATIONS FOR HRM

The context in which organizations operate today and the way in which they are designed has drastically changed during the past 20 years due to a combination of driving forces. These can be located in the areas of technology, economics, politics, and the social fabric of societies. Technological developments in the computer and information sector have enabled and accelerated the process of internationalization and globalization for all kinds of organizations. Given the new technologies and communication media such as the World Wide Web, work can now occur 24 hours a day around the globe (O'Hara-Devereaux and Johansen, 1994) in teams whose members are no longer co-located (e.g., DiStefano and Maznevski, 2000; Marquardt, 2005). Organizational members can access information regardless of hierarchy, position or expertise. They have the world at their fingertips even if they are located in the remotest area. These developments have created new kinds of work and organizational arrangements (e.g., Davidow and Malone, 1992; Pauleen, 2003; Castells, 2000, 2005) that need to be taken into consideration when dealing with human resources. Mowshowitz (2002) goes even so far as to propose that resulting virtual organizations may displace the nation-state as the main wielder of authority and provider of social services.

Increasing internationalization and globalization have produced a global marketplace for organizations and consumers, providing ample opportunities for both but also fiercer competition for organizations. This new marketplace is highly dynamic with many uncertainties for organizations. They face multiple and diverse competitors, and rapid changes in all spheres of business. To stay competitive and deal with or even exploit these new opportunities, firms have to move beyond national boundaries using different kinds of strategies such as: initiating operations in foreign locations, creating international, multinational, global or metanational firms (e.g., Doz *et al.*, 2001), using virtual work arrangements or organizations (Mowshowitz, 2002);

acquiring or merging with firms that are already established in desirable markets; forming strategic alliances and networks (e.g., Castells, 2000, Vol. 1, 2005; Conlon and Giovagnoli, 1998; Davis, 2001) or offshoring work. As a result, world export of goods and services has substantially increased since the 1990s and interdependencies and complexity have grown dramatically around the globe.

In addition, the social fabric of societies has changed during the past few decades. Studies of social value changes (e.g., Inglehart, 1985, 1997, 2002; Inglehart and Baker, 2001; von Rosenstiel and Nerdinger, 2000) indicate that the meta-trends in Western societies point toward increasing individualism, egocentrism, and diversity in values and value sets. Sociologists' characterizations of today's societies and their future development range from multi option societies (Gross, 1994) based on egocentrism (Gross, 1999) to risk society (Beck, 2003) and network societies (Castells, 2000, Vol. 1) based on a "flat world" (Friedman, 2005) in which computer literacy and access to information is replacing hierarchical ranks. These new societies are typified by individualism, changing demographics, heterogeneity or diversity, uncertainty, ambiguity and complexity, and the level of the individual, the work group, the organization and society itself.

The resultant workforces are diverse in backgrounds, including different interests, experience, training, ethnicities, religions, gender, age, nationalities, identities, and personalities. The new organizational arrangements allow them to work in different parts of the world at different times, with different contractual arrangements, in multicountry projects staffed with multinational and multicultural teams. For example, at BrainLAB, a company that develops and distributes globally software and integrated medical solutions for minimally invasive therapies, the 500 employees at the Munich Headquarters come from 26 different nations – "Multiculti pur" (Koschik, 2003: 24). The firm believes that internal globalization can help them to deal successfully with the challenges that customers bring from different cultures around the world. These new work arrangements are well captured in the following description by an Eastman Kodak executive:

> ... people of many nationalities ... lead multicultural teams, work on multi-country projects, and travel monthly outside their home countries. In any year, they may work in Paris, Shanghai, Istanbul, Moscow, or Buenos Aires with colleagues from a different set of countries.
>
> —(Cited in Delano, 2000: 77).

These contextual changes that impact the way firms operate in order to stay competitive have also implications for HRM – the role it plays in and for a firm, the way the function is organized, the kinds of services it offers, and, as a consequence, the kind of research that needs to be undertaken. If human resource management (HRM) is broadly understood as encompassing 'all management decisions and actions that affect the nature of the relationship between the organization and the employees' (Beer *et al.*, 1984: 1) covering the three areas of (1) work relations (e.g., the way work is organized and the division of labor), (2) employment relations, and (3) industrial relations (e.g., Kiessling and Harvey, 2005), then researchers in the field of IHRM need to acknowledge these new realities and take them into consideration in their research endeavors.

These new realities not only require firms to adopt a dual logic and develop local responsiveness while acting globally (e.g., Rosenzweig, 2006), they also require an understanding and consideration of culture in the research design and researchers need to be aware of the potential implications of culture for their research. Most importantly, these new realities suggest that culture can no longer be equated with nation nor can one assume that individuals hold one single and stable nation-based identity.

To get a better grasp of this elusive concept culture, I now describe three different conceptions of culture found in the literature. All three have influenced researchers with regard to the questions they consider relevant for investigation, their choice of methodology and their awareness about the implications of the results.

THREE DIFFERENT CONCEPTIONS OF CULTURE[1] AND THEIR REPRESENTATION IN IHRM RESEARCH

Management as an applied science was, and still is, a search for answers to problems that organizations and managers face in a particular time. Three major streams of research have developed in the field of international cross-cultural management research (Boyacigiller et al., 2004; Sackmann et al., 1997)[2] and have come to impact research in the field of international human resource management (IHRM). Each one of these research approaches is based on a distinct conceptualization of culture. Each one emerged in a particular context with specific political, social, economic, and intellectual contexts underpinned by different assumptions, theories and methodological approaches. Given the specific spirit of the time, each of the three approaches resulted in, and still leads to, inquiry into different research questions using different models, methodologies, and research methods. Each of them provides different insights into the phenomenon of culture and, hence, issues related to and relevant for the field of IHRM. In the following section, I describe the three perspectives that Boyacigiller et al. (2004) have identified and discuss their relevance for research in the field of IHRM.

Table 4.1 provides an overview of the specific context that drove the emergence of the three streams of research, of the respective theories, assumptions and frameworks, and of the research foci and methods that are preferred in each perspective. It also identifies some key contributors and the major contributions to knowledge gleaned from each research stream with examples of IHRM research.

THE CROSS-NATIONAL COMPARISON PERSPECTIVE[3]

Major contextual driving forces for the emergence of the Cross-National Comparison (CNC) perspective were predominantly political, economic, and academic.

---

[1]The conceptions of culture in this section are adopted from Sackmann and Phillips, 2004.

[2]The reader who is interested in an in-depth discussion of the various facets of these three streams of research is referred to this literature.

[3]This section is taken from Sackmann and Phillips (2004) and is largely based on Nakiye Boyacigiller's contribution to Boyacigiller et al. (2004). The interested reader is referred to that text for a detailed exploration and discussion of the cross-national comparison perspective.

TABLE 4.1 Three different conceptualizations of culture.

		Perspective	
Key Issues	Cross-National Comparison (CNC)	Intercultural Interaction (ICI)	Multiple Cultures (MC)
Context Driving Emergence	*Political Force* • post WW II *Economic Forces* • rise of MNC focus on how to conduct business in other countries • management recognized as means for economic development • US practices → model for other nations *Academic Research Forces* • rise of comparative management: search for universal laws • no agreed-upon definition of culture • data collection difficult because of size • management research a Western (largely U.S.) enterprise *Current Reinforcers* • globalization • nation-state as key economic actor • conservative nature of academe	*Economic Forces* • changing balance of global economic power • dramatic increase in FDI (e.g., joint ventures, subsidiaries, MNCs)	*Political Forces* • melting of national boundaries • separatist movements • regional independence *Economic Forces* • increasing globalization • growing importance of regional economic zones • increasing strategic alliances within/across borders → "borderless" organizations *Technological Forces* • enhanced communications technology *Social Forces* • growing global movement of people → socialization into different cultures • increasing workforce diversity • attention to differences in identity

Theories/ Assump- tions/ Frame- works re. culture	• nation-state = "culture" • convergence thesis • search for universally applicable dimensions • cultural identity is given, single, immutable individual characteristic – source of identity is nation/passport	• culture is socially constructed • national culture/identity of critical importance • generalized national work culture • organizational culture may be salient *Emergent/Negotiated Culture Derived from:* – organization culture research – interpretive paradigm – anthropological theories – intercultural communication model	• culture is a collective, socially constructed phenomenon • organizations house multiplicity of cultures • individuals may identify with and/or hold membership in many cultures simultaneously • salience of any cultural group/identity is empirical question • frameworks are – a priori – empirically derived – emergent
Research Focus	• How do managerial attitudes and behaviors differ across nations? • How do national cultural differences affect individual, group, and firm performance? • How can the effect of cultural differences be controlled?	• What is the nature of bi-cultural interaction and its perceived impact on organizational life? • What are the characteristics and processes of culture forma- tion/evolution/emergence from bi-national interaction?	• Many cultures are present within organizations: – which become salient? – when/why/how does this occur? • How do the various cultures interact? • How do individuals deal with multiple identities? • What are implications for managerial practice?

(continued)

TABLE 4.1 (Continued)

Key Issues	Perspective		
	Cross-National Comparison (CNC)	Intercultural Interaction (ICI)	Multiple Cultures (MC)
Research Methods	• positivistic • universal categories of culture • dimensions operationalized as scales • large-scale quantitative studies	• interpretive • anthropological ethnography "thick" description • long-term case study • primarily qualitative analysis	• interpretive, inductive methodologies • seek "insider's view" • hybrid, multiple methods/multiple paradigms • field-based data collection

Key Contributors	• comparative management:
	  – Farmer and Richman, 1965
	  – Haire et al., 1966
	  – GLOBE Project, 1993/House et al., 1999/2004
	• dimensions and constructs
	  – Triandis, 1972
	  – Hofstede, 1980a (dominant)
	  – Schwartz, 1992
	  – Smith, Peterson, and Schwartz, 2002
	  – Trompenaars, 1993
	• Country clusters
	  – Ronen and Shenkar, 1985
		Kleinberg, 1989+
		Sumihara, 1992
		Brannen, 1994+
		Salk and Brannen, 2000+
			• sociologists focusing on reality, groups and subcultures (e.g., Berger and Luckmann, 1966)
			• industrial anthropologists focusing on subcultures (e.g., Trice and Beyer, 1993)
			• organizational researchers with focus on issues of:
			  – culture and subcultures in organizational settings (e.g., Martin and Siehl, 1983; contributors to Sackmann, 1997)
			  – organizational identity (e.g., contributors to Whetten and Godfrey, 1998)
			  – professional identity (e.g., Barley 1984)
			  – social psychologists studying social identity (e.g., Tajfel, 1981)

Contribution to Know- ledge re. Culture		

• culture is tractable
  – generalizations across national units
  – cultural clustering
• cross-national testing of organizational theories, HRM policies, processes, and management/HRM practices
• motivated development of cultural dimensions and categories
• finite set of cultural dimensions allows other disciplines to use cultural variables
• increasing knowledge of management practices beyond G-7
• awareness that context matters
  – restricted to national boundaries
	• importance of contextual analysis
	• process-orientation
	• emergent "negotiated" culture
	• attention to intercultural communication in the workplace
	• "thick descriptions" of cultural contexts
	
	bridge to multiple cultures perspective but still within national boundaries
		• reveals culture as socially-constructed
		• focuses on both sensemaking process/content, as well as practical applications
		• reveals nature of shared understandings
		• reveals multi-cultral dynamics in the chosen context of organizational life including paradoxes
		• appreciative of cultural differences and similarities
		• acknowledges complexity of organizations and of personal identity
		• recognizes conflicts in organizational and individual identities
		• possibilities of achieving synergies by building on similar cultural identities
		• identifies skills needed for work in a multi-cultural environment

(continued)

TABLE 4.1 (*Continued*)

Key Issues	Perspective		
	Cross-National Comparison (CNC)	*Intercultural Interaction (ICI)*	*Multiple Cultures (MC)*
Contributions to IHRM Knowledge	• Most IHRM studies have been conducted from this perspective (single country focus as well as comparative studies across countries): – knowledge about HR policies and functions in and across different countries – knowledge about organizational and management practices relevant for HR work in and across different countries	• Above-mentioned studies have implication for IHRM practices – so far this perspective and related research methodologies have been rarely applied • Research from this perspective could yield valuable insights about the adoption and adjustment of HRM policies and practices in different countries	• Above-mentioned studies have implication for IHRM practices, but this perspective has not yet been applied in IHRM research • Research from this perspective will yield valuable insights about the adoption and adjustment of HRM policies and practices at the group level reveals HR policies, strategies, instruments and practices as socially constructed • The notion of multiple identities has implications for the design and delivery of all HRM functions and instruments

Adapted from Tables 1–3 in Sackmann, S.A., and Phillips, M.E., Contextual influences on culture research: shifting assumptions for new workplace realities, *International Journal of Cross Cultural Management*, 2004, Vol 4 (3): 371–392.

World War II strengthened the United States as a nation and led to its dominance in the Western hemisphere – politically, economically, socially, as well as psychologically. Ample opportunities existed for US-based companies to expand into other countries and to export their models of success in these areas – and especially in the economic area – to support other nations in the development of their political, social and especially economic systems. US companies and their management acted as models for how to conduct business.

With the growing expansion of companies into other countries, research soon followed regarding management and economic development (Harbison and Myer, 1959; Farmer and Richman, 1965), how to conduct business with people in other countries (Haire *et al.*, 1966), or what kind of management and also HRM practices should be adopted from economically successful countries (e.g., Pascale and Athos, 1981). In this early work, culture *per se* was not an issue – it was equated with nation or country. The focus of research concentrated on identifying similarities and differences between nations and national systems including the determinants and consequences of observed differences. Culture as such was not specified and frequently treated as a residual factor. It was assumed that it accounted for the differences observed between nations but neither postulated before the research nor explained afterwards (Child, 1981). Critical issues such as the transferability of HRM practices into other nations were rarely considered or addressed, even though Hofstede (1980b) discussed the problems of transferring American theories of motivation, leadership, and organization to other countries. Furthermore, it was assumed that individuals strongly identify with their nation of birth or citizenship and that this national culture is the sole and all-embracing source for identification.

In the field of CNC, research was guided by the quest for identifying universally applicable dimensions that would help to understand differences and similarities between countries, assist managers to navigate in different countries while doing their work, or understand the superior practices of other nations and copy them. The finite set of dimensions identified by Hofstede (individualism–collectivism; masculinity–femininity; uncertainty avoidance, power distance) and related scales developed by Hofstede (1980a,[4] 2003) and colleagues (Confucianism) gave rise to many empirical studies (e.g., Søndergaard, 1994). These research efforts are rooted in the positivistic paradigm. The developed scales allow large-scale studies across nations such as cross-national testing of organizational theories, processes, and managerial practices including HRM practices and thus building an increasing knowledge base of and for management.

Most of the existing research in the field of IHRM is rooted in this CNC perspective and paradigm with the respective assumptions and consequences for investigation. While earlier studies seemed to be driven by a universalistic model trying to identify best HRM practices, more recent research efforts tend to acknowledge contextual/cultural differences that are, however, still equated with nation (Brewster, 2006). If culture is included in a study, it is predominantly considered equivalent to nation investigating HRM policies and/or practices in various countries and/or

---

[4]The original database of Hofstede was collected in 1968 with a US company model (IBM) as base line for comparison using a comparative perspective grounded in a positivist research paradigm.

comparing them with a different nation or across different countries (e.g., Brewster, 2006; Brewster and colleagues, 1991, 1992, 1994; Dowling *et al.*, 1999; Laurent, 1986; Sackmann and Elbe, 2000; von Glinow and Chung, 1989).

As a result of this kind of research, we know more about HR policies, HR practices as well as organizational and management practices relevant for HR work in different nations (for a comprehensive review see, e.g., Schuler *et al.*, 2004). Studies include HR policies and practices in and across Europe (Brewster, 2006; Brewster and Larsen, 1992; Brewster and Mayne, 1994), and to some extent the various HR functions and related challenges that are frequently addressed in the context of multinational firms. These include HR planning from a prescriptive perspective (e.g., Wong, 2000), staffing (e.g., Peterson *et al.*, 1996), training and development (e.g., Noble, 1997), and issues around expatriate assignments (e.g., Harvey and Novicevic, 2006; Thomas and Lazarova, 2006). In regard to assignment and performance appraisal, Schuler *et al.* (2004a) point out that research has failed to fully address the impact of the international dimension and most of the work seems to have a theoretical/normative focus.

The research conducted from a CNC perspective has generated valuable knowledge about organizational and management practices relevant for HRM such as leadership (e.g., Dorfman, 2004), motivation (e.g., Steers and Sanchez-Runde, 2002), socialization (e.g., Granrose, 1997), teamwork/team performance and group effectiveness (e.g., Gibson, 1999), job satisfaction (e.g., Redding, 1993), decision making (e.g., Mitchell *et al.*, 2000), negotiation and/or conflict resolution (e.g., Leung, 1997), and organizational citizenship behavior (e.g., Moorman and Blakely, 1995).

Despite these advancements in knowledge, research results gained from the CNC perspective are limited. While they give a broad overview of a particular issue, they are limited by the country/nation focus and the underlying assumptions that culture = nation and that it consists of a rather stable set of finite dimension. A national focus may still be relevant for certain issues such as HRM policies and HRM practices as influenced by a nation's jurisdiction, e.g., in the area of taxation and labor law. These set the framework for, for example, pay and reward systems, work time issues, worker representation, employee involvement, or collective bargaining. Recent research shows, however, that even legislation and a national framework may allow for variation at the practice level between organizations located in the same nation (e.g., Sackmann, forthcoming; Harzing and Sorge, 2003).

The availability and frequent use of the scales developed by Hofstede on the basis of his culture dimensions seem to have created a reality of their own suggesting and ensuring researchers that they capture all relevant issues of culture when including these scales as part of their measurement instruments in their research endeavor. Boyacigiller *et al.* (2004) point out that these kinds of studies have overemphasized a quantitative approach neglecting valuable insights about the dynamics and multifaceted nature of culture in the context of internationally and globally operating firms. The Globe Project (House *et al.*, 2004) on endorsed leadership both at the national and organizational level offers an extended framework of culture and used a multi-method approach in its inclusion of culture. The project's focus seeks to understand culture's influence on leadership and a variety of other variables related to organizational effectiveness. This comprehensive study including 170 researchers from 62 nations can be considered a step forward in a more comprehensive treatment of culture relevant in the context of internationally and globally acting firms.

If researchers are interested in studying issues of culture that become relevant in an increasingly multicultural world and in capturing the emerging cultural realities of today's and tomorrow's work life and organizations, they need to go beyond the CNC perspective. A comparison of nations yields insights about national differences that are not necessarily – and increasingly less likely – cultural differences. The differences resulting from a comparison of values and/or practices that are collected with questionnaires distributed to employees of an American-based firm may reveal cultural differences – the question remains, however, how to interpret these differences. Are they indicative of culture at the functional level (e.g., development vs sales), the organizational level (e.g., IBM culture vs Siemens culture), the regional level (e.g., US East Coast vs US West Coast), the national level (e.g., Hungary vs Germany (here the question remains if new or old Bundesländer)), or economic regions transcending national boundaries (e.g., southern Europe vs northern Europe, or Europe vs Asia)? If researchers are truly interested in cultural, not national, differences, the CNC perspective and its underlying assumptions will no longer be the most appropriate choice of a framework for studying culture in the field of international management and IHRM.

THE INTERCULTURAL INTERACTION PERSPECTIVE[5]

The balance of global economic power started to shift in the late 1970s. The US economy was faced with problems of competitiveness, especially with regard to products from Japan. This triggered a wave of research about the Japanese way of organizing and managing (e.g., Ouchi, 1981; Pascale and Athos, 1981) based on the assumption that the uniqueness of Japanese culture (= values) contributed to their economic success. In addition, the success of Japanese "transplants", the increasing number of multinationals, and the visible degree of difference between Americans or Europeans and the Japanese created the need for and triggered interest in a better understanding of how to interact with the Japanese.

Since it was assumed that the critical success factor was culture, anthropologically-trained scholars entered the domain of intercultural management research, giving rise to the stream of research that Boyacigiller and colleagues (2004) labeled "intercultural interaction". Scholars conducting research from that perspective focused on the level of the organization. Several of them had some command of the Japanese language and were also trained in anthropological research methods (e.g., Brannen, 1994; Kleinberg, 1989). With this intellectual background and professional training, different assumptions about culture were introduced. Although national culture was considered the relevant boundary and the fundamental source

---

[5]This section is largely based on Jill Kleinberg's contribution to Boyacigiller *et al.* (2004). The interested reader is referred to that text for a detailed exploration and discussion of the intercultural interaction perspective.

of identification, that identification was not seen as persistent in the face of cross-national interactions. Hence, culture was not considered a given as in CNC research. Instead, it was conceptualized as emergent and negotiated between interaction partners within the context of organizations. This negotiated and hence socially constructed cultural reality may lead to new forms of culture due to processes of recontextualization (Brannen *et al.*, 1999) or hybridization (Shimoni and Bergmann, 2006). While national culture and identity are considered important, other emergent cultures are acknowledged at the organizational and the workplace level.

These different assumptions about the nature of culture, the professional training of these scholars, and the interface problems at daily work led to different kinds of research questions as compared to CNC. Of interest are the nature of bi-cultural (= bi-national) interaction and its perceived impact on organizational life, as well as the characteristics and processes of culture formation at the organizational level, its evolution and emergence from bi-national interaction (e.g., Brannen, 1994; Brannen and Salk 2000; Kleinberg, 1989; Sumihara, 1992). We learn, for example, from Brannen's (1994) study of a US-based Japanese takeover firm about the process by which a "bi-cultural" culture evolves at the organizational level as particular issues trigger cultural negotiations among individuals. Other research foci reveal negotiated culture in a German–Japanese joint venture (e.g., Brannen and Salk, 2000), social identity processes in the joint venture (Salk and Shenkar, 2001), and cultural issues of multinational teams (Salk and Brannen, 2000).

Given these research questions and the anthropological background, the method of choice for investigation is ethnography. This methodology is rooted in the interpretive or constructivist paradigm (e.g., Guba and Lincoln, 1994) rendering thick description (Geertz, 1973) on the basis of qualitative data analyses.

The intercultural interaction perspective has demonstrated the importance of contextual analysis and process-orientation in cultural research for certain research questions. The resulting thick descriptions reveal insights about the emergence and negotiation of culture and shed light on issues of intercultural communication in the workplace that have implications for daily work life and HRM issues. Such a research perspective could, for example, shed light on processes of implementing, adopting, using, and recontextualizing HRM systems and instruments in different locations of an international or global firm.

The CNC and intercultural interaction perspectives are both, to some extent, a product of and facilitated by the time in which they emerged, addressing questions that were pressing to organizations and their management. In that respect, both perspectives can be considered complementary in research approach and knowledge generation, even though some of their underlying assumptions about culture are contradictory (e.g., a finite set of assumptions that are universally applicable; culture as a rather stable variable vs an emergent and negotiated phenomenon). Both consider the nation-state as the relevant boundary for their research and the related culture fundamental to interaction. While the CNC perspective considers only one culture as being relevant, the intercultural interaction perspective takes a bi-cultural focus that could be extended to multicultural interactions. With its basic assumptions about culture as a socially constructed, emergent, and negotiated phenomenon, the intercultural interaction perspective seems flexible enough to acknowledge the cultural dynamics of the new business and work context. To fully acknowledge this new context, a third perspective has emerged – the multiple cultures perspective.

THE MULTIPLE CULTURES PERSPECTIVE (MCP)

As a result of the changes in the spheres of technology, economics, and the social fabric of societies – the work context, and work life as described above – the context of organizations has become increasingly dynamic, complex, changing, and truly multicultural in nature. The formation of economic zones and regions,[6] regional movements in Central, Eastern and Western Europe as well as in Asia indicate that national boundaries may not or no longer be as important as in previous decades. Former nations such as the USSR, Yugoslavia, Czechoslovakia, or Koreas no longer exist. Regionally-based separatist movements such as in Ireland (religious differences), in Great Britain, in Spain and Belgium (ethnic differences), in Italy and Germany (regional differences based on different economic drivers) indicate that the meaning and impact of "nation-state" is declining, especially in regard to personal identity economic impact.

Studies that are appropriate for capturing the new multicultural work realities call for a conceptualization of culture that allows the surfacing and identification of the various facets of cultures that may impact work life and individual identities at a given point in time, and is also sensitive to cultural dynamics and resulting cultural complexities. The multiple cultures perspective (Sackmann and Phillips, 2002, 2004) offers this needed flexibility in identifying culture(s) in a manner relevant to researchers in the field of IHRM. It is based on a conception of culture that was influenced and driven by the changes in context described above and takes these developments explicitly into account. Similar to the ICI perspective, MCP is based on a conception of culture that considers culture a collective, socially-constructed phenomenon (Berger and Luckmann, 1966) that may exist or emerge whenever a set of basic assumptions or beliefs is commonly held by a group of people. MCP is based on the following definition of culture:

> The core of culture is composed of explicit and tacit assumptions or understandings commonly-held by a group of people; a particular configuration of assumptions/understandings is distinctive to the group; these assumptions/ understandings serve as guides to acceptable and unacceptable perceptions, thoughts, feelings and behaviors; they are learned and passed on to new members of the group through social interaction; culture is dynamic – it changes over time.
>
> —(Adapted from Kleinberg, 1989; Louis, 1983; Phillips, 1994; Sackmann, 1992, and Schein 1985)

---

[6]Examples are the extension of the EU from 15 to 27 member states, EFTA, NAFTA, Mercasor, ASEAN, CARICOM, Central American Common Market, and the Andean Group.

As a consequence, organizations may be home to and carriers of several cultures – a notion that has been long acknowledged in the disciplines of sociology (e.g., Barley, 1984) and industrial anthropology (Trice and Beyer, 1993). These cultures may be separate from each other, overlapping, superimposed or nested, or interacting with each other. Hence, a multiplicity of cultural groups may develop, existing and co-existing within organizational settings at the:

- sub-organizational level, e.g., functional domain (Sackmann, 1992), ethnicity (de Vries, 1997), role (Rusted, 1986), work group (Kleinberg, 1994), plant site (Bushe, 1988), tenure and hierarchy (Martin *et al.*, 1985);
- organizational level, e.g., single business (Ybema, 1997), conglomerate (Sackmann, 1991);
- trans-organizational level, e.g., profession/occupational group or guild (Barley, 1984; Bordinger-de-Uriarte and Valgeirsson, 2002; Kwantes and Boglarsky (2004), race, project-based network (Lawless, 1980), product-based network (Moon and Sproul, 2002), regional institution (Eberle, 1997); and,
- supra-organizational level, e.g., geographic region (Jang and Chung, 1997), economic region (Hickson, 1993), industry (Phillips, 1994), ideology/religion (Aktouf, 1989), Eastern/Western civilization (Westwood and Kirkbride, 1989).[7]

The multiple cultures perspective acknowledges that individuals may identify with and hold simultaneous membership in several cultural groups (e.g., Ashforth and Mael, 1989; Pratt, 1998). Hence, the emergence as well as the salience of a specific kind of cultural group is considered an empirical question. Group membership and salience may change with changing issues, such as those revealed by Dahler-Larsen (1997) in his analysis of a strike by flight attendants at SAS and Jones (2002) in his study of identity and identification processes in Brazil. Of research interest is the unraveling of the multiple cultures and their interplay within organizations at the organizational, group, and individual level, as well as discerning the kind of impact this may have on individuals, groups, and organizations (e.g., Irrmann, 2002).

For the identification of culture from this perspective, frameworks have been used in four different ways:

1. using *a priori* frameworks (e.g., Phillips *et al.*, 1992);
2. using categories of empirically derived frameworks (e.g., Schein, 1985; Phillips, 1994);
3. based on a framework developed on the basis of their research (e.g., Sackmann, 1991);
4. using ethnographic methods, as in intercultural interaction research, and employed emerging dimensions to characterize the particular setting (e.g., Eberle, 1997; Irrmann, 2002; Lerpold and Zander, 2002; Schumacher, 1997; Sharpe, 1997).

In contrast to CNC studies, research conducted from this perspective is based in the naturalistic or constructivist research paradigm (Brett *et al.*, 1997; Guba and

---

[7]For the respective empirical work see Sackmann and Phillips (2002) and Boyacigiller *et al.* (2004).

Lincoln, 1994) or may, as in recent work, combine different paradigms (e.g., Romani and Wästfeld, 2007). For example, Irrmann (2002) concludes from his case study of a cross-border merger that the dynamics of such a situation can be best understood by using contextually sensitive methodologies, thus moving beyond a comparison of cultural differences. Hence, a wide range of methodologies and methods are applied for data collection, data analysis, and representation of data. Research efforts may be based in different disciplines and usually apply a multidisciplinary perspective. They try to unravel the insiders' view, or "emic" perspective, to get to know the understandings and social constructions of those who are central actors in the selected research context, be it at a group, organizational or supra-organizational level. In this endeavor, research methodologies and methods have been specifically tailored to be most appropriate for the chosen research question. Examples are ethnographic and quasi-ethnographic methods based on participant observation (e.g., Sharpe, 1997), consensus analysis (e.g., Caulkins, 2004), semiotics (Brannen, 2002), in-depth interviews (e.g., Phillips, 1994), analysis of perceptions and interpretations of intercultural communication (Irrmann, 2002), versions of the repertory grid technique (Langan-Fox and Tan, 1997; Krafft, 1998), concept mapping and pattern matching (Burchell, 2002), action research (Globokar, 1997) and a combination of methods that allow for comparisons (Romani and Wästfeld, 2007).

One of the major contributions to knowledge of the multiple cultures perspective is the acknowledgment of the inherent complexities, contradictions and paradoxes of the developing context in which organizations operate, the related work and cultural realties, and their meanings for organizations, work groups and individuals. As such, reciprocal and mutually influencing dynamics are considered (Mendenhall *et al.*, 1998), conflicting, contradicting, or paradoxical findings are not excluded or fine-tuned in the results section; instead, they are a vital part of the discovery process that is also reported and discussed (e.g., see contributors to Sackmann, 1997). Research efforts have characterized different cultural contexts from their constructors' point of view (e.g., Irrmann, 2002; contributors to Sackmann, 1997), unraveled the nature of shared understandings (e.g., Romani and Wästfeld, 2007), and made recommendations for organizational, managerial, and individual practice (e.g., Globokar, 1997). In addition, notions of individual and organizational identity have been expanded to include multiple and partial identities that may not necessarily build up to a homogeneous all-inclusive identity. Instead, conflicts between partial identities are accepted as part of life. Skills have been identified that are needed to work, navigate, and manage in a multicultural environment (Sackmann, 2003). And, finally, the perspective's multidisciplinary, multimethod approach can also be considered a significant contribution to research methodology in general and to the conduct of inquiry.

IMPLICATIONS FOR RESEARCH IN THE FIELD OF IHRM

The above three considerations have several implications for the research agenda in the field of IHRM. First of all, research in this field needs to recognize and acknowledge the implications of the changing business context outlined earlier in the chapter. With these developments, national boundaries will maintain some importance for firms and hence for HRM. The melting of national boundaries in an increasingly global world and the response of firms creating new forms of organizational designs with an increasingly multicultural workforce pose additional new challenges for firms and, hence, new questions as well as challenges for researchers in the field of HRM. These are summarized in Table 4.2.

Implications for the cross-national comparison perspective

Research with an international and cross-national focus will continue to be important. This kind of research will continue; however, it should be based on an informed choice that the chosen boundaries are national and not necessarily cultural. Issues of interest to be explored are, for example, the influence of national legislation and institutional arrangements on HRM policies, HR instruments and HR practices and their comparison across nations. Reward and benefit systems are, for example, framed by opportunities and constraints of national taxation. Taxation issues, in turn, may influence the choice of country in which people are officially employed, as can be observed in the banking industry in Europe. National legislation provides a framework for worker representation and employee involvement which influences, for example, the composition of boards, the way HR functions operate, and the way decisions are made about the implementation of HR instruments such as remuneration, employee representation, employee surveys, etc. Given the specific institutional environment and the importance about knowledge in the area of labor law, HR positions in Germany are, for example, frequently filled by lawyers. This practice is less the case in other countries.

   Given this nation focus, the challenge for research conducted from this perspective is likely to reinforce the notion that culture equals nation. Even if researchers depart from a universalistic model and include context specific issues, contextual considerations in existing IHRM research are restricted to nation-specific HR policies and practices (e.g., Brewster, 2006). The challenge for researchers is therefore to start including different levels of analysis at the micro, meso, and macro level. The growing influence of decisions made at a regional economic level such as the EU, NAFTA, Mercasor or ASEAN requires taking a look at potential regional/institutional influences. In Europe, for example, an increasing amount of issues relevant for HR are starting to be discussed in Brussels, such as the free movement of labor across national boundaries, minimum pay, or issues of diversity. Of interest is also a better understanding if and when culture in addition to nation matters such as in the adoption and implementation of a new legislation at different levels (the economic region, the country, and the organizational level) – within the boundaries of an organization. Furthermore, a more systematic link to outcome measures would yield additional insights (e.g., Paauwe and Farndale, 2006).

   With regard to research methodology, it is important for researchers to understand the potentials, limitations, and challenges of large-scale studies. First of all, longitudinal studies with multiple data points are a major step forward so that findings and potential changes can be compared over time (e.g., Brewster and Larsen, 2000; Ingelhart, 1997). In the recent past, cross-regional, cross-national,

TABLE 4.2 Implications for research in the field of IHRM

	Cross-National Comparison (CNC)	Intercultural Interaction (ICI)	Multiple Cultures (MC)
Research Issues of Interest	• cross-national investigation of HRM policies and instruments that are framed by country-specific legislation • cross-national comparison of HRM policies, strategies, functions, instruments and practices in and across different nations conducting large-scale comparative studies • expand focus to economic regional differences and their influence on HR policies, strategies, instruments and practices (e.g., EU, NAFTA, ASEAN, etc.) • stronger link of HR policies/strategies/practices to outcome measures	• investigation of adaptation/recontextualization/hybridization of HR policies, strategies, instruments and practices in bi-national setting expanding research questions beyond bi-national focus to multiple culture focus • unravelinging the various dynamics relevant to HRM "thick descriptions" of cultural contexts • Bridge to multiple cultures perspective but still within national boundaries	• investigation of adaptation/recontextualization/hybridization of HR policies, strategies, instruments and practices with a multicultural lense • complexities and dynamics involved in setting and implementing HR policies/strategies/instruments/work in multinational/global firms • issues of designing and practicing HR functions in a multicultural context (e.g., selection, placement, socialization, training/development/career issues, employment contracts, pay and reward systems, labor relations, etc.) • issues in implementing/using HR instruments in multicultural organizations for individuals with multiple identities • identifying skills needed for work in a multicultural environment (employees, HR professionals) • linking observations to outcome measures

(continued)

TABLE 4.2 (Continued)

	Cross-National Comparison (CNC)	Intercultural Interaction (ICI)	Multiple Cultures (MC)
Challenges for Conducting Research	• reinforces perspective that culture = nation • reinforces assumption that HR policies, strategies and practices are nation specific • expanding research to a wider range of levels of analysis • acknowledging that individuals may have multiple culture • learning to understand when culture matters to HRM • lack of mid-range theories re: how culture influences HR policies/practices and vice versa • underlying influence of colonial theory • methodological issues related to the underlying research paradigm • longitudinal studies: multiple data points	• ethnographic studies • focus research questions beyond bi-national focus to move toward multiple culture focus • research boundaries are set by issue of investigation and not limited to national boundaries • multi-case studies to allow comparisons across settings • research time frame and costs • training in ethnographic perspective and skills • publication/career issues	• expand scope of research to address issues such as – impact on organization performance and effectiveness – address reciprocal influence more explicitly (cultural dynamics) • multi-case studies to allow comparisons across settings • multi-method approaches • move toward paradigm interplay – include different paradigms • research time frame and costs • training in different paradigms and methodologies and their appropriate use • publication/career issues

cross-institutional, and, in some cases, cross-disciplinary research projects were initiated, and first results have been presented. Examples are:

- The project Best Practices in International Human Resources Management initiated by Mary Ann von Glinow, including data from several different countries (e.g., Teagarden *et al.*, 1995; Geringer *et al.*, 2002; von Glinow *et al.*, 2002).
- CRANET, or the Cranfield Project, began in 1990 to survey human resource policies and practices with a standardized survey on a regular basis, and today includes 36 nations (e.g., Brewster *et al.*, 2000).
- Project GLOBE on global leadership and organizational effectiveness was started in 1993 by Robert House (GLOBE Project, 1993; House *et al.*, 1999 and 2004) and now includes researchers from 62 nations.
- The Language and Culture project, recently initiated by Anne-Will Harzing with a team of 32 researchers located in different nations, investigates the potential effects of the language of a questionnaire on respondents' answers (Harzing *et al.*, 2002).

Existing methodological critique should be critically reflected and taken into account when organizing and designing any cross-cultural research project (e.g., Søndergaard, 1994; Earley and Singh, 2000; Mayrhofer and Reichel, this volume Chapter 3).

Implications for the intercultural interaction perspective

As mentioned above, the intercultural interaction perspective is theoretically and methodologically flexible enough to be sensitive to the new contextual requirements.

Studies conducted from this perspective could give valuable insights into the processes of adaptation, recontextualization, and/or hybridization of HR policies, HR strategies and HR practices within the boundaries of an international, multinational or globally acting firm (e.g., Brannen, 2002; Shimoni and Bergmann, 2006). However, work from this perspective has continued to emphasize national culture as a fundamental framing for interaction (e.g., Irrmann, 2002) even though recent research indicates that this may not be the case in bi-national (e.g., Dahler-Larsen, 1997, Romani and Wästfeld, 2007) or multinational work situations (e.g., Lerpold and Zander, 2002). If research is conducted from this perspective, we recommend being aware of the existence and relevance of potentially additional cultural identities.

The strength and also challenge of this perspective resides in its methodology of choice. Ethnographies and single case studies yield rich data, however they are limited in their range of applicability. One step forward would be to compare data across several cases and hence contribute to a growing body of cross-cultural knowledge. The required training of researchers, the time required for the research process and publications present additional challenges for research conducted from this perspective. Similar to research conducted from the CNC perspective, intercultural interaction needs to move beyond its focus on national culture, and recognize or include ideas from the multiple cultures perspective.

Implications for the multiple culture perspective

HRM research conducted from the multiple culture perspective could also investigate processes of adaptation, recontextualization, and/or hybridization of HR policies, HR strategies, HR instruments, and HR practices. In this perspective, the focus is, however, not restricted to intercultural interactions with a bi-national focus. Of interest is, instead, the multiple culture interplay, its evolving dynamics, conflicts, paradoxes and reciprocal influences. More specifically, the current debate of integrating global and local considerations in HRM related issues (e.g., Rosenzweig, 2006) could be translated into a research project that explores the adoption process and changing nature of HR policies, strategies, instruments, and work practices as they are implemented and disseminated into the multiple culture context of a globally acting firm and adopted by organizational units in different parts of the company.

One of the major challenges of internationally and globally acting firms is the question how to maintain the company's culture across different locations around the globe. HRM policies, systems and practices that are aligned with the firm's culture can make a major contribution in this regard. Other questions of interest are how HRM functions such as acquisition, selection, placement, socialization, training and development, remuneration, labor relations, etc., need to be designed to meet the requirements of a multicultural workforce and be effective in a multiple culture context? And what are the specific needs of different cultural groupings regarding HRM issues? The identification of skills needed by employees and HRM professionals at different levels for working in a multicultural environment are also important issues (e.g., Sackmann, 2003). Furthermore, HR managers can take the role of a strategic business partner by assisting managers in the design of organizations that fit the needs of those talented people that the firm wants to retain.

A major challenge for research conducted from the multiple cultures perspective will be to address issues of effectiveness, performance, and practice at an organizational, group, and individual level. While a link between behavior at the various levels and organizational performance is frequently implied (e.g., Globokar, 1997; Schumacher, 1997), this linkage needs to be addressed more explicitly under consideration of reciprocal influences (e.g., Sackmann, 2006a, 2006b). In addition, the transfer of cultural categories derived from one context to an international cross-cultural management setting, especially to the individual level, needs to be critically examined. We also need to learn more about the impact of multiple cultures on individuals, groups and organizations, how these can be managed at their respective levels, and how HRM can respond appropriately to the issue of multiple identities. This may eventually expand and enrich available skills and practices in dealing with cultural diversity, cultural complexity, and intercultural encounters at the various levels (Sackmann et al., 2002; Sackmann, 2003). Research could reveal additional HR strategies and HR practices for how to assist in developing synergies between cultural groups, how to change attitudes toward these cultural differences from annoyance toward appreciation, and how an organization might capitalize on those differences.

Implications for the research process

The organization of research and the research process itself have also been subject to the changing realities as indicated above. The World Wide Web allows access to a huge amount of instant information on a worldwide basis regardless of time and physical location. It allows physically dispersed research teams to stay informed and connected in real or sequential time at low cost, and researchers can even collect questionnaire data online worldwide. Processes of internationalization and globalization have increasingly internationalized professional organizations and resulted in progressively more specialized conferences and workshops held in locations around the world with participants coming from different countries, institutions, and disciplines.

Hence, the research process of IHRM has internationalized and globalized as well. The projects mentioned above show that it has become logistically easier (but methodologically still difficult, see Mayrhofer and Reichel, this volume Chapter 3) for researchers around the world to connect and work together. Given the trend that academic institutions themselves internationalize and appreciate an internationally renowned faculty, and given competitive airline prices and the possibility of internet-based conference calls at virtually no cost, as well as politically initiated funding for multinational, multidisciplinary, and multi-institution projects (e.g., ERASMUS, EU-funded research projects, US Department of Education CIBER centers), the motivation for scholars to partner among educational institutions and get involved in multinational projects has increased, and is likely to increase further.

The way the above-mentioned projects are organized and represent themselves shows, however, that the challenge for future cross-nationally organized research teams is to raise awareness about the fact that culture can no longer be equated with nation. Recent studies on a multinational strategic alliance (Lerpold and Zander, 2002), bi-national joint venture (Brannen and Salk, 2000; Salk and Shenkar, 2001), acquisition (Irrmann, 2002), multinational team (Salk and Brannen, 2000), or cross-border collaboration (e.g., Romani and Wästfeld, 2007) as well as some results of the GLOBE project (House et al., 1999) and recent work on call-centers in India show that nation or national identification is neither the only nor the strongest source for identification in a multicultural workplace.

The use of nation-state and its unreflected equation with culture continues, therefore, to reinforce the assumption that national culture is a given, single, immutable and homogeneous characteristic of both an individual and the population of a country. Instead of perpetuating this assumption, researchers will need to critically examine their research question, and make conscious choices about their research methodology including data collection methods, research design (e.g., level(s) of analysis), as well as the most appropriate cultural context for their research project. They also will need to be simultaneously aware of other potentially existing cultural influences that may impact and confound their research results in the field of IHRM.

CONCLUSIONS

In prior work along with my colleagues, I have argued that the Zeitgeist – the specific context with its unique technological, communication, political, economic, and social characteristics – has shaped conceptions of culture in international cross-cultural management research and, hence, the way culture was and is studied (Boyacigiller *et al.*, 2004; Sackmann *et al.*, 1997; Sackmann and Phillips, 2004). In this chapter I have presented the three perspectives of culture that have developed over time due to different contexts. The exploration of the changes in our societies and business world during the past few decades suggests that some of the taken-for-granted assumptions that guided the work of researchers are no longer fully appropriate.

A critical review of the state of the field reveals that the dominant perspective in both international cross-cultural and IHRM research is the cross-national comparison perspective. However, given the changes in work and research contexts, the assumptions underlying the CNC perspective do not fully capture today's and, even more critically, tomorrow's business and work realities. I have outlined some of the contributions and challenges for IHRM research conducted from this perspective.

In an increasingly multicultural and diverse society, culture can no longer be implicitly defined as a substitute for nation, and members of such societies can no longer be assumed to identify solely or most strongly with their country of national origin or citizenship. These insights and potential misfits between researchers' assumptions and their subject of study should stimulate critical discussions among researchers in the field of IHRM. Hopefully, the discussions will lead to more informed choices and more appreciative inclusion of culture in the domain of IHRM research.

HRM research conducted from an intercultural interaction and multiple culture perspective will yield relevant and complementary information about HR policies, HR strategies, HR functions, and HR practices within the boundaries of inter- and multinational as well as globally acting firms. Both perspectives represent a paradigm shift since their emergence – and especially that of the MNC perspective – was shaped by the very changes in the new work context. Consequently, its underlying assumptions are a reflection of that diverse, heterogeneous, conflicting and even paradoxical work reality. Research conducted from this perspective will yield valuable insights into the complexities and dynamics of HRM issues in a multiple culture context regardless of national boundaries or passports.

Research from the MNC perspective is, however, challenging. It involves critical questioning of and reflection on the researchers' own assumptions about the concept of culture and about their research topic. It also involves conscious choices about the level of analysis and focus of study, at the same time being aware of other elements of the research context that might influence the data and data collection process. And it involves, as in the case of a multicultural research group, awareness of and attention to the group's own cultural biases and dynamics. The application of the multiple cultures perspective to the design and operation of multicultural research teams may yield rich and useful data and insights about issues relevant to HRM in the context of multiple cultural workplaces that are the reality of 21st-century organizations. Given these developing realities, it is questionable if the use of the term IHRM will continue to be appropriate. The new challenges will require investigating issues of HRM in the context of firms that act in an increasingly global business environment and do not restrict themselves to international issues.

REFERENCES

Aktouf, O. (1989). Corporate culture, the catholic ethic, and the spirit of capitalism: A Quebec experience. In B.A. Turner (ed.), *Organizational Symbolism*. Berlin: de Gruyter, pp. 43–80.

Ashforth, B.E., and Mael, F. (1989). Social identity in the organization. *Academy of Management Review*, 14 (1), 20–39.

Barley, S.R. (1984). *The professional, the semi-professional, and the machine: The social ramifications of computer-based imaging in radiology*. Unpublished doctoral dissertation, Sloan School of Management, Massachusetts Institute of Technology, Cambridge.

Beck, U. (2003). *Risikogesellschaft* (Risk Society). Frankfurt am Main: Suhrkamp.

Beer, M., Spector, B., Lawrence, P., Mills, D., and Walton, R. (1984). *Managing Human Assets*. New York, Free Press.

Berger, P.L., and Luckmann, T. (1966). *The Social Construction of Reality*. New York: Doubleday.

Bordinger-de-Uriarte, C., and Valgeirsson, G. (2002). *Cultural disconnects among the professional institutions of American journalism: Multicultural mandates mired in monocultural newsrooms*. Paper presented at the IIB Conference "Identifying Culture" *(June)*, Institute of International Business, Stockholm School of Economics, Stockholm, Sweden.

Boyacigiller, N.A., Kleinberg, M.J., Phillips, M.E., and Sackmann, S.A. (2004). Conceptualizing culture: Elucidating the streams of research in international cross-cultural management. In B.J. Punnett and O. Shenkar (eds), *Handbook of International Management Research* (2nd edn). Ann Arbor: University of Michigan Press, pp. 99–167.

Brannen, M.Y. (1994). *Your next boss is Japanese: Negotiating cultural change at a Western Massachusetts paper plant*. Unpublished doctoral dissertation, University of Massachusetts, Amherst.

Brannen, M.Y. (2002). *When Mickey loses face: Recontextualization and the semiotics of internationalizing Walt Disney*. Paper presented at the IIB Conference 'Identifying Culture' (June), Institute of International Business, Stockholm School of Economics, Stockholm, Sweden.

Brannen, M.Y., and Salk, J. (2000). Partnering across borders: Negotiating organizational culture in a German–Japanese joint venture. *Human Relations*, 53 (4), 451–487.

Brannen, M.Y., Liker, J.K., and Fruin, W.M. (1999). *Recontextualization and Factory-to-Factory Knowledge Transfer from Japan to the United States. The Case of NSK*. New York and Oxford: Oxford University Press.

Brett, J.M., Tinsley, C.H., Janssens, M., Barsness, Z.I., and Lytle, A.L. (1997). New approaches to the study of culture in industrial/organizational psychology. In P.C. Earley and M. Erez (eds), *New Perspectives on International/Industrial Organizational Psychology*. San Francisco: New Lexington Press.

Brewster, C. (2006). Comparing HRM policies and practices across geographical borders. In G.K. Stahl and I. Björkman (eds), *Handbook of Research in International Human Resource Management*. Cheltenham: Edward Elgar, pp. 68–90.

Brewster, C., and Hogwash, A. (1994). *Policy and Practice in European Human Resource Management*. London: Routledge.

Brewster, C., and Larsen, H.H. (1992). Human resource management in Europe: Evidence from ten countries. *International Journal of Human Resource Management*, 3 (3), 409–434.

Brewster, C., and Larsen, H.H. (2000). *Human Resource Management in Northern Europe*, Oxford: Blackwell.

Brewster, C., and Mayne, L. (1994). The Changing Relationship between Personnel and the Line: The European Dimension. *Report to the Institute of Personnel and Development*, Wimbledon: IPD.

Brewster, C., and Tyson, S. (eds) (1991). *International Comparisons in Human Resource Management*. London: Pitman.

Brewster, C., Communal, C., Farndale, E., Hegewisch, A., Johnson, G., and van Ommeren, J. (2000). *HR Health Check: Benchmarking HRM Practices Across UK and Europe*. Upper Saddle River, NJ: Prentice Hall.

Burchell, R.N. (2002). *Concept mapping and pattern matching as a means of organisational culture analysis*. Paper presented at the IIB Conference 'Identifying Culture' (June), Institute of International Business, Stockholm School of Economics, Stockholm, Sweden.

Bushe, G.R. (1988). Cultural contradictions of statistical process control in American manufacturing organizations. *Journal of Management*, 14 (1), 19–31.

Castells, M. (2000). *The Rise of the Network Society*. Oxford, MA: Blackwell.

Castells, M. (2003). *Power of Identity*. (2nd ed.). Oxford, MA: Blackwell.

Castells, M. (2005). *New Network Society: A Cross-Cultural Perspective*. Cheltenham: Edward Elgar.

Caulkins, D.D. (2004). Identifying culture as a threshold of shared knowledge: A consensus analysis method. *International Journal of Cross Cultural Management*, 4 (3), 317–333.

Child, J. (1981). Culture, contingency and capitalism at the cross-national study of organizations. In L.L. Cummings and B.M. Shaw (eds), *Research in Organizational Behavior* (Vol. 3). Greenwich, CT: JAI Press, pp. 303–356.

Clark, T., Gospel, H., and Montgomery, J. (1999). Running on the spot? A review of twenty years of research on the management of human resources in comparative and international perspective. *International Journal of Human Resource Management*, 10 (3), 520–544.

Clark, T., Grant, D., and Heijltjes, M. (2000). Researching comparative and international human resource management. *International Studies of Management and Organization*, 29 (4), 6–23.

Conlon, J.K., and Giovagnoli, M. (1998). *The Power of Two: How Companies of All Sizes Can Build Alliance Networks that Generate Business Opportunities*. San Francisco: Jossey-Bass.

Dahler-Larsen, P. (1997). Organizational identity as a 'crowded category': A case of multiple and quickly shifting 'we' typifications. In S.A. Sackmann (ed.), *Cultural Complexity in Organizations: Inherent Contrasts and Contradictions*. Thousand Oaks, CA: Sage. pp. 367–389.

Davidow, W.H., and Malone, M.S. (1992). *The Virtual Corporation: Structuring and Revitalizing the Corporation for the 21st Century*. New York: Harper Collins.

Davis, S.I. (2001). *Bank Mergers: Lessons for the Future*. New York: Palgrave.

de Vries, S. (1997). Ethnic diversity in organizations: A Dutch experience. In S.A. Sackmann (ed.), *Cultural Complexity in Organizations: Inherent Contrasts and Contradictions*. Newbury Park, CA: Sage, pp. 297–314.

Delano, J. (2000). Executive commentary (to J.S. Osland and A. Bird), Beyond sophisticated stereotyping: Cultural sensemaking in context. *Academy of Management Executive*, 14 (1), 77–78.

DiStefano, J.J., and Maznevski, M.L. (2000). Creating value with diverse teams in global management. *Organizational Dynamics*, 29 (1), 45–63.

Dorfman, P.W. (2004). International and cross-cultural leadership research. In B.J. Punnett and O. Shankar (eds), *Handbook for International Management Research*, Ann Arbor: The University of Michigan Press, pp. 265–355.

Dowling, P.J., Welch, D.E., and Schuler, R.S. (1999). *International Human Resource Management*. Cincinnati, OH: South-Western.

Doz, Y.L., Santos, J., and Williamson, P. (2001). *From Global to Metanational*. Boston: Harvard Business School Press.

Earley, P.C., and Singh, H. (eds) (2000). *Innovations in International and Cross-Cultural Management*. Thousand Oaks, CA: Sage.

Eberle, T.S. (1997). Cultural contrasts in a democratic nonprofit organization: The case of a Swiss reading society. In S.A. Sackmann (ed.), *Cultural Complexity in Organizations: Inherent Contrasts and Contradictions*, Thousand Oaks, CA: Sage, pp. 133–159.

Farmer, R.N., and Richman, B.N. (1965). *Comparative Management and Economic Progress*. Homewood, IL: Irwin.

Friedman, T.L. (2005) *The World is Flat*. New York: Farrat, Straus & Giroux.

Geertz, C. (1973). *The Interpretation of Cultures*. New York: Basic Books.

Geringer, J.M., Frayne, C.A., and Milliman, J.F. (2002). In search of 'best practices' in international human resource management: Research design and methodology. *Human Resource Management*, 41 (1), 5–30.

Gibson, C.B. (1999). Do they do what they believe they can?: Group efficacy and group effectiveness across tasks and cultures. *Academy of Management Journal*, 42 (2), 138–152.

GLOBE Project (Global Leadership and Organizational Behavior Effectiveness Research Project) (1993). Haskayne School of Business, University of Calgary, Calgary, Alberta, Canada, www.ucalgary.ca/mg/GLOBE/Public, July 1, 2004.

Globokar, T. (1997). Eastern Europe meets West: An empirical study on French management in a Slovenian plant. In S.A. Sackmann (ed.), *Cultural Complexity in Organizations: Inherent Contrasts and Contradictions*. Thousand Oaks, CA: Sage, pp. 72–86.

Granrose, C.S. (1997). Cross-cultural socialization of Asian employees in U.S. organizations. In C.S. Granrose and S. Oskamp (eds), *Cross-Cultural Work Groups*. Thousand Oaks, CA: Sage Publications, pp. 61–89.

Gross, P. (1994). *Die Multioptionsgesellschaft* (The multi option society). Frankfurt am Main: Suhrkamp.

Gross, P. (1999). *Ich-Jagd im Unabhängigkeitsjahrhundert* (Ego-chase in the century of independence) (2nd edn). Frankfurt am Main: Suhrkamp.

Guba, E.G., and Lincoln, Y.S. (1994). Competing paradigms in qualitative research. In N.K. Denzing and Y.S. Lincoln (eds), *Handbook of Qualitative Research*. Newbury Park: Sage, pp. 105–117.

Haire, M., Ghiselli, E.E., and Porter, L. (1966). *Managerial Thinking: An International Study*. New York: John Wiley & Sons, Inc.

Harbison, F., and Myers, C.A. (1959). *Management in the Industrial World: An International Analysis*. New York: McGraw-Hill.

Harvey, M., and Novicevic, M.M. (2006). The evolution from repatriation of managers in MNE's to 'patriation' in global organizations. In G.K. Stahl and I. Björkman (eds), *Handbook of Research in International Human Resource Management*, Cheltenham: Edward Elgar, pp. 323–343.

Harzing, A.-W., Maznevski, M., Castro, F.B., Feely, A., Fischlmayr, I., Karlsson, C., Liberman Yaconi, L., Kong Low, J.C., Myloni, B., Romani, L., Wittenberg, K., and Zander, L. (2002) The interaction between language and culture: A test of the cultural accommodation hypothesis in seven countries. *Language and Intercultural Communication*, 2 (2), 120–139.

Harzing, A.-W., and Sorge, A. (2003). The relative impact of country of origin and universal contingencies on internationalization strategies and corporate control in multinational enterprises: Worldwide and European perspectives. *Organization Studies*, 24 (2), 187–214.

Hickson, D.J. (ed.) (1993). *Management in Western Europe*. Berlin: de Gruyter.

Hofstede, G (1980a). *Culture's Consequences: International Differences in Work-Related Values*. Beverly Hills, CA: Sage.

Hofstede, G. (1980b). Motivation, leadership and organization: Do American theories apply abroad? *Organizational Dynamics*, Summer, 42–63.

Hofstede, G. (2003). *Culture's Consequences: Comparing Values, Behaviors, Institutions, and Organizations Across Nations* (2nd rev. edn). Newbury Park, CA: Sage.

House, R.J., Hanges, P., Javidan, M., Dorfman, P, and Gupta, V. (2004). *Culture, Leadership and Organization: A GLOBE Study of 62 Societies*. Thousand Oaks, CA: Sage.

House, R.J., Hanges, P., Ruiz-Quintanilla, S.A., Dorfman, P.W., Javidan, M., Dickson, M., Gupta, V., and 170 co-authors (1999). Cultural influences on leadership and organizations: Project GLOBE. In W.F. Mobley, M.J. Gessner and V. Arnold, (eds), *Advances in Global Leadership*, Vol. 1. Stanford, CT: JAI Press, pp. 171–233.

Inglehart, R.F. (1985). New perspectives on value and change. *Comparative Political Studies*, 17, 485–532.

Inglehart, R.F. (1997). *Modernization and Postmodernization: Cultural, Economic and Political Change in 43 Societies*. Princeton, NJ: Princeton University Press.

Inglehart, R.F. (2002). Cultural cleavages in the European Union: Modernization and cultural persistence. In D. Fuchs, E. Roller and B. Weβels (eds), *Bürger und Demokratie in Ost und West: Studien zur politischen Kultur und zum politischen Prozess*. Wiesbaden: Westdeutscher Verlag, pp. 73–84.

Inglehart, R.F., and Baker, W.E. (2001). Modernization's challenge to traditional values: Who's afraid of Ronald McDonald? *The Futurist*, 35 (2), 16–21.

Irrmann, O. (2002). *Intercultural communication in international business: The case of cross-border mergers and acquisitions*. Paper presented at the IIB Conference 'Identifying Culture' (June), Institute of International Business, Stockholm School of Economics, Stockholm, Sweden.

Jang, S., and Chung, M.-H. (1997). Discursive contradiction of tradition and modernity in Korean management practices: A case study of Samsung's new management. In S.A. Sackmann (ed.), *Cultural Complexity in Organizations: Inherent Contrasts and Contradictions*. Thousand Oaks, CA: Sage Publications, pp. 51–71.

Jones, V. (2002). *Beyond black and white: Race and social identity in Brazil*. Paper presented at the IIB Conference 'Identifying Culture' (June), Institute of International Business, Stockholm School of Economics, Stockholm, Sweden.

Keating, M., and Thompson, K. (2004). International human resource management: Overcoming disciplinary sectarianism. *Employee Relations*, 26 (6), 595–612.

Kiessling, T., and Harvey, M. (2005). Strategic global human resource management research in the twenty-first century: An endorsement of the mixed-method research methodology. *International Journal of Human Resource Management*, 16 (1), 22–45.

Kleinberg, M.J. (1989). Cultural clash between managers: America's Japanese firms. In S.B. Prasad (ed.), *Advances in International Comparative Management*, Vol. 4, Greenwich, CT: JAI Press, pp. 221–244.

Kleinberg, M.J. (1994). 'The crazy group': Emergent culture in a Japanese-American binational work group. In S. Beechler and A. Bird (eds), *Research in International Business and International Relations*, Vol. 6 (Special Issue on Japanese Management). Greenwich, CT: JAI Press, pp. 1–45.

Koschik, A. (2003). Eine-Welt-Laden (A One-World-Shop). *Junge Karriere*, 3, 24–27.

Krafft, A.M. (1998). *Organisationale Identität: Einheit von Vielfalt und Differenz (Organizational Identity: Unity of Variety and Difference)*. Dissertation Nr. 2115, Universität St Gallen, Bamberg: Difo-Druck GmbH.

Kwantes, C.T., and Boglarski, C.A. (2004). Do occupational groups vary in expressed organizational culture performance? A study of six occupations in the United States. *International Journal of Cross Cultural Management*, 4 (3), 335–354.

Langan-Fox, J., and Tan, P. (1997). Images of a culture in transition: Personal constructs of organizational stability and change. *Journal of Occupational and Organizational Psychology*, 70 (3), 273–293.

Laurent, A. (1986). The cross-cultural puzzle of international human resource management. *Human Resource Management*, 25 (1), 91–102.

Lawless, M.W. (1980). *Toward a theory of policy making for directed interorganizational systems*. Doctoral Dissertation, Graduate School of Management, University of California, Los Angeles. In *Dissertation Abstracts International* (University Microfilms No. 8111245).

Lerpold, L., and Zander, L. (2002). *Making sense of changing hats: A study of cultural identities and sensemaking*. Paper presented at the IIB Conference 'Identifying Culture' (June), Institute of International Business, Stockholm School of Economics, Stockholm, Sweden.

Leung, K. (1997). Negotiation and reward allocations across cultures. In P.C. Earley and M. Erez (eds), *New Perspectives on International Industrial and Organizational Psychology*. San Francisco: Jossey-Bass, pp. 640–675.

Louis, M.R. (1983) Organizations as culture-bearing milieux. In L.R. Pondy, P.J. Frost, G. Morgan and T.C. Dandridge (eds), *Organizational Symbolism*. Greenwich, CT: JAI Press, pp. 39–54.

Marquardt, M.J. (2005). *Global Teams*. Delhi: Jaico.

Martin, J., Sitkin, S.B., and Boehm, M. (1985). Founders and the elusiveness of a cultural legacy. In P.J. Frost, L.F. Moore, M.R. Louis, C.C. Lundberg and J. Martin (eds), *Organizational Culture*. Beverly Hills, CA: Sage, pp. 99–124.

Mendenhall, M.E., Gregersen, H., and Cutright, M. (1998). Nonlinear dynamics: A new perspective on IGHRM research and practice in the 21st century. *Human Resource Management Review*, 8 (1): 5–22.

Mitchell, R.K., Smith, B., Seawright, K.W., and Morse, E.A. (2000). Cross-cultural cognitions and the venture creation decision. *Academy of Management Journal*, 43, 974–993.

Moon, J.Y., and Sproul, L. (2002). Essence of distributed work: The case of the Linux Kernel. In P. Hinds and S. Kiesler (eds), *Distributed Work*. Cambridge, MA: MIT Press, pp. 381–404.

Moorman, R.H., and Blakely, G.L. (1995). Individualism–collectivism as an individual difference predictor of organizational citizenship behavior. *Journal of Organizational Behavior*, 16 (2), 127–142.

Mowshowitz, A. (2002). *Virtual Organization: Toward a Theory of Societal Transformation Stimulated by Information Technology*. New York: Quorum Books.

Noble, C. (1997). International comparison of training policies. *Human Resource Management Journal*, 7 (1), 5–18.

O'Hara-Devereaux, M., and Johansen, R. (1994). *Global Work: Bridging Distance, Culture and Time*. San Francisco: Jossey-Bass.

Ouchi, W.G. (1981). *Theory Z*. Reading, MA: Addison-Wesley.

Paauwe, J., and Farndale, E. (2006). International human resource management and firm performance. In G.K. Stahl and I. Björkman (eds), *Handbook of Research in International Human Resource Management*. Cheltenham: Edward Elgar, pp. 91–112.

Pascale, R.T., and Athos, A.G. (1981). *The Art of Japanese Management*. New York: Warner.

Pauleen, D.J. (ed.) (2003). *Virtual Teams: Projects, Protocols and Processes*. Hershey, PA: Idea Group.

Peterson, R.B., Napier, N., and Shim, W.S. (1996). Expatriate management: The differential role of national multinational corporation ownership. *The International Executive*, 38 (4), 543–562.

Phillips, M.E. (1994). Industry mindsets: Exploring the cultures of two macro-organizational settings. *Organization Science*, 5 (3), 384–402.

Phillips, M.E., Goodman, R.A., and Sackmann, S.A. (1992). Exploring the complex cultural milieu of project teams. *pmNETwork – Professional Magazine of the Project Management Institute*, 8, 20–26.

Pratt, M.G. (1998). To be or not to be? Central questions in organizational identification. In D.A. Whetten and P.C. Godfrey (eds), *Identity in Organizations*. Thousand Oaks, CA: Sage, pp. 171–207.

Redding, S.G. (1993), *The Spirit of Chinese Capitalism*, Second edition. Berlin: Walter de Gruyter and Co.

Romani, L., and Wästfeld, M. (2007). *Paradigm interplay in cross-cultural management. Interplay applied to the study of Swedish–Japanese medical research collaborations*. Paper presented at 23rd EGOS Colloquium *Beyond Waltz – Dances of Individuals and Organizations*, Subtheme 27, *When the Cultural Context is Investigated: Toward new Knowledge Developments for the Field of Culture and Management*. Vienna, July 5–7.

Rosenzweig, P.M. (2006). The dual logics behind international human resource management: Pressures for global integration and local responsiveness. In G.K. Stahl and I. Björkman (eds), *Handbook of Research in International Human Resource Management*. Cheltenham: Edward Elgar, pp. 36–48.

Rusted, B. (1986). *Corporate entertainment as social action: The case of a service organization*. Paper presented at the International Conference on Organizational Symbolism and Corporate Culture, Montreal, Canada.

Sackmann, S.A. (1991). *Cultural Knowledge in Organizations: Exploring the Collective Mind*. Newbury Park, CA: Sage.

Sackmann, S.A. (1992). Lässt sich Unternehmenskultur 'machen'? (Can corporate culture be 'made'?). In K. Sandner (ed.), *Politische Prozesse in Organisationen* (2nd ed). Heidelberg: Springer, pp. 157–184.

Sackmann, S.A. (ed.) (1997). *Cultural Complexity in Organizations: Inherent Contrasts and Contradictions*. Newbury Park, CA: Sage.

Sackmann, S.A. (2003). Cultural complexity as a challenge in the management of global companies. In Bertelsmann Foundation (ed.), *Corporate Cultures in Global Interaction. Liz Mohn - A Cultural Forum Vol. III*, Gütersloh, Germany: Bertelsmann, pp. 58–81.

Sackmann, S.A. (2006a). *Assessment, Evaluation, Improvement: Success through Corporate Culture*. Gütersloh: Verlag Bertelsmann Stiftung.

Sackmann, S.A. (2006b). *Success Factor Corporate Culture*. Gütersloh: Verlag Bertelsmann Stiftung.

Sackmann, S.A. (forthcoming) Unternehmenskultur und Mitbestimmung – Versuch einer integrativen Perspektive. (Corporate culture and co-determination – An integrative perspective?). In K. Dörre, R. Benthin and U. Brinkmann (eds), *Unternehmenskultur und Mitbestimmung*. Frankfurt: Campus Verlag.

Sackmann, S.A., and Elbe, M. (2000). Tendenzen und Ergebnisse empirischer Personalforschung der 90er Jahre in West-Deutschland (Trends and results of empirical HRM research in the 90s in West-Germany). *Zeitschrift für Personalforschung*, 14 (2), 131–157.

Sackmann, S.A., and Phillips, M.E. (2002). *The multiple cultures perspective: An alternative paradigm for international cross-cultural management research*. Paper presented at 7th Conference of IWAM (International Western Academy of Management) (July), Challenges in the 21st Century: Opportunities, Vision and Obstacles. Lima, Peru.

Sackmann, S.A., and Phillips, M.E. (2004). Contextual influences on culture research: Shifting assumptions for new workplace realities. *International Journal of Cross Cultural Management*, 4 (3), 370–390.

Sackmann, S.A., Bissels, S., and Bissels, T. (2002). Kulturelle Vielfalt in Organisationen: Ansätze zum Umgang mit einem vernachlässigten Thema der Organisationswissenschaften (Cultural Diversity in Organizations: Ways to Deal with a Neglected Topic in Organization Science), *Die Betriebswirtschaft*, 62 (1), 43–58.

Sackmann, S.A., Phillips, M.E., Kleinberg, M.J., and Boyacigiller, N. (1997). Single and multiple cultures in international cross-cultural management research: Overview. In S.A. Sackmann (ed.), *Cultural Complexity in Organizations: Inherent Contrasts and Contradictions*. Newbury Park, CA: Sage, pp. 14–49.

Salk, J., and Brannen, M.Y. (2000). National culture, networks, and individual influence in a multinational management team. *Academy of Management Journal*, 43 (2), 191–202.

Salk, J., and Shenkar, O. (2001). Social identities in an international joint venture: An exploratory case study. *Organization Science*, 12 (2), 161–178.

Schein, E.H. (1985). *Organizational Culture and Leadership*. San Francisco: Jossey-Bass.

Schuler, R.S., Budhwar, P.S., and Florkowski, G.W. (2002). International human resource management: Review and critique. *International Journal of Management Reviews*, 4 (1), 41–70.

Schuler, R.S., Budhwar, P.S., and Florkowski, G.W. (2004). International human resource management. In B.J. Punnett and O. Shankar (eds), *Handbook for International Management Research*, Ann Arbor: The University of Michigan Press, pp. 356–414.

Schumacher, T. (1997). West Coast Camelot: The rise and fall of an organizational culture. In Sackmann, S.A. (ed.), *Cultural Complexity in Organizations: Inherent Contrasts and Contradictions*. Thousand Oaks, CA: Sage, pp. 107–132.

Sharpe, D. (1997). Managerial control strategies and subcultural processes: On the shop floor in a Japanese manufacturing organization in the United Kingdom. In S.A. Sackmann (ed.), *Cultural Complexity in Organizations: Inherent Contrasts and Contradictions*. Thousand Oaks, CA: Sage, pp. 228–251.

Shimoni, B., and Bergmann, H. (2006). Managing in a changing world: From multiculturalism to hybridization – The production of hybrid management cultures in Israel, Thailand, and Mexico. *Academy of Management Perspectives*, 20 (3), 76–89.

Søndergaard, M. (1994). Research note: Hofstede's consequences: A study of reviews, citations, and replications. *Organization Studies*, Special Issue on cross-national organization culture, 15 (3), 447–456.

Stahl, G.K., and Bjorkman, I. (eds) (2006). *Handbook of Research in International Human Resource Management*. Cheltenham: Edward Elgar Publishing.

Steers, R.M., and Sanchez-Runde, C. (2002). Culture, motivation, and world behavior. In M. Gannon and K. Newman (eds), *Handbook of Cross-Cultural Management*. Oxford: Blackwell, pp. 190–216.

Sumihara, N. (1992). *A case study of structuration in a bicultural work organization: A study of a Japanese-owned and -managed corporation in the U.S.A.* Doctoral Dissertation. Ann Arbor, MI: UMI Dissertation Services.

Teagarden, M.B., von Glinow, M.A., Bowen, D.E., Frayne, C.A., Nason, S., Huo, Y.P., Milliman, J., Arias, M.A., Butler, M.C., Geringer, J.M., Kim, N.K., Scullion, H., Lowe, K.B., and Drost, E.A. (1995). Towards building a theory of comparative management research methodology: An idiographic case study of the best international human resources management project. *Academy of Management Journal*, 38 (5), 1261–1287.

Thomas, D.C., and Lazarova, M.B. (2006). Expatriate adjustment and performance: A critical review. In G.K. Stahl and I. Björkman (eds), *Handbook of Research in International Human Resource Management*. Cheltenham: Edward Elgar, pp. 247–264.

Trice, H.M., and Beyer, J.M. (1993). *The Cultures of Work Organizations*. Englewood Cliffs, NJ: Prentice Hall.

Von Glinow, M.A., and Chung, B.J. (1989). Comparative human resource management practices in the United States, Japan, Korea, and the People's Republic of China. In I.M. Rowland and G.R. Ferris (eds), *Research in Personnel and Human Resource Management, Suppl. 1*. Greenwich, CT: JAI Press.

Von Glinow, M.A., Drost, E.A., Teagarden, M.B. (2002). Converging on IHRM best practices: Lessons learned from a globally distributed consortium on theory and practice. *Human Resource Management*, 41 (1), 123–140.

von Rosenstiel, L., and Nerdinger, F.W. (2000). Die Münchner Wertestudien: Bestandsaufnahme und (vorläufiges) Resümee (The Munich value studies: Current status and preliminary summary). *Psychologische Rundschau*, 51, 146–157.

Westwood, R.I., and Kirkbride, P.S. (1989). *Jonathan Livingston Seagull is alive and well and living in Hong Kong: Cultural disjuncture in the symbolization of corporate leadership*. Paper presented at the International Conference on Organizational Symbolism and Corporate Culture, Fontainebleau, France.

Wong, N. (2000). Mark your calendar! Important tasks for international HR workforce. *Costa Mesa*, 79 (4), 72–74.

Ybema, S.B. (1997). Telling tales: Contrasts and commonalities within the organization of an amusement park – confronting and combining different perspectives. In S.A. Sackmann (ed.), *Cultural Complexity in Organizations: Inherent Contrasts and Contradictions*. Thousand Oaks: Sage. pp. 160–186.

Part II

Managing Key Staff Groups and Individual Processes in International Organizations

5

Beyond International Experience: The Strategic Role of Cultural Intelligence for Executive Selection in IHRM

KOK-YEE NG, LINN VAN DYNE, AND SOON ANG

INTRODUCTION

International assignments are becoming more frequent and complex in organizations. Selecting individuals who are equipped to manage cross-cultural challenges therefore takes on a more significant and strategic role. Yet, selection decisions for staffing international assignments typically rely on informal and low-utility selection criteria such as international experience. This chapter advances the conceptual and applied benefits of using cultural intelligence as a selection tool to identify those with international executive potential. Specifically, we highlight the role of cultural intelligence as a set of dynamic learning capabilities that will enable individuals to transform their international experience into effectiveness. Our central thesis is that previous international experiences do not necessarily translate into learning and effectiveness; rather, the experience–effectiveness relationship is moderated by cultural intelligence, such that individuals with high cultural intelligence are more likely to leverage their experiences to enhance performance, compared to those with low cultural intelligence. Our model also explains why existing findings on international experience and adjustment have been inconsistent and weak. We conclude with a discussion on the theoretical and practical implications of our model for International Human Resource Management (IHRM).

Selecting executives who could function effectively in international joint ventures and multinational enterprises constitutes a central theme in the contemporary research and practice (Sparrow *et al.*, 2004; Schuler and Tarique, 2007; Ang and Van

Handbook of International Human Resource Management. Edited by Paul R. Sparrow
© 2009 John Wiley & Sons, Ltd

Dyne, 2008) of IHRM. An early focus of IHRM research was on the selection criteria of expatriates, due to the high rates of premature return of expatriates in the United States in the 1970s (Baker and Ivancevich, 1971; Tung, 1981; Mendenhall and Oddou, 1985). Today, the nature of international assignments has changed considerably (Collings *et al.*, 2007). Instead of relying on conventional longer-term expatriate assignments, organizations are increasingly adopting alternative forms of international assignments that are shorter in duration (Dowling and Welch, 2004; Mayrhofer *et al.*, 2004; Suutari and Brewster, this volume Chapter 7).

This growing trend has two major selection implications for organizations and their employees:

1. Challenges associated with international assignments are no longer contained within the exclusive realm of expatriate management. With the popular use of short-term, frequent-flyer international assignments, and virtual global teams in organizations (Collings *et al.*, 2007), the challenges of selecting employees who can be effective in these increasingly important roles apply to a broader group of employees – rather than a limited number of expatriates (Sparrow, 2007).
2. International assignments have also taken on more complex forms of managing cross-border alliances such as mergers and acquisitions and international joint ventures (Schuler *et al.*, 2004; Stahl and Mendenhall, 2005).

When organizations must select employees who can operate in short-term assignments set against a fast-paced and more integrated business environment (Friedman and Berthoin Antal, 2005; Morley *et al.*, 2006), the selection challenges are different from, and perhaps even more complex than, those associated with conventional expatriate assignments that deal primarily with coping and adjusting in one culture (Nardon and Steers, 2007). Moreover, many international employees in practice have to understand, adapt to and personally maintain multiple cultures (Sackmann, this volume Chapter 22).

Taken together, selection of employees equipped to deal with cross-cultural challenges takes on an even more important and significant role for managers and organizations, given the broader scope and increased cultural diversity and complexity of international assignments in today's business landscape. Yet, selection decisions for staffing international assignments have been, and continue to be, based on informal and low-utility selection strategies and criteria (Shaffer *et al.*, 2006). International experience, for instance, remains a prevalent criterion used by organizations to staff international assignments (Carpenter *et al.*, 2001; Daily *et al.*, 2000; Kealey, 1996). The justification, other than expedience, is the assumption that as experience increases, the ability to do the job also increases (Guion, 1998; Stokes *et al.*, 1994). The received wisdom is that individuals with past experiences in intercultural settings are assumed to have honed their cross-cultural skills and knowledge, and hence, will be more effective in dealing with intercultural encounters.

Empirical support, however, for the effect of international experience on expatriate adjustment and performance has been meager. The meta-analysis by Hechanova *et al.* (2003) on adjustment to overseas assignment found an estimated population correlation of 0.08 between expatriates' previous international assignment and their work adjustment. In a more recent meta-analysis by Bhaskar-Shrinivas *et al.* (2005a), previous overseas experience explained less than 1% of the variance in interaction adjustment ($\rho = 0.13$) and work adjustment ($\rho = 0.06$), prompting the authors to conclude that 'Contrary to conventional wisdom and some academic arguments, the accumulated evidence shows that prior overseas assignments are only minimally helpful for present adjustment' (p. 272).

In reflecting on the weak relationship between international experience and intercultural effectiveness outcomes such as overseas work adjustment, scholars have begun to consider other approaches. For instance Takeuchi *et al.* (2005) attributed weak results to the overly simplistic conceptualization of international experience. Building on a more sophisticated conceptualization that differentiates different types of international experience, their results enable a better understanding of the role of international experience.

The objective of this chapter is to further our understanding of the theoretical and practical utility of using international experience for selection purposes. We do this by building on the work of Ng *et al.* (2007) to explicate another rationale for the traditionally weak empirical effects of international experience. Specifically, Ng *et al.* (2007) drew on Kolb's (1984) experiential learning theory to develop the argument that individuals differ in the extent to which they benefit from international experiences. This is because some people are better able to translate and transform their experiences into useful knowledge they can use to guide future cross-cultural interactions.

Based on these arguments, we advance the argument in this chapter that the usefulness of past international experience in predicting future intercultural effectiveness depends on the individual's cultural intelligence – a set of cross-cultural capabilities that describe a person's capacity to function effectively in culturally diverse settings (Earley and Ang, 2003). Increasingly, cultural intelligence has been noted by scholars as 'an important individual characteristic that facilitates cultural adaptation and performance' (Gelfand *et al.*, 2007: 497), and 'a promising framework for understanding intercultural interactions' (Bhaskar-Shrinivas *et al.*, 2005a, b: 274). Hence, our examination of cultural intelligence as a set of dynamic capabilities that affect how individuals adapt and perform in novel cultural settings is timely and important for understanding effectiveness in contemporary international assignments. This approach also responds to recommendations for systematic research on the role of malleable competencies in predicting inter-cultural effectiveness (Shaffer *et al.*, 2006).

The theoretical model that we develop draws on Earley and Ang's (2003) multidimensional conceptualization of cultural intelligence, and more recent theorizing by Ng *et al.* (2007) on cultural intelligence as a set of learning capabilities that maximizes the developmental benefits of international assignments. Overall, we propose that culturally intelligent individuals are better able to leverage their prior international experiences in ways that enhance their effectiveness in international assignments (compared to those with low cultural intelligence). Thus, we aim to offer a novel explanation for the generally weak relationship between international experience and intercultural effectiveness.

The remainder of the chapter is structured as follows. We start with an overview of theory and research on experience and performance (Takeuchi *et al.*, 2005; Tesluk and Jacobs, 1998) as well as theory and research on cultural intelligence (Earley and Ang, 2003). We then describe experiential learning theory (Kolb, 1984), with an emphasis on how cultural intelligence enhances the four stages of experiential learning in ways that allow those with high cultural intelligence to translate and transform their experiences into effectiveness. Thus, our theoretical model proposes that cultural intelligence functions as a set of moderators that strengthen the experience–effectiveness relationship. We conclude with a discussion of the theoretical and practical implications of applying our model and using cultural intelligence as a selection tool for international staffing.

EXPERIENCE AND PERFORMANCE

The acquisition of knowledge and skills required for effective performance is the linchpin of research on experience and performance outcomes. Tesluk and Jacobs' (1998) integrated model of work experience asserts that previous experience facilitates the learning and development of knowledge and skills, motivation, as well as attitudes that are critical for effective performance in organizations. Schmidt *et al.*'s (1986) meta-analytic path model analysis supports the contention that learning and acquisition of knowledge and skills is a primary reason for the importance accorded to work experience.

In the context of international experience, Takeuchi and colleagues (2005) argued that individuals who have had more previous assignments (i.e., previous experience), or are further into their current assignments (i.e., current experience), are more likely to experience better adjustment in their international assignments because they have information that helps to overcome their initial uncertainty, and they have had more opportunities to learn appropriate behaviors through direct and vicarious modeling (Bandura, 1997). More specifically, Takeuchi and colleagues demonstrate that previous international experience acts as a buffer for expatriates in their current overseas assignment. The amount of time expatriates have into their current assignment has less impact on adjustment when expatriates have greater previous international experience. On the other hand, the amount of current experience has greater impact on adjustment when expatriates have little previous international experience. This suggests that expatriates, through their previous international experience, acquire knowledge and skills that buffer them from the challenges of adjusting to new international assignments.

Yet, research has recognized that not all individuals learn equally from their experiences. As McCauley (1986: 20) pointed out, 'Events provide a stimulus to learn; the actual response of learning itself is never a sure thing'. Likewise, Tesluk and Jacobs (1998: 333) noted that 'Learning does not often automatically follow from experience' because individual differences and contextual characteristics of the environment influence 'what is extracted from work experiences' (p. 333). We suggest that these factors moderate the experience–effectiveness relationship, which partly account for the traditionally weak results found in the domestic and international experience literatures. In the current context of international assignments, we argue that cultural intelligence is an important set of individual difference characteristics that can moderate the relationship between international experience and intercultural effectiveness, such that those with higher cultural intelligence are better able to benefit from international experiences.

CULTURAL INTELLIGENCE

Cultural intelligence (CQ) refers to an individual's capabilities to function and manage effectively in culturally diverse settings (Earley and Ang, 2003). CQ is a timely concept given the prevalence and importance of effective cross-cultural interactions and management. The conceptualization of CQ is drawn from Sternberg and Detterman's (1986) research, which integrates multiple perspectives of intelligence to propose four complementary ways of conceptualizing individual-level intelligence:

(1) metacognitive intelligence refers to awareness and control of cognitions used to acquire and understand information;
(2) cognitive intelligence refers to knowledge and knowledge structures;
(3) motivational intelligence acknowledges that most cognition is motivated and thus focuses on the magnitude and direction of energy as a locus of intelligence; and
(4) behavioral intelligence focuses on individual capabilities at the action level (behavior).

This framework is noteworthy because it recognizes multiple forms of intelligence (Ang and Van Dyne, 2008), unlike traditional research that has focused narrowly on linguistic, logical–mathematical and spatial intelligence, and ignored forms of intelligence related to self-regulation and interpersonal relations (Gardner, 1993).

Drawing on this multidimensional perspective of intelligence, Earley and Ang (2003) conceptualized CQ as a multidimensional construct with mental (metacognitive and cognitive), motivational, and behavioral components. Metacognitive CQ is the capability for consciousness and awareness during intercultural interactions. It reflects mental capabilities to acquire and understand culturally diverse situations and includes knowledge of and control over individual thought processes (Flavell, 1979) relating to culture. Relevant capabilities include planning, monitoring, and revising mental models. Those with high metacognitive CQ are consciously aware and mindful of cultural preferences and norms before and during interactions. They question cultural assumptions and adjust mental models during and after experiences (Nelson, 1996).

While metacognitive CQ focuses on higher-order cognitive processes, cognitive CQ focuses on knowledge of norms, practices, and conventions in different cultural settings acquired from education and personal experiences. This includes knowledge of economic, legal, and social systems of different cultures (Triandis, 1994). Individuals with high cognitive CQ are able to anticipate and understand similarities and differences across cultural situations. As a result, they are more likely to have accurate expectations and less likely to make inaccurate interpretations of cultural interactions (e.g., Triandis, 1995).

In addition to mental capabilities that foster understanding of other cultures, CQ also includes the motivational capability to cope with ambiguous and unfamiliar settings. Motivational CQ is the capability to direct attention and energy toward learning about and functioning in situations characterized by cultural differences, and is based on the expectancy-value theory of motivation (Eccles and Wigfield, 2002) that includes intrinsic motivation (Deci and Ryan, 1985) and self-efficacy (Bandura, 2002). Those with high motivational CQ experience intrinsic satisfaction and are confident about their ability to function in culturally diverse settings.

The fourth aspect of CQ recognizes that cultural understanding (mental) and interest (motivational) must be complemented with behavioral flexibility to exhibit appropriate verbal and non-verbal actions, based on cultural values of a specific setting (Hall, 1959). Thus, behavioral CQ is the capability to exhibit situationally-appropriate behaviors from a broad repertoire of verbal and non-verbal behaviors, such as being able to exhibit culturally appropriate words, tones, gestures, and facial expressions (Gudykunst *et al.*, 1988).

To date, CQ research has extended the conceptualization and theoretical grounding of CQ (e.g., Ng and Earley, 2006; Triandis, 2006) to examine relationships with important variables. For instance, Ang *et al.* (2006) demonstrates that the Big 5 personality, particularly openness to experience and extraversion, is associated with CQ. More recently, Ang *et al.* (2007) demonstrate in a series of studies that after controlling for cross-cultural experience, general mental ability, and other relevant individual differences, cognitive CQ and metacognitive CQ have incremental predictive validity in explaining variance in individuals' cultural judgment and decision making; motivational CQ and behavioral CQ predict cultural adaptation; while metacognitive CQ and behavioral CQ predict task performance of international executives. In another study of global professionals, Templer *et al.* (2006) found that motivational CQ predicts cultural adjustment above and beyond realistic job and living conditions previews, hence providing direct evidence of the importance of CQ for expatriates and international assignees. CQ also enhances interpersonal trust of members in multicultural teams (Rockstuhl and Ng, 2007), as well as increases joint profits of intercultural negotiating dyads (Imai and Gelfand, 2007). Taken together, these empirical findings suggest that CQ, as a distinctive individual difference, is a relevant and critical individual attribute that has implications for effectiveness in intercultural settings.

EXPERIENTIAL LEARNING AND CULTURAL INTELLIGENCE

In a recent conceptual paper on cultural intelligence and global leadership development, Ng and colleagues (2007) applied Kolb's (1984) experiential learning theory to explicate ways that global leaders can maximize the developmental benefits of international assignments. Drawing on the multidimensional conceptualization of CQ, they take a systematic approach to describe processes through which experiences are translated into learning and effectiveness, as well as the corresponding individual capabilities for effective learning from these experiences.

Recognizing the importance of CQ as a set of learning capabilities is aligned with the recent emphasis in the expatriate and international management literatures on 'ability to learn', rather than end-state competencies (Spreitzer *et al.*, 1997). Spreitzer and colleagues, for instance, argue that end-state competencies are constructed on the basis of past successes and hence may ignore competencies required for future performance. In contrast, the ability to 'learn on the fly' from experiences in today's fast-paced and dynamic multicultural environments (Nardon and Steers, 2007) is an essential attribute that distinguishes high-performing employees, managers, and expatriates from average or mediocre performers.

Experiential learning theory (ELT) provides a strong theoretical foundation for thinking about specific ways that those with high CQ can learn from their experiences and accordingly enhance their effectiveness. In essence, Kolb (1984) synthesized earlier theories on experiential learning (Dewey, 1938) to argue that effective learning from experiences requires the learner to grasp the experience and transform the experience into meaningful learning. Further, Kolb (1984) proposed two opposing modes of grasping experience (concrete experience and abstract conceptualization) and two opposing modes of transforming experience (reflective observation and active experimentation).

Together this forms a four-stage experiential cycle: concrete experience, reflective observation, abstract conceptualization and active experimentation. Thus, the ELT model portrays a learning cycle where the learner 'touches all the bases' of experiencing, reflecting, thinking and acting – in a recursive process that is responsive to the learning situation (Kolb and Kolb, 2005). Specific tangible episodes or events (concrete experiences) are the basis for descriptive processing (reflective observations) which are then assimilated and distilled into conceptual interpretations (abstract conceptualization), and become the basis for action (active experimentation). This fourth step (active testing ideas in the real world) generates new experiences for the learner and triggers another cycle of learning: concrete experiences, reflective observation, abstract conceptualization, and active experimentation.

Based on this model, Kolb and colleagues argue that individuals who are able to balance the tensions in learning styles and integrate the dual dialectics of grasping experience and transforming experience will be more effective (e.g., Kolb and Kolb, 2005; Mainemelis *et al.*, 2002). Building on this argument, Ng and colleagues (2007) position CQ as a set of learning capabilities that influence the extent to which individuals engage in the four learning modes of experiencing, reflecting, observing, and acting when exposed to cross-cultural interactions and situations. We describe links between CQ and each of the four learning modes below. The theoretical model is shown in Figure 5.1.

Concrete experience

Ng and colleagues (2007) propose that two CQ dimensions – motivational CQ and behavioral CQ – affect the amount and quality of concrete experiences that individuals seek during international assignments. Social cognitive theory (Bandura,

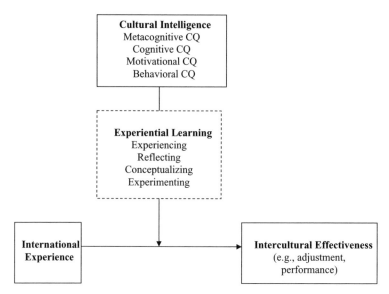

FIGURE 5.1 Theoretical model of cultural intelligence and experiential learning.

2002) suggests that individuals who are more confident of their ability to complete a particular task are more likely to initiate effort, persist in their efforts and perform better. Given that intercultural interactions are typically stressful because of unfamiliar cultural norms and cues (Mendenhall and Oddou, 1985; Oberg, 1960; Shaffer *et al.*, 2006), Ng *et al.* argue that only those with high motivational CQ – who are interested in and feel efficacious in cross-cultural settings – are more likely to actively seek cross-cultural experiences during their international assignments.

Behavioral CQ is also relevant to the amount and quality of concrete experiences that individuals seek because gaining concrete experiences requires people to engage with the environment and interactions with others (Ng *et al.*, 2007). As such, those with good interpersonal competencies (Kolb, 1984) are better able to build relationships with culturally-different individuals. This, in turn, creates more opportunities for cross-cultural contact that facilitates learning (Yamazaki and Kayes, 2004).

Reflective observations

Cognitive CQ and metacognitive CQ are important for reflective observation (Ng *et al.*, 2007). Individuals high in cognitive CQ possess elaborate cultural schemas, defined as mental representations of patterns of social interaction characteristic of particular cultural groups (Triandis *et al.*, 1984). Having elaborate cultural schemas enhances conceptually-driven information processing (Taylor and Crocker, 1981) and enables more accurate identification and understanding of cultural issues. Thus, those with high cognitive CQ are more aware of what cues to look for during intercultural encounters. They are also less likely to make negative evaluations of cultural norms and behaviors which allow them to be more objective and accurate in their observations and reflections of cross-cultural experiences (Osland and Bird, 2000).

Reflective observation also requires a high level of metacognitive CQ – thinking about thought processes related to cross-cultural experiences (Ng *et al.*, 2007). Those with high metacognitive CQ monitor and think about their own assumptions, beliefs, and emotions as well as the way they process external environment and behavioral cues provided by others. They are more active in their cognitive processing of observations as they create new categories in their memory storage and actively consider multiple perspectives in making sense of their experiences (Flavell, 1979). Hence, they are better able to engage in the learning mode of reflective observation.

Abstract conceptualization

The third stage of experiential learning requires learners to distill their reflections into more general concepts that can guide their future actions. As with reflective observation, cognitive CQ and metacognitive CQ are key to abstract conceptualization (Ng *et al.*, 2007). This is because those with more extensive knowledge of culture have better-organized knowledge structures with stronger linkages among domain-related concepts. This allows them to conceptualize problems more efficiently and effectively in terms of relevant principles (cf. Chase and Simon, 1973; Chi *et al.*, 1982). Thus, individuals with high cognitive CQ are more accurate and effective in developing general ideas and conceptual interpretations of culture. On the other hand, without a fundamental understanding of cultural concepts (low cognitive CQ), individuals are less able to integrate insights and reflections about particular experiences into coherent knowledge structures about culture. This, in turn, impedes formation of higher-order concepts and theories.

Metacognitive CQ is also directly relevant to abstract conceptualization because many cross-cultural situations do not fit typical norms or tendencies (Ng *et al.*, 2007), even when expectations are based on scientific and rigorous research (Osland and Bird, 2000). Having the metacognitive CQ capability of thinking about thinking is important for abstract conceptualization because it enables people to be open to disconfirming experiences. Thus, individuals with high metacognitive CQ are more likely to analyze new cross-cultural experiences without being biased or constrained by past experiences or expectations. They are also better able to translate their insights from a particular experience into more general concepts and accurate interpretations that can be applied to other cultural contexts.

Active experimentation

The last stage of the ELT model is actively testing and experimenting to see if enhanced understanding fits reality. Since active experimentation involves the entire person, all four CQ capabilities are important (Ng *et al.*, 2007). First, cognitive CQ and metacognitive CQ are important because they enable learners to organize and map out action plans. Action, without clear goals and plans is less likely to produce desired outcomes. Thus, those with an enhanced understanding of culture (cognitive CQ) and those who have clear plans and strategies for action (metacognitive CQ) are more likely to follow-through and test their ideas and understanding.

Motivational CQ is also important for active experimentation because those with the desire and self-efficacy to deal with cross-cultural interactions tend to seek and persist in challenging cross-cultural situations (Bandura, 2002). Moreover, given that self-efficacy is a 'generative capability in which cognitive, social, emotional, and behavioral subskills must be organized and effectively orchestrated to serve innumerable purposes' (Bandura, 1997: 37), having high motivational CQ enables learners to carry out sequences of action steps to achieve specific goals (Earley *et al.*, 2006).

Finally, since active experimentation typically involves interaction, behavioral CQ is also critical for effectiveness in cross-cultural interactions. Having the capability to adapt verbal and non-verbal behaviors to specific cultural contexts provides people with greater latitude for experimentation. In other words, those with high behavioral CQ are less constrained and better situated to implement and test their ideas.

TRANSLATING AND TRANSFORMING EXPERIENCE INTO EFFECTIVENESS

Having summarized ways in which the four dimensions of CQ are relevant to the four stages of experiential learning, we return to our opening point – that CQ can be used as a tool to identify those most likely to benefit from international experience. Specifically, we argue that particular CQ capabilities can be linked to specific stages of experiential learning and those high in all four CQ capabilities are best suited to capitalize on the learning opportunities available from international experience because they will experience the full range of experiential learning. Thus, we propose that employees need to engage repeatedly in all four stages of experiential learning (concrete experiences, reflective observation, abstract conceptualization, and active experimentation) to maximise their learning from international assignments.

This also implies that those who are low in specific CQ capabilities will have the tendency to short-circuit the experiential learning cycle. For instance, individuals with high motivational CQ and high behavioral CQ may seek many concrete experiences during their international assignments. However, without the cognitive CQ and metacognitive CQ capabilities, they lack the observational skills and conceptual understanding to transform their experiences into knowledge to guide them in future interactions. Conversely, those with high cognitive CQ and high metacognitive CQ may develop sophisticated understanding of different cultures, but without the motivation or behavioral flexibility to venture out into new cultural settings, cross-cultural learning for these individuals remains an intellectual exercise that lacks the surprises and shocks that often jolt people into discovery and growth (Hall *et al.*, 2001).

In sum, we propose an important caveat to the conventional axiom about the value of international experiences: not all individuals benefit from international experiences because they are not all capable of translating and transforming their experiences into useful knowledge to guide their future cross-cultural interactions.

Thus, based on Ng *et al.*'s (2007) positioning of CQ as a set of learning capabilities that allows individuals to enhance their learning during intercultural encounters, we argue that CQ capabilities moderate the relationship between international experience and intercultural effectiveness, such that the relationships between international experience and intercultural effectiveness is stronger for individuals with high CQ, compared to those with low CQ. This is because those with high CQ are more likely to engage in all four learning modes of experiencing, reflecting, conceptualizing, and experimenting, and they are better able to learn from and leverage their past international experiences in ways that enhance their intercultural interactions and adjustment in international assignments.

Thus far, we have explicated how cultural intelligence enhances experiential learning in ways that strengthen the link between international experience and effectiveness in international assignments. We now highlight the theoretical and practical implications of using CQ as a selection tool to identify those most likely to benefit from international experiences.

THEORETICAL IMPLICATIONS AND FUTURE RESEARCH

Although it seems intuitively logical that previous experience should have implications for future performance, empirical research on international experience and cross-cultural effectiveness has generally produced weak findings. Our goal in this chapter has been to advance a conceptual rationale that might elucidate reasons for these prior research results while providing a strong conceptual foundation for future empirical research. Thus, we have argued that individuals vary in their ability to learn from experiences. More important, we propose that cultural intelligence affects the extent to which individuals can leverage their previous international experiences through experiential learning.

Although scholars have highlighted the importance of understanding individual differences in people's ability to learn from their experiences (e.g., Tesluk and Jacobs, 1998; McCauley, 1986; Seibert, 1996), we are not aware of research that has positioned individual differences – such as CQ – as moderators to the relationship between international experience and intercultural effectiveness. Hence, little is known about the boundary conditions to the widely-accepted truism that those with greater international experience are more effective in multicultural and international settings. Our model integrates CQ and experiential learning to provide systematic explanations for why individuals differ in their ability to benefit from international experiences. Thus, the model should help to enhance the predictive validity of selection research on international experience and intercultural effectiveness such as cross-cultural adjustment and performance in culturally diverse settings.

Our model also highlights cultural intelligence as a set of learning capabilities. Thus, we go beyond prior research that has emphasized cultural intelligence as a set of performance capabilities (Ang *et al.*, 2007; Imai and Gelfand, 2007; Rockstuhl and Ng, 2007; Templer *et al.*, 2006). We suggest that viewing CQ as a set of learning capabilities has special relevance to theories and research on selection – especially to selection in the context of the changing nature of international assignments and the increasingly multicultural nature of work groups and organizations. Thus, we reinforce Spreitzer and colleague's (1997) emphasis on 'ability to learn' as a critical selection tool and predictor of international executive potential. Specifically, Spreitzer and colleagues identified three qualities that reflect a proactive approach to learning and have direct implications for international selection: seeks opportunities to learn, cross-culturally adventurous, and openness to criticisms.

Our model acknowledges and builds on existing work in two ways:

1. Rather than using an inductive list of attributes and qualities to examine individual differences in ability to learn from international experiences (Spreitzer *et al.*, 1997), we applied the cultural intelligence conceptual framework to provide a more comprehensive and theoretically-grounded basis for identifying capabilities with relevance to international selection.
2. It extends the conceptualization of experiential learning theory (Kolb, 1984) by explicating ways that cultural intelligence should enhance experiential learning.

Taken together, we aim to provide a more theoretical approach to thinking about ways that individual capabilities such as CQ enhance experiential learning and thus can enhance the conceptualization of selection processes and tools specifically for jobs with international and multicultural responsibilities.

We recommend future research that tests our predictions. This should include identification of intercultural effectiveness outcomes that are relevant to the specific study context, as well as a careful delineation of specific types of international experiences, drawing on Takeuchi and colleagues' (2005) framework.

Practical Implications

Given that organizations are increasingly emphasizing international assignments as a means of providing employees with cross-cultural experiences to equip them for the challenges of the global business environment, having a better understanding of how and whether these assignments achieve their intended goals should offer important practical insights organizations can use in selecting and training individuals for international assignments. When organizations view experiential learning and development as important components of international assignments, selecting individuals who are more likely to learn and hence, benefit from their international assignments, is critical. Thus, we recommend cultural intelligence as a selection tool that identifies those best able to benefit from international assignments.

CQ, as a malleable capability that can be enhanced over time, also has training and development implications. Based on our model, providing CQ training and development should help to prepare and equip employees with international responsibilities to do their jobs better. Our approach also has the added benefit of ensuring that real-time dynamic learning occurs during the international assignment. These sorts of programs would entail moving beyond traditional cross-cultural training methods that focus on cultural knowledge (cognitive CQ). Instead, they would also need to emphasize metacognitive CQ, motivational CQ, and behavioral CQ.

Earley and Peterson (2004) described training interventions that target these CQ capabilities. These include cognitive structure analysis for examining knowledge structures and enhancing awareness and reflection (metacognitive CQ). They also include interventions that help employees internalize the goal of getting engaged in the local culture (motivational CQ). Finally training interventions can also use dramaturgical exercises such as role-plays and simulations involving physical, emotional, and sensory processes that help employees enhance their behavioral flexibility (behavioral CQ).

Finally, Kolb's (1984) experiential learning theory, which highlights four stages of learning involving experiencing, reflecting, conceptualizing and experimenting, has important implications for the design of international assignments. Expatriate assignments entail demanding work responsibilities and often include generous pay packages with expensive cars and exclusive homes that can isolate employees from the host-country culture. Likewise, short-term overseas trips that emphasize efficient and effective travel can shelter employees in a 'bubble' that separates them from direct and meaningful contact with the local culture (Oddou *et al.*, 2000).

To avoid this sort of isolation, Kolb and Kolb (2005) emphasized the importance of providing 'space' – physical, mental, and psychological – so that employees feel they can (and should) participate actively in all four stages of experiential learning. For example, Ng and colleagues (2007) described specific organizational interventions that can promote the four modes of experiential learning during an international assignment. Organizations can emphasize developmental aspects and benefits of international assignments so that employees view assignments as more than short-term performance challenges. This should encourage them to be more culturally adventurous and curious. It also should promote more concrete and meaningful interactions with locals which should increase their sense of being engaged by the local culture (Osland and Osland, 2006).

To stimulate reflective observation after a cross-cultural experience, international assignees could be trained and encouraged to write a journal documenting their cross-cultural experiences and learning points (Oddou *et al.*, 2000). These reflections should focus on a deep examination of expectations and cultural assumptions of parties involved in interactions, rather than superficial descriptive observations of the incident. Over time, individuals can compare their experiences and learning points to gain further insights and more general cultural understanding to guide future interactions. Thus, training that helps individuals to develop inductive logic and reasoning skills to translate specific observations into more abstract and general understanding of their cross-cultural interactions is particularly important for ensuring that employees learn from their experiences and apply this to future interactions and assignments.

Finally, to encourage international assignees to test their newly acquired insights and ideas, organizations can provide incentives and resources that encourage employees to set specific and measurable developmental goals for exploration and experimentation. They also should make sure that reward systems do not contradict or dampen the importance of development. For example, if goals emphasize short-term business results, employees will be less likely to maximize experiential learning opportunities. Another organizational option would be to provide coaching and mentoring resources to support the experimentation processes and provide employees with feedback. All of these should promote active learning (e.g., McCall and Hollenbeck, 2002; Oddou *et al.*, 2000).

CONCLUSION

The nature and context of international assignments has altered significantly. With emerging alternatives (see Suutari and Brewster, this volume Chapter 7) such as short-term and frequent flyer assignments, cross-cultural challenges are no longer limited to expatriates. Moreover, these alternative forms of international assignments may create challenges that are more complex in nature. This is because many of these assignments are implemented on short notice and lack the luxury of pre-departure training that is often provided for expatriates on longer-term assignments (Nardon and Steers, 2007; Sparrow *et al.*, 2004). This further heightens the importance of selecting employees based on their ability to learn dynamically from their international experiences. In other words, this makes the role of CQ as a strategic selection tool even more promising.

Given that international experience continues to be a commonly used criterion for staffing international assignments – despite weak empirical evidence that it predicts cross-cultural effectiveness (Bhaskar-Shrinivas *et al.*, 2005a, b; Hechanova *et al.*, 2003) – this chapter seeks to provide a more in-depth understanding of methods of using CQ as a selection tool that can enhance experiential learning and thus strengthen the relationship between experience and effectiveness for employees with international responsibilities. We concur with existing research which argues that not all individuals are able to learn from and leverage their international experiences (Tesluk and Jacobs, 1998; McCauley, 1986; Seibert, 1997). Thus, we recommend the conceptual and applied benefits of using CQ as a selection tool to identify those best able to translate and transform their international experiences into effectiveness.

REFERENCES

Ang, S., and Van Dyne, L. (2008). *Handbook on Cultural Intelligence*. New York: M.E. Sharpe (forthcoming).

Ang, S., Van Dyne, L., and Koh C. (2006). Personality correlates of the four-factor model of cultural intelligence, 31, 100–123.

Ang, S., Van Dyne, L., Koh, C., Ng, K.Y., Templer, K.J., Tay, C., and Chandrasekar, N.A. (2007). Cultural intelligence: Its measurement and effects on cultural judgment and decision making, cultural adaptation and task performance. *Management and Organization Review*, 3, 335–371.

Baker, J., and Ivancevich, J. (1971). The assignment of American executives abroad: Systematic, haphazard, or chaotic? *California Management Review*, 13, 39–44.

Bandura, A. (1997). *Self-Efficacy: The Exercise of Control*. New York: Freeman.

Bandura, A. (2002). Social cognitive theory in cultural context. *Applied Psychology: An International Review*, 51, 269–290.

Bhaskar-Shrinivas, P. Harrison, D.A. Shaffer, M.A., and Luk, D.M. (2005a). Input-based and time-based models of international adjustment: Meta-analytic evidence and theoretical extensions. *Academy of Management Journal*, 48 (2), 25–281.

Bhaskar-Shrinivas, P. Harrison, D.A., Shaffer, M.A., and Luk, D.M. (2005b). Input-based and time-based models of international adjustment: Meta-analytic evidence and theoretical extensions. *Academy of Management Journal*, 48 (6), 1033–1049.

Carpenter, M.A., Sanders, W.G., and Gregersen, H.B. (2001). Bundling human capital with organizational context: The impact of international assignment experience on multinational firm performance and CEO pay. *Academy of Management Journal*, 44, 493–511.

Chase, W.G., and Simon, H.A. (1973). The mind's eye in chess. In W.G. Chase (ed.), *Visual Information Processing*. New York: Academic Press, pp. 215–281.

Chi, M.T.H, Glaser, R., and Rees, E. (1982). Expertise in problem solving. In R. Sternberg (ed.), *Advances in the Psychology of Human Intelligence*. Hillsdale, NJ: Lawrence Erlbaum Associates, pp. 7–75.

Collings, D.G., Scullion, H., and Morley, M.J. (2007). Changing patterns of global staffing in the multinational enterprise: Challenges to the conventional expatriate assignment and emerging alternatives. *Journal of World Business*, 42 (2), 198–213.

Daily, C.M. Trevis-Certo, S., and Dalton, D. (2000). International experience in the executive suite: The path to prosperity? *Strategic Management Journal*, 20, 515–523.

Deci, E.L., and Ryan, R.M. (1985). *Intrinsic Motivation and Self-Determination in Human Behavior*. New York: Plenum.

Dewey, J. (1938). *Experience and Education*. New York: Simon & Schuster.

Dowling, P.J., and Welch, D.E. (2004). *International Human Resource Management: Managing People in a Multinational Context* (4th edn). London: Thomson Learning.

Earley, P.C., and Ang, S. (2003). *Cultural Intelligence: Individual Interactions Across Cultures*. Palo Alto: Stanford University Press.

Earley, P.C., and Peterson, R.S. (2004). The elusive cultural chameleon: Cultural intelligence as a new approach to intercultural training for the global manager. *Academy of Management Learning and Education*, 3, 100–115.

Earley, P.C., Ang, S., and Tan, J. (2006). *CQ: Developing Cultural Intelligence at Work*. Palo Alto: Stanford University Press.

Eccles, J.S., and Wigfield, A. (2002). Motivational beliefs, values, and goals. In S.T. Fiske, D.L. Schacter, and C. Zahn-Waxler (eds), *Annual review of psychology*, 53, Palo Alto, CA: Annual Reviews, pp. 109–132.

Flavell, J.H. (1979). Metacognition and cognitive monitoring: A new area of cognitive inquiry. *American Psychologist*, 34, 906–11.

Friedman, V.J., and Berthoin Antal, A. (2005). Negotiating reality: A theory of action approach to intercultural competence. *Management Learning*, 36, 69–86.

Gardner, H. (1993). *Multiple Intelligence: The Theory in Practice*. New York: Basic Books.

Gelfand, M.J., Erez, M.E., and Aycan, Z. (2007). Cross-cultural organizational behavior. *Annual Review of Psychology*, 58, 479–514.

Gudykunst, W.B., Ting-Toomey, S., and Chua, E. (1988). *Culture and Interpersonal Communication*. Newbury Park: Sage.

Guion, R.M. (1998). *Assessment, Measurement, and Prediction of Personnel Decisions*. Mahwah, NJ: Lawrence Erlbaum Associates Publishers.

Hall, D.T. (1959). *The Silent Language*. New York: Doubleday.

Hall, D.T., Zhu, G., and Yan, A. (2001). Developing global leaders: To hold on to them, let them go! *Advances in Global Leadership*, 2, 327–349.

Hechanova, R., Beehr, T.A., and Christiansen, N.D. (2003). Antecedents and consequences of employees' adjustment to overseas assignment: A meta-analytic review. *Applied Psychology: An International Review*, 52, 213–236.

Imai, L., and Gelfand, M.J. (2007). *The culturally intelligent negotiator: The impact of CQ on intercultural negotiation effectiveness*. Paper presented at the 67th Annual Meeting of the Academy of Management.

Kealey, D.J. (1996). The challenge of international personnel selection. In D. Landis and R.S. Bhagat (eds), *Handbook of Intercultural Training* (2nd edn), Thousand Oaks: Sage, pp. 81–105.

Kolb, A.Y., and Kolb, D.A. (2005). Learning styles and learning spaces: Enhancing experiential learning in higher education. *Academy of Management Learning and Education*, 4, 193–212.

Kolb, D.A. (1984). *Experiential Learning: Experience as the Source of Learning and Development*. Englewood Cliffs, NJ: Prentice-Hall.

Mainemelis, C., Boyatzis, R., and Kolb, D.A. (2002). Learning styles and adaptive flexibility: Testing experiential learning theory. *Management Learning*, 33, 5–33.

Mayerhofer, H., Hartmann, L.C., Michelitsch-Riedl, G., and Kollinger, I. (2004). Flexpatriate assignments: A neglected issue in global staffing. *International Journal of Human Resource Management*, 15 (8), 1371–1389.

McCall, M.W., and Hollenbeck, G.P. (2002). *The Lessons of International Experience: Developing Global Executives*. MA: Harvard Business School.

McCauley, C.D. (1986). *Developmental experiences in managerial work: A literature review* (Technical Report No. 26). Greensboro, NC: Center for Creative Leadership.

Mendenhall, M.E., and Oddou, G. (1985). The dimensions of expatriate acculturation: A review. *Academy of Management Review*, 10, 39–47.

Morley, M.J., Heraty, N., and Collings, D.G. (2006). *New Directions in Expatriate Research*. NY: Palgrave Macmillan.

Nardon, L., and Steers, R.M. (2007). Learning cultures on the fly. *Advances in Comparative International Management*, 19, 171–190.

Nelson, T.O. (1996). Consciousness and metacognition. *American Psychologist*, 51, 102–116.

Ng, K.Y., and Earley, C.P. (2006). Culture and intelligence: Old constructs, new frontiers. *Group and Organization Management*, 31, 4–19.

Ng, K.Y., Van Dyne, L., and Ang, S. (2007). *From experience to experiential learning: Cultural intelligence as a learning capability for global leader development*. Technical Report #07-05, Center for Leadership and Cultural Intelligence, Nanyang Business School, Nanyang Technological University, Singapore.

Oberg, K. (1960). Culture shock: Adjustment to new cultural environments. *Practical Anthropology*, 7, 177–182.

Oddou, G., Mendenhall, M., and Ritchie, J.B. (2000). Leveraging travel as a tool for global leadership development. *Human Resource Management*, 2–3, 159–172.

Osland, J.S., and Bird, A. (2000). Beyond sophisticated stereotyping: Cultural sensemaking in context. *Academy of Management Executive*, 14, 65–87.

Osland, J.S., and Osland, A. (2006). Expatriate paradoxes and cultural involvement. *International Studies of Management and Organization*, 35 (4), 91–114.

Rockstuhl, T., and Ng, K.Y. (2007). A multilevel model of cultural diversity, cultural intelligence and trust in teams. In S. Ang and L. Van Dyne (eds), *Handbook of Cultural Intelligence*. New York: M. E Sharpe.

Schmidt, F.L., Hunter, J.E., and Outerbridge, A.N. (1986). Impact of job experience and ability on job knowledge, work sample performance, and supervisory ratings of job performance. *Journal of Applied Psychology*, 71, 432–439.

Schuler, R.S., and Tarique, I. (2007). International human resource management: A North American perspective, a thematic update and suggestions for future research. *International Journal of Human Resource Management*, 18 (5), 717–734.

Schuler, R.S., Jackson, S., and Luo, Y. (2004). *Managing Human Resources in Cross-Border Alliances*. London: Routledge.

Seibert, K.W. (1996). Experience is the best teacher, if you can learn from it. In D.T. Hall and Associates (eds), *The Career is Dead – Long Live the Career: A Relational Approach to Careers*. San Francisco: Jossey-Bass, pp. 246–264.

Shaffer, M.A., Harrison, D.A., Gregersen, H., Black, J.S., and Ferzandi, L.A. (2006). You can take it with you: Individual differences and expatriate effectiveness. *Journal of Applied Psychology*, 91, 109–125.

Sparrow, P.R. (2007). Globalization of HR at function level: Case studies of the recruitment, selection and assessment processes. *International Journal of Human Resource Management*, 18, 845–867.

Sparrow, P.R., Brewster, C., and Harris, H. (2004). *Globalizing Human Resource Management*. London: Routledge.

Spreitzer, G.M., McCall, M.W. Jr, and Mahoney, J.D. (1997). Early identification of international executive potential. *Journal of Applied Psychology*, 82, 6–29.

Stahl, G.K., and Mendenhall, M.E. (2005). *Mergers and Acquisitions: Managing Culture and Human Resources*. Palo Alto, CQ: Stanford University Press.

Sternberg, R.J., and Detterman, D.K. (1986). *What is Intelligence?: Contemporary Viewpoints on its Nature and Definition*. Norwood, NJ: Ablex.

Stokes, G.S., Mumford, M.D., and Owens, W.A. (1994). *Biodata Handbook: Theory, Research and Use of Biographical Information in Selection and Performance*. Palo Alto, CA: Consulting Psychology Press Books.

Takeuchi, R., Tesluk, P.E., Yun, S., Lepak, D.P. (2005). An integrative view of international experience. *Academy of Management Journal*, 48 (6), 85–100.

Taylor, S.E., and Crocker, J. (1981). Schematic bases of social information processing. In E.T. Higgins, C.P. Herman, and M.P. Zanna (eds), *Social Cognition: The Ontario Symposium*. Hillsdale, NJ: Lawrence Erlbaum, pp. 89–134.

Templer, K.J., Tay, C., and Chandrasekar, N.A. (2006). Motivational cultural intelligence, realistic job previews, and realistic living conditions preview, and cross-cultural adjustment. *Group and Organization Management*, 31, 154–173.

Tesluk, P.E., and Jacobs, R.R. (1998). Toward an integrated model of work experience. *Personnel Psychology*, 51, 321–355.

Triandis, H.C. (1994). *Culture and Social Behavior*. New York: McGraw Hill.

Triandis, H.C. (1995). Culture specific assimilators. In S.M. Fowler (ed.), *Intercultural Sourcebook: Cross-Cultural Training Methods*. Yarmouth, ME: Intercultural Press, pp. 179–186.

Triandis, H.C. (2006). Cultural intelligence in organizations. *Group and Organization Management*, 31, 20–26.

Triandis, H.C., Marin, G., Lisansky, J., and Betancourt, H. (1984). Simpatica as a cultural script of Hispanics. *Journal of Personality and Social Psychology*, 47, 1363–1375.

Tung, R.L. (1981). Selection and training of personnel for overseas assignment. *Colombia Journal of Word Business*, 16, 68–78.

Yamazaki, Y., and Kayes, D.C. (2004). An experiential approach to cross-cultural learning: A review and integration of competencies for successful expatriate adaptation. *Academy of Management Learning and Education*, 3, 362–379.

6

Mutual Adjustment of Expatriates and International Team Members: The Role of Political and Social Skill

MICHAEL HARVEY AND MILORAD NOVICEVIC

INTRODUCTION

Most expatriation research that addresses expatriate adjustment has focused on the desired fit between environmental demands and expatriate characteristics/traits in the context of the international assignment (Black *et al.*, 1991). In this research paradigm, expatriates, facing the environmental demands of work and non-work aspects of adjusting to cross-border relocation, not only adjust passively to these foreign assignment demands but also engage proactively in mutual adjustments with host country employees and international team members.

Such mutual adjustments are particularly important when expatriates are engaged as international employees in short-term assignments involving international teamwork (Sparrow, 2006, Suutari and Brewster, this volume Chapter 7). Here, mutual adjustment is viewed as the 'process by which members of different nationalities achieve a fit and reduced conflict between each other, with regard to their differences in work practices and interaction styles' (Zimmermann and Sparrow, 2008: 69). This multiple-mutualities or contextual view of expatriate adjustment emphasizes the process that evolves between members of international team in which an expatriate is a member.

Mutual adjustment of expatriates who are members of international/multicultural teams is important because it addresses a neglected issue in the expatriate literature that being, that expatriates tend to become increasingly dependent on the collaborative inputs of host country and other employees (see Reiche, Kraimer and Harzing, this volume Chapter 8; Zimmermann *et al.*, 2003). For these inputs to occur in international teams, cultural bridging between the expatriate and collaborating cohorts of different nationalities is indispensable

Handbook of International Human Resource Management. Edited by Paul R. Sparrow
© 2009 John Wiley & Sons, Ltd

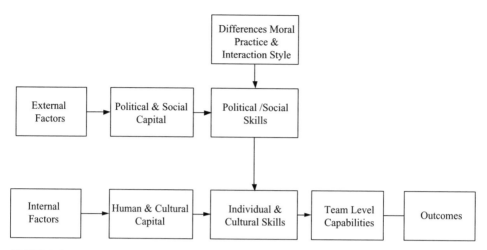

FIGURE 6.1 Model of mutual adjustments in global teams.

(Sackman and Phillips, 2004; Sackmann, this volume Chapter 4). The process of cultural bridging puts pressure upon an expatriate to assess which of their 'multiple selves' of own identity need to be retained and which ones need to be adjusted in mutual interactions with others on the international team (Berry, 1997).

In other words, expatriates involved in multicultural interactions need to assess their individual mode of adjustment relative to others. The expatriate mode of adjustment is the extent to which the expatriate needs to retain his or her standard cultural way of interacting, as well as the extent to which the expatriate expects other team members of different nationality to adjust their standard cultural way of interacting. Zimmermann and Sparrow (2008) conducted a comprehensive qualitative study of such mutual adjustments by expatriates and other members in international teams and derived the model illustrated in Figure 6.1.

The model posits that key differences in work practices and social interaction styles are the main constraints to the smooth functioning of international teams. Therefore, international team members, including expatriates, are required to make mutual adjustments to the practices and styles of 'others' on the team. The key differences in work practices refer to those related to planning, analysis, negotiation, and acceptance of change. The key differences in interaction styles are those related to explicit vs implicit expression and blaming vs non-blaming criticism.

The influence of differences in work practices and interaction styles on expatriate and others' adjustment outcomes is mediated by the levels of team conflict and the member skill set (e.g., political and social) (see Figure 6.1). The level of conflict (or mutual support) in the international teams is influenced to a large degree by the level of established political and social capital of the individual team members. In contrast, the members' skill set is influenced by the level to which they have built their human and cultural capital.

Zimmermann and Sparrow (2008) suggest that further developments of the model shown in Figure 6.1 should focus on the distribution of responsibilities and power in international teams. In particular, a very interesting research question is to examine when a greater share of responsibilities regarding the customer interface, product development and team leadership may have to be provided by other team members, such as the host country nationals: 'Expatriate adjustment research could therefore benefit from taking into account the power distribution between expatriates and other team members to examine how they affect the mode of adjustment' (Zimmermann and Sparrow 2008: 80). Evidently, the first step in addressing the problem posed by this question is to explain the concept of expatriate political capital (Harvey and Novicevic, 2004).

EXPATRIATE POLITICAL CAPITAL IN MUTUAL ADJUSTMENT WITHIN INTERNATIONAL TEAMS

Expatriate political capital reflects the expatriate capacity to control conflict between the international team members by identifying their competing interests and influencing the agenda setting for their joint programs. The legitimacy to influence agenda setting arises from the expatriate's capacity to shape credible expectations of team members about the present and future demands for the task at hand. Acting in this way as an organizational cross-border power broker, the expatriate could use his or her political influence for delegation of responsibilities to other team members.

The main purpose of this delegation is to influence them to justify the reasonableness of the proposed agenda for change. To sustain his or her political influence on the agenda addressing the team leadership, customer interface, and product development, the expatriate needs to accumulate/replenish political capital continuously. Expatriate political capital is accumulated most effectively through interactions that have occurred in prior participation in and leadership of international teams. The growing globalization of the firm's activities is likely to enhance further the importance of political capital accumulation/replenishment for the expatriate, primarily in terms of mobilizing support from team members for corporate initiatives (see Edwards, this volume Chapter 11, for a discussion of politics and reverse diffusion of practices; and Welch, Welch, and Fenwick's discussion of international project work, this volume Chapter 9).

For the accumulation and use of political capital by the expatriate to be appropriately analyzed, it is necessary to identify its distinct dimensions. An analysis can be conducted along these dimensions on how different aspects of political capital accumulate when the expatriate influences the level of conflict in an international team. As researchers, if we can develop an appropriate analytical framework it may help us to assess how variations of political capital are reflected in subsequent expatriate effectiveness in influencing other members of the international team. The development of an analytical framework should address less how the expatriate *should* use political capital to influence the team but more how this use *actually occurs*. The use of practical theory building (i.e., developing a theory and research propositions based upon observations of practice in organizations) is important in this type of situation to insure grounded research propositions. The complexity of the building and utilizing of political capital necessitates observation of behavior in the context of an organization and not from the suppositions of researchers.

The concept of political capital was originally defined by Bourdieu (1981: 192) as 'a form of symbolic capital, credit founded on credence or belief and recognition or, more precisely, on the innumerable operations of credit by which agents confer on a person (or on an object) the very powers that they recognize in him (or it)'. In recent empirical studies, political capital is used as a construct for positive analysis of policy of political reality in terms of interest-based coalition building and conflict resolution (Lopez, 2002). In contrast to Bourdieu's conceptualizations of political capital, this use of political capital assumes less communitarian values and the need for consensus building among an organization's constituents. In multinational organizations, the use of political capital is relevant because subsidiaries are engaged in a constant competition for scarce resources associated with corporate initiatives, as well as for the resources that are needed to support their own entrepreneurial initiatives (Birkinshaw *et al.*, 1998). Specifically, this competition often initiates a functional conflict among subsidiaries – the conflict that can be an important part of the problems faced by expatriates functioning in international teams.

When the subsidiaries of a multinational organization compete for new mandates, their rivalry often produces a mix of both conflict and consensus building behaviors. Facing this situation of high ambiguity, team members from subsidiaries tend to search for expatriates as coalition partners with accumulated political capital because expatriates can lobby for mandates of their subsidiaries by influencing the corporate agenda setting (Aulakh *et al.*, 1997; Birkinshaw *et al.*, 1998; Harvey and Novicevic, 2004). Therefore, the political influence of expatriates can be viewed as a critical conduit for allocation of scarce and valuable resources in a global network.

In the political realm of a global network, the most critical resources are (Zimmermann and Sparrow, 2008):

(1) the leadership authority to engage in political behavior; and
(2) the customer support and the headquarters legitimacy to engage in political behavior.

When the international team's authority is derived from the customer support and the headquarters legitimacy, political capital can be accumulated by the members involved in this collaborative exchange of international teams. For the purpose and the scope of this chapter where our analysis is focused at the individual level of an expatriate, we need to examine the expatriate's use of symbolic resources to accumulate political capital and enhance his or her reputation in international teams. To explain the expatriate's political exchange/flow of resources in the international teams, we use political resource and investment theories developed in political science research (see Figure 6.2). The use of political science theory brings benefits over more traditional IHRM theories such as institutional, resource-based view of firm, etc. (i.e., benefits and need for a broader social science view of things).

Types of Resources Used by Expatriates to Influence International Team Members

		Instrumental	Structural
Component of Expatriate Accumulated Political Capital	Reputational	Expatriate political skills to assert authority in international teams	Expatriate authority as perceived by international team members and other relevant stakeholders
	Representative	Subsidiary support for expatriates involved in international teams	Legitimacy granted by the headquarters for the expatriate role in international teams

FIGURE 6.2 Bases of expatriate power in international teams.

Birner and Wittmer (2000, 2003) argue that the concept of political capital is grounded in the political resource theory, originally introduced by Rogers (1974) and later developed by Hicks and Mishra (1993) and Leicht and Jenkins (1998). Political resource theory defines political capital as 'the resources that are used by an actor to influence policy formation processes and realize the outcomes that serve the actor's perceived interests' (Birner and Wittmer, 2000: 289). The development by Hicks and Mishra (1993: 672) makes a distinction between:

(1) instrumental resources that 'facilitate diverse actors' pursuits of their interests by empowering their actions or conditioning the effectiveness of specific instrumental resources'; and
(2) structural resources (i.e., infra-resources) which 'influence the possibilities of diverse actors to accumulate instrumental political capital and condition the effectiveness of different types of instrumental capital' (Birner and Wittmer, 2000: 6).

In the case of expatriates, instrumental resources refer to expatriate relational resources usable to lobby with the corporate top management and thus gain power in international teams; whereas, structural resources refer to expatriate centrality in the global advice network of corporate top management team, which in turn is likely to effect expatriate power in international teams.

Lopez (2002) extended the conceptualization of political capital using political investment theory originally developed by Denzau and Munger (1986). Based on this theory, an expatriate invests symbolic resources to accumulate two distinct forms of political capital:

(1) reputational political capital; and
(2) representative political capital, under the conditions of collaboration in international teams.

The reputational dimension of political capital reflects the expatriate's standing in the team members' eyes. Whereas the representative dimension of political capital reflects the members' support for the expatriate.

The relevant variables, selected from political resource and investment theories, are combined in the analytical framework shown in Figure 6.2. As Figure 6.2 indicates, this analytical framework is convenient to use for qualitative case studies to examine four expatriate power bases in international teams:

(1) expatriate political skills to assert authority;
(2) expatriate authority as perceived by the team members and other relevant stakeholders;
(3) subsidiary support for individual expatriate; and
(4) legitimacy of expatriate role in international team, as it is granted by the head-quarters.

The specific research questions or needs, which the exploration of each of these four quadrants helps to answer, include:

◆ What resources are instrumental to increased expatriate authority in international team and reputation in the organization?
◆ What structural resources may increase expatriate authority and reputation among the organization's stakeholders?
◆ What instrumental resources are positively related to subsidiary support for expatriate acceptance as a corporate representative? What structural resources are positively related to subsidiary support for expatriate legitimacy as a corporate representative?

The analytical framework shown in Figure 6.2 also can serve to guide quantitative research studies. We suggest five directions for such research:

1. Only quantitative studies can indicate whether and how the expatriate use of different types of resources (instrumental and structural variables) and the components of the accumulated expatriate political capital (reputational and representative variables) may interact. These interactions have been detected in empirical studies of political science research of politicians' behaviour (Hicks and Mishra, 1993; Leicht and Jenkins, 1998; Wohlgemuth, 1999). However, they might not be significant in case of international teams where expatriate authority is more likely to be conflicting and support becomes critical.
2. Building on the work by Leicht and Jenkins (1998) in political science, models can be developed using event history method (i.e., using international team successes as events) to explore the interactions between structural and instrumental resources as explanatory variables.
3. An alternative approach to empirical research on political capital is to use transaction cost analysis to explore why the expatriate may make trade-offs when acquiring political capital along reputational and representative

dimensions. Transaction costs could involve the costs of gathering information in, and/or the costs of monitoring international teams' activities.

4. The real options perspective can be used to address how political capital is appreciated and depreciated relative to the options in their power use, and which factors may engender path dependency of expatriate investing of symbolic resources in these options.

5. The network analysis can be conducted for evaluation and assessment of both an individual and a cadre of management's networks (see Sparrow, Brewster, and Ligthart, this volume Chapter 18). Such analysis is valuable because a shortage of expatriate leadership talent is one of the greatest barriers that multinationals encounter in their attempts to operate effectively on a global scale. As the intensifying competition increases the need for international teamwork and expatriate political capital, a strong global talent pool of expatriates will become a scarce strategic asset contributing to sustainable competitive advantage.

Eventually, the analytical framework shown in Figure 6.2 can be used to guide longitudinal studies examining the members' perceptions of expatriate adjustment across team tasks and/or time periods. In particular, variations in perceived effectiveness of expatriates relative to accumulation and investment of political capital can be examined across teams in terms of shared assumptions about social equality, homogeneity, development, and status (Gómez-Mejia and Palich, 1997). These differences may likely influence the flows of resources and support for expatriates as global employees involved in cross-border teams.

EXPATRIATE POLITICAL SKILL NEEDED FOR MUTUAL ADJUSTMENT IN INTERNATIONAL TEAMS

Expatriate political skill would appear to be an essential when one considers the level of newness, ambiguity and the complexity of most international team assignments. To gain a better understanding of the potential benefits of expatriate political skill for international team assignments, it is necessary to decompose the concept into its key dimensions.

Key dimensions of political skill

Researchers (Ferris *et al.*, 2005) have identified four basic dimensions of the political skill construct across work contexts (i.e., encompassing the associated abilities, skills, knowledge, and behaviors), which are:

1. Self and social awareness
2. Interpersonal influence and control
3. Genuineness and sincerity
4. Established Social Network Inside/Outside the Organization.

First, in relation to self and social awareness, the expatriate ability to ascertain from social interactions in the international team the meaning of a member's actions and the reactions to others in the team. If the expatriate is a keen observer of what is taking and/or not taking place in an international team, it will enable the politically astute expatriate to adjust more readily in international teams. The higher the expatriate social awareness the greater his or her likelihood of success in influencing the behavior of team members. These socially and self-aware expatriates can then translate their success into a more fluid adjustment to the foreign environment and the international team (see Ng, Van Dyne and Ang, this volume Chapter 5). Knowing how to 'read' social situations provides the expatriate with political skill level that many of his or her counterparts in the international team may not have to lead the team. It should be noted, however, that self and social awareness of the expatriate depends on expatriate cultural intelligence, which refers to the expatriate's skill to function effectively in the context of cultural diversity (Earley and Ang, 2003; Earley and Mosakowski, 2005; Ang *et al.*, 2006).

Second, in relation to interpersonal influence and control, socially skillful expatriates have the ability to get others in the international team to believe in them. This belief may be relative to the expatriate's ability to accomplish particular tasks or implicitly in their overall competency. The expatriate managers that can adapt their behavior to the team context and its behavioral/social norms will experience better adjustment. The political skill of these expatriates allows them to have influence beyond their hierarchical positions in the team.

Third, in relation to genuineness and sincerity, it is closely coupled to the level of influence an expatriate can have in a international team. The ability to merge the social norms of the international team into the personification of their actions distinguishes expatriate managers who have inordinate political skill. A key to building this type of reputation is to ameliorate the concerns of the team members that the actions of the expatriate are for their own benefit. Objectivity in dealing with other team members, so that the expatriate is viewed as being a 'straight shooter' or as being 'authentic' is a fundamental aspect of exhibiting political skill (Ferris *et al.*, 2005).

Finally, in relation to established social network inside/outside of the organization, political skill is built through the use of a pre-existing social network of managers coming into the international team. One of the fundamental problems with expatriate managers is that they are unceremoniously 'dropped' into the international team with a, more or less, 'take it or leave it' message from the domestic headquarters. Social network is the organizational 'chits' that a expatriate manager has built-up in the organization where reciprocity in assistance is expected due to past interactions. In the international team, expatriate managers will have limited social networks due to their newness to the organization and the transitory nature of their assignment. Therefore, the critical means of 'transporting' social influence is through the personal/professional networks of the expatriate manager. In other words, 'human capital is more powerful once it is leveraged through relationships to form communities and networks of engaged individusls applying their talents collaboratively' (Lengnick-Hall and Lengnick-Hall, 2006: 486).

Process benefits of political skill

If these more portable relationships can be used to have a positive impact on the members of the international team, the expatriate may influence the international team members by obtaining assistance from headquarters personnel. For example, if the expatriate has social relationships with the corporate managers who have control over scarce resources needed for the international team so that these resources are made available to the team members, expatriate political influence could quickly be built. The problem of lack of social influence in the international team can be a significant handicap to expatriate managers and one that is difficult to overcome due to their inability to effectively interface with international team members (i.e., due to language difference, cultural distance, lack of experience in the country, limited social/cultural training prior to expatriating and the like).

The social network of the expatriate managers in the headquarters organization can provide them with valuable information, resources, cooperation, and trust (Baron and Markman, 2000). From these tangible/intangible assets, expatriate managers can begin to build trust from the host country employees/managers. This trust can, over time, be elevated to political influence within the host country organization, thereby accelerating the rate at which these valuable social commodities are obtained. These social obligations become the foundation to political influence and increase the probability of the expatriate manager successfully accomplishing tasks during his or her foreign assignment in the international team.

Expatriate managers that have a high level of political skill may be invaluable in maintaining relationships between the headquarters of the home organization and the international teams. Such an expatriate plays a boundary-spanning role, bridging the control gap between the domestic and foreign organizations. The interpersonal acumen of expatriates (i.e., social awareness and self-awareness), provides the foundation of instrumental relationships with key members of the international team. This social network can be translated into obtaining commitment from decision makers at headquarters. The higher the political skill of the expatriate manager, the more likely there will be an increase in commitment from members in the international team to support the expatriate manager.

Moreover, expatriate managers who possess a high level of political skill have an equally important role when examining their impact on the international team and its members. Due to their adaptability and social acuity, such expatriate managers appear to have social knowledge and understanding beyond that of other outsiders. Therefore, higher political skill allows expatriates to build trust and confidence faster, due to their perceived genuineness and sincerity. Overall, it seems that political competence is the bedrock of building effective expatriate managers for global assignments and leadership roles.

Expatriate managers possessing political capital are likely to possess the commensurate political skill necessary for effective mutual adjustment. The concept of political capital relates to the capacity of developing political skill to influence team level capabilities (see Figure 6.1). Political capital is not the same as the 'social grease' attributed to social capital but is a capacity that rests within leaders to remove obstacles to cooperation due to their political goodwill that others perceive (Birner and Wittmer, 2000).

Meso factors as mediators or moderators

The following meso factors, which should be assessed empirically whether they act as mediators or moderators, may influence the relationship between expatriate political capital and expatriate political skill:

(1) *social approximation* – the degree of synchronicity of the expatriate interaction with the team members and those in the organization with whom the expatriate has accumulated political capital;
(2) *level/type of interaction* – access of team members to the expatriate and the type of their mutual interaction (i.e., face-to-face, electronic or other);
(3) *scope and reach* – the breadth of the network of other individuals who perceive the expatriate having political capital;
(4) *dispersion of knowledge* – the knowledge accessibility within the network of the expatriate possessing political capital;
(5) *durability* – the 'lasting' or residual capacity of the political capital of the expatriate; and
(6) *degree of formality* – the degree to which the political capital of the expatriate is legitimized in the corporate level by the position of formal authority.

The magnitude of differences in the willingness to adjust between the expatriate and the team members will influence the required level of political skill of the expatriate manager to adjust to the team's cultural context and influence the team-level capabilities. In particular, the variation in the temporal orientation among cultures of the team members is likely to influence the required rate-of-change as well as the appropriate timing for the expatriate to act appropriately. Without having the appropriate temporal perspective, the expatriate will not interact in unison with the 'natural' flow of events in the team. In other words, without culturally anchoring his or her political skill, an expatriate manager will make attempts of influence that may be misdirected, ineffectual and detrimental relative to an expatriate manager's original intent (Newman and Nollen, 1996).

The culture of a multicultural team to which the expatriate manager will be assigned may be significantly different from that of the previous domestic teams, in which the expatriate has accumulated political capital. As multicultural teams may be a composite of expatriates, local nationals, as well as third country nationals, their composition or 'mix' of employees has a hybrid culture (Lorenz, 1993; Bartlett and Ghoshal, 1989). This unique cultural setting determines the expatriate political skill needed for the expatriate as an international team member to effectively draw from his or her accumulated political capital.

Given the stickiness of political capital for transfer across organizational/team boundaries, expatriate managers' domestic political and social ties may be of limited value during foreign assignments (Burt, 1992; Brass, 1995; Coleman, 1988). Particularly, in the case of the short-term expatriate or atypical assignments addressed by

Suutari and Brewster (this volume Chapter 7), local nationals will know that they can 'outlast' any influence attempts by expatriate managers. The composite effect of the hybrid team culture and the temporary nature of expatriate assignments can dramatically increase the need for the expatriate manager's political skill in international teams (Bandura, 1982, 1995). The multicultural team settings, thereby, can reduce the political effectiveness of the transferred expatriate manager, particularly in the short-term (Reichers and Schneider, 1990).

In many foreign team assignments, expatriate managers have to manage between teams and the organizational entity to which they are assigned during the foreign assignment. Thus, the political skill of an expatriate manager needs to be attuned to both the host organization and the team environments while coordinating the other entities beyond the host country organization. These organizational/team cultures may be dramatically different, thus increasing the complexity of the political skill set needed by the expatriate manager. In addition, given the limited time for expatriates to build political capital among the international team members, expatriate managers need to employ their political skills effectively to reach the goals of the assignment. The absence of trust between the expatriate and other managers in the team reduces the team capabilities and the adjustment and effectiveness of the expatriate manager (Aulakh *et al.*, 1997; Inkpen and Currall, 1997). Given that the effective utilization of expatriate political skill is contingent on the team context, then the previous reputation of expatriate managers becomes crucial in terms of their political skill to effectively manage in a foreign context.

A central issue becomes how to assess the accumulated level of political capital, as the capacity to employ political skill of expatriates, prior to their transfer overseas. In addition, it is important not only to determine how expatriate managers will learn to adapt their political skill frame-of-reference to be effective in multicultural environments, but also how expatriate managers will develop a means to accrue social skills to improve their adjustment and acceptance in international teams.

EXPATRIATE SOCIAL SKILL NEEDED FOR MUTUAL ADJUSTMENT IN INTERNATIONAL TEAMS

Past research has indicated a strong relationship between expatriate social capital and expatriate effectiveness (Harvey and Novicevic, 2004) but a weak relationship between expatriate social capital and expatriate adjustment (Kostova and Roth 2003). However, we know little about the relationship between expatriate social capital and mutual adjustment in international teams.

Social capital is defined as an asset that is engendered via social relations and can be employed to facilitate action and achieve above-normal rents (Adler and Kwon, 2002; Baker, 1990; Hunt, 2000; Hunt and Morgan, 1995; Leana and Van Buren, 1999). In a management context, social capital has been primarily conceptualized as a resource reflecting the character of social relations within a firm (Hunt, 2000; Kostava and Roth, 2003) that extend beyond firm boundaries providing a basis for inter-firm action.

Although the term 'social capital' has received considerable attention in the literature, consensus on its theoretical domain and tenets have yet to be achieved

(Leana and Van Buren, 1999). In a review of the social capital literature, Leana and Van Buren (1999) note that the literature presents a variety of perspectives on the levels of analysis, dimensions, etc., of the concept. They further indicate that two underlying dimensions are common to existing conceptualizations of social capital:

(1) associability and
(2) trust.

Associability is defined as the willingness and ability of participants to subordinate individual level goals and associated actions to collective goals and actions (Leana and Van Buren, 1999). The inherent subordination of individual goals through participation in the collective, however, is not a relinquishment of individual goals, but rather an active mechanism that individuals employ to pursue individual goals (Leana and Van Buren, 1999). Through participation in efforts to meet group objectives, the individual is able to achieve his or her individual goals. This is not to imply a self-serving purpose, but rather through identification with the group the individual works toward the group objective, and residually toward their own goals (Leana and Van Buren, 1999). Given the nature of associability, it has both affective (i.e., collectivist feelings) and skill-based components (e.g., ability to coordinate activities).

A second component of social capital is trust. Trust is evident when one has confidence in another's reliability and integrity (Das and Teng, 1998; Leana and Van Buren, 1999; Morgan and Hunt, 1994). It has been asserted that cooperative, long-term relationships are dependent upon the fostering of trust (Das and Teng, 1998; Morgan and Hunt, 1994). Researchers have proposed that trust can be considered in terms of a risk–reward relationship (Mayer *et al.*, 1995; Williamson, 1993), where predictable actions by one party allow the relationship to operate more effectively. The value of trust is derived from a reduction in risk of opportunistic behavior on the part of one's exchange partner thus reducing the costs of the relationship (Williamson, 1993). Further, when someone is trusted, others are more willing to commit (Das and Teng, 1998; Leana and Van Buren, 1999; Morgan and Hunt, 1994). Through the development of trust in the relationship, repetitive transaction sequences occur, reducing transaction costs.

Trust extends beyond dyadic relations in international teams (Leana and Van Buren, 1999). Putnam (1993) argues that trust can reside at the generalized level via the development and adherence to generally accepted norms and behaviors in groups/teams. Thus, an individual or firm that adheres to the generally accepted norms and behaviors embedded within set social relations can be trusted even though a member joining the team does not have personal knowledge of, or interaction with, the team.

The dimensions of associability and trust are both attributes of the group as well as the individual. As such, social capital can be conceptualized as an attribute of a collective, as well as the sum of the individual relations. Leana and Van Buren (1999) argue that acts that enhance individual social capital benefit the collective directly and the individual indirectly, thus tying individual level social capital to firm/team level capital.

FUTURE RESEARCH GUIDELINES

Future research should examine how political influence of expatriates can contribute to their adjustment to international teams. Researchers of expatriate adjustment should recognize how the political capital perspective can be used to design the improved deployment of expatriate talent across the firm's cross-border relationships (Mendenhall *et al.*, 2001). In particular, researchers should examine how the effectiveness of this type of deployment can influence the organization's cultural context to delegate leadership in international teams (Beer, 1997).

The focus on the political capital perspective may reveal new approaches to assessing expatriate understanding of diversity and its role in innovative approaches to organizing and managing teams within global networks (i.e., international team-based management of diverse employees and their effective and meaningful communication in teams). Specifically, the research may focus on examining the extent to which the accumulation of expatriate capital through international team assignments may contribute to improved adjustment to facilitate knowledge integration across diverse team memberships within the global network (Harvey *et al.*, 1999).

Another suggested line for future research is to analyze political capital in terms of how it is distributed across the organization's expatriates. In this conceptualization, political capital would represent the varying capacity of expatriates to influence the way in which the power in the international teams is distributed (Dipboye, 1995). The topics of research may include the variables that influence this capacity, including expatriate political skill. This line of research may be conducted both at the individual level and at the team level (i.e., by surveying the international team members). In addition, a longitudinal research of the change in expatriate political capital during transformations of a global network may reveal the challenges faced during the change of its internal governance mechanisms.

Another interesting line of future research is to relate the level of expatriate political capital to their positioning in internal (i.e., within-organization) reputational markets. Fombrun (2001: 289) defines external reputational markets as 'winner-take-all environments in which exaggerated rewards accrue to companies that develop even marginally better reputations than their rivals'. A reputable company attracts more and better resources not only as an 'investment, supplier or neighbor of choice' but also as an 'employer of choice'. An interesting research topic to explore is the extent to which expatriate success in the internal and external reputational markets (i.e., career success) is influenced by their accumulated political capital. Perhaps the examination of such influences might reveal what really fuels participation in and leadership of international teams.

CONCLUSION

In this chapter we have provided a detailed description of the expatriate political and social capital as factors of influence for expatriate adjustment to international teams. Specifically, the expatriate influence on and adjustment to international teams in the multinational organizations of the 21st century is increasingly having implications for subsidiary development. As international teams are conducive to attempts of the symbolic political influence, it provides opportunities for the expatriates to use their political skill and assert their relevance as a critical conduit for political resource flows in the organization. In their skillful use of influence, expatriates will likely strive not only to complement the strategic efforts of top management but also enhance their own reputation inside and outside the multinational organization and its subsidiaries.

The responsiveness of the team members from subsidiaries to expatriate influence is motivated by their competition to become the champions of best practices in the global network. Therefore, the expatriate political influence might contribute to the successful transfer of knowledge and practices across subsidiaries. For example, the reproduction of best practices might be championed by expatriates as the international team leaders and members. As a positive externality of these symbolic actions, international teams-led expatriates will compete to champion corporate initiatives and enable a lateral coordination of the best-practice initiatives because expatriates are motivated to be considered for the corporate succession plans. In this way, enhanced formation and an accumulation of expatriate political capital is a critical enabler for the distributed global leadership and teamwork to flourish in the global organizations of the 21st century.

REFERENCES

Adler, P.S., and Kwon, S.-W. (2002). Social capital: Prospects for a new concept. *Academy of Management Review*, 27 (1), 17–40.
Ang, S., Van Dyne, L., and Koh C. (2006). Personality correlates of the four-factor model of cultural intelligence, *Group and Organization Management*, 31, 100–123.
Aulakh, P., Kotabe, M., and Sahay, A. (1997). Trust and performance in cross border marketing partnerships: A behavioral approach. *Journal of International Business Studies*, 27 (5), 1005–1032.
Baker, W. (1990). Market networks and corporate behavior. *American Journal of Sociology*, 96, 589–625.
Bandura, A. (1982). Self-efficacy mechanism in human agency. *American Psychologist*, 37, 122–147.
Bandura, A. (1995). Comments on the crusade against the causal efficacy of human thought. *Journal of Behavior Therapy and Experimental Psychiatry*, 26, 179–190.
Baron, R.A., and Markman, G.D. (2000). Beyond social capital: The role of social competence in entrepreneurs' success. *Academy of Management Executive*, 14 (1), 106–116.
Bartlett, C., and Ghoshal, S. (1989). *Managing Across Borders: The Transnational Solution* (1st edn). Boston, MA: Harvard Business School Press.
Beer, M. (1997). The transformation of the human resource function: resolving the tension between a traditional administrative role and a new strategic role, *Human Resource Management*, 36 (1), 49–56.
Berry, J.W. (1997). Immigration, acculturation, and adaptation. *Applied Psychology: An International Review*, 46 (1), 5–34.
Birkinshaw, J., Hood, H., and Johnson, S. (1998). Building firm-specific advantages in multinational corporations: The role of subsidiary initiative. *Strategic Management Journal*, 19, 221–224.
Birner, R., and Wittmer, H. (2000). *Converting social capital into political capital*. Paper.

Birner, R., and Wittmer, H. (2003). Using Social Capital to Create Political Capital – How Do Local Communities Gain Political Influence? A Theoretical Approach and Empirical Evidence from Thailand. In N. Dolvak and E. Ostrom (eds) *The Commons in the New Millennium, Challenges and Adaptation*. Cambridge, MA: MIT Press. pp. 291– 334.

Black, J.S., Mendenhall, M., and Oddou, G. (1991). Towards a comprehensive model of international adjustment: An integration of multiple theoretical perspectives. *Academy of Management Review*, 16, 291–317.

Bourdieu, P. (1981). *Language and Symbolic Power* (G. Raymond and M. Adamson, Trans.). Cambridge: Polity Press.

Brass, D.J. (1995). A social network perspective on human resources management, *Research in Personnel and Human Resources Management*, 13, 39–79.

Burt, R.S. (1992). *Structural Holes: The Social Structure of Competition*. Cambridge, MA: Harvard University Press.

Coleman, J. (1988). Social Capital in the Creation of Human Capital. *American Journal of Sociology*, 94, 95–120.

Das, T., and Teng, B. (1998). Resource and risk management in the strategic alliance making process. *Journal of Management* 24, 21–42.

Denzau, A., and Munger, M. (1986). Legislators and interest groups: How unorganized interests get represented. *American Political Science Review*, 80, 89–106.

Dipboye, R. (1995). How politics can destruct human resources management in the interest of empowerment, support, and justice. In R. Corpanzano and K. Kacmar (eds), *Organizational Politics, Justice, and Support: Managing the Social Climate of the Workplace*. Wesport, CT: Quorum Books, pp. 55–80.

Earley, P.C., and Ang, S. (2003). *Cultural Intelligence: Individual Interactions Across Cultures*. Palo Alto: Stanford University Press.

Earley, P.C., and Mosakowski, E. (2005). Cultural intelligence. *Harvard Business Review*, 82, 139–146.

Ferris, G.R., Treadway, D.C. Kolodinsky R.W., Hochwarter, W.A., Kacmar, C.J., Douglas, D., and Frink, D.D. (2005). Development and validation of the political skill inventory. *Journal of Management*, 31 (1), 126–152.

Fombrun, C.J. (2001). Corporate reputations as economic assets. In M. Hitt, R. Freeman and J. Harrison (eds), *Handbook of Strategic Management*, Malden, MA: Blackwell Publishers. pp. 289–312.

Gómez-Mejia, L., and Palich, L. (1997). Cultural diversity and the performance of multinational firms. *Journal of International Business Studies*, 28, 309–335.

Harvey, M., and Novicevic, M.M. (2004). The development of political skill and political capital by global leaders through global assignments. *International Journal of Human Resource Management*, 15 (7), 1173–1188.

Harvey, M., Novicevic, M.M., and Speier, C. (1999). Inpatriate managers: How to increase the probability of success. *Human Resource Management Review*, 9 (1), 51–81.

Hicks, A., and Mishra, J. (1993). Two perspectives on the welfare state: Political resources and the growth of welfare in affluent capitalist democracies, 1960–1982. *American Journal of Sociology*, 99, 668–710.

Hunt, S. (2000). The competence-based, resource-advantage, and neoclassical theories of competition: Toward a synthesis. In R. Sanchez and A. Heene (eds), *Theory Development for Competence-Based Management. Advances in Applied Business Strategy Series*. Greenwich, CT: JAI Press, pp. 177–209.

Hunt, S., and Morgan, R. (1995). The comparative advantage theory of competition. *Journal of Marketing*, 59, 1–15.

Inkpen, A., and Currall, S. (1997). *International Joint Venture Trust: An Empirical Examination*' in *Cooperative Strategies: Vol. 1. North American perspectives.* Paul W. Beamish and J. Peter Killing (eds), San Francisco, CA: New Lexington Press, pp. 308–334.

Kostova, T., and Roth, K. (2003). Social capital in multinational corporations and a micro-macro model of its formation. *Academy of Management Review,* 28 (2), 297–317.

Leana, C.R., and Van Buren, H.J. (1999). Organizational social capital and employment practices. *Academy of Management Review,* 24 (3), 538–555.

Leicht, K., and Jenkins, J. (1998). Political resources and direct state intervention: The Adoption of Public Venture Capital Programs in the American States, 1974–1990. *Social Forces,* 76 (4), 1323–1345.

Lengnick-Hall, M.L., and Lengnick-Hall, C.A. (2006). International human resource management and social network/social capital theory. In G.K. Stahl and I. Björkman (eds), *Handbook of Research in International Human Resource Management.* Cheltenham: Edward Elgar, pp. 475–487.

Lopez, E. (2002). The legislator as political entrepreneur: Investment in political capital. *The Review of Austrian Economics,* 15 (2), 211–228.

Lorenz, E.N. (1993). *The Essence of Chaos.* Seattle: University of Washington Press.

Mayer, R.C., Davis, J.H., and Schoorman, F.D. (1995). An integrative model of organizational trust. *Academy of Management Review,* 20 (3), 709–734.

Mendenhall, M.E., Kuhlmann, T., and Stahl, G. (2001). *Developing Global Business Leaders: Policies, Processes and Innovations,* Westport, CT: Quorum.

Morgan, R.M., and Hunt, S.D. (1994). The Commitment – Trust Theory of Relationship Marketing. *Journal of Marketing,* 58, 20–38.

Newman, K.L., and Nollen, S.D. (1996). Culture and congruence: The fit between management practices and national culture. *Journal of International Business Studies,* 27 (4), 753–779.

Putnam, R. (1993). The prosperous community: Social capital and public life. *American Prospect,* 13, 35–42.

Reichers, A.E., and Schneider, B. (1990). Climate and culture: An evolution of constructs. In B. Schneider (Ed.), *Organizational climate and culture.* San Francisco: Jossey-Bass, pp. 5–39.

Rogers, M.E. (1974). Instrumental and Infra-Resources: The Bases of Power. *American Journal of Sociology,* 79, 1418–1433.

Sackmann, S.A., and Phillips, M.E. (2004). Contextual influences on culture research: shifting assumptions for new workplace realities. *International Journal of Cross Cultural Management,* 4 (3), 370–390.

Sparrow, P.R (2006). International management: Key challenges for industrial and organizational psychology. In G. Hodginson and J.K. Ford (eds), *International Review of Industrial and Organizational Psychology,* Vol. 21. London: John Wiley & Sons, pp. 189–266.

Williamson, O.E. (1993). Calculativeness, trust and economic organization. *Journal of Law and Economics,* 36, 453–486.

Wohlgemuth, M. (1999). Entry barriers in politics. *Review of Austrian Economics,* 12, 175–200.

Zimmermann, A., and Sparrow, P.R. (2008). Mutual adjustment processes in international teams: Lessons for the study of expatriation. *International Studies of Management and Organization,* 37 (3), 65–88.

Zimmermann, A., Holman, D. and Sparrow, P. (2003). Unravelling adjustments mechanisms: Adjustment of German expatriates to intercultural interactions, work, and living conditions in the People's Republic of China. *International Journal of Cross-Cultural Management,* 3 (1), 45–66.

7

Beyond Expatriation: Different Forms of International Employment

VESA SUUTARI AND CHRIS BREWSTER

INTRODUCTION

Research on international mobility has so far tended to focus on long-term expatriation within MNCs (Briscoe and Schuler, 2004). The assumption has been that individuals are sent to another country for a period of time that is long enough, if they were in a long-term relationship, to justify their partner and/or family moving with them, but with the intention on both the employer and the employee side that the assignment will not last for more than a few years. In reality, other types of international assignment patterns are growing at least as fast as traditional company sponsored expatriation. These different groups involve:

- immigrants actively and passively attracted to a national labor market;
- global careerists who select a more permanent global career involving various international jobs across difference contexts;
- people working abroad who have not followed the traditional expatriate route and have been sent to another country by their employer, but have used their own initiative to seek job possibilities in foreign job markets[1] (these people can be referred to as self-initiated assignees (SEs));
- international commuters;
- short-term assignees such as project assignees;
- frequent flyers;
- people who, by contrast, never leave their home country but use modern technology to work in international teams.

[1] Being Europeans, we are conscious that the traditional (mainly US) terminology of 'overseas' seems inaccurate. It is inaccurate in the US, too, of course, but in Europe there are vast numbers of countries that can be reached without crossing any seas. We are uncomfortable with the notion of strangeness that goes with the term 'foreign' but have preferred the more accurate terminology.

Handbook of International Human Resource Management. Edited by Paul R. Sparrow
© 2009 John Wiley & Sons, Ltd

If we were reviewing 'atypical' international employees, as such, we might examine such less commonly found groups as women expatriates and expatriates coming from subsidiaries into headquarters (sometimes called, perhaps somewhat ethno-centrically, inpatriates, see Reiche, Kraimer and Harzing, this volume Chapter 8). This chapter focuses specifically on the different forms of international assignment, rather than the different types of employees in them. We review the research and literature concerning these atypical forms of international assignment, analyze the characteristics of these forms (often in comparison to standard expatriation) and examine how companies can manage the mix between these different forms. Finally we draw conclusions about future research needs related to these less-studied forms of international experience in relation to the range of HRM processes that they impact.

DIFFERENT FORMS OF INTERNATIONAL EMPLOYMENT

A number of recent analyses have pointed out the need for more awareness of the various different forms of international work experience (Mayrhofer *et al.*, 2008; Sparrow, 2006a). Briscoe and Schuler (2004: 223) too noted that the definition of international employee inside organizations continues to expand: ' . . . the tradition of referring to all international employees as expatriates – or even international assignees – falls short of the need for international HR practitioners to understand the options available . . . and fit them to evolving international business strategies.'

None of the forms of assignment that we have characterized as 'atypical' or 'different' in this chapter is new. However, there does seem to be some evidence that, for example, short-term assignment forms are growing at least as fast as, maybe faster than, standard expatriation (Dowling and Welch, 2004; PricewaterhouseCoopers, 2002; Tahvanainen, 2003). There is little empirical evidence, but a review of the different forms being identified in the consultancy surveys and the literature gives the impression that the balance is changing so that these 'different forms' are a growing proportion of the total.

There are various developments that help to explain this. Salt and Millar (2006), for example, argue that what has increased demand for these different forms of international mobility are the need for skilled expatriates to help to build new international markets (Findlay *et al.*, 2000); temporary and short-term access to specialized talent in sending countries to assist the execution of overseas projects (Minbaeva and Michailova, 2004; Hocking *et al.*, 2004; Welch, Welch and Fenwick, this volume Chapter 9); and the need for highly mobile elites of management to perform boundary-spanning roles to help to build social networks and facilitate the exchange of knowledge (Tushman and Scanlan, 2005). Others, perhaps more cynically, have pointed to the high costs of traditional expatriate assignments compared to the lower up-front costs of the alternatives (Bonache *et al.*, 2007; Peltonen, 2001).

In response, the academic community is now beginning to recognize the importance of these different kinds of international experience too. We review this work roughly in the order of its effect on the life of the individuals concerned, starting with migration and ending with virtual international teamworking where the individual may continue to live at home.

We present in Table 7.1 some of the possible advantages and disadvantages related to defined forms of international work both from the perspective of individuals and organizations. In the subsequent sections, we review the literature that leads to this analysis.

MIGRATION

Migration involves individuals in moving to a new labour market for either an indeterminate numbers of years or for the rest of their life (Salt and Millar, 2006). The earliest groups of international employees – and the most traditional form of it historically – consists of immigrants. Immigrants have been pushed out of one labor market or been actively or passively attracted to another (Salt and Millar, 2006). The United Nations estimates that 34% of immigrants go to Europe and 21% to the United States of America. And, of course, migration within regions such as Europe is now increasing considerably.

From an IHRM perspective immigrants have tended to be more commonly employed in some kind of self-employment or in lower level positions in companies – often because of inadequate language skills, lower levels of education, or limited job competencies. It is worth pointing out that the immigrant labor community tends to be bifurcated: alongside the majority working in lower level jobs there are many working in expert, highly qualified and managerial positions. In most of the developing countries the importance of this labor pool at both ends is increasing. One effect has been the increasing workforce diversity in such countries. One effect of the growing internationalization of labor markets is that organizations are now increasingly looking to spread their recruitment nets as widely as possible (this is, of course, made easier by internet recruiting). For increasing numbers of organizations, ensuring that they are attractive to the best people in the local community is no longer enough. Work and the capacity to do it cost-effectively do not always fit exactly within national borders. Thus, there has been the development of the new international division of labor with the jobs – no longer always the low-level jobs – being moved to countries where appropriate labor is available; and, concomitantly, labor being brought to where the jobs are. This is creating new demands on the recruitment experts within these organizations.

Within the diversity literature, it is argued that this growing diversity creates challenges due to the cultural differences in working habits, problems in interaction, distrust and hostility, all of which affect trust, collaboration, and decision making. Immigrants often have to face stereotyping and restriction to jobs traditionally done by non-natives.

On the other hand, there seems to be a growing body of evidence that immigrants bring real benefits to the society they join (Briggs, 2003; Mahroum, 2001; McLaughlin and Salt, 2002; Salt and Millar, 2006) and that increasingly, in the more globalized and – in certain territories such as the European Union – open society of today, employers are targeting potential immigrants as employees (for the UK, for example, see CIPD, 2005; Dench *et al.*, 2006).

TABLE 7.1 Advantages and disadvantages of different forms of international working.

Form of mobility	Advantages		Disadvantages	
	Organization	Individual	Organization	Individual
Immigrants	• New labor pool • Cost reduction • No relocation needs/costs • Other possible benefits: customer orientation, innovativeness, commitment … • No repatriation concerns/permanent contracts	• Employment and living opportunities in a new home country	• Education and skill level of average immigrants • Language and cultural skills • No experience from the company • Need for better initiation programs	• Difficulty of access to job markets • Job and career opportunities (discrimination)
Global careerists	• Skill transfer, control • Most experienced group on international business • High competency level (general and international competencies) • Lower support and training needs	• Rich and challenging job environment • High development opportunities • Global job markets • High standard of living	• High costs • Frequent relocation arrangements and career management challenges • Commitment with the employer	• Frequent relocations cause stress and adjustment challenges • Personal rootlesness • Family concerns • Personal relationships hard to keep up

Self-initiated international experiences	• Access to new international labor pool and new skills • Cost reduction (no expatriate contracts)	• Access to international job markets • Professional development in an international context • Access to attractive living environments	• Lack of experience from the company • Need for initiation programs	• Lack of organizational support and training • Future career planning and challenges on possible repatriation (no repatriation agreements)
Commuter assignment	• Skills transfer, control • Cost effectiveness • Flexibility	• Flexible • Less interruption to family than IAs (child education, careers, living) • Professional development through new experiences • No need for complete cultural integration	• Disruptions to organizational lives (at both units) • Travel logistics and administration • Cost of living, compensation and taxation issues may be difficult to identify	• Travel stress/health concerns • Disruptions to daily personal and family lives due to ongoing travel

(continued)

TABLE 7.1 (*Continued*)

Form of mobility	Advantages		Disadvantages	
	Organization	*Individual*	*Organization*	*Individual*
Short-term assignments	• Skills transfers, control • Flexibility • Simplicity • Cost effectiveness	• Personal development • Access to new type of international job experiences • Easier repatriation than on long-term IAs	• Costs sometimes difficult to define • Complex remuneration packages • Work permits and administration	• Travel stress and family life concerns • Complex taxation • Relationships with local colleagues
Virtual assignment	• Flexibility (e.g., multiple tasks from any location) • Larger recruitment pool • Cost effectiveness and easy administration (single location)	• New job possibilities • No need to travel • No repatriation challenges • Flexibility	• Investments in technology • Identification issues • Communication problems • Not suitable for all kind of jobs	• Lack of personal contacts • Problems with distant communication • Role conflicts possible

GLOBAL CAREERISTS

Global careerists are people who have a long-term commitment to working in an international context without committing themselves to another country, and as an outcome are facing frequent international relocations during their career (Mayerhofer *et al.*, 2004; Suutari, 2003). These assignees may be either technical specialists or managers: in the latter role they generally take 'country manager' posts and develop through smaller and less attractive countries to the more important and prestigious subsidiaries – sometimes to senior regional management or board level positions. Before and immediately after the Second World War, permanent expatriation was a more familiar form and is still used very effectively by some companies. Such careerist expatriates see their careers as developing outside their home country with return there, if at all, only on promotion to a senior board level position or retirement periods abroad.

The other group of global careerists similarly has several international assignments behind them but their careers involve periods in the home country between assignments, for example in headquarters or in domestic units (Suutari, 2003). In that way, their career orientation is still international but they also want to stay in contact with the home country and recognize that it is possible to have international responsibilities without staying abroad for long periods. There are other issues that may make it beneficial for the global careerists to come back to the home country periodically (e.g., strengthening of contacts to home country and headquarters, updating organizational and technical knowledge when working in less-developed contexts, and social security concerns which may require a move back to the home country after a certain period in order to stay within its social security system).

As this involves only a minority of expatriates, it is not surprising to see comparatively few theoretical insights or empirical evidence concerning these developments (see, e.g., Mayerhofer *et al.*, 2004). However, at least in some countries, such as Finland, there is survey evidence that – quite surprisingly – around 15 to 20% of highly educated expatriates report having already at least three international assignments behind them and, in addition, around 40% were already on their second assignment (Suutari and Brewster, 2000). This is probably a specific feature of small, international societies but may also indicate a wider development trend caused by the globalization of business. Clearly more research evidence is needed to understand the impact of globalization on the careers of international managers.

Some of the literature on global careers and global mindsets is relevant in this context and clearly the most extensive development of global competencies is seen to take place during more wide-ranging global careers, in which individuals go through a number of adjustment processes in different international positions and contexts (Harvey and Novicevic, this volume Chapter 6; Suutari, 2003). Each of these international moves reflects the acquisition of different skills, experiences, relationships and opportunities (Cappellen and Janssens, 2005; Ng, Van Dyne and Ang, this volume Chapter 5). Their international work experiences develop not only their ability to adjust quickly and reach proficiency in new assignments, but also develop general competencies such as management skills, social skills, leadership skills, and change management skills (Jokinen *et al.*, 2008).

Within this group of global careerists we find the people who are most experienced in managing business operations in an international context. This group is thus a very attractive labor pool for selecting employees for international positions in which such skills are needed – either in foreign affiliates or in headquarters where managers end up having global responsibilities and thus require an understanding of global business realities. They are potentially highly marketable and therefore their unusual lifestyles tend to be well compensated.

A recent study by Mäkelä and Suutari (2009) suggests that global careerists develop a new kind of career identity which has several characteristics. Due to their extensive career in challenging jobs these managers have an awareness of their high level of career capital. This creates a strong self-confidence and reliance on personal capabilities to survive in challenging job environments. At the same time, global careerists are demanding as employees: they look for new challenges in their future jobs as well, and are highly motivated to working in international environments. They have a high trust in their own employability and an extensive awareness of the global job market. Overall, through their experiences they have high level of self-understanding about their values, job interests, personal strengths and weaknesses (knowing-why career capital), and thus they have clear career identity. Such identity typically stresses internal career issues (e.g., development, new challenges, interesting job environment) over the external career success.

Organizations that have tended to rely on global careerists have generally found them to be very expensive but very efficient. There are now few organizations where this is the only method of gaining international experience: usually cost factors mean that these organizations are trying to mix global careerists with other forms of international experience. Overall, more research is still needed to understand the specifics of this group of global careerists and the implication that such specifics have for international organizations.

SELF-INITIATED INTERNATIONAL EXPERIENCES

Self-initiated international experiences (SEs) are another group that has existed for a long time but, largely because researchers have used company contacts for their databases, has only recently begun to be the focus of academic study (Inkson *et al.*, 1997; Inkson and Myers 2003; Suutari and Brewster, 2000; Tharenou, 2003). SEs are people working abroad who have not been sent to another country by their employer, but have used their own initiative to seek job possibilities in foreign job markets. SE may be seen to refer to a more specific job-related career move for a few years across borders due to job- and career-related reasons but outside corporate expatriation systems. In reality these groups may sometimes be difficult to differentiate and a self-initiated move may sometimes lead to more permanent immigration: but the individual will be, in effect, locally hired and the job will not be on expatriate terms and conditions.

There has been increasing interest in differentiating the characteristics of SEs from those on more standard expatriate contracts: exploring their individual backgrounds, their motivation and compensation principles, and developmental issues (Inkson and Myers, 2003; Suutari and Brewster, 2000; Jokinen *et al.*, 2008). At the same time, there is still much that needs to be studied in order to understand the specifics of this labor pool and the implications it has on international organizations.

Self-initiated assignees consist of a fairly diverse group of individuals (Suutari and Brewster, 2000). For example, there are young people heading to countries where visa arrangements allow them to have a prolonged period of travel and tourism (perhaps funded by low-level work), as described also by Inkson *et al.* (1997). There are SEs who have in effect been 'pushed' to look outside their own country by lack of job opportunities there (IT specialists for example) or those who have been 'pulled' by better opportunities or lifestyle (such as healthcare professionals). The group includes officials who work in international organizations such as the European Union or the United Nations. It will also include those committed to working for aid agencies or other charities (see Fenwick and McLean, this volume Chapter 19). Sometimes, the reason for a job- seeking activity is to follow a partner who may have relocated, or perhaps just a desire to find out what it is like to live and work in a particular part of the world.

What connects this fairly diverse group of individuals is still the fact that they have left home on their own initiative rather than being sent or supported by an employer. This reflects the fact that goals for SEs are different: they include different organizational goals and personal motivational factors. The motives behind such a career decision may differ, but research indicates that typically SEs are often highly motivated by a personal interest in developing international experience (Suutari and Brewster, 2000). Among a sample of highly educated people working in France and Germany at the managerial or engineering level, the 'standard' elements of external career-related motivations (such as hierarchical level, financial success) were found (Crowley-Henry, 2007), but at the same time, SEs outlined the satisfaction of his or her subjective, internal or protean career (such as personal development, learning a new language, adapting to a new culture, better work/life balance) as key influencing motivations to move internationally.

In terms of recent career literature, this group of SEs can be seen to present boundaryless careers while traditional expatriates have organizational careers (Arthur and Rousseau, 1996; Littleton and Arthur, 2000). According to Hall (1996), the traditional career – as a series of upward moves, a steadily increasing income, power, status and security – has died. Instead, individuals are experiencing lateral job movement both within and across organizational boundaries, involuntary job loss and career interruptions (Eby *et al.*, 2003; Hall, 2002; Sullivan *et al.*, 1998). As a result, we have seen a shift from 'bounded' careers prescribed by relatively stable organizational and occupational structures, to 'boundaryless' careers in which uncertainty and flexibility are prevalent. Under this paradigm, employees take charge over their careers (Banai and Harry, 2005; Hall, 1996; Yan *et al.*, 2002; Baruch, 2006). Career actors are viewed as individuals who consciously gain portable capabilities, actively construct social networks that enhance their careers, and identify their own drives and motivations and apply these in their work context (Inkson and Arthur, 2001). Individuals on self-initiated international assignments represent almost an exemplar group of people described by these new career theories. The individuals have decided to make an international career move and have searched a new job abroad through their own self-initiative. The assignees have moved not only across organizational borders but across national borders at the same time.

These international assignees are typically hired under local, host country contracts (Crowley-Henry, 2007) and thus they do not often get the extra support, allowances or insurances that assigned expatriates receive – though some may sometimes be able to negotiate such benefits to their contracts (Suutari and Brewster, 2000).

As an outcome of these different starting points, SEs are outside the traditional expatriate selection, training, and management systems and thus they typically have to find their own way through job seeking, preparation, and transfer. However, in order to attract international employees, companies may still be willing to support the SEs. For example, in a qualitative study by Crowley-Henry (2007), the educated self-initiated expatriates had often received initial organizational support (e.g., financial support for relocation; temporary accommodation paid by the organization; a budget toward language classes; and help with local practical arrangements and paperwork) However, after the initial period, the international assignee received no further support. This is in contrast to the traditional expatriate who continues to receive financial and social support from the organization for the duration of the assignment.

From the developmental perspective, self-initiated assignments appear to involve high learning possibilities similar to those found in traditional expatriation (Crowley-Henry, 2007; Jokinen *et al.*, 2008).

From a future career perspective the situation is still totally different. Since the contract is local, it does not typically involve any repatriation agreements or plans as is the case in expatriate assignments (Suutari and Brewster, 2000): the SE may or may not want that. Thus, in line with boundaryless career theory, the more long-term career management is in the hands of the individual. Our understanding of the kinds of career impacts the self-initiated assignees have, or the kinds of repatriation challenges they face on possible repatriation, is very limited due to the lack of research in this area.

From the company perspective, the fact that these employees have taken charge of their own careers may also create challenges. While this group of employees may offer an attractive alternative labor pool, it may also be a challenge to commit these people to the organization over the longer term. For example, in keeping with the boundaryless career notion, the entire sample in a study by Crowley-Henry (2007) admitted that they liked the idea of potentially moving and adapting to life in another country in the future, and not necessarily with the same organization. Having done it once, it becomes a capability open to them in the future.

Despite the widespread nature of self-initiated international experience (Suutari and Brewster, 2003), there have been very few studies of these international workers compared to the company-assigned expatriates. Again, it is a case of more research being needed.

INTERNATIONAL COMMUTERS

International commuters are commonplace in regions of the world, such as Europe, where millions of people live within a short distance of one or more national borders and have the right to work across those borders. In terms of international working, though, commuter assignments generally refer to the arrangements where people live in one country but work in another for a specified period of time (*The Economist*, 2006; Harris, 2005; Scullion and Brewster, 2001). Typically, they travel from home to their country of work on a weekly or bi-weekly basis, returning to home and family for the weekends (Dowling and Welch, 2004). Suominen (2005) notes that key to these arrangements is the fact that the commuters' permanent residence remains in the home country. Briscoe and Schuler (2004) note that some of the work might also be done in the home location.

Peltonen (2001) lists the reasons for the use of commuter assignments as skills transfer, managerial control, and management development. Companies also perceive commuter assignments as a cheaper option than (semi-)permanent relocation since the company does not have to pay for the move, children's schooling, etc. (Suominen, 2005) and they are easier to organize. The company will, of course, have to pay travel and accommodation costs. The main reason for the use of such contracts may well be as a means of resolving family constraints when the assignee or his or her family do not want to leave home.

In theory, commuter assignments create flexibility for both the employer and the employee. Neither the commuter nor his or her family is required to be relocated, and the work will not interfere in their lives. There are other advantages in the fact that extensive travel includes insight into cultures, business practices, and product ideas as well as improved sensitivity to concerns of people from different cultures (DeFrank *et al.*, 2000). The assignee therefore experiences host country insight, without having to integrate fully into that culture; thus gaining only the positive aspects of cultural integration (Mayerhofer, 2005).

For the commuter, traveling becomes a reality and a part of work. DeFrank *et al.* (2000) have identified several disadvantages that make it difficult for such people to work efficiently.

> The number of assignees willing to go is greater than in case of a permanent move... To get flexibility is the most important thing. When we use different types of internal mobility, we are also able to use much larger group of assignees for international assignments....
>
> Travelling consumes: two flights a week has to become a burden in some point... They [commuters] might do long days to get home early in the weekends and this consumes and tiredness can become a problem. There is not a lot of free time because during the weeks it goes to long work days and in the weekends there is the travelling and spending time with your family. It doesn't leave much time for you. Slowly you get more and more tired and then you will come to the point in which you have to ask how long can you continue?

There may also be problems at the host location. If the commuter is a manager, his or her subordinates will inevitably question the commitment to the country of someone who not only chooses not to live in the that country, but at every opportunity rushes to get away from it.

SHORT-TERM ASSIGNEES

Short-term assignees are generally people undertaking projects outside their own country. Some of these are recruited specifically for those contracts and some are sent from within the existing home country labor force. Projects are either technical or managerial, but with this option technical expertise is the most commonly transferred. Short-term assignments have, perhaps, always been used, but the advent of easier and cheaper travel and improvements in communications technology have seen a surge in such arrangements in recent years. They came to prominence in the 1970s when the oil and gas industries sent engineers to build refineries and wellheads. Today, such short-term assignments are widely used by industries such as construction, consulting, IT, etc. They are typically characterized by the assignees' technical skills and limited duration (Dowling and Welch, 2004).

The duration of a short-term project assignment varies, depending on purpose, company and sector. Only assignments lasting less than a year are normally categorized as short-term (Tahvanainen, 2003) and in most cases they will be much shorter than that – anything from a few weeks to six months. Whether the family relocates is decided on a case-by-case basis. This matters because the complexity of administration of project assignments is dependent on the length of the assignment: generally, assignments under six months have different rules from assignments over six months because, in most countries, assignments less than six months do not require a local contract (with associated tax implications) but a contract is required for assignments of more than six months. In many countries absence for less than six months means that people remain in their taxation, social security, pensions, and similar systems. Hence, assignments of that length are administratively much simpler (Tahvanainen, 2003). Furthermore, the main reasons for short-term assignment are skills transfer and management development, so managerial control is not as important as for long-term international assignments (Peltonen, 2001).

Thus, compared to the traditional expatriate assignments, the main advantages of project assignments are – especially in Europe where there is no need for work or residency permits – flexibility, simplicity, and cost effectiveness. Goals for short assignments are easier to set and evaluate than for longer assignments. However, remuneration and administration as well as costs associated with short-term assignments can create severe problems (Peltonen 2001). Minbaeva and Michailova (2004) found that temporary assignments (including short-term international assignments, international commuter assignments, and frequent flyers) increase the ability to share knowledge in an organization. Indeed, varying international work experience enhances a person's ability to deepen his or her knowledge and acquire globally applicable skills that make internal knowledge transfer and teaching possible.

There are costs, however. Including extensive travel, increasing risk of fatigue and even sicknesses in the assessment, someone from Ernst and Young asks whether the short-term assignments are really cheaper overall than standard expatriation (Suominen, 2005).

When doing 60 hour work week, you are exhausted in the evenings. You wouldn't have the energy to spend time with your family. These short assignments are very tough and usually the family does not join the assignee.…

You will never suffer financially on an [project] assignment. In other words, you will always earn more than when staying in Finland for different reasons. But I think that is clear that working away from home and other disadvantage . . . has to be compensated.

From the employee's perspective, a short assignment abroad might favor the family situation since other members of the family rarely have to move. Although these assignments also require multicultural adaptability and acceptance, the most important relationships remain at home. Short-term assignees take part in the everyday living in a foreign country for a short period of time but are not committed to staying there for a significant period: 'total immersion in a new culture is not required' (Mayerhofer and Hartmann, 2005: 6).

The associated disadvantages of project assignments include taxation, side effects such as alcoholism and divorce since families get separated, the assignee's relationship to local colleagues and customers, and issues related to work permits. Like commuter assignments, short-term assignments can lead to increasing stress levels and impaired personal relationships for the employee (Dowling and Welch, 2004). Non-standard international assignees are largely dependent on themselves. They should be able to fulfill their information needs themselves and find the necessary operational support. 'Self-help' books are now being produced for those left behind while their partners work abroad on short-term assignments. As opposed to very generous expatriate contracts, companies offer specially constructed compensation packages for short-term assignees. Furthermore, budgets for training are also limited due to the control of operational managers. In other words, the process of training and development of different non-standard international assignments may differ (Mayerhofer and Hartmann 2005).

FREQUENT FLYERS

Frequent flyers are not, by definition, relocating. They are people who may spend a lot of time outside their own country, but very little time in any one other country. This is a growing area of international work (Mayerhofer *et al.*, 2004; Peltonen 2001; Welch, 2003). These types of international assignments, though they do not require full relocation, may nevertheless involve extensive travel, cross-cultural work situations, and disruption of organizational and family relationships and activities (Mayerhofer and Hartmann, 2005). It is difficult to establish the costs of frequent flying mainly because the decisions on such forms of international working are generally made by line managers, or the travelers themselves, with the costs included in particular projects and little central monitoring. The benefits include an increase in international experience, flexibility, the ability to get specialists to the location of an issue in 'real time', and a limited effect on the employee's links with the home base. The negatives for the organization include a lack of knowledge of costs and even less knowledge about benefits: how much real benefit can be achieved by people flying into an environment of which they have little understanding, taking decisions largely in ignorance and not being around to see the results of their decisions? Local employees are often dubious.

There are problems for the employees too: a survey by the World Bank on the effect of frequent travel reveals that many suffer from symptoms such as depression, nervous anxiety, and sleep disturbance. Some of these may be the result of jetlag. More serious causes are separation from home, workload, and lack of back-up abroad. Another study by Hyatt Hotels shows that 18% of their sample of 500 frequent flyers believe that their absence has had a negative impact on their marriage (Dowling and Welch, 2004).

VIRTUAL INTERNATIONALISTS

Virtual internationalists are people who, by contrast, never leave their home country but use modern technology to work in international teams. Technology has recently made possible the option of working in virtual international teams (Janssens and Brett, 2006; Sparrow, 2006b), thus providing some of the characteristics of international experience without having the disruption of leaving home (Dowling and Welch, 2004). Virtual assignments use the latest technology (e-mail, videos or internet, intranet, etc.) to enable people to work in international teams. Virtual assignees travel between the target site or host location and home office but mainly work through e-mail, video, and internet meetings from their home location. This form of mobility has increased lately due to low costs and unwillingness of talented assignees to leave for traditional international assignment:

> One advantage is that there is more people available for international projects: we don't have to think if we have money to send or if the person is willing to go, what the family will say. Also, in general we don't have to think about the family or the life situation . . . the use of resources is more flexible and balanced. We have a cyclic demand and our customers are in different parts of the world. Virtual assignments will help us to balance our resources . . .
> —(Vanhanen, 2004: 5)

This has been seen as one solution to a decreasing willingness to accept long-term postings. Virtual assignments are very economical when compared to the costs of paying for the move of the assignee and his or her family (Dowling and Welch, 2004). There are also disadvantages, however. Interpersonal and work relationships mean that when people communicate virtually, the group interaction is different than in the traditional work group setting. Typically, cultural misunderstandings increase. In addition, videoconferencing, e-mail and other forms of communication media require special skills. It is difficult for virtual assignments to be successful when the international team has not met face-to-face (Dowling and Welch, 2004). Welch and Colleagues (2003) list role conflict, allegiance, identification, interpersonal relations, and communication medium as problematic issues that have an impact on the work performance in their study of the use of virtual assignments in Australian and Danish enterprises.

CONCLUSIONS

As a series of conclusions, we examine the implications that these atypical forms of international working have for various HRM processes within organizations. Overall, one form of mobility does not rule out others but internal mobility clearly can come in various forms (Vanhanen, 2004). The form of assignment is strongly dependent on the nature of the project and thus companies should develop further expertise on managing the mix of different types of international employment in order to be able to fully utilize these different employment groups beside the traditional long-term international assignments and locals. Overall, the increase of international mobility of employees challenges the organizations and HRM – experts to create necessary policies on recruitment, compensation, and training and development to fully utilize these diverse groups of employees.

The Workforce 2000 research report identifies several key reasons for such diversification of organizations (Mondy and Noe, 2004). On a global scale, traditional groups are becoming equal to untraditional groups in terms of numbers (e.g., ethnic minorities) due to labor market demographics (e.g., the age structure within Western societies). In order to find enough work capacity, companies must accordingly widen their scope of recruitment beyond traditional groups into groups such as ethnic minorities. Another reason behind cultural and ethnic diversity is the growing global activities of organizations through which global organizations face diversity every day. Through increased mobility and interaction across borders, different groups also mix more than previously. For example, international opening of internal job markets within the company through intranets promotes such transfers further. Improvements in customer service and innovativeness are also suggested as drivers of diversity since customers are also becoming more diverse (e.g., Carrell *et al.*, 1995). A good reputation as a multicultural workplace is also perceived to be a sign of commitment to social responsibility by the organization. Such a reputation may in turn help recruitment from this new diverse labor pool.

The main reasons for using each type of assignment include attempts to identify an appropriate compendium of managerial control, skill transfer, management development, international cadre, costs and family reasons. The three first reasons are the main motives for each type of assignment, although, the order of importance has slight variations (Peltonen, 2001). The purpose of the assignment is the most essential determinant of the type of assignment. Availability of assignees, and costs, also influence the choice of the form of international assignment. These different types of international assignments, of course, create differing demands for IHRM (Mayerhofer and Hartmann, 2005).

Although many companies have written policies for traditional international assignments – Peltonen (2001) finds that many companies have a separate policy for short-term assignments – they often lack the formal guidelines for non-standard international assignments. Thus, creating and managing an appropriate mix of forms becomes difficult. The more international a company becomes, the more transfers happen and the larger the company, the greater the need for common and coherent policies.

Recruitment and selection of non-standard assignees appears to be informal with little bureaucracy. Those responsible for selection often hire assignees they know from, for example, previous projects (in case of project assignment). Moreover, companies do not consider the assignee's family conditions in the candidate selection. Interestingly enough, there is evidence that some companies offer to pay for the family relocation even for short-term international assignments lasting less than a year, as this is seen as a cure for the unwanted side affects – e.g., alcoholism and divorce.

The Mendenhall and colleagues cross-cultural training model explains the need for training on many levels. It considers not only the length of training and the appropriate methods of training, but also the rigor of training (Dowling and Welch, 2004). A person who is sent from Finland to Sweden for a short period of time does not require as much pre-departure training as a person who is sent to Asia for a long-term assignment. In other words, geographical distance and length of the assignment set the approach and length of training.

Generally, even less research has been conducted on the performance effects of non-standard international assignments than the rather minimal research into performance among standard expatriates. Dowling and Welch (2004) suggest some performance management challenges concerning non-standard international assignees:

♦ The assignee's performance needs to be linked to the company's overall strategic goals. Setting, monitoring and evaluating these objectives create a challenge. Virtual international teams with dual goals are especially hard to manage.
♦ The quality of goals set influences the way performance levels are determined.
♦ The kind of cross-cultural training that is required in each non-standard international assignment is difficult to determine.
♦ Rewarding the desired performance aligned with the overall strategy is very challenging.
♦ Non-standard international assignees also have an influence on host country workers. This needs to be considered especially in assignments in which the person constantly arrives and departs (e.g., commuter assignment, virtual assignment).

Furthermore, performance criteria can be divided into hard goals, soft goals, and contextual goals. The person who is responsible for the management of the international assignee's performance presents new concerns. Dowling and Welch (2004) introduce the dilemma using an example of an expatriate whose direct supervisor is located in headquarters. The supervisor would be the most natural person to do the performance appraisal. But, how can one evaluate another person's performance from a distance of, perhaps, thousands of kilometers? Hard measures such as ROI or market share are subject to all kinds of intervening variables.

Compensation systems vary greatly from company to company: for instance, with regard to short-term assignments, some offer mobility, location or telephone allowance; some offer incentives; some offer legal advice from lawyers or taxation consultants (Tahvanainen, 2003). On a large scale, while longer term migration and external expatriate careers have complex and often non-monetary motivations together with career enhancement, financial benefits are a significant motivation for accepting commuter and short-term foreign assignments (Dowling and Welch 2004). International careerists in turn are sometimes treated in contract and compensation negotiations as expatriates, sometimes as locals (but often in combination with extra benefits and support due to relocation needs) and in some companies they may be grouped together into IB-contract group without any specification of the home country. The compensation policies then vary accordingly. With regard to SEs, local contracts are typical but at the same time some typical expatriate benefits may be offered in order to attract high-profile candidates, at least in higher organizational levels.

Overall, this increased diversity within international employment thus challenges corporate HR policies and practices. Similarly, the research tradition with the focus on long-term expatriate assignment cannot be seen to fully capture the recent changes within corporations and thus our understanding of these developments can be argued to be very limited. In the final analysis, due to the limited amount of research among these different forms of international employment (excluding traditional international assignments), there is still clearly a need to validate our literature-based observations through more large-scale empirical research.

References

Arthur, M.B., and Rousseau, D.M. (1996). *The Boundaryless Career: A New Employment Principle for a New Organizational Era.* New York: Oxford University Press.

Banai, M., and Harry, W. (2005). Boundaryless global careers: The international itinerants. *International Studies of Management and Organization*, 34 (3), 96–120.

Baruch, Y. (2006). Career development in organizations and beyond: Balancing traditional and contemporary viewpoints. *Human Resource Management Review*, 16, 125–138.

Bonache, J., Brewster, C., and Suutari, V. (2007). Knowledge, International Mobility and Careers. *International Studies of Management and Organization*, 37 (3), 3–15.

Briggs, V.M. (2003). *Mass Immigration and the National Interest: Policy Directions for the New Century*, 3rd edn. New York: M.E. Sharpe.

Briscoe, D., and Schuler, R.S. (2004). *International Human Resource Management* (2nd edn). New York and London: Routledge.

Cappellen, T., and Janssens, M. (2005). Career paths of global managers: Towards future research. *Journal of World Business*, 40 (4), 348–360.

Carrell, M., Elbert, N., and Hatfield, R. (1995). *Human Resource Management: Global Strategies for Managing a Diverse Workforce* 5th edition. Englewood Cliff, NJ: Prentice-Hall.

CIPD (2005). *Recruitment, Retention and Turnover.* Annual Survey Report. Wimbledon: Chartered Institute of Personnel and Development.

Crowley-Henry, M. (2007). The protean career. Exemplified by first world foreign residents in Western Europe? *International Studies of Management & Organization,* 37 (3), 44–64.

DeFrank, R.S., Konopaske, R., and Ivancevich, J.M. (2000). Executive travel stress: Perils of the road warrior. *Academy of the Management Executive,* 14 (2).

Dench, S., Hurstfield, J., Hill, D., and Ackroyd, K. (2006). *Employers use of migrant labour: Summary report. Home Office Report 03/06.* Brighton: Institute for Employment Studies.

Dowling, P.J., and Welch, D.E. (2004). *International Human Resource Management: Managing People in a Multinational Context* (4th edn), London: Thomson Learning.

Eby, L.T., Butts, M., and Lockwood, A. (2003). Predictors of success in the era of the boundaryless career. *Journal of Organizational Behaviour,* 24 (6), 689–708.

Economist, The (2006). Travelling more lightly. *The Economist,* 379 (8483), 99–101.

Findlay, A.M., Li, F.L.N., Jowett, A.J., and Skeldon, R. (2000). Skilled international migration and the global city: A study of expatriates in Hong Kong. *Applied Geography,* 20 (3), 277–304.

Hall, D.T. (1996). Long live the career. A relational approach. In D.T. Hall (ed.), *The Career is Dead - Long Live the Career.* San Francisco: Jossey-Bass Publishers.

Hall, D.T. (2002). *Careers in and Out of Organisations.* Thousand Oaks, CA: Sage.

Harris, H. (2005). Global careers: Work–life issues and the adjustment of women international managers. *Journal of Management Development,* 23 (4), 818–832.

Hocking, J.B., Brown, M.E., and Harzing, A.-W. (2004). A knowledge transfer perspective of strategic assignment purposes and their path-dependent outcomes. *International Journal of Human Resource Management,* 15 (3), 565–586.

Inkson, K., and Arthur, M. (2001). How to be a successful career capitalist. *Organizational Dynamics,* 30 (1), 48–60.

Inkson, K., and Myers, B. (2003). 'The big OE': International travel and career development. *Career Development International,* 8 (4), 170–181.

Inkson, K., Arthur, M.B., Pringle, J., and Barry, S. (1997). Expatriate assignment versus overseas experience: Contrasting models of international human resource development. *Journal of World Business,* 32 (4), 351–368.

Janssens, M., and Brett, J.M. (2006). Cultural intelligence in global teams: A fusion model of collaboration. *Group and Organization Management,* 31 (1), 124–153.

Jokinen, T., Brewster, C., and Suutari, V. (2008). Career capital during international work experiences: Contrasting self-initiated expatriate experiences and assigned expatriation. *International Journal of Human Resource Management,* 19 (6), in press.

Littleton, S.M. and Arthur, M.B. (2000). The future of boundaryless careers. In A. Collin and R.A. Young (eds), *The Future of Career.* Cambridge: Cambridge University Press.

Mahroum, S. (2001). Europe and the immigration of highly skilled labour. *International Migration,* 39 (5), 27–43.

Mäkelä, K., and Suutari, V. (2009). Global Careers: A Social Capital Paradox. *International Journal of Human Resource Management.* In press.

Mayerhofer, H. (2005). *Expatriate, inpatriate and flexpatriate assignments: Supporting M&A integration process.* [online][cited 23 Nov 2005]. Available from Internet: http://euram2005.wi.tum.de/index.php/Paper204.doc?page=downloadPaper_afterconference&form_id=204.

Mayerhofer, H., and Hartmann, L.C. (2005). *Three types of global assignments and their implications for global competence.* [online][cited 23 Nov 2005]. Available from Internet: http://www.handels.gu.se/ifsam/Streams/hrm/154 per cent20final.pdf.

Mayerhofer, H., Hartmann, L.C., Michelitsch-Riedl, G., and Kollinger, I. (2004). Flexpatriate assignments: A neglected issue in global staffing. *International Journal of Human Resource Management*, 15 (8), 1371–1389.

Mayrhofer, W., Sparrow, P.R., and Zimmermann, A. (2008). Modern forms of international working. In M. Dickmann, C. Brewster and P.R. Sparrow (eds), *International Human Resource Management: A European Perspective*. London: Routledge, pp. 219–239.

McLaughlin, G., and Salt, J. (2002). *Migration Policies Towards Highly Skilled Foreign Workers*. London: Home Office.

Minbaeva, D.B., and Michailova, S. (2004). Knowledge transfer and expatriation in multinational corporations: The role of disseminative capacity. *Employee Relations*, 26 (6), 663–679.

Mondy, R.W., and Noe, R.M. (2004) *Human Resource Management*, 9th edition Ed., New York: Prentice Hall.

Peltonen, T. (2001). *New Forms of International Work: An International Survey Study, Results of the Finnish Survey*. Oulu: University of Oulu, in association with Cranfield Management School.

PricewaterhouseCoopers (2002). *International Assignments Global Policy and Practice Key Trends 2002*. London: PWC.

Salt, J., and Millar, J. (2006). International migration in interesting times: The case of the UK. *People and Place*, 14 (2), 14–25.

Scullion, H., and Brewster, C. (2001). The management of expatriates: Messages from Europe. *Journal of World Business*, 36 (4), 346–365.

Sparrow, P.R (2006a). International management: Key challenges for industrial and organizational psychology. In G. Hodginson and J.K. Ford (eds), *International Review of Industrial and Organizational Psychology*, Vol. 21. Chichester: John Wiley & Sons, pp. 189–266.

Sparrow, P.R. (2006b). Knowledge management in Global organizations. In G. Stahl and I. Björkman (eds), *Handbook of Research into International HRM*. London: Edward Elgar, pp. 113–138.

Sullivan, S.E., Carden, W.A., and Martin, D.F. (1998). Careers in the next millennium: Directions for further research. *Human Resource Management Review*, 8, 165–185.

Suominen, H. (2005). Ulkomaankomennuksista tuli sukkulointia. *Helsingin*.

Suutari, V. (2003). Global managers: Career orientations, career tracks, life-style implications and career commitment. *Journal of Managerial Psychology*, 18 (3), 185–233.

Suutari, V., and Brewster, C. (2000). Making their own way: International experience through self-initiated foreign assignments. *Journal of World Business*, 35 (4), 417–432.

Suutari V., and Brewster, C. (2003). Repatriation: Empirical evidence of a longitudinal study from careers and expectations among Finnish expatriates. *International Journal of Human Resource Management*, 14 (7), 1132–1151.

Tahvanainen, M. (2003). *Short Term International Assignments: Popular Yet Largely Unknown Way of Working Abroad*. Helsinki: HeSE Print.

Tharenou, P. (2003). The initial development of receptivity to working abroad: self-initiated international work opportunities in young graduate employees. *Journal of Occupational and Organizational Psychology*, 76, 489–515.

Tushman, M.L., and Scanlan, T.J. (2005). Boundary spanning individuals: Their role in information transfer and their antecedents. *Academy of Management Journal*, 24 (2), 289–305.

Vanhanen, R. (2004). *Internal Mobility Practices: Benchmarking Report*. Outokumpu Technology Oy.

Welch, D.E. (2003). Globalisation of staff movements: Beyond cultural adjustment. *Management International Review*, 43 (2), 149–169.

Yan, A., Zhy, G., and Hall, D.T. (2002). International assignments for career building: A model of agency relationships and psychological contracts. *Academy of Management Review*, 27 (3), 373–391.

8

Inpatriates as Agents of Cross-Unit Knowledge Flows in Multinational Corporations

SEBASTIAN REICHE, MARIA KRAIMER, AND ANNE-WIL HARZING

INTRODUCTION

In the past couple of decades, multinational corporations (MNCs) have increasingly used international assignments as a key staffing mechanism to disperse knowledge resources across different organizational units (e.g., Bonache and Brewster, 2001; Kamoche, 1997; Lazarova and Tarique, 2005; Tsang, 1999). In this vein, researchers and practitioners alike have primarily adopted a unidirectional approach, focusing on staff and knowledge transfers from the corporate headquarters (HQ) to foreign subsidiaries (Welch, 2003). This 'ethnocentric approach to knowledge transfer' (Kamoche, 1997: 214) entails an exportive orientation to international staffing in general (Perlmutter, 1969; Taylor *et al.*, 1996) and reflects MNCs' traditional practice of sending parent country nationals (PCNs) abroad.

However, as MNCs attempt to capitalize on growing business opportunities in developing and emerging economies, they face the challenge of accessing, applying and leveraging local knowledge to offset their lack of experience in these culturally and institutionally more distant environments. Acknowledging that local subsidiary staff often provide a crucial source of such context-specific knowledge (Harvey *et al.*, 2000), MNCs have begun to complement the traditional expatriation of PCNs with the temporary transfer of host-country nationals (HCNs). The transfer of HCNs can occur both vertically in the form of inpatriation from the foreign subsidiary to the HQ and horizontally between peer subsidiary units (Adler, 2002; Harvey *et al.*, 2001).

With regard to inpatriation in particular, given their profound knowledge of the subsidiary context and their ability to engage in cross-unit brokerage (Harvey and Novicevic, 2004; Kostova and Roth, 2003), inpatriates may act as important

Handbook of International Human Resource Management. Edited by Paul R. Sparrow
© 2009 John Wiley & Sons, Ltd

information boundary spanners from the subsidiary to the HQ. At the same time, inpatriates learn about the HQ corporate culture and corporate routines during their HQ assignment (Bonache *et al.*, 2001) and may transfer this newly acquired knowledge back to their home unit. This chapter will examine the role of inpatriates as conduits of such bi-directional knowledge flows in more detail. Specifically, we will:

- review the recent literature on knowledge transfer through international assignments;
- discuss the role of inpatriate assignments; and
- explore the social processes that precede cross-unit knowledge sharing through inpatriation.

INTERNATIONAL ASSIGNEES AS KNOWLEDGE AGENTS

The field of international human resource management (IHRM) has recently built on the knowledge-based view of the firm (Grant, 1996) to examine the role that international assignees play as information boundary spanners and initiators of MNC knowledge flows (Bonache *et al.*, 2001; Thomas, 1994). Implicit to this research focus are two key characteristics of those knowledge resources that are relevant across MNC units:

1. Scholars increasingly recognize that knowledge is rooted in individuals (Felin and Hesterly, 2007) and therefore apply an individual-level perspective to the study of knowledge flows. In the MNC context, this involves a focus on staff movements as a key transmission channel.
2. A large part of the knowledge transferred across MNC units is highly contextual and tacit in nature (Riusala and Suutari, 2004). Contextual and tacit knowledge cannot be codified in written documents but requires personal interaction to achieve context-specific adaptation and convey meaning to its recipients (Argote and Ingram, 2000).

Based on these notions, several empirical studies have investigated international assignment-related knowledge sharing in MNCs (see Table 8.1).

The review indicates that existing literature has mainly focused on PCNs as opposed to other assignee groups as knowledge carriers. In addition, except for Tsang's (1999) study on Singaporean MNCs, research has concentrated on MNCs from the triad countries (US, Europe, and Japan). At the same time, the studies investigate different determinants of cross-unit knowledge flows, such as assignees' ability and willingness to engage in knowledge sharing (Minbaeva and Michailova, 2004), assignees' social networks (Au and Fukuda, 2002) or existing stickiness factors (Riusala and Suutari, 2004). Importantly, the authors differ in the direction of knowledge flows they consider, thereby reflecting different levels of knowledge acquisition. One group of studies cover aspects of learning and knowledge creation from an individual point of view (e.g., Berthoin Antal, 2000, 2001; Hocking *et al.*, 2004) and thus primarily focus on assignees as knowledge recipients. The

TABLE 8.1 Recent studies on knowledge sharing through international assignments.

Authors	Research objectives	Sample and research design	Main findings
Tsang (1999)	– To examine knowledge exchange and learning aspects of IHRM – To empirically evaluate the IHRM practices adopted by Singaporean MNCs from a knowledge-based and learning perspective	– 12 Singaporean MNCs (manufacturing industry) – Multiple case study – 67 semi-structured interviews (HQ managers, expatriates and local nationals)	– IHRM practices adopted by Singaporean MNCs failed to take into account expatriates' role as key agents of knowledge exchange and learning
Delios and Björkman (2000)	– To examine the control and knowledge exchange roles of expatriates in foreign subsidiaries and joint-ventures of Japanese MNCs located in China and the United States	– 797 Japanese subsidiaries in China and the US across different industries – Archival/secondary data	– Expatriates' control function was more vital in China than in the US – Expatriates played a more significant role in bilateral knowledge exchange in technology and marketing-intensive industries in China than in the US
Berthoin Antal (2000, 2001)	– To examine the types of knowledge acquired by expatriates – To explore the strategies and processes available to expatriates to embed their learning into their organizations – To identify barriers of the transfer of individual to organizational learning	– Two German MNCs (banking sector and pharmaceutical industry) – Multiple case study – 21 in-depth interviews	– Knowledge gained is of declarative, procedural, conditional, axiomatic and relational nature – Little evidence that repatriates are used in a strategic way to foster organizational learning – Organizational learning was driven by the repatriate rather than the organization itself

(Continued)

TABLE 8.1 (Continued)

Authors	Research objectives	Sample and research design	Main findings
Bonache and Brewster (2001)	– To explore the way in which characteristics of knowledge influence expatriation policies – To advance theory-building in the field of international assignments	– Spanish MNC in the financial sector – Single case study – 19 in-depth interviews (HQ managers, expatriates, local managers), documentary and archival information	– Expatriate transfer can be hypothesized as a form of knowledge exchange – International assignments will be particularly useful when knowledge to be shared is tacit – Corporate applicability and value of knowledge gained on an assignment affects repatriation and career management
Au and Fukuda (2002)	– To examine antecedents and outcomes of expatriates' boundary-spanning activities, defined as the amount of cross-unit information that expatriates exchange	– MNC subsidiaries in Hong Kong – 30 interviews with US and Japanese expatriates – Survey instrument (232 expatriates)	– Local experience and diversity of social networks promote boundary spanning – Boundary-spanning behaviour leads to a decrease in role ambiguity and an increase of role benefits, job satisfaction and power
Hocking et al. (2004)	– To explore the strategic purposes of expatriate assignments and their path-dependent outcomes from a knowledge-based perspective	– Australian subsidiary of a Swedish telecommunications MNC – Single case study – Survey instrument (71 expatriates) – 17 semistructured interviews with expatriates and HR managers – Documentary and archival information	– Strategic assignment outcomes are emergent in nature – Knowledge generation by expatriates is an underestimated strategic assignment purpose, more so than either business or organization-related knowledge applications

Minbaeva and Michailova (2004)	– To investigate how certain expatriation practices can enhance the ability and willingness of expatriates to diffuse knowledge from the HQ to subsidiaries	– 92 subsidiaries of Danish MNCs located in 11 countries – Survey instrument	– The use of long-term assignments positively influences expatriates' willingness to share knowledge across MNCs' subsidiaries – Expatriates' ability to share knowledge is enhanced through the use of short-term assignments, frequent flyer arrangements and international commuter practices
Riusala and Suutari (2004)	– To analyze the type of knowledge shared within MNCs and expatriates' role in these exchange processes – To develop and test a theoretical framework on internal stickiness factors faced by those expatriates involved in knowledge exchanges	– Polish subsidiaries of Finnish MNCs – Multiple case study – 24 semistructured telephone interviews with Finnish expatriates	– Differences exist in the type of knowledge diffused from the HQ to the subsidiary *vis-à-vis* from the subsidiary to the HQ – Expatriates hold a central role in the knowledge sharing between MNC units – Knowledge exchange is subject to stickiness factors that concern the type of knowledge as well as the social, organizational and relational context

(*Continued*)

TABLE 8.1 (*Continued*)

Authors	Research objectives	Sample and research design	Main findings
Hébert *et al.* (2005)	– To analyze the role of expatriates as agents of experience-based knowledge for the survival of acquired foreign subsidiaries	– 216 foreign acquisitions of Japanese MNCs – Archival/secondary data	– To increase the chance of subsidiary survival, expatriates need to possess relevant industry experience and host country-specific acquisition experience – Expatriation can have negative effects on subsidiary survival when the MNC possesses general host-country experience
Hocking *et al.* (2007)	– To examine how two assignment outcomes, knowledge applications and experiential learning, are influenced by expatriates' everyday knowledge access and communication activities	– Australian subsidiary of a Swedish telecommunications MNC – Single case study – Survey instrument (71 expatriates) – 12 semistructured interviews with expatriates	– Expatriates' knowledge applications result from their frequent knowledge access and communication with the HQ and other MNC units – Expatriates' experiential learning derives from a frequent access to host-unit knowledge that is subsequently adapted to the global corporate context

knowledge assignees may acquire during their assignment includes an understanding of the company's global organization, factual knowledge about the assignment culture or culture-specific repertoires. In contrast, a second group of studies concentrate on knowledge that is shared and created through the use of international assignees at the organizational level (e.g., Bonache and Brewster, 2001; Hébert *et al.*, 2005), conceptualizing assignees as senders of knowledge. Here, assignees are viewed as carriers of knowledge that streamlines cross-unit processes, creates common corporate practices and routines, and increases the chances of subsidiary survival, for example through the provision of local acquisition experience or product development know-how.

Although previous research has addressed the focal role that assignees play in cross-unit knowledge flows in MNCs, little is known about what determines knowledge sharing at the individual level. However, researchers have contended that the success of knowledge sharing through staff movements is not automatic but rather depends on social processes. For example, empirical evidence suggests that individuals being assigned to new contexts often are a minority within this new setting which affects their social influence (Gruenfeld *et al.*, 2000) and their ability to build social networks (Mehra *et al.*, 1998). Also, particularly in the case of tacit and thus less codified knowledge (Polanyi, 1966), its transfer does not necessarily occur effectively and efficiently (Gupta and Govindarajan, 2000; Szulanski, 2000). A more detailed analysis of the processes and determinants that facilitate knowledge sharing through international assignments is thus clearly warranted.

The Role of Inpatriate Assignments

In line with a knowledge-based perspective on international assignments, inpatriates can be conceptualised as a particular group of cross-unit knowledge agents in MNCs. In general, the literature understands inpatriation as the transfer of foreign nationals from the subsidiary into the MNC's HQ (Adler, 2002; Harvey, 1997) and thus distinguishes these assignments from the traditional expatriation of PCNs. Other scholars have referred to inpatriates as 'headquartered foreign nationals' (Barnett and Toyne, 1991). Conceptual differences exist with regard to the time frame of the inpatriate assignment. Harvey and colleagues, who have contributed the most to our understanding of inpatriate issues, view these assignments as semi-permanent to permanent relocations and, in doing so, primarily concentrate on the knowledge and expertise inpatriates contribute to the HQ context (Harvey and Buckley, 1997; Harvey *et al.*, 1999, 2000). Likewise, while Barnett and Toyne (1991) do not specify the duration of the relocation explicitly they seem to imply a (semi-) permanent nature of these transfers as well. In contrast, Adler (2002) adopts a broader perspective and focuses on a more temporary nature of these transfers. She understands the transfer of inpatriates as 'assignments designed to help them to learn about the headquarters' organizational culture and ways of doing business. The headquarters then returns the inpatriates back to their local culture to manage local operations' (Adler, 2002: 261). This latter view emphasizes the developmental purposes of an inpatriate assignment (Bonache *et al.*, 2001; Solomon, 1995).

We will focus on the temporary nature of inpatriate assignments for two reasons.

1. Empirical evidence suggests that the temporary inpatriation of foreign nationals seems to reflect the predominant corporate practice (GMAC Global Relocation Services, 2006; Peterson, 2003; Reiche, 2006), thus emphasizing a developmental element inherent in this assignment type. In this respect, the work by
   Harvey and colleagues addresses a particular subgroup of inpatriates. Indeed,
   by speaking of inpatriate 'managers' or inpatriate 'leaders' (e.g., Harvey and
   Miceli, 1999; Harvey and Novicevic, 2004; Harvey *et al.*, 1999), these scholars
   concentrate their arguments on staff transfers at the management level.
2. It is the temporary nature of these assignments that may be more beneficial
   to MNCs as it facilitates knowledge transfer not only into the HQ organization
   but also to other MNC units once the assignee completes the assignment and
   applies the acquired knowledge at a subsequent position, either at the origi-
   nating unit or elsewhere in the MNC (Lazarova and Tarique, 2005).

At the same time, we acknowledge that due to an increased use of inpatriates, career opportunities at assignees' home units, especially in the case of smaller foreign
subsidiaries with only few management positions, may be very restricted. As a result,
while the inpatriate assignment may initially be a temporary relocation it may evolve
into a more permanent posting (see Reiche, 2006).

Differences between expatriates and inpatriates

From an aggregate perspective, expatriate and inpatriate assignments only constitute alternative forms of establishing HQ-subsidiary linkages. Indeed, both groups
of assignees take on boundary-spanning activities (Harvey *et al.*, 2000; Thomas,
1994), help to reduce existing information asymmetries between the HQ and its
subsidiaries (Harvey *et al.*, 2001) and perceive their relocations to provide career
advancement opportunities in the wider organization (Reiche, 2006; Stahl *et al.*,
2002). However, despite their similarities expatriates and inpatriates differ along
several dimensions.

First, expatriates carry with them the status and influence that is associated with
their role as HQ representatives. Coming from the MNC's periphery, inpatriates
are, on the contrary, unlikely to encounter the same level of credibility and respect
(Harvey and Buckley, 1997; Harvey *et al.*, 2005).

Second, Barnett and Toyne (1991) delineate increased adjustment challenges for
inpatriates in comparison to expatriates. They note that inpatriates are not only confronted with the necessity to respond to acculturation pressures due to a change in
the national culture but also need to be socialized into the MNC's HQ corporate
culture. Indeed, learning the HQ corporate culture is considered an important motive for inpatriating foreign nationals (Adler, 2002). Expatriates, in contrast, often
impose elements of the HQ corporate culture upon the subsidiary they are sent
to (Harzing, 2001). In a similar vein, the HQ corporate culture can be considered
the result of a MNC's administrative heritage (Bartlett and Ghoshal, 1998) and is

therefore likely to be more deeply seated and embedded than the subsidiary corporate culture.

Third, although both inpatriates and expatriates are able to provide the HQ with sufficient knowledge to assess subsidiary behavior and performance, thus reducing existing information asymmetries, their applicability is likely to depend on the degree of goal congruency between the HQ and a given subsidiary (Harvey *et al.*, 2001). Goal congruency may reflect the extent to which the HQ and its subsidiaries share common performance expectations or requirements for inter-unit resource flows. High goal congruency decreases HQ control needs towards the subsidiary and a MNC's primary aim will be to continuously minimize information gaps between the HQ and its subsidiaries. Especially in the case of subsidiaries in culturally and institutionally more distant countries, inpatriates may be more effective in achieving this (Harvey *et al.*, 2000). In contrast, under conditions of low goal congruency, a MNC will be tempted to use PCNs in order to exert personal control over the subsidiary and enforce compliance with HQ strategies (Harzing, 2001).

Finally, it is worth noting that the use of inpatriates increases the cultural diversity and multicultural staff composition at the HQ, thereby fostering a geocentric approach to the allocation of a MNC's human resources. More specifically, a higher share of employees with diverse cultural backgrounds will be collaborating directly as inpatriates are, for instance, temporarily integrated into the HQ's management teams. In contrast, the use of expatriates reflects an ethnocentric view toward international staffing (Perlmutter, 1969) and expatriates generally continue to coordinate with their own HQ management team. Table 8.2 summarizes these distinctions between inpatriates and expatriates.

Motives for inpatriation

Recent evidence suggests that European, and US MNCs in particular, intend to increase their share of inpatriates in the future (Oddou *et al.*, 2001; Peterson, 2003).

TABLE 8.2 Distinctions between inpatriates and expatriates.

Characteristics	Inpatriate	Expatriate
Perceived status by locals	Peripheral member	HQ representative
Level of influence in host unit	Low	High
Focus of cross-cultural adjustment	Organizational and national culture	National culture
Goal congruency between HQ and subsidiary	High	Low
MNC staff composition	Geocentric	Ethnocentric

Three reasons may explain the resulting shift in the composition of international staff in MNCs.

First, growing business opportunities in developing and emerging economies have led MNCs to expand into a greater number of diverse countries. The greater cultural distance together with poor business infrastructure inherent in these new assignment destinations result in additional adjustment challenges for expatriates, thereby reducing the likelihood that these individuals successfully complete their assignment or accept the transfer in the first place. Also, growing dual-career problems make an expatriate staffing option less feasible in developing countries (Harvey et al., 1999).

Second, and perhaps more importantly, by extending their operations to developing and emerging economies, MNCs face unparalleled social, cultural, institutional, and economic differences that inhibit successful market entry and render an effective management of local business activities more difficult (Napier and Vu, 1998). In this vein, inpatriates provide the adequate social and contextual knowledge to bridge this gap and facilitate the context-specific adaptation of business strategies (see the discussion of social capital, Harvey and Novicevic, this volume Chapter 6). In addition, they serve as an important boundary-spanning mechanism that links the HQ to its subsidiaries and initiates knowledge transfer (Harvey et al., 1999). Given the intimate understanding of both the HQ and the local subsidiary context that inpatriates develop, they are able to cross existing intra-organizational, cultural, and communication boundaries to diffuse information (Thomas, 1994; Tushman and Scanlan, 1981).

Third, by socializing inpatriates into the HQ's organizational culture, the MNC establishes a more informal and subtle control mechanism toward its subsidiaries. More specifically, inpatriates' boundary-spanning role helps the MNC to exert social control that is based on acceptance by both HQ management and local nationals (Edström and Galbraith, 1977; Harvey et al., 2000).

The corporate motive for using inpatriates is thus twofold (Reiche, 2006).

1. Inpatriates are assumed to provide the required breadth of socially networked skills to successfully disseminate contextual knowledge between MNC units and facilitate a global yet locally responsive approach to MNC management (Harvey et al., 2000; Kostova and Roth, 2003). Accordingly, this knowledge transfer originates at the individual level, with inpatriates acting as *senders* of knowledge to the organization.
2. Inpatriation is motivated by developmental purposes in terms of providing inpatriates with corporate socialization and firm-specific training to prepare them for future management tasks in the MNC (Bonache et al., 2001; Evans et al., 2002).

The second motive also entails elements of knowledge transfer but views inpatriates as *recipients* of organization-rooted knowledge. Moreover, this developmental mechanism can be regarded as a way of increasing employees' competencies which, in turn, provide the firm with greater human resource flexibility needed in a global business environment (Wright and Snell, 1998). Again, it is likely that MNCs will benefit the most from this two-directional knowledge sharing if the inpatriate transfer is temporary rather than permanent, which enables the inpatriate to subsequently diffuse the knowledge developed during the assignment to other MNC units.

A SOCIAL CAPITAL PERSPECTIVE OF INPATRIATES' KNOWLEDGE SHARING

Conceptualizing knowledge at the individual level highlights the need to focus on individual-level processes that influence how knowledge is transferred in organizations. In this respect, academic research has increasingly examined the underlying social dimensions of knowledge sharing (Bouty, 2000; Harvey and Novicevic, this volume Chapter 6; Nebus, 2006; Reagans and McEvily, 2003). In the following sections, we will apply the concept of social capital to the context of inpatriate assignments and explore its value as a necessary precondition for knowledge flows through inpatriate assignments to occur. In doing so, we discuss four predictors of inpatriates' social capital building and examine the moderating effect of a MNC's HR practices. Figure 8.1 integrates all the components into a conceptual framework.

Inpatriates' social capital

Social capital can be understood as the structure and content of an individual's network ties (Adler and Kwon, 2002; Harvey and Novicevic, this volume Chapter 6). The resulting access to other actors' resources is primarily informal and personalized in nature as opposed to hierarchy- or position-based relationships (Li, 2007).

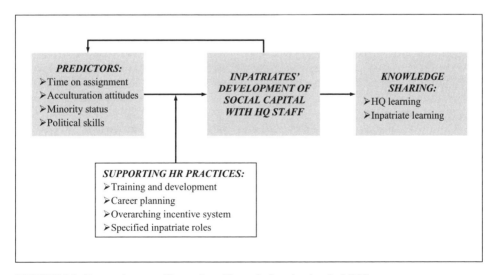

FIGURE 8.1 Determinants of inpatriates' knowledge sharing in MNCs.

In addition, building on the idea that social capital is a multidimensional construct (Putnam, 1995), scholars have extended the early research focus on structural characteristics of individuals' social networks (Burt, 1992; Coleman, 1990) to include relational and cognitive dimensions of social capital (Leana and Van Buren, 1999; Nahapiet and Ghoshal, 1998). Whereas relational social capital refers to the level of interpersonal trust between the two parties of a relationship, cognitive social capital entails common sources of understanding and identification such as shared values and goals (Tsai and Ghoshal, 1998).

Scholars have begun to discuss the concept of social capital in the context of intra-organizational boundary spanners in general and international assignees in particular. For example, it is argued that social capital is particularly important for individuals who are located at social boundaries or assume boundary-spanning positions because these roles require interaction with people from different social contexts (Raider and Burt, 1996). In a similar vein, social capital is thought to facilitate solidarity, thereby fostering compliance with local rules and reducing formal control requirements (Adler and Kwon, 2002).

This idea has important implications with regard to international staff transfers that are often subject to dual levels of organizational commitment and identification (Gregersen and Black, 1992; Reade, 2003). In addition, there is evidence that assignees' structural and relational social capital positively relates to their psychological well-being and adjustment (Wang and Kanungo, 2004). Importantly, social capital has been found to provide information benefits, both for organizational members in domestic settings (Borgatti and Cross, 2003; Seibert et al., 2001) and for international assignees (Au and Fukuda, 2002).

The boundary-spanning, solidarity, adjustment, and information benefits of social capital highlight its conceptual value in developing an understanding of the effective use of inpatriate assignments as knowledge agents in MNCs. Specifically, based on the idea that social capital serves as a main vehicle for knowledge sharing and creation (Nahapiet and Ghoshal, 1998; Perry-Smith, 2006; Reagans and McEvily, 2003), inpatriates will need to establish social capital with HQ staff in order to diffuse their local subsidiary knowledge into the HQ while, at the same time, acquiring new knowledge themselves. The more extensive their social capital with HQ colleagues, the greater the knowledge benefits for the HQ and the greater the learning outcomes for the individual inpatriate.

Determinants of inpatriates' social capital building

Building on the previous arguments, four main factors can be derived that will influence inpatriates' ability to build such social capital – time on assignment, acculturation attitudes, minority status, and political skills.

Time on assignment. The temporal character of inpatriate assignments has important implications for social capital building. For example, there is evidence that assignment duration has a positive impact on interaction adjustment which captures the assignee's ease of engaging in interpersonal exchanges with host-unit staff (Gregersen and Black, 1990; Kraimer et al., 2001). It is thus likely that inpatriates will

build more structural social capital the more time they have spent on their assignments. A similar logic applies to the relational dimension of social capital. Implicit
to Nahapiet and Ghoshal's (1998) conceptualization of relational social capital is
the notion that social capital takes time to develop. In particular, they argue that
one's relational social capital with another person is created through a series of
interactions over time. Research on trust as a main element of relational social capital indeed highlights its dynamic character (Leana and Van Buren, 1999; Rousseau
et al., 1998). As a result, inpatriates' ability to develop trustful relationships with
HQ staff will depend to a large extent on the amount of time they have spent on
the assignment. Research also shows that an individual's organizational identification and thus cognitive social capital will increase with the intensity and duration of
contacts the individual sustains with the specific organizational unit (Dutton *et al.*,
1994). While inpatriates may sustain contacts with the HQ before the relocation,
the contacts' intensity is likely to increase during the assignment due to the HQ's
proximity. Accordingly, short-term assignments such as troubleshooting fly-ins or
brief developmental transfers (Collings *et al.*, 2007; Tahvanainen *et al.*, 2005) may
provide insufficient lead time for inpatriates to develop social capital.

Acculturation attitudes. A second factor refers to extant cultural differences that
inpatriates perceive at the host culture and that may impact on their social capital
building. The process through which individuals make an effort to adjust to the
foreign cultural environment and understand its cultural elements with the aim of
reducing the effect of cultural differences is called 'acculturation' (Ward, 1996). In
this regard, the literature discusses four different acculturation attitudes that are
contingent upon an individual's need to preserve his or her own cultural identity
and the level of attraction to other cultural groups (Berry *et al.*, 1989):

(1) integration (high preservation and high attraction);
(2) assimilation (low preservation and high attraction);
(3) separation (high preservation and low attraction); and
(4) marginalization (low preservation and low attraction).

There is evidence that inpatriates differ in their choice of acculturation modes and
that these differences translate into varying degrees of contact that inpatriates seek
with HQ staff (Reiche, 2006). Whereas integration and assimilation enable individuals to interact with locals and have been shown to increase international assignees'
perceived success abroad (Tung, 1998), the other two attitudes are likely to inhibit
interaction and preserve cultural distance. Given a certain cultural distance between
inpatriates and HQ staff, we would assume that inpatriates adopting an integration
or assimilation mode are more likely to build HQ social capital than those with a
separation or marginalization mode.

Minority status. Research suggests that numerically underrepresented groups
based on attributes such as race and gender are limited with regard to the scope
of their social networks in organizational environments (Ibarra, 1995; Mehra *et al.*,
1998). Along these lines, it is important to consider that inpatriates, particularly

those from culturally and institutionally distant organizational units, are confronted with exclusionary pressures at the HQ. The extent of these pressures is contingent upon two main factors.

1. It is likely that a higher number of inpatriates from a given country transferred to the HQ at the same time reduces inpatriates' minority status. The number of international staff from a given country is subject to the orientation to international staffing prevalent in the organization (Perlmutter, 1969; Taylor *et al.*, 1996), the subsidiary's availability of and the HQ's demand for qualified staff as well as the subsidiary's size.
2. The ethnic staff composition of the HQ means that inpatriates are more likely to be confronted with exclusionary pressures if they represent a visible ethnic minority with regard to the HQ country or if local staff at the HQ is ethnically very homogenous and thus less used to dealing with foreigners and ethic minorities.

In sum, to the extent that inpatriates constitute a minority at the HQ, their ability to build and sustain social capital with HQ staff is likely to be substantially hindered.

Political skills.   Finally, inpatriates' social capital with HQ staff may be contingent upon their political skills in the MNC (see Harvey and Novicevic, this volume Chapter 6, for the relationship between social capital and political skills). Political skill is the 'ability to effectively understand others at work, and to use such knowledge to influence others to act in ways that enhance one's personal and/or organizational objectives' (Ahearn *et al.*, 2004: 311). A small body of evidence is accumulating that political skills are associated with more effective work performance and positive attitudes toward the organization (Harris *et al.*, 2007). As Harvey and Novicevic (2004) argue, these skills can be especially important for inpatriates to be able to remove obstacles of cooperation with HQ staff. In particular, politically skilled inpatriates are better able to manage interpersonal dynamics and convey a positive image with HQ staff. This positive image and ability to understand people will facilitate trusting social interactions and shared identities. Political skills should thus provide inpatriates with the ability to form and maintain social ties at the HQ.

Interrelationships and dynamics.   The four determinants are likely to be interrelated. For example, the more time inpatriates spend on their assignments, the less they will be perceived as newcomers to the HQ organization and the more opportunities they have to demonstrate their value to HQ staff, thereby reducing the role of their minority status. At the same time, the degree to which inpatriates are confronted with exclusionary pressures at the HQ may predetermine their selected acculturation mode. Strong minority problems may prompt inpatriates to focus on their own cultural identity rather than trying to integrate into the host culture which may further reduce their social capital building. Additionally, we would assume that inpatriates' political skills are related to their minority status. Indeed, the stronger their exclusionary pressures at the HQ, the more difficult it will be for inpatriates to gain legitimacy and respect among HQ colleagues and thus develop political skills.

It is also important to note that the relationship between the aforementioned factors and inpatriates' social capital building may be two-directional. For example, if inpatriates develop social capital that is to a large extent HQ-specific, they will be more motivated to accept an ongoing appointment in the HQ upon completing their original inpatriate postings, thus prolonging their assignments. The prospect of an extended stay may also encourage them to shift their acculturation attitudes toward integrating or assimilating into the host culture. Moreover, as inpatriates establish a more extensive social network at the HQ they become socialized and increase their exposure in the organizational hierarchy which will reduce their perceived minority status. Similarly, through their social capital with senior HQ managers inpatriates may advance their political skills which, in turn, can further enhance their social capital building.

The moderating effect of HR practices

The previous discussion points toward the fact that inpatriates' development of social capital with HQ staff does not occur automatically but is affected by characteristics of the assignment, the HQ, and the individual inpatriate. In this respect, the role of HR practices has been highlighted as an important means to foster social capital building. Leana and Van Buren (1999) discuss three ways in which HR practices help to create and sustain social capital.

First, they argue that long-term oriented employment relationships are essential since social capital develops slowly but can be damaged quickly, for example through trust-breaking behavior. This requires the adoption of stability-enhancing HR practices such as training and development and career planning. These arguments are supported by empirical research demonstrating that employees display more positive attitudinal and performance-based responses when the organization invests training and career development in them (Tsui *et al.*, 1997). In the inpatriate context, this may also involve the development of alternative career paths that take into account the limited career opportunities at inpatriates' home units (Reiche, 2006). The prospect of a long-term career path with the company will motivate inpatriates to build social capital. Thus, development-related HR practices should strengthen the effects of time on assignment, integration- and assimilation-oriented acculturation attitudes, and political skills on social capital building, and should weaken the effects of minority status and separation- and marginalization-oriented acculturation attitudes on social capital building.

A second role for HR practices pertains to financial incentive systems. The development of an overarching compensation system that addresses between-country differences (see Bonache, 2006) is a crucial HR practice to inpatriates, especially those from less-developed countries, when making decisions to accept inpatriate assignments (Reiche, 2006). The repatriation of inpatriates to countries with substantially lower market salaries can lead to a huge decrease of salary, a gap that is often more pronounced than in the case of expatriate assignments. In this vein, an overarching inpatriate and repatriate incentive system can be a potent tool for creating a social exchange relationship with inpatriates. A social exchange relationship is one in which there is a long-term orientation defined by mutual trust, investment and reciprocal obligations between employee and the organization (Blau, 1964; Shore *et al.*, 2006). This sense of reciprocal obligations may manifest itself in terms of inpatriates' development of social capital and knowledge sharing with HQ staff.

Existing research has indeed emphasized the importance of incentive systems for boundary spanners to create social capital and foster intra-MNC knowledge sharing (Gupta and Govindarajan, 2000; Kostova and Roth, 2003). Therefore, we would expect that a favorable overarching compensation system will provide inpatriates with the motivation to develop social capital and thus strengthen the effects of time on assignment, integration- and assimilation-oriented acculturation attitudes, and political skills on social capital building, and weaken the respective effects of minority status and separation- and marginalization-oriented acculturation attitudes.

A third way for HR practices to enhance inpatriates' social capital is through the development of specified roles that substitute relationship-based with position-based social capital and thus avoid the need to continuously manage social relationships (Leana and Van Buren, 1999). For example, an organization may institutionalize a succession planning for the inpatriation of foreign nationals into particular HQ positions and define formal, hierarchy-based communication channels to HQ staff. In this case, individual predictors such as minority status and political skill may be less relevant for developing social capital with HQ staff since inpatriates may be able to use their position power to build social capital. Thus, inpatriate roles with specified formal position power may weaken the relationship between some of the aforementioned determinants and social capital building. Overall, it has become evident that HR practices can moderate between the individual-level predictors and inpatriates' development of social capital with HQ staff and thus serve as supporting tools to leverage knowledge exchange through inpatriate assignments.

CONCLUSION

This chapter has highlighted social capital as a fruitful lens for studying international assignees as knowledge agents. Specifically, we opened up the black box of what determines knowledge flows between inpatriates and HQ staff. As Lengnick-Hall and Lengnick-Hall (2006: 486) state, the focus of social capital 'may add to our understanding of how people make a difference and why the intangible assets of a firm are so crucial to success, particularly in global, knowledge-intensive enterprises and industries'. We have argued that inpatriates provide the MNC with a unique value *because* they are able to diffuse knowledge from one unit to another. However, they can only make a difference and benefit the organization, *if* they establish social capital with HQ staff. Accordingly, the mere movement of people across intra-organizational boundaries does not automatically entail knowledge outcomes for the MNC.

The fact that inpatriates not only diffuse their local contextual knowledge into the HQ organization but also gain knowledge during their assignments which they can transfer back to their home units implies a long-term perspective to the study of inpatriates' role as knowledge agents. The organizational maintenance of inpatriates' unique knowledge and expertise then becomes primarily an issue of employee retention and demonstrates that ongoing knowledge sharing and inpatriates' career outcomes are intricately related. Although scholars have begun to address the issues inherent in knowledge sharing upon repatriation (e.g., Lazarova and Tarique, 2005), future research would clearly benefit from a more detailed analysis of how MNCs can continuously capitalize upon their assignees' knowledge resources.

References

Adler, N.J. (2002). Global managers: No longer men alone. *International Journal of Human Resource Management*, 13, 743–760.

Adler, P.S., and Kwon, S.-W. (2002). Social capital: Prospects for a new concept. *Academy of Management Review*, 27 (1), 17–40.

Ahearn, K.K., Ferris, G.R., Hochwarter, W.A., Douglas, C., and Ammeter, A.P. (2004). Leader political skill and team performance. *Journal of Management*, 30 (3), 309–327.

Argote, I., and Ingram, P. (2000). Knowledge transfer: A basis for competitive advantage in firms. *Organizational Behavior and Human Decision Processes*, 82 (1), 150–169.

Au, K.Y., and Fukuda, J. (2002). Boundary spanning behaviors of expatriates. *Journal of World Business*, 37 (4), 285–297.

Barnett, S.T., and Toyne, B. (1991). The socialization, acculturation, and career progression of headquartered foreign nationals. In S.B. Prasad (ed.), *Advances in International Comparative Management*, Vol. 6. Greenwich, CT: JAI Press. pp. 3–34.

Bartlett, C., and Ghoshal, S. (1998). *Managing Across Borders: The Transnational Solution* (2nd edn). Boston, MA: Harvard Business School Press.

Berry, J.W., Kim, U., Power, S., Young, M., and Bujaki, M. (1989). Acculturation attitudes in plural societies. *Applied Psychology*, 38, 185–206.

Berthoin Antal, A. (2000). Types of knowledge gained by expatriate managers. *Journal of General Management*, 26 (2), 32–51.

Berthoin Antal, A. (2001). Expatriates' contributions to organizational learning. *Journal of General Management*, 26 (4), 62–84.

Blau, P.M. (1964). *Exchange and Power in Social Life*. New York: John Wiley & Sons.

Bonache, J. (2006). The compensation of expatriates: A review and a future research agenda. In G.K. Stahl and I. Björkman (eds), *Handbook of Research in International Human Resource Management*. Cheltenham: Edward Elgar.

Bonache, J., and Brewster, C. (2001). Knowledge transfer and the management of expatriation. *Thunderbird International Business Review*, 43 (1), 145–168.

Bonache, J., Brewster, C., and Suutari, V. (2001). Expatriation: A developing research agenda. *Thunderbird International Business Review*, 43 (1), 3–20.

Borgatti, S.P., and Cross, R. (2003). A relational view of information seeking and learning in social networks. *Management Science*, 46 (4), 432–445.

Bouty, I. (2000). Interpersonal and interaction influences on informal resource exchanges between R&D researchers across organizational boundaries. *Academy of Management Journal*, 43 (1), 50–65.

Burt, R.S. (1992). *Structural Holes: The Social Structure of Competition*. Cambridge, MA: Harvard University Press.

Coleman, J.S. (1990). *Foundations of Social Theory*. Cambridge, MA: Harvard University Press.

Collings, D.G., Scullion, H., and Morley, M.J. (2007). Changing patterns of global staffing in the multinational enterprise: Challenges to the conventional expatriate assignment and emerging alternatives. *Journal of World Business*, 42 (2), 198–213.

Delios, A., and Björkman, I. (2000). Expatriate staffing in foreign subsidiaries of japanese multinational corporations in the PRC and the United States. *International Journal of Human Resource Management*, 11 (2), 278–293.

Dutton, J.E., Dukerich, J.M., and Harquail, C.V. (1994). Organizational images and member identification. *Administrative Science Quarterly*, 39 (2), 239–263.

Edström, A., and Galbraith, J.R. (1977). Transfer of managers as a coordination and control strategy in multinational organizations. *Administrative Science Quarterly*, 22 (2), 248–263.

Evans, P., Pucik, V., and Barsoux, J. (2002). *The Global Challenge: Frameworks for International Human Resource Management*. London: McGraw-Hill.

Felin, T., and Hesterly, W.S. (2007). The knowledge-based view, nested heterogeneity, and new value creation: Philosophical considerations on the locus of knowledge. *Academy of Management Review*, 32 (1), 195–218.

GMAC Global Relocation Services. (2006). *Global Relocation Trends 2006 Survey Report*. Woodridge, IL: GMAC Global Relocation Services.

Grant, R.M. (1996). Toward a knowledge-based theory of the firm. *Strategic Management Journal*, 17 (Winter Special Issue), 109–122.

Gregersen, H.B., and Black, J.S. (1990). A multi-faceted approach to expatriate retention in international assignments. *Group and Organization Studies*, 15 (4), 461–485.

Gregersen, H.B., and Black, J.S. (1992). Antecedents to commitment to a parent company and a foreign operation. *Academy of Management Journal*, 35 (1), 65–90.

Gruenfeld, D.H., Martorana, P.V., and Fan, E.T. (2000). What do groups learn from their worldliest members? Direct and indirect influence in dynamic teams. *Organizational Behavior and Human Decision Processes*, 82 (1), 45–59.

Gupta A.K., and Govindarajan, V. (2000). Knowledge flows within multinational corporations. *Strategic Management Journal*, 21 (4), 473–496.

Harris, K.J., Kacmar, K.M., Zivnuska, S., and Shaw, J.D. (2007). The impact of political skill on impression management effectiveness. *Journal of Applied Psychology*, 92 (1), 278–285.

Harvey, M. (1997). "Inpatriation" training: The next challenge for international human resource management. *International Journal of Intercultural Relations*, 21 (3), 393–428.

Harvey, M., and Buckley, M.R. (1997). Managing inpatriates: Building a global core competency. *Journal of World Business*, 32 (1), 35–52.

Harvey, M., and Miceli, N. (1999). Exploring inpatriate manager issues: An exploratory empirical study. *International Journal of Intercultural Relations*, 23 (3), 339–371.

Harvey, M., and Novicevic, M.M. (2004). The development of political skill and political capital by global leaders through global assignments. *International Journal of Human Resource Management*, 15 (7), 1173–1188.

Harvey, M., Novicevic, M.M., and Speier, C. (1999). Inpatriate managers: How to increase the probability of success. *Human Resource Management Review*, 9 (1), 51–81.

Harvey, M., Novicevic, M.M., and Speier, C. (2000). Strategic global human resource management: The role of inpatriate managers. *Human Resource Management Review*, 10 (2), 153–175.

Harvey, M., Novicevic, M.M., Buckley, M.R., and Fung, H. (2005). Reducing inpatriate managers' 'liability of foreignness' by addressing stigmatization and stereotype threats. *Journal of World Business*, 40 (3), 267–280.

Harvey, M., Speier, C., and Novicevic, M.M. (2001). A theory-based framework for strategic global human resource staffing policies and practices. *International Journal of Human Resource Management*, 12 (6), 898–915.

Harzing, A.-W. (2001). Of bears, bumble-bees and spiders: The role of expatriates in controlling foreign subsidiaries. *Journal of World Business*, 36 (4), 366–379.

Hébert, L., Very, P., and Beamish, P.W. (2005). Expatriation as a bridge over troubled water: A knowledge-based perspective applied to cross-border acquisitions. *Organization Studies*, 26 (10), 1455–1476.

Hocking, J.B., Brown, M.E., and Harzing, A.-W. (2004). A knowledge transfer perspective of strategic assignment purposes and their path-dependent outcomes. *International Journal of Human Resource Management*, 15 (3), 565–586.

Ibarra, H. (1995). Race, Opportunity, and diversity of social circles in managerial networks. *Academy of Management Journal*, 38 (3), 673–703.

Kamoche, K.N. (1997). Managing human resources in Africa: Strategic, organizational and epistemological issues. *International Business Review*, 6, 537–558.

Kostova, T., and Roth, K. (2003). Social capital in multinational corporations and a micro-macro model of its formation. *Academy of Management Review*, 28 (2), 297–317.

Kraimer, M.L., Wayne, S.J., and Jaworski, R.A. (2001). Sources of support and expatriate performance: The mediating role of expatriate adjustment. *Personnel Psychology*, 54 (1), 71–99.

Lazarova, M., and Tarique, I. (2005). Knowledge transfer upon repatriation. *Journal of World Business*, 40 (4), 361–373.

Leana, C.R., and Van Buren, H.J. (1999). Organizational Social Capital and Employment Practices. *Academy of Management Review*, 24 (3), 538–555.

Lengnick-Hall, M.L., and Lengnick-Hall, C.A. (2006). International human resource management and social network/social capital theory. In G.K. Stahl and I. Björkman (eds), *Handbook of Research in International Human Resource Management*. Cheltenham: Edward Elgar, pp. 475–487.

Li, P.P. (2007). Social tie, social capital, and social behavior: Toward an integrative model of informal exchange. *Asia Pacific Journal of Management*, 24 (2), 227–246.

Mehra, A., Kilduff, M., and Brass, D.J. (1998). At the margins: A distinctiveness approach to the social identity and social networks of underrepresented groups. *Academy of Management Journal*, 41 (4), 441–452.

Minbaeva, D.B., and Michailova, S. (2004). Knowledge transfer and expatriation in multinational corporations: The role of disseminative capacity. *Employee Relations*, 26 (6), 663–679.

Nahapiet, J., and Ghoshal, S. (1998). Social capital, intellectual capital, and the organizational advantage. *Academy of Management Review*, 23 (2), 242–266.

Napier, N.K., and Vu, V.T. (1998). International human resource management and transitional economy countries: A breed apart? *Human Resource Management Review*, 8 (1), 39–77.

Nebus, J. (2006). Building collegial information networks: A theory of advice network generation. *Academy of Management Review*, 31 (3), 615–637.

Oddou, G., Gregersen, H.B., Black, J.S., and Derr, C.B. (2001). Building global leaders: Strategy similarities and differences among European, U.S., and Japanese multinationals. In M.E. Mendenhall, T.M. Kühlmann and G.K. Stahl (eds), *Developing Global Leaders: Policies, Processes, and Innovation*. Westport, London: Quorum Books, pp. 99–116.

Perlmutter, H.V. (1969). The tortuous evolution of the multinational corporation. *Columbia Journal of World Business*, 4 (1), 9–18.

Perry-Smith, J.E. (2006). Social yet creative: The role of social relationships in facilitating individual creativity. *Academy of Management Journal*, 49 (1), 85–101.

Peterson, R.B. (2003). The use of expatriates and inpatriates in Central and Eastern Europe since the wall came down. *Journal of World Business*, 38 (1), 55–69.

Polanyi, M. (1966). *The Tacit Dimension*. London: Routledge & Kegan Paul.

Putnam, R.D. (1995). Bowling alone: America's declining social capital. *Journal of Democracy*, 6 (1), 65–78.

Raider, H.J., and Burt, R.S. (1996). Boundaryless and Social Capital. In M.B. Arthur and D.M. Rousseau (eds), *The Boundaryless Career: A New Employment Principle for a New Organizational Era*. New York: Oxford University Press, pp. 187–200.

Reade, C. (2003). Going the extra mile: Local managers and global effort. *Journal of Managerial Psychology*, 18 (3), 208–228.

Reagans, R., and McEvily, B. (2003). Network structure and knowledge transfer: The effects of cohesion and range. *Administrative Science Quarterly*, 48 (2), 240–267.

Reiche, B.S. (2006). The inpatriate experience in multinational corporations: An Exploratory case study in Germany. *International Journal of Human Resource Management*, 17 (9), 1572–1590.

Riusala, K., and Suutari, V. (2004). International knowledge transfers through expatriates. *Thunderbird International Business Review*, 46 (6), 743–770.

Rousseau, D.M., Sitkin, S.B., Burt, R.S., and Camerer, C. (1998). Not so different after all: A cross-discipline view of trust. *Academy of Management Review*, 23 (3), 393–404.

Seibert, S.E., Kraimer, M.L., and Liden, R.C. (2001). A social capital theory of career success. *Academy of Management Journal*, 44 (2), 219–237.

Shore, L.M., Tetrick, L.E., Lynch, P., and Barksdale, K. (2006). Social and economic exchange: Construct development and validation. *Journal of Applied Social Psychology*, 36 (4), 837–867.

Solomon, C.M. (1995). HR's helping hand pulls global inpatriates onboard. *Personnel Journal*, 74 (11), 40–49.

Stahl, G.K., Miller, E.L., and Tung, R.L. (2002). Toward the boundaryless career: A closer look at the expatriate career concept and the perceived implications of an international assignment. *Journal of World Business*, 37 (3), 216–227.

Szulanski, G. (2000). The process of knowledge transfer: A diachronic analysis of stickiness. *Organizational Behavior and Human Decision Processes*, 82 (1), 9–27.

Tahvanainen, M., Welch, D., and Worm, V. (2005). HR implications of short term assignments. *European Management Journal*, 23 (6), 663–673.

Taylor, S., Beechler, S., and Napier, N. (1996). Toward an integrative model of strategic international human resource management. *Academy of Management Review*, 21 (4), 959–985.

Thomas, D.C. (1994). The boundary-spanning role of expatriates in the multinational corporation. In S.B. Prasad (ed.), *Advances in International Comparative Management*, Vol. 9. Greenwich, CT: JAI Press, pp. 145–170.

Tsai, W., and Ghoshal, S. (1998). Social capital and value creation: The role of intrafirm networks. *Academy of Management Journal*, 41 (4), 464–476.

Tsang, E.W.K. (1999). The knowledge transfer and learning aspects of international HRM: An empirical study of Singapore MNCs. *International Business Review*, 8 (5–6), 591–609.

Tsui, A.S., Pearce, J.L., Porter, L.W., and Tripoli, A.M. (1997). Alternative approaches to the employee-organization relationship: Does investment in employees pay off? *Academy of Management Journal*, 40 (5), 1089–1121.

Tung, R.L. (1998). American expatriates abroad: From neophytes to cosmopolitans. *Journal of World Business*, 33 (2), 125–144.

Tushman, M.L., and Scanlan, T.J. (2005). Boundary spanning individuals: their role in information transfer and their antecedents. *Academy of Management Journal*, 24 (2), 289–305.

Wang, X., and Kanungo, R.N. (2004). Nationality, social network and psychological well-being: Expatriates in China. *International Journal of Human Resource Management*, 15 (4–5), 775–793.

Ward, C. (1996). Acculturation. In D. Landis and R.S. Bhagat (eds), *Handbook of Intercultural Training* (2nd edn), Thousand Oaks, CA: Sage, pp. 124–147.

Welch, D.E. (2003). Globalisation of staff movements: Beyond cultural adjustment. *Management International Review*, 43 (2), 149–169.

Wright, P.M., and Snell, S.A. (1998). Toward a unifying framework for exploring fit and flexibility in strategic human resource management. *Academy of Management Review*, 23 (4), 756–772.

9

Independent Consultants: How International Project Operations Create New IHRM Issues and Challenges

CATHERINE WELCH, DENICE WELCH, AND MARILYN FENWICK

INTRODUCTION

On February 22, 2004, a helicopter, chartered by the engineering firm, The Louis Berger Group Inc., was raked with bullets as it prepared to take off. The US-based firm had a contract from the US Agency for International Development (USAID) to build 428 kilometers of road from Kabul to Kandahar, and other projects such as rebuilding schools and clinics, in Afghanistan. On board were an Australian pilot, the firm's US construction supervisor, a British security guard, and an Afghan interpreter. They had just completed an inspection of a clinic under construction by Louis Berger. The pilot was killed. The construction engineer supervisor (a female) and the security guard were seriously wounded and later airlifted to a US military base in Germany for treatment. The interpreter had minor injuries (*Engineering News Record*, 2004: 16).

Firms operating internationally utilize a wide variety of operation modes to expand their activities. These modes (or methods of operation) include exporting, foreign direct investment, equity joint ventures, international alliances in their various forms, licensing and franchising, management contracts, international subcontracting (outsourcing, "offshoring" and contract manufacturing) and international project operations. They are not mutually exclusive: firms will combine various methods to service a particular market, such as licensing with an international joint venture. It is also recognized that firms may switch from one mode to another as circumstances in a particular market change (Petersen *et al.*, 2000).

Handbook of International Human Resource Management. Edited by Paul R. Sparrow
© 2009 John Wiley & Sons, Ltd

Existing evidence suggests that the choices for a firm's foreign operation mode have direct implications for the HR function. Yet the HR challenges associated with each operation mode have not been extensively studied. For example, success with international franchising often depends on how much support is provided to franchisees – such as McDonald's and its Hamburger University (see Dowling and Welch, 2004). However, apart from franchisee training, there has been little research into the HR management demands of international franchising. Likewise, despite early work in the 1970s and 1980s that identified the HRM implications of the management contract, there has been a paucity of academic work since the early studies that emanated predominantly from UK scholars (Holly, 1982). An exception is a recent study by Al-Husan and James (2003) of a management contract awarded to a consortium led by a French company to manage water distribution in Amman.

The bulk of IHRM research instead tends to assume that the firm is internationalizing through foreign direct investment (FDI). This has produced a wealth of literature – taking a headquarter subsidiary perspective – related to staff movements within the multinational's internal market (for a more detailed review see Clark *et al.*, 1999; Dowling and Welch 2004; Mayerhofer *et al.*, 2004; and Stahl and Bjørkman, 2006).

In this chapter, we seek to address these concerns by turning attention to a different IHRM research setting: that of international project operations. This mode of operation provides a novel IHRM setting. It requires employing and supporting project teams, composed of different specialist areas, genders, ages and nationalities, in a temporary work organization, with host country counterparts, often in remote and sometimes dangerous locations. Project firms use a range of international assignments: the traditional longer-term posting, rotational "fly-in, fly-out" arrangements and short-term assignments.

As we will discuss later, the nature of international project work raises HR issues that are different to those encountered in more traditional work settings such as wholly-owned subsidiaries. As such, the international project poses HR challenges that differ in degree and form to those generally discussed in the IHRM literature (Welch *et al.*, 2008). The Louis Berger incident at the beginning of this chapter presents a graphic, though extreme, snapshot of some of the issues involved.

As a way of demonstrating that there is no "one size fits all" approach to international staffing and management (see Suutari and Brewster, this volume Chapter 7, for a review of research on different forms of international working), and that mode of operation is an important influence, we investigate external projects in a project-intensive and internationally focused sector: international aid and development consulting. We present what our research has identified as a special group of international assignees: *the independent consultant* who is an integral part of the delivery by supplier firms of international development projects funded by multilateral institutions, such as the World Bank, and bilateral aid programs. These individuals are specialists contracted by supplier firms to provide expert consultancy input. Combined with the very nature of international project work and its context, the relationship between independent consultants and supplier firms is proving to be instructive in identifying the distinct HR challenges associated with staffing this type of project.

Our arguments in this chapter are underpinned by a commitment to a more contextualized approach to IHRM research and theory building: in other words, to account for contextual differences (in this case, the context of the firm's internationalization process) that are often assumed to be homogeneous or even erased in the march toward generalizable laws, and the goal of a more mature 'scientific' field of inquiry. By assuming that IHRM takes place solely in an FDI context, we risk being regarded as narrowly focused and somewhat disconnected from business reality.

The chapter is organized as follows: first, we relate HR activities associated with the various stages of the life of an international project. We then explain the qualitative methodology used. From the data analysis, we develop a picture of the type of individuals attracted to this line of work and related HR issues: what motivates such people, their expectations regarding career outcomes and their work context. The nature of the development project, its implications for performance, and the relationship between the independent consultant and the various parties to the project are also explored. The chapter concludes with a delineation of specific HR management implications of international project work, and suggested areas for future research.

HR Challenges of International Development Projects

International projects vary considerably in form, scope and size (Cova *et al.*, 2002). While there are consequently diverse features of projects, two are of particular relevance to this chapter: the nature of the client and of the industry. The client can be either internal or external to the firm. An example of an internal project is subsidiary R&D staff working on product development in cross-border, sometimes virtual, teams. In these cases, top management has more control over the transfer of resources and expertise. External projects can be business-to-business (as a separate contract, or as part of a strategic alliance) and business-to-government contract work. Some industries, such as construction, engineering, and consulting, are 'project intensive' in that their outputs are often delivered in the form of bespoke solutions for clients. As such, the external client tends to have a larger input into the composition of key project team composition, and project-intensive firms are heavily reliant on their ability to marshal competent teams to deliver services on time and to budget.

Given the sheer diversity of international projects, we confine our discussion to a single project-intensive sector that delivers to external clients: aid and development consulting. This sector in fact covers a very wide range of technical services, ranging from engineering and construction to health and community development; however, their objective is similar to the extent that all have the mission of improving national economic and social welfare. They also have similar institutional contexts, in that they are delivered to external clients; are all financed through aid or concessional loans administered by government or multilateral institutions, which have standardized rules and procedures; and are implemented in the often harsh, even dangerous, conditions of less-developed countries (such as Afghanistan, Iraq, Columbia, and Nigeria). In recent years, there has been a shift in funding emphasis away from the provision of 'hard infrastructure', such as roads and dams, to 'soft' infrastructure such as community development and governance. A typical input for these projects is international consulting services which, as they necessitate cross-border people movements, serve as the focus of this chapter.

International development projects follow a distinct life cycle that is prescribed by the rules of funding agencies (Welch *et al.*, 2008):

1. *Tracking.* In this phase, the start of the project cycle, potential projects are identified and monitored. Generating work is a key organizational driver, so having staff in positions where they can track potential projects is critical. This can involve frequent staff visits to host locations, and even the setting up of offshore offices to support business development and intelligence gathering.

2. *International competitive bidding process.* Firms prepare and submit tender documents to meet the specifications of the client. The bidding process is complicated by the fact that two 'clients' are involved, with their decision-making power varying according to how the project is financed: the funding agency (e.g., the World Bank or bilateral aid agency) and the host government that is the recipient of the project. In large multilateral projects, where the 'client' may be the World Bank as lender in conjunction with a host government agency, the project preparation phase and tendering process may involve years, not months.

   Successful tendering of consulting services is determined to a large extent by the qualifications of the persons nominated in the bid, so bidding firms need to stipulate the names of the consultants they are proposing and include their curriculum vitae. Some funding agencies or clients insist on interviewing the persons nominated to ensure that the face matches the curriculum vitae (CV) – that is, that staff are not substituted after the bid has been awarded. This requirement effectively locks staff into particular projects and poses a specific staffing dilemma: given the time lag between a tender notice and the signing of a contract, how do supplier firms ensure that the named personnel are available when required? A further complication is that most bids fail and even those that win can be subject to delays to the start of the project. The HR issues at the preliminary stages of tracking and bidding center around maintaining contact with the independent consultants who are nominated in each bid and keeping CV databases up-to-date.

3. *Implementation* (project delivery). This stage is staff intensive. A large project is normally led by a Project Director, located either at headquarters or in a regional or country office. The project director will make frequent visits to the project site, and liaise with the client and host country stakeholders. The Team Leader handles the day-to-day operations and team maintenance. Team membership commonly is fluid, with people joining the project at different stages, and for different lengths of time, across the lifecycle of a project.

Teams are then typically diverse in their composition. From the supplier firm, team members may be a mix of PCNs, TCNs, and local hires (HCNs). In addition, they typically include independent consultants hired specifically for that project. Funding agencies distinguish between 'international' and 'domestic' consultants, with the former providing world-class expertise and the latter referring to local professionals.

Team composition is further complicated by the number of organizations that may be involved. Supplier firms often form alliances to win a tender, with these partners then involved in staffing the delivery of the project, and, in addition, staff from the client government may be heavily involved in the implementation phase. As we will demonstrate later in this chapter, in international aid and development projects, interaction between team members and their local counterparts, and with funding agency staff, has critical performance implications. Despite this, personnel in supplier firms generally have little involvement in aspects relating to team maintenance, conflict resolution and safety that may arise during this stage. HR, as a consequence, faces relevancy issues. Its role is often regarded as one of administrative support.

4. *Post-Completion*. During the fourth and final stage, this temporary organization that was the project is disbanded, although the relationships formed may continue (Hadjikhani, 1996). For firms hiring independent consultants, the traditional repatriation situation is replaced by a need to handle the cessation of contractual obligations in a manner that keeps a positive relationship with those who will be required on future projects. Obviously, how this is handled will affect the firm's ability to win future work. There is also the question of how the firm can harvest knowledge, given that key individuals may not be prepared, or available, to share their knowledge (see Harvey and Novicevic, this volume Chapter 6; Welch *et al.*, 2008).

While the project cycle in this industry is very much shaped by funding rules and specific client demands, it nevertheless exhibits what have been identified as the key features of project business (Davies and Hobday, 2005):

- ◆ temporary organizations,
- ◆ discontinuity in terms of client demand,
- ◆ a high degree of uncertainty over project timelines and technical complexity.

This lack of continuity presents challenges both for firms (in terms of the staffing of projects) and for individuals (in terms of career management). Studying how firms and individuals coped with operating in an environment of enhanced uncertainty, in somewhat atypical organizational structures, allowed us to identify a separate category of international assignees, and a range of HR and general management issues that result from international project work that are different to those in the more 'mainstream' IHRM context. However, before we describe these factors, it is important to explain our research approach.

METHODOLOGY

Interest in the topic arose from a study aimed at understanding the internationalization of Australian firms that deliver international development projects for multilateral institutions (for further details about this study see Welch, 2005a, 2005b). Organizations included in the study were from the public as well as private sector and ranged from small (under 20 employees) to large (over 3000). Their degree of experience of international development projects varied – from those with over 30 years through to new entrants. While the firms were all consulting providers, they represented a range of sectors – engineering, health, education, and public sector reform – although most provided consulting expertise across a range of sectors. A consistent theme that emerged from the study was the critical role of staffing in the successful delivery of international development projects, particularly the management of a high proportion of independent specialist consultants who were not permanent employees.

The initial study provided a picture of HR issues from the perspective of the supplier firm. However, in order to fully appreciate the HR aspects of international development work, it was deemed necessary to obtain the perspectives of the international project workers who are mainly responsible for implementation. To this end, a second round of interviews was conducted. Individuals who had experience in international development work were contacted, using a snowballing technique. Initial approaches were made to consultants who had worked with some of the firms in the initial study. These persons became key informants, providing data and assisting in gaining access to others through their personal and work-related networks. They also acted as data verifiers in terms of critiquing interview questions, commenting on a report of the initial study, and offering additional insights post interview.

Sixteen people agreed to participate in this follow-up study. They came from a range of backgrounds, but were skewed toward senior positions and age, due to the nature of the development work. As one interviewee explained, the clients (usually the World Bank and aid agencies) placed emphasis on experience as a criterion for winning the bid and this has resulted in a dearth of younger people being available as they do not have a chance to develop the requisite track record (see the discussion of social capital, Harvey and Novicevic, this volume Chapter 6). As a consequence, interviewees had a wealth of experience upon which to draw, as careers spanned several decades on average, and a range of different positions in connection with development projects: from bid writer, team leader, technical adviser, project director through to official evaluator. Interviewees were permanent staff members, senior managers or independent consultants – with most having even held two or even all three positions during the course of their careers.

Interviews took place either in the person's office or via telephone hook-up. They ranged from half an hour to one hour in duration, based on semistructured questions. Interviews were recorded (with the interviewee's permission) using a digital voice recorder. These were transcribed and checked for accuracy. Given the small sample size, the data was analyzed manually, using the following research questions as a general organizing template:

- What attracts individuals to work as external contractors?
- How are employment relationships between the parties managed?
- What role does the HR function perform?

The next section provides a summary of key findings and accompanying discussion.

Defining a New Research Population

Global assignment trends indicate that, due to cost constraints and demographic changes such as dual career couples, multinationals are trying to reduce their reliance on the more traditional international assignment of three or more years. 'Non-traditional' assignments identified in the academic literature include short-term assignments (Fenwick and Di Cieri, 2004; Tahvanainen *et al.*, 2005), assignments involving frequent travel without relocation (Mayerhofer *et al.*, 2004; Welch *et al.*, 2007), and even virtual assignments (Welch, 2003).

Accompanying the change in focus has been the identification of different types of individuals who are attracted to non-standard international assignments, or who fall somewhat outside the traditional category of expatriate (see Suutari and Brewster, this volume Chapter 7). Mayerhofer *et al.* (2004), for example, coined the term 'flexpatriate' to describe their sample of assignees working on commuter-type and other more flexible arrangements that avoid the need to relocate to another country for a considerable length of time. Banai and Harry (2005: 100), when discussing boundaryless global careers, describe a group they term international itinerants: 'professional managers who over their careers are employed for their ability, by at least two business organizations that are not related to each other, in at least two different foreign countries'. Another identified group is that of self-initiated expatriates, who find their own international assignment positions as external hires, rather than being sent abroad by their existing employer (Suutari and Brewster, 2000). These authors identify subgroups: young opportunists; job seekers; officials; localized professionals; and international professionals (or mercenaries).

We found that the supplier firms in the aid and development sector tend to rely more heavily on a high proportion of temporary employees than is the case with organizations generally studied in international management. Hence a common (although slightly pejorative) descriptor within the international development sector of such a firm is 'body shop'. While not all supplier firms are so-called body shops, they share a common characteristic of being heavily dependent on attracting sufficient numbers of skilled external contractors in often highly competitive circumstances. This was even the case for the large firms in our study, which were typically not able to field a team just with permanent hires, given the highly specialized technical qualifications and prior international experience demanded by funding agencies. It is not surprising therefore that, during the data collection and analysis stages, it became evident that international development work involved a special category of international assignees hitherto ignored by extant IHRM literature: *the independent consultant.*

On the surface, this may seem a semantic rather than substantive distinction: 'independents' share some of the characteristics of the international itinerant, the self-initiated international professional, and the traditional expatriate. There are common concerns among all these groups related to factors such as compensation, family issues, organizational support and career outcomes. There may be shared motives for accepting international work. However, as we will demonstrate, our data suggests sufficient distinct differences to warrant their own category. We argue that these differences relate above all to the loosely coupled nature of the independents' relationships with supplier firms. The distinctive characteristics of this group are explored in the next section.

The Independent Consultant: Profile and Perspective

A strong advantage of the qualitative approach taken in our study is the ability to allow the data to drive the analysis, rather than researchers predetermining factors or variables. It requires an open mind so that emerging, often unexpected, themes are recognized. Possible links between themes become building blocks for theoretical development. Another advantage is that the process of iteration between the data and theory forced us to 'revisit' concepts outside the expatriate literature. Having a team of researchers from different scientific backgrounds is also an advantage. As this section illustrates, our data revealed themes of motivation, power, career outcomes and the role of project partners, which we now discuss.

Motivation

Independents actively seek international work – it is essential to their livelihood – rather than being presented with a choice to accept or reject an international assignment, as is generally the case with traditional expatriates. They are thus highly internationally mobile. Asked what type of people are attracted to such work, an interviewee remarked that they could be divided into three groups – what he referred to as the '3 Ms: missionaries, mercenaries and misfits', though he then added a fourth category: that of 'escapee'. The interviewee explained that he would see himself as mercenary, though not driven solely by chasing money but rather enjoying the short-term challenges international projects posed, and the fact that 'on-shore' (i.e., domestic) work did not lend itself to the same level of variety and buzz:

> Like in Nigeria, I've been on a US$55 million micro enterprise program. Here in Australia, how often do you do that? And that is just taking the team in for four weeks.

There was some consensus about this categorization, in that some consultants were considered to be missionaries in the sense of being attracted to development work because they were able to contribute in a meaningful way: 'seeing what they could put in', as opposed to 'seeing what they could take out'. One of the interviewees was from a less-developed country, so had personal experience of being 'the local beneficiary of somebody's intervention there'. Typically, the categories of 'mercenary' and 'missionary' were not seen as absolute or fixed: people could start out with high ideals and expectations but later the money becomes important; others regarded the categories of mercenary and missionary as extremes, with most consultants somewhere in the middle:

> ... a large proportion of people are not zealots ... They are development focused and they have a concern and working in these sorts of organizations, it's their way of expressing their concerns. So I wouldn't call them missionaries but they certainly are concerned individuals but nor are a lot of them mercenary.
>
> A lot of people get into it [development work] just because of feeling good ... that you're doing something. .. [They] get rewarded, I guess when they see things working ... people have always said to me that they have been astounded by how rapidly things – once things get moving – how rapidly they can take place, much faster than ... at home. That's very stimulating, it's quite rewarding ... There's no question that money's a factor. Big salaries to go places, particularly tax-free salaries, keep a lot of people in it.
>
> I think there is a bit of all three in all of us.

Therefore, there were differences between our sample and the international professional subcategory of the self-initiating expatriate – they were not just mercenaries. There were intangible aspects that contributed: the degree of autonomy and independence that it offers; combined with the sense of adventure, a way to gain valuable work experience, or as a convenient way to experience a particular country or culture:

> I think in the first instance, it's the adventure, you know. Clearly one had sort of a value system [to contribute] but I'm not sure if that was the primary motivator. It was more just [the work] sounded like an exotic and adventurous sort of activity ... but with a safety net.
>
> Many people go into the field because they want to get experience and develop [skills]. So it is not only money ... [but] money drives some – about 50 per cent of the consultants.
>
> I think the other part for some people anyway is always wanting – which is sort of the stimulation thing – but for a number of people who had an interest in a particular country or a particular language or a particular region, it's still quite difficult to find work over in those places ... but [development work] is a way of getting work, adding another path.
>
> People prepared to go [to] places others don't want to go.

However, the uncertainty of development projects and future job prospects had an impact – moving people from the missionary end of the spectrum to that of mercenary. A comment made by the Director Global HR of the US construction firm, Bechtel, in a presentation to the IHRM conference, Cairns, June 17, 2005 reflects this: 'you have to find work...you have to eat'. It is not surprising to find that project workers generally 'follow the work, not the company'.

As one interviewee whose experience spanned both hiring consultants and being one herself put it, ultimately, independents have to be 'loyal to themselves', and this reinforced the tendency to be individualistic. The mercenary aspect was reflected in instrumental behavior provoked by the very nature of international development project work and their independent external status which meant a focus on the transactional side of the employment relationship.

Loyalty emerges as a factor in the relationship between the independent consultant and the supplier firm which, in turn, is a consequence of the nature of development work, coupled with the non-permanency of the employment contract. The tendency for 'self-preservation' made it challenging for supplier firms to generate commitment and loyalty. The former co-owner and managing director of one supplier firm recalled that even when his firm grew to a sufficient size to warrant the employment of a dedicated HR manager, many of the initiatives introduced were not as successful as he had hoped. The company experimented with training programs, career development and additional support measures for project staff in the field. However he felt that even among his permanent staff, the level of interest in such initiatives was not as high as might have been anticipated. He attributed this to the fact that international development experts saw themselves as 'solo people' or 'free traders', with self-reliance very much part of their professional image. Thus, the motivation and self-image of the 'independent' is quite different to that of the traditional expatriate

Power

Like self-initiated expatriates, independent consultants are externally hired contract employees. However, the situation – the international development project – shapes the power base of this group. Independents are key to commercial success, given that the funding agency and/or client rates the bid on the basis of the consulting expertise that is put forward. As a project director of a supplier firm explained:

> You have to have people who have got CVs [that] will be approved [by the funding agency]. Quite often now on projects, in evaluating bids, the team will be upwards of 700 points out of 1,000...so you have to have really good people with really good CVs that can be marked highly.

In other words, the supplier firm's hands are effectively tied by the bidding process, the stipulations of the client/funding agency, and their ability to retain good consultants in a loosely coupled arrangement. They do not drive staff selection as is typically the case with other modes of operation such as FDI or management contracts.

The bargaining power exhibited by *independents* stems from three bases:

- the ability to control a resource,
- the technical power, and
- expert power derived from their specialist skill and knowledge.

As Mintzberg (1983) explains, to serve as a basis of power, the resource, skill and knowledge must satisfy the following conditions: be essential to the supplier firm, in short supply, and nonsubstitutable. The bidding process places *independents* in a strong bargaining position, as success of the bidding process is partly determined by the quality of the consultants named. Those who have gained good reputations have strong resource power: they can provide or withhold their names to the supplier firm's bid. Specialist knowledge and technical skills that are in short supply enhance the independent's bargaining power as they are sought after by competing supplier firms.

Senior, very experienced independents will have built up a strong reputation with the funding agency, or local client (often a host government agency) or both. In some cases, their specific participation is a prerequisite to the supplier firm being awarded the tender – that is, nonsubstitutability is formalized. Such independents are in a strong position when negotiating the terms of their fees with supplier firms and are often able to dictate terms and conditions even after the commencement of the project. One interviewee related a recent experience when visiting a development project in an African country. The team leader was frustrated with the performance of a team member but was unable to do anything about it:

> Because he [the team member] was the key to winning this job, he just named a very high price and after [the supplier firm] got the job...said: 'Oh, I think I'll work 8 months instead of 12, same monthly rate but we'll just spread it across the year', so he's spent 4 months a year here in Australia.

The strong bargaining position means that some are free to pick and choose project work, with a 'take it or leave it' approach:

> I have a network of about 12 different people who email me to do work and basically... all my work now comes from email... I don't play the game. I just say, this is my price.

These are individual, independent specialists. They're not just on your bid, they're on several other jobs, they've got several other commitments.

The senior, more experienced consultants described above form an inner circle of independents who are a tight-knit group – they tend to know each other (even being described as 'mates'), with strong relationships that have been developed over, in some cases, decades. Not all *independents* have the same level of bargaining power as they lack the conditions required to influence the situation. Those outside the inner circle have yet to reach the high level of resource power and/or face fiercer competition: 'there are lots of consultants who want to do development work'. The outer-circle independents lack expertise, and/or their specific skills or knowledge are not in demand, so their power base is comparatively restricted. Our interviews with permanent staff in supplier firms suggest that senior independents who command a high fee, and enjoy a tax-free status, can unsettle permanent staff working alongside them at the field site due to a perceived lack of parity in terms and conditions. This was expressed in terms of 'when I have the experience, I would like to go out on my own'.

Power is an important aspect in the organizational context, yet there is a dearth of treatment of power in the IHRM literature (see, however, Harvey and Novicevic, this volume Chapter 6). The exception is subsidiary and international joint venture management where discussion tends to center on Hofstede's (1980a, b) concept of power distance to explain differences between work groups and MNC management. In contrast, the examination of international development project work revealed the influence of power in terms of work relationships in difficult environments. The concept of power and its various bases may be a fruitful avenue for explaining elements of cross-cultural group dynamics beyond Hofstede's cultural dimensions.

Career outcomes

'Independents' are similar to Banai and Harry's (2005) international itinerants in that they hold a career identity that is independent of the employer and are active in managing their own careers. However, career management entails considerable challenges due to the work context. While the bidding process may tilt bargaining power in favour of at least the 'inner circle' of experienced consultants, it also exposes them to considerable uncertainty. The bidding system was likened to a 'lottery' by one industry veteran: in a competitive bidding process most bids will fail since only one can win, and even then the project may not go ahead on schedule. Due to this uncertainty, *independents* will often simultaneously have their names associated with bids from numerous supplier firms, usually for different projects. As two experienced interviewees explained:

> [The project] timing keeps moving. So you keep saying yes to more people than you could ever hope to do work for. That juggling becomes a big issue and it can lead to difficulties with the client in that you've said I'll be there to do it but you haven't finished [the current one] . . . it is the nature of the work.
>
> [I]n this competitive work you've always got to be in three or four bids at any time if you're going to keep working . . . To give you an idea, I'm starting on a job tomorrow – that job was supposed have started in February this year, then it was definitely going to be June and we are finally getting on with it now [November].

While some independents may have a degree of commitment to a particular supplier firm, the necessity to ensure a continuous stream of work can lead them to feel mixed loyalties, having worked with different supplier firms 'and been satisfied with both', but are forced to place concern for self above other considerations. Thus, the high level of uncertainty affects the independent's future career prospects and sets up the countering behavior outlined above: loyalty to oneself, concern for reputation and standing, and networking within funding bodies and agencies.

One of the dilemmas independents faced was the potential of disqualifying themselves from work in their home country, with offshore experience in a developing country potentially not rated as relevant. Just as the skills that experts gained in a management position at home did not necessarily qualify them to lead the team on a development project, the skills gained on a development project (such as managing a cross-cultural team) were not always regarded as relevant to the industry context at home. In this sense, the independent consultants shared similar concerns to that of Suutari and Brewster's (2000) international professionals who were less than optimistic about their job prospects if they returned to their home country.

Another dilemma in terms of career outcomes was that being on the 'international treadmill' too long could potentially cut them off from cutting edge innovations and changes in their field of expertise – effectively 'technically redundant', thus also reducing their effectiveness on international projects. The bargaining power of the international consultant was therefore seen as having a 'use by' date, with distinct implications for future career outcomes.

The uncertain environment in which *independents* operate is perhaps extreme in relation to other types of international assignments. However, the trend of not guaranteeing repatriate positions for traditional expatriates appears to continue, along with a swing toward short-term assignments (Tahvanainen *et al.*, 2005). These trends are occurring against the backdrop of changing workplace relationships, such as the lessening of loyalty and continuous career paths with one employer. It would therefore seem that the experiences of our cohort of *independents* may have relevance to the way in which firms approach international assignments, should the use of traditional forms continue to decline.

Successful assignments: the role of project partners

Success, in the discussion of most international assignments, is framed in terms of the assignee's relationship with the firm:

- ◆ whether the firm supports the assignee's transition to the new location,
- ◆ how the assignee is able to adjust to the new working environment in the host country, and
- ◆ the cooperation that develops between local and expatriate staff.

However, as has been discussed, the international consultant's relationship with the contracting supplier is a relatively loose one and may not last beyond the duration of the assignment. This relationship can be made even more tenuous by the fact that the supplier firm may well not have an office at, or even in the same country as, the project site. The project team will in that case be alone 'in the field', with only occasional visits from the project director. On the other hand, some supplier firms will have established local or regional offices that can play an active role in the delivery of the project. They may complement the project team with its own permanent

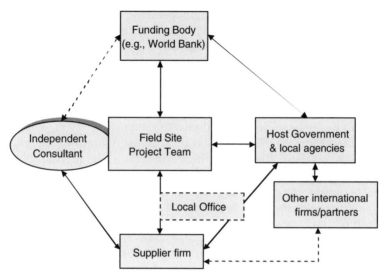

FIGURE 9.1 Independents and project partners.

staff in some cases. Yet even in these situations, the project team is required to operate with a high degree of self-sufficiency. Consequently, in order to survive an assignment, consultants need to be 'independent, practical sort of people . . . because you don't get a lot of support, you're on your own quite a lot'.

While the consultant's relationship with the contracting firm is potentially not so central to the assignment experience, other parties may have a considerable role to play (see Moingeon, Lumineau, and Perrin, this volume Chapter 13, for a discussion of knowledge transfer across organizational boundaries). Figure 9.1 highlights other parties likely to be part of an international development project, and who feature strongly in interviewees' accounts of their assignments. Perhaps the organization most often referred to is the recipient government (i.e., the government receiving the loan or aid) and its related local agencies, that may provide project staff (termed counterparts) to complement those provided by the supplier firm. Building solid relationships with government officials was seen as critical to the project's success, but often an elusive goal to achieve. As well as cross-cultural communication problems, consultants may well encounter corruption in government agencies, tension between the funding agency and client government, and a lack of support for the project aims. As a result, consultants are likely to need considerable political skills in navigating around the demands and interests of multiple parties (see Harvey and Novicevic, this volume Chapter 6) and the ability to deal with the 'frustrations' involved, particularly the slow pace of progress.

Other relevant parties consist of the other firms involved in the project (shown in Figure 9.1). The supplier firm may be part of an alliance or consortium that will also have input into project team composition, including their own independent consultants and/or permanent staff. The supplier firm will also likely be partnered with a local consulting firm, as funding agencies have policies to encourage such partnerships. The local firm will then be involved in recruiting local consultants: as one interviewee explained, 'we try to use local knowledge to hire local consultants'. This means that the project team will involve international consultants working alongside local colleagues. The interviewees agreed that the quality of local consultants was often very high, but obviously being paid a fraction of the rates of an international consultant.

In this situation, international consultants are expected to be transferring expertise to their local colleagues (see Moingeon, Lumineau, and Perrin, this volume Chapter 13, for a discussion of interorganizational communities of practice). This can be a double-edged sword: the consultant shares the knowledge but in so doing may forgo a distinct competitive advantage that may influence bargaining power in later project negotiations. However, as one interviewee explained, one ingredient of a successful assignment is the recognition that the knowledge transfer needs to be two-way: 'Look at them as an equal … , as equal as you are, because you learn from them. They learn but you learn from them as well.'

CONCLUSION: IMPLICATIONS FOR HRM

The above analysis highlights the relationship between the independent consultant and the supplier firms involved in international development projects as being simultaneously loosely coupled and interdependent. It is therefore not surprising that the former co-owner of a consulting firm we interviewed described HRM as a 'constant topic of discussion at a senior management level'. Managing this special group of international assignees therefore presents supplier firms with distinct management challenges, centered around four major issues: work continuity, loyalty, compensation, and on-site support. As indicated in Table 9.1, these are common to both firms and independents, though the action taken to address these may differ.

The unpredictable pipeline of projects is just as much a challenge for firms as for the individual consultants discussed in the previous section. The uncertainty

TABLE 9.1 Issues and associated actions for independents and supplier firms.

Issue	Independents	Supplier firms
Work continuity	Network maintenance Safeguarding reputation	Market intelligence CV database
Loyalty	To self but some attachment to firms	Enduring relationships with 'inner circle' consultants
Compensation	Bargaining power often high	Parity between permanent staff, and independents
On-site support	Self-reliance and experience	Reliance on local agencies Use of project management systems Morale boosting

that prevails in this project context places considerable constraints on the supplier firm due to its reliance on often powerful independents who are physically removed during the delivery phase. Its options are further limited by rules on recruitment, assignment conditions and performance that are, to a large extent, set by its external clients. In this fluid environment, HR activities need to be seen in the wider context of the firm's project partners, rather than confined to the employment relationship it has with its permanent staff.

The challenge of work continuity is met by firms putting considerable effort into market intelligence, so that they can ensure a steady pipeline of projects that fit the skills sets of existing staff, and obtain sufficient early warning to contact desirable independents ahead of the competition. HR activities in this discontinuous environment also involve building and maintaining a database of independents. This database does not just consist of CVs, but also the unwritten, tacit knowledge about which consultants are reliable team members, with interviewees unwilling to rely on an independent they did not already know. Senior independents can be a valuable resource in terms of market intelligence. This group's inner circle extends beyond other independents. It includes senior managers of other supply firms, key representatives in funding agencies and recipient organizations in host countries.

Loyalty to an 'inner circle' of consultants was also shown by firms, with interviewees revealing that maintaining ties with top independents was a priority. While repatriation services for independents were not an issue, many firms made a considerable effort to reuse talent on subsequent projects. A senior manager (who had himself been an independent and now manages a workforce of both permanents and independents) described it as being able to successfully manage 'a very complicated process of social interaction and behavior [that is] built on long-term relationships and trust and intimate knowledge of each other'. Given that this 'inner circle' has considerable power when negotiating compensation, supplier firms had to consider carefully how they could deal with inequities between independents and their own permanent staff. The perceived attractiveness of the independents' lifestyle, particularly their tax-free status, was a factor in staff retention.

Supplier firms also need to think about providing on-site support – not just to ensure that projects were delivered on time, but also to ensure that independents would want to maintain ties with the firm beyond the duration of the project. The use of project management systems can provide warning signs, even from a distance, of team breakdown or adjustment problems. One avenue is to provide logistical support so that team members feel they are not on their own but have the support of the company. This was easier to provide if the firm had the necessary local presence or good relationships with local agencies. But if there was no local presence, a simple but effective form of support was morale boosting through regular phone calls and even visits to the project team to reassure them that they had not been forgotten. Such support tended to be recognized by independents and acted as a factor when later deciding which supplier firm to work for.

We commenced this chapter by arguing that a 'one size fits all' approach to IHRM overlooks variations that are related to an internationalizing firm's choice of operation mode. We have provided empirical support for this argument by tracing how the nature of a development project shapes the relationship between supplier firm and its staff, as well as resulting in distinctive career outcomes for individuals. This has allowed a fuller exploration of international assignees that share certain characteristics of the self-initiated assignees, a hitherto under-researched group. Changes in the global environment, accompanied by multinational firms' attempts to reduce traditional expatriates, indicate that various types of work arrangements in international business are likely to increase. Further research into non-traditional assignees is therefore warranted.

In addition, while our sample size is modest, the study has indicated the value of looking at other types of international assignees in order to expose a broader range of issues associated with changes in the way internationalizing firms approach their operations. As mentioned earlier, strategic decisions and actions taken by a firm's top management to further international growth and market expansion have HR consequences. It is clear that the variety of modes of foreign operation utilized by internationalizing firms has not been matched by studies which explore the HR issues and challenges that accompany each mode. We would suggest that studies into other operation modes under-represented in existing literature would provide a fruitful avenue for future research in IHRM.

REFERENCES

Al-Husan F.B., and James, P. (2003). Cultural control and multinationals: The case of privatized Jordanian companies. *International Journal of Human Resource Management*, 14 (7), 1284–1295.

Banai, M., and Harry, W. (2005). Boundaryless global careers: The international itinerants. *International Studies of Management and Organization*, 34 (3), 96–120.

Clark, T., Gospel, H., and Montgomery, J. (1999). Running on the spot? A review of twenty years of research on the management of human resources in comparative and international perspective. *International Journal of Human Resource Management*, 10 (3), 520–544.

Cova, B., Ghauri, P., and Salle, R. (2002). *Project Marketing: Beyond Competitive Bidding*. Chichester: John Wiley & Sons.

Davies, A., and Hobday, M. (2005). *The Business of Projects: Managing Innovation in Complex Products and Systems*. New York: Cambridge University Press.

Dowling, P.J., and Welch, D.E. (2004). *International Human Resource Management: Managing People in a Multinational Context* (4th edn), London: Thomson Learning.

Engineering News Record (2004). Afghan attack on helicopter kills pilot, wounds engineer. *Engineering News Record*, 252 (9), 16.

Fenwick, M., and De Cieri, H. (2004). Interorganizational network participation: Implications for global career management. *Journal of Management Development*, 23 (9), 798–817.

Hadjikhani, A. (1996). Project marketing and the management of discontinuity. *International Business Review*, 5 (3), 319–336.

Hofstede, G (1980a). *Culture's Consequences: International Differences in Work-Related Values*. Beverly Hills, CA: Sage.

Hofstede, G. (1980b). Motivation, leadership and organization: Do American theories apply abroad? *Organizational Dynamics*, Summer, 42–63.

Holly, J. (1982). Management contracts. In M.Z. Brooke and P.J. Buckley (eds), *Handbook of International Trade Issue 2*. Brentford: Kluwer.

Mayerhofer, H., Hartmann, L.C., Michelitsch-Riedl, G., and Kollinger, I. (2004). Flexpatriate assignments: A neglected issue in global staffing. *International Journal of Human Resource Management*, 15 (8), 1371–1389.

Mintzberg, H. (1983). *Power in and Around Organizations*. Englewood Cliffs: Prentice-Hall.

Petersen, R.B., Welch, D., and Welch L., (2000). Creating meaningful switching options in international operations. *Long Range Planning*, 35 (5), 688–705.

Stahl, G.K., and Bjorkman, I. (eds) (2006). *Handbook of Research in International Human Resource Management*. Cheltenham: Edward Elgar Publishing.

Suutari, V., and Brewster, C. (2000). Making their own way: International experience through self-initiated foreign assignments. *Journal of World Business*, 35 (4), 417–432.

Tahvanainen, M., Welch, D., and Worm, V. (2005). HR implications of short term assignments. *European Management Journal*, 23 (6), 663–673.

Welch, C. (2005a). International consulting providers and multilateral institutions: Networks and internationalization. *Advances in International Marketing*, 15, 175–197.

Welch, C. (2005b). Multilateral organisations and international project marketing. *International Business Review*, 14 (3), 289–305.

Welch, C., Welch, D., and Tahvanainen, M. (2008). Managing the HR dimension of international project operations. *International Journal of Human Resource Management*, 19 (2), 205–222.

Welch, D.E. (2003). Globalisation of staff movements: Beyond cultural adjustment. *Management International Review*, 43 (2), 149–169.

Welch, D.E., Welch, L.S., and Worm, V. (2007). The international business traveller: A neglected but strategic resource. *International Journal of Human Resource Management*, 18 (2), 173–183.

10

Gender Issues: Women in International Management

HELEN DE CIERI

INTRODUCTION

Globalization has brought remarkable developments in the diversity and complexity of international business and multinational corporations (MNCs). Geopolitical, social, economic, and technological changes have created opportunities for managers and employees to interact with diverse populations. Concomitant with these developments has been increasing awareness that the management of a global workforce is a critical dimension of international human resource management (IHRM). Research and practice in IHRM has developed and increased in importance; as more markets internationalize, more nations become integrated with the global economy, and more businesses expand their operations across national borders, issues around the management of people become more critical to the success of MNCs (Brewster and Suutari, 2005; Schuler *et al.*, 1993).

Research in IHRM has been characterized by three broad foci (Dowling, 1999):

1. Early work in IHRM with early work emphasizing cross-cultural management issues (e.g., Laurent, 1986; Sackmann, this volume Chapter 4).
2. Developments in comparative HRM research (e.g., Hendry, 2003; Mayrhofer and Reichel, this volume Chapter 3).
3. Aspects of HRM in MNCs (Brewster *et al.*, 2005; Schuler *et al.*, 1993; Sparrow, Brewster and Ligthart, this volume Chapter 18).

It is the third area that is most widely recognized as IHRM, involving the same elements as HRM within a single country, yet with added complexities due to the diversity of national contexts and the inclusion of different national categories of workers. Early research in IHRM focused overwhelmingly on issues around the management of expatriate workforces and managing local employees in subsidiary

Handbook of International Human Resource Management.   Edited by Paul R. Sparrow
© 2009 John Wiley & Sons, Ltd

operations (Dowling and Welch, 2004). Indeed, a major focus of IHRM research has been on developing our understanding of the HR practices (Sparrow *et al.*, 1994) and individual-level variables related to the cross-national transfer of employees and management practices (Caligiuri, 2000).

Focusing on gender issues, there is some debate as to whether HRM policies and practices utilized in MNCs provide equal benefits to men and women (Harris, 2002; Ely, 1995; Woodall, 1996). For example, Hearn *et al.* (2006) argue that diversity policies implemented by Western MNCs in developing (host) countries have perpetuated and reproduced gender and social inequalities. Further, there has been substantial discussion and debate around the concept of gender and its implications for management (see also Adler, this volume Chapter 22). This chapter will not enter into this debate (for detail, see Hearn *et al.*, 2006); instead, it examines issues for women in international management. A variety of forms of participation by women in international management are identified, explanations for women's under-representation in international management are discussed, and implications for policy makers, employers, individuals, and researchers are presented.

PARTICIPATION OF WOMEN IN INTERNATIONAL MANAGEMENT

The participation of women in international management can take several forms, including but perhaps not limited to:

- board membership of multinational companies;
- experience of international (expatriate) assignments;
- experience of other forms of international work, such as frequent flyer assignments, and global project teams.

Much of the research has focused on female employees sent overseas on expatriate assignments for multinational firms. However, many other women engage in international work, such as those on what Suutari and Brewster (2000: 435) call 'self-initiated foreign experiences' (see also Suutari and Brewster, this volume Chapter 7). Women who have chosen to travel overseas to find work have received some research attention (Myers and Pringle, 2005; Napier and Taylor, 1995), although they have not been studied to the same extent as corporate expatriates. Women also participate in and are influenced by international management where they are employees in MNCs, and possibly in other employment arrangements around the world.

Women and board membership

Governance is a major strategic concern for organizations, and the composition of the board of directors is key to the quality of governance and corporate decision making. However, as Schein (2007: 7) has observed: 'Barriers to women in management exist globally and the higher the organizational level, the more glaring the gender gap.'

For at least two decades, management scholars have suggested that companies would benefit from greater diversity in board membership, as it would signal recognition of a variety of stakeholders (Westphal and Stern, 2007). This applies particularly to MNCs. Demographic diversity on boards is argued to bring improved corporate governance via broader representation of views and experience (Singh *et al.*, 2001). Focusing on the gender composition of boards of directors, numerous scholars have proposed that inclusion of women directors on boards brings benefits to companies (Burke, 1997a, 2003). Having female board members improves the reputation of a firm, improves strategic direction such as better understanding of relevant women's issues, and contributes positively to the attraction and retention of female employees (Burgess and Tharenou, 2002). The inclusion of women on a company's board sends a message to employees that advancement to senior positions is possible; further, female board members may be able to serve as role models and mentors to other women.

However, it should be noted that women may choose not to push the 'women's agenda', and men may also serve as role models and mentors to women; it could be argued that an overall change in mind-set, toward inclusivity will bring the most substantial benefits (Burke, 1995). Research has also suggested that inclusion of women on boards is positively related to firm performance (Catalyst, 2004), although the evidence supporting link is inconclusive (Bilimoria, 2006).

Despite the recognized benefits of utilizing women directors on company boards, research continues to show evidence of a relatively low proportion of female directors on boards; the studies typically include large firms that are multinational in their operations (e.g., Catalyst, 2007a; Dimovski and Brooks, 2006). Worldwide, women are disproportionately under-represented with regard to members of company boards. In the USA in 2006, around 15% of board members in Fortune 500 firms were female; women were only 1% of the Fortune 500 CEOs (Catalyst, 2007a). According to a study conducted by the European Professional Women's Network (2006), Scandinavian countries are increasing the representation of female members (executive and non-executive) on boards, due to some extent to proactive policies and quotas. Countries with relatively greater representation of women on boards include Norway (29%), Sweden (23%), Finland (20%), and Denmark (18%). However, other European countries have less representation of women on boards. According to Harris (2002: 176), 'in the UK, for instance, women comprise only 2% of executive directors and 9.6% of non-executive directors in FTSE 100 companies'. Overall, women occupy 8.5% of European corporate boardroom seats, or 385 of the 4535 positions considered in this survey. It is interesting to note that this survey found that companies are showing more change in increasing the national diversity of boards (23% of board directors were not the same nationality as their company) (European Professional Women's Network, 2006).

The representation of women on boards in other parts of the world is typically lower than in Europe or in the USA, according to available data. Adams and Flynn (2005) present collated statistics on women as a percentage of members on corporate boards around the world. These statistics vary from 13.6% in the US top 500 firms in 2003, 8.4% of top 200 firms in Australia in 2003, 4.6% of the Top 300 firms in Spain in 2002, 7.1% of all state and public owned companies in South Africa in 2004, to 3.0% of 2396 companies in Japan in 1998.

Women's employment around the world

Globalization has resulted in increased participation of women in the labor force in almost all regions of the world (ILO, 2007; Yukongdi and Benson, 2005). Concomitantly, women have increased their participation in higher education and in the labor force, there are worldwide shortages of managers and professionals, and equal opportunity legislation has been introduced in many countries. Across developed and developing economies, the increase in labor force participation includes an increase in the proportion of women with family responsibilities who are in the workforce. Women are increasingly engaged in lower-level management (Adler and Izraeli, 1994), service work, and part-time and contingent work, the higher the level of management, the fewer women to be found (Catalyst, 2007a; Linehan and Walsh, 1999). Consistent with the evidence for female membership of boards, women are disproportionately under-represented with regard to participation in senior management.

Worldwide, women represent a minority (28%) in senior official or managerial positions, although there has been noteworthy progress in recent years, as women's representation in senior official or managerial positions has increased in all regions of the world (ILO, 2007). In Africa, according to a United Nations (2000) report including 26 African countries, women's participation in management and administrative positions is 15%, on average. The most growth is evident in the South Asian region, where demand for managers has increased dramatically over the past decade (Yukongdi and Benson, 2005). However, this remains the region where women hold the lowest share of senior official or managerial positions; in some countries, such as the Republic of Korea and Sri Lanka, women hold less than 10% of senior official and managerial positions (ILO, 2007).

In China over 50% of women are in full-time employment, comprising almost 40% of the total workforce (*China Statistics Yearbook*, 2003). Women's participation in the labor force and in higher education in China is largely due to the government's social equality policy. Over the past 50 years, the Chinese government has placed the removal of gender inequality in all aspects of life as a major priority (Cooke, 2005). 'However, these achievements in gender equality in employment are mostly in quantity rather than quality, when measured against the proportion of women in management and pay equity between men and women' (Cooke, 2005: 151). While there have been several advances for women in China in pursuing managerial careers, these are inconsistent across sectors and many women continue to face the dual burdens of work and family commitments (Bowen *et al.*, 2007).

In the Middle East, as in other regions where Islam predominates, women's participation in the labor force has shown significant increases in recent years, although participation levels in general, and participation in management in particular, are low when compared to other parts of the world (Metcalfe, 2007; Sidani, 2005). An Islamic perspective of gender issues in the workplace views women and men as equal but different; equal opportunity policies are typically not included in HRM policies. Indeed, 'the lack of concern for equal opportunity organization development, limited provisions for women's professional training, combined with patriarchal and religious gender codes provide difficult terrain for both women themselves and HR strategists to navigate' (Metcalfe, 2007: 67).

Many women (and men too) experience work–life conflict, or difficulty in reconciling paid work with parenthood and other non-work responsibilities. As noted by the ILO (2007: 73):

> As women still shoulder the bulk of family responsibilities in most societies, these responsibilities are a source of gender inequality. Work–family tensions reduce women's options as to whether to work, where and in what types of jobs. This, in turn, affects their seniority and work experience, as well as their training and career prospects, thus contributing to keeping their earnings down.

Numerous scholars have argued that globalization is empowering for some, yet disempowering and impoverishing for others, particularly unskilled employees in developing countries. This applies particularly to women (Guillén, 2001; ILO, 2007).

Women as expatriates in multinational corporations

Evidence of under-representation of women as international assignees has been suggested by a comparison of the numbers of female managers in general with female expatriate managers. Harris (1995) reported this comparison as: in the USA, around 40% of managers and in the UK around 27% of managers are female, compared with between 3 and 5% of expatriate managers from the US and the UK being female.

Female participation in managerial and professional roles has increased over the past decade, with several studies reporting that female managerial expatriates are around 12 to 15% of all expatriates managers (Caligiuri *et al.*, 1999). According to a report by GMAC Global Relocations Services (2008), women represent 19% of the international assignee community (which may include non-managerial positions). The peak figure was 23% in 2005. However, it remains the consensus that women are disproportionately under-represented in international assignments, with numerous studies of expatriation reporting low proportions of women with access to international experience (Adler, 2002).

Early research on HRM in MNCs was principally concerned with expatriate selection and training, usually for expatriate management assignments (Dowling and Welch, 2004). Expatriates on long-term assignments remain an important aspect of MNC staffing strategies. However, recently the focus of research has broadened to recognize the increasing diversity of international work assignments. Organizations may utilize extended international assignments (up to one year), or short-term (up to three months and usually for project supervision or as a fill-in while awaiting a more permanent arrangement), or some combination of these. Indeed, many MNCs are moving away from long-term expatriation toward more flexible forms of international work, such as transnational project teams, short-term assignments, and virtual assignments. International assignments, particularly the more flexible (and usually less expensive) types, are also increasingly being undertaken by employees outside the senior levels of management (Welch *et al.*, 2007). Yet, many MNCs still choose to use expatriates to varying degrees and most organizations utilize a mix of employees and managers from differing cultural backgrounds.

While research has begun to examine the flexible forms of international assignments, there has been little attention to gender issues relevant to these forms of employment. While it may be assumed that women engaged in any form of international work may encounter similar issues with regard to selection and discrimination, more research is needed to understand the gender issues here. It may be the case that more flexible forms of international work, such as short-term project work, or global teams, may address some of the gender discrimination encountered by expatriates on long-term assignments.

Women in self-initiated foreign experience

Much of the research in the field of international human resource management has focused on expatriates who are sent on international assignments as a step in their career in an MNC (De Cieri *et al.*, 2005; Suutari and Brewster, this volume Chapter 7). However, many individuals are self-initiating international careers, by moving between countries as part of their job search (Myers and Pringle, 2005). Expatriate experience is usually organization-mediated and linked to an organization-bound career, while self-initiated foreign experience is usually characterized as an 'individual odyssey', associated with a boundaryless career (Inkson *et al.* 1997: 352). Suutari and Brewster (2000) have applied the term 'self-initiated expatriates' to overseas experience that is not company initiated, and several scholars have investigated the growing number of those on self-initiated foreign experiences, or self-initiated expatriates (Inkson and Myers, 2003; Myers and Pringle, 2005; Richardson and Mallon, 2005).

Self-initiated expatriates often have existing language and cultural knowledge skills and are often recruited by MNCs in a host country. These managers and professionals are typically less costly for employers than expatriates on compensation packages. It is feasible that self-initiated expatriates form a substantial segment of the global labor market, yet there has been relatively little research about these individuals, and little is known about any potential gender issues related to their experience of international management (Myers and Pringle, 2005). Recent research suggests that women are more highly represented among self-initiated expatriates than in the corporate expatriate sector. This may be because self-initiated expatriates include professional groups not typically included in IHRM research, such as health professionals, researchers, and academics.

Theoretical Explanations for Women's Under-Representation in International Management

As discussed above, women represent half the population in most countries, the evidence supports the inclusion of women in international management, and there is recognition of the importance of international assignments and international forms of work. However, research continues to show that women remain under-represented in international management (Schein, 2007; Tung, 2004).

Despite increases in the participation of women in the labor force over the past two decades in most developed countries and in many developing economies, it remains evident that there are barriers to women's career advancement. Evidence of barriers for women's career advancement is quite consistent in research (see Schein, 2007; Sheridan, 2002; Yukongdi and Benson, 2005). Rindfleisch's (2000) study of senior women in Australia found that the majority of women believe barriers exist to women's advancement into management, although there is a lack of consensus with regard to the nature of those barriers (also see Davidson and Burke, 1994; Schein, 2007). At least some of these barriers may be forms of discrimination, whether overt and intentional or unintentional and subtle.

While several writers have sought to explain the under-representation of women on boards, there has been relatively 'little theory development in the context of women's poor representation on boards internationally' (Sheridan and Milgate, 2005: 853). By comparison, numerous scholars have offered explanations for the under-representation of women in international assignments (Harris and Brewster, 1999; Smith and Still, 1996; Paik and Vance, 2002); it is also feasible to apply these explanations to the broader issue of women's participation in international management.

Based on a review of the literature, explanations for the glass ceiling and glass border, and hence for the low participation of women in international management, are considered here in four broad categories:

* social, cultural, structural, and systematic discrimination against women, including social and economic barriers;
* biases in organizational decision making and structures, including gender stereotyping of women and of managerial roles; and
* individual or person-centered factors.

Social, cultural, and structural barriers

Social or cultural barriers for career advancement include gendered communication styles and personal (male) networks and social exclusion (Sheridan, 2002). For instance, Sheridan (2002) has suggested that under-representation may be due to women having insufficient influence and/or networks with chairmen or other existing board members. Singh and Vinnicombe (2004) apply social networks (see also Harvey and Novicevic, this volume 6; and Sparrow, Brewster, and Ligthart, this volume Chapter 18) and social cohesion theory to explain the low levels of women's membership of corporate boards. The importance of networks is recognized in many societies; in China, 'existing evidence suggests that women, more so than men, tend to enter their managerial careers by a route dependent on personal/family network, or "Guanxi" as it is called in Chinese' (Cooke, 2005: 158).

Further, it seems that industry plays an influential role in career advancement for women and female board membership. Hyland and Marcellino (2002) have suggested that male-dominated industries such as construction and manufacturing are less likely to utilize women directors. In contrast, firms in industries such as retailing, banking, health, and media, with relatively higher levels of female employees, are more likely to have women on boards (Singh *et al.*, 2001).

Considering economic as well as social barriers against women's participation in international management, it is important to note that:

> [a] country's stage of economic development does not seem to play a key role in determining the percentage of women in such jobs. Many other factors, such as anti-discrimination laws and policies, national job classifications and codification systems, the share of women in non-agricultural paid work and cultural norms, help to explain variations in the female share of the [senior official or managerial positions].
>   —(ILO, 2007: 19; also see Anker, 2005, cited in ILO, 2007).

A particularly controversial topic is the impact of globalization on inequality and wage disparities across and within countries; on average, women work for lower pay than their male counterparts, even when women advance in their education and careers and occupy senior positions. This points toward the existence of discrimination in remuneration (ILO, 2007). The evidence shows gender inequalities in pay are widespread and significant. Several studies have sought to determine which proportion of gender pay inequity is due to discrimination and which part is due to objective factors, such as education, years of work experience and hours spent on paid work. As reported by the ILO (2007: 23):

> Most studies concur that discrimination, which is equated with the unexplained part of the gender pay gap, accounts for a not insignificant portion of the gender pay gap, although it varies considerably depending on the country and the methodology used.

Organizational barriers

The evidence suggests that women face barriers to their career advancement that men do not encounter. This has been described as an enduring form of the 'glass ceiling' for women (Caligiuri and Tung, 1998), or, more relevant to international management, a 'glass border' (Linehan and Walsh, 1999), which refers to stereotyped assumptions by senior management about female managers and their interest in and suitability for international work. The two phenomena are related: 'the glass ceiling in home countries is a contributory factor to the low participation rate of women in international management' (Linehan and Walsh, 1999: 271). Burke (1997b) found that a key predictor of lack of career advancement for women was lack of experience. Similarly, Daily *et al.* (2000) found that women encounter difficulties in obtaining international experience, which is increasingly viewed as a step toward senior management. With respect to international assignments, '[w]hether single or married, the situation for a female going abroad is seen to be more problematic than for a male assignee' (Harris, 1995: 28). Stereotypes of expatriates as male managers with a dependent female spouse may lead to female expatriates being viewed as 'risky' and 'atypical'. Organizational barriers include informal and hidden selection and senior promotion processes (Alimo-Metcalfe, 1995; Harris, 2002), lack of appropriate career development (Ragins *et al.*, 1998) and pay inequity for women (Oakley, 2000).

Several theories have been suggested to explain the reasons for these barriers; here, we discuss:

◆ identity theory and gender stereotyping,
◆ token theory, and
◆ selection systems.

Identity theory and social categorization.   To understand predictors of women's involvement in international management, it can be useful to draw upon identity theory, which conceptualizes the self as a social construct that is 'a collection of identities that reflects the roles that a person occupies in the social structure' (Terry *et al.*, 1999: 226). A core notion in identity theory is that, to predict behavior, we first need to recognize that the self and the social context are linked. There is a lack of consensus about the meaning and definition of identity; to some degree, identity is complex, enigmatic, and multidimensional (Albert *et al.*, 2000; Ashforth and Mael, 1989; Pratt and Foreman, 2000). Identity theory proposes that 'an individual's identities are at least partially composed of the roles he or she plays' (Pratt and Foreman, 2000: 19). A role can be defined as 'a set of expectations as to what constitutes role-appropriate behavior' (study cited in Terry *et al.*, 1999: 227). Engaging in role-appropriate behavior reinforces or validates one's role status. For women engaged in international work, we suggest that one's identity roles, in addition to gender, might include one's professional and familial roles, national identity and roles related to one's age or other demographic characteristics.

The notion of social categorization, or stereotyping, based in identity theory (Varma *et al.*, 2006), can be applied to the reported phenomenon of gender stereotyping of managerial positions. It has been argued that there is an intractable 'think manager – think male' attitude among males in management (Schein *et al.*, 1996). Schein (2007: 16) concludes that three decades of research on gender stereotyping with regard to the requisite characteristics for management positions shows that 'males continue to see women as less likely than men to possess characteristics necessary for managerial success'. Such stereotyping leads to unfounded biases against women when decisions are being made with regard to selection, promotion, and professional development opportunities.

Several researchers have investigated the importance of managerial attitudes in influencing women's participation in international assignments (e.g., Harvey and Novicevic, 2001; Paik and Vance, 2002). The attitudes of managers who make and influence selection decisions have been identified as influential in selection processes (Harris and Brewster, 1999). In Linehan's (2002) study of female assignees, women perceived that their managers may believe family commitments could negatively influence women's interest in international assignments, or that international assignments would lead to work–family conflict for women. Managers' unfounded selection biases have been found to influence expatriate selection decisions to the detriment of female candidates (Paik and Vance, 2002). Social categorizations and stereotyping may also explain negative reactions by host country nationals toward female expatriates. However, surprisingly, Varma *et al.* (2006) found that both male and female host country nationals in India preferred female expatriates to male expatriates. This finding appears to contradict the self-categorization theory, which would predict that male host country employees would favor male expatriates.

Token theory.   Another perspective that helps to provide understanding of women's low participation in international management is provided by token theory (Kanter, 1977; also see Varma *et al.*, 2006). When women are in a minority, such as in senior management in large multinational firms, these women are viewed as 'tokens', according to Kanter (1977). Token theory suggests that when representation of a minority group within a community (such as women in management) is less than 15%, those in the minority group are seen as representing their category rather than being seen as individuals. As the representation increases, for example to between 30 and 40%, although the population is seen as 'tilted', the minority group are less isolated and often provide social support for others. However, as Singh and Vinnicombe (2004: 481) explain, there is a toll on those women who are in management or senior positions: '[t]oken individuals in senior positions have to give attention and make decisions about how to behave in order to fit in the group, using energy that those in the dominant category (males) do not have to expend.'

This theory suggests that women in gender-balanced organizations will have more access to career advancement opportunities such as international assignments, than will women in male-dominated organizations and/or occupations.

Selection systems and processes.   Previous research suggests that formal and informal organizational processes, such as selection systems used for international managers, may present barriers for women (Harris, 1995; Harris and Brewster, 1999). Harris and Brewster (1999) have presented a typology of selection systems for international assignments. Their typology identifies four international assignment selection systems: open/formal, open/informal, closed/formal and closed/informal. These authors propose that the prevalence of informal selection systems, which rely on personal informal networks, at least partially explains the lower representation of women in international assignments, as women are less likely than men to have those informal networks that positively influence selection. In contrast, women are viewed as more likely to be selected for an international assignment in an open/formal system, in which selectors assess candidates against formal criteria and bias is reduced by the application of equal opportunity principles (Harris and Brewster, 1999; also see Harris, 2001).

Person-centered barriers

Numerous studies have explored individual factors that might influence selection and experience of international assignees (e.g., Caligiuri, 2000; Fischlmayr, 2002; Riusala and Suutari, 2000). It has been suggested that women's interests in and attitudes toward international assignments may influence participation rates (Lowe *et al.*, 1999; Stroh *et al.*, 2000; Tung, 1998); further, van der Velde and colleagues (2005) found that the importance a woman placed on her career explained her willingness to participate in an international assignment. However, several studies have shown that women and men are equally interested in international assignments (Stroh *et al.*, 2000).

Janssens and colleagues (2006: 146) used identity theory to explore the strategies used by successful female expatriates; they concluded that, even when women are successful as expatriates, 'their success does not necessarily alter the power relations that make it difficult for women to be international managers'.

Empirical research on women and international assignments

In applying these theories to aid our understanding of the participation of women in international management, it is helpful to consider the substantial body of research that has focused on women on international assignments. Research on women and international (expatriate) assignments can be placed in three categories (Caligiuri *et al.*, 1999).

First, a stream of research has investigated differences between men and women with respect to their attainment of global assignments. Within this category, the seminal work by Adler (1984) identified and questioned three myths:

1. women do not want expatriate assignments;
2. companies do not want to send women overseas; and
3. prejudice against women makes them ineffective expatriates in some host countries.

Subsequent research has been inconclusive with respect to these three myths. With regard to the first myth, there is now a substantial body of research showing that women do want international assignments, although there are complex dynamics underlying decisions to expatriate (see Mathur-Helm, 2002). For example, Myers and Pringle (2005) found women to have a propensity to seek out less risky locations in their pursuit of career development.

With regard to the second myth, that companies do not want to send women overseas, the espoused views of managers are that they do not discriminate against women. While there is overwhelming evidence that men are more likely than women to be sent by multinational corporations on international assignments, women are increasingly engaging in international work (Adler, this volume Chapter 22; Harris, 2002; Janssens *et al.*, 2006).

With regard to the third myth, while Adler (1987) found that female expatriates did not experience prejudice when assigned to several Asian countries, other researchers found that female expatriates were more likely than their male counterparts to encounter negative attitudes from host country nationals (e.g., Caligiuri and Cascio, 1998). There is an enduring assumption that Western women will not be accepted as managers in host locations such as some Asian countries, because of the exclusion of women at managerial levels in those countries (van der Boon, 2003). Despite such assumptions, the overwhelming evidence to date shows that women can be successful as expatriates, even in host countries that might be perceived as unwelcoming (Napier and Taylor, 2002; Selmer and Leung, 2003; Taylor *et al.*, 2002; van der Boon, 2003).

Overall, it seems likely that levels and expressions of prejudice vary between societies. Further, it seems likely that factors other than host country attitudes will influence whether women are effective expatriates. Company and managerial support, and the personal competencies of the female assignee, are likely to play important roles in expatriate success.

A second research stream has explored whether there are different outcomes for men and women from expatriation assignments. Caligiuri and Tung (1998) found that female expatriates in host country locations with low female workforce participation and a lower percentage of female managers were less cross-culturally adjusted than were male expatriates in these locations. However, they found no gender differences in either desire to terminate an assignment or supervisor-rated performance.

It is interesting to note that several studies have identified counter–intuitive findings that suggest that further investigation is required. For instance, while much of the research has assumed that cultural distance between home and host countries exacerbates the likelihood for perceived and experienced prejudice, Tung (2004) reported that women from the UK faced gender-based discrimination while on expatriate assignment in the US, and American women faced similar discrimination while on assignment in the UK. Considering the many similarities between the UK and the US, not least of which is language, this finding is intriguing.

The third research stream has focused on differences between men and women with respect to the antecedents, or predictors, of their international assignments (Caligiuri, 2000; Caligiuri *et al.*, 1999). Caligiuri and Cascio (1998) proposed a model of antecedents for the success of female expatriates, identifying the following four predictors: personality traits; organizational support; family support; and host nationals' attitudes toward women expatriates. Numerous studies have explored personality factors; for example, Guthrie *et al.* (2003) found that gender-based dispositional differences may actually place women at an advantage with regard to international assignments. Other researchers have tested multiple influences on expatriate experience. For example, Culpan and Wright (2002) showed the importance of organizational, individual, and cultural characteristics as antecedents of job satisfaction of expatriate women managers.

It has also been suggested that dual-career issues are relevant to an individual's access to and experience of international management. Konopaske and colleagues (2005) applied family systems theory and literature on dual-career/dual-income couples to explore familial antecedents by investigating the influence of spouse willingness to relocate internationally on the manager's willingness to undertake a global assignment. Valcour and Tolbert (2003) investigated both antecedents and outcomes of intra-organizational and inter-organizational mobility for dual-earner couples. They found significant gender differences: women experience more inter-organizational mobility, while men experience more intra-organizational mobility. They also found that marital instability increased intra-organizational mobility among women, but had no effect for men. Indeed, several studies have suggested that 'gender boundaries in the family are most challenged when the female partner is more successful in career terms, or earns more than her partner' (e.g., Linehan and Walsh, 1999: 268). Moore (2002) reports on a survey conducted by Catalyst, which found that female expatriates are much more likely to have a spouse who is working full or part time (91%) than are male expatriates (50%). Overall, while having dual careers does present challenges, the evidence shows that dual-career couples can and do relocate.

Overall, growing awareness of the problems associated with underutilization of the human capital pool available for international management, combined with community and legislative pressure for equal opportunity in the workplace, have led to recognition of the need for theoretical analysis and empirical research, to identify barriers and to provide guidance for practical improvements to be implemented. The conceptual and empirical research in this area to date suggests that a multitheoretical and multilevel approach is necessary to understand the factors that influence women's participation in international management.

ENHANCING THE PARTICIPATION OF WOMEN IN INTERNATIONAL MANAGEMENT

In theoretical and practical terms, and in business and ethical cases, it makes sense for all qualified employees have equal opportunity to engage in the various forms of international work that may be available; discrimination against any segment of the human resource pool is in neither the individual's nor the organization's interests. As noted by the ILO (2007), discrimination is both wrong and inefficient.

The economic, or business, case for greater inclusion of women in management argues for equal opportunity in representation by proposing 'that discrimination is sub-optimal for the firms in question, rather than immoral' (Brammer *et al.*, 2007: 395). In contrast, although not in contradiction, an ethical, or social, case for equality of opportunity argues that 'it is wrong for individuals to be excluded from the highest echelons of the business world purely on the grounds of gender or race and regardless of ability' (Brammer *et al.*, 2007: 394). Clearly, these cases can be equally applied to women in *international* management. There are potential social benefits for candidates, organizations, and society at large in increasing the participation of women in international management. For instance, international assignments provide opportunity for personal and professional development of the individual employee, as well as leading to organizational outcomes such as organizational development and knowledge transfer. International assignments can serve an important function in career development for employees in MNCs, as these assignments can be important steps toward promotion and career advancement into global leadership positions (Black *et al.*, 1999; Harris, 2002). International experience has been associated with the development of international management knowledge, skills and careers (Dickmann and Harris, 2005; Vance, 2005).

Implications for policy-makers

In order to develop a full understanding of the participation of women in international management, there is a need for better, more reliable, valid and comprehensive data. According to a report by the United Nations (2006, cited in ILO, 2007: 13) on the world's women, 'the limited availability of data on gender equality indicators is a reflection of poor national statistical capacity, lack of gender mainstreaming in public policies and inadequate concepts and methods'.

Some progress has been made in policy development and legislative reform to encourage women's career advancement. Several governments around the world have initiated policies to improve the presence of women on company boards. For example, in 1993 Israel introduced affirmative action legislation for government-supported firms (Izraeli, 2000). In Norway, a quota system has been imposed on female board representation (study cited in Adams and Flynn, 2005).

To achieve improvements in women's workforce and managerial participation, legislative reform is necessary in many countries. However, this is not sufficient; also required are improvements in women's education levels, economic and industrial reforms, and recognition of the inefficiencies created by discrimination against women. As Benson and Yukongdi (2005: 291) argue, until

> ... there are major shifts in the role perceptions of women by individuals, organizations and society it is likely that change will occur only gradually and women will remain disadvantaged and underrepresented in management.

Even where progress is evident, as in China, there remains much need for further developments as Cooke (2005: 149) has said,

> ... although a series of equal opportunity legislation has been introduced by the state, the fairness of these regulations and the effectiveness of their implementation are highly debatable. This is worsened by the absence of equal opportunity initiatives at the organizational level aimed to improve women's career prospects.

In countries such as China and India, where the 'liberalization of the economy, and the extra competition from overseas firms, has put a lot of pressure on the personnel function of ... domestic companies to prepare and develop their human resources' (Budhwar and Baruch, 2003: 701), the impact of foreign direct investment has been the subject of considerable debate. For HRM professionals in MNCs, there are opportunities to contribute to professional development and career opportunities for women in developing countries via initiatives such as the introduction of vocational training programs and career planning and management, the facilitation of cross-national technology and knowledge transfers, and the provision of advice to governments, trade unions, consumers and communities, as well as employers in developing countries. It must be noted, however, that such initiatives have been criticized for assuming the appropriateness of universal application of Western approaches to HR development.

Implications for employers

There are numerous implications for employers to enhance the participation of women at board level, in management, and to enhance the overall experience of work in a global context.

Representation of women on boards. Adams and Flynn (2005) advocate more open and public nomination and selection processes as a means to increase the presence of women in the boardroom. Taking the point further, Rindfleish (2000) has suggested that comprehensive, substantive policies at organizational and governmental level are necessary to increase female membership of boards. For instance, Goldman Sachs designed a Senior Women's Initiative to increase the number of women business leaders globally. Strategies for recruitment, engagement, advancement, and retention were designed to support women in their career growth. The initiative is aimed to eliminate potential barriers to advancement and to enhance networking opportunities for senior women. Globally, the number of female partners at Goldman Sachs has doubled from 2001 to 2006 (Catalyst, 2007b).

Factors that might encourage or facilitate female representation on boards include scrutiny by the general public, media, and investors; this may help to explain why larger firms and firms with higher public profiles (e.g., Fortune 500 firms are more likely to have women on boards – Dimovski and Brooks, 2006).

Women and international assignments. Three decades of literature has highlighted the vital importance of MNCs providing comprehensive expatriate management strategies and practices (Dowling and Welch, 2004). While IHRM has in many ways transformed from a focus on the specifics of expatriation, nonetheless it remains important to understand the core IHRM practices relevant to managing international assignments and a global workforce.

Experience in international management is widely and increasingly recognized as important for managerial career advancement in global firms (Tung, 2004; Varma *et al.*, 2006). Organizational strategies and HR strategies to enhance female participation include the use of formal/open systems for selection of international assignees (Harris and Brewster, 1999). International HR policies should encourage the selection and support of women (Culpan and Wright, 2002). The design and application of comprehensive HR systems that include performance management that informs and encourages individuals to indicate interest in international assignments, is a potential factor in enhancing women's participation in international work (Culpan and Wright, 2002). During an international assignment, managers should be supported in maintaining regular contact with the home location (Linehan and Walsh, 1999). Linehan and Scullion found that the repatriation may be even more stressful than expatriation, as 'female international managers experience more difficulties than their male counterparts because of their pioneering roles' (Linehan and Scullion, 2002: 254). These authors suggest that more attention should be directed toward identifying and implementing strategies to enhance the social and organizational readjustment of repatriated women and their spouses/families. It is also suggested that female executive repatriates can act as role models and mentors to other women who wish to undertake international assignments (Linehan and Scullion, 2002). Overall, employers need to understand that their workforce will have a diverse range of needs, and the employer should provide a supportive infrastructure to address the needs of those they seek to engage in international work (Moore, 2002).

HRM strategies and practices. Several researchers (Culpan and Wright, 2002; Linehan, 2002) have noted that organizations may need to tailor HR support to take into account the needs of single women, women in dual-career couples, and women with families. For example, Adler (2002) has suggested that organizations should offer encouraging and supportive compensation and benefits packages to meet the needs of single females, dual-career females, and females with families. As noted earlier, ongoing pay inequity suggests 'the need for continued efforts aimed at promoting equal opportunities for women in employment, tackling direct and indirect sex discrimination in remuneration and enabling them to juggle paid work and family responsibilities' (ILO, 2007: 23).

Diversity management. Diversity management initiatives may be an important part of IHRM practices to encourage women's participation in international management, as such initiatives enhance appreciation of sociopolitical and cultural differences and similarities. Diversity management initiatives are specific activities, programs, policies, and any other formal processes designed to improve management of diversity via communication, education and training, employee involvement, career management, accountability, and cultural change. For example, diversity initiatives may include practices such as training programs to reduce stereotyping and to improve cross-cultural sensitivity and skills (Wentling, 2000). Some transnational firms have developed global approaches to diversity initiatives. For example, Thomas (2004) reported that IBM developed a global strategy to better address diversity issues facing the company around the world. However, researchers have suggested that diversity management initiatives typically require a decentralized approach (Egan and Bendick, 2003), because diversity initiatives are required to be responsive to local cultural and institutional factors, such as equal employment opportunity laws. Further, Egan and Bendick's (2003) research shows that differing attitudes to diversity management across national contexts have led some MNCs to emphasize local responsiveness for diversity management initiatives.

Organizational and managerial support. Research has indicated that a positive organizational context, with managerial and organizational support, will be important organizational elements to enhance perceptions of women's opportunities, HR strategies to encourage gender balance in organizations, and to provide opportunities for women to develop networks with senior managers who are likely to offer support. Strategies such as the provision of networking, mentoring, and coaching programs for international work could be helpful. HRM policy development at the organization level should specifically address the issue of women's management training, and gender issues should be incorporated in policy planning and development in MNCs (Metcalfe, 2007; van der Boon, 2003). There have been high profile cases of gender discrimination; awareness of these should be part of education for management (Schein, 2007). 'It is imperative that legal pressures are maintained and serious attention given to restructuring managerial work' (Schein, 2007: 16). Achieving and maintaining equality of opportunity for women in management requires an ongoing and comprehensive process.

Implications for individuals

While recognizing that many women face structural and relational constraints that limit their choices with regard to employment and career advancement (e.g., Hearn *et al.*, 2006; Lewis *et al.*, 2007), there may be some suggestions to be made at an individual level. For example, individuals may seek to develop strategies to build networks to generate contacts that will lead to international work (Harris, 2005; Harris and Brewster, 1999). The European Professional Women's Network (www.europeanpwn.net) and the Women's Foundation in Hong Kong (www.thewomensfoundation.org) are examples of useful resources and supports for women.

Further, as suggested earlier in this chapter, it is feasible that self-initiated foreign experience provides an alternative entry point to international management that is more accessible than via the corporate experience. Myers and Pringle (2005: 430) conclude that self-initiated foreign experience may:

> provide an opportunity for accelerated development and a way of enhancing individual career capital in a global environment for men and women ... Thus, [self-initiated foreign experience] provides women with a de facto expatriate career experience and a gateway into global careers.

Implications for future research

There have been noteworthy developments in the recognition of gender issues in IHRM, in both theoretical and empirical terms (e.g., see Hearn *et al.*, 2006). Despite such progress, much remains to be explored. IHRM scholars and practitioners should seek to understand and appreciate diverse perspectives, for example by including non-Western theory, research, and practice in the development of our work.

Numerous studies have focused on women from developed countries, particularly the US, on international assignment (e.g., Adler, 1987). By comparison, there has been little research on European women as expatriates, or Asian women, or women from less-developed countries (see Varma *et al.*, 2006 for an interesting exception).

Much of the research exploring international HRM issues has focused on large Western profit-based companies, particularly those headquartered in the US or Europe. However, there is a growing literature examining organizations operating in non-Western regions, and in emerging and transition economies (Ramamurti, 2004). Also, there is emerging research into organizational forms, such as small multinational enterprises (Sparrow and Brewster, 2006), inter-organizational networks (Fenwick and De Cieri, 2005), cross-border alliances (Schuler and Tarique, 2005), and international non-profit organizations, including relief and development organizations (Fenwick and McLean, this volume Chapter 19). Recent research also explores issues such as HRM initiatives for host country nationals (Bartlett *et al.*, 2002) and the extent to which transnational firms may seek to localize their HRM practices (Aycan, 2005). Our conceptualizations of phenomena related to international management are still developing. For example, Hartl (2004) presents a framework of expatriate experiences as career transitions. This is particularly useful, as it helps to move the focus of research and practice away from the expatriate assignment in isolation, in an endeavor to understand it in the context of the career dynamics. While this research to date has raised awareness of the complexities and challenges of IHRM, more could be done to examine the experiences of women and implications for their participation in international management.

CONCLUSION

Scholars and practitioners of IHRM have paid increasing attention to gender issues. Women may participate in international management in a variety of ways, yet they continue to be under-represented. It is evident that multiple theoretical perspectives can be applied to build understanding of the factors that influence women's participation in international management. It is in the best interests of scholars, managers, employees, and communities to make sense of, and address, the phenomena related to the participation of women in international management.

REFERENCES

Adams, S.M., and Flynn, P.M. (2005). Local knowledge advances women's access to corporate boards. *Corporate Governance: An International Review*, 13 (6), 836–846.

Adler, N.J. (1984). Women do not want international careers: And other myths about international management. *Organizational Dynamics*, 13 (2), 66–79.

Adler, N.J. (1987). Pacific basin managers: A *gaijin*, not a woman. *Human Resource Management*, 26 (2), 169–191.

Adler, N.J. (2002). Global managers: No longer men alone. *International Journal of Human Resource Management*, 13, 743–760.

Adler, N.J., and Izraeli, D.N. (eds) (1994). *Competitive Frontiers: Women Managers in a Global Economy*. Oxford: Basil Blackwell.

Albert, S., Ashforth, B.E., and Dutton, J.E. (2000). Organizational identity and identification: Charting new waters and building new bridges. *Academy of Management Review*, 25, 13–17.

Alimo-Metcalfe, B. (1995). Leadership and assessment. In S.M. Vinnicombe and N.L. Colwill (eds), *The Essence of Women in Management*. Hemel Hempstead: Prentice Hall.

Ashforth, B.E., and Mael, F. (1989). Social identity in the organization. *Academy of Management Review*, 14 (1), 20–39.

Aycan, Z. (2005). The interplay between cultural and institutional/structural contingencies in human resource practices. *International Journal of Human Resource Management*, 16 (7), 1038–1119.

Bartlett, K.R., Lawler, J.J., Bae, J., Chen, S.-J., and Wan, D. (2002). Differences in international human resource development among indigenous firms and multinational affiliates in East and South East Asia. *Human Resource Development Quarterly*, 13, 383–405.

Benson, J., and Yukongdi, V. (2005). Asian women managers: Participation, barriers and future prospects. *Asia Pacific Business Review*, 11 (2), 283–291.

Bilimoria, D. (2006). The relationship between women corporate directors and women corporate officers. *Journal of Management Issues*, 18 (1), 47–61.

Black, J.S., Gregersen, H.B., Mendenhall, M., and Stroh, L.K. (1999). *Globalizing People through International Assignments*. Boston MA: Addison-Wesley.

Bowen, C.C., Wu, Y., Hwang, C., and Scherer, R.F. (2007). Holding up half of the sky? Attitudes toward women as managers in the People's Republic of China. *International Journal of Human Resource Management*, 18 (2), 268–283.

Brammer, S., Millington, A., and Pavelin, S. (2007). Gender and ethnic diversity among UK corporate boards. *Corporate Governance: An International Review*, 15 (2), 393–403.

Brewster, C., and Suutari, V. (2005). Global HRM: Aspects of a research agenda. *Personnel Review*, 34 (1), 5–21.

Brewster, C., Sparrow, P.R., and Harris, H. (2005). Towards a new model of globalising HRM. *International Journal of Human Resource Management*, 16 (6), 949–970.

Budhwar, P., and Baruch, Y. (2003). Career management practices in India: An empirical study. *International Journal of Manpower*, 24 (6), 699–721.

Burgess, Z., and Tharenou, P. (2002). Women board directors: Characteristics of the few. *Journal of Business Ethics*, 37, 39–49.

Burke, R.J. (1995). Do women on corporate boards make a difference? Views of women directors. *Corporate Governance: An International Review*, 3 (3), 138–143.

Burke, R.J. (1997a). Women directors: Selection, acceptance and benefits of board membership. *Corporate Governance: An International Review*, 5 (3), 118–125.

Burke, R.J. (1997b). Women on corporate boards of directors: A much-needed resource. *Journal of Business Ethics*, 16 (9), 909–915.

Burke, R.J. (2003). Women on Corporate Boards of Directors: the Timing is right. *Women in Management Review*, 18, 346–348.

Caligiuri, P.M. (2000). Selecting expatriates for personality characteristics: A moderating effect of personality on the relationship between host national contact and cross-cultural adjustment. *Management International Review*, 40 (1), 61–80.

Caligiuri, P.M., and Cascio, W.F. (1998). Can we send her there? Maximizing the success of western women on global assignments. *Journal of World Business*, 33 (4), 394–416.

Caligiuri, P.M., and Tung, R.L. (1998). Comparing the success of male and female expatriates from a US-based multinational company. *International Journal of Human Resource Management*, 10, 763–782.

Caligiuri, P.M., Joshi, A., and Lazarova, M. (1999). Factors influencing the adjustment of women on global assignments. *International Journal of Human Resource Management*, 10 (2), 163–179.

Catalyst (2004). *Study of 353 Fortune 500 companies connects corporate performance and gender diversity*. News release, January 26, 2004, New York, NY: Catalyst, (http://www.catalystwomen.org/).

Catalyst (2007a). *2006 census of women corporate officers, top earners, and directors of the Fortune 500*. Press release, February 21, 2007, New York, NY: Catalyst, (http://www.catalyst.org).

Catalyst (2007b). *Catalyst honors initiatives at Goldman Sachs, PepsiCo, PricewaterhouseCoopers, and Scotiabank*. Press release, January 24, 2007, New York, NY: Catalyst, (http://www.catalyst.org).

China Statistics Yearbook (2003). Beijing: Ministry of Statistics of China.

Cooke, F.L. (2005). *HRM, Work and Employment in China*. London: Routledge.

Culpan, O., and Wright, G. (2002). Women abroad: Getting the best results from women managers. *International Journal of Human Resource Management*, 13 (5), 784–801.

Daily, C.M. Trevis-Certo, S., and Dalton, D. (2000). International experience in the executive suite: The path to prosperity? *Strategic Management Journal*, 20, 515–523.

Davidson, M., and Burke, R. (1994). *Women in Management: Current Research Issues*. London: Paul Chapman.

De Cieri, H., Fenwick, M., and Hutchings, K. (2005). The challenge of international human resource management: Balancing the duality of strategy and practice. *International Journal of HRM*, 16 (4), 584–598.

Dickmann, M., and Harris, H. (2005). Developing career capital for global careers: The role of international assignments. *Journal of World Business*, 40 (4), 399–408.

Dimovski and Brooks, R. (2006). The gender composition of boards after an IPO. *Corporate Governance*, 6 (1), 11–17.

Dowling, P.J. (1999). Completing the puzzle: Issues in the development of the field of international human resource management. *Management International Review*, 39 (4), 27–43.

Dowling, P.J., and Welch, D.E. (2004). *International Human Resource Management: Managing People in a Multinational Context* (4th edn), London: Thomson Learning.

Egan, M.L., and Bendick, M. Jr (2003). Workforce diversity initiatives of U.S. multinational corporations in Europe. *Thunderbird International Business Review*, 45, 701–727.

Ely, R.J. (1995). The power in demography: Women's social construction of gender identity at work. *Academy of Management Journal*, 38 (3), 589–634.

European Professional Women's Network (2006). *EuropeanPWN BoardWomen Monitor 2006*, http://www.europeanpwn.net/files/boardwomen_present_large120606.pdf.

Fischlmayr, I.C. (2002). Female self-perception as a barrier to international careers? *International Journal of Human Resource Management*, 13 (5), 773–783.

GMAC Global Relocation Services. (2008). *Global Relocation Trends 2008 Survey Report*. New York: GMAC Global Relocation Services.

Guillén, M. (2001). Is globalisation civilising, destructive or feeble? A critique of five key debates in the social sciences literature. *Annual Review of Sociology*, 27, 235–260.

Guthrie, J.P., Ash, R.A., and Stevens, C.D. (2003). Are women 'better' than men? Personality differences and expatriate selection. *Journal of Managerial Psychology*, 18 (3), 229–243.

Harris, H. (1995). Women's role in (international) management. In A.W. Harzing and J. Van Ruysseveldt (eds), *International Human Resource Management*. London: Sage, pp. 229–251.

Harris, H. (2001). Researching discrimination in selection for international management assignments: The role of repertory grid technique. *Women in Management Review*, 16 (3), 118–125.

Harris, H. (2002). Think international manager, think male: Why are women not selected for international management assignments? *Thunderbird International Business Review*, 44 (2), 175–203.

Harris, H. (2005). Global careers: Work–life issues and the adjustment of women international managers. *Journal of Management Development*, 23 (4), 818–832.

Harris, H., and Brewster, C. (1999). The coffee-machine system: How international selection really works. *International Journal of Human Resource Management*, 10 (3), 488–500.

Hartl, K. (2004). The expatriate career transition and women managers' experiences. *Women in Management Review*, 19 (1), 40–51.

Harvey, M., and Novicevic, M.M. (2001). Selecting expatriates for increasingly complex global assignments. *Career Development International*, 6 (2), 69–86.

Hearn, J., Metcalfe, B., and Piekkari, R. (2006). Gender and international human resource management. In I. Björkman and G. Stahl (eds), *Handbook of International Human Resource Management*, London: Edward Elgar, pp. 502–522.

Hendry, C. (2003). Applying employment systems theory to the analysis of national models of HRM. *International Journal of Human Resource Management*, 14, 1430–1437.

Hyland, M.M., and Marcellino, P.A. (2002). Examining gender on corporate boards: A regional study. *Corporate Governance*, 2 (4), 24–31.

Inkson, K., and Myers, B. (2003). 'The big OE': International travel and career development. *Career Development International*, 8 (4), 170–181.

Inkson, K., Arthur, M.B., Pringle, J., and Barry, S. (1997). Expatriate assignment versus overseas experience: Contrasting models of international human resource development. *Journal of World Business*, 32 (4), 351–368.

International Labour Office (ILO) (2007). Equality at Work, Tackling the Challenges. Global Report under the follow-up to the ILO Declaration on Fundamental Principles and Rights at Work. *International Labour Conference, 96th Session, Report I (B). Geneva: International Labour Office*.

Izraeli, D. (2000). The paradox of affirmative action for women directors in Israel. In R.J. Burke and M.C. Mattis (eds), *Women on Corporate Boards of Directors: International Challenges and Opportunities*. Boston: Kluwer Academic, pp. 75–96.

Janssens, M., Cappellen, T., and Zanoni, P. (2006). Successful female expatriates as agents: Positioning oneself through gender, hierarchy, and culture. *Journal of World Business*, 41, 133–148.

Kanter, R.M. (1977). *Men and Women of the Corporation*. New York: Basic Books Inc.

Konopaske, R., Robie, C., and Ivancevich, J.M. (2005). A preliminary model of spouse influence on managerial global assignment willingness. *International Journal of Human Resource Management*, 16 (3), 405–426.

Laurent, A. (1986). The cross-cultural puzzle of international human resource management. *Human Resource Management*, 25 (1), 91–102.

Lewis, S., Gambles, R., and Rapoport, R. (2007). The constraints of a 'work-life balance' approach: An international perspective. *International Journal of Human Resource Management*, 18 (3), 360–373.

Linehan, M. (2002). Senior female international managers: Empirical evidence from Western Europe. *International Journal of Human Resource Management*, 13 (5), 802–814.

Linehan, M., and Scullion, H. (2002). Repatriation of European female corporate executives: An empirical study. *International Journal of Human Resource Management*, 13 (2), 254–267.

Linehan, M., and Walsh, J.S. (1999). Senior female international managers: Breaking the glass border. *Women in Management Review*, 14 (7), 264–272.

Lowe, K.B., Downes, M., and Kroeck, K.G. (1999). The impact of gender and location on the willingness to accept overseas assignments. *International Journal of Human Resource Management*, 10 (2), 223–234.

Mathur-Helm, B. (2002). Expatriate women managers: At the crossroads of success, challenges and career goals. *Women in Management Review*, 17 (1), 18–28.

Metcalfe, B.D. (2007). Gender and human resource management in the Middle East. *International Journal of Human Resource Management*, 18 (1), 54–74.

Moore, M. (2002). Same ticket, different trip: Supporting dual career couples on global assignments. *Women in Management Review*, 17 (2), 61–67.

Myers, B., and Pringle, J.K. (2005). Self-initiated foreign experience as accelerated development: Influences of gender. *Journal of World Business*, 40, 421–431.

Napier, N.K., and Taylor, S. (1995). *Western Women Working in Japan: Breaking Corporate Barriers*. Greenwich, CT: Quorum.

Napier, N.K., and Taylor, S. (2002). Experiences of women professionals abroad: Comparisons across Japan, China and Turkey. *International Journal of Human Resource Management*, 13 (5), 837–851.

Oakley, J.G. (2000). Gender-based barriers to senior management positions: Understanding the scarcity of female CEOs. *Journal of Business Ethics*, 27, 321–334.

Paik, Y., and Vance, C.M. (2002). Evidence of back-home selection bias against US female expatriates. *Women in Management Review*, 17 (2), 68–79.

Pratt, M.G., and Foreman, P.O. (2000). Classifying managerial responses to multiple organizational identities. *Academy of Management Review*, 25, 18–42.

Ragins, B.R., Townsend, B., and Mattis, M. (1998). Gender gap in the executive suite: CEOs and female executives report on breaking the glass ceiling. *Academy of Management Executive*, 12, 28–42.

Ramamurti, R. (2004). Developing countries and MNEs: Extending and enriching the research agenda. *Journal of International Business Studies*, 35, 277–283.

Richardson, J., and Mallon, M. (2005). Career interrupted? The case of the self-directed expatriate. *Journal of World Business*, 40, 409–420.

Rindfleish, J. (2000). Senior management women in Australia: Diverse perspectives. *Women in Management Review*, 15 (4), 172–183.

Riusala, K., and Suutari, V. (2000). Expatriation and careers: Perspectives of expatriates and spouses. *Career Development International*, 5 (2), 81–90.

Schein, V.E. (2007). Women in management: Reflections and projections. *Women in Management Review*, 22 (1), 6–18.

Schein, V.E., Mueller, R., Lituchy, T., and Liu, J. (1996). Think manager – think male: A global phenomenon? *Journal of Organizational Behavior*, 17, 33–41.

Schuler, R.S., and Tarique, I. (2005). Alliance forms and HR issues, implications and significance. In O. Shenkar and J. Reuer (eds), *Handbook of Strategic Alliances*. Thousand Oaks, CA: Sage, pp. 219–240.

Schuler, R.S., Dowling, P.J., and De Cieri, H. (1993). An integrative framework of strategic international human resource management. *Journal of Management*, 19 (2), 419–459.

Selmer, J., and Leung, A. (2003). Expatriate career intentions of women on foreign assignments and their adjustment. *Journal of Managerial Psychology*, 18 (3), 244–258.

Sheridan, A. (2002). What you know and who you know: 'Successful' women's experiences of accessing board positions. *Career Development International*, 7 (4), 203–10.

Sheridan, A., and Milgate, G. (2005). Accessing board positions: A comparison of female and male board members' views. *Corporate Governance: An International Review*, 13 (6), 847–855.

Sidani, Y. (2005). Women, work, and Islam in Arab societies. *Women in Management Review*, 20 (7), 498–512.

Singh, V., and Vinnicombe, S. (2004). Why so few women directors in top UK boardrooms? Evidence and theoretical explanations. *Corporate Governance: An International Review*, 12 (4), 479–488.

Singh, V., Vinnicombe, S., and Johnson, P. (2001). Women directors on top UK boards. *Corporate Governance: An International Review*, 9 (3), 206–16.

Smith, C.R., and Still, L.V. (1996). Breaking the glass border: Barriers to global careers for women in Australia. *International Review of Women and Leadership*, 2 (2), 60–72.

Sparrow, P.R., and Brewster, C. (2006). Globalizing HRM: The growing revolution in managing employees internationally. In C. Cooper and R. Burke (eds), *The Human Resources Revolution: Why Putting People First Matters*. London: Elsevier.

Sparrow, P.R., Schuler R.S., and Jackson, S.E. (1994). Convergence or divergence: Human resource practices and policies for competitive advantage worldwide. *International Journal of Human Resource Management*, 5, 267–299.

Stroh, L.K., Varma, A., and Valy-Durbin, S.J. (2000). Why are women left at home: Are they unwilling to go on international assignments? *Journal of World Business*, 35 (3), 241–255.

Suutari, V., and Brewster, C. (2000). Making their own way: International experience through self-initiated foreign assignments. *Journal of World Business*, 35 (4), 417–432.

Taylor, S., Napier, N.K., and Mayrhofer, W. (2002). Women in global business: Introduction. *International Journal of Human Resource Management*, 13 (5), 739–742.

Terry, D.J., Hogg, M.A., and White, K.M. (1999). The theory of planned behaviour: Self-identity, social identity and group norms. *British Journal of Social Psychology*, 38, 225–244.

Thomas, D.A. (2004). Diversity as strategy. *Harvard Business Review*, September, 98–108.

Tung, R.L. (1998). American expatriates abroad: From neophytes to cosmopolitans. *Journal of World Business*, 33 (2), 125–144.

Tung, R.L. (2004). Female expatriates: The model global manager? *Organizational Dynamics*, 33 (3), 243–253.

United Nations (2000). *The World's Women 2000: Trends and Statistics*. New York, NY: United Nations.

Valcour, P.M., and Tolbert, P.S. (2003). Gender, family and career in the era of boundarylessness: Determinants and effects of intra- and inter-organizational mobility. *International Journal of Human Resource Management*, 14 (5), 768–787.

Van Der Boon, M. (2003). Women in international management: An international perspective on women's ways of leadership. *Women in Management Review*, 18 (3), 132–146.

Van Der Velde, E.G., Bossink, C.J.H., and Jansen, P.G.W. (2005). Gender differences in the determinants of the willingness to accept an international assignment. *Journal of Vocational Behaviour*, 66, 81–103.

Vance, C.M. (2005). The personal quest for building global competence: A taxonomy of self-initiating career path strategies for gaining business experience abroad. *Journal of World Business*, 40 (4), 374–385.

Varma, A., Toh, S.M., and Budhwar, P. (2006). A new perspective on the female expatriate experience: The role of host country national categorization. *Journal of World Business*, 41, 112–120.

Welch, D.E., Welch, L.S., and Worm, V. (2007). The international business traveller: A neglected but strategic resource. *International Journal of Human Resource Management*, 18 (2), 173–183.

Wentling, R.M. (2000). Evaluation of diversity initiatives in multinational corporations. *Human Resource Development International*, 3, 435–450.

Westphal, J.D., and Stern, I. (2007). Flattery will get you everywhere (especially if you are a male Caucasian): How ingratiation, boardroom behaviour, and demographic minority status affect additional board appointments at U.S. companies. *Academy of Management Journal*, 50 (2), 267–288.

Woodall, J. (1996). Human resource management and women: The vision of the gender blind. In B. Towers (ed.), *Handbook of Human Resource Management*. Oxford: Blackwell.

Yukongdi, V., and Benson, J. (2005). Women in Asian management: Cracking the glass ceiling? *Asia Pacific Business Review*, 11, (2), 139–148.

Part III

MANAGING GLOBALIZATION PROCESSES AT THE LEVEL OF THE FIRM

11

Multinational Companies, National Business Systems, and Reverse Diffusion

INTRODUCTION

The last quarter of a century has witnessed a marked strengthening of the linkages between national economies. Levels of foreign direct investment and trade have risen sharply; technological change and the removal of restrictions on capital mobility have facilitated vast increases in international financial flows; and the reach and influence of international institutions has grown. For some observers, this process of globalization has led to a convergence across countries in the way that organizations operate as firms make attempts to emulate the practices that they perceive to be at the root of the success of strongly performing companies in other countries.

While there may be some indicators of convergence, there is much countervailing evidence that points to persistent differences across borders in the way that companies operate. For example, the large MIT study of competitive strategies in firms in different countries confirmed the existence of 'a variety of strategies that companies use to compete successfully in the same industries' and went further in arguing that 'this diversity is not disappearing and that there is no convergence on a single best practice model' (Berger, 2005: 145). Accordingly, it is well established

*I am particularly grateful to Anthony Ferner for the permission and encouragement to use, in this chapter, concepts and arguments that we developed jointly. The three research projects were as follows. First, the study of British MNCs was part of Tony Edwards' doctoral studies. Second, the research into German MNCs was funded by the Anglo-German Foundation and involved Anthony Ferner, Matthais Varul and Javier Quintanilla. Third, the project examining US MNCs was funded by the Economic and Social Research Council in the UK and involved Phil Almond, Peter Butler, Ian Clark, Trevor Colling, Tony Edwards, Anthony Ferner, Len Holden and Michael Muller-Carmen.

Handbook of International Human Resource Management. Edited by Paul R. Sparrow
© 2009 John Wiley & Sons, Ltd

that there are lasting national differences in the institutional context in which firms operate. Some writers have conceptualized the interlocking nature of institutions in areas such as corporate governance, training, and employment regulation as giving rise to distinctive 'national business systems' (Whitley, 1999).

For multinational companies (MNCs) this national distinctiveness simultaneously creates opportunities and presents constraints. By definition, MNCs are linked into multiple national systems and their experience of cross-national diversity in business practice increases their scope for organizational learning. Thus MNCs may be able to observe practices that are in operation in one part of the company and transfer them to other parts. Unsurprisingly, the issue of knowledge transfer in MNCs has attracted considerable attention in the academic literature (e.g., Gupta and Govindarajan, 2000). However, while national distinctiveness creates this scope for learning it also constrains the extent to which people are able to absorb new knowledge. For example, Lam (1997) argues that the different 'knowledge structures' that characterize national systems constrain the ability of individuals to learn from those in other parts of the firm. Moreover, HR practices are to varying extents dependent on a supportive institutional context, meaning that attempts by MNCs to diffuse practices across borders may be met with resistance in the new context.

There is abundant evidence that MNCs are oriented toward the home country system as the source of practices that are spread across their operations (see Edwards and Ferner, 2002 for a review). This has been termed 'forward diffusion' in the sense that the direction of diffusion flows with the hierarchy of the firm. In recent years a different strand of the research in this area has addressed 'reverse diffusion' in which practices that originate in the foreign subsidiaries are transferred to the rest of the company, including the domestic operations.

This is a potentially significant phenomenon for two main reasons. The first relates to the way in which reverse diffusion can contribute to an ongoing process of 'hybridization'. For example, there is a wealth of evidence that the business systems in countries such as France and Germany are changing in character, partly because of the investments made by institutional shareholders and foreign MNCs (e.g., Clift, 2004; Goyer, 2006). An additional way in which elements of other business systems can be introduced into a country is through domestic MNCs observing practices in their foreign operations that they subsequently transfer back to the home country. As we will see, there is substantial evidence of this happening in German MNCs in particular.

The second reason is linked to the first. We also know that despite the apparent popularity of the 'networked' firm (e.g., Bartlett and Ghoshal, 1998) most MNCs retain a strong hierarchical element involving a corporate HQ that possesses many sources of power, such as the authority to determine the character of international HR policies. Reverse diffusion can change the expectations of organizational actors concerning the legitimacy of groups at a range of levels to influence the policy formation process. More specifically, where reverse diffusion occurs it may change a perception that practices will naturally flow from the corporate center out to the operating units, and if this expectation changes then this may lead to a lasting impact on power relations with the firm.

This chapter reviews the evidence on reverse diffusion, examining two dimensions:

(1) the extent to which it is conditioned by national business systems and
(2) the impact it has on relations between actors in different parts of a multinational.

Throughout the chapter, for illustrative purposes, evidence is drawn from three linked research projects that examined British, German, and American MNCs.

PATTERNS IN PREVIOUS RESEARCH

The literature on the transfer of HR practices across sites has tended to focus strongly on how practices that are established in the domestic operations are spread cross-nationally to other parts of the firm. This is referred to above as 'forward diffusion' and is found in firms that have what Perlmutter (1969) called an 'ethnocentric' element to their approach in which the center of gravity of the firm is its original home base. A large number of studies have indicated that this is a widespread feature of US MNCs (e.g., Almond and Ferner, 2006), many of which have sought to ensure that their overseas operating units are union-free, have 'variable' pay for a large proportion of workers and have taken steps to increase workforce diversity. Similarly, a raft of studies of Japanese firms have confirmed that they commonly implement in their foreign sites the practices associated with lean production, such as teamwork and employee involvement in quality issues (e.g., Elger and Smith, 2005).

As noted in the introduction, there is now a growing body of work that sheds light on reverse diffusion. One approach to this issue has been concerned with establishing the orientation of management that is necessary if the firm is to engage in learning from its sites across countries (see also Moingeon, Lumineau, and Perrin, this volume Chapter 13). An example of this line of work is Bartlett and Ghoshal's (1998) analysis of the 'transnational' firm in which the operating units are linked with each other through an 'integrated network' in which sites are interdependent, having a role that is distinct from those in other countries. Such firms rely on a flow of knowledge and resources that is multidirectional as opposed to the flow being from the corporate center to foreign sites and is, therefore, the sort of company in which reverse diffusion will occur. Bartlett and Ghoshal (1998) argue that for this to happen effectively the firm must be characterized by high trust relations between operating units and what they call 'stretch', by which they mean the setting of ambitious goals that are to be achieved through a set of common values. In other words, they emphasize the importance of the mentality of key figures in the organization in creating an organizational culture that is conducive to innovations being spread across the firm.

A related strand of this work examines the mechanisms that facilitate the transfer of knowledge across sites. This 'information processing' perspective focuses on how information is diffused from one 'receptacle' to another (Gourlay, 2006). One distinction that is commonly drawn upon is the difference between codifiable and tacit knowledge (Kogut and Zander, 2003). The former refers to knowledge that can be clearly articulated and stored in written form; the latter relates to knowledge that can only be understood by a person who is familiar with the context. There is some evidence to demonstrate that codifiable knowledge concerning HR practices can effectively be reverse diffused through such mechanisms as manuals, databases, and systematic management audits (e.g., Sewell and Wilkinson, 1993; Coller, 1996; Ferner and Varul, 1999). Such formal ways of transferring knowledge are much less likely to be effective for tacit knowledge, for which 'people-based' mechanisms such as multidisciplinary teams, cross-national workshops and international assignments are better suited (Harzing, 2001; Martin and Salomon, 2003). The extent to which such mechanisms exist and are effective is, therefore, a factor that distinguishes MNCs from each other in their ability to engage in reverse diffusion.

These approaches are useful insofar as they point to the type of organizational culture and the different organizational mechanisms that shape the likelihood that reverse diffusion will occur. However, there is a need to go beyond this, since both of these strands of research risk playing down the challenges that are involved in the process. In particular, there are two fundamental challenges to firms that seek to engage in reverse diffusion:

(1) those that arise from national institutional differences and
(2) those from the organizational politics involved.

I explore each of these in turn.

NATIONAL INSTITUTIONS AND REVERSE DIFFUSION

In analyzing the impact that reverse diffusion brings it is useful to make a distinction between two types of the phenomenon (Edwards and Ferner, 2004). It can be 'evolutionary' in that it involves a firm seeking to achieve an optimal mix of practices within an existing *modus operandi*. That is, the multinational retains its basic identity and culture but refines and adapts this through adopting practices that originate in the foreign operating units. In contrast, it can be 'transformative' in that it has the effect of moving the firm to a new *modus operandi*. In this scenario the diffusion of practices from countries outside the original base has the effect of bringing about radical change in the orientation of the firm.

One way in which this distinction is linked to national business systems is through the concept of 'dominance effects' (Smith and Meiksins, 1995). These arise out of differences between countries in economic performance; at any one time, Smith and Meiksins argue, there is a hierarchy of economies according to their economic performance with the country at the top serving as the national model that firms in other countries look to emulate. Thus for much of the 1980s the strength of the Japanese economy led to considerable interest among firms in other countries in emulating the practices associated with the 'lean production' regime of many successful companies in Japan. During the last two decades or so the conventional wisdom has changed somewhat as the Japanese economy has faltered and the

American economy has become resurgent. In this period it appears that many firms have expressed interest in a characteristically American approach to issues such as performance management and variable pay, seeing them as important components to succeeding in international markets. While the concept of dominance effects in its simplest form can be criticized – it has been argued, for example, that it risks implying that national systems are made up of one form of organization and management when there is, of course, considerable diversity in most countries – it is nevertheless useful in capturing widely held beliefs about the success or otherwise of various national models.

The concept of dominance effects is instructive in indicating the form that reverse diffusion is likely to take, and how this varies with the nationality of the firm. At its simplest level, MNCs that originate in a dominant country are likely to model their international operations on the form of organization that is characteristic of the home country. Thus they may not use the practices in place in their foreign operating units at all and if they do then it is likely to take the form of minor adaptations to an existing approach. In other words, it is likely that reverse diffusion will be limited in its extent and primarily evolutionary in its impact where it does occur. In contrast, MNCs from non-dominant countries are more likely to be actively searching for a new operating model as they internationalize. Therefore, they are more open to making major changes to the way they function by drawing on practices from quite different national systems. In our terms, these are the MNCs most likely to engage in reverse diffusion, including that which is transformative in nature, as a way of catching up with firms from dominant countries.

A more refined application of dominance effects to the issue of reverse diffusion is to see national systems as having strengths in some areas of HR and employment relations and weaknesses in others. Thus national systems may achieve a degree of dominance with respect to particular management practices rather than having this status across the board. For instance, a multinational in the engineering sector that is looking to build new forms of work organization may be drawn to 'lean production' as developed most famously by some Japanese firms or the 'diversified quality production' of German companies, while the same firm that is seeking new forms of 'variable' pay is more likely to look to the British and especially American economies where such practices have been well established for a considerable period of time.

The literature provides some evidence that is consistent with this. One illustration of transformative reverse diffusion was in a case study of a British multinational, Engineering Products (Edwards, 1998). During the 1980s and 1990s this firm was producing automotive components in increasingly competitive markets and perceived the UK to lack a production model on which to base an internationally integrated approach. Thus senior management sought to implement Japanese style practices, using their overseas subsidiaries as sites from which practices were diffused across the firm. One example is that of cellular production, which one of the foreign operating units developed and subsequently spread across the firm. This brought about major changes in the organization of work in the domestic sites, from a linear production layout to one based on teams. Within these teams, operators were required to work flexibly, interchanging their position in the cell with others with whom they shared responsibility for quality issues.

Another illustration is that of German MNCs and the structures that they have used to control their international operations (e.g., Ferner and Quintanilla, 1998; Lowendahl, 1999). A body of evidence into German firms shows that growing internationalization has been associated with a shift away from traditionally German decision-making structures which are characterized by hierarchical reporting relationships and 'dual' forms of control to both 'commercial' and 'line' managers. In their place have come the devolved business units that have characterized large American and British firms that tended to internationalize at an earlier stage in their development. These business units involved responsibility for 'bottom line' results residing at lower levels in the hierarchy than is typical in Germany. In HR terms, this shift has often been accompanied by the greater use of 'Anglo-Saxon' practices such as performance-related pay and share options for managers (Buck *et al.*, 2004; Kurdelbusch, 2002). These changes constituted a significant shift in the character of control of operating units and reward for senior staff. However, the significant qualification here is that these Anglo-Saxon practices were amended in form as they were introduced into the German system, leading Buck *et al.* (2004) to conclude that we should see this process as one of practices being 'translated' rather than simply diffused.

Some evidence relating to Chinese MNCs in Britain is also indicative of transformative reverse diffusion, at least on the face of it (Zhang *et al.*, 2006). Of course, Chinese firms originate in a domestic system which was closed to the international economy for most of the second half of the 20th century and which in recent years has gone through a process of rapid economic reform. The study of six firms in Zhang *et al.*'s study revealed that the UK is used as a base for the accumulation of knowledge concerning international management in general and international human resource management (IHRM) in particular. In all six companies young Chinese managers were given developmental assignments in Britain, something that was motivated partly by an attempt by senior managers to expose them to the 'rules of the game' in Western forms of capitalism. In addition, some British staff were sent on short assignments to China, sometimes with an explicit brief of transferring to the domestic sites practices that operate in the UK. One example is in the area of recruitment, where the British operations of one of the firms pushed a model of recruiting staff which was taken up in China. The model was based on a form of identifying competencies in job applications that represented a significant shift away from the reliance on personal contacts in recruitment that had been the norm in the firm. Such instances of reverse diffusion have the potential to make a transformative impact on firms that are seeking to 'catch-up' with their Western counterparts.

However, this latter case also raises the issue of how apparently transformative cases of reverse diffusion sometimes have a more modest impact in practice. The new recruitment model operated in a different way in China from the way it had functioned in Britain; the sheer weight of job applications meant that it was not used in full and recruitment continued to be shaped by personal contacts, demonstrating the continuing influence of *guanxi*. As one respondent in China put it, 'before the interviews the candidates for most posts have been decided already'. This instance demonstrates the importance of exercising caution in judging the practical impact of a practice that is transferred across quite different business systems.

This highlights a quite different way in which reverse diffusion is influenced by business systems – namely, the way that national distinctiveness shapes the operation of a practice after it has been diffused to a new context. The ease with which a practice can be transferred across borders is determined in part by the existence of supportive and distinctive extra-firm structures. These structures include the legal and institutional framework of the labor market and the attitudinal and behavioral norms that characterize employment relations in a particular country. All employment practices are in some way or other dependent on these legal, institutional, and cultural 'props' and the ease with which a practice can be transferred to another country is influenced by the extent of this dependency. In some cases it may even be that a practice changes so significantly that it is no longer really helpful to continue to regard it as the same practice after diffusion compared with how it operated in its original context.

In the field of work organization, for example, some practices are highly dependent on supportive props. One instance is a system of production in Sweden that differed markedly from Japanese-style lean production or of the variants of lean production that were deployed in the American firms trying to emulate the Japanese. According to Berggren (1993), 'post-lean human-centered production', which was most famously developed at Volvo's Uddevalla site, involved a focus on autonomous work groups with no first-line supervisors and was distinctively Swedish in as much as it rested on an open management style and collaborative tenor to employment relations that characterized the country. The differing context in other countries was one of the factors that limited the international spread of this form of work organization.

The characteristics of national business systems in which MNCs operate can also limit the transfer of a practice in a slightly different sense. As well as lacking the institutional 'props' that might be necessary for the operation of a practice, a national system may also present institutional or cultural 'constraints' to transfer. Organizational actors in the unit to which the practice is targeted may use their legal powers or rights provided by institutions to prevent a practice being implemented in their operating units. In this sense, practices may be diffusible because they come up against nationally distinct constraints.

One illustration of how these constraints are influential is in the area of numerical flexibility. To some extent, the way that firms seek to achieve this is governed by prevailing labor market regulations and norms in each country. The role of part-time workers in meeting fluctuations in demand, for example, is dependent on there being a pool of workers willing to accept such jobs. Other forms of numerical flexibility, such as annualized hours, temporary contracts and changes in shift patterns, have to be negotiated with employee representatives in many countries and, therefore, a multinational's ability to transfer them across its sites is clearly influenced by the attitudes and strengths of organized labor (Hayden and Edwards, 2001).

An illustration of how institutions and norms in the home country impede reverse diffusion is evident in Edwards *et al.*'s (2005) study of US MNCs in which the authors argued that the American system presented a number of barriers to this process. For example, the British subsidiary of one of the firms, FMCG, had developed a significant innovation in the form of 'broad-banding', which involved the reorganization of the pay structure to suit the site's new emphasis on team-working. Specifically, the change meant that the main British site moved from having 20 pay grades to six broader 'bands' that were related to skill sets. British managers tried to push this innovation to the American operations, but were unsuccessful. The explanation for this failure lay in the fierce ideological commitment to keeping unions out of the firm that is found in many American firms, of which FMCG is one. In the context of an ongoing struggle to keep unions at bay in the firm's large manufacturing sites, the British practice of broad-banding looked unattractive to managers. In contrast to the British emphasis on the link between pay and skills, the pay structure in the US contained seniority provisions and multiple job grades in an apparent attempt to emulate the payment structures and improve upon the levels of pay in unionized firms. In the eyes of American managers, to introduce the British pay structure would risk creating a situation in which some workers perceived themselves to be losing out, creating favorable conditions for a union organizing drive. In this sense, the emphasis on keeping unions out, which has become an institutionalized feature of the American system of employment relations, constrains the ability of US MNCs to engage in reverse diffusion.

These constraints rarely close off all scope for the diffusion of practices, however; in many cases they are partial rather than absolute, especially where powerful MNCs have the ability to influence local institutions in such a way that leaves open some scope for diffusion. The partial nature of constraints means that a practice may be diffused but operate in a different manner. In this way national differences can lead to a process of 'transmutation' in which practices change in character as they are implemented in a new context (Edwards and Ferner, 2004). For reverse diffusion, this means that, while the impact can sometimes be transformative as the above cases demonstrate, the impact is often evolutionary.

Indeed, research in this area has provided numerous illustrations of reverse diffusion that are evolutionary. One example is the way that many German firms that have significant operations in the UK and the US have developed explicit statements of 'corporate culture' and 'mission statements', which are common in large British and American MNCs. Ferner and Varul (1999) show that when German MNCs take such steps, often under pressure from international investors, these statements encompass rather than transcend the traditional German concept of *Betriebsgemeinschaft*, or 'works community', which stresses the role of the workers' interests. In doing so, these statements have a particular Germanic trait, distinguishing them from the greater Anglo-American emphasis on 'shareholder value'.

Another illustration of transmutation of practices that are the subject of reverse diffusion is evident in Edwards *et al.*'s (2005) study of US MNCs referred to above. On the face of it, we might expect the tendency in American firms to make radical and rapid changes in their strategy, which has been documented by authors such as Hall and Soskice (2001) to be conducive to transformative reverse diffusion. Certainly, the evidence in the US firms was one of the basic strategies and structures changing markedly and repeatedly, in part because the American business system (particularly the financial system) creates pressures and incentives to do so. For instance, one of the companies, ITco, had made some dramatic changes in its strategy in response to a corporate crisis, including the reversal of a move toward decentralizing responsibility for operating matters and a shift into quite different products and services. However, rather than favorably disposing the companies that made these type of changes to reverse diffusion, the evidence indicated that the fluidity in strategy appears to impede the international coordination that is necessary for reverse diffusion to flourish. The building of close links between site level actors across borders takes time and involves a lengthy process of coalition building and cross-national learning. Thus the American institutional context appears to limit the impact of reverse diffusion. This is consistent with the evidence in ITco, where there was evidence of evolutionary – a refinement of the appraisal system that related to goal-setting – but not transformative reverse diffusion.

This section has examined the role of distinctive national business systems in shaping the process of reverse diffusion, showing how national institutions both influence the incentives for firms to engage in it and also their ability to do so. It has also raised the issue of the role of coalition building that is central to cross-national learning in MNCs and this points to the importance of considering the political dimension to this phenomenon, and this is the focus of the next section.

THE ORGANIZATIONAL POLITICS OF REVERSE DIFFUSION

While national business systems condition the process of reverse diffusion, whether it occurs or not is strongly shaped by the preferences and influence of various groups of organizational actors. Therefore, we might see a condition for reverse diffusion taking place as various groups have an interest in engaging in it. In this section I make a broad distinction between actors at foreign subsidiary and HQ levels.

A major incentive for those in the foreign operating units to engage in reverse diffusion is the enhanced status and stronger claim on resources that might result from being the source of new innovations that are adopted in other parts of the firm. As we have seen above, studies of German MNCs have revealed that the British subsidiaries have been at the heart of corporate-wide policy initiatives in areas such as payment structures, performance management systems and the development of explicit statements of corporate culture. Ferner and Varul (2000) use the term 'vanguard' subsidiary to refer to the elevated position of such sites, which in effect generate a role for themselves that went beyond their borders. Given this, the sites' security in terms of future investment from the center was inevitably strengthened. This notion has much in common with that of subsidiaries taking on the status of 'center of excellence' that is widely used in the international business literature (e.g., Birkinshaw *et al.*, 1998).

As well as benefiting the site as a whole, being the source of reverse diffusion may bring gains for certain individuals. Illustrations of this are evident in Edwards' (2000) study of British MNCs. One case involved the French site of an engineering company that had developed a way of organizing the factory that involved the creation of 'internal customers' with each stage in the production process being designated as a semi-independent unit with its own budget and support services. This was spread across the firm by one of the French managers who became an internal consultant, roaming around the company with a brief to advise on how best to operate the practice (see Harvey and Novicevic, this volume Chapter 6, for a discussion of the benefits of political capital for international managers). Another case was in a chemicals firm in which the American unit had attracted the attention of the corporate HQ for its training and development work. As a consequence, the American manager responsible for some of the initiatives was promoted to be the worldwide Director of Training.

Turning to the perspective of actors in the corporate center, there are incentives for some at this level to ensure that reverse diffusion takes place, the most obvious of which is that it may raise the productivity and efficiency of the firm as a whole. Beyond this, those that have responsibility for overseeing the foreign operating units may well see reverse diffusion as a way of emphasizing the profile of the international in relation to the domestic sites. One illustration of this was found in an American engineering company which had begun to place greater importance on its overseas operating units as part of its 'global' strategy (Edwards *et al.*, 2005). The International HR Director, who was nominally at a similar hierarchical level to the US HR Director, saw the identification of practices from outside America as a way in which his role could be enhanced within the function. Accordingly, he played a key role in championing a competency-based form of appraisal that had been developed initially in the UK and liaised closely with the British manager responsible for this, arranging for him to spend an assignment at the corporate HQ with a brief to get the practice incorporated into the company's policies world wide.

In this way, alliances may be formed between some actors at the corporate HQ and those at foreign subsidiary level. Another illustration involves the study of German MNCs in which the introduction of performance-related remuneration based on the practices of the British and American operations created a new role at the corporate center that those in the HR function could claim as a new functional responsibility (Ferner and Varul, 1999). In addition, of course, reverse diffusion of new forms of pay such as share options along Anglo-American lines can bring substantial material benefits to those at senior level, further strengthening alliances between actors at the sites on which the new policies are modeled and those at the corporate HQ.

While there are grounds for expecting some organizational actors to see clear incentives in engaging in reverse diffusion, others may not consider it to be in their interests. In this sense, whether it occurs or not is not just a matter of making sure that there are mechanisms capable of absorbing the knowledge effectively. In other words, reverse diffusion is not simply a technical issue of establishing the organizational architecture through which it may occur, nor is it solely a cultural matter of establishing an organizational mindset that values cross-national collaboration. Rather, it is also a political matter in which material interests are at stake and active resistance may prevent it occurring.

This resistance may take place at subsidiary level. A primary reason why actors in the operating units may wish to block reverse diffusion is that engaging in it may undermine their competitive position within the multinational. There is abundant evidence that the HQs of many MNCs set up internal benchmarking systems that systematically compare the performance of sites against one another, with the outcome of these 'coercive comparisons' being tied to future investment decisions (Marginson and Sisson, 2004). Where this is the case there is a clear tension in the eyes of managers at site level between being subject to competition for investment funds with other sites on the one hand, and being expected to identify the practices that contribute to the performance of the site on the other. This reluctance to share their innovations with other sites with whom they are in competition may lead them to conceal the true nature of their own practices. Of course, it may not be easy for actors at this level to disguise what they are doing since some practices are easily observed and the HQ of many MNCs places expatriate managers in their foreign subsidiaries who subsequently act as the 'eyes and ears' of the corporate center.

A further reason why those in the operating units may not want to engage in reverse diffusion is that it may draw unwelcome attention to the site in other respects. That is, in identifying a practice developed within the subsidiary that the HQ may be interested in diffusing across the firm, managers at operating units may unwittingly provoke a fuller examination of the nature of other practices. This is likely to be a concern among managers in those sites that are not fully complying with the corporate policies. As one manager in the project on US MNCs referred to above put it, there is a reluctance to invite this level of corporate interest when they had been 'flying underneath the radar' on other issues.

Resistance to reverse diffusion may also stem from those at the HQ. It might be that actors in the HQ see reverse diffusion as threatening their legitimacy in formulating corporate policies. That is, if initiatives in the multinational are generated from across the company then the privileged claim on resources of those at the center might be weakened. An illustration of this was in the study of German MNCs in which many British respondents argued that if their initiatives were to be taken up by those at the center they needed to try to play by the corporate 'rules of the game' and even then the practices they were pushing were met with a high degree of skepticism by a layer of managers below the director level (Ferner and Varul, 1999).

A further obstacle to reverse diffusion arises less from deliberate resistance by those at the HQ and more from a type of organizational inertia. In MNCs with a strong centralized tradition this way of operating may endure even where there are attempts to move away from it. One example is an engineering company studied in the American MNCs project. In this company there had been widespread calls among those in the foreign operating units for more scope to enable them to exert influence over international policy making in general, and for the practices developed at their level to be spread across the firm in particular. Eventually, this message was acted upon by senior corporate HR staff who set up a new form of corporate policy-making in which consultation and participation of HR leaders from across the company was a key feature. Thus the development of any new policies to apply across the firm had to involve an international HR team generally of eight people, with no more than two of these coming from the US. For a while this approach seemed to represent a major departure from the previous way of doing things and led to an instance of reverse diffusion (the competency-based appraisal system described above). However, this participative approach to policy making was short-lived; a downturn in the product market led to a bout of cost-cutting, including a ban on non-essential travel. In this context, the policy-making groups ceased to meet and virtual forms of communication were not seen as an adequate replacement, meaning that the company reverted to type in the sense that the corporate HQ once again came to dominate policy making (Edwards *et al.*, 2005). In essence, the center reasserted control not as the result of a plot but rather through taking advantage of circumstances.

CONCLUSION

The arguments in this chapter have implications for both academics and practitioners. For the former, the chapter has indicated various analytical approaches that might be used to study the way in which MNCs use new practices that develop in their foreign operating units. Much previous research has examined the type of organizational culture or orientation that is most conducive to aiding companies in tapping into the diversity of practice that exists across the firm and the type of mechanisms that are more or less adept at transmitting knowledge across borders. To these two additional factors can be added.

1. Variations in national business systems shape the process of reverse diffusion in fundamental ways. These national differences create the diversity on which the process depends, of course, but their impact goes further. The country in which the firm originates influences whether it is likely to use reverse diffusion as a way of catching up with firms in other countries, and national differences influence the practices that are likely to be the subject of diffusion and how they operate in the new context.
2. The process of reverse diffusion is highly political and should be seen as more that simply a matter of establishing an appropriate organizational culture and set of mechanisms to transfer expertise, important as these are. If it is to occur, it must be in the interests of different groups of organizational actors. We have seen that while there are incentives for these various groups to initiate and engage in the process, there are also numerous grounds for expecting there to be resistance too.

What, then, are the implications of the chapter for practitioners? In essence, it suggests that, while there are very good reasons for companies to seek to engage in reverse diffusion, there are a number of barriers to be overcome. Following the logic of the arguments advanced, these barriers relate not only to establishing an appropriate organizational culture and a set of mechanisms to transfer expertise, but they also arise in the form of national differences in institutional context. Those seeking to push reverse diffusion should be aware, for example, of the way in which practices change in character, or go through a process of 'transmutation', as they are implemented in a new national context. Perhaps most importantly of all, if senior staff in MNCs want to use reverse diffusion as a way of tapping into the diversity of practice across their operations then they must look to overcome potential resistance. More specifically, they must look to structure the incentives of different groups of actors so that these groups see it as in their interests to engage in the process.

REFERENCES

Almond, P., and Ferner, A. (eds) (2006). *American Multinationals in Europe: Managing Employment Relations Across National Borders.* Oxford: Oxford University Press.

Bartlett, C., and Ghoshal, S. (1998). *Managing Across Borders: The Transnational Solution* (2nd edn). Boston, MA: Harvard Business School Press.

Berger, S. (2005). *How We Compete: What Companies Around the World are Doing to Make it in Today's Global Economy.* New York: Doubleday.

Berggren, C. (1993). *The Volvo Experience.* London: Macmillan.

Birkinshaw, J., Hood, N., and Jonsson, S. (1998). Building firm-specific advantages in multinational corporations: The role of subsidiary initiative. *Strategic Management Journal,* 19, 221–241.

Buck, T., Shahrim, A., and Winter, S. (2004). Executive stock options in Germany: The diffusion or translation of US-style corporate governance. *Journal of Management and Governance,* 8 (2), 173–186.

Clift, B. (2004). Debating the restructuring of French capitalism and Anglo-Saxon institutional investors: Trojan horses or sleeping partners? *French Politics,* 2 (3), 333–346.

Coller, X. (1996). Managing flexibility in the food industry: A cross-national comparative case study of European multinational companies. *European Journal of Industrial Relations,* 2 (2), 153–172.

Edwards, T. (1998). Multinationals, employment practices and the process of reverse diffusion. *International Journal of Human Resource Management,* 9 (4), 696–709.

Edwards, T. (2000). Multinationals, international integration and employment practice in domestic plants. *Industrial Relations Journal,* 31 (2), 115–129.

Edwards, T., and Ferner, A. (2002). The renewed "American Challenge": A framework for understanding employment practice in US multinationals. *Industrial Relations Journal,* 33 (2), 94–111.

Edwards, T., and Ferner, A. (2004). Multinationals, reverse diffusion and national business systems. *Management International Review,* 44 (1), 49–79.

Edwards, T., Almond, P., Clark, I., Colling, T., and Ferner, A. (2005). Reverse diffusion in US multinationals: Barriers from the American business system. *Journal of Management Studies,* 42 (6), 1261–1286.

Elger, T., and Smith, C. (2005). *Assembling Work: Remaking Work Regimes in Japanese Multinationals in Britain.* Oxford: Oxford University Press.

Ferner, A., and Quintanilla, J. (1998). Multinationals, national business systems and HRM: The enduring influence of national identity or a process of 'Anglo-Saxonisation'? *International Journal of Human Resource Management,* 9 (4), 710–731.

Ferner, A., and Varul, M. (1999). *The German Way? German Multinationals and the Management of Human Resources in their UK Subsidiaries.* London: Anglo-German Foundation.

Ferner, A., and Varul, M. (2000). Vanguard subsidiaries and the diffusion of new practices: A case study of German multinationals. *British Journal of Industrial Relations,* 38 (1), 115–140.

Gourlay, S. (2006). Knowledge management and international HRM. In T. Edwards and C. Rees (eds), *International Human Resource Management: Multinational Companies, Globalisation and National Systems*. Harlow: Pearson.

Goyer, M. (2006). Varieties of institutional investors and national models of capitalism: The transformation of corporate governance in France and Germany. *Politics and Society*, 34 (3), 399–430.

Gupta A.K., and Govindarajan, V. (2000). Knowledge flows within multinational corporations. *Strategic Management Journal*, 21 (4), 473–496.

Hall, P., and Soskice, D. (eds) (2001). *Varieties of Capitalism: The Institutional Foundations of Comparative Advantage*. Oxford: Oxford University Press.

Harzing, A.-W. (2001). Of bears, bumble-bees and spiders: The role of expatriates in controlling foreign subsidiaries. *Journal of World Business*, 36 (4), 366–379.

Hayden, A., and Edwards, T. (2001). The erosion of the country of origin effect: A case study of a Swedish multinational company. *Relations Industrielles/Industrial Relations*, 56 (1), 116–140.

Kogut, B., and Zander, U. (2003). A memoir and reflection: Knowledge and an evolutionary theory of the multinational firm 10 years later. *Journal of International Business Studies*, 34 (6), 505–515.

Kurdelbusch, A. (2002). Multinationals and the rise of variable pay in Germany, *European Journal of Industrial Relations*, 8 (3), 325–349.

Lam, A. (1997). Embedded firms, embedded knowledge: Problems of collaboration and knowledge transfer in global cooperative ventures. *Organization Studies*, 18 (6), 973–996.

Lowendahl, H. (1999). Siemens' 'Anglo-Saxon' Strategy: Is globalising business enough? *German Politics*, 8 (1), 89–105.

Marginson, P., and Sisson, K. (2004). *European Integration and Industrial Relations: Multi-level Governance in the Making*. Basingstoke: Palgrave Macmillan.

Martin, X., and Salomon, R. (2003). Knowledge diffusion capacity and its implications for the theory of the multinational corporation. *Journal of International Business Studies*, 34 (4), 356–373.

Perlmutter, H.V. (1969). The tortuous evolution of the multinational corporation. *Columbia Journal of World Business*, 4 (1), 9–18.

Sewell, G., and Wilkinson, B. (1993). Human resource management in 'Surveillance' companies. In J. Clark (ed.), *Human Resource Management and Technical Change*. London: Sage.

Smith, C., and Meiksins, P. (1995). System, society and dominance effects in cross-national organizational analysis. *Work, Employment and Society*, 9 (2), 241–267.

Whitley, R. (1999). *Divergent Capitalisms: The Social Structuring and Change of Business Systems*. Oxford: Oxford University Press.

Zhang, M., Edwards, T., and Edwards, C. (2006). Internationalization and developing countries: The case of China. In T. Edwards and C. Rees (eds), *International Human Resource Management: Multinational Companies, Globalisation and National Systems*. Harlow: Pearson.

12

Performance Management Across Borders

INGMAR BJÖRKMAN, WILHELM BARNER-RASMUSSEN,
MATS EHRNROOTH, AND KRISTIINA MÄKELÄ

INTRODUCTION

One of the essential questions facing a multinational corporation (MNC) overseas is the extent to which the management of human resources is – and in fact should be – adapted to local conditions. The answer is far from self-evident. Several studies have analyzed the extent to which subsidiary HRM practices resemble those of local firms ('localization') versus those of the foreign parent organization ('standardization'), the latter entailing a transfer of practices within the MNC (e.g., Rosenzweig and Nohria, 1994; Rosenzweig, 2006; Hannon *et al.*, 1995; Björkman and Lu, 2001). MNCs engage in the internal transfer of organizational practices for many reasons, the two main ones in relation to performance management being that:

1. such practices are valuable resources that firms seek to replicate and exploit throughout the organization (Szulanski, 1996; Zaheer, 1995); and
2. the consistency achieved through their transfer also contributes to equity enhancement within the MNC and the management of its external legitimacy (Kostova and Zaheer, 1999).

However, despite their clear strategic value, planned transfers of practices do not always work out in the way intended by the headquarters. Previous research has shown that there are significant differences in the achieved extent of transfer even between different subsidiaries belonging to the same MNC (Edwards, this volume Chapter 11; Kostova and Roth, 2002). Important questions to be addressed thus include the extent to which home country human resource practices are and/or can

Handbook of International Human Resource Management. Edited by Paul R. Sparrow
© 2009 John Wiley & Sons, Ltd

be adopted by MNC subsidiaries, and why the extent of adoption differs between units.

In this chapter we outline a model of MNC internal factors that influence the transfer of HRM practices from headquarters to foreign units, focusing on the internal transfer of performance management systems. In line with the arguments put forward by Kostova (1999) and Kostova and Roth (2002) we suggest that it is important to make a distinction between:

- the *implementation* of the policies, tools, and practices associated with performance management, and
- the extent to which subsidiary managers and other employees have *internalized* its underlying principles on the other.

Our model suggests that human, social, and organizational capital (Wright *et al.*, 2001), both at headquarters and at the foreign subsidiary, influence the extent to which performance management policies and practices are implemented and internalized in the subsidiary. Although there has been a surge of studies concerning the effect of the different forms of capital, and social capital in particular, on a range of organizational issues (see, e.g., Harvey and Novicevic, this volume Chapter 6; Sparrow, Brewster and Ligthart, this volume Chapter 18; Youndt *et al.*, 2004), the whole range of 'capitals' appears not to have been used to examine subsidiary adoption of HRM practices within the MNC.

PERFORMANCE APPRAISAL IN MNCS – KEY ISSUES

Performance management is a major item on many Western companies' strategic human resource management (SHRM) agenda. It has been defined as a 'strategic and integrated approach to increasing the effectiveness of organizations by improving the performance of the people who work in them and by developing the capabilities of teams and individual contributors' (Armstrong and Baron, 1998). Several HRM practices – especially those associated with the concept of a high-performance work system – could ultimately be seen as part of an organization's performance management system. An essential element of the latter is the process of systematically and regularly establishing the employee's performance goals in line with those of the organization, monitoring and measuring performance, giving feedback on behavior and results, providing rewards based on performance, agreeing on and facilitating development, and offering promotion and career development advice and opportunities (for reviews of different performance management models, see Hartog *et al.*, 2004; Molleman and Timmerman, 2003). The fact that knowledge about performance management for and by host country managers is limited makes the issue particularly intriguing and important to pursue in the MNC context (Cascio, 2006). This is not least because performance management systems, along with talent management systems, are often among the first tier of strategically important HR practices that MNCs attempt to coordinate globally (Sparrow *et al.*, 2004).

At the heart of the performance management process is the *performance appraisal*, which typically takes place once or twice per year. It includes an analysis of a person's current performance, overall capabilities and future potential, and facilitates informed decisions concerning the setting of future performance goals, compensation, promotion, and development, all for the purposes of improving motivation and performance (adapted from Bratton and Gold, 2007). The focus in this chapter is on performance appraisal given that the dual challenges of standardization and localization are particularly strong in relation to this practice.

Research in Western (domestic) settings has established several facts about performance appraisal (for a comparative review of performance management systems see Varma *et al.*, 2008). First, the appraisal process comprises two key elements focusing on:

(1) performance assessment and
(2) future development or potential of the employee (in addition to these, the question of pay might also form part of an appraisal discussion).

The performance assessment element focuses on feedback and goal setting, the purpose being to enhance future performance and to reach decisions on compensation and promotion. The challenges associated with the assessment of employee performance are numerous and well documented (e.g., Townley, 1994): depending on how well it is carried out, it may significantly enhance the future performance of an individual, or alternatively demotivate him or her and therefore have a very negative influence. The developmental element of the appraisal process, in turn, includes discussion about upcoming challenges, competence requirements, career opportunities and support. Furthermore, judgments are often made about potential future performance.

A key challenge concerns how these two main elements are integrated. This is important because less-than-good news during the first part of the discussion around current performance and compensation may have a very negative influence on how fruitful the subsequent developmental part of the discussion will be. Indeed, it has been argued that '[n]o other management tool is more critical to productivity than effective performance appraisals, yet they can actually impair employee performance' (English, 1991: 53), and research indeed indicates that poor compliance or usage is a significant barrier to system effectiveness (Cascio, 2006).

Secondly, these challenges are further amplified within MNCs striving for a degree of global standardization across subsidiary units embedded in very different national cultures and institutional contexts (Cascio, 2006; Geppert and Mayer, 2006). Recent research has provided evidence of a range of resistance tactics that subsidiaries may use against standardized corporate-driven systems and policies (Ferner *et al.*, 2004; Kristensen and Zeitlin, 2005; Blazejewski, 2006; Tempel *et al.*, 2006; Mohan, 2006).

According to Kostova (1999) and Kostova and Roth (2002), the adoption of parent organization performance management systems by foreign subsidiaries comprises two central elements:

(1) the *implementation* of a corporate system in the foreign subsidiaries, and

(2) its *internalization* by the subsidiary managers and employees.[1]

While implementation is necessary for a subsidiary to successfully adopt parent organization performance appraisal practices and policies, it is crucial for the users of the system also to have internalized its underlying principles. Indeed, the most challenging element is often this internalization, referring to the 'state in which the employees at the recipient unit view the practice as valuable for the unit and become committed to the practice' (Kostova and Roth, 2002: 217). A 'textbook' approach to performance appraisal suggests that the underlying principles that need to be internalized involve:

(1) general commitment to the importance of the discussions;

(2) the understanding that managers should support employees in a constructive way;

(3) an appreciation of the fact that understanding the perspective of the employee is as important for managers as the understanding of the organizational performance requirements is for employees; and

(4) acknowledgment that the developmental focus is crucial.

While headquarters may, to some extent, impose policies and practices through various control systems, there are no simple means available of positively influencing the attitudes of subsidiary employees toward a system (see Edwards, this volume Chapter 11, for a discussion of the challenges of practice diffusion). Thus, we argue that as Western MNCs pursue the standardization and diffusion of a globally cohesive performance appraisal system, they need to pay attention to both the implementation *and* the internalization of practices at the subsidiary level.

A lack of attention to the underlying principles of a certain practice may lead to it being adopted only ceremonially (Meyer and Rowan, 1977; Kostova and Roth, 2002), or even to resistance, open conflict and rebellion (Blazejewski, 2006). The enforced adoption of a practice if there is no belief in its value is, at best, likely to lead to superficial obligation and a low level of commitment. Indeed, most previous research has focused on the aspect of implementation (e.g., Rosenzweig and Nohria, 1994; Hannon *et al.*, 1995; Björkman and Lu, 2001), and although some studies in institutional sociology have emphasized the reshaping and reinvention (Lervik and Lunnan, 2004), or 'hybridization' (Ferner *et al.*, 2005) of transferred practices, there is very little research on the internalization of HRM practices in general, and performance management/appraisal in particular.

---

[1]A third element in addition to the implementation and internalization of practices concerns their *integration* into other relevant and related subsidiary practices (see Björkman and Lervik, 2007). Integration in this context refers to the linkages and connections that are developed between the focal practice and the culturally and institutionally established set of other processes and practices in the subsidiary (Lervik, 2005). However, although integration is another important sign of successful transfer, it falls outside the scope of this chapter.

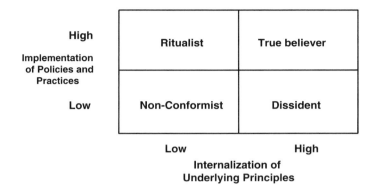

FIGURE 12.1 Four archetypes of subsidiary adoption patterns.

A FRAMEWORK OF SUBSIDIARY ADOPTION PATTERNS

As indicated earlier, MNCs differ in the extent to which they implement a standardized parent organization practice on the one hand, and internalize its underlying principles on the other. In the following we identify four different adoption patterns, which we refer to as four ideal types, or archetypes, of foreign subsidiary adoption. Figure 12.1 represents a conceptualization of these, based upon different combinations of high versus low levels of implementation and internalization. This is in line with Kostova and Roth's (2002) finding of four clusters of adoption patterns, and further contributes to that line of inquiry by exemplifying how the level of implementation and internalization defines the four adoption archetypes. Obviously, the 'perfect' replication (implementation) and internalization of parent organization practices is unlikely to happen in a foreign subsidiary due to differences in the cultural and institutional environments, among other things. Hence, we focus on the distinction between high vs low internalization/implementation, and would accept that units classified as having high levels of both may still exhibit some degree of local adaptation.

In what follows we illustrate each type with examples from a study of the performance management systems of four Finnish MNCs. In all four cases, the Finnish parent organization followed a relatively standard performance appraisal system according to which the employees and their superiors were required to partake in yearly discussions. The principles underlying the systems were reminiscent of the 'textbook' elements outlined above. Efforts had been made in all four companies to introduce performance management systems in their foreign subsidiaries, but our interviews revealed significant differences in the implementation and internalization of the appraisal systems. The four observed archetypes are described below.

The true believer

In our typology, a 'true believer' is a subsidiary (or indeed a manager who might be able to control the performance management climate within a particular unit) that has implemented the system and believes in its underlying principles, as illustrated by the quotation below. As discussed, some local adaptation may be required due to cultural and institutional issues, for instance, but this is done in accordance with the principles and to support the implementation of the practice. In fact, the key characteristic of a 'true believer' is that even if minor adaptations are made, they are within the spirit of the parent system and do not alter the fundamental design principles and logic of the practice.

> I have such [performance appraisal] dialogues. In principle I should have them once a year, but in reality we have them once a quarter because we have a quarterly bonus system in our subsidiary. I decided that if we're having a discussion anyway, let's make an interpretation of the development at the same time. We have a short discussion quarterly on both performance and development, maybe 30 minutes, maybe 40 minutes. Once a year we have a longer one. We discuss the best cases and the worst cases. And it helps a lot... For me the goal of these discussions is to understand where a person is, and how I motivate him or her.

The ritualist

A 'ritualist' is a unit (manager) scoring high on the implementation of policies and practices but low on the internalization of the underlying principles. Performance appraisals are typically formally implemented, but there is little belief in the principles, as the following quotations illustrate:

> I as the manager just put marks for every employee and then announce what needs to be improved.
> For people who come to an appraisal, just one thing is important: what mark will be put by the manager on the appraisal form.

In such situations, the subsidiary often reports to headquarters that the system is being implemented, but in reality the adoption may only be ceremonial. The concerns related to this kind of ceremonial adoption are well illustrated in the following quotation from an HR manager at headquarters:

> We have a timetable for the subsidiary appraisal discussions, and they should be done by the end of April. We keep statistics; we ask the subsidiary managers how many appraisal discussions they have actually had... But I don't see it as important because I don't really trust... the reports that they send to headquarters.

The non-conformist

A 'non-conformist' is a subsidiary (manager) scoring low on both dimensions. Non-conformist behavior may be driven by a complete lack of interest or even overt opposition towards such systems, as illustrated in the following quotation from a subsidiary manager expressing a very negative attitude toward the system and its underlying principles:

> I think that the only thing we must do is to create profit for our company. When my subordinates understand what they must do but cannot do it, I have only one discussion in that case. The second discussion is only about when you leave our company – because I'm not a teacher and we're not at school.

The dissident

A 'dissident' is a subsidiary (or a manager) that has internalized the underlying principles but, by and large, has not implemented the practices and policies. In other words, the underlying principles are deemed worth while, but it has not been considered appropriate to introduce the system used at the parent organization in that particular unit. The perceived lack of usefulness of centralized systems is well illustrated in the following quotation:

> I tried to have the appraisal discussion with every employee, including workers throughout the company. At least we tried, but I can't say it was a good experience in the sense that it was efficient. It created much more confusion than efficiency. So, the next year we decided that they are simply not ready. . . For manager level employees it was actually much easier. . . In multinational companies, people just blindly copy what is done elsewhere. . . Maybe the top management might think yes, it works, but it's not the case.

In research terms, the key challenge in establishing 'dissident' status is that there has to be evidence that the principles have been truly understood and internalized, and that shortcomings and alterations in implementation are not just an excuse, but are a legitimate alternative to abiding by the same principles.

The focus of our discussion now shifts to how the notion of human, social and organizational capital (Wright *et al.*, 2001; Youndt *et al.*, 2004), within both the focal unit and the corporate headquarters, can help to explain the extent to which the transfer of practices from the parent to the foreign unit takes place. We propose that the comprehensive conceptual framework offered by these four types of capital will shed new light on the challenges in terms of attempts by MNC headquarters to transfer performance management practices and policies. We concentrate in the following analysis on the aggregate subsidiary level, although we recognize that individual subsidiary managers and employees may differ considerably in the extent to which they personally internalize and implement such practices. We then develop a set of propositions related to how human, social and organizational capital influence the extent to which subsidiary managers:

(1) implement parent organization practices and policies, and
(2) internalize their underlying principles.

HUMAN CAPITAL PROPOSITIONS

Theorists have been stressing the importance of human capital for the success of corporate operations for a long time (Becker, 1964). The term commonly refers to the combined stock of knowledge and skills among a company's employees that have value for the firm (Wright *et al.*, 2001). Indeed, there has been considerable debate around how firms should analyze the returns they get on the investments they make in developing the skills and knowledge of their employees (Bhattacharya and Wright, 2005). For instance, Lepak and Snell (1999) argue that the uniqueness and strategic value of a firm's human capital is associated with certain employment modes. Here we leave considerations of strategic value aside, and consider the role that human capital plays in the transfer of performance management systems within the MNC. We should also point out that while we focus on human capital as a necessary input in the effective transfer of practices, an increase in such capital is also a goal and an outcome of the pursuit of transferring performance appraisal systems.

We posit that the human capital of both the MNC parent organization attempting to transfer practices, and of the receiving unit, is likely to affect the outcome of the transfer process. Below, we elaborate on the following three key contributions human capital makes to the implementation–internalization matrix[2]:

1. Knowledge of the context in which the system is to be implemented.
2. Knowledge of performance management systems in general.
3. Skills related to the transfer process and change management.

Knowledge of the focal context

There has been a longstanding debate concerning the extent to which HRM practices need to fit the local environment, with most of the discussion centering on arguments for and against adaptation to local cultural and institutional conditions (Rosenzweig, 2006). Going beyond this debate, and given that the issue addressed in this chapter is the transfer of parent organization practices, we posit that the more knowledgable the parent organization managers involved in the transfer process are about local conditions at the recipient unit, the more likely are the practices and policies to be implemented and internalized.

We need to explain two issues.

1. How might such parent organization insight be arrived at?
2. What are the mechanisms through which such insight impacts the implementation–internalization matrix?

---

[2]It is worth noting that this knowledge resides within the sender (corporate HQ managers) and within the recipients (subsidiary managers). This means that there may be complex combinations, mutual interdependencies, and potential conflicts between the knowledge held by the two sides, with possible consequences for the effectiveness of the transfer process. Furthermore, the different types of knowledge are also likely to influence each other interdependently. However, for the sake of analytical clarity, we focus our discussion on the different types of human capital and leave the issue of interdependence for future research.

Parent organization managers may have augmented their understanding of the local context during expatriate assignments, for instance, through extensive visits to the focal country or formal and/or informal training and coaching, or they may originate from the country in question. Mechanisms through which such insights influence the design and implementation of systems include the following:

1. These managers might be better equipped to explain how the proposed policies and practices could contribute to subsidiary operations within the constraints of the local cultural and institutional environment.
2. They may also be able to make minor adaptations in keeping with the overall goals of the system, so as to improve the contextual fit.
3. Decision makers at the subsidiary may consider parent organization managers with a thorough understanding of the local context more trustworthy advocates of the proposed system, thereby enabling more honest discussion and transparency in terms of devising alterations on their behalf.
4. Corporate managers who understand the current HRM system of the recipient subsidiary, and the extent to which different actors are satisfied with various aspects of the existing systems, may be better equipped to present the value added of a proposed new system.
5. They may also be more likely to better understand the potential resistance toward the introduction of a new system that stems from a commitment to other existing subsidiary practices.

Therefore, we put forward the following propositions:

PROPOSITION 1A: *The implementation of the MNC performance appraisal policies and practices in a subsidiary is positively associated with the level of knowledge about the subsidiary and its context among the key managers in the parent organization.*

PROPOSITION 1B: *The internalization of the MNC performance appraisal policies and practices in a subsidiary is positively associated with the level of knowledge about the subsidiary and its context among the key managers in the parent organization.*

Turning to the knowledge of the subsidiary managers, we posit that when the foreign subsidiary is staffed predominately with expatriates, the management team is likely to know less about the local context than if it comprised host country nationals. Expatriates have often used the parent organization's performance management systems, and are therefore likely to attempt to introduce similar practices at the subsidiary level. Indeed, recent research has pointed to their role in transferring knowledge and organizational practices from headquarters to subsidiaries (Bonache and Brewster, 2001; Mäkelä, 2007; Minbaeva and Michailova, 2004), and has found a positive relationship between the number of expatriates and the degree to which subsidiary HRM practices resemble those of the parent (Rosenzweig and Nohria, 1994; Björkman and Lu, 2001). Hence, we would expect there to be a negative relationship between the subsidiary management's local understanding – as reflected in the number of expatriates in top management – and the implementation of parent organization practices.

The relationship between the use of expatriate managers and the internalization of the performance management policies and practices of the parent organization is less clear. Although expatriates may be closely involved in deciding which policies and practices should be implemented in the subsidiary, local employees may have a more cautious or even a negative attitude toward systems imposed by expatriates (and, possibly, MNC headquarters).

PROPOSITION 1C: *The implementation of MNC parent organization performance appraisal policies and practices in a subsidiary is positively associated with the number of expatriate managers in the subsidiary.*

PROPOSITION 1D: *Compared with the level of implementation, the internalization of the MNC parent organization performance appraisal policies and practices in the subsidiary is less positively associated with the number of expatriate managers.*

Knowledge of performance management

Our second proposition relates to the knowledge of the performance management system itself. Someone seen as an expert is more likely to be able to influence the views and behavior of the recipient, as an expert is typically perceived to be credible (Szulanski, 1996). Furthermore, MNC headquarters managers with extensive knowledge of performance management – involving the setting of goals, the provision of feedback, and dealing with the interpersonal conflicts that may arise – are in a better position to explain how the parent organization system works and contributes to superior performance, and similarly to argue for its contribution to the subsidiary's performance. Therefore, we would expect there to be a positive association between the level of professional knowledge regarding performance management among key headquarters managers and the levels of subsidiary implementation and internalization.

PROPOSITION 2A: *The implementation of the MNC parent organization performance appraisal policies and practices in a subsidiary is positively associated with the level of knowledge about performance management among the key managers in the parent organization.*

PROPOSITION 2B: *The internalization of the MNC parent organization performance appraisal policies and practices in a subsidiary is positively associated with the level of knowledge about performance management among the key managers in the parent organization.*

However, the relationship between knowledge about performance management and the implementation and internalization of the parent organization's systems is less straightforward on the receiver's side. On the one hand, according to the absorptive capacity argument (Cohen and Levinthal, 1990; see also Szulanski, 1996; Lane and Lubatkin, 1998; Lane *et al.*, 2006), the better informed the people in the focal subsidiary are about performance management systems, the easier it should be for them to understand and therefore also to implement such a system in their own organization. Furthermore, line managers in the subsidiary are more likely to adopt new HRM practices if they respect the professional capabilities of the subsidiary HR managers responsible for their introduction. This typically means that the HR function plays a strategic role in the unit (Truss *et al.*, 2002).

On the other hand, a high level of knowledge about performance management is more likely to be found in units that have already invested in a system. In such cases, subsidiary managers may be more reluctant to implement and internalize the system transferred from the parent organization without evidence of improved results. While there is a lack of empirical research to guide us in formulating propositions, it seems that the former absorptive capacity argument may be more persuasive than the latter not-invented-here one. We therefore propose the following:

PROPOSITION 2C: *The implementation of the MNC parent organization's performance appraisal policies and practices in a subsidiary is positively associated with the level of knowledge about performance management among key subsidiary managers.*

PROPOSITION 2D: *The internalization of the MNC parent organization's performance appraisal policies and practices in the subsidiary is positively associated with the level of knowledge about performance management among key subsidiary managers.*

Transfer process and change management skills

Our third proposition relates to knowledge of the process of transfer and that of change management: the way in which transfer to foreign subsidiaries is managed is likely to influence its outcome. Martin and Beaumont (2001) developed a process model of strategic HRM change in MNCs, and suggested a number of key factors that contribute to the successful transfer of HRM policies. They emphasized the role of change management champions at headquarters and subsidiaries, the importance of constructing a persuasive discourse around why certain changes are needed, and the key role of presenting an attractive image of the future state of the organization. Empirical case studies on the transfer of practices within MNCs have also emphasized the role of initiative, change management, and rhetorical devices (Geppert *et al.*, 2003; Martin and Beaumont, 1998).

Furthermore, the importance of due process has been stressed in the context of MNC operations (Kim and Mauborgne, 1993), and this is likely to be equally important in the successful transfer of practices to foreign subsidiaries. Foreign subsidiary managers are more likely to accept decisions on HRM practice implementation if they have been involved in the design and decision-making process. Likewise, if subsidiary managers are given an in-depth rationale for the decisions, they are more likely to implement them (Kim and Mauborgne, 1993). Indeed, perceptions of fair process are likely to influence subsidiary management attitudes toward standardized HRM policies and practices. Although empirical research in this area is limited, existing findings indicate that the use of international project teams may be beneficial for the development and diffusion of 'best HRM practices' within the MNC (Martin and Beaumont, 1998). Thus, knowledge of and an ability to adhere to the principles of due process are likely to contribute positively to the subsidiary adoption of parent company practices. We see the management of the transfer process as a collective phenomenon, and argue that the skills held by the managers of the parent organization will positively influence subsidiary management interpretations of and attitudes toward performance management policies and practices. Consequently, we put forward the following propositions:

PROPOSITION 3A: *The implementation of the MNC parent organization's performance appraisal policies and practices in a subsidiary is positively associated with the level of transfer skills among key managers in the parent organization.*

PROPOSITION 3B: *The internalization of the parent organization's performance appraisal policies and practices in a subsidiary is positively associated with the level of transfer skills among key managers in the parent organization.*

However, according to our observations on the transfer of performance management practices in Finnish MNCs, the change management skills of the subsidiary managers committed to the transfer project are likely to be at least as important for the widespread implementation of parent-company practices and, in particular, for their internalization. Specifically, skills associated with change management may have a significant and positive effect on the implementation and internalization of practices. As Martin and Beaumont (1998) emphasized, the role of change management champions at the subsidiaries is the key to the successful transfer of HRM policies. We argue that, in the context of transferring a performance management system, the more the key subsidiary managers are perceived to hold a belief that the proposed HRM practices will enhance performance, and to have superior change management skills, the more effective will be both the implementation and the internalization. Therefore, we propose the following:

PROPOSITION 3C: *The implementation of the MNC parent organization performance appraisal policies and practices in a subsidiary is positively associated with the level of change management skills among key managers in the subsidiary.*

PROPOSITION 3D: *Compared with the level of implementation, the internalization of parent organization performance appraisal policies and practices in a subsidiary is more positively associated with the level of change management skills among key managers in the subsidiary.*

SOCIAL CAPITAL PROPOSITIONS[3]

Social capital theory has been proposed as a fruitful framework for explaining knowledge transfer within the MNC (e.g., Nahapiet and Ghoshal, 1998; Tsai and Ghoshal, 1998). We draw upon this theory to examine how the relationship between headquarters and the subsidiary may influence the transfer of HRM practices. Nahapiet and Ghoshal (1998: 243) define social capital as 'the sum of the actual and potential resources embedded within, available through, and derived

---

[3]This section builds on arguments put forward in Björkman and Lervik (2007).

from the network of relationships possessed by an individual or social unit', and distinguish three interrelated dimensions:

1. The structural dimension concerns the physical linkages between people or units, such as the existence of interaction ties between actors, the structure of the various ties, and their density and connectivity.
2. The focus in the relational dimension is on the personal relationships, friendships, and relations of mutual respect that have developed through a history of interactions; and includes trust as a key concept.
3. The cognitive dimension encompasses shared representations, interpretations, language, codes, narratives, and systems of meaning.

While there is some overlap between these three dimensions, they are sufficiently distinct to be treated as separate constructs (Nahapiet and Ghoshal, 1998). As these authors argue, each one has a direct impact on internal knowledge sharing within a firm. Tsai and Ghoshal (1998) provided an empirical application of the social capital concept in the MNC context, concluding that interaction ties and shared cognitions influence resource exchange and combination within the MNC both directly and through the inter-unit trust that develops. We follow the arguments put forward by Nahapiet and Ghoshal (1998) in proposing that each of the three dimensions is likely to have a direct influence on the transfer of performance management practices to overseas affiliates.

The structural dimension

The structural dimension of social capital is closely related to what is usually termed in international management research normative (or social) integration mechanisms (Martinez and Jarillo, 1989). Through the use of informal integration mechanisms operating between MNC headquarters and foreign subsidiaries, individuals are likely to develop interpersonal networks (see Harvey and Novicevic, this volume Chapter 6), as well as open and positive attitudes toward other nationalities and cultures (Edström and Galbraith, 1977; see Ng, Van Dyne and Ang, this volume Chapter 5). Previous research results indicate that the creation and transfer of knowledge within MNCs builds on lateral and horizontal relationships between its units (Ghoshal and Bartlett, 1988; Gupta and Govindarajan, 1991; Moingeon, Lumineau, and Perrin, this volume Chapter 13) and individuals (Tsai and Ghoshal, 1998). Therefore, specifically in situations with at least some degree of uncertainty among the subsidiary actors concerning what constitutes efficient and appropriate performance management, intensive interaction ties are likely to be associated with mimetic motives for adopting practices from headquarters. The headquarters management may also use existing interaction ties to persuade the subsidiary to take certain practices on board.

Furthermore, the existence of headquarters–subsidiary interaction ties is likely to lower the costs of practice transfer, as the key actors already know the relevant people in the other unit, or at least they know whom to contact so as to facilitate the implementation. However, we consider it less likely that the mere existence of inter-unit interaction ties will positively influence subsidiary attitudes toward HRM practices. In fact, the use of existing ties to put pressure on the subsidiary to adopt policies and practices may even provoke negative attitudes among the actors in the subsidiary (Kostova and Roth, 2002).

PROPOSITION 4A: *The implementation of MNC parent organization performance management practices and policies is positively associated with the intensity of the interaction ties between the focal subsidiary and headquarters.*

PROPOSITION 4B: *The internalization of MNC parent organization performance management practices and policies in the subsidiary is not significantly associated with the intensity of interaction ties between the focal subsidiary and headquarters.*

The relational dimension

The notions of risk and vulnerability are at the center of most conceptualizations of organizational trust described in the literature (Mayer *et al.*, 1995). Indeed, in the absence of risk, trust is irrelevant because there is no vulnerability. In the MNC context, adopting a new practice from headquarters may have adverse consequences in that the subsidiary may see a risk that headquarters do not have the ability, integrity or benevolence (Mayer *et al.*, 1995) to ascertain efficient practices. Instead, the subsidiary actors may believe that its efforts at adopting parent organization performance management practices will lead to high transfer costs and/or a post-transfer situation in which the subsidiary is less efficient than with its old practices. A high level of trust in the headquarters management may foster the perception that the focal practice is indeed efficient, and the subsidiary may therefore contribute to its implementation (Kostova and Roth, 2002; Tsai and Ghoshal, 1998).

Several studies have confirmed that the existence of a trustful relationship between the 'sender' and the 'receiver' of knowledge tends to enhance intra-MNC knowledge transfer and exchange (e.g., Nahapiet and Ghoshal, 1998; Szulanski, 1996). Kostova and Roth (2002) also found that a subsidiary's trust toward and identification with the parent organization was positively related to the transfer of organizational practices to foreign subsidiaries. Therefore, we put forward the following propositions:

PROPOSITION 5A: *The implementation of the MNC parent organization performance management practices and policies in a subsidiary is positively associated with the level of trust between the focal subsidiary and headquarters.*

PROPOSITION 5B: *The internalization of the MNC parent organization performance management practices and policies in a subsidiary is positively associated with the level of trust between the focal subsidiary and headquarters.*

The cognitive dimension

In our treatment of the cognitive dimension of social capital we follow Nahapiet and Ghoshal (1998) in focusing on the extent to which subsidiary and headquarters management share a language, vocabulary, and narratives. The sharing of a common language and vocabulary makes it easier for subsidiary managers to gain access to and obtain information from people at headquarters, and thereby to recognize the value of the proposed HRM practices. It also enhances the subsidiary's capacity to gain relevant insights from the other party that will facilitate the assimilation of the policies and practices in their own organization (Nahapiet and Ghoshal, 1998). The ability to communicate in a shared natural language, such as English, is important (Marschan *et al.*, 1997; Marschan-Piekkari *et al.*, 1999; Barner-Rasmussen and Björkman, 2007; see Piekkari, 2006 for a review), as is overlap in terms of vocabulary and the meaning attached to highly specialized terms in any one language. As in our discussion on human capital, we note the following mechanisms through which social capital should influence systems design and implementation:

1. MNC scholars have pointed out that the existence of shared company-specific communication codes may serve as valuable assets facilitating the transfer of knowledge among individuals and units (Kogut and Zander, 1996).
2. Stories about the successful use of a performance management practice in the parent organization or other units may motivate the decision makers in the subsidiary to implement it and to be persuasive in terms of explaining how and why to carry it out – thereby influencing both implementation and internalization.
3. There is a growing body of literature suggesting that while subsidiaries may draw on local resources to resist parent company HRM practices perceived as undesirable or not congruent with the local culture, the inverse effect also appears to hold true – the better the parent company practice matches the subsidiary environment and local ways of thinking, the more likely it is to be adopted (Ferner *et al.*, 2004; Myloni *et al.*, 2004; Blazejewski, 2006; Mohan, 2006; Tempel *et al.*, 2006; Edwards, this volume Chapter 11).

We therefore propose the following:

PROPOSITION 7A: *The implementation of MNC parent organization performance management practices and policies in a subsidiary is positively associated with the level of shared cognition between the focal subsidiary and headquarters.*

PROPOSITION 7B: *The internalization of MNC parent organization performance management practices and policies in a subsidiary is not significantly associated with the level of shared cognition between the focal subsidiary and headquarters.*

ORGANIZATIONAL CAPITAL PROPOSITIONS

The organizational capital of a firm has been defined as the 'institutionalized knowledge and experience stored in databases, routines, parents, manuals, structures, and the like' (Youndt *et al.*, 2004: 338), and it is created in different ways. Investments in databases or computerized systems acquired from external suppliers constitute one such way, and even more important is the learning that takes place concerning the kind of policies and practices that are successful. As organizational learning theorists (e.g., Levitt and March, 1988) have argued, when the experiential lessons of organizational history, including interpretations of what works well and what does not, are discussed and debated, they will in time become codified in manuals, checklists and computerized tools, and institutionalized in organizational routines.

However, there are some inherent problems in drawing inferences from history. For instance, the frequently ambiguous nature of cause–effect relationships may lead managers to misread information and engage in superstitious learning (March and Olsen, 1976). It has also been shown that managers often attribute good organizational performance to their own actions, further strengthening existing routines and strategies (Fiske and Taylor, 1991). In the organizational context, the question of who does the learning is crucial. Not only do different groups in the firm have access to different types of information, focus on different issues, and therefore tend to learn about different things, they may also evaluate the outcome of a certain action differently and have different interpretations of what led to it (Huber, 1991).

Furthermore, the impact that learning has on organizational decision making is dependent on the ability of individuals, units, and coalitions to implement what has been learned (Huber, 1991). Actors who pursue their own interests are likely to be selective in terms of the learning points that they share with and adopt from others in the organization. Finally, organizational learning could be said to depend on memory (Levitt and March, 1988; Walsh and Ungson, 1991): what has been learned at a certain point in time may not be available for retrieval at a later stage. Reorganizations and personnel turnover may further aggravate the availability of historical insights into what 'works' and what does not. Learning is most likely to have a positive impact on organizational performance when the actors collectively engage in the process of first explicitly sharing and then critically discussing and articulating what worked and what did not, and when these lessons are codified in tools, databases, and blueprints (Zollo and Winter, 2002; Zollo and Singh, 2004).

At least two aspects of organizational capital are relevant as far as the adoption of MNC parent organization performance management systems in the subsidiary is concerned:

1. *Codification*: The existence of manuals, tools, and computerized systems that have already proved successful is likely to facilitate the transfer. A proven success record makes it easier to induce recipients to engage in the transfer process (Szulanski, 1996). The more the various elements of the performance management system are codified, the less burdensome it is likely to be to explain the parent organization's practices, which in turn will make the process of transfer easier and less costly (Kogut and Zander, 1992).

2. *Organizational learning related to the international transfer of practices*: There are a considerable number of studies on how organizations become more proficient through processes of learning. For example, research has shown that corporations investing in critical reflection on their experiences, and in the codification of their interpretations of what constitutes successful practices,

are better at integrating acquired units (Zollo and Singh, 2004). Although we are unaware of similar research in the context of MNC-internal transfers of organizational practices in general, and of performance management systems in particular, we consider it likely that a similar mechanism is also at play here.

We therefore put forward the following propositions concerning the relationship between the level of codification of the performance management system and the experience of transferring HRM policies and practices on the part of the MNC on the one hand, and the implementation and internalization of the system in the foreign subsidiary on the other:

PROPOSITION 8A: *The implementation of the MNC parent organization's performance management practices and policies in a subsidiary is positively associated with the level of codification in the system and in the transfer process.*

PROPOSITION 8B: *The internalization of the MNC parent organization's performance management practices and policies in a subsidiary is positively associated with the level of codification in the system and in the transfer process.*

PROPOSITION 8C: *The implementation of the MNC parent organization's performance management practices and policies in a subsidiary is positively associated with its experience of transferring HRM policies and practices to its foreign subsidiaries.*

PROPOSITION 8D: *The internalization of the MNC parent organization's performance management practices and policies in a subsidiary is positively associated with its experience of transferring HRM policies and practices to its foreign subsidiaries.*

CONCLUSION

In this chapter we have developed a model of the MNC internal factors that influence the adoption of the parent organization's performance management practices and policies in a subsidiary. The focus of the model is on how human, social, and organizational capital – in both the headquarters and in the focal subsidiary – influences a subsidiary's implementation and internalization of the policies and practices. It is our hope that the model will inspire researchers to conduct further conceptual and empirical research on this important topic. Of the three forms of capital discussed in this chapter, most of the empirical work carried out to date has concentrated on the impact of social capital on the transfer of knowledge and/or organizational practices. We encourage scholars with an interest in international HRM to also examine how human and organizational capital within the MNC might be related to the adoption of corporate practices.

In encouraging work of this nature, we should also point out some of the issues that researchers may have to deal with. One of the limitations of our model is its focus on MNC internal issues. Previous studies have considered the effect of external factors such as the cultural and institutional distance (Kostova and Roth, 2002) between the host country and the MNC home country, and these findings should be integrated with MNC internal factors, including the consideration of possible interaction effects. Additional MNC internal variables, such as the mode of subsidiary establishment (Nohria and Rosenzweig, 1994) and the level of subsidiary autonomy (Björkman and Lervik, 2007), may also need to be included. Finally, we encourage scholars to go beyond the subsidiary level of analysis that we have examined in this chapter, and to analyze individual level differences among users of performance management systems.

REFERENCES

Armstrong, M., and Baron, A. (1998). *Performance Management. The New Realities.* Chartered Institute of Personnel and Development (CIPD).

Barner-Rasmussen, W., and Björkman, I. (2007). Language fluency, socialization and inter-unit relationships in Chinese and Finnish subsidiaries. *Management and Organization Review*, 3 (1), 105–128.

Becker, G.S. (1964). *Human Capital: A Theoretical and Empirical Analysis.* Chicago; University of Chicago Press.

Bhattacharya, B., and Wright, P.M. (2005). Managing human assets in an uncertain world: Applying real options theory to HRM. *International Journal of Human Resource Management*, 16 (6), 929–948.

Björkman, I., and Lervik, J.-E. (2007). Transferring HRM practices within multinational corporations. *Human Resource Management Journal*, 17 (4), 320–335.

Björkman, I., and Lu, Y. (2001). Institutionalization and bargaining power explanations of HRM practices in joint ventures – the case of Chinese–Western joint ventures. *Organization Studies*, 22 (3), 491–512.

Blazejewski, S. (2006). Transferring value-infused organizational practices in multinational companies. In M. Geppert and M. Mayer (eds). *Global, National and Local Practices in Multinational Companies.* Hampshire: Palgrave Macmillan, pp. 63–104.

Bonache, J., and Brewster, C. (2001). Knowledge transfer and the management of expatriation. *Thunderbird International Business Review*, 43 (1), 145–168.

Bratton, J., and Gold, J. (2007). *Human Resource Management. Theory and Practice* (4th edn). Hampshire: Palgrave Macmillan.

Cascio, W.F. (2006). Global performance management systems. In G.K. Stahl and I. Björkman (eds), *Handbook of Research in International Human Resource Management.* Cheltenham: Edward Elgar.

Cohen, W.M., and Levinthal, D. (1990). Absorptive capacity: A new perspective on learning and innovation. *Administrative Science Quarterly*, 35 (1), 128–152.

Edström, A., and Galbraith, J.R. (1977). Transfer of managers as a coordination and control strategy in multinational organizations. *Administrative Science Quarterly*, 22 (2), 248–263.

English, G. (1991). Tuning up for performance. *Training and Development Journal*, April, pp. 56–60.

Ferner, A., Almond, P., and Colling, T. (2005). Institutional theory and the cross-national transfer of employment policy: The case of 'workforce diversity' in US multinationals. *Journal of International Business Studies*, 36 (3), 304–321.

Ferner, A., Almond, P., Clark, I., Colling, T., and Edwards, T., Holden, L., and Muller-Carmen, M. (2004). The dynamics of central control and subsidiary anatomy in the management of human resources: Case study evidence from US MNCs in the UK. *Organization Studies*, 25 (3), 363–391.

Fiske, S.T., and Taylor, S.E. (1991). *Social cognition* (2nd edn.). New York: McGraw Hill.

Geppert, M., and Mayer, M. (eds) (2006). *Global, National and Local Practices in Multinational Companies.* Hampshire: Palgrave Macmillan.

Geppert, M., Matten, D., and Williams, K. (2003). Change management in MNCs: How global convergence intertwines with national diversities. *Human Relations*, 56 (7), 807–838.

Ghoshal, S., and Bartlett, C.A. (1988). Creation, adoption, and diffusion of innovations by subsidiaries of multinational corporations. *Journal of International Business Studies*, 19 (3), 365–388.

Gupta, A.K., and Govindarajan, V. (1991). Knowledge flows and the structure of control within multinational corporations. *Academy of Management Review*, 16 (4), 768–792.

Hannon, J., Huang, I.-C., and Jaw, B.-S. (1995). International human resource management and its determinants: The case of subsidiaries in Taiwan. *Journal of International Business Studies*, 26 (3), 531–554.

Hartog, D.N. Den, Bosalie, P., and Paauwe, J. (2004). Performance management: a model and research agenda. *Applied Psychology: An International Review*, 53 (4), 556–569.

Huber, G. (1991). Organizational learning: The contributing processes and the literatures. *Organization Science*, 2, 88–115.

Kim, W.C., and Mauborgne, R. (1993). Procedural justice, attitudes, and subsidiary top management compliance with multinationals' corporate strategic decisions. *Academy of Management Journal*, 36 (3), 502–526.

Kogut, B., and Zander, U. (1996). What firms do? Coordination, identity and learning. *Organization Science*, 7 (5), 502–518.

Kostova, T. (1999). Transnational transfer of strategic organizational practices: A contextual perspective. *Academy of Management Review*, 24 (2), 308–224.

Kostova, T., and Roth, K. (2002). Adoption of an organizational practice by subsidiaries of multinational corporations: Institutional and relational effects. *Academy of Management Journal*, 45 (1), 215–233.

Kostova, T., and Zaheer, S. (1999). Organizational legitimacy under conditions of complexity: The case of the multinational enterprise. *Academy of Management Review*, 24 (1), 64–81.

Kristensen, P.H., and Zeitlin, J. (2005). *Local Players in Global Games: The Strategic Constitution of a Multinational Corporation.* Oxford: Oxford University Press.

Lane, P.J., Koka, B.R., and Pathak, S. (2006). The reification of absorptive capacity: A critical review and rejuvenation of the construct, *Academy of Management Review*, 31: 833–863.

Lane, P.J., and Lubatkin, M. (1998). Relative absorptive capacity and interorganizational learning. *Strategic Management Journal*, 19, 461–477.

Lepak, D.P. and Snell, S.A (2002). The strategic management of human capital: Determinants and implications of different relationships. *Academy of Management Review*, 24 (1), 18.

Lervik, J.E. (2005). Managing matters: Transferring organizational practices within multinational companies. Dr. oecoon dissertation, BI.

Lervik, J.E., and Lunnan, R. (2004). Contrasting perspectives on the diffusion of management knowledge – performance management in a Norwegian multinational. *Management Learning*, 35 (3), 287–302.

Levitt, B., and March, J.G. (1988). Organizational learning. In W.R. Scott and J. Blake (eds), *Annual Review of Sociology*. Palo Alto: Annual Reviews, pp. 319–340.

Mäkelä, K. (2007). Knowledge Sharing through Expatriate Relationships: A Social Capital Perspective. *International Studies of Management and Organization*, 37 (3), 108–126.

March, J.G., and Olsen, J.P. (1976). *Ambiguity and choice in organizations.* Bergen: Scandinavian University Press.

Marschan, R., Welch, D.E., and Welch, L.S. (1997). Language: The forgotten factor in multinational management. *European Management Journal*, 15, 591–598.

Marschan-Piekkari, R., Welch, D.E., and Welch, L.S. (1999). In the shadow: The impact of language on structure, power and communication in the multinational. *International Business Review*, 8, 421–440.

Martin, G., and Beaumont, P.B. (1998). Diffusing 'best practice' in multinational firms: Prospects, practice and contestation. *International Journal of Human Resource Management*, 9 (4), 671–695.

Martin, G., and Beaumont, P.B. (2001). Transforming multinational enterprises: Towards a process model of strategic human resource management change. *International Journal of Human Resource Management*, 12 (8), 1234–1250.

Martinez, J.I., and Jarillo, J.C. (1989). The evolution of research on coordination machanisms in multinational corporations. *Journal of International Business Studies*, 20 (Fall), 489–514.

Mayer, R.C., Davis, J.H., and Schoorman, F.D. (1995). An integrative model of organizational trust. *Academy of Management Review*, 20 (3), 709–734.

Meyer, J.W., and Rowan, B. (1977). Institutional organizations: Formal structure as myth and ceremony. *American Journal of Sociology*, 83, 340–363.

Minbaeva, D.B., and Michailova, S. (2004). Knowledge transfer and expatriation in multinational corporations: The role of disseminative capacity. *Employee Relations*, 26 (6), 663–679.

Mohan, A. (2006). Variation of practices across multiple levels within transnational corporations. In M. Geppert and M. Mayer (eds). *Global, National and Local Practices in Multinational Companies*. Hampshire: Palgrave Macmillan, pp. 105–145.

Molleman, E., and Timmerman, H. (2003). Performance management when innovation and learning become critical performance indicators. *Personnel Review*, 32 (1), 93–113.

Myloni, B., Harzing, A.W., and Mirza, H. (2004). Host country specific factors and the transfer of human resource management practices in multinational companies. *International Journal of Manpower*, 25 (6), 518–534.

Nahapiet, J., and Ghoshal, S. (1998). Social capital, intellectual capital, and the organizational advantage. *Academy of Management Review*, 23 (2), 242–266.

Nohria, N., and Rosenzweig, P. (1994). Influences on human resource management practices in multinational corporations. *Journal of International Business Studies*, 25 (2), 229–251.

Piekkari, R. (2006). Language effects in multinational corporations: A review from an international human resource management perspective. In G.K. Stahl and I. Björkman (eds), *Handbook of Research in International Human Resource Management*. Cheltenham: Edward Elgar, pp. 536–550.

Rosenzweig, P.M. (2006). The dual logics behind international human resource management: Pressures for global integration and local responsiveness. In G.K. Stahl and I. Björkman (eds), *Handbook of Research in International Human Resource Management*. Cheltenham: Edward Elgar, pp. 36–48.

Rosenzweig, P.M., and Nohria, N. (1994). Influences on human resource management practices in multinational corporations. *Journal of International Business Studies*, 25, 229–251.

Sparrow, P.R., Brewster, C., and Harris, H. (2004). *Globalizing Human Resource Management*. London: Routledge.

Szulanski, G. (1996). Exploring internal stickiness: Impediments to the transfer of best practice within the firm. *Strategic Management Journal*, 17, 27–43.

Tempel, A., Wächter, H., and Walgenbach, P. (2006). The comparative institutional approach to human resource management in multinational companies. In M. Geppert and M. Mayer (eds), *Global, National and Local Practices in Multinational Companies*. Hampshire: Palgrave Macmillan, pp. 17–37.

Townley, B. (1994). *Reframing Human Resource Management. Power, Ethics and the Subject at Work.* London: Sage Publications.

Truss, C., Gratton, L., Hope-Hailey, V., Stiles, P., and Zaleska, J. (2002). Paying the piper: Choice and constraint in changing HR functional roles. *Human Resource Management Journal*, 12 (2), 39–63.

Tsai, W., and Ghoshal, S. (1998). Social capital and value creation: The role of intrafirm networks. *Academy of Management Journal*, 41 (4), 464–476.

Varma, A., Budhwar, P.S., and De Nisi, A. (eds) (2008). *Performance Management Systems: A Global Perspective.* London: Routledge.

Walsh, J.P., and Ungson, G.R. (1991). Organizational Memory. *Academy of Management Review*, 16 (1), 57–91.

Wright, P.M., Dunford, B.B., and Snell, S. (2001). Human Resources and the Resource-Based View of the Firm. *Journal of Management*, 27, 701–721.

Youndt, M.A., Subramaniam, M., and Snell, S.A. (2004). Intellectual capital profiles: an examination of investments and returns. *Journal of Management Studies*, 41 (2), 335–361.

Zaheer, S. (1995). Overcoming the liability of foreignness. *Academy of Management Journal*, 38 (2), 341–363.

Zollo, M., and Winter, S.G. (2002). Deliberate learning and the evolution of dynamic capabilities. *Organization Science*, 13, 339–351.

Zollo, M., and Singh, H. (2004). Deliberate learning in corporate acquisitions: Post-acquisition strategies and integration capability in U.S. bank mergers. *Strategic Management Journal*, 25, 1233–1256.

13

Managing Knowledge Across Boundaries: A Learning Mix Perspective

BERTRAND MOINGEON, FABRICE LUMINEAU, AND
ALEXANDRE PERRIN

INTRODUCTION

At the beginning of the 21st century, we are witnessing a new phase of international integration, driven by the growing interconnectedness of economic activity. As globalization intensifies, organizations face new challenges to sustain and enhance their competitiveness. Moreover, a wider range of forms of international working become possible (see Suutari and Brewster, this volume Chapter 7). The management of human resources is confronted with new issues in cross-national settings where different cultural, political, economic, and legal systems are involved. Sparrow *et al.* (2004) argue that most academic work has concentrated on firms, rather than other interesting global operations or organizations. International HR professionals need to promote innovative ways of working that transcend the boundaries of firms as well as nations (see, for example the discussion of international project teams by Welch, Welch, and Fenwick, this volume Chapter 9). Among the key challenges faced by international human resources management (IHRM), Brewster *et al.* (2005) identify information exchange and knowledge transfer as two of the most prominent drivers of change.

In similar vein, Eunni *et al.* (2006) also point out that doing business in an international setting makes more complex creation, transfer, and application of knowledge. Given that most failures observed in knowledge management initiatives are attributed to a lack of integration, we advocate an integrative perspective. The literature on knowledge management underlines the fact that fragmented initiatives coexist in those organizations which implement knowledge management tools or processes (Choi and Lee, 2003), such as the implementation of knowledge-sharing tools, the creation of a knowledge base, or actions aimed at identifying the organization's competencies. The difficulty lies in articulating these different actions and incorporating them into an integrated approach that can capitalize upon them.

In order to address this problem, in this chapter we take up the challenge of analyzing the management of an inter-organizational community of practice (ICP) through a comprehensive framework (subsequently called the 'Learning Mix'). Attention has been given to the role of networks and the use of social network analysis as a way of understanding the operation of such networks (see also Harvey and Novicevic's discussion of social capital, this volume Chapter 6; Sparrow, Brewster, and Ligthart, this volume Chapter 18).

Communities of practice are more than networks, however. Communities of practice (CoPs) are mechanisms through which collective knowledge can be created, held and transferred. They have been the subject of much recent debate (Handley *et al.*, 2006; Roberts, 2006). Communities of practice bring together, on a voluntary basis, individuals sharing the same interests (for a vocation, product, technology, and so forth). They make an ideal place for knowledge management to take place (Brown and Duguid, 1991; Wenger, 1998; Wenger *et al.*, 2002). Sparrow (2006) argues that attention has focused on unstructured, spontaneous, self-managing and emergent groups, and the social interactions within and outside them, that surround learning, the ways in which meaning is negotiated and materializes through processes of participation and engagement, and the development of shared repertoires of knowledge. Although the extent to which such processes can be managed is open to debate, managers (and their organizations) are assumed to be able to identify the networks that might constitute a community of practice at any one point of time and facilitate the development of such communities in two ways:

(1) by encouraging the alignment of new practices that result; and
(2) by promoting the lateral processes and organizational forms that might assist their operation.

Inter-organizational communities of practice (ICPs) bring another layer of complexity. In addition to the above, they challenge us to revisit the notions of organizational boundaries (Moingeon *et al.*, 2006). In this chapter we bring conceptual analysis of ICPs and knowledge management together with some exploratory empirical research that we have been undertaking on an *international* ICP (AUGI – Autodesk User Group International). We have conducted an exploratory empirical study of a user group and have applied the 'Learning Mix' – an integrative model that was initially designed to approach knowledge management within companies in a comprehensive way – to the study of this ICP. The AUGI community brings together more than 100 000 voluntary individuals worldwide that share a common professional usage of Autodesk's software designed to enable 2D and 3D drawing on a PC (e.g., AutoCad).

The chapter is organized as follows: in the first part we present the integrative model of the 'Learning Mix' and its four facets. In the second part we explain the methodology that we used for the study. In the third part we analyze the AUGI case in depth. Finally, we draw some lessons for HR managers in managing international inter-organizational communities of practice.

THE LEARNING MIX: AN INTEGRATIVE MODEL

Key characteristics of a learning organization include the collective capacity of its members to capitalize on experience gained, to share knowledge, to acquire new knowledge, to innovate, to solve problems, particularly sensitive ones, instead of seeking to cover them up (Levitt and March, 1988). In operational terms, we argue that this means that four different dimensions of the Learning Mix need to be managed:

1. *Strategic*: The identification and management of the firm's knowledge domain, that is, both its existing knowledge and the knowledge it needs to acquire to maintain or improve its competitive advantage.
2. *Technological*: The management of information systems, particularly tools devoted to knowledge sharing.
3. *Organizational*: Implementation and management of an organization whose mode of functioning enhances knowledge creation and sharing.
4. *Identity*: Development of a learning identity, which requires, in many cases, a complex approach involving the reassessment and the remodeling of values and reasoning processes.

We outline each of these in turn by laying out the relevant theory.

Strategic dimension: the management of a knowledge portfolio

The first facet of the Learning Mix concerns the firm's knowledge portfolio. The resource-based view of the firm brought to light the key role of these intangible assets in the creation of a competitive advantage (Peteraf, 1993). Although certain knowledge can be easily formalized (explicit knowledge), other knowledge, often referred to as tacit knowledge, is difficult to render explicit and codify. As Polanyi (1966) stresses, we know more than it is possible to express orally. This type of individual expertise, know-how or collective capability is based on tacit knowledge and can be a source of competitive advantage because it is rare, difficult to imitate or to substitute (Barney, 1991). The management of this portfolio must be guided by the quest to achieve a balance between knowledge exploitation and exploration (March, 1991), exploitation facilitating the capitalization of the acquired knowledge base, and exploration leading to the acquisition of new knowledge. However, the logic behind knowledge exploitation has its limitations: a company can become trapped by its own competencies (Levitt and March, 1988). In other words, it will tend to use those that it masters, even if they may not be the most efficient. In this case, what was once a 'core competence' becomes a 'core rigidity' (Leonard-Barton, 1992). These phenomena are often reinforced by the 'not invented here' syndrome, with employees refusing to learn from the external environment, and can ultimately cause the knowledge portfolio to become limited to its existing patrimony.

The work of Davenport and Prusak (1999) contends that knowledge transfer involves two actions:

(1) transmission (sending or presenting knowledge to a potential recipient), and
(2) absorption by that person or group.

It follows that if knowledge has not been absorbed, it has not been transferred. The concept of 'absorptive capacity' has mainly been used to signify a company's ability to recognize, assimilate, and apply external knowledge to commercial ends (Cohen and Levinthal, 1990). Several studies on the knowledge flows of multinational corporations suggest that the absorptive capacity of the receiving unit is the most significant determinant of internal knowledge transfer in multinational corporations (Gupta and Govindarajan, 2000).

First, a company needs to clearly identify existing knowledge, a task that can be quite challenging. The expression 'if only my company knew what it already knows' (O'Dell and Grayson, 1998) is frequently used by managers wishing to better 'know the knowledge' in order to identify the existing patrimony in a precise and reliable manner. As a result of the difficulties firms encounter in attempting to identify and transfer what is known, knowledge is wasted through lack of use. The use of knowledge, unlike that of other resources, does not lead to a reduction in its quality or quantity. On the contrary, it can result in the creation of new knowledge. On the other hand, a lack of use can cause the available knowledge base to shrink. This is also true at the individual level, for example when one does not speak a language or practice a sport over a long period of time.

For companies to innovate, knowledge sharing is not enough. They have to create new knowledge. New organizational knowledge can be created in several ways: by combining the company's knowledge and know-how (Nonaka and Takeuchi, 1995) or by obtaining and integrating external knowledge. It can even come from 'double loop learning' (Argyris and Schön, 1978, 1996), that is, by questioning values, fundamental hypotheses and norms that help to define the knowledge to be mobilized.

Technological dimension: IT systems

The technological dimension of the Learning Mix – arguably the most tangible of the four elements – is the one that has attracted the most attention from companies over the past few years (see also Bondarouk and Rüel, this volume Chapter 14). Certainly, many companies have allocated significant resources to the implementation of information technology (IT) systems related to knowledge management.

First, it is important to note that information and knowledge can be seen as having a hierarchical relationship to each other. Information is data to which an individual attributes significance. As for knowledge, it is necessary for the individual to first structure available information and then to appropriate and incorporate it. From this perspective, managing knowledge is a matter for individuals or groups, and not just a question of management tools themselves. Nevertheless, recent technological evolutions have led to spectacular growth, both in the capacity of IT to handle and stock information and in the different possibilities for communications. For example, customer relationship management is based on the computerized collection and exploitation of extremely large consumer databases, containing information on customer profiles, buying habits and so forth. They help marketing specialists to acquire new knowledge, and thereby increase efficiency. Generally speaking, databases, search engines, expert systems, and other decision-making tools all provide people with information that they cannot otherwise obtain due to the limitations of their memories and cognition. Thus technology can be seen as a source of knowledge (see Bondarouk and Rüel, this volume Chapter 14).

In addition, the internet has led to unprecedented growth in the possibilities for communication and its use has enabled us to overcome some of the constraints imposed by time and space. Information systems play a key role in the sharing of knowledge. However, the significance of IT depends on the knowledge management strategy the company adopts. Hansen *et al.* (1999) highlight the existence of two strategies:

(1) codification, and
(2) personalization.

In the first case, the IT systems, as well as the employees responsible for them, are at the heart of the knowledge management approach. The main stakes lie in identifying knowledge, codifying it and making it available through the IT tool. This strategy is suited to situations in which knowledge can easily be made explicit. In a personalization strategy, the IT system plays a much less central role. The stakes lie in enhancing the capacity of available structures and operational processes for sharing predominantly tacit knowledge: frequent meetings, transversal project teams, and so forth.

Nevertheless, even when the company opts for a codification strategy, the knowledge management tool must remain just that, and not become an end in itself. In other words, knowledge management must not on any account be reduced merely to its technological dimension.

Organizational dimension: a learning structure

'Who does what' when it comes to knowledge management? What are the organizational patterns that favour knowledge sharing and creation? The third facet of the Learning Mix focuses on these questions.

There are relatively few publications devoted to the organization of the knowledge management function and those that exist mainly take a managerial stance (for an exception, see Phillips and Bonner, 2000). This situation attests to the relatively recent nature of this concern among companies (Earl and Scott, 1999). Much of the research in this field is also inspired by knowledge-intensive organizations (e.g., consulting firms). In these types of organizations, whose very existence depends on knowledge management, the role of knowledge management tends to be more clearly defined and specialized. Since the early 1990s, functions such as Chief Learning Officer, Chief Knowledge Officer or Intellectual Capital Director have emerged. According to the companies that use them, these titles address different realities. In short, the Chief Learning Officer is responsible for training programs, the Chief Knowledge Officer, for knowledge sharing tools, and the Intellectual Capital Directors, for patent management. From a broader perspective, these directors must encourage and coordinate actions related to the creation and sharing of knowledge such as implementing specific tools, improving the identification and exploitation of the existing knowledge base, enriching this base by identifying and formalizing the best practices and avoiding 'knowledge loss' – which may occur when employees leave the company (retirement, lay-offs, and voluntary departures). At the divisional level, we see specific roles, such as Knowledge Manager (in charge of the deployment of knowledge management initiatives), or Knowledge Editors responsible for identifying and codifying new knowledge and ensuring that it is updated – for example, by choosing knowledge that must be acquired at the end of a consulting mission, validating it and making it accessible via the IT system.

As Nonaka and Takeuchi (1995) demonstrate, knowledge management requires knowledge conversion processes: the passage from tacit to explicit, from the individual to the collective, and inversely. The management of these processes is one of the main missions entrusted to knowledge management specialists. In addition to formally identifying roles devoted to knowledge management, the company's entire structure and operations must be reconsidered so as to facilitate knowledge sharing and creation (Garvin, 1993; Pedler et al., 1991; Goh and Richards, 1997). A learning structure has several characteristics, including project-based and transversal teams (see Welch, Welch, and Fenwick, this volume Chapter 9), few hierarchical levels (flat structure), a limited number of formal procedures as well as employee networks which favor collaboration.

The cultural dimension: a learning identity

This facet is unquestionably the most difficult to grasp as it relates to the least tangible aspects of a company. Indeed, to study an organization's identity is to consider everything that contributes to making it specific, different from others (Larçon and Reitter, 1984; Albert and Whetten, 1985). Beyond identifying managerial procedures, employee behavior, and 'symbolic products' (rituals, organization of time and space, etc.), it is necessary to explore the value system that guides individual behavior and lies behind the official practices and procedures, without people necessarily being aware of it; that is, one must go to the roots of the firm's identity (Moingeon and Ramanantsoa, 1997).

The identity of a company can be said to have five different facets (Soenen and Moingeon, 2002):

(1) professed,
(2) projected,
(3) experienced,
(4) manifested, and
(5) attributed.

On the one hand, top management may state that 'innovation is a critical factor for the company' (professed identity) and communicate it in the Annual Report (projected identity). On the other hand, employees (experienced identity) as well as external stakeholders (attributed identity) may not consider the company as being truly innovative. Moreover, the observation of existing routines and procedures (manifested identity) may support their views.

The analysis of the experienced as well as the manifested identity of a learning firm generally reveals the existence of:

(1) a willingness to make informed choices based on valid information and knowledge (Argyris and Schön, 1974; Argyris, 2004);

(2) a high level of inter-individual trust; this trust is two-fold, as it concerns both colleagues' intentions (e.g., 'When I share knowledge with colleagues, I am not worried because I know that they will not use it against me and my interests') and their competencies (e.g., 'I can ask him to meet my important clients for me; I know that everything will go well. He is an excellent people person') (Moingeon and Edmondson, 1998);

(3) a collective capacity to confront the 'real problems' in a constructive manner, that is, without adopting defensive arguments when the problem discussed is potentially sensitive (Argyris, 1993, 2004); and

(4) the right to make mistakes and a 'psychologically safe' environment when problematic situations arise (Edmondson, 1999).

On the road to building a learning identity, there can be numerous obstacles to overcome. For instance, employees can develop the 'not invented here' syndrome without even being aware of doing so. This leads them to refuse external knowledge, which is knowledge from outside their company or even their division or team. This syndrome can be attributed to there being too much emphasis placed on technical excellence, which makes it difficult to accept and give recognition to external technical expertise. Some companies have decided to fight this syndrome by actively rewarding the use of knowledge coming from other firms or entities (e.g., British Petroleum's 'Thief of the Year' award).

Another significant hurdle is the system of wages, status, and power. While isolated initiatives have their limitations, managing a company's identity involves implementing a range of different measures and practices that could help to overcome such obstacles: including knowledge management in the objectives and remuneration policy (especially by rewarding those who acquire new knowledge *and* share it with others); recognizing the right to make mistakes – given their value for learning; and inviting key managers to be role models (the executive committee should be recognized by all as an opportunity to share and create knowledge).

RESEARCH SETTING, METHODS, AND DATA

Research setting

Our research was focused on the study of AUGI, the Autodesk User Group International. Autodesk is the world leader in Computer Aided Design (CAD) software. This is an inter-organizational community of practice (ICP) that operates across international boundaries. As such, it represents an under-researched form of international work (see Suutari and Brewster, this volume Chapter 7, for an analysis of different forms of international working). Autodesk's products (which have six million users worldwide) help designers, engineers, and video games developers to design and draw complex objects in two dimensions (2D) or in three dimensions (3D). AUGI has two main goals.

1. To assist its members by issuing them with programs and information that will enhance their use of Autodesk products. The use of CAD software is complex by nature. Users need to devote a lot of time improving their skills with the software before they can be considered experts. In the case of AUGI, the relevant knowledge is not limited to the software's technical functions, but covers a set of frameworks, ideas, tools, information, styles, languages, stories, and documents shared by members of the community to help with the actual use of the software.
2. To be the voice of the user community in relation to Autodesk, thereby assisting Autodesk in product development and giving users a say in the process.

AUGI was chosen as the object of study for three reasons.

1. Its community crosses boundaries in many respects: AUGI members belong to different organizations, different countries and different industries such as building, manufacturing, infrastructure engineering, media, and entertainment. Members can be employed in companies that compete on the same market or can be self-employed.
2. It attracts individuals that use Autodesk's products for professional activities. Unlike traditional user groups, AUGI is a community directly managed by its members; it is an autonomous and independent community. Members share some common practices or problems related to the use of Autodesk's software. Given that AutoCAD's native file format (.DWG) has become the *de facto* standard for the exchange of 2D CAD data, many professionals are required to have a good level of knowledge of the software.
3. It is a mature structure. It was founded in 1989 in North America, and is now present worldwide. The community brings together more than 100 000 volunteers with common professional usage of the Autodesk software. Membership is free. AUGI offers programs and services such as a website with many forums, newsletters, and training sessions created by peers – called 'CAD Camps' – which give the Autodesk user community access to the knowledge of others.

Our unit of analysis is the AUGI community as a whole. However, our study has included different sub-communities: the Product Communities – which provide member-focused content regarding specific Autodesk products, and the Local Chapters – which exist for specific regions or cities. It also includes the productions of the community (the publications – such as the *wish list* and the *tips and tricks* – and the training sessions), and finally AUGI's internal rules.

Methods

The goal of this research was to analyze the management of ICPs. In order to grasp as finely as possible each of the four dimensions of the Learning Mix, the research was conducted using qualitative research methods (Miles and Huberman, 1994) based on a single case study (Eisenhardt, 1989; Yin, 2003). The Learning Mix was used to define the different categories for coding the data collected.

Data collection

Our data collection was based on a complementary set of four approaches: a 'netnography', an analysis of archival data, interviews of community volunteers and direct observations of meetings organized by the community.

First, the study was initiated by using a 'netnographic' approach (Kozinets, 1998). Netnography, a technique used by marketers to analyze cybercultures, is described as the textual output of internet-related fieldwork and is in essence an interpretative methodology (Jeppesen and Frederiksen, 2006). We became members of the community and browsed the website. This gave us access to questions and answers posted on online forums. The objective was to improve our understanding of the 'local language' used by the community, user interests, and knowledge exchanged.

Second, we collected secondary and archival data – both internal and external to AUGI – on the community, its environment, and its members. This was derived from a speech made by a former president of the community who explained, year after year, the different highlights or events that had marked AUGI's evolution between 1989 and 2005. In addition to the AUGI's history, we gathered many documents exchanged by users. These included tips and tricks for using AutoCAD, questions and answers posted on the website, and newsletters sent to AUGI members.

Third, to further our understanding of AUGI, 24 interviews were conducted. We interviewed 12 volunteers face-to-face (six in 2005 and six in 2006) that devote time to the organization of AUGI. These people are past and current members of the board of directors. In addition, we carried out telephone interviews of three former AUGI presidents. We also interviewed three consultants who were in charge of structuring the governance of the AUGI community. Finally, we did face-to-face interviews of six Autodesk users who are also members of AUGI. The interviews were semistructured and conducted according to a protocol. All interviews were recorded and transcribed. A total of 24 hours and more than 60 pages of interviews were analyzed. The facets defined in the Learning Mix helped us to code different categories in the data collected. The analysis software NVivo was used to code our data.

Fourth, we observed face-to-face interactions between the members of the community. It was possible to carry out this observation at the Autodesk University, an event which brought 7600 Autodesk users and employees to Las Vegas. During this event, AUGI had its own booth where members could meet and talk. We spent several days observing this booth and discussed informally with many participants about the value of being part of the community. Memos were written to capture our feelings and thoughts on what we observed during meetings and social events.

CASE STUDY: THE AUTODESK USER GROUP INTERNATIONAL

Our case study, designed to address the issue of knowledge management in inter-organizational communities of practice, is presented in four parts. We look at:

(1) how the portfolio of practices evolves;
(2) the use of information sharing tools;
(3) governance of the community; and
(4) the creation of shared identities.

We would note that these underlying processes become particularly important in the study of communities of practice that span international – and not just inter-organizational – boundaries. Throughout the data analysis process, findings were grouped into the four categories outlined earlier reflecting the facets of the Learning Mix.

An evolving portfolio of practices

In AUGI, the evolution of the knowledge portfolio is made according to

(1) a set of issues,
(2) the development of common practices, and
(3) the quality of the available content.

In relation to the first of these – issues raised by members are related to the efficient use of Autodesk's products. This preoccupation is related to the complexity, flexibility, and huge potential of the AutoCAD software. In theory, any user could rely on the manual that accompanies the software. In reality, users often feel the need to ask for support from peers. AUGI offers them the opportunity to tap into a portfolio of user practices through, in particular, an online forum. Members of the community post their problems on the online forum, and their peers offer solutions whenever possible. In that way, they obtain solutions to problems relatively quickly and they also have the pleasure of helping others because the issue is relevant to other members.

> At night, some people read a book or watch television … I prefer going on AUGI because when I need help, I always find a buddy that can help me right away. 80% of the questions raised are answered in less than two hours, 90% in less than one day.
>
> (An AUGI member)
>
> AUGI Forum members commit themselves to helping their fellow members in whatever way they can, and as fast as they can.
>
> (AUGI website guideline)

In relation to the development of common practices, what guides the actual learning of the community is an insider's view of the knowledge portfolio. Every member compares her or his own practices to the available ones in AUGI. Members can assess what they can learn from the community and what they can bring to others. Participation in the community thus enhances the quality and the quantity of the portfolio. It is true that a practice is built up from social activities which take place when participating in the community (Brown and Duguid, 1991; Lave and Wenger 1991; Wenger 1998). AUGI gives members a sense of belonging, of having access to a place where members solve problems together and where they learn from each other's perspectives. This participation is supported by the question/answer process and monitored by the forum moderator.

> If a member is asking something that has already been answered, it is the role of the forum moderator not to put the question online. We send a mail to the requester explaining where he can find the existing answer. It enables us to reduce the redundancy of information.
>
> (An AUGI forum moderator)

Finally, in relation to the quality of the portfolio, the forum moderator ensures that the quality of the knowledge portfolio is maintained; issues are up-to-date and solutions offered are accurate. Moderators are identified from within the community. They are unpaid volunteers who receive no compensation for the time they devote to AUGI. Moderators play an important role in enriching the available content because they have the ability to assess the quality of a better practice. In some cases, the best practices identified by the moderator can become official 'AUGI Tips and Tricks'. In that case, the tip is codified on an electronic document according to a specific template. In the short term, this active participation is rewarded formally by the publication of the Trick. In the long term, an active participant can become recognized as an expert within the community. This type of appointment is perceived by AUGI members as an achievement.

> If a member is recognized as a main contributor of AUGI Tips and Tricks, he can be identified as a potential forum moderator. He is interviewed and appointed by the Board of Director. Many active members of AUGI have moved into better positions in their own corporations because they have been officially considered within AUGI as expert. This is a kind of personal achievement!
>
> (An AUGI director)

> A user group is not a television: we only get out of this organization what we put into it.
>
> (A former AUGI president)

The information sharing tools

In AUGI, the portfolio of practices is available on a website. The information sharing tools serve two purposes:

1. Gathering different sources of information.
2. Acting as a robust information system.

In relation to different sources of information, the AUGI's ability to connect members worldwide is based on strong relationships enhanced by the website. So far, the AUGI website, created in the 1990s, has always been the backbone for the exchange of practices. Using a website implies identifying knowledge, codifying it, and making it available through a database. The AUGI forums, for example, build a searchable knowledge base by maintaining a database record of all communications posted to them. In this way, the portfolio is readily available to the members. This codification of member practices is suited to situations in which knowledge can easily be made explicit. The codification of knowledge on the website is relevant to the software community. Indeed, members are familiar with IT tools because they are part and parcel of their professional practice. This ease of use enables the community to provide various forms of knowledge, like Tips and Tricks, Publications (newsletters such as *AUGIWorld*), FAQ, Questions and Answers, and a wish list of improvements to Autodesk. On the AUGI website, information is not only pulled from users but also pushed to members according to their interests, language or country. For example, three country chapters (such as Japan or Scandinavia) were created in the last few years.

> Our website reflects our organization: it's all about users helping users.
>
> (AUGI website)

> *AUGIWorld*, the official publication of AUGI, is a bimonthly magazine designed to help readers to improve their use of Autodesk products and learn new techniques. Every issue is packed with product tips and tricks and other technical fare, CAD management issues, and education trends.
>
> (AUGI website)

In relation to the development of a robust information system, the AUGI website has been highly successful: the number of hits on the website skyrocketed over the last few years. More than 12 million pages have been viewed in the last year. AUGI has gone from being a community of 10 000 users six years ago to having more than 100 000 registered members today. This was made possible by having a robust technological backbone. Between 2000 and 2002, this mind-boggling increase in membership caused chaos. In fact, the technological facility was simply underpowered to handle the number of members. Due to technical problems, a full-time webmaster was appointed in 2001. This investment was supported financially through paid training events organized by AUGI volunteers. Money is generated from face-to-face meetings, such as CAD Camps or Conferences. The website owes its existence to the physical meetings that take place.

> The website and e-mail (+ directory) became the backbone for knowledge sharing in 2000. Email became the definitive means by which AUGI maintained contact with its membership (instead of the older published newsletter or through snail mailings).
>
> (A former AUGI president)

Clear governance of the community

Analysis of the community's governance reveals the importance of three issues:

(1) the existence of an elected board of directors,
(2) the use of an external/neutral consulting company, and
(3) independence from Autodesk.

The AUGI Board of Directors was created in 1989. The Board of Directors defines the internal rules for the community. The AUGI President is elected every two years and rules are changed every three or four years. For example, the Board of Directors appoints forum moderators every three years. As mentioned previously, forum moderators play a critical role in ensuring the quality of the knowledge portfolio is maintained. The Board also has the capacity to exclude members from the community, although it has only done so twice in the history of AUGI. It is necessary to have management experience to become a member of the Board of Directors. The rules for joining the Board were defined year after year, very intuitively. Becoming a member of the Board is also seen has an achievement within the community.

> In 1989, the first Board of Directors was voted into office, and the first Bylaws were voted into place. I don't think most people realise how much effort the first Board of Directors poured into the first draft of the Bylaws.
>
> (A former AUGI president)

> What does it mean to be a member of the Board of Directors? Members new to the Board of Directors rarely had any idea what their duties and responsibilities were, let alone what they could and could not expect in the way of required travel, and days off for AUGI business. There really was no manual for being a Board Member, and it made sense to put one together so that members could know what they were really volunteering for.
>
> (A former AUGI president)

> I think it was my duty and my responsibility to give back to the community what it gave to me.
>
> (A former AUGI president)

The use of an independent consulting company (SolidVapor) is another reason why AUGI managed to define a clear governance structure. The consultancy has provided a methodology to manage AUGI's day-to-day processes. The consultancy is monitored by the Board of Directors, and its main mission is to support the community as a whole. This is done by using leadership, creating excitement, and marketing efforts (gifts, mugs, and t-shirts) at the grassroots level. In addition, the consulting firm provides a methodology for launching local communities in different countries. Thus the firm is providing 'backstage' guidance to the community but it will never appear frontstage before its members.

Without organizational help, a community is only a group of professionals who share what they know sporadically. With an appropriate amount of guidance, such communities can flourish. With a set of rules and structures that encourage critical evaluation of existing knowledge, the participation of members can become fruitful and long-lasting across the boundaries of the company users are working for.

(A consultant)

In relation to the independence from Autodesk. Ten years after AUGI was formed, the organization managed to gain budgetary independence through the help of Autodesk and the Board of Directors. The relationships between AUGI and Autodesk are complex and ever-changing. On the one hand, AUGI provides Autodesk with feedback from users and requests for modifications to the products; on the other hand, Autodesk controls and modifies AutoCAD software. In that reciprocal relationship, the consulting company creates a bridge between Autodesk and AUGI. In that sense, the role of the consultancy is to ensure there are no political games between the two entities.

In 1997, for the first time ever the organization had to deal with dangerous misrepresentations on the account of certain individuals on the Board, and although most of the troubles eventually got ironed out, the fiasco forever changed the way Autodesk viewed the organization's potential to be dangerous if certain members on the board were not careful when representing them in public.

(A former AUGI president)

In 1999, still financially supported by Autodesk, third-party developers, and by membership dues, the Board of Directors worked with Autodesk's legal department this year to set up AUGI as a financially independent organization truly in control of its budget.

(A former AUGI president)

The last few years, 80% of the 'wish list' has been covered by Autodesk and included in the development of the software. Every month they have feedback on the top 5 and top 10 requests from users. Autodesk releases now a new version every year. It was not the case before (every two years).

(A former AUGI president)

A shared identity

Analysis of the creation of a shared identity at AUGI shows that it has grown up through the:

(1) mutual trust of its members and the friendly atmosphere,
(2) clear goal of the community from the beginning, and
(3) possibility to modify the software itself.

In AUGI, there is a high level of inter-individual trust. This trust is linked both to members' intentions and their competencies. This trust enables people to overcome the fear of exchanging knowledge outside the boundary of their own company or organization. A common language and stories have grown up within AUGI. Some private jokes and references to the different speeches made by the AUGI presidents can be found. These references started to appear as a result of the friendship heralded by the volunteers and by the community members.

> When I share knowledge with colleagues [within AUGI], I am not worried because I know that they will not use it against me and my interests.
>
> (An AUGI member)

> AUGI is in my life. I work with it daily. I am not afraid to share what I know with potential competitors because I increase my productivity faster than if I don't share.
>
> (An AUGI member)

> We say that 'In AUGI, everybody is your buddy!' I like sharing in AUGI because the volunteers in charge of AUGI are happy people. They are smiling. I believe they are doing the best they can to help me. I really do.
>
> (An AUGI member)

The professed identity of AUGI – i.e., the objective assigned to the community – has always been clear; this community was created in order for people to help each other. This aim is manifested in the motto, the logo, and the tools used within the community.

> In 1996, the organization needed a motto of some kind for its marketing and the Board of Directors voted on the now familiar AUGI battle-cry 'Educate! Enlighten! Enhance! Empower!'
>
> (A former AUGI president)

> Our motto is now 'Users Helping Users.' Our goal is to implement programs that are lacking in the Autodesk community rather than compete with programs already available to users. We work very hard to promote our membership as a community working together to strengthen each other and the community in general.
>
> (AUGI Website)

The possibility to modify software – the concurrent evolution of AUGI and Autodesk – is also leading to the emergence of a knowledge sharing identity. Since its creation in 1989, this strong sense of belonging has been reinforced by the possibility to modify the software itself. As mentioned above, practices were shared more freely because members felt that they were able to change the final product they were using.

> In the 90s, users discovered that their opinions, expertise, war stories and wish lists mattered to Autodesk, and that AUGI was the vehicle which made this

possible. Autodesk also took AUGI meeting seriously, making sure that users were given every opportunity to express their concerns, and to let them know that their input was valuable to the future of AutoCAD.

(A former AUGI president)

We both need each other. We are conveyers of information in both directions. Autodesk needs to ask end users and the end user needs to ask for modifications to Autodesk.

(A former AUGI president)

Conclusions

Throughout this volume attention has been given to a series of emergent forms of international work, which, by their nature, require novel forms of management (see in particular Welch, Welch, and Fenwick's discussion of international project teams in Chapter 9, and Bondarouk and Rüel's analysis of the use of e-enablement in Chapter 14). We now draw a series of conclusions for International HRM (IHRM) professionals.

Sparrow and colleagues (2004) gave attention to the role of knowledge management processes inside internationalizing organizations. However, our research helps to identify some of the difficulties faced by international HRM managers in helping to define knowledge management policies. With the increased globalization of the economy, managing knowledge within and across boundaries becomes a key challenge for international HR professionals. It requires a comprehensive view that integrates people, context, and process.

A first set of conclusions relate to the gap between the rhetoric and the reality in the management of this form of working. While all companies today agree that knowledge is of paramount importance, few have truly implemented an integrative approach for knowledge management. We support Davenport and Prusak's view that 'when people talk about knowledge management, the conversation often devolves into highly abstract and philosophical statements ... but there is a real world of knowledge management – a world of budgets, deadlines, office politics, and organizational leadership' (Davenport and Prusak, 1999). Thus, one frequently notes a gap between the knowledge management policy that firms profess and their 'theory-in-use' (Argyris and Schön, 1978; Argyris, 2004). Very often, the speeches delivered by the CEOs and the policies stated at the corporate level do not correspond with the practices and behavior observed. The difficulties encountered by HRM practitioners tempted by the knowledge management adventure on the one hand, and by researchers seeking to study this phenomenon, or even by consultants hoping to propose improvements on the other hand, can be explained by the absence of an integrative vision and instead the parceling out of the different approaches.

In this context, the Learning Mix can be a useful analytical tool to diagnose knowledge management in all its complexity: technological, strategic, organizational, and cultural dimensions. In this chapter, we have studied AUGI – an inter-organizational community of practice (ICP) – using the Learning Mix's four dimensions. AUGI appears to be a truly learning structure for four reasons:

(1) its portfolio of knowledge is constantly evolving as a result of members' contributions,
(2) its tools for spreading information are robust,
(3) its governance is clear and well accepted by its members, and
(4) its shared identity facilitates knowledge management.

In other words, this ICP can be seen by HR professionals as a benchmark for managing knowledge in an inter-organizational setting.

A second set of conclusions relate to the observation that ICPs have significant limits. Although ICPs represent exemplary forms of knowledge management, such organizations are, however, not ideal. First, they seem to essentially generate incremental-type innovations and merely extend an already existing practice. ICPs often turn out to be extensions of the practice rather than a break from its fundamental concepts. Second, in the wake of Roberts (2006) who underlines the limits of communities of practice in the field of knowledge management, we extend her view to warn against ICPs' potential downsides. In fact, as noted by Wenger *et al.* (2002), communities of practice are not safe from narcissistic propensities and can even hinder learning. They can be narrowing and create blinders focusing on a given domain, leading to inertia and rigidity (Leonard-Barton, 1992). This is all the more crucial in ICPs, where the vitality of cross-boundary exchanges is a real keystone. Thus, ICPs have to be able to regularly add new members in order to maintain enthusiasm. With poor ICP management, there is a serious risk of breeding an arrogant attitude, where the community then tries to act as a 'thought police' on a given practice.

A third set of conclusions relate to the challenges that face ICPs. Our study explains how ICPs contribute to the gradual overcoming of the different exchange barriers. If advances in communication means have enabled to do away with some spatiotemporal boundaries (cross-border exchanges, asynchronous exchanges, etc.), ICPs are an original way to free knowledge creation from traditional organizational limits. Although they contribute to reducing some constraints, they do not eliminate cultural, sociocognitive, or psychological barriers (see Sackmann's discussion of culture in the context of globalization, this volume Chapter 4). By contributing to the reduction of distances and by making frontiers more and more gradual, permeable, flexible, and dynamic, ICPs lead to a reassessment of the notion of boundaries.

Actually, if the notion of 'community' involves members of a group having something in common with each other, what they share distinguishes them in a significant way from members of other possible groups (Cohen, 1985: 12). In that way, ICPs imply both similarity and difference. ICPs gather people around a practice, but they also emerge from an opposition to others or to other social entities. Thus, it must be noted that if ICPs enable to transcend many traditional boundaries, they also create boundaries of their own. In fact, a boundary places some people within, and some beyond the line. The definition of a community can therefore become an exclusionary act, because the benefits of belonging to a particular group are denied to non-members.

If, in the traditional sense, boundaries may be marked on a map, or in law, or by physical features, ICPs shift the relevant criteria to define boundaries by driving us to focus more on human factors. As noted by Cohen (1985: 118), 'people construct community symbolically, making it a resource and repository of meaning, and a referent of their identity'. As such, ICPs may be seen in very different ways, not only by people on either side, but also by people on the same side, according to how people experience the community. In this regard, ICPs that cross international boundaries represent challenging opportunities for future research in the IHRM field.

REFERENCES

Albert, S., and Whetten, D.A. (1985). Organizational identity. In L.L. Cummings and B.M. Staw (eds), *Research in Organizational Behavior*, 7, 263–295.
Argyris, C. (1993). *Knowledge for Action: A Guide for Overcoming Defensive Behaviors*. San Francisco: Jossey-Bass.
Argyris, C. (2004). *Reasons and Rationalizations. The Limits to Organizational Knowledge*. Oxford: Oxford University Press.
Argyris, C., and Schön, D. (1974). *Theory in Practice*. San Francisco: Jossey-Bass.
Argyris, C., and Schön D. (1978). *Organizational Learning: A Theory of Action Perspective*. Reading, MA: Addison-Wesley.
Argyris, C., and Schön D. (1996). *Organizational Learning II: Theory, Method, and Practice*. Reading, MA: Addison-Wesley.
Barney, J.B. (1991). Firm resources and sustained competitive advantage. *Journal of Management*, 17, 99–120.
Brewster, C., Sparrow, P.R., and Harris, H. (2005). Towards a new model of globalising HRM. *International Journal of Human Resource Management*, 16 (6), 949–970.
Brown, J.S., and Duguid, P. (1991). Organizational learning and communities-of-practice: Toward a unified view of working, learning, and innovation. *Organization Science*, 2 (1), 40–57.
Choi, B., and Lee, H. (2003). Knowledge management enablers, processes, and organizational performance: An integrative view and empirical examination. *Journal of Management Information Systems*, 20 (1), 179–228.
Cohen, A.P. (1985). *The Symbolic Construction of Community*. London: Tavistock.
Cohen, W.M., and Levinthal, D. (1990). Absorptive capacity: A new perspective on learning and innovation. *Administrative Science Quarterly*, 35 (1), 128–152.
Davenport, T., and Prusak, L. (1999). *Working Knowledge: How Organizations Manage What they Know*. Boston: Harvard Business School Press.
Earl, M.E., and Scott I.A. (1999). What is a Chief Knowledge Officer? *Sloan Management Review*. Winter, 29–38.
Edmondson, A. (1999). Psychological safety and learning behavior in work teams. *Administrative Science Quarterly*. 44, 350–383.
Eisenhardt, K.M. (1989). Building theories from case study research. *Academy of Management Review*, 14 (4), 532–550.
Eunni, R.V., Kasuganti, R.R., and Kos, A.J. (2006). Knowledge management processes in international business alliances: A review of empirical research, 1990–2003. *International Journal of Management*, 23 (1), 34.

Garvin, D. (1993). Building a learning organization. *Harvard Business Review*. July–August, 78–91.

Goh, S.C., and Richards, G. (1997). Benchmarking the learning capability of organizations. *European Management Journal*, 15 (5), 575–583.

Gupta A.K., and Govindarajan, V. (2000). Knowledge flows within multinational corporations. *Strategic Management Journal*, 21 (4), 473–496.

Handley, K., Sturdy, A., Fincham, R., and Clark, T. (2006). Within and beyond communities of practice: Making sense of learning through participation, identity and practice. *Journal of Management Studies*, 43 (3), 641–53.

Hansen, M.T., Nohria, N., and Thierney, T. (1999). What's your strategy for managing knowledge? *Harvard Business Review*, 106–116.

Jeppesen, L.B., and Frederiksen, L. (2006). Why do users contribute to firm-hosted user communities? The case of computer-controlled music instruments. *Organization Science*, 17 (1), 45–63.

Kozinets, R.V. (1998). On netnography: Initial reflections on consumer research investigations of cyberculture. *Advances in Consumer Research*, 25 (1), 366–372.

Larçon, L., and Reitter, R. (1984). Corporate imagery and corporate identity. In M. Kets de Vries (ed.), *The Irrational Executive: Psychoanalytic Explorations in Management*. Madison, CT: International Universities Press.

Lave, J., and Wenger, E. (1991). *Situated Learning: Legitimate Peripheral Participation*. Cambridge: Cambridge University Press.

Leonard-Barton, D. (1992). Core capabilities and core rigidities: A paradox in managing new product development. *Strategic Management Journal*, 13, 111–125.

Levitt, B., and March, J.G. (1988). Organizational learning. In W.R. Scott and J. Blake (eds), *Annual Review of Sociology*. Palo Alto: Annual Reviews, pp. 319–340.

March, J.G. (1991). Exploration and exploitation in organizational learning. *Organization Science*, 2 (1), 71–87.

Miles, M., and Huberman, M. (1994). *Qualitative Data Analysis: An Expanded Sourcebook*. London: Sage Publications.

Moingeon, B., and Edmondson, A. (1998). Trust and organizational learning. In N. Lazaric and E. Lorenz (eds), *The Economics of Trust and Learning*. London: Edward Elgar Publishers, pp. 247–265.

Moingeon, B., and Ramanantsoa, B. (1997). Understanding corporate identity: The French school of thought. *European Journal of Marketing*, 31 (5/6), 383–395.

Moingeon, B., Quélin, B., Dalsace, F., and Lumineau, F. (2006). *Inter-Organizational Communities of Practice: Specificities and Stakes*. Working Paper, HEC Paris School of Management.

Nonaka, I., and Takeuchi, H. (1995). *The Knowledge-Creating Company. How Japanese Companies Create the Dynamics of Innovation*. Oxford: Oxford University Press.

O'Dell, C., and Grayson, J. (1998). If only we knew what we know: Identification and transfer of internal best practices. *California Management Review*, 40 (3), 154–174.

Pedler M., Burgoyne, J., and Boydell T. (1991). *The Learning Company*. London: McGraw Hill.

Peteraf, M.A. (1993). The cornerstones of competitive advantage: A resource-based view. *Strategic Management Journal*, 14 (3), 179–191.

Phillips, J.J., and Bonner, D. (eds) (2000). *Leading Knowledge Management and Learning*. Alexendria: ASTD.

Polanyi, M. (1966). *The Tacit Dimension*. London: Routledge & Kegan Paul.

Roberts, J. (2006). Limits to communities of practice. *Journal of Management Studies*, 43 (3), 623–39.

Soenen, G., and Moingeon B. (2002). The five facets of collective identities: Integrating corporate and organizational identity. In B. Moingeon and G. Soenen (eds), *Corporate and*

Organizational Identities: Integrating Strategy, Marketing, Communication, and Organizational Perspectives. London: Routledge, pp. 13–34.

Sparrow, P.R. (2006). Knowledge management in Global organizations. In G. Stahl and I. Björkman (eds), *Handbook of Research into International HRM.* London: Edward Elgar, pp. 113–138.

Sparrow, P.R., Brewster, C., and Harris, H. (2004). *Globalizing Human Resource Management.* London: Routledge.

Wenger, E. (1998). *Communities of Practice: Learning, Meaning, and Identity.* New York: Cambridge University Press.

Wenger, E., McDermott, R., and Snyder, W. (2002). *Cultivating Communities of Practice.* Boston: Harvard Business School Press.

Yin, R. (2003). *Case Study Research: Design and Methods.* Thousand Oaks: Sage.

14

Structuring the IT-enabled Transformation of HR: An HRM Frames Analysis in an International Company

Tanya Bondarouk and Huub Ruël

Introduction

This chapter aims to conceptualize and explore the linkages between the normative foundation underlying the IT-enabled transformation of HR and insights out of sociology in order to bridge the gap between the intentions of IT-enabled human resource management (HRM) and its organizational reality. We start from the theory of structuration (Giddens, 1984), which suggests that social phenomena are dual. They can be understood as shaping human actions whilst also being shaped by them. We apply this belief to explain the dynamic development of HR transformations in organizations, and the relationship of this development with organizational structures.

   We explain how structuration theory may be applied to understand IT-enabled HR transformation. More specifically, we introduce the notion of 'HRM frames' where the HR transformation in organizations (whether IT-enabled or not) influences employees' behaviors at the same time as it is influenced by human actions. This framework allows us to step beyond traditional polarities in HR research (such as debates about individual-level vs macro-level performance outcomes, subjective vs objective, deterministic vs phenomenological, and quantitative vs qualitative). As a result, we aim to analyze the underlying assumptions, values, and interpretations that employees have about the IT-enabled HRM transformation in organizations. We argue that such an analysis is central to understanding the role of the IT-enabled change in the HR processes and their transformation (e.g., role changes,

Handbook of International Human Resource Management.   Edited by Paul R. Sparrow
© 2009 John Wiley & Sons, Ltd

competency modifications, restructuring, and globalization of the HR function). Where the interpretations of key groups of people involved (HR professionals, line managers, and employees) differ significantly, we draw attention to the difficulties and conflicts around the HR transformation that might arise.

After developing this framework, we offer an example of its use in HRM research. We use the findings of an empirical study to illustrate how different stakeholders interpreted the intentions, nature, value and the HR transformation process, resulting in outcomes that deviated from those that were expected. We argue that interpretations of meanings, built on structuration theory, provide a useful analytic perspective for explaining and anticipating such actions and that such insights are not easily obtained using other HRM theoretical lenses.

IT-ENABLED HRM: CURRENT RESEARCH AND RESEARCH QUESTIONS

Modern HRM is one arena in which the dictum *'there is nothing constant but change'* is particularly relevant. One of the recent key drivers of this everlasting change is the application of information technology (IT), supporting its everyday activities, personnel administration, policy development, and decision making. More and more working organizations have been introducing IT for HRM, using a variety of names, for example electronic HRM, digital HRM, virtual HRM. It is probably not surprising therefore that IT is highly praised for its potential positive impact on the ways in which HRM is organized, allocated, and accomplished.

In the literature there is a strong belief that IT should facilitate the role of HRM as a strategic partner, allowing it to undertake critical people management activities (Lepak and Snell, 1998). A number of benefits are expected from the introduction of IT-enabled HRM in organizations (Reilly and Williams, 2003; Ruël *et al.*, 2004):

- ◆ integrated 'total solution' approach to problems through the recentralization of the HR function;
- ◆ more selective and strategic contribution from HRM by freeing staff from the burdens of administration;
- ◆ greater efficiency and professional provision of HR services through simplification and providing a single point of contact for clients;
- ◆ cost-effectiveness;
- ◆ more efficient resourcing through economies of scale in staffing;
- ◆ improved cross-group learning and sharing good practices through having a common information base;
- ◆ better management of information, provided more consistently across the organization as a whole;
- ◆ improved career development for HR staff;
- ◆ higher customer satisfaction through better service specification; and
- ◆ greater transparency of cost of services and easier monitoring of budgets.

Despite the growth of implementation of IT-enabled HRM, organizations continue to experience mixed results. Recent studies, for example, indicate that in nearly half of the companies with a completely integrated HR Information System (HRIS), HRM was not viewed as a strategic partner (Lawler and Mohrman, 2003), but re-alignment of the HRM function led to an increase of the line managers' work stress (Bondarouk and Ruël, 2006).

Academics are devoting more and more attention to examining IT-enabled HRM in attempts to explore this contradiction. Within the last decade, several conclusive notions have been proposed about its goals (Legnick-Hall and Moritz, 2003; Cober *et al.*, 2004; Ruël *et al.*, 2004), its types (Lepak and Snell, 1998), the effectiveness of different applications (Buckley et al, 2004; Hustad and Munkvold, 2005), and the implementation of HRIS (Ball, 2001; Hussain *et al*, 2007). However, The ex-isting research into IT-based HRM has continued using the factor-based approach of analyzing a few variables that influence IT-HRM adoption (Marler *et al.*, 2006), HR competencies (Bell *et al.*, 2006), changes in HRM roles or IT-HRM effectiveness (Bondarouk and Ruël, 2006). Such studies are very useful in sensitizing researchers to issues of importance and help to develop guidelines to overcome constraints to this organizational change, but have been criticized on two grounds. These studies:

- ◆ tend to adopt cross-sectional survey methods, with little consideration of the *dynamics* of the HRM transformation process;
- ◆ are inclined to consider HRM practices as a communication from the em-ployer to employees (Guzzo and Noonan, 1994; Bowen and Ostroff, 2004), with little thought given to the social constructions of HRM by the employees themselves.

Therefore, our chapter aims to make a contribution to the research into IT-enabled HRM transformation by adopting a process approach. It provides an example of HRM transformation attempted with the help of IT in a large international organi-zation. Two key questions motivating our research were:

- ◆ How do social and technological issues explain the IT-enabled HRM transfor-mation?
- ◆ To what extent do beliefs and perceptions influence the IT-enabled HRM trans-formation in a large international organization?

To answer these questions we draw on structuration theory and HRM frames anal-ysis. We demonstrate that IT-enabled HRM transformation is a dynamic process in which stakeholders frame and reframe their perceptions and, thus, actually con-struct the transformation of the HRM function.

STRUCTURATION THEORY

Our research starts from the belief in the importance of subjective meanings as sym-bolic actions in the process through which humans construct and reconstruct their reality. This requires the use of field studies of humans in their social settings so as to understand the social world from the participants' perspectives (Barrett, 1999).

The first step in understanding the basics of structuration theory is to recognize its objectives and driving forces. Giddens (1984) states that the basic domain of social science study is neither the experience of the individual nor the existence of any form of societal totality, but social systems referring to regular patterns of enacted conduct by actors who interact with each other in situations with specific conditions. Giddens proposes to view 'objective' structures and subjective interpretations not as independent (even conflicting) elements but as a mutually interacting duality (Jones and Karsten, 2003). Therefore, social structures can be viewed as created by human agents through their actions, while those actions produce and reproduce the social structures. Structuration is understood as a social process that involves the reciprocal interaction between human agents and structural features of organizations: human actions are enabled and constrained by structures, yet these structures are the result of previous actions.

More specifically, Giddens proposes three dimensions of structures: signification, domination, and legitimation. Attempting to apply the concept of structuration to organizational life, Taylor *et al.* (2000: 79) state that a structured organization implies that

- ◆ there is an established system of domination;
- ◆ the system is legitimated;
- ◆ it is inscribed in the framework of its members, as part of their normal interpretive sense-making.

These dimensions are linked with corresponding dimensions of power, sanction, and communication through modalities of facilities, norms, and interpretive schemes (Figure 14.1).

The recognition that human agents are knowledgable and reflexive is one of the central premises in the theory. Reflexivity is not simply self-consciousness, but mostly the ability of human agents to continuously monitor physical and social contexts and activities. Actions always incorporate all three dimensions. Modalities are

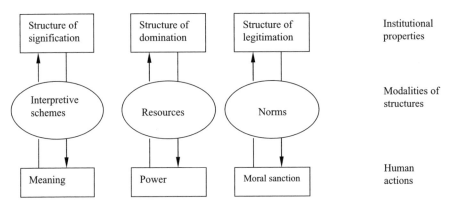

FIGURE 14.1 The interactions of human agents and institutional properties, mediated by modalities of structures. (Adapted from Giddens 1984: 29.)

considered as the locus of interaction between the knowledgable capacities of actors and the structural features of the system (Jones and Karsten, 2003). However, splitting the duality of structures into these dimensions serves more as an analytical procedure: in practice, all three are interlinked.

Structuration theory and HRM research

Giddens frequently stated that structuration was not intended as a concrete research program and that his principles 'do not supply concepts useful for the actual prosecution of research' (Giddens, 1990: 312). He is also very critical of those who 'have attempted to import structuration theory *in toto* into their given area of study' (Giddens, 1991: 213), and prefers those who use his concepts in a sparing and critical fashion. Among scientists who have put considerable effort into clarifying Giddens's theory of structuration, the common opinion is that structuration is 'fundamentally non-propositional' (Archer, 1990) and that it 'does not give us anything to test or to find out' (Craib, 1992: 108). Gregson (1989) views structuration as a second-order theory concerned not with explaining events or contingencies but with conceptualizing the general constituents of human society. In Giddens's view, structuration should be seen as a generic theory, meaning a meta-theory, a way of thinking about the world rather than as an empirically testable explanation of human behavior (Giddens, 1989).

Table 14.1 provides an overview of 10 key points of structuration that should serve, in Giddens's view, as guidelines for the social studies.

Based on these points, empirical HRM research always has ethnographic, cultural aspects. And any HRM field of inquiry has its constituted meanings before the study. An 'entry' to such fields means interventions in already existing meanings. Therefore, concepts in HRM are considered as 'secondary-order' concepts as they are always built on existing knowledge and interpretations. HRM researchers, therefore, have a role of communicators, introducing frames of meaning associated with certain contexts.

IT-ENABLED TRANSFORMATION OF HR: MAKING SENSE THROUGH THE HRM FRAMES

The structuring HRM transformation is influenced by the participants' interpretations of their work, social context, HRM policies, and the information technology used to enable the HRM transformation; their access to HRM, organizational and technological resources, and the normative rules that guide their organizational performance.

Participants draw on existing HRM organizational (institutional) properties of meaning, power, and moral structures and on the existing HRM frames to build assumptions about HRM transformation (IT-enabled). These assumptions are always culturally embedded, meaning appreciating the assumptions hold for participants of a given group (Geertz, 1973; Prasad, 1997).

TABLE 14.1 Key points of the structuration theory for empirical research. (Adapted from Giddens, 1984: 281–284.)

1 All human beings are knowledgable agents.
2 The knowledgability of human agents is always bounded on the one hand by the unconscious and on the other hand by the unacknowledged conditions and unanticipated consequences of action.
3 The study of day-to-day life is integral to the analysis of the reproduction of institutionalized practices.
4 Routine, psychologically linked to the minimizing of unconscious sources of anxiety, is the predominant form of day-to-day social activity.
5 The study of context, or of the contextualization of interaction is inherent in the investigation of social reproduction.
6 Social identities, and the position–practice relations associated with them, are 'markers' in the virtual time-space of structure.
7 No unitary meaning can be given to 'constraint' in social analysis.
8 Among the properties of social systems, structural properties are particularly important, since they specify overall types of society.
9 The study of power cannot be regarded as a second-order consideration in the social sciences.
10 There is no mechanism of social organization or social reproduction identified by social analysis which lay actors cannot also get to know about and actively incorporate into what they do.

HRM MENTAL FRAMES

In recent years, there has been a growing recognition in the managerial literature that, ultimately, it is the actors' perceptions of organizational processes, filtered through existing mental frames, which form the basis for the formulation and inter-pretation of organizational issues (Hodgkinson, 1997: 626). Further, social cognitive research shows that people act on the basis of their interpretations of the world, and in doing so they enact particular social realities through giving them meaning (Bartunek and Moch, 1994; Goodhew et al., 2005; Weick et al., 2005). Mental frames (representations) of reality are seen to preclude and challenge the processing of information (Eden, 1992; Hodgkinson, 2001) through sense-making and sense-giving processes, when people face new actions, and interpret and communicate their thoughts about them (for an overview, see Hodgkinson and Sparrow, 2002).

Borrowing the concept of 'frames' from cognitive psychology (Bandura, 1986), it has been described as a 'repertoire of tacit knowledge that is used to impose structure upon, and impart meaning to, otherwise ambiguous social and situational information to facilitate understanding' (Gioia, 1986: 56). In a less profound way, frames are defined as organized knowledge structures that allow individuals to in-teract with their environment (Mathieu et al., 2000: 274).

We assume that HRM frames are unlikely to be shared across the three differ-ent groups, or subcultures, in HRM transformation (line managers, HR specialists, and employees). For example, HR specialists may be assumed to have a longstanding perspective on the HRM transformation, expecting it to facilitate business and contribute to human capital development. In contrast, employees may have a short-term, more focused view on HRM policies, looking for immediate task-specific benefits, for example, the introduction of IT tools for HR practices. And line managers may expect overloading with HR tasks devolved from the HR specialists to them.

Following Orlikowski and Gash (1994) we articulate the notion of *congruence* in HRM frames as referring to the alignment of frames across subcultures. By congruence, we do not mean identical, but related in content, values, and categories. Congruent HRM frames would, for example, imply similar expectations about the role of HRM in organizations, ideas behind the HRM transformation, HR practices in the organizational reality, the nature of IT tools for HRM processes, or the type of HRM support (Bondarouk, 2006).

Incongruence, on the other hand, would mean crucially different, or even opposite, assumptions about the key aspects of the HRM transformation. To the extent that frames differ across subcultures, problems such as misaligned expectations, contradictory actions, resistance, and skepticism may occur (Orlikowski and Gash, 1994).

Globalization triggers for HRM framing

Change in interpretive processes and understanding of HRM systems (IT-enabled) can be triggered by many other factors if incongruence among social groups' frames is not the crucial one (Davidson, 2006). The background of such circumstances is not always clear for the actors. In large international and global companies, external triggers like the development of new technologies, IT-market changes for HRM purposes, everlasting race for 'the best IT solution' may result in interpretive shifts within an organization and, thus, impact HRM outcomes. Also, when IT developers or central HRM departments bring new ideas and priorities to the IT-based HRM project, they trigger interpretive frames that in the end influence the change program. Global companies often experience organizational restructuring and IT-related turbulences, and may go through episodic shifts in frames.

Further, contextually specific HRM frames may be drawn from an organizational field in which an organization operates, e.g., IT suppliers, regulatory agencies, global stakeholders and other institutions that produce similar services or products (Davidson, 2002).

Globalization presents at least two important issues for IT-enabled HRM systems:

1. As IT services and functionalities increasingly involve inter-organizational coalitions and even whole industrial sectors, structuring of IT-enabled HRM frames extends beyond one single organization (see Moingeon, Lumineau, and Perrin, this volume Chapter 13).
2. In an unstable environment of global and international companies, episodic shifts in HRM frames (IT-enabled) might lead to dissatisfaction with IT-HRM projects.

RESEARCH STUDY

The field study was conducted in 2002–2003 within a global chemical company Iris (a pseudonym). We described the general findings of the e-HRM developments in this company previously (Ruël *et al.*, 2004), within a framework of comparative analysis with four other large international companies. For the purpose of this chapter, we chose quotes from interviews and documents to illustrate the new theoretical analysis done here.

The data we gathered came from interviews held with 23 Iris employees: members of the works council, coaches, team leaders, HR professionals. We also studied instruction guides to the e-HRM applications, materials from external presentations, HR policy documents, and the e-HRM system itself.

Research site

With about 50 000 employees the Iris company is one of the largest chemical companies in the world. This US-based company (Midland, Michigan) is now active in 33 different countries around the globe.

Until the mid-1990s Iris was a country-oriented company, with quite autonomous sites around the world to which it was loosely coupled. Then Iris decided to become a global company with the globally dispersed sites turned into more business-oriented units. Before the 1990s Iris was mainly a 'blue collar/manual work' organization. It offered employees job security. Working at Iris meant a lifelong career for an employee, but mainly in the same functional area. From management's point of view, the workforce was a 'load on the budget'.

A decade ago, the company made financial losses. A new strategic plan was developed – the organizational structure was reduced from 10 layers to a maximum of six between the shop floor and the CEO, a model chosen on purpose to bring responsibility/accountability as close as possible to the shop floor level. This need for change led to the development of a new global HR strategy that 'broke up' the job security tradition and made a switch to *career* security.

Management realized that the competencies of its employees are a competitive advantage. This basic assumption and the focus on offering employees career security became the foundation of the new HR philosophy, called the People Strategy. From now on Iris wants to facilitate its employees' personal development optimally, but the responsibility for this development is in the hands of the employees.

In 1997 Iris started introducing the product People Soft–People Success System (PSS), to replace earlier electronic HR applications. The crucial differences with PSS were:

- ◆ the idea to have one global database, and
- ◆ a completely new HR philosophy, enabled by PSS.

PSS had to become accessible for every employee at any place on the globe via Iris's Intranet on one of the 26 000 planned workstations. The philosophy 'behind' PSS is based upon the value that people are the source of Iris's success. Senior management therefore adopted the following principles: diversity of thought, style, skills, etc., pay for performance, long-term careers, and contributions of employees.

RESEARCH FINDINGS

Four HRM frame domains were identified to characterize the interpretations that participants made about the PSS-enabled HRM at Iris and its role in supporting the HRM transformation:

- *Nature of the IT-enabled HRM transformation* – refers to actors' images of the HRM transformation process and their understanding of its business value.
- *Strategy of the IT-enabled HRM transformation* – refers to reasons people postulated of why their organization decided to implement the IT-enabled HRM.
- *Implementation of the IT-enabled HRM* – refers to people's views on how the IT-enabled HRM system is used in their daily work life.
- *Globalization issues* – actors' understandings of the contribution of the IT-enabled HRM to the globalization of the company.

Three social groups were identified: HRM professionals including people working in the HR Department responsible for different HR fields (recruitment, competence management, career development); managers including team coaches and line managers; employees.

Nature of the IT-enabled HRM transformation

All groups noticed that the introduction of PSS led to the establishment of the team leaders, coaches who became responsible for training other employees in computer skills and explaining the new concepts of HRM at Iris. The job tasks of coaches were mainly social ones like team support, learning support, or training. The company established the network of coaches operating around the globe – coaches exchanged their experience on training employees.

Enhanced communication with employees was noticed as a second important HRM transformation. Communication became faster and easier, both globally and within each location. Every department, division, plant received its own internal distribution list, and all respondents commented that e-communication improved the exchange of information.

The competence system has changed the culture of Iris dramatically: employees expressed that they take responsibility now for their own competence paths, that the average educational level has increased due to this development as everybody in the company is able to look for and choose his/her career line within Iris for several years ahead, and therefore to plan training courses.

Regarding HR task division, HR specialists and line managers noted that with the introduction of the PSS technology, much of the HR work is transferred to the line managers, and even the support personnel is involved in HR tasks:

> We don't have many HR people (40–45 people before), they are in the departments. The official HR department is about 10–12 people. Now we see this transformation, even Works Council does HR work. People want to talk about personal situations. We support this transformation. (Man-4)

The number of HR specialists has decreased, and the role of the HR Department has changed: from being the police to being advisers:

> Responsibilities were shifted from HR department to the managers. HR dept changed the role – we became more the consultancy instead of the police office. We had to learn not to play the role of the police office to be more a consultant. In the compensation part there were 5–6 people, with fewer countries. Now – only 2–3 people, with more countries. (HR-4)

The analysis of the frames around the *Nature of the IT-enabled HRM transformation* is shown in Table 14.2.

Strategy of the IT-enabled HRM transformation

The document analysis revealed that *Iris*'s top management introduced PSS as part of the organizational change process. For example, employees new to Iris received a brochure about PSS, explaining that PSS was 'a global, integrated competency-based human resources'. It also stated that PSS was an essential mechanism for bringing business and personal success while reflecting and supporting the

TABLE 14.2 Nature of the IT-enabled HRM transformation: HRM frames of HR specialists, line managers, and employees.

HR specialists (N = 8)	Line managers (N = 8)	Employees (N = 7)
– Establishment of coaches (team leaders) network – Transparency of HR policies – Enhanced communication with employees – Equalizing and simplifying compensation levels – Devolution of the HRM tasks to the line managers – HR department has changed its role: from the police to the consultant – Greater empowerment – Employees' self-management of careers – Awareness of employees' competencies – Greater software skills and knowledge of English	– Communication is very fast and easy – Fewer compensation levels – Life-long learning possibilities – People are managers of their own careers – Fewer HR specialists – Everybody is involved in HR work, even the Works Council	– Appraisal system is now based on social skills – Competence system is oriented fully toward social skills, ignoring technical (chemical) expertise – the culture has changed – you have to take responsibility for your career path, and you have to have a higher education level for almost all functions

company's goals of decreased hierarchies, decreased bureaucracy, and increased accountability.

We extracted the following five statements reflecting on the strategy of the IT-enabled HRM transformation published in different documents:

- enabling globalization,
- supporting strategies and goals,
- providing the employees with greater control over their own professional destinies,
- empowering the employees, supporting a delayered organization, self-directed teams, and creating a change-ready workforce.

All respondents believed that the IT-based HRM transformation aimed to empower people.

> I really don't know why was it introduced. When I started, the HRM department was rather big – with a lot of people, they did a lot of things in promotion, education, training, etc. Probably the new idea was to facilitate the leaders to do it in their own way. To bring HR responsibilities to the team leaders. An employee was considered responsible himself for his development. I think that was the main reason. Reducing costs?... I don't know, but I think that philosophy was to transfer the responsibility from the HR department to employees themselves. (Empl-1)

The director of HRM at Iris explained that he saw the role of the intranet-based system in improving the strategic role of HRM. In his view, it created the possibility to reach every employee at any time anywhere around the globe. He believed that IT also provided optimal opportunities to personalize information (through personalized portals) and more advanced instruments for employees.

Table 14.3 summarizes the HRM frames of the three groups around the strategy of the IT-enabled HRM transformation.

TABLE 14.3 Strategy of the IT-enabled HRM transformation: HRM frames of HR specialists, line managers, and employees.

HR specialists (N = 8)	Line managers (N = 8)	Employees (N = 7)
– Globalization of the company – Empowerment of the employees	– Cost efficiency – Empowerment of the employees – Centralization of the company and its HRM work – No idea	– Empowerment of the line managers and employees – Restructuring of the company – No idea

Implementation of the IT-enabled HRM

An important issue concerning the implementation of IT-enabled HRM is to know enough about its possibilities to appropriate and operate it in line with its ideas. Such knowledge is usually acquired through training, education and providing people with documents. Initially, PSS was paper-based. Then, quite suddenly in the employees's opinion, the intranet-based version was introduced. Such a sudden proposal for such a big change was unusual for the company. The Workers' Council gave their approval, however. The Council especially focused on the question of whether everything was in accordance with the law. Extra responsibilities were delegated to the team coaches to clarify the characteristics of the system. Coaches experienced at the beginning that it was quite difficult for employees (in the plant mostly) to get used to the system, to know what was available, which tools were optimal, and the background for specific aspects. In 2001/2002 the coaches prepared a presentation of about 50 pages dedicated to 'unlocking the system'. It was meant to make the use of PSS easier and to give some keys to employees.

In the beginning there were a lot of discussions about PSS and the HRM transformation during which future users could propose changes in the design of the technology. HRM specialists believed that the first reaction about PSS from people working in the plants was hesitation, while people working on the supporting staff were also hesitant but more open. There were three aspects explaining this difference: level of computer skills (experience), new language to work with PSS, and availability of computers in the company.

The most sensitive and popular aspect at the beginning became the application of compensation management: it had the most information. The compensation system change attracted a lot of attention; it was simpler and less rigid than the former system, provided more possibilities to reward performance and allowed more people to have same level skills in one shift. It also caused management to set the current salary level as the new average, which had a negative psychological effect. Employees who earned a salary at the top of their salary scale suddenly experienced this level as 'just' the average that employees in similar functions earned. Also, employees who had just started work were psychologically returned to a pre-starter's salary level.

As the system became more sophisticated, the enthusiasm for the use of the system itself improved. HR specialists believed that the 'Job Announcement System' became the most successful application:

> The JAS showed up to be a main success story of People Success in the beginning and still is. Line managers had to publish job vacancies on the JAS and employees from the very first beginning used the opportunities offered to apply for an internal job. Some line managers were not pleased by the fact that their employees 'walked out' and cried to HR: 'Help, my people are walking out.' HR's reply in these cases was: 'Then you got a problem.' It meant that in these cases line managers had to work on the way they managed their people.

The latter quote demonstrates some HRM outcomes on closer inspection: line managers were forced to improve or take care with their people management policies in the department.

Although, most of the people were 'open-minded' about the new system, the one-day training course was not felt to be appropriate by some respondents.

Employees perceived the process of implementation as not successful. They saw it as very top-down, without clear instructions and help only in emergencies. Some employees felt they were left on their own to study the system.

Furthermore, the main parts of the texts in the new system were in English. For many employees this was problematic, because they lacked the skills to read in English. However, from the beginning PSS contained important and relevant information for everybody (especially regarding the new compensation system), and therefore it was important for all employees to be able to work with it. HR specialists noted, the problems everybody experienced with the implementation of the system were not exceptional in comparison to other changes:

> ... at the beginning employees had a lot of questions about the system, but after some time this decreased. The big resistance to using PSS is similar to resistance during other change processes. (HR-8)

We summarized HRM frames about the implementation process of PSS in Table 14.4.

Globalization issues

All respondents experienced that two IT-supported HRM domains were globalized the most: the compensation and recruitment applications. The global compensation system received a lot of hits in the beginning, and people were surfing the most in this application, as an HR specialist commented:

> The global compensation system provided information about salaries at all job levels at all company sites around the world. People could compare between countries and between job levels. We even know cases where employees wanted to move to another country within the company because of the attraction of a higher salary. But then, after comparison of other labor conditions, they preferred to stay in the Netherlands. (HR-4)

HR specialists and line managers believed that this contributed to the open culture, part of the HR change at Iris. The new HRM policy also concerned the idea that compensations had to be comparable between all Iris sites.

Another popular HRM field was recruitment. Through the IT-based HR applications (Job Announcement System), Iris posted job openings in eight languages. During the interview, one HR manager proudly remarked to us – referring to the internal documents – that:

> Our placement statistics is consistently higher by 10–15% when benchmarking to external companies. In June 2002 the JAS celebrated its fifth birthday. Since 1997, 12 792 jobs were posted on the JAS and filled over 7100 job opportunities. (HR-3)

TABLE 14.4 Implementation of the IT-enabled HRM: HRM frames of HR specialists, line managers, and employees.

HR specialists (N = 8)	Line managers (N = 8)	Employees (N = 7)
– 'Normal' resistance to change experienced with other organizational changes – Three key aspects disturbed implementation at the beginning: differences in PC skills, English writing-reading skills, and availability of computers – Availability of information played a double role: was appreciated by the people but also discouraged them opening PSS – In the beginning the most popular application was 'compensation management' – After it became institutionalized, the most popular became 'Job Announcement System'	– User participation in the design phase through discussions – Sensitivity of the compensation transformation – Contrasting opinions about usefulness of training – Lack of personal computers disturbed implementation process – Lack of software skills – Active role of the Works Council in the implementation of PSS – Helpful support from the team coaches	– The implementation went top-down – No real help – Employees felt they were left on their own to get used to PSS

HR specialists explicitly expressed that going global restructured the HRM Department and HR processes. There were only three HR roles left for the Department:

> With the presentation of the Strategic Blueprint our HR Department was restructured. HR's new structure is based upon three different roles that HR has to fulfill. Now there is a HR business center, a strategic center and a resource center. The business center acts as the sparring partner of strategic management, the strategic center develops new HR products that fit the business needs. The resource centre implements them. (HR-5)

HR specialists believe that they moved to a more strategic role with the IT-based HRM transformation. Non-HR professionals felt that with the introduction of PSS, Iris became more bureaucratic than ever before: lots of standard procedures, papers, applications.

Table 14.5 summarizes the HRM frames of the three social groups around globalization issues.

TABLE 14.5 Globalization issues: HRM frames of HR specialists, line managers, and employees.

HR specialists (N= 8)	Line managers (N= 8)	Employees (N= 7)
– Popularity of the global compensation – Enhancing of the open culture through the IT-enablement of HRM – Harmonization of the HR policies in all company sites – Job Announcement in eight languages – Restructuring and centralization of the HRM department – Strategic role of HR specialists	– Popularity of the global compensation – Enhancing of the open culture through the IT-enablement of HRM – Team coaches international network	– Open culture – Possibilities to compare the labor conditions in other countries – Growth of bureaucracy

OUTCOMES OF THE IT-ENABLED HRM TRANSFORMATION

Although the implementation of the IT-based HRM transformation within Iris was complete and people adapted to the new organizational and HRM developments and worked with the IT, the nature and extent of their understanding, perceptions, and attitudes toward those changes sometimes differed from the official Iris policy and beliefs of top management. Such differences in expectations and action between HR specialists, line managers, and employees can be traced to the differences in their HRM frames. Cognitive incongruence existed in four HRM frame domains to different extents.

Nature of the IT-enabled HRM transformation

All groups emphasized three main organizational changes at Iris forced by the IT-enabled HRM change:

1. They acknowledged the introduction of the new job function: team coaches who had mostly social team-leading responsibilities.
2. The competence system had changed the culture of Iris towards the empowerment of people: all interviewees expressed that they take responsibility for their own career paths. Life-long learning was also noticed as one of the major foci of the HRM transformation.
3. The increased communication and transparency of information were interpreted by all groups as an organizational change.

HRM specialists observed the increase in the average educational level as everybody in the company was able to choose his or her career line within Iris for several years ahead, and therefore could plan training courses.

Regarding HR task division, HR specialists and line managers noted that with the introduction of the PSS technology, much of the HR work goes to the line managers, and even the support personnel is involved in HR tasks. The number of HR specialists has decreased, and the role of the HR Department has changed: from the police into advisers.

In principle, all social groups saw the nature of the HRM transformation in similar ways, with minor differences in accents. This *alignment* of frames shaped similar assessments of the value of the IT-enabled HRM transformation and led to similar responses to it. It is not surprising then, that at the time of this study, HR specialists, line managers, and employees supported the organizational HRM transformation. At the same time we noticed that HR specialists operating PSS and dealing with HRM changes did so in support of the organizational, HRM, and individual employee level work, while employees were concerned mostly with their own individual work.

Strategy of the IT-enabled HRM transformation

Official documents expressing the HRM policies revealed that the IT-enablement would strongly contribute to the globalization of the company and empowerment of its employees. However, an analysis of interpretations of its goals given by line managers and employees showed some confusion, deviation from the official policy documents, and diversity in the clarity of seeing the strategic choices, and the content of the goals.

HR specialists were again the closest group in their interpretations of the strategic goals, but still their expressions covered too many aspects that could be referred to the first-order change, assembling modes of operations by exercising incremental organizational changes: offering up-to-date information, relevant electronic links, relevant instruments to work with, electronic database management, online recruitment, online training, and online assessment tools.

Implementation of the IT-enabled HRM

HR specialists perceived the implementation process as a 'normal' change process for Iris. They felt that the resistance shown was not stronger than for any other changes implemented in the company. They saw three factors hindering this implementation: differences in PC skills, low English writing–reading skills, and lack of computers. The line managers also pointed to the lack of personal computers and software skills as disturbing factors, but they did not notice problems with the mastering of English.

HR specialists believed that the increased amount of information for employees played a double role: it was appreciated by the people as a good source, but they were also discouraged from opening PSS as a result of information overload.

We discovered contrasting opinions regarding user participation in the implementation process. For the line managers, employees were invited to take part in the design phase, and team coaches helped them a lot in getting acquainted with the system. However, the employees themselves felt that they did not get any real help and were left on their own to get used to PSS.

Globalization issues

All groups of interviewees assumed that the organizational culture had become more open with the IT-enablement of HRM. Also, they all noticed that the most popular element was the global compensation application; employees even directly expressed that they highly appreciated the possibility to compare labor conditions at different sites. The recruitment global application turned out to be the most successful field.

At the same time we observed opposite assumptions regarding organizational and HRM restructuring. For HR specialists, HR policies seemed harmonized at all company sites, and the HRM function was perceived as strictly centralized with enough freedom for the country-based HRM. They saw themselves as developing toward strategic partners. Employees, on the other hand, sensed a growth of bureaucracy in all these changes, seeing organizational priorities in the restructuring rather than in the people themselves.

We examined the use of the PSS technology as an enabler for the HRM transformation at Iris some years ago. We acknowledge that because the actors' interpretations could have an episodic character (Davidson, 2002), the changes may have occurred recently.

IMPLICATIONS FOR RESEARCH AND PRACTICE

Our assumption behind HRM frames is essentially structurational (Davidson, 2002): employees perform according to the meanings that HRM systems have for them, and their actions shape the meaning of HRM for others and for the organization as a whole. As such, HRM frames both facilitate and restrain.

We identified four HRM frame domains that can serve as the basis for articulating actors' interpretive schemes about the IT-supported HRM transformation: its nature, its strategy, its implementation, and globalization issues. While we believe that these domains are general, much could be learnt in other or cross-organizational settings.

We saw that the HRM frames at Iris became facilitators when they were congruent across three groups of employees: HR specialists, line managers, and employees. The highest level of congruency was observed around the nature of the HRM transformation. The similarity in frames reduced uncertainty and made it possible for different people to understand each other with respect to the HRM changes.

HRM frames were constraining when they pushed people into different directions in their interpretations of the HRM change. Thus, assumptions about the strategic goals or reasons behind the IT-enabled HRM transformation revealed contrasting interpretations: it was seen by the HR specialists as an enabler of the globalization of the company and by the line managers as a cost-reducing opportunity. Differences in the clarity of the strategic goals became a limitation in the process of implementing the HRM transformation globally. However, all three groups had similar ideas about empowerment and the competence system at Iris.

Understanding of the implementation process differed to a larger extent across the three groups. While HRM professionals did not observe exceptional difficulties in employees' resistance to this change, employees themselves felt they were left on their own in learning and adapting to a new situation. The 'mediating' group of team coaches felt responsible for helping employees and perceived the latter as receiving a lot of assistance in this change.

We believe that after HRM rules and policies are introduced and symbolized by the organizational policy makers, employees will influence their working meanings through HRM frames. We argue that a real meaning is given to the HRM practices only during organizational practices, guided by the frames of HR specialists, line managers, and employees. HRM transformation therefore develops from prescribed toward situated practices. We saw that people do draw on their prior HRM and IT experience, skills, power, and educational level that has already been shown in IT research to have great significance in the situated use of the technology (Orlikowski and Gash, 1994; Orlikowski, 2000).

Research might further focus on identifying the conditions that sharpen congruency in the HRM frames. We observed that the systematic training and timely communications with employees helped to reduce uncertainty and misunderstandings, and to improve the self-efficacy of those who were the targets of the HRM transformation. Employees' participation also became an important issue in the ongoing changes.

By adopting a process approach we believe that the IT-based HRM transformation is always situated and emergent. However, this does not imply that such transformation is always unique. As suggested by Orlikowski (2000), because regular use of an introduced change tends to be recurrent, people tend to enact similar HRM frames over time. In this way HRM frames even become routine under certain circumstances. Such institutionalizations might allow for identifying generalizable HRM frames that are likely to be enacted by particular organizational actors.

Figure 14.2 suggests some provisional generalizations of the HRM frames for the IT-enabled HRM transformation, based on these two types of generalizations. By focusing on the emergent, embedded HRM practices instead of only embodied ones, we have temporarily generalized the structuring process of the IT-enabled HRM transformation. Three social groups – HR specialists, line managers, employees – draw on existing HRM organizational (institutional) properties (arrow 1) and on the existing HRM frames (arrow 2) to build assumptions about the IT-enabled HRM transformation. In working 'within' the HRM transformation situation, participants develop HRM frames including four domains (arrow 3) and enact a set of organizational properties as a combination of: the improvement of the IT support for HRM processes, restructuring of the HRM Department, establishment of the global network of team leaders, enhancement of the open culture, harmonization of the HR policies in all company sites, division of HR responsibilities among HR specialists,

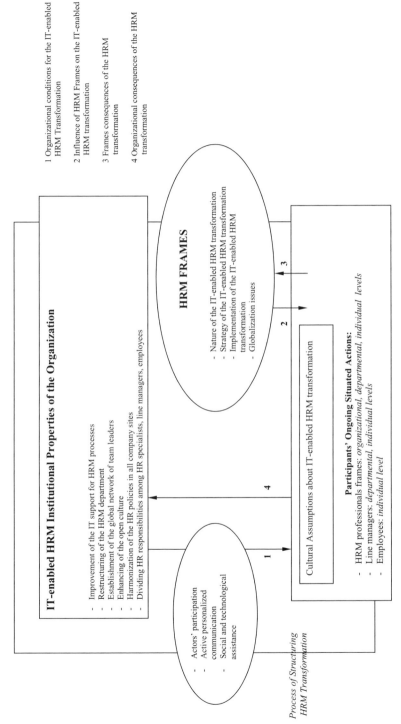

1 Organizational conditions for the IT-enabled HRM Transformation

2 Influence of HRM Frames on the IT-enabled HRM transformation

3 Frames consequences of the HRM transformation

4 Organizational consequences of the HRM transformation

IT-enabled HRM Institutional Properties of the Organization

- Improvement of the IT support for HRM processes
- Restructuring of the HRM department
- Establishment of the global network of team leaders
- Enhancing of the open culture
- Harmonization of the HR policies in all company sites
- Dividing HR responsibilities among HR specialists, line managers, employees

HRM FRAMES

- Nature of the IT-enabled HRM transformation
- Strategy of the IT-enabled HRM transformation
- Implementation of the IT-enabled HRM transformation
- Globalization issues

Cultural Assumptions about IT-enabled HRM transformation

Participants' Ongoing Situated Actions:
- HRM professionals frames: *organizational, departmental, individual levels*
- Line managers: *departmental, individual levels*
- Employees: *individual level*

Process of Structuring HRM Transformation

- Actors' participation
- Active personalized communication
- Social and technological assistance

FIGURE 14.2 Generalizations for the structuring of the IT-enabled HRM transformation.

line managers, employees, globalization of the recruitment and compensation policies (arrow 4).

Conclusion

In conclusion, our research has shown that the early articulation, reflection, proper communication about and possibly modification of inconsistencies may reduce the likelihood of unintended misunderstandings around the IT-enabled HRM transformation. Attempts to bring the common assumptions, expectations, and knowledge to the surface must be welcome in the organizational life. Early identification of inconsistencies in HRM frames may prevent some difficulties during the implementation process and reduce resistance to change, even if it is usually perceived as normal.

References

Archer, M. (1990). Human agency and social structure: A critique of giddens. In J. Clark, C. Modgil, and J. Modgil (eds), *Anthony Giddens: Consensus and Controversy*. Brighton, UK: Falmer Press, pp. 73–84.

Ball, K.S. (2001). The use of human resource information systems: A survey. *Personnel Review*, 30, 677–693.

Bandura, A. (1986). *Social Foundations of Thought and Action: A Social Cognitive Theory*. Englewood Cliffs, New Jersey: Prentice-Hall.

Barrett, M. (1999). Challenges of EDI adoption for electronic trading in the London insurance market, *European Journal of Information Systems*, 8 (1), 1–15.

Bartunek, J.M., and Moch, M.K. (1994). Third-order organizational change and the Western mystical tradition. *Journal of Organizational Change Management*, 7, 24–41.

Bell, B.S., Lee, S.-W., and Yeung, S. (2006). The impact of e-HR on professional competence in HRM: Implications for the development of HR professionals. *Human Resource Management*, 45, 295–308.

Bondarouk, T. (2006). Action-oriented group learning in the implementation of information systems: Results from three case studies. *European Journal of Information Systems*, 15, 42–53.

Bondarouk, T., and Ruël, H.J.M. (2006). E-HRM effectiveness in a Dutch ministry: Results of survey and discursive exploration combined. In T. Bondarouk and H. Ruël (eds), *Proceedings of the 1st European Academic Workshop on e-HRM*, October 25–26, 2006. Enschede, The Netherlands, pp. 1–17.

Bowen, D.E., and Ostroff, C. (2004). Understanding HRM-firm performance linkages: The role of the 'strength' of the HRM system. *Academy of Management Review*, 29, 204–221.

Buckley, P., Minette, K., Joy, D., and Michaels, J. (2004). The use of an automated employment recruiting and screening system for temporary professional employees: A case study. *Human Resource Management*, 43, 233–241.

Cober, R.T., Brown, D.J., and Levy, P.E. (2004). Form, content, and function: An evaluative methodology for corporate employment web sites. *Human Resource Management*, 43, 201–218.

Craib, I. (1992). *Anthony Giddens*. London, UK: Routledge.

Davidson, E. (2002). Technology frames and framing: A socio-cognitive investigation of requirements determination. *MIS Quarterly*, 26, 329–358.

Davidson, E. (2006). A technological frames perspective on information technology and organizational change, *The Journal of Applied Behavioral Science*, 42 (1), 23–39.

Eden, C. (1992). On the nature of cognitive maps. *Journal of Management Studies*, 29, 261–265.

Geertz, C. (1973). *The Interpretation of Cultures*. New York: Basic Books.

Giddens, A. (1984). *The Constitution of Society*. Cambridge, UK: Polity.

Giddens, A. (1989). A reply to my critics. In D. Held and J.B. Thompson (eds), *Social Theory of Modern Societies: Anthony Giddens and his Critics*. Cambridge, UK: Cambridge University Press, pp. 249–301.

Giddens, A. (1990). *The Consequences of Modernity*. Cambridge, UK: Polity.

Giddens, A. (1991). *A Modernity and Self-Identity*. Cambridge, UK: Polity.

Gioia, D.A. (1986). Symbols, scripts, and sense-making: Creating meaning in the organizational experience. In D.A. Gioia (eds), *The Thinking Organization: Dynamics of organizational Social Cognition*, San-Francisco, California: Jossey-Bass, pp. 317–335.

Goodhew, G.W., Cammock, P.A., and Hamilton, R.T. (2005). Managers' cognitive maps and intra-organizational performance differences. *Journal of Managerial Psychology*, 20, 124–136.

Gregson, N. (1989). On the ir(relevance) of structuration theory to empirical research. In D. Held and J.B. Thompson (eds), *Social Theory of Modern Societies: Anthony Giddens and his Critics*. Cambridge University Press, Cambridge, UK, pp. 235–248.

Guzzo, R.A., and Noonan, K.A. (1994). Human resource practices as communications and the psychological contract. *Human Resource Management*, 33, 447–462.

Hodgkinson, G.P. (1997). The cognitive analysis of competitive structures: A review and critique. *Human Relations*, 50, 625–654.

Hodgkinson, G.P. (2001). The psychology of strategic management: Diversity and cognition revisited. In C.L. Cooper and I.T. Robertson (eds), *International Review of Industrial and Organizational Psychology*, Volume 16. Chichester: John Wiley & Sons, Ltd.

Hodgkinson, G.P., and Sparrow, P.R. (2002). *The Competent Organization: A Psychological Analysis of the Strategic Management Process*. Buckingham: Open University Press.

Hussain, Z., Wallace, J., and Cornelius, M.E. (2007). The use and impact of human resource information systems on human resource management professionals. *Information & Management*, 44, 77–89.

Hustad, E., and Munkvold, B.E. (2005). IT-supported competence management: A case study at Ericsson. *Knowledge Management*, Spring, 78–88.

Jones, M., and Karsten, H. (2003). *Review: Structuration theory and information systems research*. Research Papers in Management Studies, University of Cambridge, Judge Institute of Management WP 11/2003.

Lawler, E.E., and Mohrman, S.A. (2003). HR as a strategic partner: What does it take to make it happen? *Human Resource Planning*, 26, 15–29.

Lengnick-Hall, M.L., and Moritz, S. (2003). The impact of e-HR on the human resource management function. *Journal of Labor Research*, 24, 365–379.

Lepak, D.P., and Snell, S.A. (1998). Virtual HR: Strategic human resource management in the 21st century. *Human Resource Management Review*, 8, 215–234.

Marler, J.H., Liang, X. and Dulebohn, J.H. (2006). Training and effective employee information technology use. *Journal of Management*, 32, 721–743.

Mathieu, J.E., Goodwin, G.F., Heffner, T.S., and Cannon-Bowers, J.A. (2000). The influence of shared mental models on team process and performance. *Journal of Applied Psychology*, 85, 273–283.

Orlikowski, W.J. (2000). Technology and constituting structures: A practice lens for studying technology in organizations. *Organization Science*, 11, 404–428.

Orlikowski, W.J., and Gash, D.C. (1994). Technological frames: Making sense of information technology in organizations. *ACM Transactions on Information Systems*, 2, 174–207.

Prasad, P. (1997). Systems of meaning: Ethnography as a methodology for the study of information technologies. In A.S. Lee, J. Liebenau, and J.I. DeGross (eds), *Information Systems and Qualitative Research*. London: Chapman & Hall, pp. 101–118.

Reilly, P., and Williams, T. (2003). *How to Get the Best Value from HR: The Shared Service Option*. Aldershot: Gower.

Ruël, H.J.M., Bondarouk, T.V., and Looise, J.C. (2004). *E-HRM: Innovation or Irritation. An Exploration of Web-based Human Resource Management in Large Companies*. Utrecht: Lemma Publishers.

Taylor, J.R., Groleau, C., Heaton, L., and Van Every, E. (2000). *The Computerization of Work*. San Francisco, CA: Sage Publications.

Weick, K., Sutcliffe, K.M., and Obstfeld (2005). Organizing and process of sensemaking. *Organization Science*, 16, 409–421.

15

Employer Branding and Corporate Reputation Management in an International Context

GRAEME MARTIN AND SUSAN HETRICK

INTRODUCTION

In this chapter, we examine the phenomenon of employer branding, a concept whose time may have come given the global interest shown by practitioners (Barrow and Mosely, 2005; Sparrow *et al.*, 2004; CIPD, 2007a, b). Although it has attracted some academic criticism and practitioner scepticism (CIPD, 2007a; Edwards and Kuruvilla, 2005), employer branding began to take off in the USA, the UK, continental Europe and, most recently, Asia during this first few years of this millennium (Economist Panel Survey, 2003; Hatch and Schultz, 2001; Martin and Beaumont, 2003a; Martin and Hetrick, 2006; Rao and Baid, 2006; Schultz *et al.*, 2005; Zhang *et al.*, 2008). Driven by the progressively more heated and global 'talent wars' (Boudreau and Ramstad, 2007; CIPD, 2007c; *The Economist*, 2006, 2007a; Michaels *et al.*, 2001), international human resource management (IHRM) researchers are beginning to sense a trend among international and multinational organizations to use employer branding as an important tool for creating a sense of 'corporateness' among often decentralized multinational corporations (MNCs) and as a key means of differentiating themselves in overseas labor markets (Sparrow *et al.*, 2004; Sparrow, 2006a, b). 'Corporateness' is a term coined by Balmer and Geyser (2003) to describe trends among organizations to achieve a greater sense of corporate identity, corporate governance, corporate leadership and corporate social responsibility (see also Martin and Hetrick, 2006).

Despite the interest shown in employer branding by such organizations, there has been little research into what it means in practice and into the effectiveness of employer branding (Martin and Beaumont, 2003b), especially as a means for reconciling a key tension faced by international organizations – balancing the

Handbook of International Human Resource Management. Edited by Paul R. Sparrow
© 2009 John Wiley & Sons, Ltd

needs for corporate integration, control, and legitimacy on the one hand with local differentiation, autonomy and initiative on the other (Deephouse and Carter, 2005; Roberts, 2004).

This chapter sheds some light on these issues in an international context by examining how employer branding works in theory and practice by:

1. Developing a simplified model of the process, theorizing the key variables and their linkages, and discussing some critical success factors and potential problems that organizations face in establishing effective employer brands.
2. Setting out the available evidence on employer branding to address the questions: does it work in practice and can it work in international contexts? The evidence, such as it is, indicates that employer brands that focus on the symbolic and culturally authentic meanings for potential and existing employees are more likely to be effective than those that stress purely instrumental benefits or global corporate messages.
3. Illustrating some of the problems of employer branding in a multinational context using insights from ongoing action research into the development of a global HR strategy and employer branding proposition for one of the world's largest financial services companies. This case highlights the problems of establishing a global employer brand in potentially unreceptive contexts for change, i.e., where MNC subsidiaries in different countries hold markedly different and somewhat negative views of corporate headquarters' leadership, HR and people management policies, and company image and positioning (see also Edwards, this volume Chapter 11, on the challenges of practice diffusion). The case shows how the company is proposing to deal with these problems in an innovative way by applying IHRM theory to the employer branding process.

We conclude by discussing lessons from the IHRM literature for the company, for our model and for further research.

Toward a Theory of Employer Branding

Drawing on our previous work on corporate reputations and corporate branding (Martin and Hetrick, 2006; Martin, 2007) and the work of others (e.g., Davies *et al.*, 2003) we capture the key variables and links in the process of employer branding (see Figure 15.1).

Corporate and organizational identity

The storyline of this model is predicated on the twin aims of employer branding: to attract talented individuals and ensure both they and existing employees identify with the organization, its brand, and mission in order to produce desired outcomes for organizations. These outcomes include brand advocacy and enhanced organizational reputations (Lievens *et al.*, 2007; Martin and Hetrick, 2006), which, as Thorne (2004) has cogently argued, are two of the three principal assets of knowledge-based

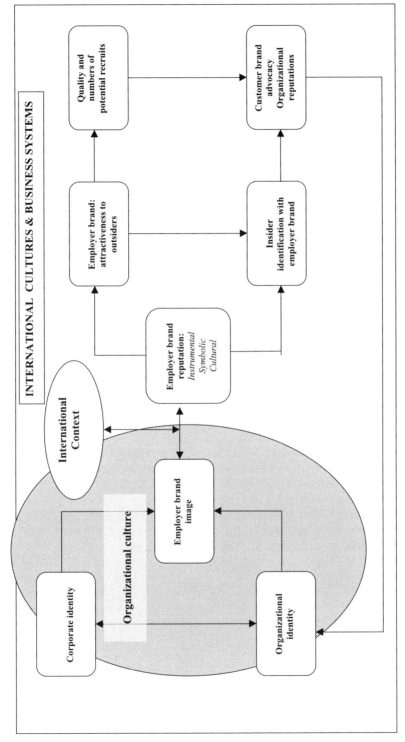

FIGURE 15.1 Model of the employer branding process in international context.

enterprises and knowledge-based economies. The two key antecedents or drivers of employer branding are *organizational identity* and *corporate identity*.

Organizational identity is best thought of as the collective answer by employees and managers to the 'who are we?' question, revealed in the organization's shared knowledge, beliefs, language, and behaviors (Whetten and Mackey, 2002; Sparrow and Cooper, 2003). This organizational self-concept is not just a collection of individual identities but has a metaphorical life of its own, independent of those who are currently employed in it.

In contrast, corporate identity is an organization's projected image of 'who we want to be', expressed not only in the form of tangible logos, architecture, and public pronouncements, but also in its communication of mission, strategies, and values (Balmer and Geyser, 2003).

Both antecedents are rooted in the more deep-seated notion of *organizational culture* – the often hidden values, assumptions, and beliefs that shape external adaptation and internal integration, which has formed the basis of much of the 'culture-excellence' writing during the previous decades (Hatch and Schultz, 2004; Schein, 2004). As we will discuss, this notion of culture is becoming an important concept in marketing and brand management, reflecting earlier developments in HRM and organization studies. In one sense, employer branding can be seen as little more than a derivative of the culture-excellence literature – but with a few important twists and turns (Martin and Beaumont, 2003a; Storey, 2007).

In an MNC context, however, this notion of organizational culture is complicated by the often acute differences between headquarters and subsidiaries which are sometimes embedded in a myriad of national cultures and national institutional frameworks (Brewster, 2007; Martin and Beaumont, 2001; Sackmann, this volume Chapter 4; Sparrow, 2006a, Whitley, 1999). Such national cultures and institutions influence HRM and people management practices in MNCs in subtle and uncertain ways – although recent evidence suggests that the effects of national culture alone on values may be quite small (Gerhart and Fang, 2005). National effects are often difficult to disentangle in their effects from organizational cultures.

1. They shape choices over HRM architectures and practices emanating from corporate headquarters (Brewster, 2007). From an institutional perspective Ferner and Varul (1999), Reich (2007) and Edwards (this volume Chapter 4) have shown how the organizational and HR practices of US-owned MNCs are embedded in the American business system and American Business Model.
2. National cultures and institutions act as a moderating influence in affecting the strength or direction of the relationship between organizational cultures and how employees and managers perceive HRM practices (Ostroff and Bowen, 2000; Stiles *et al.*, 2006), in this case employer brand images. However, this moderating relationship is not just one way; employees and managers in these subunits may also 'enact' (Weick, 1988) their national cultures in their day-to-day sense-making and articulations of their behaviors, or at least enact limitations on the influence of the national cultures on their local organizational culture and HR practices.

Thus, in our modeling, we have to allow for the two-way and dynamic processes involved in the relationship between national cultures and organizational cultures and practices (Erez and Gati, 2004; Sackmann, this volume Chapter 4), in this case employer brand images and reputations.

Employer and employee authorship of employer brands

These antecedents drive the construction of an *employer brand image* and *employer brand reputation*. The employer brand image can be defined as what an organization's senior managers want to communicate about its package of functional, economic and psychological benefits; its *autobiographical account* of the employer brand promise or employment proposition (Martin and Hetrick, 2006). It also aims to influence wider public perceptions of an organization's reputation since both potential and existing employees' attitudes and emotions are shaped by what they believe significant others feel about the organization (Lievens *et al.*, 2007). This rationale underlies the establishment of corporate communications departments in institutions as diverse as financial services, universities, and healthcare, and for developing employer of choice schemes (Van Riel, 2003).

If the employer brand image is the self-authored account of what the organization wants to be known for as an employer, employer brand reputations are the multiple *biographical accounts* of what an image holds for potential and existing employees who, along with others, begin to write different stories and form themselves into distinct segments of interest and lifestyles. What people see depends on where they stand and what they value (Morgan, 1997), and different groups of people expect, and attribute different values to, particular aspects of the employer brand image. However, these reputations are sometimes aggregated statistically to give an overall score, which often suits the needs of organizations for trend analysis and as a benchmark (Fombrun and Van Riel, 2003). In the context of IHRM, this issue of aggregation is something that comes to the fore and risks giving rise to a sense of misplaced concreteness that leads practitioners toward unwarranted conclusions, as we shall highlight in our case.

These ideas of employee authorship and plural reputations mirror a debate in branding practice and theory more generally, prompted by the often asked question in marketing circles: Are the best brands created by marketers or consumers? (Holt, 2006). The answer has important implications for understanding employer branding and how firms create employer brands, mirroring an earlier debate over the sources and management of organizational cultures (Martin, 2002).

A popular perspective is that strong consumer brands are the product of cynical groups of consumers, many of whom resent the 'spin' of big business and public relations machines and who use the power of the internet and the street to 'discover' their own 'cool' brands (Gladwell, 1997). Thus marketing departments have become involved in 'coolhunting' – intense searches for brands that have meaning 'on the street' before they become embraced by mass culture. Given that cool brands are unlikely to be susceptible to corporate messages and image management, marketing departments use *viral branding*, drawing on the power of below-radar marketing to influence key consumers to 'own' the brand and help it to spread like a virus throughout the community. The problems associated with this perspective on brand management, whether aimed at consumers or employees, is that the origins of such brands are often highly local in origin, and what is 'cool' in one community is not necessarily so in others. Two examples suffice:

1. The declining influence of American brands on the rest of the world, especially in Muslim countries and communities, and the mixed reception of the American icons such as Wal-Mart and Disney as employers in Germany and France (Fishman, 2006; Martin, 2007).
2. The different reputation ranking that the same MNC attracts in countries as close in national culture and institutional make-up as, for example, Sweden, Norway, and Denmark, and the different criteria used to evaluate such companies in these same countries (Apéria et al., 2004).

A related and more fruitful perspective is Gilmore and Joseph-Pine's (2007) search for *authenticity* in brands. These writers argue that in an 'experience economy' consumers seek authentic experiences from goods and services which reflect and help to project their self image – 'real offerings from genuinely transparent sources' (p. 5). Rendering authenticity can be managed more effectively by allowing consumers to provide input into the design of the experience 'not only for their own pleasure but for the enjoyment of others' (p. 15), citing the success of internet brands such as YouTube, Facebook, and MySpace, and even simple product brands such as Build-a-Bear. Following this line of argument, by giving current and potential employees greater voice and input into the design stage, employer brands could and may need to be rendered more authentic. We pick up this thread when discussing employer brands and segmentation later in this chapter.

While acknowledging the importance of this marketing debate over the source of brand value and the notions of culturally-specific and co-created brand reputations, we would not want to take this imagery and agency argument too far, especially in the context of employer brands, for two reasons:

1. Even though the ideas of unitary cultures have long since been challenged as the dominant perspective from which to view organizations, the unitary perspective offers a useful analysis of periods of organizational stability. Organizational cultures may be described at certain stages in their history as characterized by common values, attitudes and ways of 'doing things around here' (Hatch and Schultz, 2004; Martin, 2002). So, too, employer brand reputations. While authored by employees and potential employees, they are not written in a social vacuum; and are the product of a two-way, interactive relationship in which images influence reputations and vice versa.
2. Employer brands may be strong and weak, paralleling arguments over strong and weak organizational cultures.

In relation to the second point, most organizations have an employer brand in the weak sense, containing an image and message that holds meaning (or is intended to hold meaning) for a group of core knowledge and creative employees only (Lepak and Snell, 2002; Martin and Hetrick, 2006) – typically managers and other senior employees, who have most to gain from identification with a projected image. In contrast, strong employer brands hold similar meaning for all, or nearly all, segments of the extended organization and its HR supply chain, including full-time lower grade workers, temporary workers, contractors, external consultants, and business partners. Such meaning is also carried over into the wider society, allowing potential recruits to attribute reputations to companies as being among the best places to work in their national business systems, though, as we have noted, there are limitations on the extent to which images are perceived in the same way across national boundaries (Andersen, 2007; Apéria *et al.*, 2004).

INSTRUMENTAL, SYMBOLIC, AND CULTURAL AIMS OF EMPLOYER BRANDING

In discussing meaning, a further important feature of current employer brand reputations is that they are intended to fulfill three levels of needs and meaning: instrumental, symbolic, and cultural. These distinctions parallel developments in the more general branding literature (Holt, 2004; Lievens *et al.*, 2007).

Instrumental and symbolic branding

The first level concerns the *instrumental* needs of people for objective, physical, and tangible attributes that an organization may or may not possess (Lievens *et al.*, 2007). These might include the ability to provide rewarding jobs, high salaries, opportunities for career advancement, job security, job satisfaction, etc. – all items that might form the expectations calculus of employees' views of their psychological contract (Conway and Briner, 2005).

The second level concerns the *symbolic* needs of people for meaning. These broadly translate into their perceptions and emotions about the abstract and intangible image of the organization; for example, employees' feelings of pride in the organization, the extent to which it gives them a sense of purpose, beliefs about its technical competence and honesty in dealing with clients and employees, the extent to which it is an exciting or innovative place to work, and the extent to which it is seen as chic, stylish and/or as aggressively masculine or competitive (Davies and Chun, 2007; Lievens *et al.*, 2005).

Distinguishing between instrumental needs and symbolic meaning mirrors recent trends in branding models. These models have moved away from a focus on so-called *mind-share approaches*, which refers to a brand's capabilities to occupy a central, focused appeal to individuals (through specific employee value propositions on rewards, career development, etc.) to an *emotional* level, in which the brand interacts and builds relationships with people (Holt, 2004).

Cultural branding

Qualitative research has recently pointed to the emergence and effectiveness of celebrity brands (Rindova *et al.*, 2006) and iconic brands (Holt, 2004). Both ideas refer to high profile, global corporate brands working beyond the level of mind-share and emotions to achieve iconic status through the satisfaction of strong, culturally influenced needs. Not surprisingly, Holt describes these as *cultural brands*, which are 'performers of and containers of important identity myths for individuals'. Drawing on in-depth studies of global corporate brands such as Coke, Apple, Nike, and Volkswagen, he argues that iconic brand images are largely driven from the inside out; such organizations 'look deeply inward to truly understand their identity and then inculcate their brand spirit into everything they do. ... When a brand is communicated with such supercharged emotion, a deep bond will form with customers' (p. 22).

Similarly, Rindova *et al.* (2006) describe such firms as having achieved 'celebrity' status by taking bold or dramatic steps to express an identity that captures important societal changes or tensions in society. These organizations become natural targets for the business press to create 'dramatized realities'; witness the portrayal of US brands such as Google, Apple and, from a specifically employer branding perspective, Southwest Airlines and Yahoo! in putting employees before customers (Miles and Mangold, 2005; Sartain, 2005). Southwest Airlines CEO was quoted as saying that she wasn't really interested in stock prices but had as her number one goal the satisfaction and motivation of employees (Liden, 2007) – perhaps a case of doing well by doing good and/or a message made for the business press hungry for quotable quotes?

Such iconic, cultural brands, according to Holt, represent the pinnacle of branding achievement in both a customer and employee sense, which is borne out by research into the superior power of global corporate branding by companies such as Toyota in contrast to Ford's more localized strategies (Quelch, 2007). However, there is a warning here. Even icons such as Toyota will not remain so – according to *The Economist* (2007b), its brand reputation suffered during 2007 because of it failure to sustain its reliability record and its 'green credentials' – unless they are able to continuously tap into what Holt calls 'myth markets' and reinvent themselves to reflect changes in these markets.

Myth markets are those in which certain corporate stories compete with others to resolve important contradictions between national ideologies that allow societies as a whole to function and populist, local cultural groups that are either disenfranchised from the dominant national cultures or choose to disenfranchise themselves for specific reasons. Apple originally achieved (then lost and recently regained) its iconic or authentic status because of its appeal to individualist 'free agents' who no longer wanted to work with or buy from staid, large bureaucratic organizations; instead they saw themselves as creative consumers and employees in a new knowledge economy who could pursue their essential, artistic selves in a largely shareholder-driven US business system (Gilmore and Joseph-Pine, 2007; Holt, 2004). Google has achieved the status of a cultural brand both in consumer and employer terms in much the same way, by creating a *sustainable corporate story* that is novel, credible, compelling, and sustainable (Barry and Elmes, 1997; Martin and Hetrick, 2006; Fombrun and Van Reil, 2003). Brands achieve cultural status by creating identity myths that are *authentic* in the sense of portraying the populist world in which the company is a real participant rather than a stage-managed one and *charismatically aesthetic* by telling a novel and compelling story to all stakeholders, including employees and customers.

Thus far we have set out the beginnings of a theoretical model of how employer branding is meant to work. Borrowing from the branding literature, we have discussed the levels at which employer branding can work in satisfying instrumental and symbolic and, most importantly, cultural needs.

In the next section we examine some of the evidence on employer branding in practice and raise some key questions and tensions that are relevant to employer branding in an international context.

DOES EMPLOYER BRANDING WORK IN PRACTICE AND CAN IT WORK IN AN INTERNATIONAL CONTEXT?

One of the problems of the extant research into employer branding is that it is largely based in a domestic context in which national cultures and institutions play a limited role. For IHRM researchers and practitioners, a central question is whether the principles and practices developed domestically can be transferred to different national labor markets? Our case study addresses the question: Do the same corporate messages and mechanisms that are effective in the headquarters of a UK-based MNC transfer to different overseas subsidiaries?

Research into employer branding in a domestic context makes hard evidence difficult to find. The corporate communications literature has focused on image management and how images of organizations are portrayed by organizations and in the media (Miles and Mangold, 2005; Van Riel, 2003). Arnold *et al.* (2003) showed how important media influences were in shaping existing and potential employee views of the UK-based National Health Service as an employer. However, most research focuses on the distinction between instrumental and symbolic benefits to recruits and existing employees.

Table 15.1 shows an emerging consensus on the potential effectiveness of employer branding, particularly over the importance of symbolic dimensions and emotional appeal. As Lievens *et al.* (2007) warn: '. . . if organizations only focus on instrumental job and organizational attributes . . . an important part of what makes an organization attractive is ignored' (p. S55). There is some evidence that viral employer branding techniques, such as word-of-mouth, interaction with potential recruits and securing endorsements by potential recruits, are more likely to communicate the symbolic and emotional attributes of organizations, and are more effective in the recruitment phase. Nevertheless, as Brewster *et al.* (2007) point out, recruitment media, messages, and selection criteria are embedded in national cultural and institutional settings. What is acceptable and works in one setting, for example, extensive word-of-mouth recruitment in countries such as Turkey and Greece, may be less acceptable in institutional environments in which discrimination on the basis of race, ethnicity, and gender are major issues, for example, in the USA and the UK.

Where we lack hard evidence, both in a domestic and international setting, is on the power of cultural employer brands in creating important identity myths and telling aesthetically compelling, novel, and authentic stories to potential recruits and existing employees. This is important because the aspirations of some organizations in the long term may lie in creating such iconic employer brands, especially MNCs which operate in global labor markets for talent (Sparrow *et al.*, 2004) but

TABLE 15.1 Key findings from recent employer branding studies.

	Key findings	Authors
Attracting potential recruits	Certain kinds of recruitment practices can be used to market employer brands better than others. Engineering students' employment intentions and actual decisions were influenced by two dimensions of employer brand image: general attitudes toward the company and perceived job attributes. The relationships between word-of-mouth endorsements and the two dimensions of brand image were found to be particularly strong, though they worked in interaction with publicity, sponsorship and advertising.	Collins and Stevens (2002)
	(a) A recent Danish study involving 10 000 graduates showed they were more interested in the prospects of professional development than either workplace conditions (autonomy, work–life balance, work hours, and so on) or the corporate communication of leadership and performance or products and ethics. (b) Pharmaceutical companies and consulting firms were much more highly rated as employer brand images than retailing, telecommunications or oil and gas companies. (c) Familiarity with the employer brand was not closely correlated with its reputation. (d) Direct communications of the employer brand (through advertising, fairs, and so on), has less impact on employer brand image than more interactive methods (for example companies hosting events) and endorsement approaches (having students endorse the company, hosting research, placements, and so on).	Andersen (2007)
	Early recruitment and advertising had beneficial effects on increasing the quantity and quality of applicants.	Collins and Han (2004)

	Symbolic attributes of the employer brand image were more important than instrumental (job and organizational) attributes in helping potential recruits to differentiate among banks.	Lievens and Highhouse (2003)
	Students tended to be attracted to organizations that had personality traits similar to their own.	Slaughter et al. (2004)
	Research on 231 potential recruits to nursing and allied professions in NHS in the UK suggested that prior images of operational difficulties, work pressure and understaffing primarily gained through media and personal experience had a significant effect on willingness to become employed. Research also suggested that such images were very difficult to manage	Arnold et al. (2003)
Employee identification and organizational performance	(a) Those instrumental and symbolic factors that were important in attracting applicants to the Belgian Army were also important to those individuals pursuing a career in it.	Lievens et al. (2007)
	(b) Perceived competence of the organization was the most important factor in explaining employees' identification with the army.	
	(c) Organizational identification is more related to pride and respect than to material (instrumental) benefits, such as advancement, travel, pay and job security.	

(Continued)

TABLE 15.1 (Continued)

Key findings	Authors
Canadian research on employer of choice policies. . . (a) Agreeableness (friendly, supportive, honesty) of the employer brand image was seen by 870 managers in 17 UK organizations as the best predictor of their job satisfaction and affinity (identification with the organization). However, perceived differentiation (uniqueness) and loyalty were influenced by quite different dimensions. (b) The perceived competence of the organization was not found to influence managers' perceptions of its uniqueness, their loyalty to it, job satisfaction or affinity with it. (c) Managers had a greater affinity to employer brands which were seen to be arrogant, aggressive, authoritarian and controlling!	Davies (2007)
Employer branding policies of top 100 US companies were associated with not only stable and highly positive workforce attitudes but also performance advantages over the broad market, and in some cases, over the matched group, with beneficial effects on organizational performance.	Fulmer *et al.* (2003)

also domestic organizations which recruit internationally, such as the UKs largest employer, the National Health Service (Sparrow, 2007). We are also short on evidence on the potential of organizations to influence or leverage cultural brands through informal techniques equivalent to viral branding. In MNCs this becomes an especially difficult proposition because cultural brands rely on corporate stories being seen as locally authentic and charismatically appealing to employees in settings that may be marked by large cultural and institutional distances between headquarters and subsidiaries (Martin and Beaumont, 2001; Kostova, 1999).

Our conclusions from current theory and evidence on employer branding are that the process is more complicated than most practitioners acknowledge and the evidence so far is piecemeal but supportive of promising practices in particular contexts (hence the contradictions in Table 15.1). Our model and discussion of the process of employer branding is necessarily simplified for the purposes of this chapter, but has shown potential points of fracture at which the theory and practice can break down and where the theory (and therefore practice) is underdeveloped.

So, in an international context, does it therefore make sense to speak about – or indeed to try to create – an employer brand image in the singular? It does and it doesn't. On the one hand, there is a good case for iconic global employer brands that contain strong identity myths, emotional links, and symbolism for employees in many different countries. Technology companies such as HP, Microsoft, Google, Cisco, and IBM are good examples, and though many of these employer brands are American in origin and speak to American myths, their appeal is often worldwide. On the other hand, there is a strong argument and some evidence that employer brands are, or need to be, locally authored or co-created to be contextually authentic, if they are to achieve the cultural authenticity that some organizations seek from investment in employer branding. This may apply particularly to firms in certain kinds of industries, such as retailing and to those operating in experience goods markets, such as tourism, personal services, financial services, and even healthcare and education, arguably all of which are characterized by a grater degree of culture-boundedness than technology. The initial problems experienced by Disney in France and the failure of Wal-Mart in Germany are good illustrations of this point.

These developments towards co-creation and the search for authenticity of employer brands reflect another, more prosaic lesson – the need to segment the customer base, i.e., dividing customers into groups of individuals that are similar in specific ways relevant to marketing, such as age, gender, interests, spending habits, and so on. Using segmentation allows organizations to target groups effectively, and allocate marketing resources to best effect (Copeland et al., 2000). Some organizations, for example large motor vehicle producers, have adopted a strategy of mass customization to achieve the benefits of customer segmentation while mass producing goods and, increasingly, services with differing individual specifications through the use of 'components' that may be assembled in a number of different configurations.

These segmentation approaches are beginning to find their way into the HR literature and practice in the form of specific employer value propositions (EVPs) designed for different groups of employees, especially where organizations are able to use sophisticated data analysis to arrive at meaningful, evidence-based but changing segments. Indeed, as Huselid *et al.* (2005) have argued, one-size-fits-all employer of choice schemes that fail to segment internally produce an inevitable mediocrity among the workforce because organizations often over-deliver to those that they don't want to keep and under-deliver to those that they do want to keep.

Choices in international employer branding

The message is well documented by writers in the field of international management (Roberts, 2004) – we need a 'both/and' solution. In employer branding terms both/and translates into embracing sustainable corporate stories and specific/local employee value propositions that reflect the inevitable tensions in international organizations between the needs for 'being the same' and 'being different' (Deephouse and Carter, 2005). Increasingly, MNCs seek to reconcile their simultaneous but sometimes conflicting needs for *corporate governance, international legitimacy* and *organizational learning* across subunit and national boundaries with *differentiation* in local product and labor markets (Martin and Hetrick, 2006). Adapting the classic Perlmutter model, we propose four stylized choices for an international employer brand, which can be contrasted with a *reactive* weakly branded position that many organizations in the early stages of internationalizing find themselves in (Figure 15.2).

Organizations, especially those that have grown internationally through rapid acquisition, often find themselves adopting a local/domestic employer brand strategy, analogous to what marketing specialists label a 'house of brands'. Employer branding would typically be locally created and managed, with little centralized governance. Such a position allows MNCs to retain the advantages of authenticity and

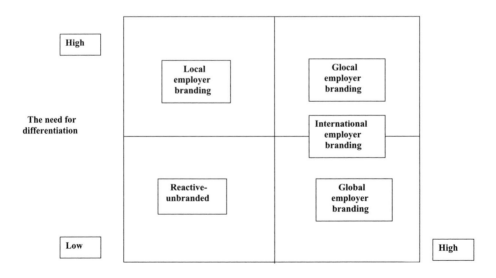

FIGURE 15.2 Choices in international employer branding strategies.

maximum potential to tap into local employee voice and psychological contracts. As firms grow their operations beyond domestic markets, however, they face the classic problems of establishing corporate integration and global legitimacy on issues such as strategy, leadership, governance, and ethical standards (Martin and Hetrick, 2006). They seek to leverage and create strong corporate cultures, and build on the benefits of standardized recruitment, development, employment practices and, increasingly, common HR technology platforms (Martin *et al.*, 2008).

We propose they have a choice among three positions, distinguished by how they wish to balance the needs for local authenticity and global leverage in relation to the product-market environment taking into account their stage in the internationalization process.

1. If organizations perceive the balance of benefits lies in leveraging their global brand, culture, and HR practices and technologies, they will settle for a *global employer brand* (in marketing terms, a 'branded house'). Typically, such a strategy would be centrally determined and implemented, with little influence from local HR teams.
2. If organizations strive to maximize the benefits primarily of the global brand, culture, and HR practices but secondarily seek (or are required to by local labor law) to achieve a degree of local relevance and authenticity, they may adopt an *international employer brand* strategy. In marketing terms, this is an endorsed brand, but with a twist in which the local brand will be used to endorse the global brand to help to make it more authentic in local labor markets. Typically, such a strategy would be developed by headquarters HR teams in consultation with local management and HR functions. Recent case study evidence supports this – most MNCs studied were following this path toward corporateness, finding little differences in their HR architectures and practices in the different countries in which they operated (Stiles *et al.*, 2006; Stiles, 2007).
3. If organizations seek to optimize global branding with local authenticity and relevance, they may strive for a *glocal employer brand*. What distinguishes this strategy from others lies not so much in what it looks like but in how it is developed. To promote authenticity, such an employer brand strategy has to maximize employee voice and the views of local HR teams in all international and organizational contexts, but at the same time, balance these with a sustainable corporate story that has transnational appeal.

From our previous discussion of cultural brands, the third strategy holds out the most promise in the long run for MNCs which seek to differentiate themselves in international labor markets by becoming a cultural, iconic or authentic employer brand, though what this might look like in practice is still open to question.

To illustrate some of the points raised so far, we now outline the initial attempts of one large UK-based financial services company (Finco), which has grown rapidly through acquisitions overseas, to theorize and implement an international branding strategy. This ongoing story describes the early stages of what will be a long journey, given its ambitions to become a world-renowned company in its industry and leader in international management.

FINCO AND EMPLOYER BRANDING

Finco's history

Since the 1990s Finco has grown fast to become one of the largest banks in the world, which, at the time of writing, ranks fifth in the world in market share and capitalization. From its small provincial banking origins in the UK in 1727, it now has 135 000 employees in 30 countries (or national jurisdictions as it calls them) throughout Europe, America, and Asia. Finco's recent strategy has been based on growth through sometimes spectacular and hostile acquisitions into related markets, though it established its reputation as a major UK player in the 1980s by growing organically through developing some innovative enterprises with new business models for the industry – for example, an online car insurance company, the UK's first comprehensive online banking service over the internet, a joint financial services ventures with a major UK-based retailer, and another with a well-known company that had developed its online operations. In 2000, Finco's acquisitions began by successfully bidding for an under-performing UK bank nearly three times its size, which was the largest acquisition in the history of UK banking at the time. This purchase, in contrast to many acquisitions, has turned out to be highly successful according to financial analysts since every original business goal promised by Finco during the acquisition contest has been delivered. It also saw Finco begin to develop internationally, since part of this major acquisition included taking on responsibility for some regional US banks.

Finco, branding strategy and employer branding

During this period of rapid acquisition, Finco followed a typical 'house of brands' marketing strategy, retaining the brands of the original businesses. On the one hand, this strategy had the benefits of retaining customer loyalty, identification and authenticity among its customers and employees with the original brands in the different countries and lines of business in which it operated; on the other hand, it resulted in the company selling broadly similar products through different divisions under different brands, which was confusing for customers. Gradually, Finco moved toward an endorsed, external branding strategy, in which the external communications of the acquired businesses are branded with Finco's corporate brand and logo. These companies began to cross-sell products and services across the range of line-of-business brands.

By 2007, however, the organizational structures and cultures of the different brands, divisions and lines of products and services was increasingly perceived by the headquarters senior leadership team as detrimental to the development of a globally branded business. There was a growing recognition among the senior leadership team that developing a globally 'branded house' strategy, embracing a global corporate identity and image, would meet client demands for a more unified product and service portfolio, especially given the global branding industry recipe (Spender, 1989; Stiles, 2007) adopted by most of the major competitors. Such pressures to adopt a more global strategy were not only customer-driven; increasingly, senior leaders have seen these moves as necessary in meeting institutional demands from the international financial and regulatory communities for such a strategy.

These pressures toward a growing 'corporateness' in Finco's external branding and governance strategies have been mirrored internally by an increasingly influential HR function in corporate headquarters. It became evident to this global HR team that duplication of HR resources and services, coupled with fragmentation of people management policies and processes, were impacting on the organization's needs to balance corporate and local interests. There were significant differences in the way employees were managed and employed both by division and within the different country jurisdictions, which the senior team believed to be harmful to the needs for effective corporate governance, HR management, and a global brand image. An internal report on Finco's three businesses operating in Germany exemplified many of the problems. Each of these German businesses had its dedicated HR team creating mainly local HR policies and practices to suit their respective needs. There was little evidence of coordination among them at national level over issues such as leadership development or disciplinary policies, which were agenda items that, in a German context, would normally be expected to be integrated nationally. Nor was there any evidence of sharing of good HR practices or other forms of knowledge – one of the often made justifications for mergers and acquisitions. This state of affairs was not purely accidental: when these three businesses were forced to adopt corporate policies – for example, Finco's code of conduct and international payroll policies – the local HR teams expressed a degree of resentment that these polices did not take account the scale of their businesses and forced them to submit time-consuming management information that was perceived to be of little value.

A further piece of evidence forced the case for some fresh thinking on employer branding and the employment proposition. Internal survey evidence collected through the company's highly sophisticated human capital management system across all Finco's country jurisdictions revealed highly varied patterns of responses to its engagement survey (see Table 15.2). So, for example, Finco's Dutch, Italian, Belgian, German and even American employees were significantly more likely to hold negative perceptions of Finco's management, HR and people strategies, and sense of Finco's image and positioning than employees in Finco's other subsidiaries in countries including the UK. Though patterns of variation are to be expected in international surveys of this nature – employees in different countries systematically differ in attitudes to questions on job satisfaction and the like – the pattern in this table is not the one that might be expected from other similar surveys. Moreover, this data has been standardized to a degree by being reported as deviations from norms for high-performing global companies, data for which is collected by the survey consultants that assist Finco. So, for example, the survey consultants have comparable data for high-performing companies operating in Finco's country jurisdictions across engagement criteria such as perceptions of senior headquarters leadership, divisional leadership, people management, communications, the extent to which the business was customer-focused, efficient and innovative, levels of workload and work–life balance, job security, etc.

The data in Table 15.2 further reinforced the perceptions of headquarters HR team that much more work was needed on bedding down the global employer brand promise across the company.

TABLE 15.2 Finco's international engagement performance.

A Finco Group Leadership
B Division Leadership
C Managing People and Change
D Customer Focus
E Communication
F Efficiency
G Innovation
H Workload and Work–Life Balance
I Cooperation and Working Relationships
J Respect and Diversity
K Performance Management and Development
L Recognition and Reward
M Job Satisfaction and Engagement
N Image and Competitive Position
O Employment Security

	A	B	C	D	E	F	G	H	I	J	K	L	M	N	O
Global High-Performing Norm 2006 (N=149 193)	74	66	73	83	70	66	71	57	75	79	63	60	79	70	75
UK (N=90,114)	0	-1	+2	-3	+8	-2	+4	+1	+3	+2	-1	+2	-9	-4	+11
Italy (N=763)	-25	-18	-6	-10	-9	-2	-10	-1	-5	-5	-18	-5	-12	-20	-3
Germany (N=880)	-15	-11	-9	-7	-4	-3	-10	0	-2	-9	-15	-12	-5	-20	0
Belgium (N=83)	-34	-14	-4	-7	+2	-6	+11	+7	-6	+4	-6	-14	+2	-22	-4
Netherlands (N=83)	-38	-33	-20	-18	-15	-14	-12	+8	-15	-10	-23	-26	-13	-39	-17
Switzerland (N=512)	-9	-8	-3	-5	-3	0	+11	+22	+3	-5	-4	+2	+2	-22	+3
France (N=205)	-15	-9	-7	-9	-4	-6	-17	-4	-3	-8	-12	-15	-10	-22	-5
Jersey (N=963)	+2	+3	+5	-1	+13	+1	+9	+8	+5	+5	+3	+2	-3	-7	+12
Guernsey (N=217)	+13	+12	+8	+5	+17	+12	+14	+15	+10	+10	+12	+15	+2	+4	+14

TABLE 15.2 (*Continued*)

Isle of Man (N=572)	+4	+4	+4	+1	+14	+2	+10	+10	+8	+6	+4	+3	-2	-4	+14
Gibraltar (N=145)	+14	+16	+15	+10	+16	+9	+16	+16	+13	+12	+14	+1	+8	+16	+16
Other Europe (N=4 554)	-12	-9	-7	-11	-2	-9	-6	-5	-4	-4	-10	-6	-12	-18	+7
USA (N=24 840)	-20	-3	-4	-4	-8	-1	-4	-2	+1	-1	-4	-5	-6	-12	-10
China (N=19)	-8	-8	-2	-5	-6	+2	-11	-7	+13	-7	-6	-13	-9	-6	-14
Singapore (N=382)	-3	-2	+2	-6	0	+1	+1	+7	+4	+3	-1	-3	-1	-17	-1
Hong Kong (N=333)	-4	-3	-1	-3	-5	+1	-4	-7	+4	+5	-2	-8	-2	-18	-1
Japan (N=191)	-15	-9	-6	-13	-4	-4	-10	-10	-9	-7	-15	-15	-5	-30	-20
India (N=291)	-8	-8	-3	-6	-3	+6	-3	+14	0	-4	-6	-5	-3	-12	-2
Other Asia (N=65)	+8	+9	+6	+4	+5	+10	+12	+10	+16	+11	+3	-9	+9	+2	+9

Shaded box = a statistically significant difference

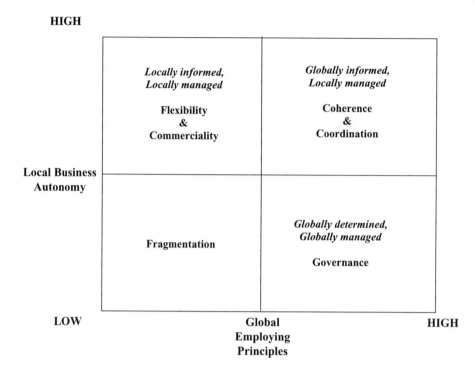

HIGH

Locally informed,
Locally managed

**Flexibility
&
Commerciality**

Globally informed,
Locally managed

**Coherence
&
Coordination**

**Local Business
Autonomy**

Fragmentation

Globally determined,
Globally managed

Governance

LOW   **Global**   **HIGH**
                        Employing
                        Principles

FIGURE 15.3 The Finco global employing framework.

The HR team in Finco set themselves the problem of how to reconcile the two po-tentially contradictory demands inherent in global businesses discussed in the main body of this chapter: How could Finco ensure local business autonomy, and flexibil-ity *and* gain the benefits of corporate integration? Their answer lay in the two-by-two framework in Figure 15.3 they produced that drew on the classic Perlmutter matrix.

Accordingly, and in common with many MNCs (Stiles *et al.*, 2006), their starting position was that certain HR and people management policies, particularly those that relate to *governance* issues, are sacrosanct and need to be globally determined and globally managed. In contrast, where the needs for local autonomy in HR policy making are high and the needs for global employer branding are low, for example, where businesses need to be able to respond flexibly to local labor market condi-tions to achieve a commercial advantage or to meet local labor legislation, certain HR and people management polices can be locally informed and locally managed. In the quadrant entitled 'Coherence and Coordination', global principles inform policies across divisions and country jurisdictions. However, the actual process of implementation or delivery is locally managed to meet country-specific business or regulatory requirements. Currently, work is focused on two critical processes in the development of the global vision for HR, employer branding, and the employment propositions.

The first is the articulation of the framework to each of the HR divisions that make up Finco's global HR team, which are resourcing, reward, development, and policy and employment relations. In turn local HR teams have been asked to 'populate' the framework with their policies as a starting point for a discussion to the global–local tensions embodied in it.

Second, following the acquisition of a large European bank with interests in the USA in late 2007, the headquarters HR team have to ensure that the Finco 'Employing Principles' (see Table 15.2) and its 'People Strategy' are implemented consistently in the new acquisition according to the criteria underlying the strategic framework in Figure 15.3 and the population of that framework with HR and people management policies.

Work has also commenced on articulating Finco's global employing principles, which forms the basis for a global employer brand proposition (see Table 15.3). These include standards of professional behavior and conduct detailed in a Global Code of Conduct, polices on rewards and core benefits, and employee and contractor screening. They also include a competency-based selection system, structured assessments, performance reviews, access to learning and development, and the rights to expect the company to identify and develop talented people.

Conclusions

In this chapter we have developed the beginnings of a model of employer branding in an international context, examined the evidence on the success of employer branding, which indicates that a focus on the symbolic and cultural dimensions are likely to be critical, and illustrated some of the problems of employer branding in an international context using the Finco case. So what can we learn from this work? First, in the spirit of action research into Finco's journey, there are some lessons that might be of value to practitioners and academics. Second, we reflect on our model in Figure 15.1, and the matrix of choices in international employer branding in Figure 15.2, and raise some important questions for the future of employer branding.

Regarding the Finco case, there are at least four lessons for the IHRM literature.[1] The first is a positive one for IHRM practitioners. Cross-national data and evidence on how companies devise and implement HR policies used to be the preserve of comparative HRM researchers and used in a purely descriptive way, for example, that HR in certain countries tends to be more centralized than in others. However, the Finco case illustrates how practitioners are beginning to use such data to theorize about what practices can be centralized and what practices need to be localized, and use these ideas and frameworks to negotiate with HR teams and their employees to establish workable employment propositions and employer brands. For example, Finco is now in a better position than it was a few years ago to answer the question of how best to manage the tensions between the needs for a global corporate identity and sensitivity to local needs. Nevertheless, as we have pointed out, there is still much work to be done to assess where this balance may lie in different

[1]We are grateful for the editor in shaping our thinking in this section.

TABLE 15.3 Finco's global employing principles.

We treat all our employees with dignity and respect, and are committed to valuing and promoting inclusion and to the following employment principles:

- Employees are employed (on one employing entity per country) based on the Group employment template. Certain policies will be Group-wide irrespective of country, others tailored to fit local operations. Local variations will meet unique legal. Regulatory, and/or commercial reasons.
- Our overall employee proposition will be determined by the Group and benchmarked to global high-performing companies. It will be implemented in accordance with country norms. The employee proposition will always meet minimum legislative requirements;
- Employees are expected to maintain high standards of professional behavior and conduct at all times as detailed in our Global Code of Conduct;
- Reward packages will be market competitive and will be differentiated by individual performance. Reward practices will allow for customisation with a core benefits offering;
- All employees and contractors are pre-employment screened to a minimum standard in accordance with our Group, legal and regulatory requirements. Additional screening will be carried out on a country by country basis;
- Selection for all job roles within Finco is done on a merit-based approach using competency based methods and more structured assessment where circumstances require;
- All internal and external recruitment is in accordance with the Group's recruitment guidelines to ensure consistency with the Finco Employer Brand;
- Every employee has regular performance reviews using the Finco performance management system, and has access to learning and development opportunities via Finco learning systems and products;
- Employee talent is identified, managed and developed;
- All employees are expected to contribute toe continuous improvement in their area using the Work-Out approach.

international and organizational contexts, should it seek greater competitive advantage through glocalization. There is unlikely to be one organizing principle of HR that suits all circumstances and all contexts at all times, and perhaps their theorization or practices into global determined/informed and locally managed/informed needs to reflect this.

The second lesson relates to the notion raised earlier that recruitment and selection processes are culturally embedded, so what is seen as appropriate and what works in one international context may be alien to another (Brewster *et al.*, 2007; Collings and Scullion, 2006). This point raises a key question regarding the suitability of some of Finco's proposed global employment principles (see Table 15.3), especially those that focus on the desire to use standardized selection criteria based on merit, standardized recruitment and selection methods, and performance management based on individual performance. The IHRM literature has been very prominent in highlighting the cross-national differences in assumptions and approaches on selection in particular, thus any attempt to set out a global approach on these issues has to take such differences into account.

The third concerns the question of how Finco's talent management and employer branding policies might play out in practice. National cultural differences typically do not influence work attitudes and behaviors directly, but do so through interlinked organizational cultures, HR architectures, and people management practices at the level of the firm or local subsidiary (Sparrow, 2006c). Thus the data regarding Finco's international engagement performance in Table 15.2 must be treated with some caution beyond the points made in the case above. Although there may be systematic national cultural differences in how employees respond to survey items such as diversity and job satisfaction, it is equally plausible that the data in Table 15.2 reflect local organizational cultures, HR and people management practices, and competences of local managers. Indeed, earlier cited evidence of the low impact of national cultures on values by Gerhart and Fang (2005) suggest that this is more likely to be the case. So, our example of Finco's three German sites suggests that local organizational factors may have been more important here than anything specific to German national culture.

The final lesson is more subtle and concerns the two-way, recursive relationship between national cultures and employee attitudes and behaviors. The vast majority of IHRM literature stresses the role of national cultures in influencing employees, albeit mediated by organizational cultures. However, as we have pointed out, some researchers have observed how employees *enact* national cultural differences in their reactions to the application of standard HR practices. From this perspective, national cultures, as we observe them in comparative HRM, are not objective phenomena but are more likely to be the product of bottom-up employee sense-making of imposed policies and practices. Employees and managers socially construct these structures through their actions, beliefs and needs for local identity, autonomy and a desire for a voice in matters that affect and/or threaten them. So, for example, in the Finco case, rather than being a cause, it is possible that German national culture may have been enacted to explain and legitimize why local HR staff in the three German companies found the policies on codes of conduct and payroll to be inappropriate, with a view to limiting further incursions into their autonomy. This point speaks to the importance of cultural branding and authenticity in our model.

Finally, we make some reflections on theory. In our attempts to construct a model of employer branding in an international context and to frame our choices in international employer branding strategies, we have stressed the importance of symbolic branding, which deals with emotional responses to corporate messages, and of cultural branding, which, to borrow Holt's (2004) terms, is an attempt to make employer brands more authentic and charismatically aesthetic. The core of our argument has been that sustained competitive advantage in labor markets and high levels of existing employee identification are more likely to be achieved by organizations that can create and maintain cultural brands by continuously reinventing themselves to marry changes in national ideologies with populist local cultures. Employer brands that rest on instrumental needs for tangible benefits and even symbolic meanings can be imitated by other organizations – and frequently are (Stiles *et al.*, 2006).

In our view the potential of cultural employer branding lies not so much in telling the charismatically appealing novel and compelling story but in continuously tapping into local employee voice to determine what that story should be. In other words, as the two-way relationship between cultures and actions in our model suggests, employer branding is, and should be, both top-down and bottom-up. This is especially so for firms operating in markets that deal mainly in experience goods and personal services, in which national cultures and business systems usually play an important role in shaping customer and employee views. However, it is probably equally so for firms operating in dynamic market environments where they find it difficult to defend or sustain long-term advantages and can, at best, stay ahead of the game through continuous experimentation and strategic maneuvering to secure their future (Dyer and Ericksen, 2007). Yet, the weight of evidence and even our case suggests that the top-down, corporate global message continues to be the dominate one, which often represents considerable previous investment in ideas and program and, hence, an inbuilt reluctance to change course or experiment. And, as we have noted, there are strong institutional and rational pressures to remain top-down, including the desire to build global customer-facing brands, pressures to meet international governance standards and to transfer best practice, including developing global performance standards and HR business process so that they can be adapted to technological solutions and outsourcing (Martin *et al.*, 2008; Stiles, 2007).

So, given the evidence of what global enterprises believe works best for them – which seems to be a growing corporateness – and our arguments for more locally authentic and dynamic employer brands, where should the balance lie? On this question, we are inclined to agree with Hamel (2007), who argues that the innovation agenda for modern businesses requires them to move beyond the 'unavoidable trade-offs that have been the unhappy legacy of modern management … to build organizations where discipline and freedom aren't mutually exclusive' (p. 9). Innovative products and services are built on innovative management practices, which change the traditional business models of organizations and their organizational forms from those designed to deliver efficiencies through standardization to those that make innovation a systemic feature of their progress. Translated into the language of employer branding, this argument can be interpreted as changing the balance from global integration to local authenticity and maximum employee voice. Indeed, three of Hamels's examples of radically innovative organizations – Google, Whole Foods, and W.L. Gore – have drawn heavily on values and HR practices that reflect this notion.

Where does this lead in terms of further research? Perhaps the first and key question is: To what extent do international organizations in general and MNCs in particular see their future as tied up with a movement toward the local? Second, and contingent on a desire to move toward a more glocal employment strategy and employer branding position, what such a change poses for international HR departments, particularly in how to learn from and capitalize on the ideas and desires of those 'at the fringe' in what attracts them to the organization and what engages them when they are in it? Third, given the dynamics of global labor markets, the questions of how centralized HR departments can adapt, relearn, and recapitalize on changing employee and potential employee expectations, desires, and needs also becomes a fruitful area for further investigation in this field. These questions are certainly relevant to Finco and, on grander scale, might form a relevant future agenda for international HRM research in this developing field.

References

Andersen, K. (2007). *Workplace reputations: Lessons from Scandinavia.* Paper presented to the 11th Annual Conference of the Reputation Institute, Norwegian School of Management, Oslo, June 1–3.

Apéria, T., Simcic Brønn, P., and Schultz, M. (2004). A reputation analysis of the most visible companies in the Scandinavian countries, *Corporate Reputation Review*, 7, 218–230.

Arnold, J., Coombs, C., Wilkinson, A., Loan-Clarke, J., Park, J., and Preston, D. (2003). Corporate images of the United Kingdom National Health Service: Implications for the recruitment and retention of Nursing and Allied Health professional staff. *Corporate Reputation Review*, 6 (3), 223–238.

Balmer, J.T., and Greyser, S.A. (2003) *Revealing the corporation: Perspectives on Identity, Image, Reputation, Corporate Branding and Corporate-Level Marketing.* London: Routledge.

Barrow, S., and Mosley, R. (2005). *The Employer Brand®: Bringing the Best of Brand Management to People at Work.* Chichester: John Wiley & Sons Ltd.

Barry, D., and Elmes, M. (1997). Strategy retold: Toward a narrative view of strategic discourse. *Academy of Management Review*, 22 (2), 429–452.

Boudreau, J.W., and Ramstad, P.M. (2007). *Beyond HR: The New Science of Human Capital.* Boston: Harvard Business School Press.

Brewster, C. (2007). HRM: The comparative dimension. In J. Storey (ed.), *Human Resource Management: A Critical Text.* London: Thomson, pp. 195–212.

Brewster, C., Sparrow, P.R., and Vernon, G (2007). *International Human Resource Management.* London: Chartered Institute of Personnel and Development.

CIPD (2007a). *Employer Branding: The Latest Fad or the Future of HR?* London: Chartered Institute of Personnel and Development.

CIPD (2007b). Designs on the dotted lines. *People Management*, October 18, 36–39.

CIPD (2007c). *Talent Management.* London: Chartered Institute of Personnel and Development.

Collings, D.G., and Scullion, H. (2006). Approaches to international staffing. In H. Scullion and D.J. Collings (eds), *Global Staffing.* London: Routledge.

Collins, C.J., and Han, J. (2004). Exploring applicant pool quantity and quality: The effects of early recruitment practices, corporate advertising and firm reputation. *Personnel Psychology*, 57, 687–717.

Collins, C.J., and Stevens, C.K. (2002). The relationship between early recruitment-related activities and the application decisions of new labor-market entrants: A brand equity approach to recruitment. *Journal of Applied Psychology*, 87 (6), 1121–1133.

Conway, N., and Briner, R.B. (2005). *Understanding Psychological Contracts at Work: A Critical Evaluation of Theory and Research.* Oxford: Oxford University Press.

Copeland, T., Koller, T., and Murrin, J. (2000). *Valuation: Measuring and Managing the Value of Companies* (3rd edn). New York: John Wiley & Sons.

Davies, G. (2007). Employer branding and its influence on managers. *European Journal of Marketing.*

Davies, G., and Chun, R. (2007). To Thine Own Staff Be Agreeable, *Harvard Business Review*, 85, 30–32.

Davies, G., Chun, R., da Silva, R.V., and Roper, S. (2003). *Corporate Reputation and Competitiveness.* London: Routledge.

Deephouse, D.L., and Carter, S.M. (2005). An examination of differences between organizational legitimacy and reputation. *Journal of Management Studies*, 42, 329–360.

Dyer, L., and Ericksen, J. (2007) Dynamic organizations: Achieving marketplace agility through workforce scalability. In J. Storey (ed.), *Human Resource Management: A Critical Text.* London: Thomson, pp. 263–281.

The Economist (2003). Unpublished panel survey of HR directors of major companies in North America, Asia and Europe. Personal communication (May).

The Economist (2006). Talent Management. A Special Survey. *The Economist*, October 6, London.

The Economist (2007a). Talent Wars in Asia. *The Economist,* August 18, pp. 58–60.

The Economist (2007b) A Wobble on the Road to the Top: Economist Briefing on Toyota. *The Economist*, November 10.

Edwards, T., and Kuruvilla, S. (2005). International HRM: National business systems, organizational policies and the international division of labour in MNCs. *International Journal of HRM*, 16 (1), 1–21.

Erez, M. and Gati, E. (2004). A dynamic, multi-level model of culture: From the micro level of the individual to the macro level of a global culture. *Applied Psychology: An International Review*, 53 (4), 583–598.

Ferner, A., and Varul, M. (1999). *The German Way? German Multinationals and the Management of Human Resources in their UK Subsidiaries.* London: Anglo-German Foundation.

Fishman, A. (2006). *The Wal-Mart Effect: How an Out-of-Town Superstore became a Superpower.* London: Allen Lane.

Fombrun, C.J., and Van Riel, C.B.M. (2003). *Fame and Fortune: How Successful Companies Build Winning Reputations.* Upper Saddle River, NJ: Financial Times/Prentice Hall.

Fulmer, J.S., Gerhart, B., and Scott, K.S. (2003) Are the 100 best better?: An empirical investigation of the relationship between being 'the best place to work' and firm performance. *Personnel Psychology*, 56, 965–993.

Gerhart, B., and Fang, M. (2005). National culture and human resource management: Assumptions and evidence. *International Journal of Human Resource Management*, 16 (6), 971–986.

Gilmore, J.H., and Joseph Pine II, B. (2007). *Authenticity: What Consumers Really Want.* Boston, MA: Harvard Business School Press.

Gladwell, M. (1997). The coolhunt. *New Yorker.* May 17.

Hamel, G. (2007). *The Future of Management.* Boston: Harvard Business School Press.

Hatch, M.J., and Schultz, M. (2001). Are the strategic starts aligned for your corporate brand? *Harvard Business Review,* Jan–Feb, 129–134.

Hatch, M.J., and Schulz, M. (2004). *Organizational Identity: A Reader.* Oxford: Oxford University Press.

Holt, D.B. (2004). *How brands become icons.* Boston, MA: Harvard Business School Press.

Holt, D.B. (2006). Jack Daniel's America: Iconic Brands as Ideological Parasites and Proselytizers, *Journal of Consumer Culture*, 6 (3), 355–77.

Huselid, M.A., Becker, B.E., and Beatty, R.W. (2005). *The Workforce Scorecard: Managing Human Capital to Execute Strategy.* Boston: Harvard Business School Press.

Kostova, T. (1999). Transnational transfer of strategic organizational practices: A contextual perspective. *Academy of Management Review*, 24 (2), 308–224.

Lepak, D.P., and Snell, S.A. (2002). The strategic management of human capital: Determinants and implications of different relationships. *Academy of Management Review*, 24 (1), 18.

Liden, R. (2007). Doing well by doing good in the employee–organization relationship: Current knowledge, future promise. *Academy of Management All Academy Symposium*, Philadelphia, August 5–9.

Lievens, F., and Highhouse, S. (2003) The relation of instrumental and symbolic attributes to a company's attractiveness as an employer. *Personnel Psychology*, 56, 75–102.

Lievens, F., Van Hoye, G., and Anseel, F. (2007). Organizational identity and employer image: Towards a unifying framework. *British Journal of Management*, 18, S45–S59.

Lievens, F., Van Hoye, G., and Scheurs, B. (2005) Examining the relationship between employer knowledge dimensions and organizational attractiveness: An application in a military context. *Journal of Occupational and Organizational Psychology*, 78, 553–572.

Martin, D. (2007). *Rebuilding Brand America: What we must do to Restore our Reputation and Safeguard the Future of American Business Abroad*. New York: American Management Association.

Martin, G., and Beaumont, P.B. (2001). Transforming multinational enterprises: Towards a process model of strategic human resource management change. *International Journal of Human Resource Management*, 12 (8), 1234–1250.

Martin, G., and Beaumont, P.B. (2003a). *Branding and HR: What's in a Name?* London: Chartered Institute of Personnel and Development.

Martin, G., and Beaumont, P.B. (2003b). *What's in a name? Building the relationship between people management and branding*. London: Chartered Institute of Personnel and Development.

Martin, G., and Hetrick, S. (2006). *Corporate Reputations, Branding and Managing People: A Strategic Approach to HR*. Oxford: Butterworth Heinemann.

Martin, G., Reddington, M., and Alexander, H. (eds) (2008). *Technology, Outsourcing and Transforming HR*. Oxford: Butterworth Heinemann.

Martin, J. (2002). *Organizational Culture: Mapping the Terrain*. Foundations for organizational science series. Newsbury Park, CA: Sage.

Michaels, E., Handfield-Jones, H., and Axelrod, B. (2001). *The War for Talent*. Boston, MA: Harvard Business School Press.

Miles, S.J., and Mangold, W.G. (2005). Positioning Southwest Airlines through employee branding. *Business Horizons*, 48, 535–545.

Morgan, G. (1997). *Images of Organization*, 2nd ed. Thousand Oaks: Sage Publications.

Ostroff, C., and Bowen, D.E. (2000). Moving HR to a higher level: HR practices and organizational effectiveness. In J.K. Klein and S.W.J. Kolzlowski (eds), *Multilevel Theory, Research and Methods in Organizations. Foundations, Extensions and New Directions*. San Francisco: Jossey-Bass, pp. 211–266.

Quelch, J. (2007). *How Brand China Can Succeed*. Boston, MA: Harvard Business School Publishing.

Rao, B.A., and Baid, P. (2006). *Employer Branding: Concepts and Cases*. Hyderabad, India: Icfai University Press.

Reiche, B.S. (2007). Knowledge sharing through inpatriate assignments in multinational corporations: a social capital perspective. PhD thesis, Department of Management and Marketing, University of Melbourne.

Rindova, V.P., Pollock, T.G., and Hayward, M.L.A. (2006). Celebrity firms: The social construction of market popularity. *Academy of Management Review*, 31, 50–71.

Roberts, J. (2004). *The Modern Firm: Organizational Design for Performance and Growth*. Oxford: Oxford University Press.

Sartain, L. (2005). Branding from the inside out at Yahoo!: HR's role as a brand builder. *Human Resource Management*, 44 (1), 89–93.

Schein, E.H. (2004). *Organizational Culture and Leadership* (3rd edn), New York: John Wiley & Sons.

Schultz, M., Antorini, Y.M., and Csaba, F.F. (2005). *Corporate Branding: Purposes, People and Processes*, Copenhagen: Copenhagen Business School Press.

Slaughter, J.E., Zickar, S., Highhouse, S., and Mohr, D.C. (2004). Personality traits inferences about organisations: Development of a measure and assessment of construct validity. *Journal of Applied Psychology*, 89, 85–103.

Sparrow, P.R (2006a). International management: Key challenges for industrial and organizational psychology. In G. Hodginson and J.K. Ford (eds), *International Review of Industrial and Organizational Psychology*, Vol. 21. London: John Wiley & Sons, pp. 189–266.

Sparrow, P.R. (2006b). Knowledge management in Global organizations. In: G. Stahl and I. Björkman (eds), *Handbook of Research into International HRM*. London: Edward Elgar, pp. 113–138.

Sparrow, P.R. (2006c). *International recruitment, selection and assessment*. London: Chartered Institute of Personnel and Development.

Sparrow, P.R. (2007). Globalization of HR at function level: Case studies of the recruitment, selection and assessment processes. *International Journal of Human Resource Management*, 18, 845–867.

Sparrow, P.R., Brewster, C., and Harris, H. (2004). *Globalizing Human Resource Management*. London: Routledge.

Sparrow, P.R., and Cooper, C.L. (2003). *The New Employment Relationship*. Oxford: Butterworth – Heinemann.

Spender, J.C. (1989). *Industry Recipes: The Nature and Sources of Managerial Judgement*. Oxford: Blackwell.

Stiles, P. (2007). A world of difference. *People Management*, November 15, pp. 36–41.

Stiles, P., Trevor, J., Paauwe, J., Farndale, E., Wright, P., Morris, S., Stahl, G., and Bjorkman, I. (2006). *Best practice and key themes in global human resource management: Project report*. Accessed November 17, 2007 http://www.jbs.cam.ac.uk/research/subject_groups/downloads/ghrra_report.pdf.

Storey, J. (2007). Strategic HR. In J. Storey (ed.), *Human Resource Management: A Critical Text*. London: Thomson, pp. 59–78.

Taylor, J.R., Groleau, C., Heaton, L., and Van Every, E. (2000). *The Computerization of Work*. San Francisco, CA: Sage Publications.

Thorne, K. (2004). Employer Branding, Personnel Today Management Resources, Surrey: Reed Publishing.

Van Riel, C.B. (2003). The management of corporate communications. In J.M.T. Balmer and S.A. Geyser (eds), *Revealing the Corporation: Perspectives on Identity, Image, Reputation, Corporate Branding and Corporate-Level Marketing*. London: Routledge.

Weick, K. E. (1988). Enacted sense making in crisis situations. *Journal of Management Studies*, 25 (4), 305–317.

Whetten, D., and Mackey, A. (2002). A social actor conception of organizational identity and its implications for the study of organizational reputations. *Business and Society*, 41, 393–414.

Whitley, R. (1999). *Divergent Capitalisms: The Social Structuring and Change of Business Systems*. Oxford: Oxford University Press.

Zhang H., Liu G., and Zhao P. (2008). *China Employer Brand Management*. Beijing: Post & Telecom Press.

16

Developing a Theory of Skills for Global HR

DAVID ASHTON, PHIL BROWN, AND HUGH LAUDER

INTRODUCTION

The United Nations Conference on Trade and Development (UNCTAD) defines a transnational corporation (TNC) as 'an enterprise comprising entities in more than one country which operate under a system of decision making that permits coherent policies and a common strategy. The entities are so linked, by ownership or otherwise, that one or more of them may be able to exercise a significant influence over the others and, in particular, to share knowledge, resources, and responsibilities with the others.' A multinational corporation (MNC), in contrast, is more bounded by the location of its operations. MNCs have production facilities or other fixed assets in at least one foreign country and make their major management decisions in a global context, but in a number of functions such as marketing, production, research and development, and human resource management, for example, these decisions must be made in terms of host country customs and traditions.

This chapter argues that TNCs are now operating *outside* the boundaries of national systems (hence our preference to use the term TNC rather than MNC). We are currently witnessing a major transformation of the process of skill formation in which the process is being 'freed' from the constraints of national vocational education and training (VET) and industrial relations systems and is taking on a global character.

The chapter outlines the changes taking place in the production of skill in relation to economic globalization and explains why this process is becoming central to organizational competitiveness. There is a gap in the literature, however. In the context of globalization, the HR literature does not focus on the issue of skill. To rectify this shortcoming, in this chapter we outline some of the key arguments and concepts that are necessary to develop a broader conceptual framework for understanding the role that skills play in the strategies of TNCs.

Handbook of International Human Resource Management. Edited by Paul R. Sparrow
© 2009 John Wiley & Sons, Ltd

Although there is no literature that is centrally concerned with the process of skill acquisition and use and the changes that are taking place in the process at the global level, there are two schools of thought which deal with aspects of the process, namely the national systems approach and the international human resource management (IHRM) literature.

Over the last two decades there have been a number of studies, from what we call the 'national systems' approach, which focus on the impact of national systems of education and training on the competitiveness of national economies (Ashton and Green, 1996; Crouch et al., 1999; Brown et al., 2001; Thelen, 2004) These have argued for the importance of national institutions both in shaping what has been described as the process of skill formation within societies and explaining variations in national competitiveness. This tradition has made a powerful intellectual case for the primacy of national institutional frameworks and cultures in shaping the process of skill formation and the competitive strategies of companies in the private sector. Indeed, it was the belief in the efficacy of public policy in shaping business strategies that led to the advocacy of Western governments adopting the 'High Skills Route' to economic growth.

Understandably the main focus of empirical work has been on the role of public policy rather than on the role of business. However, this research tradition has close affinities to the 'business systems' approach to the analysis of the companies championed by Whitley (1999) and others (see also Edwards, this volume Chapter 11). Here the argument is that the structure of the business enterprise, and its behavior, are fundamentally influenced by the institutional and cultural context within which they were established and grew. When this approach was extended to the study of international businesses, the same argument was adopted. Thus Morgan (2003: 1) argues that multinational firms have to be seen as social constructions '... in particular they are built out of specific national contexts that shape how they internationalize'. The assumption is that firms will not converge toward a single model of the 'global firm' but that divergence and diversity will persist. The challenges of operating across national boundaries and in different local contexts is seen to present TNCs with new problems and the opportunities to establish new patterns of behavior and procedures. However, the impact of these new patterns of behavior and practices for the process of skill formation have not been examined – a task this chapter intends to start.

The one school of thought that has explored the question of skill acquisition among TNCs directly is the human resource management (HRM) literature. Here researchers have produced a wealth of evidence on HRM practices in the areas of selection, recruitment, training and development, payment systems, and industrial/employee relations. However, what globalization has meant to some of these scholars is a view that argues that these practices have simply been transferred from a national or local level to the international stage. In one of the standard texts on international human resource management (IHRM), Briscoe and Schuler (2004) argue that firms 'internationalize' their business in response to the development of global markets. They see the internationalization of business resulting in the internationalization of staffing (finding the best and lowest cost employees anywhere in the world), executive development (ensuring that the management group has the knowledge and ability to operate anywhere in the world), compensation (being globally competitive), and labor relations (which vary from country to country), thereby transforming HRM into IHRM. They see IHRM as the '...process of managing human resources in enterprises throughout the global environment...' (Briscoe and Schuler, 2004: 21), a process which has involved the introduction of new activities such as the management of international assignees, working alongside HR professionals from other countries and adapting HR practices to multicultural and cross-cultural environments (Briscoe and Schuler, 2004: 27).

Other scholars in the field of IHRM have moved beyond this tendency to see IHRM as just an international version of HRM. For example, Sparrow and Brewster (2006) recognize that IHRM is confronted with new developments and problems that cannot be adequately handled by treating IHRM in this way. They point out that only a few multinational companies (MNCs) have penetrated markets across the globe in that they have the capability to locate, source, and manage resources anywhere in the world. While they consider that most MNCs are still operating within their own national systems they do acknowledge that firms who have moved to an international orientation are confronting new HR issues and problems. They see new global business structures overriding country-based HR processes. In global MNCs, HR becomes focused on all human resources not just the mobile internationals, on the new opportunities and challenges presented by new technologies of e-enabled HRM, on the benefits of knowledge transfer through techniques such as centers of excellence, as well as on the need to ensure the affordability of staff. In addition, central to the new role of HR is the need to develop organizational capability in the areas of R&D, production centers, logistics networks, and new HR processes and systems. Here we see the emergence of a new agenda with HR becoming involved in the wider business processes such as knowledge management and supply chain management. In this respect it marks a major shift in intellectual perspective from the 'old' IHRM tradition.

The strength of this literature is that it points to some of the new skills associated with the emergence of the globally oriented MNCs, the skills required to manage knowledge through centers of excellence, to negotiate and manage alliances with other companies and institutions as well as the skills to manage talent at a global level and so on. Whereas the old tradition saw IHRM merely as an extension of the conventional HR agenda, this new agenda is pointing to the fact that there is something different in the ways in which skills issues, and their management, are handled by firms at the transnational level.

The problem with the IHRM literature is that it still remains focused primarily on the agenda of the HR professionals. While acknowledging that there are new issues to be addressed in these TNCs, the analysis remains locked into developing an understanding of how these issues affect the HR manager. In this respect the academic agenda is closely tied to the requirements of professional organizations such as the CIPD which provide certification of professional competence. Harris *et al.* (2003) reiterate this central concern with identifying strategies and practices aimed at ensuring the most effective use of human resources.

To fully understand the changes that are taking place in TNCs, especially those concerning the creation and use of skills, we must first step outside this perspective and locate the analysis of HR issues in the wider national and global context within which these firms operate. We must ask why such companies approach the process of skill creation and use in different ways and how the wider institutional and market conditions within which they operate shape their responses. This means exploring how the local or international supply of labor, the national origins of the company, as well competitive conditions shape the ways in which firms create and utilize skills through their broader management practices. The important point is that in order to understand these issues we have to look at the firm in the context of the wider relationships within which it is embedded and which it seeks to shape. We would note that the use of the term 'international' in the HRM literature suggests that firms are operating between nations, modifying their behavior in the light of national differences. However, the firms we interviewed in our research (outlined below) were clearly operating across nations and in crucial respects, were not moderating their behavior.

THE RESEARCH

Our research, funded by the UK's Economic and Social Research Council, was designed to open up this broader agenda. Between 2004 and 2007 we interviewed 180 senior managers and chief executive officers in 20 multinationals operating in the financial services, automobiles, and the electronic/communications sectors, in seven countries to establish their approaches to skill formation. While the main focus of our research was on these three sectors we also interviewed employers in other sectors such as retail to provide additional contrasts. This provided data on the changes that were taking place in their business strategies, the problems they faced in the global markets within which they were operating and the implications this had for the ways they developed and used skills within their own enterprises. It also generated significant insights into the challenges they faced in operating in global markets.

To tackle the issue of the impact of national institutional and contextual factors on their behavior, and the ways they responded to and utilized the new opportunities they encountered in global markets, we conducted interviews with policy makers and academics in seven of the countries within which these multinationals operated, namely the UK, the USA, Germany, Singapore, South Korea, China, and India. This enabled us to examine current changes that are taking place in the ways in which these companies use skills as well as the relationships between them and the national education and training institutions that provide some of skills they utilize. The results reported in this chapter are based on a first analysis of the data from these interviews.

One of the first outcomes of this research was to force us to reconceptualize our approach to skill. The notion of skill typically applies to individuals and refers to expertise, experience, and attributes acquired by individuals and sometimes identified through qualifications. This has been the dominant approach informed by human capital theory (Becker, 2006). However, there has been a competing theory of the creation and use of skill that sees it as determined by social context (Maurice *et al.*, 1986) in which skills are seen as, in part, the outcome of struggles for power and the distribution of rewards in the labor market (Ashton and Green, 1996). This theory has generally been termed that of skill formation. Yet, with the emergence of TNCs we have witnessed a series of developments concerning the organization of production for high-quality goods and services, electronic communications and the resources that such companies have at their disposal, which has meant that the processes related to the creation and use of skills has fundamentally changed, rendering both these theories of skill production problematic.

SKILL FORMATION VERSUS HUMAN CAPITAL THEORY

The new theory of skill development and utilization that we sketch in this chapter is intimately related to *the capacity for TNCs to develop a portfolio of skill strategies*. Human capital theory makes the assumption that human beings, as rational egoists, will pursue educational qualifications because they enhance returns in the labor market over those with lower or no educational qualifications. In particular, the theory has been used to explain the returns to education in terms of the enhanced productivity that educated labor generates and hence higher incomes. It is assumed, also, that employers will respond to increases in the supply of educated labor by upgrading technology and organizational structures in order to make the most productive use of it. By this mechanism the supply and demand will notionally reach a point of equilibrium.

Many criticisms have been made of human capital theory (Ashton and Green, 1996; Brown *et al.*, 2001). For the purposes of this chapter we highlight two. The first is that it is not a theory that has universal application. Many of the criticisms have focused on the point that skills require institutional structures for their development, realization, and reward. These institutions have been shown to vary between countries and indeed regions, such that particular locales can generate unique skill sets: the production of engineers for the Mittelstand in Germany through the dual system of training is an example. In other words, criticisms of human capital theory have argued that skills for particular productive purposes cannot be generated anywhere. Moreover, in terms of motivation, more than simple rational egoism is required to understand the creation of these unique skill sets. The force of such criticisms has been encapsulated in skill formation theory (Maurice *et al.*, 1986).

However, there is a further criticism relevant to this chapter that can be made. That is, that as a guide to policy human capital theory has had a historically limited shelf life. This is because the new form skill creation and utilization we refer to above has broken the connection between educated labor and income. In the second half of the twentieth century human capital theory guided the expansion of education, because as the supply of educated labor increased so did the rewards. However, we have argued elsewhere that various elements of globalization have now made the link between all educated labor and rewards tenuous at best for all but those graduating from elite universities (Brown and Lauder, 2006).

The reason for this is that TNCs have now developed a series of global strategies to exploit differences in the cost of educated labor, with a consequent decline in its value. Because graduates across the world can be of a similar standard, cost becomes the lever by which TNCs maintain profitability and competitiveness. In effect, what the globalization of skill strategies has done is to dislocate the national equilibrium between the supply and demand for educated labor.

However, if there are problems in human capital theory as a theory explaining the development and utilization of skills, then its competitor, skill formation theory, also has problems.

The term 'skill formation' is now widely used but it has more of an institutional and contextual connotation. It is used to refer to the ways in which institutions, whether they are the family, school or company, socialize members and shape their skills. In the case of companies, it is the decisions by managers and others about how to organize work that determines the 'skill' content of the job and their decisions about who to allocate to jobs that determines who has the opportunity to acquire skills. We would note for the sake of brevity that this observation is something of an oversimplification. Individuals may become active agents in the process, sometimes through their influence in shaping the job, but also through their actions in securing specific jobs . Nonetheless, the power of institutions to shape the nature of skill formation can be seen to be a dominant influence.

The problem with this concept is that it has passive connotations which are the product of the national systems within which skills were generated prior to the emergence of TNCs. In the mid to late 20th century, as long as MNCs were either manufacturing products or delivering services (still within the confines of national markets) or exporting to different national markets, the company's decisions and their impact on the process of skill formation was contained within and shaped by national boundaries. For example, when British Leyland decided on a new car or truck for the UK market they would design the vehicle in the UK, source the components parts within the UK and assemble the vehicle in one of their UK plants. The companies were run along bureaucratic lines with a rigid hierarchy and a command and control system of authority. The knowledge work was largely confined to the R&D staff and senior management. The manufacturing process was designed to take out the high level skills and, while it still involved some skilled maintenance workers, the vast majority of employees were semi-skilled. The low skilled work was a function of the design of the (mass) production process, while the knowledge work was monopolized by senior staff. Staff were recruited locally and rewarded according to national agreements negotiated with the union. The local sourcing of supplies led to the geographical clustering of suppliers around the assembly plants utilizing similar organizational forms and division of labor to that found in the main manufacturer. This meant that all the skills required for the production process, for employees at all levels, were acquired from institutions within the national boundary.

In such societies there was a tight bond between the national VET and industrial relations systems and the home-based MNC in their respective contributions to the process of skill formation. It is no surprise, therefore, that this gave rise to the 'societal approach' to skill formation. Through their comparative studies of France and Germany Maurice et al. (1986) highlighted the reciprocal relationship, between the national VET system, the organization of work within the firm and the national industrial relations systems, in structuring the process of skill formation. In France these relationships generated company-specific skills through the firms internal labor market while in Germany a different combination of institutions generated occupation-based skills.

Given its origins, it is not surprising then that the concept of skill formation inevitably draws attention to the ways in which these institutions and contexts shape the formation of skills. Yet what our research found was that TNCs were now operating *outside* the boundaries of these national systems (hence our preference to use the term TNC rather than MNC) and forging skills and capabilities that could only be understood in this new global context. Whereas institutions related to skill formation were nationally or locally grounded, it is now TNCs operating across much of the globe that can determine the nature of skills, their utilization and reward. Where skill generation was rooted in particular national contexts, elements of the process of globalization have ensured that they are no longer necessary. In order to understand this new process of skill utilization and use as developed by the TNCs, we must first identify the conditions that gave rise to it.

THE NEW GLOBAL CONTEXT

The most obvious of these new conditions is the extension of global markets that have taken place over these last three or four decades. The reduction of tariff barriers has led to a substantial increase in the number of countries that form the global market and the size of that market. In addition, the processes of deregulation and privatization have resulted in new industries such as telecommunications and financial services being incorporated into the global economy. As a result TNCs, while still retaining the imprint of their country of origin, are operating across the globe. For example, one of our companies, while of German origin, had 80% of its business overseas while operating in 190 countries worldwide.

A second important development has been the creation of new information and computing technologies which have had a profound impact in a number of areas. It has facilitated the decomposition of the production process, sometimes referred to as modularization (Berger, 2005). The different components can then be sourced wherever there are cost and business advantages to the company, providing there is a basic infrastructure and education service. Just as important has been the way in which the new technology has been used to control product specifications and manage the supply chain. By providing the means to specify technical requirements and deliver information almost instantaneously across the globe, it has enabled companies to utilize the supply chain to ensure the seamless integration of the different functions without regard to geographical considerations (Berger, 2005: 76).

This ability to break down the process of production into small units and source their production across the globe is not confined to manufactured goods. The commoditization of knowledge work, through the use of technological innovation involving the standardized of processes, what we call digital Taylorism, has enabled innovations to be translated into sets of routines that might require some degree of education but not the kind of creativity and independence of judgment that is often associated with the knowledge economy (Brown *et al.*, 2007). This enables companies such as those in the financial and business services to engage in skills arbitrage, and outsource and offshore a great deal of their white collar work to take advantage of lower labor costs.

In reality this process of offshoring and outsourcing is far more complex than we can depict here (see Cooke and Budhwar, this volume Chapter 17), requiring as it does a whole series of prior decisions about the organizational design and remit of the other aspects of the business in order that these activities can be effectively integrated into the overall business strategy. For example, at the most elementary level there need to be standard procedures in place to ensure that when you compare the costs of producing skills production in different localities you are comparing like with like. These issues are dealt with in greater detail by Sparrow and Braun (2008). Some of these decisions form an integral part of what we identify later as the emergent global skills webs.

A third and equally important development has been the emergence of a global market in initial skills. For many years the developing countries have provided low-cost low-unskilled labor but more recently the entry of China, India, and Russia into the global market has transformed the opportunities available to TNCs. Not only has it extended the pool of unskilled labor available for global production but it is increasingly providing a new source of highly qualified labor (Brown *et al.*, 2006). Universities in developing and redeveloping nations such as China, India, and Russia, have maintained high standards despite poverty and social upheaval. There is now a significant supply of graduate labor which enables TNCs to engage in a skills arbitrage where, if the costs are too high in one location, they can simply 'buy in' from another. This provides TNCs not only with the opportunity to move their low value-added forms of mass production to take advantage of lower labor costs, but also with the opportunity to transfer higher value-added activities such as research and R&D.

THE RESPONSE OF THE TNCs: CREATING AND UTILIZING SKILLS IN THE GLOBAL CONTEXT

Skill strategies – how companies take advantage of the opportunities for skills arbitrage

We use the concept of skills strategy to refer to the ways in which companies acquire, generate, and use the skills available to them to create a competitive advantage in the market. In the industrial era of Fordist mass production, these strategies were designed to concentrate the knowledge required to design and build products in the hands of management while deskilling the production workers. They were strategies designed within the confines of national labor and product markets. In the new global context this is no longer the case; there are far more opportunities available to employers to generate knowledge and utilize and configure the labor and skills of employees.

Skills are now available globally, in India and China, as well as in older industrial countries. In addition the opportunities to generate new knowledge are also more diverse, through the use of local R&D teams, alliances with other companies, and higher education institutions and so on. In the new area, therefore, these skills strategies become much more complex and difficult to manage, although the potential business pay-off is greater. To take advantage of the opportunities to source skilled labor and develop knowledge and products provided by global markets decisions where to produce, how to produce and what forms of organization to use, are now taken on a global basis.

There are of course a variety of ways in which this can be done. In some cases the headquarters of the company functions as a governor of a global producer-driven supply chain. Here the headquarters traditionally specifies the product details and coordinates the output of numerous suppliers and assembles and delivers the final product to the customer. This has often been the case in capital-intensive high-technology sectors such as aerospace, computers, and automobiles. In other sectors such as retail, the headquarters of the company act as governors of a buyer-driven supply chain, controlling decentralized production networks in a variety of countries where labor-intensive products such as clothes and footwear can be sourced using low-cost labor (UNIDO, 2001).

While in the past much of this outsourcing was confined to the production of labor-intensive items using low-cost low-skilled labor, our interviews revealed that this is no longer the case, the opportunity for skills arbitrage now extends to the whole of the labor force. Whereas in the recent past these TNCs retained much of the R&D in their central hub, in the automobile and electronics and telecommunications sectors much of this is now undertaken across the globe in order to secure added value. The hub of the company is now increasingly decentralized. In the clothing industry, this decentralization has been extended to the management of the supply chain. Bitran *et al.* (2006) report that companies such as Li and Fung, based in Hong Kong and servicing private clothing firms in Europe and North America, provide the expertise for managing the supply chain and deliver the product to the customer's specification. In the business and financial services sectors we found that some research and consultancy work has already been relocated from the head office to specialist companies in countries such as India. Also in the financial services sector we found that the process of digital Taylorism has enabled the banks and other companies to relocated much of their white collar work to India and other low-labor-cost countries where graduates have a proficiency in the English language. All this serves to highlight the fact that we are witnessing a rapid process of experimentation by TNCs as they search to seek out new ways of adding value and making profit through the implementation of a global skills strategy.

The emergence of skill webs

Given the myriad of ways in which production can be organized the notion of skill webs highlights significant differences in the ways in which companies approach this task. It is a concept that enables us to focus on the ways in which companies chose to generate and use the skills and knowledge they require. For example, the kind of core capabilities they seek to develop, whether these are seen as a series of skills that can be bought in or whether they are capabilities that have to be built over time, whether they source their new knowledge or skills internally or seek to generate it in collaboration with partners through joint ventures. Their importance derives from the attempts by TNCs to develop consistency in the management of the relationships involved in the creation of these webs across the globe as part of their overall business strategy. The form taken by these webs reflects how companies understand the relationship between people and profits – the extent to which they see the company as existing just for profit, or the extent to which they try to balance the influence of different stakeholders – including employees, shareholders, and national governments in their decision-making processes. Skill webs also shape how they relate to their suppliers and the level of trust they generate in the relationships they establish, for example, whether they seek to protect their core capabilities or share them with suppliers in order to improve their performance.

Our interviews led us to distinguish four main types of skill web:

(1) the traditional,
(2) transformative,
(3) transactional, and
(4) transitional.

Traditional.   The traditional refers to companies that remain multinational rather than transnational. The home base retains its traditional roles in terms of recruitment to senior and executive positions where positions are filled from a domestic talent pool. Virtually all 'mission critical' work including R&D remain concentrated in the home economy with little attempt to transform the corporate culture to reflect its global business. Traditional companies may own global brands but the home base remains the center of power with little attempt to 'localize' high-skill, high-value activities within its global operations. These companies often use 'ex-pats' or 'flying executives' to run overseas operations and rely on established suppliers throughout the value chain. These companies have not developed strategic skill webs requiring extensive capacity building beyond the home base.

Transactional.   The transactional is characterized by a business strategy based on cost reduction through exploiting international differences in labor and business costs. There is an emphasis on buying in talent through careful recruitment rather than developing it internally, on participating in the 'war for talent' rather than cultivating a wealth of talent. They seek to create value through the use of market relationships and exhibit low levels of trust in their relationships. Relationships with suppliers are likely to be short term with little transfer of skill involved as the supplier may be replaced if they fail to meet the cost and quality requirements of the TNC. It assumes a transactional relationship with employees based on a model of the 'free agent' mind set and contingent careers.

Transformative.   Transformative webs are characterized by companies that attempt to balance immediate competitive pressures to reduce costs and increase profits with an eye on the medium term. The emphasis is on building competitive capacity that require the organization to go 'beyond contract' in its commitment to workers, suppliers, customers and its overseas operations. Globalization involves investing in employee development over the long term in return for loyalty, commitment, and performance irrespective of location. These are 'high' trust organizations in which a much larger proportion of employees are involved in developing core capabilities, although these capabilities are more highly developed among senior management. Links with suppliers are also likely to be centered on a long-term relationship in which some core capabilities are readily transferred in order to improve performance.

Transitional.   These are the new form of skill webs which are emerging from the domestic economies of India and China. In many respects they include elements of both transactional and transformative approaches. On the one hand, they are driven by the need to produce 'quality' goods and services and increasing market share beyond the domestic economy based on a 'low cost' model. This will lead them to adopt an arbitrage model including moving operations to other low-wage countries or regions. On the other hand, rapid expansion requires them to gain the strategic and operational knowledge required to succeed in global markets and access new technologies. This is leading these companies to acquire foreign companies and enter alliances based on trust. However, they are relatively new TNCs and it is difficult at this stage to determine all the characteristics of their webs, hence the name transitional.

Before explaining how these skills webs impact the process of skills creation and utilization, we make a few generic observations about them.

First, while these four categories reflect the overall configuration of the skill web, companies do have some degree of choice on terms of the extent to which the different types of relationships they embody are utilized throughout the company. For example, some companies may be characterized by transformative relationships throughout the organization, including their relationships with suppliers, as in the case of some Japanese companies, while other companies in the retail trade may utilize transformative relationships for the core staff but transactional relationships with their suppliers. All this serves to highlight the fact these webs are evolving in a dynamic manner as companies struggle to develop their competitive advantage in global markets.

Second, these skill webs have not appeared overnight, as companies have developed them in the light of their previous experience. As a result, and as the 'Business Systems' literature has emphasized (Whitley, 1999; Morgan, 2001) they still carry the imprint of the national cultures within which they originated. Thus the 'transactional' webs are more characteristic of companies of US and UK origin, the 'transformative' webs are more frequently observed in companies of German and Japanese origin, the 'tradition' webs are more frequently observed in companies of Korean origin while the 'transitional' webs are more frequently found in companies of Chinese and Indian origin. However, they are all in the process of detaching themselves from their national origins, as they convert into more globally oriented TNCs, so that over time the influence of their culture of origin is likely to lessen.

Third, in addition to their country of origin, the other factor that conditions these different types of webs is the sector within which they operate. Of the sectors we studied, companies in electronics/telecommunications are the most advanced in terms of the extent to which production is organized on a global basis. Those in the automobile industry are rapidly moving toward a more global form of organization while those in financial services are largely operating from their home base, although some are rapidly emerging as global players.

The existence of these different types of skill web has important implications for the creation and utilization of skills. What it means is that at the heart of these webs are very different ways of using and managing skills. On the one hand, there are those TNCs with transformative webs concerned with building long-term relationships with their own employees, creating high skill levels and securing high levels of commitment to the company. This approach also extends to their suppliers, partners in their alliances as well as collaborative R&D projects. It also extends to their links with national institutions. Thus, while they may still be capable of manufacturing anywhere in the world, they nevertheless attempt to build long-term relationships with the national institutions such as universities and colleges.

On the other hand, there are those companies, characterized by transactional webs and concerned with maximizing short-term gains, who are willing to collaborate with other companies on research and new products as long there are immediate business benefits, but carefully guarding their own skills and knowledge. Similarly, they will work with national institutions such as universities and colleges providing there is an immediate pay-off. However, once the immediate business benefits are no longer evident then the relationships are terminated. There is little concern with or incentive in these companies to transfer skill either to suppliers or national economies.

These are very different ways of managing the global process of skill creation and use, although both can be equally effective in producing high levels of return to capital.

The internalization of skill creation and use

One major consequence of the emergence of these global skill webs is the internalization of skill creation and use. As they move from a national to a global orientation, TNCs cease their dependence on national institutions for their skill supply and start to exert greater control over it, in order to take advantage of the opportunities offered by global markets. This becomes possible only when they have loosened their bonds with their home institutions and national culture. For the companies we interviewed, decisions about what to produce, where to produce, how to produce, and what forms of organization to use, are no longer taken within the confines of national boundaries. The supply of skilled labor is no longer a given, determined by the national institutions and government policies but is now just another area of choice for managers.

As production has become fragmented, and new technology provided the means of controlling activities at a distance, this has created new opportunities for companies to change the ways in which they approach skills issues. Operating as the

German TNC cited earlier does in 190 countries, and with the ability to break down the process of production into discrete components, it can chose to obtain its supply of unskilled labor from a number of low-wage-cost countries, its supply of intermediate level skills from different countries and to locate its R&D in a range of other countries that provide high-quality graduate labor. What was once a given with regard to labor supply is now a variable. If the national system of industrial relations is a hindrance to the company in achieving the level of wages it is prepared to pay, it can make a realistic threat to move production to another, with a more compliant industrial relations system.

This means that once the companies had become global in their orientation, then the links with the national VET system were transformed. They no longer rely on the universities within their old 'home' base, they now recruit globally, sourcing graduates from wherever the supply is abundant and the cost is low. Neither are they dependent on their 'home' based universities as a source for new ideas and innovation as they could now source new ideas from universities anywhere in the world where they have operations. They were no longer tied to the national VET system as a source for their intermediate level skill workers, as they could now train them themselves.

Faced with such an array of national training providers and institutional arrangements for the rewarding of employees, the managers of the globally oriented TNCs can now chose which they might use and how they might combine them. This has provided new opportunities for TNCs and allowed them to shape the skills they use rather than relying on the national institutional systems or context to provide them. In responding to these new opportunities TNCs have taken a more proactive role in shaping their own skills. They have internalized the process of skill creation and use, creating links between employees across the globe.

This process of internalization has gone further in some companies than others, for example Japanese companies such as Toyota were among the first to develop a whole series of techniques designed to enhance the workplace skills of their employees, ranging from sophisticated froms of on-the-job training to Total Quality Management to Continuous Improvement. The impact of these and similar techniques in raising employee skills and enhancing productivity has been well documented in the work of Koike and Inoki (1990). As other companies sought to compete with the Japanese in world markets, these and other 'lean' techniques were adopted in varying degrees by competitors through the process of benchmarking. Our interviews provided examples of US companies in the automobile industry still struggling to adopt forms of 'lean' production while other global companies were using alliances and joint ventures to acquire knowledge of how to implement such 'new' management practices.

This is a process that is now well established. However, the important point with regard to skill creation and use, is that acquisition of these techniques enables companies to take greater control over the process of skill creation and use within their own labor forces.

One consequence of this is that these companies are able to establish their production bases in almost any country with a basic economic infrastructure. For example, when we asked a US company in the automobile components industry whether they were able to locate their production anywhere in the globe, their response was that 10 years ago they would have been restricted to the US and Europe because of the availability of skilled labor, whereas now they could locate anywhere with a basic educational and economic infrastructure. Shortly after the interview they announced the establishment of plants in China and India. We had the same response to this question in many of our firms. This provides them with substantial control of the process of skill creation, so much so that one company operating in India described the process of moving from one of being 'outside in' where the skills are created outside and then used within the company, to one in the developing countries of being 'inside out' where the company takes the labor and provides the skills even when surrounded by dire poverty.

By internalizing the process of skill creation, companies have not only loosened their bonds with national systems of VET but they are also actively engaged in creating the basic institutional infrastructure for global markets. For example, many of the companies we interviewed are seeking to recruit from what they believed was only a small group of elite graduates, whose abilities would enable them to maintain their competitive advantage in the market, the so-called 'War for Talent'. This was leading them to forge links with an equally small group of elite universities in Europe, Asia, and Russia where it is believed such talent is to be found. Such is the impact of this on national systems of education and training that governments in the UK and Germany, Singapore and China are actively supporting the ability of their elite universities to compete in this new global market, thereby differentiating them from the remaining national universities and intensifying positional competition within their own societies.

The increasing importance of skills within the business agenda

The internalization of skills creation and use is resulting in skills issues becoming more central to business success. There are four main reasons for this.

The first, and perhaps most important, is because questions about what skills to create and how to reward them are no longer given by the national institutional conditions but are now part of the company's own decision making process. As we have seen, in the Fordist industrial economy's precisely because the use of manual workers' skills was minimized, skills issues were accorded low priority in the business agenda. In manufacturing the whole purpose of the mass production system was to minimize the skills required by the majority of the labor force in order to reduce labor costs. Management's decisions about what labor to use, the availability of skill and their cost were largely determined by the national VET and industrial relations system.

Now these decisions about skills use all provide opportunities to add value and therefore become more central to business success. The availability of low-cost labor in the developing economies, such as those of India and China, provides new opportunities for reducing labor costs. Initially the gains were in the use of unskilled labor, but with the expansion of graduates in these countries, decisions about the location of knowledge-intensive work as well that requiring intermediate level skills offers the same opportunities to add value – a process aided and abetted by governments eager to attract TNCs through the provision of free training and other incentives.

The second reason is that senior managers' decisions about the type of skills they develop also determines the extent to which the company will devote resources to developing their staff. Each of these skill webs offers the choice of the type of skills to be developed and the level of resources to involved in generating them. Should skills be developed over the long term and an attempt made to commit employees to company values, as in the transformative web, or should skills be bought in where possible, as with the transactional webs, devoting less resources to developing them internally? Should they use transformative relationships throughout the web or just for core employee? Whichever path is taken, skills issues have to be confronted.

The third reason is that the increase in the speed at which knowledge is changing and the ability to introduce digital Taylorism also provides opportunities to add value in different ways. Companies can now seek a competitive advantage through speeding up the development process but skills issues are central to this. Given the speed at which knowledge is developing, especially in areas such as telecommunications where the barriers between technologies such as the telephone, computer and internet are breaking down, single companies are no longer able to source all the knowledge they need to develop new products. The result is that many of the TNCs we interviewed are continually involved in forming alliances with competitors to develop new products or services. Here skills issues are crucial as decisions have to be made about where best to access the appropriate skills and knowledge.

The fourth reason why skills issues become central is through the opportunities that globalization generates to speed up design and R&D activities. By dispersing their R&D across the globe, companies can speed up the creation of new ideas and products through the use of virtual teams. Thus one German automobile manufacturer we interviewed is operating virtual design teams with members located in R&D centers in different time zones, enabling the work to continue 24 hours a day. R&D work conducted in China and India was transferred at the end of the working day to colleagues in Europe who then worked on it and transferred it to the US center, which in turn then transferred it back to their colleagues in India and China. Not only were they able to speed up the design and development process, they could also access a source of cheap knowledge production. In addition, the local centers also provided the means to adapt products to markets in the emerging economies of China and India. As Lynn and Salzmann (2005) found, some such local centers have now also become of global significance for the companies as they develop new products and ideas in these local centers that can be used globally. Here then was another crucial area of innovation in the management of skill knowledge where issues relating to the use of skills could be potential sources of added value.

For all these reasons, the important questions relating to skills and knowledge that have to be understood by researchers are:

- How are skills created within the company?
- How are they combined and used?
- Where are they sourced?
- How are they to be developed?

The answers in relation to these questions all provide opportunities for adding value and thereby pushing the importance of skills issues up the business agenda.

However, we do acknowledge that this process is in its early stages. At this point in time, many of the business leaders we interviewed could not necessarily articulate their strategies in a clear and unambiguous manner, but that was because many of the components of such strategies were still in the early stages of development. As we have already said, 5 to 10 years ago there was no option available to locate the manufacturing of vehicle components anywhere in the world, 10 years ago there was no internet to facilitate the outsourcing of routine service jobs. We did not have the computer and internet-based technology to enable companies to control the specification of their product requirements, and so control production anywhere in the globe, and neither did they have access to a huge pool of highly skilled graduate labor across the globe. It is no wonder that business leaders are still learning how to utilize these opportunities to add value and enhance their competitive strategy.

Many of the senior business personnel were therefore experimenting with new ideas, learning on a day-to-day basis as they sought to exploit new opportunities, exploring new ways of collaborating with competitors and seeking new ways of enhancing the performance of their staff. Under these conditions they were struggling to establish clear strategies but what is clear is that the components of such a strategy were starting to emerge: for example, the utilization of highly skilled low-cost graduate labor in the emerging economies, the emergence of new management practices for sustaining innovation and the management of knowledge, the diffusion of R&D across the globe to accelerate process, the establishment of links with elite universities for recruitment, and so on.

Conclusion: The Globalization of Skills and IHRM

What we have documented throughout this chapter is the globalization of the process of skill acquisition and use. There is a fundamental transformation of the process in two respects: first, in the loosening of the bonds that tied traditional MNCs operating in national markets to the national systems of education and training; second, in the internalization of the process of skill creation and use, providing TNCs with greater control over it. In so doing it has created the conditions for the creation of skill webs through which companies seek to gain a competitive advantage, thereby raising skills issues to a more central role in their business strategies.

This has important implications for the national systems and business systems approaches in that it represents a new phase in HRM – a phase in which the process of skill acquisition and use now transcends the national institutions. As such it signifies a reduction in the influence that national systems of VET can exert over the behavior and skill levels of TNCs. Once having secured control over the process of skill acquisition and use, companies can then move their production or components to wherever they see a competitive advantage can be gained. This in turn provides them with more influence over governments and nationally based trades unions, as they are able to ignore the challenge from organized labor and relocate production to more company-friendly environments.

This transformation of the process of skill acquisition and use also creates new conditions within which, and under which, IHRM functions. We have argued that the dual concept of skill strategies and skill webs enables us to move outside the conventional HR management frameworks used to think about IHRM. This concept highlights the transformation of the broader context within which the recent developments in IHRM are located. The concept of skill strategy highlights the ways in which skills issues have moved up the business agenda of these companies, playing a more important part in their overall competitive strategy. This is a change that is not evident in the IHRM literature because of its focus on the more immediate practical issues facing IHRM practitioners. Yet this is a crucial development in the sphere of people management, as decisions about sourcing skills now provide an important component of the company's ability to add value. Similarly, the emergence of what we have referred to as digital Taylorism and its significance for the process of skill formation and use, especially in the service sector, does not appear in the IHRM literature. Yet this development, with its potential to reduce the cost of knowledge work and lead to the relocation of white collar work is arguably another of the most important developments that is stemming from the process of globalization.

When we turn to the concept of skill webs, this can be seen to broaden the IHRM agenda in terms of the impact of these webs both within the firm and in its external relations. We use two examples to demonstrate the contribution that can be made to IHRM research agendas, namely talent management and knowledge management.

By focusing on skill webs, attention is directed at how these webs are transforming the process of recruitment, as the behavior of companies generates a new global institutional framework in the form of globally competitive elite universities. This in turn generates pressures on governments to divert resources to selectively support their national champions. Within the companies, it sensitizes us to the fact that in the process of selection, and in the management of the 'talent pipeline', companies are actively seeking to reproduce their skill webs, which means that they are constructing some skills rather than others – for example, producing leaders who will emphasize the importance of trust and commitment in the transformational webs, as opposed to the need for immediate performance outcomes in the transactional webs.

In the case of knowledge management, the focus on skill webs helps again in directing attention to the fact that knowledge management networks in transformative webs will focus more on the importance of sharing knowledge with suppliers and building knowledge that will add value in the long term (see Moingeon, Lumineau, and Perrin, this volume Chapter 13), whether in the form of new products or greater sensitivity to customer demands. In the transactional webs, the focus of knowledge management is more on the immediate requirements of production, securing intellectual property rights and buying in specialist expertise. In other words, our focus on skill webs helps to highlight the fact that we should be concerned not just with the mechanics of knowledge management – namely, centers of excellence, global management systems, expatriate advice networks, communities of practice, and the use of globally distributed teams (Sparrow, 2006) – but also with the types of knowledge and skills they are delivering.

Finally, the concept also directs attention to the external consequences of the development of knowledge management systems, namely the increasing integration of the economies of the developing and developed world in the creation of high value-added goods and services. The dispersion of knowledge in the form of R&D across such companies facilitates the transfer of knowledge across national boundaries. In so doing, it allows companies to take advantage of the cheaper graduate labor in countries such as India and China. This also means that graduates from the older industrial countries are competing directly with those from China and India as sources of knowledge and skills, with all the implications that has for the future salaries of those in the older industrial countries. In short, the concepts of skill strategies and skill webs point to the fact that IHRM is intimately involved not only in the process of relocating unskilled jobs but also in the process of relocating and deskilling white collar jobs and in developing the conditions whereby many of the high-skilled knowledge-intensive jobs traditionally located in the older industrial countries are moving to lower wage countries.

In conclusion, we do not see our approach as challenging the validity of the existing IHRM literature, but we do see it as providing a framework within which new questions can be asked about the nature of skills that are being developed in TNCs as well as sensitizing us to the impact that the globalization of skills has on national economies and institutions. In opening up these issues we see it as contributing to a theory of global HR.

REFERENCES

Ashton, D., and Green, F. (1996). *Education, Training and the Global Economy*. Cheltenham: Edward Elgar.

Becker, H. (2006). The age of human capital. In H. Lauder et al. (eds), *Education, Globalization and Social Change*. Oxford: Oxford University Press.

Berger, S. (2005). *How We Compete: What Companies Around the World are Doing to Make it in Today's Global Economy*. New York: Doubleday.

Bitran, G.R., Gurumurthi, S., and Sam, S.L. (2006). *Emerging trends in supply chain governance.* MIT School of Management, Working Paper. Center for eBusiness@MIT.

Briscoe, D., and Schuler, R.S. (2004). *International Human Resource Management* (2nd edn). New York, and London: Routledge.

Brown, P., and Lauder, H. (2006). Globalisation, knowledge and the myth of the magnet economy. *Globalisation, Societies and Education*, 4 (1), 25–51.

Brown, P., Green, A., and Lauder, H. (2001). *High Skills*. Oxford: Oxford University Press.

Brown, P., Lauder, H., and Ashton, D. (2007). Towards a high skills economy: Higher education and the realities of global capitalism. In D. Epstien (ed.), *Education World Year Handbook*. London: Routledge.

Brown, P., Lauder, H., Ashton, D., and Tholen, G. (2006). Towards a High-Skilled, Low-Waged Economy? A Review of Global Trends in Education, Employment and the Labour Market. In S. Porter and M. Campbell, (eds.) *Skills and Economic Performance*, London: Caspian Publishing, pp. 55–90.

Crouch, C., Finegold, D., and Sako, M. (1999) *Are Skills the Answer?: The Political Economy of Skill Creation in Advanced Industrial Countries*. Oxford: Oxford University Press.

Harris, H., Brewster, C., and Sparrow, P.R. (2003). *International Human Resource Management*. London: CIPD.

Koike, K., and Inoki, T. (eds) (1990). *Skill formation in Japan and Southeast Asia.* Tokyo: University of Tokyo Press.

Lynn, L., and Salzman, H. (2005). *The 'new' globalization of engineering: How offshoring of advanced engineering affects competitiveness and development.* Paper presented at 21st European Group for Organizational Studies (EGOS) Colloquium 'Unlocking Organizations' Berlin, June 2005, 21pp.

Maurice, M., Sellier, F., and Silvester, J.J. (1986). *The Social Foundations of Industrial Power.* Cambridge, Mass: MIT Press.

Morgan, G. (2001). The multinational firm: Organizing across institutional and national divides. In G. Morgan, P.H. Kristensen and R. Whitley (eds), *The Multinational Firm: Organizing Across Institutional and National Divides.* Oxford: Oxford University Press, pp. 1–24.

Morgan, G. (2003). Hayek, Habermas, and European integration. *Critical Review,* 15 (1–2), 1–22.

Sparrow, P.R. (2006). Knowledge management in Global organizations. In G. Stahl and I. Björkman (eds), *Handbook of Research into International HRM.* London: Edward Elgar, pp. 113–138.

Sparrow, P.R., and Braun, W. (2008). HR strategy theory in international context. In M. Harris (ed.), *The Handbook of Research in International Human Resource Management.* Mahwah, NJ: Lawrence Erlbaum, pp. 77–106.

Sparrow, P.R., and Brewster, C. (2006). Globalizing HRM: The growing revolution in managing employees internationally. In C. Cooper and R. Burke (eds), *The Human Resources Revolution: Why Putting People First Matters.* London: Elsevier.

Thelen, K. (2004). *How Institutions Evolve: The Political Economy of Skills in Germany, Britian, the United States, and Japan.* Cambridge: Cambridge University Press.

UNIDO (2001). *Integrating SMEs in Global Value Chains: Towards Partnership for Development.* Vienna: UNIDO.

Whitley, R. (1999). *Divergent Capitalisms: The Social Structuring and Change of Business Systems.* Oxford: Oxford University Press.

17

HR Offshoring and Outsourcing: Research Issues for IHRM

Fang Lee Cooke and Pawan Budhwar

Introduction

The continuous globalization through offshoring skilled employment from developed countries such as the US and the UK to emerging markets such as India and China has become a major topic of debate. While some prescribe global sourcing as an important management strategy to sustain competitive advantage, critics question the societal and organizational benefits of this trend (see, for example, Pickard, 2007a). In relation to this, there is a bourgeoning body of literature on HR outsourcing, much of it comes from practitioners' sources (see, for example, Beaman, 2004). HR outsourcing can be defined as 'placing responsibility for various elements of the HR function with a third-party provider' (Turnbull, 2002: 11). By contrast, HR offshoring, which is the relocation of one or more aspects of the HR function from the home country to a foreign country (both captive and outsourced), is an area that has so far received relatively little attention in the IHRM literature. This is in spite of the fact that HR offshoring as part of the internationalization process creates 'a new set of pressures on HRM specialists' (Brewster *et al.*, 2005: 966) and makes 'the need to understand how HRM is delivered in different country contexts more important' (Brewster *et al.*, 2005: 950).

This chapter addresses some of the issues related to HR offshoring and outsourcing in its five main sections. The first two sections review firms' motives of HR offshoring and outsourcing and patterns of the global trend of HR outsourcing. This is followed by a more specific summary of modes of HR offshoring by multinational companies (MNCs). The fourth section outlines the implications of HR offshoring for an MNC's global HR structure and strategy. The fifth section then provides a more detailed discussion on the role of the in-house HR team in the decision-making process of HR offshoring/outsourcing and their subsequent role in managing the outsourcing relationship. In addition, pitfalls of HR outsourcing

Handbook of International Human Resource Management. Edited by Paul R. Sparrow
© 2009 John Wiley & Sons, Ltd

that may affect the corporate HR strategy are highlighted and particular attention is drawn to the need to manage organizational and societal cultural differences. Finally, implications of HR offshoring for international HR professionals' skills needs and career paths are assessed.

While the chapter touches upon HR outsourcing in general and covers HR offshoring in both captive and outsourced forms, the discussion focuses more on HR offshored outsourcing as this is an area that is least covered in existing literature and yet a strategy that is most challenging to the HR function and professionals due to the combined complexity of international HRM and HR outsourcing. Given the fact that India and China are two of the most popular outsourcing host countries, with the former leading by some distance, the discussion of this chapter focuses relatively more on these two countries. The cultural and institutional environments of these two countries not only differ from each other but also differ from that of the Western developed countries in significant ways.

FIRMS' MOTIVES OF HR OFFSHORING AND OUTSOURCING

There are a number of strategic and operational reasons why organizations decide to outsource their HR activities (Cook, 1999; Greer *et al.*, 1999, Klaas *et al.*, 2001; Lilly *et al.*, 2005; Oates, 1998; Pickard, 2006; Sparrow and Braun, 2008a, b). Three major strands of theoretical arguments have been developed to explain the strategic decision for adopting an outsourcing strategy. The first is the 'core' and 'periphery' model advanced by Atkinson (1984). Broadly speaking, core activities are those that the firm does best and/or are crucial to the firm's competitive advantage. These are the activities that must be kept in-house. By contrast, 'non-core' or peripheral activities are considered to have a lower impact on the overall performance of the organization and can therefore be outsourced to external providers who can perform the tasks more efficiently and/or professionally. This model is supported by advocates of the resource-based view of the firm. They believe that outsourcing can be a productive way to develop the core competence of the organization – by implementing strategies that exploit their internal strengths and external opportunities, while at the same time avoid internal weaknesses (Conner, 1991; Hunter, 2006; Oliver, 1997).

A second strand of argument on the decision-making process relates to Williamson's (1985) transaction cost economic model of whether to 'make or buy' (goods) or 'supply or buy' (services). According to this model, the decision as to whether to provide goods and services internally or to outsource rests upon the relative costs of production and transaction. In other words, if the costs of coordinating and managing the outsourcing relationship outweighs that of supplying the goods/services through internal mechanisms, then outsourcing should be used and vice versa.

A third strand of theoretical argument on strategic HR outsourcing relates to Ulrich's (1998) influential thesis of the four roles of HR in which he proposed that HR should be a strategic partner, an administrative expert, an employee champion, and a change agent. Ulrich (1998) argues that HR professionals must embrace four new proactive roles as champions of competitiveness in creating and delivering value. In this context, outsourcing is seen as a way of liberating the in-house HR professionals to perform a more consultative and strategic role, designing and implementing programs aimed to retain the workforce and enhance its performance by releasing the inherent value intrinsic in HR. This is a role where arguably HR can add the greatest value to the organization that is difficult to be measured quantitatively (also see Arkin, 2007).

In addition to these three strands of theoretical arguments, Lilly *et al.* (2005) apply Sutcliffe and Zaheer's (1998) analysis of environmental uncertainty to the HR outsourcing context. According to Sutcliffe and Zaheer (1998), environmental uncertainty comprises three distinct components – primary, competitive, and supplier. Primary uncertainty relates to uncertainty arising from external environment (e.g., change of regulation); competitive uncertainty arises from the actions of competitors, both actual and potential; and supplier uncertainty refers to the possible opportunism by the supplier. In the HR context, Lilly *et al.* (2005: 65) argue, 'primary and competitive uncertainty create a situation in which the firm must react', HR outsourcing specialist firms are better able to respond to the changes than an internal HR department, hence firms will benefit from obtaining HR services from these specialist outsourcing providers. By contrast, the opportunistic behavior of HR outsourcing providers will have a negative impact on the HR performance of the client firm (Lilly *et al.*, 2005). This analysis goes some distance in explaining why MNCs operating in a host country that has a significantly different institutional and cultural environment are more likely to outsource some of their HR functions. The desire to minimize the negative impact of environmental uncertainty leads MNCs to tap into outsourcing providers' local knowledge, even though the cost to outsource may exceed that in-house. As we will see in the next section, Western MNCs operating in Asia Pacific region are the main users of HR outsourcing, whereas indigenous firms tend to keep their HR functions in-house.

GLOBAL TRENDS OF HR OUTSOURCING

Empirical evidence from various sources, mostly through survey studies conducted by professional consultancy firms, points to the continuing growth of HR outsourcing as a global trend. This growth is pushed by organizations' needs to acquire outsourcing services, as well as pulled by international HR outsourcing provider firms that are keen to expand their services in different business areas and geographical locations. According to Quisenberry (2006), the number of HR outsourcing agreements occurring globally had increased by 32% in 2005. The global HR outsourcing market is estimated to grow by 11% in 2008, reaching an estimated value of US$33 billion (SBPOA, 2004). In addition, there appears to be a growing trend for multiprocess HR Business Process Outsourcing (BPO), that is, the provision of multiple HR services by one provider. According to the Shared Services and Business Process Outsourcing Association (SBPOA, 2004), the worldwide market for multiprocess HR BPO is estimated to grow at 21% annually, reaching US$7 billion by 2008. Meanwhile, outsourcing providers are increasingly acquiring competitor firms in order to broaden their service delivery capabilities across various HR areas, such as organizational and people development, employee data management, workforce planning and human capital services (SBPOA, 2004). Large MNCs are the main user firms of HR outsourcing.

However, the growth of HR outsourcing has not followed the anticipated speed predicted by some commentators. Nor has the scope of the outsourcing been as radical as some may assume. For example, only 3% of organizations surveyed by SBPOA in 2005 reported that they outsourced the entire HR function (Pickard, 2006). It is reported that the diversity of the HR function makes it difficult for firms to outsource its HR function as a whole to a single service provider to gain economies of scale. Instead, they tend to outsource single processes to different service providers to take advantage of their unique strengths. Single-process outsourcing is therefore believed to be the main growth area (Pickard, 2006).

In addition, differences exist in the use of HR outsourcing in different parts of the world, from the developed economies to the less-developed economies such as China and India. These differences arise from the size of the businesses, the degree of sophistication of the HR function, the extent of development of the HR outsourcing market, cultural norms and other institutional factors in specific countries and regions. Below are some examples of research evidence on a number of regions and countries in the world.

North America

It is reported that North America is the main market of HR outsourcing (Pickard, 2006), where super-large organizations make up a relatively large proportion of businesses and where the HR function is arguably more sophisticated. These conditions provide the strategic need for, as well as the economies of scale of outsourcing. It is also reported that external HR service providers are seeking super-large manufacturing firms as the main clients for the services (Pickard, 2006). A recent survey conducted in the US by Hewitt Associates (Zagata-Meraz and Frighetto, 2005) found that organizations are satisfied with their HR outsourcing decisions and plan to outsource more HR activities by 2008. This survey was conducted on 129 large US organizations representing nearly two million employees. The most commonly outsourced activities, either partially or totally, include outplacement services, employee assistance programs, defined contribution plans and defined benefit (pension) plans. This study further revealed that US organizations also plan to outsource leave management, learning and development, payroll, recruiting, health and welfare, and global mobility by 2008.

Europe

The Cranet survey on HR policies and practices conducted by the Cranfield School of Management and William M. Mercer Inc. in 1999 (Vernon *et al.*, 2000) revealed that there was an increasing trend of outsourcing HR in Europe. This survey was based on responses from HR directors and managers in 3964 organizations (employing over 200 employees) across Europe. From the organizations surveyed, 97%

stated using HR outsourcing for at least one HR activity, while 40% reported increased usage of HR outsourcing during the period 1996–1999. The major HR activities outsourced include training and development (77%), recruitment and selection (59%), pay and benefits (30%), and workforce outplacement/reduction (29%). In particular, France, Belgium, and the Netherlands showed increased levels of HR outsourcing, leading to the conclusion that HR outsourcing is influenced by national forces as well as the industry sector and organizational size (Vernon *et al.*, 2000).

Asia

Similarly, HR outsourcing activities are found in Asia, albeit to a considerably smaller extent than that in Europe and the US. The majority of outsourcing user firms appear to be Western MNCs. According to Hewitt Associates (2004), the trend toward outsourcing HR services in Asia-Pacific had achieved an annual growth of 17.52% between 1999 and 2004. In addition, the 'Outsourcing in Asia-Pacific' survey (Hewitt Associates, 2004) conducted in 2003 on 524 firms in Asia revealed that 39% of participants are already using outsourcing for their HR processes. Perceived benefit of cost reduction and the desire to focus on core competencies are the main reasons for outsourcing the HR function. Social security benefits, payroll processing, recruitment, and training and development are the main HR activities to be outsourced. Similarly, research finding from the Gartner Group shows that the most commonly outsourced HR functions in Asia-Pacific are: recruitment, training and development, payroll, and legal compliance (cited in Beaman and Eastman, 2003: 5). Recruitment is the first and most common HR process to be outsourced by MNCs in Asia-Pacific countries because it is an area in which they rarely have core competency (Beaman and Eastman, 2003) and can benefit from the specialist services from well-established HR outsourcing provider firms (e.g., recruitment agencies).

It is apparent that the degree of development of the HR outsourcing market in a country plays an important role in shaping the HR outsourcing pattern, disregarding the degree of its economic development. This is found in the case in Asia; for instance, research conducted by Khatri and Budhwar (2001) on strategic HR issues in Singapore revealed that organizations do not extensively consider HR outsourcing due to the perceived poor quality of service and competency level of consultants in the market. However, potential HR activities for outsourcing include:

(1) mundane, administrative, and non-value added activities,
(2) recruitment of contract workers and sourcing of high executive positions and specialists, and
(3) specialized or one-day training courses (Khatri and Budhwar, 2001: 182).

Similarly, according to the Watson Wyatt's Greater China e-HR survey of 268 firms in the region (cited in *China Staff*, November 2002), a major reason for the lack of outsourcing and shared services of the HR function is the lack of options for outsourcing and shared services. Hewitt Associates' (2004) survey also found that while a small number (6.5%) of companies in Southeast Asia expressed their intent to evaluate the outsourcing strategy in the future, many are reticent to outsource HR activities due to a perceived lack of qualified suppliers in the market.

China

The same survey by Hewitt Associates (2004) further revealed that many companies in China are either unfamiliar with the processes and procedures of HR outsourcing or are unfamiliar with the players in the market. In China, HR outsourcing is still a new concept unfamiliar to the majority of Chinese organizations. Their target user companies are primarily Western MNCs. In addition, it may be difficult for Chinese companies to justify a decision to outsource on the basis of potential cost reductions because administrative labor is still relatively cheap in China and it may actually cost more to outsource the function than to keep it in-house. By contrast, Western MNCs are the main drivers of HR outsourcing in the Chinese market both as user firms and as supplier firms. A number of international HR outsourcing operators have moved into the Chinese market, including Towers Perrin and Affiliated Computer Services (McDougall, 2005).

It must be noted that although the concept of HR outsourcing is novel to the Chinese organizations, using external providers for certain HR activities is by no means a new practice. Chinese firms have started to use external providers for their training and development activities since the early 1980s (Cooke, 2005a, b). There has also been an increasing use of external providers for recruitment since the 1990s, especially for headhunting managerial and professional staff. Given the rapid growth of the number of recruitment and headhunting agencies in China in recent years, some of them large MNCs such as Manpower, recruitment is undoubtedly one of the major outsourcing activities (Cooke, 2005a, b).

It can be predicted that the HR outsourcing market targeted at MNCs is going to expand in China, partly due to increasing labor cost and the emergence of new types of employee benefits (for example, retention-oriented employee saving plans, flex benefits) (see Hewitt Associates, 2007). The Chinese government is in the process of enacting a series of industrial policy to boost service industries, with outsourcing being listed as one of the industries in which investment is most encouraged. Industrial policy interventions include financial support to enterprises and the launch of a project by the Ministry of Commerce with an annual budget of at least US$12.5 million to set up 10 bases for service outsourcing over the coming three to five years. The Ministry hopes to persuade 100 multinational corporations to transfer their partial outsourcing businesses to China, as well as creating 1000 large-scale international service outsourcing enterprises. It is hoped that this will help to improve domestic outsourcing services. The Ministry plans to focus on 10 enterprises with over 10 000 employees, which will carry out international service outsourcing. Although currently trailing well behind India, China aims to become the main international outsourcing service base within the next five to 10 years (*People's Daily Online*, 2006).

India

Contrary to its bourgeoning business process outsourcing (BPO) market, HR outsourcing in India has not developed in the expected momentum that is in line with the global trend. Nevertheless, HR outsourcing in India is projected as the fastest growing segment of BPO over the next three years with large-scale offshoring already taking place and larger international players like Fidelity, Exult and Hewitt have set-up their delivery centers in India. The revenue from HR outsourcing in India is expected to increase to US$3.5 billion by 2008, according to a Nasscom–McKinsey survey (see Rediff.com, 2005; Singh, 2007). Indian firms share the same view as their Chinese counterparts that it is more effective to manage their HR processes in-house due to cost factors and potential risks in confidentiality, quality, security breaches, ethics and control.

The most common HR processes outsourced include: training, payroll processing, surveys, resume management services, online performance management solutions, benefits administration, travel and expense management, compensation consulting, benchmark studies, and statutory compliance (Rediff.com, 2005; Sehgal, 2004). Very small and very large firms are the main outsourcing users, the former due to the absence of in-house expertise and/or capacity, whereas the latter outsource routine HR processes in order to focus on core businesses (Jasrotia, 2003). Mathew's (2005) survey study of Indian and foreign-owned firms operating in India similarly revealed that recruitment and training delivery were the most common HR processes that are outsourced, followed by HR climate and compensation surveys and payroll processing. Lack of in-house expertise is the main reason for HR outsourcing. Nevertheless, experts in the field believe that HR outsourcing in India is going through a transitional phase regarding its acceptance and movement from a corporate domain (mainly MNCs) to public sector undertakings. Hunter (2006), highlighting the Indian offshore advantage, predicts that India will be a significant HR outsourcing venue for the majority of Western MNCs. However, the challenge this sector faces to flourish in India rests with the quality, sustained cost advantage, and security of information.

Two tentative conclusions can be made from this review of the global trend of HR outsourcing:

1. The primary motives of HR outsourcing are to gain access to external expertise and cost efficiency. In other words, transformational HR outsourcing has not yet taken root. Nevertheless, Sako and Tierney (2005) observed that firms seeking HR outsourcing services are no longer satisfied with cost efficiency alone. Instead, they are beginning to look for providers who will transform their existing HR function. In parallel developments, HR outsourcing providers are focusing on value-added solutions by 'bundling HR consulting and systems integration with outsourcing, and introducing gain sharing associated with

total HR spend versus transactional fees for delivery' (Sako and Tierney, 2005: 26). While what 'transformation' exactly means is debated, transformational outsourcing claims to support the raised aspirations of in-house HR teams rather than threatening them and 'provide sustainable competitive advantage by aligning human capital strategies with business objectives through robust measurement systems and analytics' (Sako and Tierney, 2005: 27).

2. HR outsourcing is more likely to be adopted by MNCs than by local firms, especially in emerging markets such as China and India. Offshoring HR function to developing countries may have strong implications for Western MNCs' corporate HR structure and strategy.

In the next section, we will focus on the modes of HR offshoring by MNCs before we contemplate how existing patterns of HR offshoring and outsourcing may impact on their global corporate HR structure and strategy.

MODES OF HR OFFSHORING BY MNCS

There are various ways through which MNCs can source their HR services, both internally and externally, onshore as well as offshore (see Figure 17.1). In this section, we focus on modes of HR offshoring.

HR offshoring can be achieved in two ways.

1. Through captive offshoring, or offshore insourcing, through the establishment of a wholly- or partly-owned foreign affiliate in a foreign country. The parent group is either a direct employer or an indirect employer (CIPD, 2006). Offshore insourcers are typically large MNCs that have the resource

	Onshore	Offshore
Insourcing	1. In-house onshore (traditional and arguably shrinking)	2. In-house (captive) offshore in overseas subsidiaries (growing)
Outsourcing	3. Onshore outsourcing (growing)	4. Offshore outsourcing, either directly by client firm or offshored by international HRO provider (growing)
Co-sourcing	5. A combination of in-house and outsourced HR services that are delivered onshore and offshore (increasingly adopted by MNCs)	
	Best-shore	

FIGURE 17.1 Methods of sourcing HR services.

and economies of scale to set up fully-fledged in-house HR functions, drawing on corporate or regional resource back up.

2. The other way of HR offshoring is through outsourcing services to external providers. This can take place either by:

   (a) outsourcing directly to HR service providers operating in offshore countries, especially where the MNC has subsidiary operations in the host countries; or by

   (b) outsourcing to an HR outsourcing service provider onshore who then offshores some of the processes to other countries for strategic and operational reasons.

Offshoring and outsourcing are sometimes (mis)treated as the same thing in part because companies seem to choose them for similar reasons, such as to focus on core competencies, to increase flexibility and to realize cost savings. 'However, offshoring cannot be regarded as purely interchangeably with outsourcing' (Gorp *et al.*, 2006: 7). As we can see from the categorization above, there are important differences between these two approaches. In the case of captive offshoring, a level of direct control is possible. In the case of offshore outsourcing, especially in scenario (b), it is more difficult for client firms to control/coordinate the outsourcing process and relationship when the HR function is both externalized and internationalized through a third party.

The precise volume of HR offshoring that is occurring is unknown. According to Teicher (2003), some 5% of HR jobs had moved offshore in 2002 and it was estimated that by 2007 the number would rise to at least 15%. We can reasonably suggest, based on the evidence of increases in global HR outsourcing and BPO in general, that HR offshoring is on the increase as part of this broader trend.

Offshoring is taking place typically from a developed economy to a developing country where wages are significantly lower than in the former. It is a phenomenon associated with cost, quality, productivity, flexibility, speed, and innovation in the context of heightened global business competition. It was reported that captive offshoring is the dominant type of offshoring, suggesting that firms choose to relocate their business activities to foreign countries under direct control (Gorp *et al.*, 2006). According to the analysis of McKinsey Global Institute, it was estimated that 'for every dollar of spending that American companies transfer to India, $1.46 in new wealth is created. India received 33 cents' (Farrell, 2005: 676). 'In the USA, companies save $0.58 for every dollar of spending on jobs they move to India. German companies save €0.52 for every euro of corporate spending they offshore to India' (Farrell, 2005: 676). It is estimated that 1000 British jobs offshored to India can help to save up to 10 million annually (see Budhwar *et al.*, 2006). India offers two advantages. One is the '*people attractiveness*' – India produces over two million English-speaking graduates every year who are ready to work at up to 80% less salary than their Western counterparts. This availability of technical and computer literate human resources who can offer lower response time with efficient and effective service makes India a magnet for MNCs. A second advantage is the '*location attractiveness*'. Enormous savings are possible for foreign firms by offshoring their processes to India because of the availability of a relatively inexpensive but strong and established infrastructure that offers telecom services, improved international bandwidth, technology parks, a well-developed software industry, and an existing base of blue-chip companies already operating there (for more details see Budhwar *et al.*, 2006).

The A.T. Kearney Offshore Location Attractiveness Index 2004 (A.T. Kearney, 2004) revealed that India, China, Malaysia, the Czech Republic, Singapore, Philippines, Brazil, Canada, Chile, and Poland were the top 10 offshore locations, with India well ahead as the most favourite country because of its strong mix of low costs and rich level of human capital (e.g., IT and language skills and management competence). China's vast labor pool and low costs made it the second most favorite place, although it lags behind India in terms of its experience as an outsourcing provider country, level of human capital, and concerns of intellectual property rights. Firms offshore to India and China for different reasons. They offshore to China for its manufacturing capacity, product design and development, and access to the vast market opportunities both within China and in the Asia-Pacific region. By contrast, firms offshore to India for IT development and maintenance and other service provisions. These different offshoring motives and business contexts give rise to different implications for the MNCs' HR strategy and HR offshoring/outsourcing.

It is unlikely that HR offshoring will take on the same rage as call center and business process offshoring. Instead, HR offshoring tends to be part of the firm's internationalization plan. MNCs may be seeking local HR oursourcing providers to provide part of the services while delivering the rest in-house in a co-sourcing mode. Co-sourcing refers to 'the action of allowing an organization's HR generalist to work with external vendors on some activities, or to the action of allowing HR specialists to work as consultants to line managers who actually perform HR duties' (Lilly *et al.*, 2005: 57). In principle, co-sourcing takes advantage of best-shore and is seen as best-sourcing. HR offshoring has implications for the control, coordination and delivery of the HR function as a whole, be it in the form of insourcing, outsourcing or co-sourcing. It is to this issue that we now turn.

IMPLICATIONS OF HR OFFSHORING FOR THE MNCs' GLOBAL HR STRUCTURE AND STRATEGY

As we have noted earlier, MNCs often outsource certain elements of their HR function in offshore countries where they operate in order to tap into local expertise and to focus on core competence. This practice enables firms to acquire the necessary expertise resource in a relatively short period of time without having to go through the traditional life cycle stages assumed for internationalizing firms. However, this 'short-cut' to acquiring HR competence requires a corporate HR structure that is different from one that may evolve through in-house development. Indeed, the advent of HR outsourcing and shared services centers enabled by ICT has led to significant changes in the corporate HR structure for many firms as

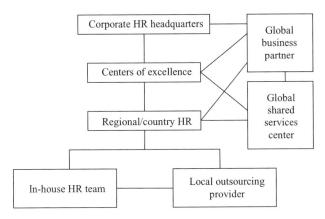

FIGURE 17.2 A model of a global HR structure with HR offshoring/outsourcing.

a prerequisite for adopting these services. The new structure often includes: an elite corporate HR team at the headquarters, centers of excellence, business partners, and shared services centers/HR outsourcing services (Ulrich, 1998; Cooke *et al.*, 2005; Cooke, 2006; Tamkin *et al.*, 2006). Captive offshoring and offshored outsourcing of the HR function adds further challenges to the complexity of centralization, decentralization, control, and coordination that are exhibited in managing HR in MNCs and the outsourcing relationship. A global HRM structure that involves offshoring and outsourcing may take, or be similar to, the form shown in Figure 17.2.

The *corporate HR headquarters* is usually 'responsible for the strategic direction of the function, with a broad policy overview. A governance role is nearly always included' to ensure adherence to broadly the same corporate standard of and approach to people management (Tamkin *et al.*, 2006: 2). *Centers of excellence* tend to specialize in specific HR aspects. They 'give professional support to business partners' by 'developing detailed policy for corporate HR and acting as a reference point for shared services agents dealing with complex issues raised by clients' (Tamkin *et al.*, 2006: 2). More importantly, 'they take on a strategic role in the global organization that reaches beyond their local undertakings' (Sparrow *et al.*, 2004: 51). In the *global shared services center*, 'activities performed locally by divisions or business units are re-engineered, streamlined and centralized, so that the various business units pool resources and 'share' in the service delivery solution' (Tamkin *et al.*, 2006: 2). *Global business partners* are often highly experienced HR professionals knowledgeable of the organization's business and HR strategy. They are expected to provide consultancy advice and support to their line clients 'in strategic development, organizational design and change management', to broker 'the delivery of transactional services from the shared services operation', and to act 'as the conduit with corporate HR' (Tamkin *et al.*, 2006: 2).

It has been argued that different internationalization strategy adopted by an MNC (see Bartlett and Ghoshal, 1989 for typologies) will have different implications for the role of the HR function (Farndale and Paauwe, 2005). Therefore, the choice of HRM strategy and the specific role and influence of each of the stakeholders outlined in Figure 17.2 'is largely dependent on the internationalization strategy adopted by the firm:

◆ *Multi-domestic*: Subsidiaries are seen as an independent business, therefore the adaptive approach to HRM systems is most appropriate.
◆ *Global*: Subsidiaries are managed as dependent businesses, therefore an exportive approach to HRM systems is most appropriate.
◆ *Transnational*: Subsidiaries are managed as interdependent businesses, therefore an integrative approach to HRM systems is most appropriate' (Farndale and Paauwe, 2005: 8).

Farndale and Paauwe (2005: 8) further define the adaptive, exportive and integrative models of an IHRM system as:

◆ *Adaptive*: Low internal consistency with the rest of the firm and high external consistency with the local environment – little transfer of practices.
◆ *Exportive*: High integration of subsidiary HRM systems across the company – replicating practices developed at head office.
◆ *Integrative*: Substantial global integration with an allowance for some local differentiation – two-way transfer of HRM practices between head office and subsidiaries.

Tensions exist in the continuing needs to maintain a dynamic balance on issues of global vs. regional/local control (centralization vs decentralization) and in-house vs outsource provision. These issues are often manifestations of the more fundamental challenges facing MNCs – the need to achieve both cost-efficiency and quality and the need to ensure a consistent corporate global strategy as well as responsiveness to local circumstances (Bartlett and Ghoshal, 1998; Doz and Prahalad, 1986; Evans *et al.*, 2002; Pucik, 1997; Sparrow *et al.*, 2004). As Brewster *et al.* (2005: 963) argue; a driving force for 'most global HR functions' recent restructuring efforts has been the need to deliver global business strategies in the most cost-efficient manner possible. Both people and activities are examined to identify their added value.' While it is true that cost efficiency is a primary motive for HR offshoring/outsourcing, some argue from a more critical perspective that such a decision is an outcome of an organization's broader strategy to maintain power and control that is aimed to 'raise market barriers to protect their core assets and capabilities' and to 'constrain the ability of unions to challenge the process of international economic restructuring' (Levy, 2005: 692). Since an HR system is embedded in a wider institutional and social relations context, different internationalization strategy and the resultant HR offshoring/outsourcing strategies adopted by MNCs are likely to have different impacts on the global HR outcome. Nevertheless, the role of the HR professionals remains central in ensuring the alignment between the global HR strategy and the local/offshored/outsourced HR function and between the corporate business strategy and the HR strategy.

Managing HR Offshoring/Outsourcing: the Role of and Implications for International HR Professionals

Writers on international HRM have identified a number of new roles of HR departments operating in MNCs 'based on different HRM strategies for internationalization' (Taylor *et al.*, 1996, cited in Farndale and Paauwe, 2005: 3). These include: 'effective influencer' (Novicevic and Harvey, 2001: 1260), 'network leadership' and 'process champion' (Evans *et al.*, 2002: 472), 'constructive fighting' (*ibid.*: 487), 'guardian of culture' (Sparrow *et al.*, 2004: 27) and 'knowledge management champion' (*ibid.*: 24) (cited in Farndale and Paauwe, 2005: 3). These roles are particularly important in managing HR offshoring and the offshored outsourcing relationship.

The role of HR professionals in the decision of HR offshoring

It has often been reported that HR personnel are not involved sufficiently or early enough in the decision making of HR offshoring and outsourcing. According to a survey of more than 500 senior finance and HR leaders on their firms' offshoring decisions, 'companies often underestimate HR related organizational impact and costs when making global sourcing decisions' (cited in Robinson, 2004: 30). Almost two-thirds of HR professionals reported maintaining corporate culture and values as their top offshoring challenge. These were followed by talent management (57%) and legal and regulatory challenges (56%). The cost of training and managing cultural differences amounts to the biggest hidden and unexpected cost occurred in the process (cited in Robinson, 2004).

Similar findings are revealed by a survey conducted by the UK's Chartered Institute of Personnel and Development (CIPD).

According to a survey on 589 HR professionals conducted by CIPD (2006), 70% of the HR professionals who had experience of offshoring believe that HR should play a central part in managing the change process when offshoring projects are being implemented. However, less than half of them report this as being the case in practice. The same survey also found that the most common role played by HR once offshoring has been completed is in contributing to internal communication messages, a function carried out by HR at 42% of organizations that have experience of offshoring. However, two-thirds of respondents believe that HR should play an ongoing role in internal communications to help to integrate offshoring operations once they are in place. HR is also involved in recruiting and retaining employees in the new overseas locations in about a third of organizations. Other functions typically carried out by HR once offshoring projects are in place include: identifying training needs (36%), managing ongoing training (30%), and developing HR policy in the new locations (36%). In contrast, about half of respondents believe that HR should play a central role in all these activities once offshoring projects have been completed. Four in 10 of those surveyed think HR should help to develop the employer brand in the new overseas location, though, in reality, this only happens in less than one-fifth of organizations.

It has been widely noted by HR writers that the HR function is not regularly seen as a strategic partner, despite the increasing need for a more strategic and influential role for the HR department in the accelerating pace of internationalization and globalization (Evans *et al.*, 2002; Novicevic and Harvey, 2001; Scullion and Starkey, 2000; Farndale and Paauwe, 2005). Therefore, it is important for HR professionals to ensure their full involvement in the HR offshoring decision-making process to enable them to 'carefully address issues such as skill and language requirements, labor costs by market, alternative talent pools, workforce training, retention, and change management at both ends of the global sourcing spectrum – those being displaced and those receiving the work' (Robinson, 2004: 30). In addition, HR managers need to clarify the type of HR supply chain model they are using, for example, insourcing vs outsourcing, in order to make strategic HR sourcing decisions and develop related HR competencies to match those required to operate the models effectively without 'relinquishing power and control over critical HR functions' (Kosnik *et al.*, 2006: 671; also see Sparrow and Braun, 2008a on future development and challenges of HR outsourcing).

Impact of HR offshoring/outsourcing on corporate HR

As discussed earlier in this chapter, payroll and benefits, legal issues, recruitment, and training and development are the most common HR activities to be outsourced by MNCs in host countries. Outsourcing transactional activities (e.g., payroll) and specialist HR activities (e.g., legal compliance) enables client firms to gain cost efficiency and access specialist knowledge with relatively little negative impact to the corporate HR. However, outsourcing human capital activities (e.g., recruitment and training and development) may present additional challenge to the maintenance of corporate culture and value, which is already a difficult task to manage for MNCs. For example, a regional HR director of a highly reputable MNC who oversees the HR function in the Asia Pacific region revealed in an interview with the first author that the recruitment agency firm the MNC deployed in China systematically screened out female graduate job candidates, even though their quality was as high as, and in some cases higher than, that of their male counterparts. The MNC had a global corporate policy of equal opportunity and imposes a gender ratio in recruitment target. As a result, the Chinese subsidiary's gender ratio statistics consistently fell below that of the corporate target. When this intervention of the recruitment agency firm was discovered, the HR director drew the attention of the staff from the agency firm to the corporate policy and requested them not to discriminate against female candidates. This request was brushed aside by the Chinese recruitment staff, who tried to convince the HR director that this was a common practice in China as women employees were deemed less productive due to their family commitment. Providing HR services in a professional and fair manner has a direct impact on the employees' perception about the organization and is 'crucial in developing corporate strategies concerning employee retention, employee value to the organization and employee productivity' (Lilly *et al.*, 2005: 60). Divergence from the corporate value by the outsourcing provider not only creates a distorted image about the MNC in the host country, but may also undermine the implementation of a global HR strategy.

At a broader level, problems encountered by MNCs in the recruitment and retention of talent in countries such as China and India reflects significant differences in the institutional and cultural environment and levels of economic development between the Western countries and developing countries and among developing countries. These differences may render a Western approach to the high commitment HRM model irrelevant, even in the management of knowledge workers, and jeopardize the MNC's business success in the host countries. It is reported that employee turnover in offshore countries is considered to be one of the highest risks by companies that are offshoring. Firms may not be aware of the high attrition rate in offshore countries until after the problem has occurred (Lewin and Peeters, 2006). For instance, the high attrition rate in the IT industry in India has had a negative impact on both the demand and supply of BPO (Budhwar *et al.*, 2006; Human Resources Outsourcing Association Europe, 2007). The intensifying competition for Indian IT talent is largely based on wage levels rather than initiatives of high commitment oriented HRM, such as empowerment and employee involvement. It is also noted that group loyalty is important in India. Traditionally, it 'comes before individual ambition and eccentricity, and hierarchy is highly respected among Indian managers. Further, Indians enjoy negotiation but will take offence at arrogance or conceit, most particularly if it comes in the patronizing manner' (*Human Resource Management International Digest*, 2005: 37; also see Budhwar, 2001).

The availability of talent pools and work attitudes of young graduates vary across emerging markets. According to a study of 28 low-wage countries by McKinsey Global Institute, there were about 6.4 million young professionals suitable for offshore jobs in 2003. 'Suitable' professionals are university graduates with up to seven years of experience who have the skills and attributes that are sought after by MNCs. However, the percentage of suitable professionals varies across countries (cited in Farrell, 2006: 87). For example, 10% of engineers in China are suitable for employment in an MNC, compared with 20% of Filipino engineers in spite of China's much larger population (Farrell, 2006). In addition, compared with their Russian counterparts, Chinese graduates are more willing to migrate from their hometown to cities where MNCs are located to take up career opportunities (Farrell, 2006). Outsourcing the recruitment function may therefore take away the opportunity for MNCs to gain an in-depth understanding of the local labor market and culture, an area in which they are already weak, and to design an effective HR policy to suit local needs.

Managing HR offshoring/outsourcing relationships

The need for boundary spanners from both the supply and client sides to monitor and coordinate outsourcing relationships in order to ensure satisfactory service delivery is well recognized (Lane and Bachmann, 1998; Williams, 2002; Marchington *et al.*, 2005). The importance of having a global HR team that spans across national boundary is also recognized in managing MNCs (Brewster *et al.*, 2005; Pucik, 1997; Sparrow *et al.*, 2004). Given the added complexity of HR offshored outsourcing, HR professionals, particularly those in the business partner role, can and should play a pivotal role in managing the inter-organizational and cross-border relationships. In fact, the need for HR professionals to act as the guardian of corporate culture by managing the cultural differences as a result of organizational and societal differences is particularly important. According to Lewin and Peeters' (2006) survey of offshoring work, poor service quality and lack of fit of corporate culture and values are the two most important perceived risks by offshoring firms. They also found that cultural challenges appear to be higher with offshoring to China than to India or the Philippines. Beaman and Eastman (2003) identified four key cultural aspects that have the greatest impact on the HR outsourcing situation in Asia-Pacific. These are:

- relationship management that aim for a longer-time span;
- 'introduction fees' which is considered normal in China and India but may be seen as unethical or illegal in the UK and the US;
- collective decision making as the norm so that no individual takes the responsibility; and
- the need for control due to the lack of trust of supplier firms.

It is therefore important for the boundary spanning HR professionals to develop a 'relational' approach to managing the HR outsourcing relationship so that their corporate vision, culture and values are enforced, or, better still, shared by the outsourcing provider (Conkline, 2005).

HR offshoring/outsourcing and career implications for the HR professionals

Globalization has led to radical changes in the role and structure of the in-house HR function that depart from the traditional model. According to Pucik (1997: 167), there are three major challenges to the HR function as it 'strives to become the champion of globalization'. These include:

1. Developing a global mindset inside the HR organization, including a deep understanding of the new global competitive environment and the impact it has on the management of people worldwide.
2. Aligning core human resource processes and activities with the new requirements of competing globally while simultaneously responding to local issues and requirements.
3. Enhancing global competencies and capabilities within the HR function so it can become a borderless business partner in rapidly exploiting business opportunities worldwide (Pucik, 1997: 167).

In the HR offshoring/outsourcing context, this requires the in-house HR department to make strategic change to realign its function with offshoring/outsourcing in order to achieve the transformational effect (see Pickard, 2007b). It also requires the HR professionals to develop new skill sets and advance their career in a different route. The need for HR professionals to become a strategic business partner has been well articulated (e.g., Pucik, 1997; Ulrich, 1998; Sparrow *et al.*, 2004). The key questions are:

- What is a business partner?
- What do we mean by being more strategic?
- How do we transform an operational HR function into a strategic role?
- How do we redesign the career path for HR professionals in an outsourcing context where the HR function is segmented into seemingly discrete units under separate organizations with different skill requirements for the HR professionals?

Existing research studies of HR shared service center (e.g., Cooke, 2006) and HR offshoring (e.g., Tamkin *et al.*, 2006) have revealed the different skill requirements and resultant fragmentation of HR professionals' career paths, as well as the gap between the aspiration for HR professionals to become business partners and the ability to develop individuals into these roles. The increasing demarcation between transactional and transformational reduces the opportunities for individuals to develop a broad range of HR skills and channels them into a more distinct specialists or generalists career. This is especially the case 'in large organizations where there are centers of expertise and business partners' (Tamkin *et al.*, 2006: ix). 'These distinct HR communities can sometimes become quite separated in location, leadership, philosophy, aims and stakeholder interactions, and these divisions may mean that ideas, approaches, views and talent are not shared', making it more difficult to develop HR professionals (Tamkin *et al.*, 2006: ix). International exposure opportunities to gain awareness of different HR environments and mobility across different functions, sectors, and organizations to gain wider experience seem to be the way forward to move up the HR career ladder (Tamkin *et al.*, 2006).

Conclusions

This chapter has reviewed the motives and growth of global HR outsourcing and offshoring and its implications for the HR function and HR professionals. While total outsourcing remains rare, payrolls and benefits, legal compliance, recruitment and training are the main activities that firms outsource to local providers. It is often assumed that recruitment and training are discrete HR functions that can be outsourced easily without any negative impact. However, the process of performing the recruitment and training functions is also a process of projecting the culture of the organization to its employees. As such, the outsourcing of a seemingly simple and discrete HR activity may have a knock-on effect on the soft aspect of the corporate HR and sends a negative signal to its employees, if the activity is handled in a way that departs from the corporate culture and values.

Managing HR offshored outsourcing reflects similar issues to that of managing HR in MNCs, but has added challenges. Communication can be more difficult when there is geographical, organizational, as well as cultural separation. National and organizational cultural differences, specificities of employment legislation and unique characteristics of the labor market of each country all make the process of HR outsourcing more challenging. Global HR professionals need to adopt a flexible approach to locate, source, and manage human capital and the HR process in different parts of the world to respond to local differences. They also need to constantly review, if what are classified as 'non-core' HR activities are really non-core activities to be outsourced to avoid oversimplification of the complexity of the real business situation (Klaas *et al.*, 2001).

In addition, there are a number of important issues that the in-house HR team needs to address if it is to secure its strategic role in the organization. How will the in-house HR department manage its multi-sourced HR functions? What control mechanisms should be in place to operate such a system successfully? How can it ensure that the HR input reaches the strategic level when the HR functions are delivered by a potentially large and growing collection of specialized and self-contained units that are both internal and external to the organization across the world? How should the two-way relationships be developed and maintained effectively among the stakeholders in the HR structure? How should the corporate culture and value be embedded into that of the outsourcing provider? Given the fact that most outsourcing relationships incur more problems than anticipated, some of which have serious implications, how can the in-house HR team disassociate itself from these operational problems and diffuse discontent from its 'clients' on the one hand, and try to enhance its strategic position on the other? Finally, the reconfiguration of the HR structure as a result of offshoring and outsourcing raises important questions of how HR professionals are to be trained and what career patterns are available for them.

REFERENCES

Arkin, A. (2007). *Free to Fly: The Guide to HR Outsourcing.* London: Chartered Institute of Personnel and Development, February, pp. 18–22.

Atkinson, J. (1984). Manpower strategies for flexible organizations. *Personnel Management*, August, pp. 28–31.

Bartlett, C., and Ghoshal, S. (1989). *Managing Across Borders: The Transnational Solution* (1st edn). Boston, MA: Harvard Business School Press.

Bartlett, C., and Ghoshal, S. (1998). *Managing Across Borders: The Transnational Solution* (2nd edn). Boston, MA: Harvard Business School Press.

Beaman, K., and Eastman, S. (2003). *HR outsourcing in Asia/Pacific*, Internet source: http://www.jeitosa.com/resources/karen_beaman/HROinAsiaPacific.pdf, accessed on May, 4th 2007.

Beaman, K.V. (ed.) (2004). *Out of Site: An Inside Look at HR Outsourcing.* New York: Reactor-Duncan, Inc.

Brewster, C., Sparrow, P.R., and Harris, H. (2005). Towards a new model of globalising HRM. *International Journal of Human Resource Management*, 16 (6), 949–970.

Budhwar, P. (2001). Doing business in India. *Thunderbird International Business Review*, 43 (4), 549–568.

Budhwar, P., Luthar, H., and Bhatnagar, J. (2006). Dynamics of HRM systems in BPOs operating in India. *Journal of Labor Research*, XXVII (3), 339–360.

Chartered Institute of Personnel and Development (2006). *Offshoring and the Role of HR: Survey Report.* London: CIPD.

China Staff, November 2002, 8 (11), 34.

Conkline, D. (2005). Risks and rewards in HR business process outsourcing. *Long Range Planning*, 38, 579–98.

Conner, K. (1991). A historical comparison of resource-based theory and five schools of thought within industrial organizational economics: Do we have a new theory of the firm? *Journal of Management*, 17, 121–54.

Cook, M. (1999). *Outsourcing Human Resources Functions.* New York: Amacom.

Cooke, F.L. (2005a). *HRM, Work and Employment in China.* London: Routledge.

Cooke, F.L. (2005b). Women's managerial careers in China in a period of reform. *Asia Pacific Business Review*, 11 (2), 149–162.

Cooke, F.L. (2006). Modeling an HR shared services center: Experience of an MNC in the United Kingdom. *Human Resources Management*, 45 (2), 211–227.

Cooke, F.L., Shen, J., and McBride, A. (2005). Outsourcing HR: Implications for the role of the HR function and the workforce. *Human Resource Management*, 44 (4), 413–32.

Doz, Y.L., and Prahalad, C. (1986). Controlled variety: A challenge for human resource management in the MNC. *Human Resource Management*, 25 (1), 55–71.

Evans, P., Pucik, V., and Barsoux, J. (2002). *The Global Challenge: Frameworks for International Human Resource Management.* London: McGraw-Hill.

Farndale, E., and Paauwe, J. (2005). *The role of corporate HR functions in MNCs: The interplay between corporate, regional/national and plant level.* International Programs Visiting Fellow Working Papers. US: Cornell University.

Farrell, D. (2005). Offshoring: Value creation through economic change. *Journal of Management Studies*, 42 (3), 675–683.

Farrell, D. (2006). Smarter offshoring. *Harvard Business Review*, June, 86–92.

Gorp, D., Jagersma, P., and Ike'e, M. (2006). *Offshoring in the service sector: A European perspective.* The Nyenrode Research Group (NRG) Working Paper Series, NRG Working Paper No. 06-06, The Netherlands.

Greer, C., Youngblood, S., and Gray, D. (1999). Human resource management outsourcing: The make or buy decision. *The Academy of Management Executive*, 13 (3), 85–96.

Hewitt Associates (2004) Time to focus. *Hewitt Quarterly Asia Pacific*, 3 (2), Internet source: http://was4.hewitt.com/hewitt/ap/resource/rptspubs/hewittquart/HQ_10/time_to_ focus.html, accessed on March 12, 2006.

Hewitt Associates (2007). China Opens the Door to HR Outsourcing. http://www.hewittassociates.com/Intl/AP/en-CN/KnowledgeCenter/ArticlesReports/ hr_outsourcing.aspx, accessed on October 22, 2007.

Human Resource Management International Digest (2005). International outsourcing, *Human Resource Management International Digest*, 13 (3), 30–32.

Human Resources Outsourcing Association Europe (2007). India: An attractive BPO destination marred by alarming attrition, Internet source: http://www.hroeurope .com/file/3557/conference-board-cautions-on-labor-cost-benefits-of-offshoring, accessed on May 6, 2007.

Hunter, I. (2006). *The Indian Offshore Advantage: How Offshoring is Changing the Face of HR.* Aldershot: Gower Publishing.

Jasrotia, P. (2003). Why HR outsourcing has few takers. *IT People.* Internet source: http://www.itpeopleindia.com/20030428/cover.shtml, accessed on May 10, 2007.

Kearney, A.T. (2004). *A.T. Kearney's 2004 Offshore Location Attractiveness Index: Making Offshore Decisions.* Chicago: A.T. Kearney.

Khatri, N., and Budhwar, P.S. (2001). A study of strategic HR issues in an Asian context. *Personnel Review*, 31 (2), 166–88.

Klaas, B., McClendon, J., and Gainey, T. (2001). Outsourcing HR: The impact of organizational characteristics. *Human Resource Management*, 40 (2), 125–138.

Kosnik, T., Wong-Ming Ji, D., and Hoover, K. (2006). Outsourcing vs insourcing in the human resource supply chain: A comparison of give generic models. *Personnel Review*, 35 (6), 671–683.

Lane, C., and Bachmann, R. (1998). *Trust within and between Organizations: Conceptual Issues and Empirical Applications*. Oxford: Oxford University Press.

Levy, D. (2005). Offshoring in the new global political economy. *Journal of Management Studies*, 42 (3), 685–93.

Lewin, A., and Peeters, C. (2006). Offshoring work: Business hype or the onset of fundamental transformation? *Long Range Planning*, 39, 221–39.

Lilly, J., Gray, D., and Virick, M. (2005). Outsourcing the human resource function: Environmental and organizational characteristics that affect HR performance. *Journal of Business Strategies*, 22 (1), 55–73.

Marchington, M., Grimshaw, D., Rubery, J., and Willmott, H. (eds) (2005). *Fragmenting Work: Blurring Boundaries and Disordering Hierarchies*. Oxford: Oxford University Press.

Mathew, M. (2005). *HR outsourcing in India: The organised and the unorganised sector*. Paper presented at the 23rd International Labour Process Conference, UK: Strathclyde.

McDougall, P. (2005). EDS likely to open HR centre in China, *InformationWeek*. Internet source: http://www.informationweek.com/story/showarticle.jhtml?articleID=60401263, accessed on March 12, 2006.

Novicevic, M., and Harvey, M. (2001). The changing role of the corporate HR function in global organizations of the twenty-first century. *International Journal of Human Resource Management*, 12 (8), 1251–68.

Oates, D. (1998). *Outsourcing and the Virtual Organization: The Incredible Shrinking Company*. London: Century Business.

Oliver, C. (1997). Sustainable competitive advantage: Combining institutional and resource-based views. *Strategic Management Journal*, 18, 697–713.

People's Daily Online (2006). China to Promote Outsourcing Biz, Internet source: http://english.people.com.cn/200607/eng20060727_287154.html, accessed on May 6, 2007.

Pickard, J. (2006). Multiple choice. In: *The Guide to HR Outsourcing*. London: Chartered Institute of Personnel and Development, February, 7–11.

Pickard, J. (2007a). Spring in its step. In: *The Guide to HR Outsourcing*. London: Chartered Institute of Personnel and Development, February, 6–10.

Pickard, J. (2007b). One giant leap. In: *The Guide to HR Outsourcing*. London: Chartered Institute of Personnel and Development, February, 16–17.

Pucik, V. (1997). Human resources in the future: An obstacle or a champion of globalisation? *Human Resource Management*, 36 (1), 163–7.

Quisenberry, J. (2006). Outsourcing IT to get the most out of your HRO, The Shared Services and Business Process Outsourcing Association, February 16, 2006, Internet source: http://www.sharedservicesbpo.com/file/3169/outsourcing-it-to-get-the-most-out-of-your-hro-.html, accessed on March 14, 2006.

Rediff.com (2005). HRO, the Next Big Opportunity for India. http://inhome.rediff.com/money/2005/mar/23inter.htm, accessed on October 20, 2007.

Robinson, K. (2004). Study: HR needs larger role in 'offshoring'. *HR Magazine*, May, 30.

Sako, M., and Tierney, A. (2005). *Sustainability of business service outsourcing: The case of human resource outsourcing (HRO)*. AIM Research Working Paper Series: 019-June-2005, Advanced Institute of Management Research.

SBPOA (2004). NelsonHall Forecasts 21 percent Annual Growth in Multi-process HR BPO Market by 2008, The Shared Services and Business Process Association (SBPOA),

August 2, 2004, Internet source: http://www.sharedservicesbpo.com/file/2036/21-percent-annual-growth-forecasted-in-multi-process-hr-bpo-market-by-2008.html, accessed on March 14, 2006.

Scullion, H., and Starkey, K. (2000). In search of the changing role of the corporate human resource function in the international firm. *International Journal of Human Resource Management*, 11 (6), 1061–81.

Sehgal, M. (2004). *The new mantra is HR outsourcing*. Internet source: http://in.rediff.com/money/2004/may/03bpol.htm, accessed on May 6, 2007.

Singh, J. (2007). Asymmetry of knowledge spillovers between MNCs and host country firms. *Journal of International Business Studies*, 38, 764–786.

Sparrow, P.R., and Braun, W. (2008a). HR strategy theory in international context. In M. Harris (ed.), *The Handbook of Research in International Human Resource Management*. Mahwah, NJ: Lawrence Erlbaum, pp. 77–106.

Sparrow, P.R., and Braun, W. (2008b). HR sourcing and shoring: Strategies, drivers, success factors and implications for HR. In M. Dickmann, C. Brewster and P.R. Sparrow (eds), *International Human Resource Management: A European Perspective*. London: Routledge, pp. 39–66.

Sparrow, P.R., Brewster, C., and Harris, H. (2004). *Globalizing Human Resource Management*. London: Routledge.

Sutcliffe, K.M., and Zaheer, A. (1998). Uncertainty in the transaction environment: An empirical test. *Strategic Management Journal*, 19 (1), 1–23.

Tamkin, P., Reilly, P., and Hirsh, W. (2006). *Managing and Developing HR Careers: Emerging Trends and Issues*. London: Chartered Institute of Personnel and Development.

Taylor, S., Beechler, S., and Napier, N. (1996). Toward an integrative model of strategic international human resource management. *Academy of Management Review*, 21 (4), 959–985.

Teicher, S. (2003). White-collar jobs moving abroad. *The Christian Science Monitor*, Internet source: http://www.csmonitor.com/2003/0729/p01s03-usgn.html, accessed on May 6, 2007.

Turnbull, J. (2002). Inside outsourcing. *People Management: Connected HR*, 10–11.

Ulrich, D. (1998). A new Mandate for human resources. *Harvard Business Review*, January–February, 124–34.

Vernon, P., Phillips, J., Brewster, C., and Ommeren, V.J. (2000). *European Trends in HR Outsourcing*. UK: Cranfield School of Management & William M. Mercer Inc.

Williams, P. (2002). The competent boundary spanner. *Public Administration*, 80 (1), 103–24.

Williamson, O.E. (1985). *The Economic Institutions of Capitalism*. New York: Free Press.

Zagata-Meraz, S., and Frighetto, J. (2005). *HR outsourcing continues to boom as organizations gain experience and reap benefits*. Hewitt Associates, April 18, USA. Internet source: http://was4hewitt.com/hewitt/resource/newsroom/pressrel/2005/04-18-05.pdf, accessed on March 14, 2006.

18

Globalizing Human Resource Management: Examining the Role of Networks

PAUL SPARROW, CHRIS BREWSTER, AND PAUL LIGTHART

INTRODUCTION

Research and practice in the field of international human resource management (IHRM) has advanced significantly in recent years. Schuler and Tarique (2007) argue that throughout this period, writing about IHRM has focused on the worldwide management of human resources (Briscoe and Schuler, 2004; Brewster and Suutari, 2005; Schuler and Jackson, 2005; Sparrow and Brewster, 2006; Stahl and Björkman, 2006; Sparrow and Braun, 2008a, b). The purpose of IHRM is to enable the firm to be successful globally and this entails being: competitive throughout the world; efficient; locally responsive; flexible and adaptable within the shortest of time periods; and capable of transferring knowledge and learning across their globally dispersed units. In achieving this, however, there is a continual tension between the requirement to standardize and the requirement to be sensitive to local circumstances.

Four academic debates are shaping much IHRM research:

- the nature of IHRM structures and strategies and the ensuing IHRM research agenda;
- the changing technological context and the impact of developments in shared services, e-enablement, outsourcing and offshoring;
- the role of line managers and business partners in the effective conduct of IHRM;
- the role of knowledge management, networking, and social capital processes.

We outline some of the key issues in each of these four areas, and then explore the latter topic in more depth through some exploratory research inside a single case study organization.

Handbook of International Human Resource Management. Edited by Paul R. Sparrow
© 2009 John Wiley & Sons, Ltd

THE NATURE OF IHRM STRUCTURES AND STRATEGIES

It is widely accepted that within international business, HRM is the most likely activity to be localized (Rozenweig and Nohria, 1994). However, recent research has demonstrated that largely as a result of technology 'a new line in the sand' is being drawn between standardized and localized HR practices (Sparrow *et al.*, 2004). As Evans and his colleagues have put it, organizations are faced with a 'duality': they have to be good both at standardizing and at respecting the local environment (Evans and Lorange, 1989; Evans and Doz, 1992; Evans and Genadry, 1999). Even this may understate the complexity. Organizations often split HR responsibilities in these areas between a global HR department, country management, and business stream leaders. In addition, arising from research which identified a trend toward the regionalization of businesses and HRM, there is yet another layer of complexity in the mix. Definitions of the geographical nature of regions, their scope, their resources and their capabilities vary from organization to organization. An important contribution still to be made is to explain *how* organizations manage this complexity. What is the role of the regional coordination processes and structures in the way people are managed within global organizations? Research is needed to understand the trends in IHRM structures and strategies; the antecedents of those trends; the factors that are pushing organizations in one direction or pulling them in another; and the practical implications that flow from these developments.

IHR Directors also face a series of inward-facing and "operational" – yet equally challenging to answer – questions. Global organizations today are presented with multiple choices as how to structure and organize their HR organizations. The answers are unlikely now to rest in a series contingencies, but rather require us to understand what is pushing organizations in one direction or pulling them in another and with what practical implications? IHRM academics need to help global HR functions to position themselves inside the rest of the organization so that they can best achieve the needs of their (many and diverse) stakeholders. If we are to understand and advise on the positioning of global HR functions, at a pragmatic level, we need to help to advise on who should have the responsibility for the HR policies and the practice? Having considered who should have responsibility, how should such responsibility be integrated with the organizational strategy at a global and local level? What conflicts of interest can be expected between these areas and how can they be resolved? HR specialists now manage through multi-line reporting relationships, but what is really meant by the business partner role in this global context?

CHANGING TECHNOLOGICAL CONTEXT: THE IMPACT OF DEVELOPMENTS IN SHARED SERVICES, E-ENABLEMENT, OUTSOURCING, AND OFFSHORING

Questions about IHRM structures and strategies cannot be fully understood, however, without also examining the combination of a series of parallel and technologically-enabled changes – shared services, e-enablement, outsourcing, and offshoring. The combination of developments in technology, process streamlining, and sourcing are moving the focus of the IHRM function away from managing a global set of managers toward becoming a function that can operate a series of

value-adding HR processes within the business internationally. Yet, these developments are in most instances impossible to disentangle from the parallel debates
about specialization, core capability, and the technological enablement of service
delivery that makes some of these developments easier to implement.

Historically, considerable energy has been spent translating central initiatives into
what works within different countries. Now, however, there is a much stronger focus
on cross-country and cross-business border implementation issues. HR is moving
toward a world where it has to satisfy line-of-business – and not just country – needs,
and this is beginning to shift the way that HR professionals think about problems
(Sparrow *et al.*, 2004). Brewster and colleagues (2005) have drawn attention to three
distinct, but linked, enablers of high-performance that are creating a new set of
pressures on IHRM specialists:

(1) HR affordability (the need to deliver global business strategies in the most cost
    efficient manner possible);
(2) central HR philosophies (the need to ensure a common philosophy and co-
    herent practice across disparate countries and workforces); and
(3) e-enabled HR knowledge transfer (the use of networks and technology to assist
    organizational learning).

E-enablement of HRM is a significant and developing trend in international organizations (Martin, 2005) and it is already evident that there will undoubtedly be a
considerable impact on the role and activities of global HR departments, centrally
and locally.

However, the implementation of e-enablement has been fraught with problems,
in part because practitioners lack a sound body of theory and evidence on which
to proceed, particularly in the area of innovation, absorptive capacity, technology
acceptance, and change management. The pursuit of this process across countries
is also a relatively under-theorized one, and the consequences of ICT enablement
for HR specialists, line managers and other employees is not well understood, with
researchers highlighting both significant benefits and problems for these stakeholders (Cooke, 2006). This will likely affect the credibility and authority of such departments, in turn having significant implications for the roles and activities of line
managers. There will also be extensive resourcing implications for global HR functions given that e-enablement is often associated with shared service structures and
adjustments in terms of global outsourcing or insourcing of HR activity. Research
therefore needs to address the following questions: What is the usage of e-enabled
HRM? What are the implications of technical developments and process streamlining for the design and conduct of international activity? What are the specific
challenges of operating shared services on a regional or a global basis? What are
the implications for the role of HR departments and line managers?

THE ROLE OF LINE MANAGERS IN THE CONDUCT OF IHRM

In order to help to answer these questions, we also need to address a third
puzzle that faces HR functions, which is how best to build upon the role of line

managers in the conduct of IHRM and how to best achieve the HR business partner role. The role and responsibility of the line manager has been much debated over the years (Schuler, 1990; Blyton and Turnbull, 1992). There is now considerable evidence that this role varies in a significant and consistent manner across countries (Brewster and Larsen, 2000; Brewster and Mayne 1994; Paauwe, 1995; Brewster and Scullion, 1997; Gennard and Kelly 1997; Brewster and Larsen (2000); Larsen and Brewster, 2003). The opportunities and the difficulties this creates for organizations are obviously magnified across international boundaries (De Cieri, Fenwick, and Hutchings, 2005). There are many unresolved questions about the distinctions about HR work is conducted within the "line management" category: responsibilities at the different levels will vary considerably; there may well be HQ/subsidiary differences.

Despite there being clear specifications about the nature of the business partner role, '. . . the challenge lies in creating the contexts and practices through which the strategic partner role can be realized' (Smethurst, 2005: 25). In his original conception, Ulrich (1997) outlined four HR roles of employee champion (which were later split into two roles of employee advocate and human capital developer), administrative expert (later re-termed functional expert), strategic partner, and change agent (later combined into a broadened strategic partner role and accompanied by a new leader role). In all of these roles HR acted as a business partner but the practical realization of the job title "business partner" became that of "strategic partner" or "strategic business partner". Exactly what was involved in this role was unclear. The boundaries between the attention given simply to business issues (i.e., working with line management but with an HR background, and focusing therefore on strategic execution) as opposed to higher level strategy formulation advice, has once more become vague. The strategic business partner role has become opportunistic in its delivery.

While the complexities and strategic centrality of the international business partner role often affords the necessary context to create understanding, demonstrate value and relevance and acquire support from line managers, it also risks removing strategic influence of HR previously exerted by a central board-level role and subsuming it in a decentralized and more anonymous line relationship, dependent on the idiosyncratic skills and unplanned opportunities negotiated by HR practitioners. Clearly there is an opportunity now to address a number of important questions. Who has the responsibility, authority and accountability to set HR policies, and at what level? Who is responsible for carrying out the policies through into practice? How are we to understand the responsibilities of the different levels of line management that may be involved in these processes?

THE GROWTH OF NETWORKING TO MANAGE DEMANDS ON IHRM FUNCTIONS

The fourth and final strand of research that needs to be understood results from the growth of networking as a way of managing the extensive demands of HRM in international organizations. One component of these demands clearly concerns that of knowledge management. Bonache and Dickmann (2007) have argued that knowledge management is still loosely defined in the literature. They characterize the field as focusing on three issues: the generation of new knowledge through processes of acquisition and creation; taking stock of and understanding knowledge assets through processes of knowledge capture and storage; and the capacity of the firm to distribute knowledge flows among parts of an international network through processes of knowledge diffusion and transfer. The resource-based view of the firm and institutional theory have been used as dominant theoretical frameworks (Kostova, 1999; Martin and Beaumont, 2001; Kostova and Roth, 2002). Five main forms of global knowledge management, or integration mechanisms, have featured in the literature (Sparrow, 2006b), namely: organizational design and the specific issue of centers of excellence; managing systems and technology-driven approaches to global knowledge management systems; capitalizing on expatriate advice networks; coordinating international management teams; and developing communities of practice or global expertise networks.

The developments noted earlier – such as real and/or virtual shared service centers and centers of excellence – draw particular attention to the need to understand the role of networks in enabling many of these knowledge management mechanisms. Global organizations can pursue different models to organize and manage their formal and informal international networks. It is clear that network and project-based structures also have a range of significant impacts beyond knowledge transfer, such as on the conduct and quality of international HR interventions and on the career trajectories of HR professionals (Fenwick and De Cieri, 2004). Harvey and Novicevic (2004) observed that global leaders must possess a complex amalgamation of technical, functional, cultural, social, and political competencies (see also Harvey and Novicevic, this volume Chapter 6). They made a distinction between human, social, and political capital. Human capital leads to competencies. This is an area that is well researched and is quite well understood, but less well understood are the areas of social and political capital. Social capital leads to trust. It is typically reflected in the standing the manager has in the organization and his or her ability to use that standing to influence others. It helps to build on and meld the many cultural norms that exist in a foreign subsidiary. Political capital by contrast leads to legitimacy. Global leaders have to accumulate political capital – which as subsets includes reputational capital (i.e., being known in the network for getting things done) and representative capital (the capacity to effectively build constituent support and acquire legitimacy by using traditional forms of power) simply in order to be in a position to remove obstacles to cooperation.

Recent empirical work has helped to explain the role of these networks in IHRM and a fair amount is now known about the extent to which networking is used by international organizations and the field has also developed frameworks and taxonomies to describe how they conceive of and use networks. Tregaskis *et al.* (2005) described the function, structure, and process typically associated with international HR networks, which may be run through top-down or more collaborative remits and operate through leadership, project or special event team structures. They can serve a range of functions including policy development and implementation, information capture, exploitation of knowledge, sharing of best practice, achieving political buy-in and socialization of members. Face-to-face contact is important in the process of relationship and reputation-building but is often supplemented by virtual working as a way of signaling more global cultures. The level of localization is generally driven by the politics of acquisition, size, expertise, and level of resistance in subsidiaries. HR leadership through networks can facilitate more collaborative solutions, but this depends on the strategic capability of the function, board-level support and strength of international HR networks.

Given that different types of networks can be categorized, we now need to understand how protocols for managing these networks may be established, and how such protocols impact the other areas explored in the symposium – i.e., international HRM structures and strategies; the potential impact of the technological context: shared services, e-enablement, outsourcing and offshoring; the role of line managers in the effective conduct of IHRM; and the role of knowledge transfer and social capital processes.

THE ADVANTAGES OF USING SOCIAL NETWORK ANALYSIS RESEARCH METHODS

Given the above analysis, we believe that a useful avenue of research is to explore the conduct of IHRM through the analyses of social networks. Before doing so, we briefly review some key principles of social network analysis as a research tool.

Social network analysis serves a powerful role in helping to model complex real world phenomena (Borgatti and Foster, 2003). Over time, however, various forms of network theory have been imported into the social sciences. The earliest work looked at interpersonal influence and the way that people think about relationships (their cognitions). Sociologists then introduced more mathematical approaches to graph the social structures of such relationships, moving the study of social network beyond description and into a more analytical mode. Anthropologists then began to look at the emergence of these social structures inside organizations. Throughout these developments, the range of algorithms, programs, and procedures used to map networks expanded massively.

The essence of network approaches is to look at the patterns that exist within relationships and to see if these patterns relate to other important factors such as power, knowledge or capital. A range of factors can be considered to be related to social capital and its development (Kilduff and Tsai, 2003). Typically these have included the centrality of an actor to a network, which in turn may be analyzed through:

- ascribed qualities (for example, how competent they may be perceived as being);
- their betweenness (acting as a go-between for others not directly connected); or
- their eigenvector (the extent to which they are connected to others who are highly central).

Social network analysis in essence serves to analyze social structures and the role of people within these structures (Cheuk, 2007). The social structure of a network is also important. Networks may be analyzed to look at (Freeman, 1979; Wasserman and Faust, 1994):

- the nature of cliques (blocks of actors with a tendency to interact with people similar in some way);
- the overlaps, symmetry or density (tightness) of connections between and within cliques; and
- the role and nature of important dyadic (paired) relationships within the network.

Indeed, a number of recent studies have started to address the role of social networks to research generic IHRM issues. For example, Singh (2007) used patent citation data to examine the bi-directional knowledge flows between foreign multi-national companies and host county organizations in 30 countries. They used micro-level observations to explain macro-level knowledge diffusion patterns by assessing the career history of patent inventors. As a matter of general interest to the IHRM literature, they considered patterns if interfirm mobility as a driver of knowledge inflows and outflows, and found that these indeed appeared to track personnel flows within the organizations. Cheuk (2007) examined the role of social network analysis as a support tool for the British Council's knowledge management program, analyzing the social networks of 30 global leaders, while M'Chirgul (2007) examined the complete network structure of smart card firms, the strategic value of interfirm collaborations, and how these networks evolved over time.

The value of social network analysis to the field of international HRM, then, lies in its ability to look at both micro- and macro-level linkages between individual actions and institutional outcomes, and vice versa. For this to be the case, a plausible set of hypotheses must be developed to link micro individual actions to successively macro organizational or institutional outcomes. It is an approach, therefore, that can be used to link social capital theory with institutional theory and knowledge management theory – all approaches that have recently begun to influence the IHRM field (see Stahl and Björkman, 2006; Lengnick-Hall and Lengnick-Hall, 2006; and Sparrow, 2006b).

RESEARCH METHODOLOGY

Case study organization

The case study organization is a global information company providing information tailored for professionals in the financial services, media, and corporate markets. In 2006 its revenues were £2.6 billion. The information provided drives decision making across the globe. More than 90% of revenues are derived from financial services businesses. The organization has grown through acquisitions. It employs 16 900 staff in 94 countries with nearly 200 in-country sites and establishment. It has a population of over 800 expatriates, which at around 5% of the workforce signifies the high levels of international mobility needed. There are three regional headquarters in: Europe, Middle East and Africa (Switzerland); the Americas (the USA); and Asia-Pacific (Singapore). The organization has been transforming its core business after completing a major change program. Strategic issues concern improvements in time to market, product quality, network resilience, and customer service. It has been concentrating its product development into fewer centers; continuing to improve the timeliness and breadth of data by streamlining content management, modernizing customer administrator, and simplifying its network of data centers. It operates through business divisions, a series of geographic sales and service channels and shared resources. The business divisions are aligned with the user communities and cover sales and trading; research and asset management, enterprise, and media.

Interviews

A sample of 13 interviewees was preselected by the organization to represent their significant lines of business, the main corporate HR functions and the regional layers of HR coordination. The interviews, which were tape recorded, and lasted on average for one hour each, were with senior managers (Global Heads or equivalent level) with the roles shown in Table 18.1.

Eight of the 13 interviewees were senior line managers responsible for running key global businesses within the case study organization. Two were leaders of corporate HR functions and three held roles at the regional HR level.

Each interview focused on five key themes – the respondent's perceptions of: evolving HR strategies and structures (in the context of your business); the role of line managers; the role of e-HR; the management of diversity; and finally (to help to interpret the subsequent social network analysis exercises) the role of networks and knowledge management. For each theme we explored: the business rationales behind the five core research issues, via the link to organizational strategy and

TABLE 18.1 Role of 13 interviewees.

Line Functions	*Corporate HR*
Head of Asian Development	Global Head of HR Operations
Global Head of Customer Service	Global Head of Performance and Reward
Global Head of Divisional Technology Group	
	Regional HR
Managing Director, Global Sales and Service Operations	Head of HR EMEA
Global Head of Finance, Group and Shared Services	Head of Human Resources Japan
Senior Company Officer, Pacific	Senior VP Human Resources, Americas
Senior Company Officer Japan	
Managing Director Italy and Iberia	

effectiveness (value creation, value improvement, value protection) and the criteria for success; and the political, process and technical skills that have to be brought to bear to manage these interventions.

Social network analysis instrument

The social network analysis exercise uses analysis of egocentric data (Kilduff and Tsai, 2003), i.e., we are collecting data from the same sample of HR and line managers who were made available for our interview. The exercise had two parts. In exercise one respondents listed all the key people/units that formed part of their network. In exercise two, for each person or unit they identified, respondents provided some key information (in the form of ratings) about the dyadic relationship. Respondents spent up to 5 minutes generating a list of (up to 10) people/units/stakeholders that they dealt with (each person/or unit was called a *node*). They were asked the following questions:

- ◆ In order to execute your HR strategy, who is the target, i.e., with whom do you interact?
- ◆ Why do you interact with them?
- ◆ How important is the relationship?

In the second exercise respondents were asked to select their top five interactions and to answer the following 13 questions for each one:

1. How *frequently* do you interact with this node? (1 = not very frequently; 5 = very regular contact)
2. To what extent do you *transfer expert knowledge* to/from this node? (1 = not very frequently; 5 = very frequently)
3. To what extent do you *broker information* to/from this node? (1 = not very frequently; 5 = very frequently)
4. To what extent do you *provide consulting support* to/from this node? (1 = not very frequently; 5 = very frequently)
5. To what extent do you *have to persuade* this node to do something? (1 = not very frequently; 5 = very frequently)
6. How *deep is the relationship*? (1 = surface level; 5 = very deep)
7. How much *power* do you have in the relationship? (1 = very little; 5 = considerable)
8. What would happen if interaction *never took place*! How serious would the consequence be for international HRM? (1 = we could find a work-around; 5 = very serious impact)
9. To what extent is *value added or created for the HRM function* from this relationship? (1 = low; 5 = high)
10. To what extent is *value protected through this relationship* (e.g., brand/reputation, corporate social responsibility, risks controlled); (1 = low; 5 = very high)
11. What is the *level of reciprocation* in this relationship? (1 = very low; 5 = very high)

12. Who *most influences what is delivered?* (1 = I do; 2 = joint negotiation; 3 = they do)
13. How *central to (the case study's) strategy* is the relationship? (1 = very central; 5 = of some importance to the strategy).

To summarize, the social network analysis is based on a dataset consisting of the questionnaires filled in by 13 managers (*egos*) of the case study organization. Each manager was asked to list from 5 to 10 others (*alters*) with whom they interacted. Furthermore, additional questions were asked about the relationship between the *egos* and their five most important *alters*.

Plotting the network

The first observation that has to be made is the complexity of network actors involved in practice in the delivery of IHRM (Table 18.2). The social networks necessary to enact HR for just 13 *egos* involved 76 significant *alters*. These included 11 nodes covering corporate HR roles and functions, 21 nodes covering corporate business roles, 2 corporate leadership nodes, 4 regional HR roles, 7 country business roles, 8 country HR roles, 6 HR business partner roles, 9 strategic teams, and 10 external advisers. The second observation is that the majority of these *alters* are not part of formal HR structures. They include external advisers, and a very high proportion of line management roles.

In order to best convey the structural features of these networks, the usual practice is to develop some form of visual display. In social network analysis, two options tend to be used to assist visualization (Huisman and van Duijn, 2005). The first is to use UCINET. This is probably the best known and most frequently used software package for the analysis of social networks and other proximity data. The program contains a large number of network analytic routines for the detection of cohesive subgroups (such as completely mutual cliques, or clans) and regions (components, cores). These may be used for centrality analysis, for ego network analysis, or for structural holes analysis. A centrality analysis can plot the in- and out-farness from a node to and from every other node. The program finds the most central subgroup of fixed size, or tests the (degree) centrality of a specified group.

A second option is to use Pajek, which is a network analysis and visualization program specifically designed to handle large datasets. Large networks are hard to visualize in a single view. Therefore meaningful substructures have to be identified, which can be visualized separately. Pajek uses six different data structures:

(1) networks (nodes and arcs/edges),
(2) partitions (classifications of nodes, where each node is assigned exclusively to one class),
(3) permutations (reordering of nodes),
(4) clusters (subsets of nodes),
(5) hierarchies (hierarchically ordered clusters and nodes), and
(6) vectors (properties of nodes).

TABLE 18.2 Network nodes.

Corporate HR roles	Corporate business roles	Corporate leaders	Regional HR roles	Country business roles	Country HR roles	HR business partner roles	Strategic teams	External advisers
1. Group HR Director	1. Group Legal Counsel	1. Chairman	1. Head of HR Europe, Middle East and Africa	1. Manager Sales Japan	1. HR Manager Italy	1. Head of HR Business Divisions	1. HR Administration	1. Consulting Firm Advising Remuneration Committee
2. Global Head of HR Operations	2. Group Diversity Counsel	2. Chief Executive Officer	2. Head of HR Asia	2. Head of Account Management Japan	2. HR Manager Spain	2. Divisional Technology Group HR Support	2. Avian Flu Steering Group	2. Consulting Firms Advising on Methodology for Business Integration processes
3. Global Head of Performance and Reward	3. Managing Director, Global Sales and Service		3. Head of HR Pacific	3. Head of Specialist Sales Japan	3. HR Manager Portugal	3. Business Unit HR leads	3. Merger Integration Team	3. External consultants work-life balance
4. HR Executive Team	4. Channel Review Team, Global Sales and Service		4. HR Manager South Asia	4. Lead Business Head	4. HR Manager Thailand	4. Global HR Business Partner Data	4. Indian HR Team Start Ups	4. Best in class thinking but independent external consultants
5. HR Operations Team	5. Group Finance Team			5. Head of Technical Support Japan	5. Bangkok HR Team	5. High reputation HR Business Partners	5. Channel Review Team	5. Learning and Development specialist
6. Head of Remuneration	6. European Middle East and Africa Business Leadership Team			6. Head of Finance Japan	6. Head of HR China	6. Ask HR e-enabled support centre	6. Key Talent Forum	6. Organization development and organization effectiveness consultants
7. Head of Talent Management	7. Head of Asian Development			7. Head of Business Development Japan	7. Head of HR Japan		7. HR specialist Roadmap Teams in organization development	
8. Remuneration Committee Chairman	8. Business Leadership Team				8. Review Manager Japan		8. HR specialist Roadmap Teams in Remuneration	
9. Legal HR	9. Senior Company Officer Pacific						9. HR Specialist Roadmap Teams in Management Development	
10. Head of UK and International Graduate Programs								
11. Learning and Development in UK HR								

(Continued)

TABLE 18.2 (Continued)

Corporate HR roles	Corporate business roles	Corporate leaders	Regional HR roles	Country business roles	Country HR roles	HR business partner roles	Strategic teams	External advisers
	10. Global Head Divisional Technology Group 11. Global Head of Customer Service 12. Head of Operations Bangalore 13. Bangalore Leadership Team 14. Remote line managers Bangalore 15. Data Management Team 16. Operational Centres Leadership Team 17. Managing Director Italy and Iberia 18. Leadership Team for Italy and Iberia 19. Senior Company Officer Japan 20. Managing Director, Asia 21. Head of Financial Information Division Asia						7. External HR colleagues 8. Important customers 9. High performing companies 10. Business schools	

We have included in Figure 18.1 a single visualization of the HRM network within the case study organization, which for ease of interpretation is the smaller network based on the 13 *egos* and their five most important *alters*. The legend is shown in Figure 18.2.

We have categorized the actors, i.e., *egos* and *alters*, with respect to two dimensions:

(1) Geographical/internal structure (the actor's activities are primarily Global/HQ, (sub)continental, regional/national, or external/not applicable); and

(2) HR being the focus of the actor's activities: (yes/no).

The nodes shown in Figure 18.1 are mostly a person (by name, sometimes only a job title, such as head of . . .), sometimes only a team or group.

FINDINGS

In the following section we present some exploratory analysis of the features of the networks involved. It is important to note here that we have to refer to specific roles, positions or teams, and to the external reader the importance of these teams is difficult to assess. In order to appreciate the utility of a social network analysis, one has to be able to imagine that the organization is capable of looking at these actual (realized) interactions, and be able to assess this pattern against a master-view of what interactions were intended by the organization structure. Put simply, are the brokerage roles, structural holes, centrality, and importance those that would be expected, and if not, what is the consequence on the efficiency and effectiveness of the structure-in-practice?

Centrality measures

This first task of course can be attempted by analyzing three positional attributes of the network. In this ongoing research we use a positional analysis of the first seven out of the total 13 *egos* in the HRM network dataset to demonstrate the potential utility of social network analysis to explain the relative prominence of actors (centrality), their degree of closeness, and the level of betweenness. In the following sections, we present some of the main findings that can be derived from the analysis. In the final section we relate these back to more generic observations about the utility of such social network analysis in IHRM research.

The prominence or importance of an actor is indicated by the centrality of his or her position in the network. There are a number of different centrality measures. The best known, and used in this analysis, are the degree centrality, closeness and betweenness (Wasserman and Faust 1994). The centrality measures of the actors in the HRM network are based of the reversed rankings of the (maximally) five most important *alters* by the first seven *egos* (data taken from Exercise 2).

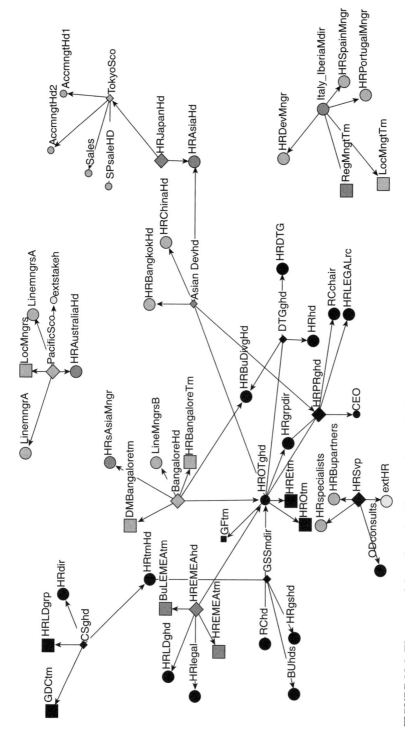

FIGURE 18.1 The network based on the 13 *egos* and up to 5 *alters*.

Legend:

NODES

(shape represents type of actor):

◆ Diamond (*egos*)

● Circles (*alters* in person)

■ Boxes (*alters* as team or unit)

(shade represents the geographical/internal dimension):

■ globally operating actors/Headquarters

▨ (sub)continental actors

▥ regional/national actors

▦ external actors, i.e. outside Reuters, e.g. consultants/not applicable

(size of node represents HR activity of the actor):

Large sized nodes: HR activity

Small sized nodes: non-HR activities

TIES

(dashed lines; no size):   ties included in the initial ranking of max. 10 *alters*, but not assessed in Exercise 2

(solid lines; size):   short list based on Exercise 2, 5 sizes based reversed ranking on Exercise 2: thin (low ranking) to **thick** (high ranking)

FIGURE 18.2 Legend for the social network analysis.

A high level of degree centrality indicates the presence of highly valued ties between an actor and his first-order *alters*. On average, the HRM-network has a degree centrality of 6.25 (min. 3.125, max. 25). Within the group of *egos*, two (the Global Head of HR Operations and Head of Asian Development) are particularly well connected. The Global Head of Customer Service and Global Head of the Divisional Technology Group have relatively low levels of degree centrality. Within the group of *alters*, a high level of degree centrality exists for the Group HR Director, the Business Partner for development transformation, the Global Head of HR Business Divisions and the HR Operations Team. All the other *alters* have equally lower levels of degree centrality.

Closeness refers to the nearness of an actor to all *alters* in the network. On average, the HRM network has a closeness centrality of 11.3 (min. 3.4, max. 14.9). Within the group of *egos*, the Global Head of HR Operations has a relatively short path distance to the *alters* in the HRM network, the Global Head of Customer Service has a relatively lower level of closeness. Within the group of *alters*, the Group HR Director, HR Operations Team, Global Finance Team, and HRET have relatively high levels of closeness, whereas some teams (Group Diversity Counsel, Group Learning and Development, and Head of Talent Management) have low levels of closeness.

Betweenness measures the extent to which an actor lies 'between' the various other actors in a network. On average, the HRM network has a betweenness of 5.1 (min. 0, max. 56.7). Within the group of *egos*, again the Global Head of HR Operations has an important 'intermediary' position in the HRM network, whereas the Global Head of Customer Service is relatively at the periphery. Within the group of *alters*, the HR Operations Team is relatively central. Every other *alter* has a low level of betweenness.

Brokerage analysis

The second task is to identify who are the most important brokers of exchange within this HRM network. A brokerage-analysis of the different roles that *egos* can have connecting groups shows that only the Global Head of HR Operations appears to be a representative broker between the central division of the case study organization and the organization's foreign groups (notably Geneva and Bangkok). The analysis of the structural holes in the smaller HRM network also points to the Global Head of HR Operations (as well as the Managing Director Global Sales and Service Operations) being the one who is the least constrained by the HRM *alters*.

Component analysis of the HRM network

The third task is to see if comment can be made about the key components within this HRM network? Centrality of the complete HRM network is 14.53% (expressed as a proportion of the possible ties that are actually present in the network). The HRM network contains two completely connected cliques. One clique has the Global Head of Asian Development, Global Head of HR Operations and Global

Head of Performance and Reward as members. The other clique, which largely overlaps the first, includes the Group HR Director, the Global Head of HR Operations and the Global Head of Performance and Reward.

Statistical findings

Finally, a fourth task, based on the correlations between the tie-characteristics, is to see if any important statistical relationships can be established within the network data. Indeed, some important relationships could be seen:

- The Frequency (Q1) and Deepness of the Relationship (Q6) appear to be the two most important characteristics. The frequency characteristic affects to a high level most of the other characteristics. Frequency is highly correlated with the Deepness (Q6) of the relationship, which has a similar coverage, but on average lower correlation coefficients and a less clear-cut meaning.
- Frequency (Q1) almost equals transferring information to the *alters* (Q7). They correlate extremely highly, i.e., 0.911.
- The higher an *alter* is ranked by an *Ego* (Exercise 2), the deeper (Q6) is the relationship, the more serious the effect on IHRM (Q4), and the more information that is received (Q8) from the *alter*. The ranking based on Exercise 2 is significant and negatively correlated with these three characteristics.
- The less central (Q3) the relationship with the *alter* is, the more support that is provided to (Q9) the *alter* (or vice versa).
- The characteristics referring to providing expert knowledge to/from, information to/from, and support to/from are highly correlated (except for receiving expert knowledge and providing support).
- The easiness to get what the *ego* needs (Q13) is highly correlated with helping to achieve objectives (Q14).
- The extent of created HRM value from the relationship (Q14) is positively correlated with the centrality of the relationship to the case study organization's strategy (Q3).
- Protection of the case study's reputation through the relationship (Q15) is positively correlated with providing expert knowledge (Q5)/information (Q7)/support (Q8), and the effect of absence of interaction in the relationship (Q4).

With regard to a Reliability analysis of the tie-characteristics, based on the responses of the *egos*, the tie-characteristics (Q1 to Q12) show a high level of consistency/reliability (Cronbach's Alpha is 0.85; 13 items, number of ties: 33). Based on regression analyses of the rankings in Exercise 2 (the smaller HRM network), the deepness of the relationship has the largest effect on the ranking of the *alters* in Exercise 2. This effect is significant (Deep $F_{(1,31)}$: 5.0; $p < 0.032$). R-square is 11.2%. On entering this characteristic in the regression model, the other characteristics do not have additional explanatory effects.

DISCUSSION

For Kilduff and Tsai (2003) a number of concepts – each of which may in turn be considered as an important structural or design feature for an organization – lie at the heart of social network analysis. We draw upon six of these features in this discussion: social capital; structural holes; density of connections; level of centralization; reachability; and the level of reciprocity.

The first concept used to discuss the findings is social capital, which may be individual or collective. For Kilduff and Tsai (2003) social capital reflects the potential set of resources inherent in the social ties that an individual holds and the advantages that may be created (be this advantage in terms of economic outcomes, value creation or other specified outcomes) by the activation of particular links (to individuals, groups, units, etc.) in a social network. Although the activation of these links may not always be in the control of individuals and may be dependent upon the actions of others, this potential is still regarded as capital because it may be traded for other forms of capital (such as money or career advancement). The reality that activation may be dependent on others means that it is the configuration of the social network that produces different levels of social capital at the individual level. Moreover, at a collective level (for example the social capital of an HR function) it is the maintenance of effective relationships that determines the level of capital. We caution that our findings have to be seen as exploratory at this stage, but the statistical analysis of the tie qualities showed just how important social capital was. Frequency of ties is the main capital being traded, affecting most all other qualities, and having a dominant effect on the level of knowledge transfer. The depth of ties has independent effects on the amount of information received and the seriousness of consequence for IHRM provision.

The second concept that we use is structural hole theory (Burt, 1992). This theory explains how the bridging or liaising across disconnected networks may be important. Therefore it is the kind of ties that connect networks that may best be used to classify the type of structure that the network represents. The same principle applies to bridging roles, where the notion of centrality becomes important. In the act of go-between, how central is any one actor? This centrality reflects the level of reciprocated interactions or connections to others who have beneficial ties. Looking at Figure 18.1 it is clear that there are two structural holes, both of which in fact have no brokerage roles to cross the divide, creating structural islands with regard to IHRM. In both instances, there is poor coordination at regional level. The first structural island concerns the Pacific–Australian operations, and the second the Iberian regional operations. It could be hypothesized that there are relatively low levels of HR standardization within these regions and a highly devolved, autonomous form of IHRM. One other region, that of Asia (Japan and China) is only connected to the mainstream HR network via the spanning role of Head of Asian Development. It is clear from this analysis that the health of regional layers of IHRM regional coordination may be examined via such social network analysis. In the case of this organization, the structural ties are weak.

A third important concept is that of density. Density may be seen in terms of the number of connections between actors as a proportion of the total number of connections that could mathematically exist. Loose networks have low density, tightly-knit networks have high density. The role of important dyads can take on especial importance in this context. In some instances, the nature of an important relationship – say, between an HR Director and a senior line Director – can only be understood by examining the network of relationships that surround the pair. Based originally on studies of married couples, the use of mutual dependence on loosely-knit networks, where organizational actors may be '. . . thrown on each others' resources', has been understood as an important way of coping with and reducing significant role differences (Kilduff and Tsai, 2003: 50).

Where loosely knit networks that are relatively unconnected exist around both members of the dyad, the two members of the dyad become more reliant and dependent on each other than if they were surrounded by relatively unconnected (independent) but tightly-knit surrounding networks. If surrounding networks are tightly-knit, members of the dyad can reduce their mutual dependence by relying on their respective networks (and the role differences they may sustain). In short, the embeddedness of a relationship may also depend on the looseness and tightness of surrounding networks. A useful avenue for research on the effectiveness of HR–line management relationships therefore would be to examine the network qualities that surround important dyadic relationships.

The likely significance of this for the effectiveness of IHRM in this case study organization can be seen by an examination of some loose, but important, ties evidenced in Figure 18.1. Consider that the relationship between the Global Head of Customer Service (CSghd) and the Head of Talent Management (HRtmHd) provides some very important brokerage, tying the more distant concerns of the diversity counsel and learning and development into the mainstream network. Similarly, the relationship between the Global HR Operations Director (HROTghd) and the Head of HR EMEA brings the HR capabilities associated with legal and learning and development activities into the central fold. Finally, the Global Head of Performance and Reward (HRPRghd) brokers contacts from the spider-in-the-web HR Operations Director to the CEO.

A fourth concept is the level of centralization that exists within a network. This is the extent to which interactions are focused around one or two actors, or the extent to which coordination is around a single center or multiple centers. We would note that this concept could be important to judge, for example, whether a center of excellence established within an HR structure (Sparrow, 2006b) is indeed a real center of excellence. Do the bulk of interactions naturally gravitate to a few central points of reference? Is a center of excellence formally constituted as an organizational unit, or is it more the case that such centers are charismatic (Moore and Birkinshaw, 1998) – focused around a handful of individuals (talent) who operate as spiders-in-the-web? The data analyzed in this study did not manage to assess the networks surrounding the few (newly established) formal centers of excellence in this case study organization. However, the presence of at least one charismatic spider-in-the-web, to whom many interactions gravitate, is clearly evident in

Figure 18.1. The Global HR Operations Director has network arms reaching out into the Asia region (China and Japan), EMEA region, and to South Asia (Bangalore), and these powerful regional webs are supported by similar network arms extended out into two important business partners, the Divisional technology Group and Global Sales and Service.

A fifth related concept is that of reachability. Reachability reflects the proportion of people who may be interacted with through a "friend" (an immediate and proximal linkage), or through a "friend of a friend" (a linkage that is one-removed). High reach structures are considered to be more efficient as there is less message distortion in the transmission across ties. The spider-in-the-web role associated with the Global HR Operations Director would seem to have very high reachability in this organization, suggesting little message distortion between the regions and business functions connected via this reach.

Finally, the sixth construct used to discuss the impact of networks on IHRM is that of the level of reciprocity, whereby relations may be mutual (symmetric) or non-reciprocated (asymmetric). We found that the less central the relationship with the *alter*, the more support that was provided to the *alter* (or vice versa). Providing expert knowledge to/from the *alter*, information to/from the *alter*, and support to/from the *alter* were all highly correlated and clearly operate on a reciprocal basis. There were two exceptions to this – where there is a much more asymmetric relationship, and these were the receiving of expert knowledge and the provision of support. This seems to make eminent sense – those attributes of networks that are concerned with capability building activity (and providing expert knowledge and support reflect this) understandably operate on a one-way basis. The comments made about reverse transfer (see Edwards, this volume, Chapter 11) may be seen is this context. Asymmetric transfer in IHRM may need to happen by design, a process handled by network structure. Of course, it is still possible that asymmetric networks, as observed in this case study, simply reflect a blindness, whereby reverse capability transfer is possible but is structurally ignored.

Kilduff and Tsai (2003) draw attention to some other important concepts, that while not discussed here, may have important implications for IHRM. The first of these additional concepts is the notion of embeddedness (where work-related transactions may be seen to overlap with other forms of social relations which might not initially be the purpose of study). They showed, for example, that knowledge communicated between business units in a large food company in reality flowed around a small central network of family-led business units, i.e., in this instance knowledge transfer was embedded in kinship ties. The strength of ties may also be expected to be important for IHRM. Strength may be judged on different grounds or criteria, such as the temporal, emotional, communicational, or reciprocal qualities. Weak ties may, however, still facilitate knowledge transfer (Hansen, 1999). Finally, another potentially useful construct for future exploration is the level of multiplexity (the extent to which a tie between actors might be judged differently depending on the range of particular stakeholder perspectives), i.e., the stability of a tie across different social arenas.

CONCLUSIONS

We believe that the use of social network analysis in IHRM research has the potential to open up very valuable new streams of theoretical development. We have
discussed the role that social networks in this case study organization play with regard to IHRM through examination of six structural features. We noted at the beginning of the section that examined the structural features of the HRM network
that such analysis might be focused on what interactions were intended by the organization structure, the identification of key brokerage roles or the existence of
structural holes, the centrality and importance that would be expected from key
roles, and the consequence on the efficiency and effectiveness of the structure-in-
practice. However, future research should be able to move beyond such pragmatic
analysis toward a deeper theoretical understanding of the capabilities that such networks help to create for the organization.

Sparrow (this volume Chapter 1) argues that the field of IHRM would benefit
from theoretical extension at the micro-level, but only where that extension aids
and assists the understanding of international phenomena. We have noted that social network analysis helps to bring together theoretical perspectives driven by social
capital, knowledge transfer and institutional explanations of organization-level behavior. We would note also that the analysis of these networks could be looked at
from a social cognitive perspective. What do the networks say, for example, about
the level of sense-making within international strategy, the role of information markets in helping to execute appropriate strategy and structure within international
organizations, and the existence (or not) of any collective cognition within the organization? The rather old and tired global–local debates about international strategy and structure may be enriched by a more realistic understanding of how networks not only provide the glue between structures, but also create mindsets that
are more appropriate to the complexity that surrounds current globalization processes. We briefly signal some social cognitive theoretical perspectives that might
help researchers to understand the conditions that effective global networks need
to create inside organizations.

The first perspective is that of sensemaking. Sensemaking is the process whereby
members of an organization confront surprising or confusing events, issues, and
actions (Gioia and Chittipendi, 1991). It both precedes decision making and also
follows it, but it is still a relatively unexplored social process (Maitlis, 2005). Pfeffer
(2005) has recently argued that HR needs to help to manage this process inside organizations, i.e., help to manage the mental models in the organization. Strategies
– and global strategies and structures are no exception – are the product of a negotiated order, in turn associated with a process of sensemaking. This sensemaking
of course is a collective process. There has been discussion in the IHRM literature
about the role in particular of expatriates as sensemakers, but also the importance
of reverse knowledge flows provided by inpatriates (Reiche, Kraimer and Harzing, this volume Chapter 8) or via practice transfer (Edwards, this volume Chapter
11). This role of collective sensemaking is also now provided by multiple forms of
international working (see Suutari and Brewster, this volume Chapter 7). Global

networks are in some sense just one very important vehicle through which these insights are provided. From this perspective, a global mindset might just reflect the ability of key individuals to be able to ensure and enable collective dialogue; either by:

(1) possessing the appropriate social and political capital that their position in the network affords them (see Harvey and Novicevic, this volume Chapter 6); or
(2) having the ability to be able to understand and model the connections and interactions revealed by the social network analysis, thereby short-circuiting learning about appropriate execution of strategies.

The analysis of social networks may show that relevant social and political capital resides at singular points or at several levels of the organization. However, in future, such research might examine the linkages between actual networks (structures-in-practice), the sensemaking advantages that this provides key global leaders, and the sensegiving messages that these individuals have to convey through their knowledge and insight into the reality of global operations.

A second conceptual development could be to link analysis of social networks with an understanding of the information markets that they create inside organizations. The scarcest resource in organizations is attention to information in what is an overloaded environment – the various nodes revealed through the social network analysis in this chapter are in competition with each other for the attention of line managers. Organizations are therefore considered to be designed around markets because there are distinct sets of suppliers of information (practice groups, networks, functions, etc.), but these suppliers have to compete for attention in a crowded space. Both information suppliers and users have to receive rewards to participate in this market. For Kang *et al.* (2007), knowledge brokering within these information markets gains access to divergent knowledge that is valuable or unknown to important parts of the organization. The ability to control and manage the quantity and quality of information that flows through these markets is central to organizational survival (see, for example, Hansen and Haas, 2001). Considerable strategic importance is now attached to the brokering of information across internal (intra-) and external (inter-) organizational information markets necessitated by a global operating model.

To conclude, social network analysis can provide some very powerful insights into the reality of IHRM-structures-in-practice. Moreover, the structural qualities that such analysis reveals can provide useful insight into the underlying levels of capability that an IHRM might (or might not) truly possess. Future research must move on to examine the extent to which networks serve to merely glue together existing capabilities, or to create new and previously untapped ones. Do networks serve to correct deficiencies in formal IHRM structures, do they create their own deficiencies, or do they, via the connectivity they can bring, offer the opportunity for new modes of IHRM delivery? To answer such questions, in addition to understanding the structural benefits and knowledge transfer properties that these networks bring, we believe it will also become necessary to understand the social and cognitive capabilities that these networks create for their members.

REFERENCES

Blyton, P., and Turnbull, P. (1992). *Reassessing Human Resource Management.* London: Sage.

Borgatti, S.P., and Foster, P.C. (2003). The network paradigm in organizational research: A review and typology. *Journal of Management*, 29 (6), 991–1013.

Brewster, C., and Mayne, L. (1994). The Changing Relationship between Personnel and the Line: The European Dimension. *Report to the Institute of Personnel and Development.* Wimbledon: IPD.

Brewster, C., and Larsen, H.H. (2000). *Human Resource Management in Northern Europe.* Oxford: Blackwell.

Brewster, C., and Scullion, H. (1997). A review and agenda for expatriate HRM. *Human Resource Management Journal*, 7 (3), 32–41.

Brewster, C., and Suutari, V. (2005). Global HRM: Aspects of a research agenda. *Personnel Review*, 34 (1), 5–21.

Brewster, C., Sparrow, P.R., and Harris, H. (2005). Towards a new model of globalising HRM. *International Journal of Human Resource Management*, 16 (6), 949–970.

Briscoe, D., and Schuler, R.S. (2004). *International Human Resource Management* (2nd edn). New York and London: Routledge.

Burt, R.S. (1992). *Structural Holes: The Social Structure of Competition.* Cambridge, MA: Harvard University Press.

Cheuk, B. (2007). Social networking analysis: Its application to facilitate knowledge transfer. *Business Information Review*, 24 (3), 170–176.

Cooke, F.L. (2006). Modeling an HR shared services center: Experience of an MNC in the United Kingdom. *Human Resources Management*, 45 (2), 211–227.

De Cieri, H., Fenwick, M., and Hutchings, K. (2005). The challenge of international human resource management: Balancing the duality of strategy and practice. *International Journal of HRM*, 16 (4), 584–598.

Evans, P., and Doz, Y. (1992). Dualities: A paradigm for human resource and organizational development in complex multinationals. In V. Pucik, N. Tichy and C. Barnett (eds), *Globalising Management: Creating and Leading the Competitive Organization.* New York: John Wiley & Sons, Inc.

Evans, P., and Genadry, N. (1999). A duality-based prospective for strategic human resource management. In P.M. Wright, L.D. Dyer, J.W. Boudreau and G.T. Milkovich (eds), *Strategic Human Resource Management in the Twenty-First Century (vol. 4, Research in Personnel and Human Resource Management).* Stamford, Conn: JAI Press.

Evans, P., and Lorange, P. (1989). The two logics behind human resource management. In P. Evans, Y. Doz, and P. Lorange (eds), *Human Resource Management in International Firms, Change, Globalization, Innovation.* London: Macmillan, pp. 144–161.

Fenwick, M., and De Cieri, H. (2004). Interorganizational network participation: Implications for global career management. *Journal of Management Development*, 23 (9), 798–817.

Freeman, L.C. (1979). Centrality in social networks: Conceptual clarification. *Social Networks*, 1, 215–239.

Gennard, J., and Kelly J. (1997). The unimportance of labels: The diffusion of the personnel/HRM function. *Industrial Relations Journal*, 28 (1), 27–42.

Gioia, D.A., and Chittipeddi, K. (1991). Sensemaking and sensegiving in strategic initiation. *Strategic Management Journal*, 12, 433–48.

Hansen, M.T. (1999). The search-transfer problem: The role of weak ties in sharing knowledge across organizational sub-units. *Administrative Science Quarterly*, 44, 82–111.

Hansen, M.T., and Haas, M.R. (2001). Competing for attention in knowledge markets: Electronic document dissemination in a management consulting company. *Administrative Science Quarterly*, 46 (1), 1–28.

Harvey, M., and Novicevic, M.M. (2004). The development of political skill and political capital by global leaders through global assignments. *International Journal of Human Resource Management*, 15 (7), 1173–1188.

Huisman, M., and van Duijn, A.J. (2005). Software for social network analysis. In P.J. Carrington, J. Scott and S. Wasserman (eds) *Models and Methods in Social Network Analysis*. Cambridge: Cambridge University Press.

Kang, S-C., Morris, S.S., and Snell, S.A. (2007). Relational archetypes, organizational learning, and value creation: Extending the human resource architecture. *Academy of Management Review*, 32 (1), 236–256.

Kilduff, M., and Tsai, W. (2003). *Social Networks and Organizations*. London: Sage Publications.

Kostova, T. (1999). Transnational transfer of strategic organizational practices: A contextual perspective. *Academy of Management Review*, 24 (2), 308–224.

Kostova, T., and Roth, K. (2002). Adoption of an organizational practice by subsidiaries of multinational corporations: Institutional and relational effects. *Academy of Management Journal*, 45 (1), 215–233.

Larsen, H.H., and Brewster, C. (2003). Line Management Responsibility for HRM: What's happening in Europe? *Employee Relations*, 25 (3), 228–244.

Lengnick-Hall, M.L., and Lengnick-Hall, C.A. (2006). International human resource management and social network/social capital theory. In G.K. Stahl and I. Björkman (eds), *Handbook of Research in International Human Resource Management*. Cheltenham: Edward Elgar, pp. 475–487.

M'Chirgul, Z. (2007). The smart card firms' network positions: A social network analysis. *European Management Journal*, 25 (1), 36–49.

Maitlis, S. (2005). The social processes of organizational sensemaking. *Academy of Management Journal*, 48 (1), 21–49.

Martin, G. (2005). *Managing People in Changing Contexts*. Harlow: Pearson Education.

Martin, G., and Beaumont, P.B. (2001). Transforming multinational enterprises: Towards a process model of strategic human resource management change. *International Journal of Human Resource Management*, 12 (8), 1234–1250.

Moore, K., and Birkinshaw, J.M. (1998). Managing knowledge in global service firms: Centers of excellence. *Academy of Management Executive*, 12 (4), 81–92.

Paauwe J. (1995). Personnel management without personnel managers: Varying degrees of outsourcing the personnel function. In P. Flood, M. Gannon and J. Paauwe (eds), *Managing Without Traditional Methods*. Wokingham: Addison-Wesley.

Pfeffer, J. (2005). Changing mental models: HR's most important task. *Human Resource Management*, 44 (2), 123–128.

Rosenzweig, P.M., and Nohria, N. (1994). Influences on human resource management practices in multinational corporations, *Journal of International Business Studies*, 25, 229–251.

Schuler, R.S. (1990). Repositioning the human resource function: Transformation or demise. *Academy of Management Executive*, 4 (3), 49–60.

Schuler, R.S., and Jackson, S. (2005). A quarter-century review of human resource management in the US: The growth in importance of the international perspective. *Management Revue*, 16 (1), 11–35.

Schuler, R.S., and Tarique, I. (2007). International human resource management: A North American perspective, a thematic update and suggestions for future research. *International Journal of Human Resource Management*, 18 (5), 717–734.

Singh, J. (2007). Asymmetry of knowledge spillovers between MNCs and host country firms. *Journal of International Business Studies*, 38, 764–786.

Smethurst, S. (2005). The long and winding road. *People Management*, 11 (15), 25–29.

Sparrow, P.R. (2006b). Knowledge management in Global organizations. In G. Stahl and I. Björkman (eds), *Handbook of Research into International HRM*. London: Edward Elgar, pp. 113–138.

Sparrow, P.R., and Braun, W. (2008a). HR strategy theory in international context. In M. Harris (ed.), *The Handbook of Research in International Human Resource Management*. Mahwah, NJ: Lawrence Erlbaum, pp. 77–106.

Sparrow, P.R., and Braun, W. (2008b). HR sourcing and shoring: Strategies, drivers, success factors and implications for HR. In M. Dickmann, C. Brewster and P.R. Sparrow (eds), *International Human Resource Management: A European Perspective*. London: Routledge, pp. 39–66.

Sparrow, P.R., and Brewster, C. (2006). Globalizing HRM: The growing revolution in managing employees internationally. In C. Cooper and R. Burke (eds), *The Human Resources Revolution: Why Putting People First Matters*. London: Elsevier.

Sparrow, P.R., Brewster, C., and Harris, H. (2004). *Globalizing Human Resource Management*. London: Routledge.

Stahl, G.K., and Björkman, I. (eds) (2006). *Handbook of Research in International Human Resource Management*. Cheltenham: Edward Elgar Publishing.

Tregaskis, O., Glover, L., and Ferner, A. (2005). *International HR Networks in Multinational Companies*. London: CIPD.

Ulrich, D. (1997). *Human Resource Champions: The Next Agenda For Adding Value To HR Practices*. Boston: Harvard Business School Press.

Wassermann, S., and Faust, K. (1994). *Social Network Analysis: Methods and Applications*. New York: Cambridge University Press.

Part IV

ORGANIZATIONAL ACTION IN CONTEXT

19

IHRM in Non-Governmental Organizations: Challenges and Issues

Marilyn Fenwick and Margaret-Ann McLean

Introduction

International human resource management (IHRM) researchers have stressed the importance of context in developing an accurate understanding of the field (Wright and McMahan, 1992; Brewster, 1999; Teegen *et al.*, 2004; Brewster *et al.*, 2005; Fenwick, 2005). The aim of this chapter is to examine non-governmental organizations, a significant IHRM context that remains under-researched. The term 'international' or 'transnational non-governmental organization' covers an array of not-for-profit and non-public sector organizations with activities and assets that extend outside their domestic bases. These organizations often have long histories of transnational operations and of formal or informal IHRM. They play an increasingly vital role in global civil society and governance, the global economy and, importantly for the comprehensive understanding of IHRM, they are significant employers.

Although the study of NGOs has spanned several disciplines, including, most recently, international business (see the work by Teegen and colleagues, 2003, 2004). relatively little is known about NGO international management and HRM practices. In this chapter:

1. International NGOs are defined and a brief background of their nature, role and emergence is provided.
2. Major external and internal environmental issues currently impacting HRM in international NGOs are discussed.
3. The example of strategic staffing in World Vision International (WVI), a multinational relief and development organization is presented. As organizational action in context, this example is used to illustrate existing academic understanding of international NGOs and to highlight the means by which one large international NGO seeks to meet the challenges of its HRM environment.
4. Conclusions are drawn with implications for future IHRM research.

Handbook of International Human Resource Management. Edited by Paul R. Sparrow

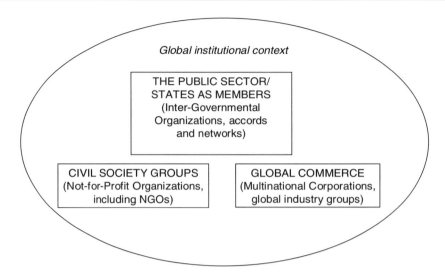

FIGURE 19.1 The global institutional context. (Adapted from Teegen *et al.*, 2004).

A commonly agreed definition of NGOs is lacking due to the sector's diversity of form and purpose, and multidisciplinary streams of research, resulting in a lack of consensus and clarity about the definition and nature of NGOs (Vakil, 1997; Dichter, 1999). Consequently, various labels have been attached to this one group of organizations belonging to civil society, and some distinctions need to be made in the terminology often applied to them. 'Civil society' broadly refers to those organizations existing between the level of the family and the state, having a degree of autonomy from the state and from the market. Civil society enables the interests of individual and collectives of citizens to be represented, offsetting state power and market forces (Oakley, 2003; Teegen *et al.*, 2004). Alternative terms of *'third sector'* and *'non-profit'* are commonly used in Europe (Anheier and Seibel, 1990) and in the US, the UK, and Australia, respectively (Drucker, 1990; Lyons, 2001).

Figure 19.1 shows the three sectors active in the global institutional context; public, commercial, and civil society. NGOs can be considered one of the largest subsets of not-for-profit organizations in civil society (Sogge, 1996).

NGOs can be classified by the benefits they create:

- membership or club NGOs produce benefits geared toward their members,
- social-purpose NGOs promote broader social interests.

The latter may be further classified according to their principal activities. Advocacy NGOs work on behalf of others who lack the voice or access needed to promote their own interests and operational NGOs provide critical goods and services to clients in need. NGOs engaging in both purposes are common and these are classified as hybrids (Parker, 2003). In addition to providing specific, legally defined goods or services, NGOs are prohibited from distributing profits to persons in their individual capacities, they are voluntary because they are created, maintained, and terminated according to voluntary decision and they exhibit value as opposed to economic rationality. These defining characteristics exclude sacramental elements of religious organizations, various types of government agencies and for-profit organizations (Hudson and Bielefeld, 1997).

This chapter will focus on one of the most visible types of social-purpose international NGO – intermediate private aid and development organizations. 'Intermediate' organizations are those whose chief calling is to relieve suffering and promote development by transferring material or financial resources internationally (Hudson and Bielefeld, 1997). Social-purpose NGOs have been defined as (Teegen *et al.*, 2004: 466):

> private, not-for-profit organizations that aim to serve particular societal interests by focusing advocacy and/or operational efforts on social, political and economic goals, including equity, education, health, environmental protection and human rights.

International NGOs (INGOs) are social-purpose NGOs in operating globally and the term 'INGO' will be used in the rest of this chapter to refer only to them.

THE ROLE AND EVOLUTION OF INGOs IN SOCIETY AND DEVELOPMENT POLICY

Concomitant with the rapid development of multinational corporations from the 1960s, but much less visible, INGOs emerged from developed economies. Between 1977 and 1992, according to the *Yearbook of International Organizations,* INGOs increased globally by 122% (Anheier and Cunningham, 1994).

The proliferation of not-for-profits was prompted by a shift in the perspectives of for-profit, corporate entities, and in particular nation states, toward international relief and development activities (Dichter, 1999; Lindenberg, 1999). Although their role in welfare provision differs across regions and even countries, the increasing reliance on NGOs can be linked to the declining state provision of social services (Agg, 2006), particularly, the trend of state withdrawal from provision of development programs in developing economies (Vakil, 1997). For example, by the mid-1990s in Sub-Saharan Africa, following the effects of structural adjustment policies, church-based INGOs provided over 40% of education services in Kenya and 35% of health services. Agg (2006: 4) notes that development discussion during the 1980s and 1990s:

> implicitly portrayed NGOs as innovative, value-driven organizations with access to the people who needed help the most, in comparison to governments, which were seen as bureaucratic, inherently inefficient, and possibly corrupt... and ... fully supported by the development community as a cushion between the state and individual.

Globalization has affected the environments of INGOs through the growth and proliferation of supra-territorial social relations, global corporations, global civil society and global regimes; the internationalization of major financial markets, technology,

and important sectors of manufacturing and services; and, the acceleration of globalization following the break-up of the Soviet Union in 1991 (Lindenberg and Dobel, 1999). Globalization of INGOs is evidenced by the increasing diversity and distribution of their activities and staff.

Perhaps the most significant indicator of the role and evolution of INGOs has
been the degree of influence world wide now exerted by them (Lindenberg,
1999). The three sectors shown in Figure 19.1 interact; with INGOs affecting governments and corporations directly and indirectly by moderating or mediating
business–government interaction, or becoming '. . . full participants in a complex
web of business–government–societal relationships' (Doh, 2003: 2). By the early
1990s, Salamon (1994) suggested that the immensity of scope and scale of this
global movement might prove to be of equivalent significance to the late 20th century as the rise of the nation state was to the late nineteenth. By mobilizing and
elaborating around world-cultural principles of universalism, individualism, volun-
taristic authority, rational progress and world citizenship, ". . . INGOs lobby, criticize and convince states to act on those principles, at least in some sectors and with
respect to some issues" (Boli and Thomas, 1997: 187). Potentially, the impact of IN-
GOs can extend much further than the goods and services they provide, as they may
permanently change the relationship between citizens and states (Salamon, 1994).

MANAGEMENT AND STRUCTURAL ISSUES IN INGOS

The complex management environment and strategic management of not-for-
profit organizations has received considerable attention from development and welfare perspectives (Anheier and Cunningham, 1994). Often more difficult to manage than for-profits, yet long overlooked in organization management literature, the
management of not-for-profits and INGOs is increasing as a focus in economics (for
example, Speckbacher, 2003), accounting (for example, Oster, 1996) and international business (see, for example, Teegen and colleagues, 2003, 2004; and Fenwick,
2005).

A review and analysis of 66 empirical studies of strategic management in the
not-for-profit sector, including NGOs, reported in international academic journal
articles between 1977 and 1999, focused on strategy formulation, content, and implementation, the major elements of strategic management (Stone *et al.*, 1999). It
concluded that, in *strategy formulation*, determinants for the use of strategic planning
were organizational size, board and management characteristics, and prior agreement on organizational goals. The findings emphasized the influence on NGOs of
funders and inter-organizational systems, often in conflict with each other, and that
strategic planning was used to cope with critical resource dependencies. In particular, whether or not funding sources required submission of action plans was the
most compelling external determinant of the use of formal strategic planning.

Further, in relation to *strategy content*, the type of strategy followed by NGOs will
be affected by the structure of various funding environments. Inter-oganizational
cooperative strategies have been relatively widely documented in studies of NGOs
and there is some evidence that this is on the increase. Many more organizations are

adopting these strategies to develop commercial income sources as compensation for declining levels of other revenues; for example, private and government funding. In contrast to managers in for-profit multinationals that have found it difficult to accept the need for cooperative alliances across their organizational boundaries, INGO managers have struggled with developing and implementing effective competitive strategies necessary in such a market (Fenwick, 2005).

According to Stone *et al.* (1999), *strategy implementation* in NGOs has received the least attention from researchers. The focus has been on the impact of organizational values on strategy implementation; with the acknowledgment that not-for-profits are especially inclined to the imposition of values from external others due to their relatively permeable boundaries. Of concern in IHRM terms is the evidence that professionals enter NGOs with values acquired through professional and often educational or religious socialization and that the foci of commitment for these professionals are often not the employing organization. Line-level staff also share this susceptibility to the influence of external values when they act as boundary spanners with commitments to user groups and to other organizations (Stone *et al.*, 1999; Fenwick, 2000). These values are often competing and are likely to influence the formulation and content, but little is known about the nature of their impact.

INGO structures range from independent to unitary enterprises, according to differences in rights and responsibilities held by central units and affiliates, and effective control (Hudson and Bielefeld, 1997; Lindenberg and Dobel; 1999). At the 'independent' end of the continuum, there is little or no formal central coordination. At the mid-point, in federation or confederation structures, either strong centers (federation) or strong members (confederation) allocate some coordination, resource allocation and standard setting activities to the other. At the 'unitary' end, there is a single global enterprise, with only one board and central headquarters, responsible for resource acquisition and allocation, and program decisions. Contemporary INGOs have moved toward more coordinated confederative or federative structural models. Further, reflecting the growth in popularity of inter-oganizational cooperative strategies, the sophisticated intra- and inter-organizational network structures adopted by many INGOs are at the leading edge of structural innovation recently advocated for for-profit organizations (Fenwick, 2005).

RECENT DEVELOPMENTS IN THE EXTERNAL ENVIRONMENTS OF INGOS

We argue that it is the features of NGOs laid out throughout this chapter that make them a particularly organizational context for IHRM researchers to study. The context of NGOs means that they are coordinated by trust, by values, by inter-organizational relationships and by professional logics. These coordination mechanisms become particularly important in several other forms of international working (see, for example, Welch, Welch, and Fenwick's discussion of project work, this volume Chapter 9; Moingeon *et al.*'s discussion of inter-organizational communities of practice, this volume Chapter 13; and Martin and Hetrick's discussion of employer branding, this volume Chapter 15). They also rely considerably on developed capabilities, multiple stakeholder views about their purpose, federal structures, and considerable voluntarism in expatriation. These, too, are becoming increasing important features of much international working.

In addition to the reduction of private and government funding for aid mentioned above, worldwide, recent developments in the external and internal environments present significant challenges to HRM in INGOs. The major external impacts have been the evolution of local NGOs in developing economies and the complexity of relationships between them and NGOs from developed economies; and the pressure for greater efficiency and accountability with regard to relief and development outcomes.

The evolution of local NGOs

There is some argument as to whether the current upsurge in NGO numbers is new or just the rediscovery of a long overlooked sector, due to the diversity of NGO function, type and terminology used to define the sector. However, it seems that evidence of the growth of the not-for-profit sector in developing economies globally is compelling (Salamon, 1994). Before the 1970s, there were virtually no not-for-profits outside the developed economies. Now, however, any discussion of the role and activities of INGOs must consider the emergence and current rapid growth of NGOs in nation states with developing economies. This division is referred to as the 'northern' ('developed') and 'southern' ('developing') economies (Sogge, 1996: 3) respectively. While cautioning that size estimates of southern NGOs are often unrealizable, Lindenberg (1999) indicates that by the late 1990s, there were more than 250 000. These organizations seek to found globalized concepts like sustainable development in their own local contexts.

The relationship between northern and southern NGOs began as paternalistic, with resources flowing from the northern organizations to the south. This was often actively encouraged by the southern not-for-profits because they sought to learn from the more experienced and better resourced northerners. More recently the trend in north–south relationships is for inter-organizational partnerships and network structures, as noted previously; similar to relationships between for-profit multinationals. Issues of balancing competition and cooperation, and trust and control have been raised with regard to north–south relationships (Lindenberg, 1999; Sogge, 1996). Southern partner organizations and affiliates are increasingly expecting board representation and control over resources in their northern partnerships. In addition to generating some management tensions in the sector, this has resulted in globalization of staff, including boards of directors, and of funding sources.

Increased 'professionalization' and pressure for performance management

At the organizational level, parallel with the strengthening of calls for increased *corporate* social responsibility, and increased levels of competition for resources and markets, INGOs are being pressured to demonstrate greater accountability and efficiency, via increased formalization and 'professionalization'. Managers of INGOs have looked to the applicability of for-profit management issues and approaches to meet these environmental pressures. Related to this is the need for INGOs to reconcile calls for increased professionalism and 'corporate'-style management with maintaining their ideological frameworks. 'Management' has often been considered a business concept, and therefore to taint not-for-profit organizations with commercialism. However, the blurring of boundaries between for-profit and not-for-profit organizations is increasingly evident as INGOs adopt strategies that include competition and commercialism.

An important underlying issue driving this is that INGOs rely heavily on trust and legitimacy to attract funding and indeed to access 'markets' for their activities. It seems that these necessities can be undermined if constituencies cannot assess INGO performance. Performance management is a core business management activity, and although it is a challenge for all organizations, it is arguably easier in multinational corporations because they share the characteristics of owner primacy, homogeneity and measurability of owners' interests, and a shared currency for evaluation and delegation (Speckbacher, 2003).

Salm (1999: 101) suggests that the challenge for many INGOs is the need to 'deeply consider just what this sector's bottom line is – for values-based organizations, the bottom line cannot be unit price or benefit-cost ratios alone', yet determining the overall measure of whether the sector is making a difference or not, is daunting. This is because, in INGOs, there is no clearly defined primary group with homogeneous interests and goals that can be readily expressed through a performance measure transferable for evaluation throughout the organizations.

While academics have begun to search for economic models that might be applicable to not-for-profit organizations (see, for example, Speckbacher, 2003), an influential intergovernmental organization; the Organization for Economic Cooperation and Development (OECD), has introduced an attempt to measure the impact of international development involving INGOs. The Paris Declaration on Aid Effectiveness is an initiative that seeks to have signatory members measure, via a set of indicators and targets shown in Table 19.1, their success or failure to make aid more effective. It is also an attempt "to enable [partner countries'] citizens and parliaments to hold governments accountable for the use of those resources" (OECD, 2007: 1). It seeks to address the United Nations Millennium Declaration and the Millennium Development Goals. The five thematic headings of the Declaration are ownership [1], aid alignment [2a–8], aid harmonization [9–10], managing for results [11], and mutual accountability [12] (OECD, 2007). Three country-level monitoring rounds were set for 2006, 2008, and 2010.

More than 100 governmental, intergovernmental, developed and developing economies, and 14 civil society organizations have signed the declaration. Signatories include Australia, the location of the author's office, and the United States, the headquarters location of WVI, and several countries in which WVI operates. Therefore, with regard to the INGO described later in this chapter, although WVI itself is not a signatory, the declaration influences the criteria upon which eligibility for government funding is determined.

For INGOs, implicit in theses criteria is the importance of managing their interorganizational relationships generally and partnerships between northern and southern NGOs in particular.

TABLE 19.1 Indicators of aid effectiveness and 2010 targets in the Paris declaration.

	Paris indicators of aid effectiveness	Targets for 2010
1	Ownership – Operational Poverty Reduction Strategies	At least 75% of countries have operational development strategies
2a	Quality of Public Financial Management systems	**Half of partner countries** significantly increase the quality of their systems
2b	Quality Procurement systems	**One-third of partner countries** significantly increase the quality of their systems
3	Aid reported on budget	At least **85%** of aid flows reported on budget
4	Coordinated capacity development	**50%** of technical cooperation through coordinated programs
5a	Use of country Public Financial Management systems	**90–100%** of donors use country systems in countries with sound systems
5b	Use of country procurement systems	**90–100%** of donors use country systems in countries with sound systems
6	Parallel Project Implementation Units	**Reduce by two-thirds** the stock of parallel Project Implementation Units
7	In-year predictability	**Halve the proportion** of aid not disbursed within the fiscal year
8	Untied aid	More aid is untied
9	Use of program-based approaches	**66%** of aid flows are provided in a coordinated manner
10	Joint missions and country analytic work	**40%** of donor missions are joint
11	Sound performance assessment framework	**Reduce by one-third** the countries without sound performance assessment
12	Reviews of mutual accountability	**All partner countries** have reviews of mutual assessment in place

Source: Adapted from www.oecd.org/dataoecd/0/2/37463394, 2006.

STRATEGIC INTERNATIONAL HUMAN RESOURCE MANAGEMENT ISSUES IN INGOS

The capacity of any organization to manage external environmental pressures is a key concern of strategic international human resource management (SIHRM). It is generally held responsible for performance management of individuals and groups in multinational enterprises. SIHRM has been defined as 'human resource management issues, functions, and policies and practices that result from the strategic activities of multinational enterprises and that impact the international concerns and goals of those enterprises' (Schuler *et al.*, 1993: 422). More recently, as this field has developed in research and practice, the terms 'strategic HRM in multinational enterprises' (De Cieri and Dowling, 2006) and 'global HRM' have been adopted to distinguish between an integrated versus a quarantined organizational HRM function in organizations operating in a global rather than international context (Brewster *et al.*, 2005).

The importance of a strategic approach to managing people in INGOs has been recognized (Cunningham, 2000; Kellock Hay *et al.*, 2001), yet HRM research lags practice in INGOs. Yet there is evidence to suggest that those who work in not-for-profit organizations have different assumptions, values, and beliefs than corresponding members of for-profit organizations (Wilensky and Hansen, 2001). The development literature indicates that INGO staff exhibit values that are highly participatory, with a strong ideological drive (Stark Biddle, 1984). Participation is not just a management style, it is inherent in the ideology of development (Sheehan, 2003), and volunteerism is central to the creation, maintenance, and termination of INGOs (Hudson and Bielefeld, 1997).

We argue that there is an important future research agenda to understand not just the advantages, but also some of the disadvantages of relying on values-based coordination. The following analysis is also relevant to those researching any other workgroups or organizational forms that are (potentially) values-based.

It is important to note that the presumption that INGOs like the not-for-profit sector generally are values-driven, and that executives and staff are bound to their organizations because of shared values derived from altruism, religion, and/or humanitarianism does not mitigate the need for effective IHRM policies and practices. The myths of 'pure virtue' and of 'voluntarism' have romanticized INGOs (Salamon, 1994) and those who work in them. Just as in other organizations, dissatisfaction with pay and other employment conditions can override attachment to organization mission and intention to stay with the not-for-profit employer. For example, where pay is concerned, this is despite the value held by many not-for-profit employees that money is "a means to accomplish larger objectives and not as an end in itself, either personally or organizationally" (Brown and Yoshioka, 2003: 6).

INGOs, like for-profit multinationals, also struggle to balance global integration and local responsiveness in staffing. INGOs have a long history of using expatriates (Fenwick, 2005) but have an agenda toward building local capacity that results in reliance on staffing with host country nationals (HCNs), depending on the type of their relief and development work (Salm, 1999). Just as is often claimed in multinational corporations, the use of expatriates and the discrepancies in pay between this group and local employees generates tension, but so does the hiring of locals if they are paid international rather than local rates. This can then diminish local capacity (Agg, 2006). Again, as in multinational corporations, INGO staff can be caught in conflicts of interest between headquarters and affiliates such as field offices. The former want to be accountable to donors and the latter want to be accountable to project participants (Fenwick, 2005; Merlot *et al.*, 2006).

Implicit in the preceding discussion of INGOs is the centrality of the staffing function of strategic IHRM to managing the environmental complexities of these organizations. A number of issues challenge the procurement and allocation of suitably qualified staff, such as:

- ◆ balancing global integration and local differentiation,
- ◆ resource dependencies, and
- ◆ balancing cooperation and competition in interorganizational relationships.

The next part of this chapter aims to illustrate the strategic response of one large INGO to these particular challenges.

STRATEGIC STAFFING AT WORLD VISION INTERNATIONAL

WVI is a Christian relief, development and advocacy organization dedicated to working with children, families, and communities to overcome poverty and injustice. Established in 1950 to care for orphans in Asia, WVI has grown to embrace the larger issues of community development and advocacy for the poor in its mission to help children and their families to build sustainable futures. Working on six continents, WVI is one of the largest relief and development INGOs. Central to WVI's work is supporting communities to build stronger and healthier relationships. Almost 80% of WVI's funding comes from private sources, including individuals, corporations, and foundations. The remainder comes from bilateral, government-to-government, and multilateral agencies including the United Nations. In addition to cash donations, WVI accepts gifts-in-kind, typically food commodities, medicine, and clothing donated through corporations or government agencies. Currently, WVI employs 28 630 staff. This includes 800 international staff and 185 Partnership Office staff; the remaining 27 645 are HCNs.

History

WVI began through a child sponsorship program, supported by Americans, to help orphaned children as a result of the Korean War. The response was so great that the US Founder, Bob Pierce, could not manage it alone so in 1950 the World Vision organization was formed with Bob Pierce as its first President. From there, the organization expanded its operations to meeting the needs of refugees in Indochina and those recovering from disasters in Bangladesh and several African countries. In the 1970s World Vision broadened its focus again, toward focusing on community development principles which included having a more collaborative approach with partner organizations and local communities. This expansion coincided with offices being set up in other Western countries such as Australia, Canada, New Zealand, United Kingdom, and parts of Western Europe. At around this time, the name was changed from World Vision to World Vision International, to reflect its growing geographic dispersion. While other similar INGOs have opted for franchise or equity-share based expansion, WVI has remained a wholly owned organization (Oster, 1996).

The evolution of structure and IHRM at World Vision

A governance structure evolved to allow for greater levels of affiliate participation in decision-making through WVI's 1970s and 1980s internationalization initiative and growth. In INGOs generally, accountability to the central organization starts high and gradually decreases, as power is devolved back to the membership (Foreman, 1999). Whether or not power is devolved depends on the affiliate, national board demonstrating over time the capacity and commitment to uphold the organizational mission. It was essential for WVI to find a mechanism for increasing mission ownership consistent with the Christian philosophy at the national level, and with achieving a manageable, decentralized global structure (Foreman, 1999).

If we take out the word Christian there is a generalizable requirement here for INGOs – i.e., a need to build a consistent philosophy in what is a centralized global structure. The decision as to whether or not to shift away from federalism, or to learn how to manage globally through a federal structure, we would argue, is a general challenge for many internationalizing organizations.

In this regard, WVI moved to a "global bumblebee federation" structure during the late 1990s, with partners such as World Vision Australia having comparable global governance and equivalent governance roles via participation in the two senior levels of governance, the WVI Council and its Regional Forum (Foreman, 1999: 186). Characteristics of this type of structure include a partnership basis of mutual benefits, legitimacy and complexity reduction; a council of all members meets every three years with the executive committee or board meeting at least twice a year; control rests with the board and executive committee; representative membership is based on non-resource acquisition criteria like commitment to core partnership documents; full membership through council and headquarters staff; more mutual control and sanctions; common systems; some common resource acquisition with added pressure for all members to find resources; central allocation with increasing budget control as each member receives board certification (Foreman, 1999).

Figure 19.2 shows the global bumblebee structure of World Vision. The organization functions as a network, a partnership of interdependent national offices, overseen by their own boards or advisory councils. A common mission statement and shared core values bind the partnership. By signing the Covenant of Partnership, each partner agrees to abide by common policies and standards. Partners hold each other accountable through an ongoing system of peer review. According to this process, each National Office is reviewed every three years to determine the level of alignment with the Partnership mission, values, and strategy. A self-review is conducted internally and then a Peer Review team containing representatives from the two or three National Offices visits other National Offices in turn to meet with stakeholders and confer about whether or not the activities of that office are in overall alignment.

The Global Center, or headquarters, is located in Los Angeles. It, together with Regional Partnership offices, located in Bangkok, Nairobi, Cyprus and San Jose, and other offices in Geneva and Costa Rica, coordinate the strategic operations of the organization, and represent WVI in the global arena.

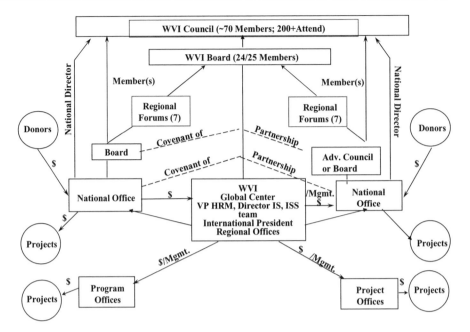

FIGURE 19.2 World Vision Partnership structure.

IHRM therefore has a key strategic role in the strategic HRM function, as indicated by the presence of the Vice President of Human Resources, the Director of International Services and the International Services Specialists team in the Global Center. Operationally, each National and Regional Partnership office has an HRM function.

Each National Office, regardless of the size of its programs, enjoys equal voice in Partnership governance, erasing a common distinction between the developed and developing world. Globalization has enabled WVI to engage in advantageous resource gathering and service delivery via transfer programming, transfer emergencies and transfer fundraising, adaptations of 'transfer pricing' in multinational corporations. For example, for WVI, transfer fundraising involves opening offices in countries where the matching grant ratios are better, investing in fundraising at a lower cost and requesting a match to the donor-raised funds. Smillie provided this example in 1996: "World Vision raised less than $[US]1 per head in the United States in 1991, but $[US]1.50 in Australia and $[US]1.78 in Canada" (Smillie, 1996: 53).

IHRM has been an enduring part of WVI's HRM strategy since its inception. Strategic IHRM in WVA is characterized by:

♦ values-based employee and volunteer selection,
♦ values-based employee self-selection,
♦ development and maintenance of relational rather than transactional psychological contracts, and
♦ an important role for expatriation.

Expatriation is often seen as the initial staffing strategy, either when skills gaps exist locally or when new operations requiring knowledge transfer are established. The primary strategy is, however, to hire host country nationals wherever possible in each location.

Staff within the founding offices of America, Canada, and Korea were Host Country Nationals (HCNs) recruited within their home bases to work within their domestic geographic boundaries. Volunteers were heavily utilized in National Offices to help to support the fledgling organization. In the 1970s the work expanded into Africa and Latin America and with the introduction of long-term development activities as well as relief work in Bangladesh, Ethiopia, Thailand, and Vietnam, the need arose to recruit international staff who were prepared to work outside their home countries for longer periods of time. These staff were generally HCNs and Parent Country Nationals (PCNs).

Larger scale relief efforts in the 1980s and 1990s such as those in Ethiopia, Somalia, Cambodia, Romania, Sudan, and Mozambique saw a significant expansion in the relief work of WVI. This was resourced through a combination of national (sourced at the national level and responsible to national offices) and international teams (recruited and selected by WVI). A greater level of professionalism was being sought for relief efforts and a greater diversity of staff was needed to manage programs which covered a range of sectors from: Food security, agriculture, water/sanitation, food distribution and health.

With this expansion, the area of general management and support services grew to ensure that quality in delivery of aid and processes matched donor and other requirements such as those of the Paris Declaration. This change in professionalism and the need to meet increasing donor requirements drove an increase in the numbers of staff being required to fill roles with less traditional 'humanitarian' titles such as: Finance Manager, Grant Accountant, HR Manager, and Administration Manager.

Thus, the IHRM function has evolved with WVI's changing role and geographic expansion. In response to the growing need for professional staff from a wide range of sectors, many offices, particularly in countries such as America, Canada, United Kingdom, and Australia, recognized the need to have a dedicated staffing function for sourcing, hiring, and supporting expatriates in the field.

Preparing for a staffing plan for an emergency situation was also viewed as a growing priority, as well as meeting the growing demand for staff in development situations. World Vision Australia (WVA) recognized this need in the 1980s with a part-time resource dedicated to this function. In the 1990s this became a full-time role, particularly in the wake of the Rwanda and Romanian crises and other ongoing needs globally. WVA believed it was not only important to hire good people but it was also essential to provide them with good support, care and follow-up on return from the field. Over the past 10–15 years they have led the way within WVI in providing support to expatriate staff and families from a practical, spiritual, and psychological perspective. Despite the resource constraints imposed by their internal and external environments, these programs are well developed and extensive, compared with reports of IHRM in many multinational corporations (Fenwick, 2005), including some of those engaged in international development projects (see Welch, Welch, and Fenwick, this volume Chapter 9).

Similarly, other World Vision offices that were considered to have good hiring pools established an IHRM resource. The resourcing for these positions varied as did the key focus of the role.

However, one of the failings of this process was that each entity with an International Recruiter was managing and directing its activities *independently*, recruiting for domestic positions, and without a common strategic direction. This is an issue that can also affect ill-considered inpatriation processes (see Reiche, Kraimer, and Harzing, this volume Chapter 8). It was therefore a process inconsistent with the need for internal alignment. In some cases priorities for these staff were changed and those affected by the results, largely the National Offices in field countries, were unable to have any direct influence over the decision or the resource. Although the functions were largely doing the same work for the whole partnership, the resources were managed very independently, with little coordination but greatly diverse processes and procedures.

With a growing number of international jobs needing to be filled in increasingly difficult and complex locations, there was no central management or coordination to ensure that all jobs were given appropriate attention and that some jobs were not favored over others. Inevitably, it led to managers in some international locations having larger pools of candidates from which to select, and other more demanding locations with harsher conditions may have had small or poor quality candidate pools. This led to obvious difficulties with program implementation and management due to lack of staff.

The 'Our Future' strategy

The increasing demands of donors, fundraising offices, and complexity in the humanitarian aid and development sector, in general, has added greater responsibility to the work of individuals in the field. For example, the Area Development Program is a complex, integrated program of community development funded by several WVI offices world wide. Often, funding originated from several different external donors, each with their own reporting requirements. Area Development Program managers, usually HCNs, were spending increasing amounts of time on meeting administration and reporting requirements and therefore less time on core activities. This delayed progress on the programs.

The problem was recognized by WVI management and concern was being expressed about how staff would cope with the organizations' rapid growth and inadequate structure and systems to support such growth. Therefore, a large-scale internal change process called 'Our Future' began at the triennial council meeting, a gathering of all senior leadership from Partnership offices, in 2003.

'Our Future' is a strategy to reconfigure the decision-making structure in WVI to enable greater connectivity, flexibility and efficiencies throughout the organization. This initiative will fundamentally change the way the Partnership is organized, the way it makes decisions and the way work is done. It is a means of refining and realigning the global bumblebee structure described earlier, and it is the largest change initiative WVI has ever undertaken.

In addition to other key areas of WVI such as Information Technology, 'Our Future' would have a big impact on the way some aspects of HRM in WVI, particularly international staffing, would be conducted in the future. 'Our Future' relies substantially on e-enabled HRM and knowledge transfer to build the global HRM presence (Brewster *et al.*, 2005; see also Moingeon, Lunineau, and Perrin, this volume Chapter 13; Bondarouk and Rüel, this volume Chapter 14). Expected outcomes of the change process will result in greater centralization of work for some activities such as purchasing of supplies and staffing, while maximizing the resources and influence the partnership has with other key stakeholders. 'Our Future' has four key objectives:

- ◆ have more impact on the lives of children;
- ◆ free up more resources, energy, and capacity to transform more lives;
- ◆ improve the quality, service, efficiency, and effectiveness of our work;
- ◆ provide staff with more job satisfaction.

The 'Our Future' change process was divided into two parts. Phase 1 saw the collection of data across the partnership to build the 'business case' for change. Phase 2, since December 2005, has been the time of building the change process and the beginning of many new initiatives.

The change design team sought to evaluate areas which, with some minor adjustments, would be good role models for change. These were named the 'Quick Wins' teams. These initiatives were those considered simple to achieve or already ongoing but that needed an additional boost to get some immediate results; that is, within a 12-month time frame. The International Recruitment system was one of these teams as it was currently operating at a global level with some centralization of function while also thinking locally. International Recruitment required greater coordination and efficiency but was operating informally as a virtual team but with direct reporting to individual offices even though the functions of the recruiters were largely identical. With changes made to the formal reporting lines, consolidation of budgets and some changes to the job descriptions and focus areas, a new team was formed called the *International Staffing Solutions Center of Expertise* (ISS COE).

Current structure

Since October 2006, the International Staffing Solutions (ISS) team has been operating as a virtual team around the world. There are 19 International Staffing Specialists based in key locations including Australia, Asia, United Kingdom, South Africa, Germany, Netherlands, Cyprus, and the Americas.

The main role of the International Staffing Specialists is to:

- ◆ participate in workforce planning for designated hiring offices,
- ◆ source candidates from designated countries, and
- ◆ assist Hiring Managers in filling specified roles as they arise and support the expatriate staff while on assignment and upon their return.

The ISS staff now have designated countries from which they source candidates as well as designated countries they support with expatriates. The latter function is a major change as now, field-based staff who are hiring internationally have one major point of contact who will manage the hiring process with them. This will allow the development of specialist knowledge of the countries for which they are responsible and a greater understanding of operational needs in these. As a result, field-based staff can rely on this person to find the best match possible between operational needs and job candidates.

Anecdotal feedback indicates that this process is proving worth while and that recruitment briefs are being acted on more quickly and with greater success. This requires team members to work more closely together, as ISS staff may need to enlist greater support from their colleagues in sourcing and interviewing candidates for their respective positions.

World Vision has recognized that communication is vital in this process. The ISS team designates many formal methods to ensure that communication is strong within the entire global network as well as between individual staff and the Director of International Staffing. Individual ISS staff meet with the Director monthly via telephone to discuss their key performance indicators, challenges, successes, and latest developments. Performance is managed through a standardized World Vision Performance Management system. This system includes a Performance Agreement through which goals and targets to be achieved each year are established, and an Individual Development Plan. Each Regional team meets via a monthly conference call along with the Director to discuss issues within that region and provides updates on vacant roles. Lastly, a quarterly conference call occurs across the global team to connect people with changing practice, policy and other relevant issues of common concern.

All ISS staff gather for a week in an annual conference for training and team-building, to review common practices, to share common challenges and to determine the goals for the year ahead. These regular formal practices are enhanced by informal communications which occur daily by e-mail, phone, and real-time messaging systems like 'Skype'. Advances in technology have seen great changes in the way this team can function, particularly in a disaster situation. Communication during a disaster or humanitarian crisis is greatly increased with more regular e-mail updates and more frequent telephone communication with key stakeholders.

Other e-tools to facilitate increased communication and improved processes are Lotus Notes computer databases which have been built to manage candidate flows, as well as process toolkits. The candidate database is not only an applicant tracking system but also assists in the evaluation of aspects of recruitment such as: source of candidates, number of days a vacancy is open, measures activity by individual recruiters as well as acts as a candidate pool for future searches. The latter toolkit has been built in-house to meet the particular needs of the global team and has helped to standardize the recruitment system, and to give all staff access to the same tools and information wherever their location. Information can now be accessed quickly and without constant e-mail exchanges across the globe.

Another change to the way hiring is managed is through the introduction of a Service Level Agreement. This agreement forms the basis for the partnership between key parties in managing the hiring process. The Service Level Agreement clearly outlines the responsibilities of the ISS staff member and also that of the Hiring Manager to clearly delineate roles and expectations as well as time frames. This ensures goal alignment, a major step forward, which will assist in keeping people accountable and help reduce the time in trying to fill critical roles.

The ISS team is one of a few teams operating virtually within World Vision. These teams focus more on the Initial Emergency response as well as future information technology systems that will support the organization. There is some corporate learning, used informally, which has helped management to develop and support this new ISS structure. For example, the International Staffing Director sought assistance with managing virtual teams by contacting the Emergency Response Team Leaders, to learn from their experiences. Particular emphasis was on systems that would support virtual teamwork and also understand the demands of managing a team of culturally diverse people. This learning is not yet documented formally within the organization, but this is one of the challenges that have been identified as a future need.

Evaluating the lessons from global structural change in an INGO

At this stage in the team development there has been no formal evaluation of the structural change. However, as indicated earlier, preliminary feedback shows that it has brought greater responsiveness to the recruitment process for key roles, greater relationship-building across the offices and more consistency of practice; and hence more efficiency within the international staffing area. Further evaluation will take place as each team member's performance is evaluated at the conclusion of his or her performance management cycle.

The WVI scenario outlined above demonstrates similar difficulties to those experienced by maturing multinational corporations. The complex global marketplace, with its features of increasing levels of competition, rapid pace of change, and high levels of uncertainty and ambiguity, makes it difficult to continually realign for fit. According to the Director of International Staffing:

> . . . any kind of change is always a challenge for people and keeping the reason for change at the forefront with the appropriate resources (human and financial) is a struggle. The change process is well underway but still requires time for consolidation. The seemingly apparent 'Quick Win' may not be as quick as expected, so the challenge is to keep up the momentum and to journey with people as they see the benefit of the change.

Two key issues with the internationalization process currently specific to this form of organization, but also likely now of wider generalizability, can be observed. The need to:

- relinquish resources for the benefit of the broader group;
- manage a large, culturally diverse virtual team without a strong background of corporate knowledge.

Some initial problems and issues associated with the change have been related to encouraging people to see the global, partnership view rather than their local view;

thereby relinquishing a resource (budget or staff member) for the benefit of the broader group. This has necessitated a lot of time being spent with individuals to work through the benefits of the change as well as assuring them that their commitment to the change will make a big difference to the overall outcome in the National Offices.

Another obvious challenge is managing a large, culturally diverse virtual team without a strong background of corporate knowledge in this area. For ISS, being one of the first teams to head in this direction, it has not been without its challenges. This is not surprising as research into virtual teams has found that successful virtual teams concentrate more on building interpersonal relationships to increase trust (Maznevski and Chudoba, 2000); so demands on resources for this can often compete with the urgency with which an INGO must fulfill its mission. Also message complexity increases with task complexity and complex messaging requires a rich communication medium such as face-to-face communication and extensive telephone conferencing. The size and cultural diversity of the 19-member ISS team at WVI makes virtual teamwork an ongoing challenge, but according to those involved, the benefits have certainly outweighed the concerns.

CONCLUSION: IMPLICATIONS FOR IHRM RESEARCH

This chapter has drawn attention to some challenges and issues for HRM in INGOs; a neglected yet increasingly influential organizational context in IHRM research and theory building. To date, little guidance from IHRM scholars has been available to human resource managers and practitioners in INGOs as these organizations globalize. To extend a point made by Stone *et al.* (1999), details of the competitive environment and its influence on HRM in INGOs are missing from research. INGOs compete for personnel and board members in addition to funds, users, and legitimacy. As evidenced in World Vision, competition for these resources is impacting on IHRM strategy and structure. The potential to *exchange* knowledge between INGOs and multinational corporations often faced with similar challenges has also not been realized. For example, the requirement in INGOs for more competitive, commercial strategies, and in multinational corporations for more collaborative, interorganizational networking suggests an ideal opportunity for each to learn from the other. Management through shared values and commitment common in the not-for profit sector reflects the ethos in contemporary HRM, but the for-profit sector has struggled with this. Again, perhaps insights might be gained by for-profits in researching not-for-profits.

Challenges to the nature of IHRM from recent developments in the external and internal environments of INGOs – such as declining levels of government funding, the emergence of local NGOs in developing economies, increased pressures for professionalization of organizational practices and staff, and for performance management – also signal the need to focus IHRM research on addressing the concerns of those working in INGOs. Little is known abut the impact of these challenges on strategic HRM in INGOs.

The section on WVI was presented as a means of highlighting the extent to which the need to realign for strategic fit requires innovative changes to the IHRM function and to practices such as global staffing. The organizational context of an INGO is made more complex than that of multinational corporations because they rely heavily on trust and legitimacy to attract funding and access to markets. The need for more effective performance management is increasing, yet this activity is more difficult in INGOs because they lack the characteristics of owner primacy, homogeneity and measurability of owners' interests, and a shared currency for evaluation and delegation evident in multinational corporations.

An important part of framing an IHRM agenda for INGOs, therefore, is the issue of definition and clarification. Vakil (1997) has made much progress in consolidating the not-for-profit literature and proposing a taxonomy of NGOs in order to clearly identify groupings of NGO types, yet she acknowledges that her work does not clearly differentiate the NGO sector from the not-for-profit sector, nor does it include management attributes like HRM.

There may be an argument for relabeling the non-profit sector. Although widely used, 'non-profit' portrays an end state rather than a reflection of purpose and the term 'not-for-profit' more accurately represents the true nature of these organizations. Thus it has been used throughout the chapter, but it still says virtually nothing about these organizations. In a similar vein, according to Teegen *et al.* (2004), the term 'non-governmental' is not particularly helpful because it merely says what an organization is *not*, rather than clarifying what it *is*. They persist, however, with using 'NGO', probably because it is widely applied and recognized in some sources and locations.

By way of highlighting what NGOs *are*, the term 'multinational not-for-profit enterprise' might be considered. The term 'multinational enterprise' used to describe the organizational context of mainstream IHRM includes all organizations in the not-for-profit sector including INGOs, despite the narrow application of its definition to multinational corporations within the management and IHRM disciplines (Fenwick, 2005).

The need for more IHRM research into NGOs is clear. The type of research needed is also reasonably clear. Identifying and examining categories of NGO by sector would be valuable to gain understanding of IHRM in these different contexts; social purpose versus advocacy and member-based NGOs, for example. Theory building about the interplay between key actors and the impact of it on IHRM in the global institutional context of NGOs is needed through multilevel (national, organizational and individual), multi-method designs (see Wright and van de Voorde, this volume Chapter 2). The conduct of more qualitative case studies would surface the issues for IHRM, and quantitative theory testing would determine the explanatory and predictive power of extant theory, and 'mainstream' HRM concepts and frameworks for those managing and working in NGOs.

Based on the preceding discussion, several theories appear relevant to understanding HRM in INGOs; resource dependence, institutional, network, and stakeholder theories for example. If IHRM is to be more than rhetoric, if it is to lead as well as reflect practice, then it must include the not-for-profit sector as a significant organizational context.

REFERENCES

Agg, C. (2006) Trends in government support for non-governmental organizations: Is the "golden age" of the NGO behind us? Civil society and social movement programme Paper 23. United Nations Research Institute for Social Development.

Anheier, H.K., and Cunningham, K. (1994). Internationalization of the nonprofit sector. In R.D. Herman (ed.), *The Jossey-Bass Handbook of Nonprofit Leadership and Management.* San Francisco, CA: Jossey-Bass, pp. 100–116.

Anheier, H.K., and Seibel, W. (eds) (1990). *The Third Sector: Comparative Studies of Nonprofit Organizations.* Berlin: de Gruyter.

Boli, J., and Thomas, G.M. (1997). World culture in the world polity: A century of international non-governmental organization. *American Sociological Review,* 62 (2), 171–190.

Brewster, C. (1999). Different paradigms in strategic HRM: Questions raised by comparative research. In P. Wright, L. Dyer, J. Boudreau and G. Milkovich (eds), *Research in Personnel and HRM.* Supplement 4. Greenwich, CT: JAI Press.

Brewster, C., Sparrow, P.R., and Harris, H. (2005). Towards a new model of globalising HRM. *International Journal of Human Resource Management,* 16 (6), 949–970.

Brown, W., and Yoshioka, C. (2003). Mission attachment and satisfaction as factors in employee retention. *Nonprofit Management and Leadership,* 14 (1), 5–18.

Cunningham, I. (2000). Sweet charity! Managing employee commitment in the UK voluntary sector. *Employee Relations,* 23 (3), 226–239.

De Cieri, H., and Dowling, P. (2006). Strategic international human resource management in multinational enterprises: Developments and directions. In G.K. Stahl and I. Bjorkman (eds), *Handbook of Research in International Human Resource Management.* Cheltenham: Edward Elgar Publishing Limited, pp. 15–35.

Dichter, T.W. (1999). Globalization and its effects on NGOs: Efflorescence or a blurring of roles and relevance? *Nonprofit and Voluntary Sector Quarterly,* 28 (4), 38–58.

Doh, J.P. (2003). Nongovernmental organizations, corporate strategy and public policy: NGOs as agents of change. In J.P. Doh and H. Teegen (eds), *Globalization and NGOs: Transforming Business, Government and Society.* Westport, USA: Praeger Publishers, pp. 1–18.

Drucker, P.F. (1990). *Managing the Non-Profit Organization: Principles and Practices.* New York: Harper Business.

Fenwick, M. (2005). Extending strategic international human resource management research and pedagogy to the non-profit multinational. *International Journal of Human Resource Management,* 16 (4), 497–512.

Foreman, K. (1999). Evolving global structures and the challenges facing international relief and development organizations. *Nonprofit and Voluntary Sector Quarterly,* 28 (4), 178–197.

Hudson, B.A., and Bielefeld, W. (1997). Structures of multinational nonprofit organizations. *Nonprofit Management and Leadership,* 8 (1), 31–49.

Kellock Hay, G., Beattie, R.S., Livingstone, R., and Munro, P. (2001). Change, HRM and the voluntary sector. *Employee Relations,* 23 (3), 240–255.

Lindenberg, M. (1999). Declining state capacity, voluntarism, and the globalization of the not-for-profit sector. *Nonprofit and Voluntary Sector Quarterly,* 28 (4), 147–168.

Lindenberg, M., and Dobel, J.P. (1999). The challenges of globalization for Northern international relief and development NGOs. *Nonprofit and Voluntary Sector Quarterly,* 28 (4), 4–24.

Lyons, M.S. (2001). *Third Sector: The Contribution of Nonprofit and Cooperative Enterprise in Australia.* Sydney: Allen & Unwin.

Maznevski, M., and Chudoba, K.M. (2000). Bridging space over time: Global virtual-team dynamics and effectiveness. *Organizational Science,* 11, 473–492.

Merlot, E., Fenwick M., and De Cieri, H. (2006). Applying a strategic international human resource management framework to international non-governmental organisations. *International Journal of Human Resources Development and Management*, 6 (2–4), 313–328.

Oakley, P. (2003). Strengthening civil society: Concept and approaches. In B. Pratt (ed.), *Changing expectations? The Concept and Practice of Civil Society in International Development*. Oxford: International NGO Training and Research Centre, pp. 31–42.

Oster, S.M. (1996). Nonprofit organizations and their local affiliates: A study in organizational forms. *Journal of Economic Behavior and Organization*, 30, 83–95.

Parker, A. (2003). Prospects for NGO collaboration with multinational enterprises. In J.P. Doh and H. Teegen (eds), *Globalization and NGOs: Transforming Business, Government and Society*. Westport, USA: Praeger Publishers, pp. 81–106.

Salamon, A. (1994). The rise of the nonprofit sector. *Foreign Affairs*, 73 (4), 109–122.

Salm, J. (1999). Coping with globalization: A profile of the northern NGO sector. *Nonprofit and Voluntary Sector Quarterly*, 28 (4), 87–103.

Schuler, R.S., Dowling, P.J., and De Cieri, H. (1993). An integrative framework of strategic international human resource management. *Journal of Management*, 19 (2), 419–459.

Sheehan, J. (2003). *NGOs and participatory management styles: A case study of CONCERN Worldwide, Mozambique*. Centre for Civil Society International Working Paper Series, 2, 1–33.

Smillie, I. (1996). Interlude: The rise of the transnational agency. In D. Sogge, K. Biekhart and J. Saxby (eds), *Compassion and Calculation: The Business of Private Foreign Aid*. London: Pluton Press.

Sogge, D. (1996). Settings and choices. In D. Sogge, K. Biekhart and J. Saxby (eds), *Compassion and Calculation: The Business of Private Foreign Aid*. London: Pluton Press.

Speckbacher, G. (2003). The economics of performance management in nonprofit organizations. *Nonprofit Management and Leadership*, 13 (3), 267–281.

Stark Biddle, C. (1984). *Management Needs of Private Voluntary Organizations*. Springfield, USA: Office of Private and Voluntary Cooperation, Agency for International Development, US Department of Commerce.

Stone, M., Bigelow, B., and Crittenden, W. (1999). Research on strategic management in nonprofit organizations: Synthesis, analysis, and future directions. *Administration and Society*, 31, 378–423.

Teegen, H. (2003). International NGOs as global institutions: Using social capital to impact multinational enterprises and governments. *Journal of International Management*, 9, 271–285.

Teegen, H., Doh, J.P., and Vachani, S. (2004). The importance of nongovernmental organizations (NGOs) in global governance and value creation: An international business research agenda. *Journal of International Business Studies*, 35 (6), 463–484.

Vakil, A.C. (1997). Confronting the classification problem: Toward taxonomy of NGOs. *World Development*, 25 (12), 2057–2070.

Wilensky, A., and Hansen, C. (2001). Understanding the work beliefs of nonprofit executives through organizational stories. *Human Resource Development Quarterly*, 12 (3), 223–239.

Wright, P.M., and McMahan, G. (1992). Theoretical perspectives for strategic human resource management. *Journal of Management*, 18 (2), 295–320.

20

The Role of IHRM in the Formulation and Implementation of Ethics Programs in Multinational Enterprises

ABIHIJEET VADERA AND RUTH AGUILERA

INTRODUCTION

Organizations across the globe are implementing ethics programs but with mixed results. This issue becomes more complex for multinational enterprises operating in several different economies simultaneously. In this chapter, we review the literature on ethics programs in the US and the international context to suggest ways of better understanding the role of international human resource management (IHRM) in the success of ethics programs in multinationals. We propose that the ethics programs should be fully integrated with the human resource practices for their successful formulation, designing in terms of content, and communication of ethics programs. We also suggest that this integration should be examined along with institutional, industry- and country-level, and organizational forces affecting the success of ethics programs to garner a holistic view of the role of IHRM in the formulation and implementation of ethics programs in multinational enterprises.

According to the 2005 National Business Ethics Survey, more than half of the American workers have observed at least one type of ethical misconduct in the workplace, but only 55% of these employees reported it to the management, despite an increase in workers' awareness of formal ethics programs in their organizations. The ethics programs adopted by organizations include written standards of conduct, training on ethics, mechanisms to seek ethics advice or information, means to report misconduct anonymously, discipline of employees who violate ethical standards, and evaluation of employees' performance based on ethical conduct.

Handbook of International Human Resource Management. Edited by Paul R. Sparrow
© 2009 John Wiley & Sons, Ltd

Additionally, five of these six elements of formal ethics and compliance programs, as suggested by the Federal Sentencing Guidelines for Organizations, increased in 2003 consistently from 1994. Research also suggests that most of these initiatives have been placed under the responsibility of ethics or compliance departments, ethics officers, general counsels of organizations, or even corporate communications and corporate secretaries in some cases (Weaver *et al.*, 1999b). Largely missing from this listing is the role of human resources policies and practices in the formulation and successful implementation of ethics programs in organizations (Weaver and Trevino, 2001).

In this chapter, we suggest that for the above-mentioned statistics to drastically improve, organizations need to orient their human resource practices and systems to embrace ethics programs of various kinds. We particularly focus on multinational companies (MNCs) due to the recent increase in their numbers as a result of globalization. We define MNCs as "any enterprise that carries out transactions in or between two sovereign entities, operating under a system of decision making that permits influence over resources and capabilities, where the transactions are subject to influence by factors exogenous to the home country environment of the enterprise" (Sundaram and Black, 1992: 773). The increase in MNCs necessitates the understanding of cultural and national differences in how organizations grasp the:

(1) formulation,
(2) content,
(3) communication of, and
(4) effectiveness of ethics programs.

We therefore review extensively the literature on ethics programs in the US and the international context against these four criteria, with key studies summarized in Table 20.1. We then propose two major ways through which scholars and researchers can study the role of International Human Resource Management (IHRM) in the formulation and implementation of ethics programs in corporations operating in the international context.

Ethics Programs in Organizations

Prior research on ethics programs in organizations primarily looks at the formulation, content, communication, and effectiveness of ethics programs. As noted, organizations adopt ethics programs in various forms. Some organizations may adopt a code of ethics and ensure that all organizational members understand and follow these codes. On the other hand, other organizations may circulate codes of ethics without explaining the content or communicating the importance of the codes to its members. Similarly, ethics training may range from filling out short surveys online to intense workshops with regular feedback and counseling. Therefore, organizations differ largely on how they form, design, and communicate ethics programs.

Below, we review the literature on each of these dimensions to put forth the current state of research on ethics programs. In brief, research on the formulation of

TABLE 20.1 Current research on ethics programs.

Reference	Key concepts	Key predictions and findings	Method and sample
Bailey and Spicer (2007)	National identity; international business ethics; integrative social contracts theory	Russian and American respondents expressed similar attitudes toward organizational practices that violated the ethical standards of "hypernorms" and "local norms".	Experimental data from 1998 until 2001, using the same six survey scenarios and procedures, but different respondent samples.
Brenner (1992)	Corporate ethics programs and its dimensions; founder values; competitive pressures; and leadership	Defines corporate ethics programs, provides a set of dimensions which would allow categorization of ethics programs and their components, and examines a variety of influences on such programs.	Propositions based on a case study
Farrell and Farrell (1998)	Corporate code of ethics; grammatical structures; Australia	The codes in Australia use language that adopts an authoritarian tone and communicate a strong sense of obligation and powerlessness.	Five international companies- a chemical manufacturing company and a health, beauty and medical manufacturer; Australian bank; an Australian federal government business agency; and an Australian mining company.

(Continued)

TABLE 20.1 (*Continued*)

Reference	Key concepts	Key predictions and findings	Method and sample
Felo (2001)	Ethics programs; board composition; insider participation on compensation committees; and director compensation practices	Firms with ethics programs have a lower percentage of inside directors, have more independent boards, and compensate outside directors with equity.	137 firms included in the 1995–1996 AIMR Annual Review of Corporate Reporting Practices
Jackson (2000)	Management ethics; corporate policies; cross-cultures	The clarity of corporate policy has little influence on managers' reported ethical decision making and the perceived behavior of managers' colleagues is far more important in predicting attitudes toward decision making of managers across the nationalities surveyed.	Managers in France, Germany, Britain, Spain and the USA working in over 200 companies operating in these countries.
Langlois and Schlegelmilch (1990)	Corporate codes of ethics; national character; Europe; United States	There exist significant differences between European countries and also between firms in Europe and the United States, in particular with regard to employee conduct, supplier and contractor relations as well as political interests.	The data were collected during 1988 via 600 mail questionnaires dispatched to the chairmen of the 200 largest French, British and West German companies, respectively.

McKendall *et al.* (2002)	Ethical compliance programs; corporate illegality; corporate sentencing guidelines	Ethical compliance programs do not lessen legal violations. Instead, ethics programs may serve as "window dressing" to deflect attention and or culpability resulting from illegal actions. Lower firm profitability results in a greater number of willful and repeat OSHA violations.	Surveys were sent to 315 companies with responses from 108- return rate of 34%. The number of OSHA violations was obtained by searching the Enforcement Action Data Base that is maintained by OSHA and available through their web site.
Melé *et al.* (2006)	Corporate ethical policies; corporate ethics statements; Argentina; Brazil; Spain	The primary responsibility for ethical issues in the company rests with the CEO and the main differences between the countries concern the emphasis given to specific aspects, such as avoiding misconduct or taking ethical criteria into account when selecting personnel.	In Spain, the questionnaire was sent to 500 companies (with responses from 106), in Argentina the survey covers the 555 largest Argentinean commercial companies ranked by number of employees (with responses from 126), and the 500 largest in Brazil (with responses from 100).
Montoya and Richard (1994)	Code of ethics; Health Care facilities; Energy utilities	Neither the Health Care facilities nor Energy companies has encountered much success with a codes of ethics program and the ways in the codes are communicated is highly related to the priority given to it in the organization.	The sample consists of 10 energy companies and 10 health care facilities all located in a large metropolitan area in the Southwest, USA. Data were collected over a four-week period through ethnographic interviews.

(Continued)

TABLE 20.1 (*Continued*)

Reference	Key concepts	Key predictions and findings	Method and sample
Nijhof *et al.* (2000)	Ethics programs; ethical decision making	There exist two alternative ways – monological and dialogical approaches – of stimulating responsible behavior in the organization.	
Palazzo (2002)	Business ethics; US-American companies; German companies; national cultures	Although many US corporations have introduced formal business ethics programs, German companies are very reluctant to address normative questions publicly due to different cultural backgrounds.	
Pelletier and Bligh (2006)	Perceptions of ethics programs; public sector organization; leadership	The perceived importance of awareness of formal ethics codes, decision-making techniques, availability of resources and ethical leadership theorized to be critical for ethics program effectiveness were examined.	The sample was randomly selected from a total of 1000 employees (with 458 responses) in a southern California government agency to participate in the survey process.

Robertson and Schlegelmilch (1993)	Institutionalization of ethics; United States; Great Britain	There exist some important differences between US and UK firms in perceptions of what are important ethical issues, in the means used to communicate ethics policies, and in the issues addressed in ethics policies and employee training.	Of the 3481 questionnaires mailed in the US and UK, 860 were returned, yielding a response of 25%.
Singh (2006)	Content of code of ethics; Canada	In 2003, as in 1992, more of the codes of conduct in Canadian firms were concerned with conduct against the firm than with conduct on behalf of the firm. However, there were a significant increase in the frequency of mention of environmental affairs, legal responsibility as the basis of codes and enforcement/compliance procedures.	A total of 80 codes, representing a broad cross section of Canada's largest firms, were analysed for 2003 and 75 for 1992.

(Continued)

TABLE 20.1 (*Continued*)

Reference	Key concepts	Key predictions and findings	Method and sample
Singh *et al.* (2005)	Content of codes of ethics; Australia; Canada; Sweden	The contents of the Australian and Canadian codes were similar, but the contents of the Swedish codes were found to be very different from the Australian and Canadian codes in some areas, reflecting the cultural differences between Sweden and the other two countries.	490 Canadian, 125 Australian, and 74 Swedish surveys were used.
Snell *et al.* (1999)	Code of ethics; Hong Kong; moral climate of adopters	In Hong Kong, content analysis of codes of ethics suggests that the prime motive was corporate self-defense and companies appear to have imposed their codes top-down, emphasizing disciplinary procedures rather than ethics training, and appointing neither ethics counsellors nor ombuds-people.	The research involved questionnaire surveys, longitudinal questionnaire-based assessments, interviews, and content analysis of company codes of conduct.

Stevens et al. (2005)	Ethics codes; Financial decision-making	Pressures from stakeholders, belief of positive external image, and integration of ethics programs into daily activities of the company influences financial executives to integrate company's ethics codes into their strategic decision-making.	414 firms were randomly selected from the Fortune 1000 and those firms that were smaller, and an equal number from manufacturing and service sectors.
Trevino and Weaver (2001)	Organizational justice; ethics program "follow-through"; employees' behaviors	Employees' perceptions of general organizational justice, and their perceptions of ethics program follow-through, in relation to unethical behaviour that harms the organization, and to employees' willingness to help the organization by repotting ethical problems and issues to management are considered.	A survey of ethics/compliance management in four companies: a utility company, a telecommunications company, and two energy-related companies. The response rate was 29%.
Tulder and Kolk (2001)	Corporate ethics; multinationality; Sporting goods industry	The reasons why individual companies or clubs in the global sporting goods industry adopted were investigated.	60 codes of firms belonging to the 1997 global Fortune 500 ranking were adopted- approximately 30% of which were from European firms

(*Continued*)

TABLE 20.1 (*Continued*)

Reference	Key concepts	Key predictions and findings	Method and sample
Weaver and Trevino (2001)	Ethics programs orientations; employees' attitudes and behaviors	This field survey in a large financial services company investigates the relationships of the values and compliance orientations in an ethics program to a diverse set of outcomes such as commitment, integrity, etc.	A survey of employees in a financial services company in which four hundred and twenty employees responded, for a 21% response rate.
Weaver and Trevino (2001)	Ethics/compliance management; human resources; fairness	Relying on research on fairness in organizations and corporate ethics practices, the article explains why the extensive involvement of HR in corporate ethics programs is important to the perceived fairness, and thus the likely outcomes, of those programs.	
Weaver et al. (1999a)	Corporate ethics practices; Fortune 1000	A high degree of corporate adoption of ethics policies, but wide variability in the extent to which these policies are implemented by various supporting structures and managerial activities.	Fortune 500 industrials and 500 service corporations, as listed in 1994 were surveyed during late 1994 and early 1995, for a 26% response rate.

Weaver *et al.* (1999a)	Corporate ethics programs; control systems; executive commitment; environment	Investigates why corporations introduce formal programs to manage ethics and why those programs display varying characteristics. Environmental factors were the stronger influences on scope, but management commitment was the stronger determinant of control orientation.	Fortune 500 industrials and 500 service corporations, as listed in 1994 were surveyed during late 1994 and early 1995, for a 26% response rate.
Weaver *et al.* (1999a)	Integrated and decoupled corporate social performance; management commitments; external pressures; corporate ethics practices	External pressures for social performance encourage easily decoupled processes but that top management commitments can encourage both easily decoupled and integrated processes.	Fortune 500 industrials and 500 service corporations, as listed in 1994 were surveyed during late 1994 and early 1995, for a 26% response rate.

ethics programs mainly includes all organizational and environmental characteristics that contribute toward designing and creating ethics programs such as the code
of ethics in organizations. Content of the ethics programs research entails understanding the factors that influence the language and structure of these programs.
Scholars interested in the communication of ethics programs have adopted a comparative perspective (between industries or nations) to comprehend the differences
between successful and unsuccessful ethics programs (see Mayrhofer and Reichel,
this volume Chapter 3, for a discussion of comparative analysis of HR). Finally, effectiveness of ethics programs has mostly been understood in conjunction with various
organizational factors that make these programs valuable.

Formulation of ethics programs

Several organizational and environmental factors have been suggested as antecedents to formulation of ethics programs in organizations. Prominent among
the organizational factors are the roles of various actors such as organizational leaders, board of directors and top management of the organization. Brenner (1992),
in propositions based on a case study, argues that the founders' values, competitive
pressures, leadership, and organizational problems are some of the major sources
that influence the corporate ethics programs. Other studies have also provided evidence for these factors. For instance, Felo (2001), while analyzing data from 137
firms included in the 1995–1996 AIMR Annual Review of Corporate Reporting Practices, shows that the composition of the board of directors influences the adoption
of ethics programs such that firms with ethics programs have a lower percentage
of inside directors on their compensation committees than do firms without ethics
programs. This is so because outside directors are expected to exercise their monitoring role and in that regard, have lesser incentives to collude with managers
(Fama and Jensen, 1983). One way to signal their monitoring role is by designing
ethics programs in the corporations on whose board they sit. Additionally, Melé *et al.*
(2006), through surveys sent to a large number of companies in Argentina, Brazil,
and Spain from 2000 to 2001, find that most respondents believe that the CEO
of a company has the greatest responsibility for the company's ethical issues and,
thus, for maintaining and enforcing ethical corporate practices. Similarly, Weaver
and colleagues (1999c, 1999d), in their multiple studies on ethics programs, analyze data from surveys and archival sources for 254 of all the Fortune 500 Industrial
and Fortune 500 Service companies listed for 1994. They find that organizations,
in which the top management is committed to ethics, are more likely to have formal and integrated ethics programs practices such as ethics-oriented performance
appraisals.

Regarding environmental influences, the forces of various stakeholders and the
organization's perceptions of its external image are influential in the formulation
and adoption of ethics programs in organizations. Stevens *et al.* (2005), in a survey of 407 firms from Fortune 1000 and smaller firms from the manufacturing and
service sectors, uncover that financial executives are more likely to integrate their
company's ethics code into their strategic decision processes when three different

exogenous and endogenous forces occur: First, if they perceive pressure from market stakeholders to do so (suppliers, customers, etc.); if they believe the use of ethics codes creates an internal ethical culture and promotes a positive external image for their firms; and if the code is integrated into daily activities through ethics code training programs. The effect of market stakeholder pressure is further enhanced when executives also believe that the code will promote a positive external image. Tulder and Kolk (2001) examine corporate codes for 60 firms belonging to the 1997 global Fortune 500 ranking in the sporting goods industry and find that individual companies tend to adopt codes that are less distinct instead of those that are designed as a result of interaction with other stakeholders. In comparison to individual companies, clubs such as the Business Support Groups generally provide weaker incentives for credible codes, due to the weak possibilities of excludability and appropriability of club goods. Similarly, in another study in the international context, Snell et al. (1999), using multiple methods and sources, study companies in Hong Kong to find that while a mixture of prudential and altruistic reasons were given for code of ethics adoption, content analysis of the codes suggests that the prime motive was corporate self-defense against bribery, conflict of interest, insider information, gambling, moonlighting, accuracy of records, and misuse of corporate assets, while wider social responsibility tend to be neglected.

Weaver et al. (1999c, 1999d), in their studies, investigate both- environmental and organizational factors that influence formulation of ethics programs. They find that environmental factors (such as the government policies, media attention, conference board ethics meetings) and management's ethical commitment influence an organization's ethics program's scope and its orientation toward compliance- and values-based control. Environmental factors were the stronger influence on scope, but management commitment was the stronger determinant of control orientation. Additionally, they show that these factors are influential only if the ethics programs adopted are decoupled or integrated with the organization's policies and systems.

Thus, research on the formulation of ethics programs in organizations has mainly examined how organizational factors, such as top management commitment, and environmental factors, such as the forces of stakeholders and perceptions of organizational image, influence formulation of ethics programs in organization. However, largely missing from the literature is the effect that institutional policies and norms have on the types of ethics programs formulated by organizations. Design of the programs could also be affected by country-level factors, whereby certain programs may be more effective in some countries than others. We later propose how understanding the effects of these forces enables researchers to gain a holistic perspective of the factors that play a role in the creation and formulation of ethics programs in organizations.

Content of ethics programs

The content of any ethics program should include features that aid employees in making ethical decisions in the workplace. The language and structure of content of the ethics programs should, therefore, be clear and easily understood by organizational members. Also, corporations may adopt ethics programs in several forms including (Weaver *et al.*, 1999b):

- ethics-oriented policy statements;
- formalization of management responsibilities for ethics;
- free-standing ethics offices;
- ethics and compliance telephone reporting/advice systems;
- top management and departmental involvement in ethics activities;
- usage of ethics training and other ethics awareness activities;
- investigatory functions; and
- evaluation of ethics program activities.

However, most research on the content of ethics programs does a comparative analysis of mainly one type of ethics program, that is, the code of ethics in different countries, and proposes ways in which the codes would be similar or different based on Hofstede's (1983) cultural dimensions. For example, Singh *et al.* (2005) examine corporate codes of ethics from Australian, Canadian, and Swedish firms along a number of criteria: policy area, authority, and compliance procedures. They find that the contents of the Australian and Canadian codes were similar on these dimensions, reflecting the similar histories and cultures (as measured by Hofstede's dimensions) of these two countries. Further, the contents of the Swedish codes were found to be very different from the Australian and Canadian codes in some areas, reflecting the cultural differences between Sweden and the other two countries. On similar lines, Langlois and Schlegelmilch (1990) investigate the differences between the content of the codes of ethics of European (French, British, and West German) and American companies to find significant differences between Europe and the United States, in particular with regard to employee conduct, supplier and contractor relations as well as political interests. They also show that the differences in the contents of codes exist between the three European countries. France, for example, stands out through the high proportion of codes that address customer relations (93%), while German codes address innovation and technology more frequently (60%) than the codes in any other country. Melé *et al.* (2006), while studying the codes in Argentina, Spain, and Brazil, demonstrate that the main differences between these countries concern the emphasis given to specific aspects, such as avoiding misconduct or taking ethical criteria into account when selecting personnel. The emphasis is greatest in countries where corruption seems most prevalent.

Another aspect of the ethics programs that has received attention is the language used in the code of ethics in organizations in various countries. Farrell and Farrell (1998) examine the codes of ethics of five large enterprises in Australia and find that the language used in the corporate codes examined construct an authoritarian position in the writer/reader relationship from the overuse of grammatical structures such as relational clauses, the passive, nominalization, grammatical metaphor, and modality. Collectively, these structures communicate a strong sense of obligation and even powerlessness since a strong authoritarian tone is established which does not give the addressees the possibility of discretionary decision making. Moreover, Palazzo (2002) suggests that in comparison to US corporations, fewer German companies have introduced ethics programs since the latter are very reluctant to address normative questions publicly. This difference can be explained by the different cultural backgrounds in both countries and by defining these different 'habits of the heart' (which are described by analyzing the way corporations deal with norms and values within their organizations) underlying German and American business ethics.

Lastly, to our knowledge, only one article examines how the content of the code of ethics of organizations has changed over time. Singh (2006) compares a total of 80 codes, representing a broad cross-section of Canada's largest firms in 2003 to 75 codes adopted by Lefebvre and Singh (1992). Singh (2006) finds that in 2003, as in 1992, more of the codes were concerned with conduct against the firm than with conduct on behalf of the firm. Among the changes from 1992 to 2003 were a significant increase in the frequency of reference to environmental affairs, legal responsibility as the basis of codes and enforcement/compliance procedures.

Thus, research on the content of ethics programs has primarily focused on only one type of ethics program – the code of ethics in organizations, and on understanding how corporations operating in different countries differ on the content (language and structure) of these programs due to the cultural differences between the countries. Lacking in the literature on the content of ethics programs is the focus on exploring how and why other practices such as ethics training and formation of free-standing ethics offices differ between organizations. Also overlooked is the role of human resource practices in designing the content of the ethics programs. Therefore, we propose the integration of IHRM policies with the ethics program practices in organizations below.

Communication of ethics programs

Effective communication of ethics programs can be considered as the main determinant of success of these programs in any organization. An ethics program may be regarded as successful if organizational members are suitably socialized to view the ethics program as legitimate and vital for the benefit of the organization, and if organizational members internalize these programs such that they view ethical conduct as an integral part of their workplace behavior. This can be achieved through effective communication of the ethics programs. However, prior research in this regard has largely focused on the negative consequences of inappropriate methods of communications, and the differences in communication styles of managers in different companies or different industries. Consider, for example, the study by McKendall et al. (2002) who, using survey and archival methods for 108 firms from the Wards Business Directory which lists the largest 1000 US-based firms, determine whether ethical codes, communication about ethics, ethics training and incorporating ethics into human resources practices would result in fewer Occupational Safety and Health Administration (OSHA) violations. The results indicate that communication of the ethical compliance programs also did not have any effect on OSHA violations, and ethical compliance programs themselves did not lessen legal violations. Nijhof et al. (2000), in their theoretical framework on ways of stimulating responsible behavior in organizations, suggest the adoption of a dialogical approach for communication of ethics programs. In a dialogical approach, the communications between decision makers and other stakeholders involved are the foundations for determining a responsible solution. They suggest that this dialogical approach of communication would facilitate the success of an ethics program. In the international context, Snell *et al.* (1999), in their multi-method, longitudinal study of companies in Hong Kong, find that companies tend to impose their codes top-down, emphasizing disciplinary procedures rather than ethics training, and appointing neither ethics counselors nor ombuds people. However, this style of communication and implementation of ethics programs resulted in a decline in moral ethos without any change in the overall standards of perceived conduct over a seven-month period.

From a comparative perspective, Montoya and Richard (1994) conduct ethnographic interviews in 10 Health Care and 10 Energy companies in the US. Data was collected over a four-week period using focus group and structured individual interviews. They discover that neither the Health Care facilities nor Energy companies encounter much success with the codes of ethics program. Further, companies that distribute copies of their code of ethics seldom ensure that the process is completed or that employees understand the purpose of the document, and staff responsible for the code give it a low priority relative to their overall responsibilities. On the other hand, Robertson and Schlegelmilch (1993) survey a total of 860 companies in the US and the UK, and show that UK companies tend to be more likely to communicate ethics policies through senior executives, whereas US companies tend to rely more on their Human Resources and Legal Departments. Additionally, US firms consider most ethical issues to be more important than do their UK counterparts, and are especially concerned with employee behavior that may harm the firm. In contrast, the issues that UK managers consider more important tend to be concerned with external corporate stakeholders rather than employees.

Thus, research on the communication of ethics programs suggests that inappropriate communication of ethics programs may have negative consequences for the organization, and that organizations in different environments communicate their ethics programs differently to their members. However, lacking in the literatures is a process model of how the communication of ethics programs leads to the success or failure of such programs. Communication and implementation of ethics programs could be a negotiated process whereby only particular types of programs may work better in organizations depending on the involvement the employees of the organization in the communication and implementation of the programs. Future research needs to focus on such processes of communication of ethics programs.

Effectiveness of ethics programs

Current research advocates that ethics programs are effective depending on their type, and the perceptions of employees and managers regarding the organizational context. For instance, Weaver *et al.* (1999a) conducted a field survey in a large financial services company to investigate the relationships of the values and compliance orientations in an ethics program to a diverse set of outcomes such as commitment, integrity, etc. Employees' perceptions that the company ethics program is oriented toward affirming ethical values are associated with seven outcomes of reporting violation, commitment, integrity, ethical awareness, better decision making, seeking advice, and observing ethical behavior. Perceptions of a compliance orientation are associated with the latter four of these outcomes. The interaction of values and compliance orientations is associated with employees' willingness to report misconduct. In another study of a utility company, a telecommunications company and two energy-related companies, Trevino and Weaver (2001) show that when employees perceive general organizational justice and ethics program follow-through, there is less unethical behavior and a greater willingness to report problems. General justice and ethics program follow-through also interact with each other, showing that the impact of ethics initiatives is influenced by the organizational context. Pelletier and Bligh (2006), in a California government agency, examine the perceived importance of three organizational preconditions (awareness of formal ethics codes, decision-making techniques, and availability of resources) theorized to be critical for ethics program effectiveness, and the importance of ethical leadership and congruence between formal ethics codes and informal ethical norms in influencing employee perceptions. Results suggest that employee perceptions of organizational preconditions, ethical leadership and informal ethical norms were related to perceptions of ethics program effectiveness.

Regarding ineffectiveness of ethics programs, McKendall *et al.* (2002), in the above-mentioned study, indicate that ethical compliance programs do not lessen legal violations. In fact, lower firm profitability results in a greater number of willful and repeat OSHA violations. Similar results were attained by Jackson (2000), whose data encompass managers in France, Germany, Britain, Spain, and the US working in over 200 companies operating in these countries. Jackson (2000) presents evidence that, despite national differences in areas of gift giving and receiving, loyalty to company, loyalty to one's group, and reporting others' violations of corporate policy, the clarity of corporate policy about management ethics has little influence on managers' reported ethical decision making, and also finds that the perceived behavior of managers' colleagues is far more important in predicting attitudes toward decision making of managers across the nationalities surveyed. Thus, effectiveness of ethics programs is largely influenced by not only the type of ethics programs but also the perceptions of the usefulness of such programs by various organizational members.

FUTURE AVENUES FOR RESEARCH: PRACTICE INTEGRATION

To better understand the role of IHRM in the formulation and implementation of ethics programs in MNCs, we propose that the practices and policies of IHRM should be fully integrated with the formulation, content and communication of ethics programs reviewed above. Additionally, multilevel forces affecting the ethics programs in MNCs should also be considered during their formulation (see Wright and van de Voorde, this volume Chapter 2, for a discussion of research issues associated with multilevel analysis). We elaborate on each of these ideas below.

Previous research suggests that the human resources management in a MNC administers the policies and practices of (a) human resource planning, (b) staffing, (c) training and development, and (d) performance evaluation, and compensation (see Schuler *et al.*, 2002, for a review). However, this research does not explicate how these practices may be administrated to ensure that ethics programs in MNCs are successful. We suggest that each of these IHRM practices plays a key role in how MNCs formulate, design in terms of content, and communicate ethics programs for high effectiveness. We argue that the staffing and training should aim at facilitating the formulation, content and communication of ethics programs, whereas the performance appraisals and compensation of top organizational leaders should be linked to the successful implementation of these programs.

Human resource planning

Human resource planning entails synchronizing the staffing, appraisal and compensation subsystems of IHRM (Schuler *et al.*, 2002). Bartlett and Ghoshal (1998) suggest that such planning should be cognizant of, and responsive to, the MNC's industry characteristics, product market, global structures, and competitive strategies. However, we contend that this planning should also be attentive to the ethics programs in the MNCs. We explore this proposal in detail below.

Staffing

The staffing policies of MNCs can influence both the formulation and communication of ethics programs. Brewster and Scullion (1997) suggest that traditionally, MNCs sent parent country nationals abroad to ensure that the foreign operations carried out the policies and procedures of the home office. However, as the costs of hiring and retaining these managers became inflated, MNCs increasing hired from the host country or a third country to satisfy their international staffing needs (Black *et al.*, 1999). The above review suggests that this practice can be characterized as being detrimental to the formulation of ethics programs in organizations since organizational leaders and high-level managers are some of the important forces in the creation and adoption of ethics programs in organizations. This issue is further complicated for US firms in comparison to other firms such as those from Japan since the former are less likely to staff higher management vacancies in foreign operations with parent-country nationals than Japanese MNCs who frequently staff senior and middle management positions with expatriates (Tung, 1982). On the other hand, Bailey and Spicer (2007), through data collected via two experiments from 1998 until 2001, find that American expatriate respondents who were highly included in the Russian community expressed ethical attitudes similar to those of the Russian respondents, even though differences may have been expected due to cultural and national differences. Furthermore, Cappelli and McElrath (1992) suggest that ethnocentric forces may compromise an MNC's ability to appreciate the cultural synergies between the parent and host country operating units. Therefore, it may be preferable to engage more host country managers than those from the parent company since the former may be expected to have been previously socialized in the culture of the units in the host country.

We propose that to ensure the optimal formulation and communication of ethics programs, MNCs should be staffed with both, parent and local company managers, such that the former, with the aid of the local company managers, are primarily responsible for creating and formulating ethics programs that highlight the concerns of the parent company. Similarly, the local company managers may be responsible for effectively communicating the benefits of the ethics programs to the other members of the MNCs since they may be more versed with the mode and cultural norms of communicating these policies.

Training and development

Research on training and development in IHRM has mostly focused on the predeparture (expatriate) training extended to parent company nationals and their families (Schuler *et al.*, 2002). Lack of or inadequate training has been shown to lead to higher expatriate failure rates (Tung, 1982). Research has also adopted comparative analyses of training programs offered by MNCs in different countries. For instance, US multinationals have been found to engage in less training than European and Japanese firms (Tung, 1982), and multinationals in different countries have been shown to provide divergent training to their managers (Noble, 1997). However, missing from the literature is the importance of *ethics* training for the expatriates, including the need of ethical behavior by the managers themselves. We contend that managers in MNCs need to receive additional training, regarding ways to increase ethical behavior among employees in MNCs, in addition to monitoring their own behaviors. This training would encourage the managers to act as role models, thereby ensuring a successful formulation, appropriate content, and clearer communication of ethics programs. Weaver and Trevino (2001) propose that organizational leaders need to receive ethics training so that they can convey the ethics message through their involvement in delivering training and through daily role modeling, and suggest that "the HR function is uniquely situated to insure that a values orientation is emphasized in training, that training occurs frequently and across levels, and that training related to ethics and fairness is incorporated into leadership and management development activities in appropriate ways" (p. 123).

The language used to describe situations can also influence people's ability to recognize and act on ethical concerns (Butterfield *et al.*, 2000). Thus, the language used by the organizational leaders can facilitate the formulation and adoption of ethics programs in organizations. As noted in the review above, the language of the code of ethics adopted by firms in different countries varied noticeably (Langlois and Schlegelmilch, 1990; Melé *et al.*, 2006; Singh *et al.*, 2005). Training and development of expatriate managers should, therefore, include understanding the cultural and national differences in language between their parent and host countries. This training can provide the managers with knowledge that could be used to improve or change the content and communication of the ethics programs.

Performance evaluation and compensation

Performance evaluations of expatriates is mostly related to the operation of the unit and how it relates to other locations (Evans, 1986), unless they are exclusively assigned for technical projects or short-term stays. Peterson *et al.* (1996) compare the British, German, Japanese, and US multinationals to find that expatriates were evaluated either quantitatively or qualitatively entailing numerous job performance dimensions. However, missing from the list are criteria such as cross-cultural interpersonal qualities, sensitivity to foreign norms, laws and customs, and the host country's integration with the MNC's other units (Schuler *et al.*, 2002), that are not directly related to performance. Also missing is the evaluation of the success of the ethics programs in the MNC unit. Including dimensions that evaluate the ethics programs of a MNC unit would ensure the indisputable formulation and implementation of ethics programs in MNCs.

Research on compensation in MNCs has mainly looked at the patterns of compensation and benefits received by the managers. For instance, Towers-Perrin (1987), in their report on worldwide total remuneration, demonstrate that American and Japanese multinationals tend to provide their parent company nationals with home country entitlements, but limit host company nationals to fringe benefits. However, European companies extend home country benefits to both groups. We suggest that irrespective of the compensation packages given to either groups, each must be awarded additional benefits when their units have created and adequately communicated ethics programs to the MNCs' employees. These benefits should also be linked to the success of the ethics programs, whereby success is measured by a reduction of, and increase in reports of, unethical behavior of the employees.

Thus, we propose that the comprehensive staffing and training of organizational members can facilitate the formulation, content and communication of ethics programs, and performance appraisals and compensations should be linked to the implementation and success of these programs.

FUTURE AVENUES FOR RESEARCH: MULTILEVEL ISSUES

Another way to grasp the role of IHRM in the success of ethics programs in MNCs is by focusing on a more comprehensive picture of the influences of institutional, industry or country level and organizational pressures affecting ethics programs in MNCs. As Figure ?? illustrates, factors that influence the success of ethics programs at one level will also have an affect at another level. We propose that an integrative, multilevel view of the forces behind the formulation and implementation of ethics programs can add to our knowledge of the role of IHRM in ensuring the success of these programs. Let us consider some probable relationships herewith.

Institutional factors

Institutional theory emphasizes the role of social factors such as external conformity pressures from regulatory bodies or parent organizations, pressures from other organizations with ties to the focal organization, and collective social construction processes, instead of economic and organizational factors on the adoption of practices by organizations (Baron *et al.*, 1986; Burns and Wholey, 1993; Meyer and Rowan, 1977; Scott, 1995). These normative pressures contribute to isomorphism, that

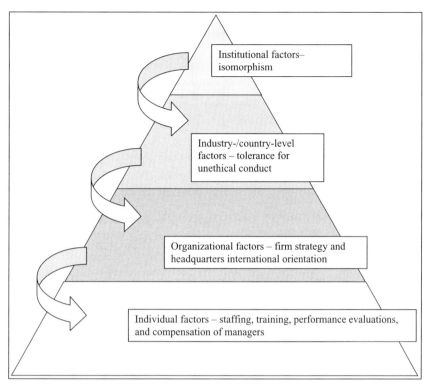

FIGURE 20.1 Multilevel issues in understanding the role of IHRM in formulating and implementing ethics programs.

is, the emergence of common organizational practices over time (DiMaggio and Powell, 1983). Therefore, it is essential that the reasons behind the adoption of ethics programs by organizations – whether the programs are implemented for efficiency gains or simply to gain legitimacy – are investigated (see Westphal *et al.*, 1997). This insight should be the first step in exploring and explicating the role of IHRM in the success of ethics programs.

Industry- and country-level factors

Institutional pressures may vary according to the industry or the country in which the organization is embedded. Institutional pressures may, thus, influence the industry- or country-level factors affecting the formulation of ethics programs in MNCs. For instance, in some industries such as the pharmaceutical industry, there may be a higher institutional pressure to adopt ethics programs than in, say, the sporting goods industry. Similarly, in countries such as India, the attitudes toward, and pressures for, successful implementation of ethics programs are significantly lower than those in, say, the US (see Christie *et al.*, 2003). In such situations, the human resource practices and policies in MNCs in the pharmaceutical industry, and in the US, may have a greater role to play in the formulation, content, communication and implementation of ethics programs. On the other hand, in countries such as India, MNCs may need better understanding of the cultural factors that influence employees attitudes toward ethics programs. MNCs may, hence, need to be more strategic in developing the content of ethics programs and also in communicating the need of these programs to employees in these MNCs.

Organizational factors

This leads us to examine the organizational factors that have an effect on the ethics programs in MNCs. As noted in the review, foremost among them is the role of the CEO and other top leaders in the organization. Other factors include the firm strategy and the headquarters international orientation (Schuler *et al.*, 2002). These organizational factors may differ by the industry or country in which the MNC operates. Consider the Japanese-owned auto firms in the US in the 1980s. The US has shown particular concern in the equal employment opportunity (EEO) posture to foreign subsidiaries. However, Japanese auto plants were generally situated in areas that had lower black-to-white populations than were the norm for the US auto plants (Cole and Deskins, 1988). The Japanese auto plants, therefore, received much criticism for these actions. Hence, even though the firm strategy for the Japanese auto plants in the US would be to market cheaper cars to the US population, this policy would be highly influenced by the industry- and country-level factors. We suggest that the human resources policies and practices may play a role in such scenarios by communicating the programs required to ensure ethical conduct in the host country by the foreign firm. This again suggests that the parent company should play the lead in formulating and monitoring the ethics programs in MNCs, but with the aid of the local units since the latter may be more successful in developing the content and communicating the ethics programs.

The organizational factors, in turn, have an effect on the staffing decisions, the training and development, and compensation of managers in the MNCs discussed above. In summary, research on the role of IHRM in formulating and implementing ethics programs in MNCs should look at all the factors comprehensively to gain a holistic picture of the forces affecting these programs.

CONCLUSION

This chapter explicates the role of IHRM practices and policies in the formulation and implementation of ethics programs in multinational enterprises. We have conducted an extensive review of the literature on ethics programs. We find that the impact of human resource practices and policies on ethics programs is largely ignored in the literature. We, therefore, suggest ways in which scholars interested in understanding the human resource practices or the ethics programs in organizations can advance both literatures. We propose that we should look at how ethics programs and human resource practices can be integrated such that the formulation, content and communication of ethics programs are incorporated into the staffing, training and development, and performance appraisals and compensation practices of MNCs. We argue that staffing and training decisions may influence the formulation, content and communication of ethics programs, whereas the performance appraisals and compensation of top managers in MNCs will have an effect on the successful implementation of these programs.

We also propose that the role of the IHRM should be understood by comprehending the multilevel issues affecting the formulation and implementation of ethics programs. We contend that the institutional, industry- or country-level and organizational factors all influence each other and have an impact on the ethics programs of MNCs. We advocate understanding the institutional forces first to assess the importance of ethics programs in organizations. The industry- and country-level forces should then be accounted for while formulating and communicating ethics programs. Lastly, organizational factors should also be considered since they play a pivotal role in the successful implementation of ethics programs. We have, therefore, put forth several ways in which the fields of ethics programs and IHRM can progress so that ethics programs are successfully formulated and implemented in MNCs.

REFERENCES

Bailey, W., and Spicer, A. (2007). When does national identity matter? Convergence and divergence in international business ethics. *Academy of Management Journal*, 50 (6), 1462–1480.

Baron, J.P., Dobbin, F., and Jennings, P.D. (1986). War and peace: The evolution of modern personnel administration in U.S. industry. *American Journal of Sociology*, 92, 250–283.

Bartlett, C., and Ghoshal, S. (1998). *Managing Across Borders: The Transnational Solution* (2nd edn). Boston, MA: Harvard Business School Press.

Black, J.S., Gregersen, H.B., Mendenhall, M., and Stroh, L.K. (1999). *Globalizing People through International Assignments*. Boston MA: Addison- Wesley.

Brenner, S.N. (1992). Ethics programs and their dimensions. *Journal of Business Ethics*, 11, 391–399.

Brewster, C., and Scullion, H. (1997). A review and agenda for expatriate HRM. *Human Resource Management Journal*, 7 (3), 32–41.

Burns, L.R., and Wholey, D.R. (1993). Adoption and abandonment of matrix management programs: Effects of organizational characteristics and interorganizational networks. *Academy of Management Journal*, 36, 106–138.

Butterfield, K.D., Trevino, L.K., and Weaver, G.R. (2000). Moral awareness in business organizations: Influences of issue-related and social context factors. *Human Relations*, 53, 981–1008.

Cappelli, P., and McElrath, R. (1992). *The transfer of employment practices through multinationals: Working paper*. Wharton School, University of Pennsylvania.

Christie, P.M.J., Kwon, I.-W.G., Stoeberl, P.A., and Baumhart, R. (2003). A cross-cultural comparison of ethical attitudes of business managers: India, Korea and the United States. *Journal of Business Ethics*, 46, 263–287.

Cole, R.E., and Deskins, D.R. (1988). Racial factors in site location and employment patterns of Japanese auto firms in America. *California Management Review*, 31, 9–21.

DiMaggio, P.J., and Powell, W.W. (1983). The iron cage revisited: Institutional isomorphism and collective rationality in organizational fields. *American Sociological Review*, 48, 147–160.

Evans, P. (1986). The context of strategic human resource management policy in complex firms. *Management Forum*, 6, 105–107.

Fama, E.F., and Jensen, M.C. (1983). Separation of ownership and control. *Journal of Law and Economics*, 26 (June), 301–325.

Farrell, H., and Farrell, B.J. (1998). The language of business codes of ethics: Implications of knowledge and power. *Journal of Business Ethics*, 17, 587–601.

Felo, A.J. (2001). Ethics programs, board involvement, and potential conflicts of interest in corporate governance. *Journal of Business Ethics*, 32, 205–218.

Hofstede, G. (1983). National cultures in four dimensions. *International Studies of Management and Organization*, 13 (2), 46–74.

Jackson, T. (2000). Management ethics and coporate policy: A cross-cultural comparison. *Journal of Management Studies*, 37 (3), 349–369.

Langlois, C.C., and Schlegelmilch, B.B. (1990). Do corporate codes of ethics reflect national character? Evidence from Europe and the United States. *Journal of International Business Studies*, 21 (4), 519–539.

Lefebvre, M., and Singh, J. (1992). The content and focus of Canadian corporate codes of ethics. *Journal of Business Ethics*, 11, 799–808.

McKendall, M., DeMarr, B., and Jones-Rikkers, C. (2002). Ethical compliance programs and corporate illegality: Testing the assumptions of the corporate sentencing guidelines. *Journal of Business Ethics*, 37, 367–383.

Melé, D., Debeljuh, P., and Arruda, M.C. (2006). Corporate ethical policies in large corporations in Argentina, Brazil, and Spain. *Journal of Business Ethics*, 63, 21–38.

Meyer, J.W., and Rowan, B. (1977). Institutional organizations: Formal structure as myth and ceremony. *American Journal of Sociology*, 83, 340–363.

Montoya, I.D., and Richard, A.J. (1994). A comparative study of codes of ethics in health care facilities and energy companies. *Journal of Business Ethics*, 13, 713–717.

Nijhof, A., Fisscher, O., and Loosie, J.K. (2000). Coercion, guidance and mercifulness: The different influences of ethics programs on decision-making. *Journal of Business Ethics*, 27, 33–42.

Noble, C. (1997). International comparison of training policies. *Human Resource Management Journal*, 7 (1), 5–18.

Palazzo, B. (2002). U.S.– American and German business ethics: An intercultural comparison. *Journal of Business Ethics*, 41, 195–216.

Pelletier, K.L., and Bligh, M.C. (2006). Rebounding from corruption: Perceptions of ethics program effectiveness in a public sector organization. *Journal of Business Ethics*, 67, 359–374.

Peterson, R.B., Napier, N., and Shim, W.S. (1996). Expatriate management: The differential role of national multinational corporation ownership. *The International Executive*, 38 (4), 543–562.

Robertson, D.C., and Schlegelmilch, B.B. (1993). Corporate institutionalization of ethics in the United States and Great Britain. *Journal of Business Ethics*, 12, 301–312.

Schuler, R.S., Budhwar, P.S., and Florkowski, G.W. (2002). International human resource management: Review and critique. *International Journal of Management Reviews*, 4 (1), 41–70.

Scott, W.R. (1995). *Institutions and Organizations*. Thousand Oaks, CA: Sage.

Singh, J. (2006). A comparison of the contents of the codes of ethics of Canada's largest corporations in 1992 and 2003. *Journal of Business Ethics*, 64, 17–29.

Singh, J., Carasco, E., Svensson, G., Wood, G., and Callaghan, M. (2005). A comparative study of the contents of corporate codes of ethics in Australia, Canada and Swedan. *Journal of World Business*, 40, 91–109.

Snell, R.S., Chak, A.M.-K., and Chu, J.W.-H. (1999). Codes of ethics in Hong Kong: Their adoption and impact in the run up to the 1997 transition of Sovereignty to China. *Journal of Business Ethics*, 22, 281–309.

Stevens, J.M., Steensma, H.K., Harrison, D.A., and Cochran, P.L. (2005). Symbolic or substantive document? The influence of ethical codes on financial executives' decisions. *Strategic Management Journal*, 26, 181–195.

Sundaram, A.K., and Black, J.S. (1992). The environment and internal organization of multinational enterprises. *Academy of Management Review*, 17, 729–757.

Towers-Perrin (1987). *Worldwide Total Remuneration*. New York: Towers Perrin, Foster, and Crossby.

Trevino, L.K., and Weaver, G.R. (2001). Organizational justice and ethics program "follow-through": Influences on employees' harmful and helpful behavior. *Business Ethics Quarterly*, 11 (4), 651–671.

Tulder, R. v., and Kolk, A. (2001). Multinationality and corporate ethics: Codes of conduct in the sporting goods industry. *Journal of International Business Studies*, 32 (2), 267–283.

Tung, R.L. (1982). Selection and training procedures of US, European, and Japanese multinationals. *California Management Review*, 25, 57–71.

Weaver, G.R., and Trevino, L.K. (2001). The role of human resources in ethics/compliance management: A fairness perspective. *Human Resource Management Review*, 11, 113–134.

Weaver, G.R., Trevino, L.K., and Cochran, P.L. (1999a). Compliance and values oriented ethics programs: Influences on employees' attitudes and behavior. *Business Ethics Quarterly*, 9 (2), 315–335.

Weaver, G.R., Trevino, L.K., and Cochran, P.L. (1999b). Corporate ethics practices in the mid-1990's: An empirical study of the Fortune 1000. *Journal of Business Ethics*, 18, 283–294.

Weaver, G.R., Trevino, L.K., and Cochran, P.L. (1999c). Corporate ethics programs as control systems: Influences of executive commitment and environmental factors. *Academy of Management Journal*, 42 (1), 41–57.

Weaver, G.R., Trevino, L.K., and Cochran, P.L. (1999d). Integrated and decoupled corporate social performance: Management commitments, external pressures, and corporate ethics practices. *Academy of Management Journal*, 42 (5), 539–552.

Westphal, J.D., Gulati, R., and Shortell, S.M. (1997). Customization and conformity? An institutional and network perspective on the content and consequences of TQM adoption. *Administrative Science Quarterly*, 42, 366–394.

21

The Ethnic Factor in IHRM: A Research Agenda

STEPHEN NYAMBEGERA

INTRODUCTION

The field of human resource management (HRM) pertains to the way individuals, groups and organizations act to create products and/or services for the organization (Erez and Earley, 1997). Brewster *et al.*, (2007) point out that in international organizations or multinational corporations (MNCs) human resource management is a key to success. They argue that there is a cost–benefit element in using the human resource. On both sides of the equation, HRM is crucial to the survival, performance and success of the enterprise. Business organizations today operate in an increasingly global environment leading to dramatic changes in the nature and structure of organizations in response to new opportunities and the shift of labor-intensive activities to low-wage countries. This creates a challenge to organizations operating internationally as they have to respond to an increasingly wider set of country-specific challenges in both the political and socio-economic spheres (Brewster *et al.*, 2007). The challenge of dealing with multicultural assumptions in international organizations is ever present. Those Human Resource (HR) Managers who make no attempt to learn to adapt to recent changes in the global environment often find themselves reacting rather than innovating. Thus, HRM decision making needs to identify the most important factors that influence the individual within the organizational context.

Kihlstrom and Canto (1987) point out that one of the factors that influence individual decision making in organizations is their identity as a form of diversity. Individual identity is rooted within the social environment, and is a reflection of the external policies of the larger group or organization. In the social sphere this creates the challenge of successful diversity management in organizations (Cassell and Biswas, 2000). This diversity is usually conceptualized in terms of the difference of relevant issues of identity, such as gender, age, ethnicity, disability, and sexual

Handbook of International Human Resource Management. Edited by Paul R. Sparrow
© 2009 John Wiley & Sons, Ltd

orientation. The literature is awash with research on approaches to deal with cultural and other contextual factors like age, gender, education levels and so forth. However, this literature contains very little about the importance of ethnicity, or indeed on developing approaches to ethnicity that fit international human resource management (IHRM).

Some attention has been given to the growing issues of ethnic discrimination in domestic contexts, with, for example, Debbie Andalo in the article "Ethnic minorities blocked from top jobs" appearing in *The Guardian* of April 30, 2007 reporting that employees from ethnic minorities in managerial and professional jobs earn up to 25% less than their white colleagues. The article further reveals that comparable pay scales for black African and Bangladeshi men were likely to face the greatest pay discrimination. In the paper of January 20, 2007, Martin Jacques in his article 'British society is dripping in racism (read ethnicity)' reports that racism is widespread in Britain but no one admits it. However, studies on employee relations in Europe often make little mention of ethnic diversity despite the fact that there are, for example, large numbers of people of Afro-Caribbean and Asian origin working in the United Kingdom. It is evident that many countries are multi-ethnic – witness the recent upsurge in migration and its use as one source of international resourcing (Mayerhofer *et al.*, 2008) but in the main analysis of the influence of ethnicity continues not to be an issue in IHRM research.

International management researchers have called for a broadening of the scope of cross-cultural analysis to incorporate the social and cognitive processes that underpin culturally embedded behavior (see Sackmann, this volume Chapter 4). As societies globalize and become more plural they have to come to terms with phenomena such as *intra-cultural diversity* and growing *intercultural communalities*. Sackmann and Phillips (2004) call this the multiple cultures perspective. They point out that social-cognitive theorists argue that we need to understand:

- how individuals deal with multiple and shifting identities inside organizations;
- how they manage these shifts; and
- what the implications are for the managers who have to deal with this self-management by employees.

This chapter focuses on the issue of ethnicity in IHRM research, specifically by examining the nature of ethnicity in organizations in Africa, United States of America, and Britain. It is hoped that the chapter will lay out an agenda for research on the implications of ethnicity in IHRM. Further, it is hoped that it will also contribute to an understanding of ethnicity in organizational life.

PERSPECTIVES ON ETHNICITY

There is no universally accepted definition of ethnic origin itself. Although the term "ethnicity" is criticized by some theorists for its lack of precision, it is widely recognized and used in preference to the largely discredited concept of "race" (Mason, 2000). However, ethnicity is a culturally derived term often used to denote populations who have some common ancestry, common "cultural heritage" and who are considered by others to be from the same or similar "grouping" (Smith, 1981). Ever since the 1960s the definition of ethnicity has changed considerably; however the most outstanding feature is the consideration of ethnicity as a community in which the members are aware of the identity of their community, as well as the different identities of other ethnic groups around. Ethnicity definitions are based upon a variety of factors including language, religion, national origin, and race (Simpson and Yinger, 1985).

Osaghae (1995: 11) defines ethnicity as the employment and mobilization of ethnic identity or difference to gain advantage in situations of competition, conflict or cooperation. Deng (1997: 28) defines ethnicity as an "embodiment of values, institutions, and patterns of behavior, a composite whole representing a people's historical experience, aspirations, and worldview". Ethnic classification, either externally imposed or intrinsically engendered, often defines people's membership to a group. Ethnicity is innately more central to human experience and identity than race. This understanding then leads to the conclusion that an ethnic group is one whose members share a common identity and affinity based on a common language, culture, myth of common origin, and territorial homeland, which becomes the basis for differentiating "us" from "them" and upon which people act. Rather than perceiving ethnic categories as primitive and rigid, many commentators therefore argue that they are socially constructed and dynamic, enabling them to adopt different identities in different circumstances (Pilkington, 2003).

This concurs with the situational approach to ethnicity advocated by Banton (2000), which argues that individuals have many different potential bases for collective action, which may be used if it suits the particular situation in which they find themselves. Ethnic distinctiveness is more likely to invoke an innate sense of people mood. Ethnic uniqueness thus provides an immediate identity marker both within a group and between groups. Ethnic categories are often perceived or discussed as though they are fixed and unchanging entities. However, because ethnicity incorporates language, religion, demarcations of territory, and other cultural traits, changes in people's affinity with any of them can occur over time.

Erez and Gati (2004), reflecting the multiple cultures perspective of Sackmann and Phillips (2004) mentioned above, called for a shift in research focus, moving away from approaches that view culture as a stable entity toward approaches that examine dynamic phenomena, and in particular the interplay between different levels of culture: "... very few studies have examined the effect of culture on change, or recognized that culture itself changes over time" (Erez and Gati, 2004). A number of researchers have therefore argued that globalization, as a macro level of culture, produces behavioral change in members of various cultures through top-down structural processes, but that reciprocal individual level behavioral changes are also created through bottom-up processes that modify culture at the macro level (Sparrow, 2006; see also Sackmann, this volume Chapter 4).

Roosens (1989) and Marger (1994) assert that it was believed that ethnicity as an element of culture would gradually disappear as an organizational form, but from available literature it seems that ethnic groups are becoming even stronger. Nyambegera (2002) argues that in multi-ethnic societies, ethnic group is a key source of attachment and serves as an important referent of self-identification which impacts heavily on people behavior. Coughlan and Samarasinghe (1991) indicate that ethnicity is an important element in cultural studies, emanating from deep historical roots that could affect the present. People of different ethnic backgrounds possess different attitudes, values and norms. Cultural differences, rather than a numerical minority status, determine the observed differences in work attitudes relative to the "white" employees.

One area of cultural differences is the contrast between individualism and collectivism. Collectivists emphasize the needs of the group, social norms, shared beliefs and cooperation with group members. In general, Asians, Hispanics, and blacks have roots in nations with collectivist traditions, while Anglos have roots in the European tradition of individualism (Hofstede, 1980). The extent of people's cultural beliefs of individualism or collectivism has been used to predict the effectiveness of many management practices. People from cultures that view relationships in terms of hierarchy have a preference for highly structured teams. Those from cultures that see relationships in terms of groups want teamwork to be the norm, and societies that emphasize the individual feel most comfortable with voluntary and informal teams. Mixing these culture types can have a significant impact on an organization (Perkins, 1993).

An organization's culture determines the ability of members from other groups to perform within the organization. Individuals from minority groups face challenges every day dealing with prejudice, discrimination, and stereotyping (Healey, 2003). In order for minority group members to overcome these challenges, organizations must set realistic goals for its leaders as well as its employees to work toward. Although widely used, the term "minority ethnic" is imperfect. Within the UK, Mason (2000) argues that the term is usually understood to refer to "visible" minority groups rather than minority ethnic as a whole, thus ignoring the significant communities who also have their own cultural traditions such as Polish and Ukrainian communities. A similar term "ethnic minority" is sometimes used. Despite these problems and their current usage, the terms ethnicity, minority ethnic, tribe, and race will be used in this chapter. One reason minority groups are important is that they are associated with the general patterns of inequality in society. Minority group membership can affect access to jobs, education, wealth, health care, and housing. It is associated with a lower proportional share of valued goods and services and more limited opportunities for upward mobility in employment.

Organizations and their cultures, therefore, are a function of the kind of people in them, who are as a result of an A–S–A (attraction–selection–attrition) cycle (Schneider, 1987). As the world is shrinking through globalization, more and more people live and work in foreign countries and therefore continually come into contact with the people coming from much diversified cultural origins, involving language, norms, and lifestyles. Improvement and management of the people on a global scale inevitably requires dealing with diversity and the problems regarding matters of motivation, leadership, productivity, and authority. Due to their complex nature, MNCs must perform a delicate balancing act when developing their IHRM policy (Hannon *et al.*, 1995; Mayrhofer *et al.*, 2008).

ETHNICITY FROM A CROSS-NATIONAL PERSPECTIVE

Hannon *et al.* (1995) define multinational enterprise as a group of geographically dispersed and goal diverse organizations, including headquarters, domestic operations, and foreign ventures. As Rosenzweg and Nohria (1994) suggest, the need to strive for consistency among units in the way they manage international employees (global integration) often conflicts with the need to adapt to local domestic management practices and cultural norms (local adaptation), resulting in a conflict over the intended use of people as organizational resources. The need for human resource specialists to adopt an increasingly international orientation in their functional activities is widely acknowledged and becoming ever clearer.

Ethnicity is commonly believed to be an African and other developing countries problem, but evidence shows that is not the case. Research into discrimination, both on grounds of ethnic origin, and other characteristics such as gender reveals the many forms unequal treatment may take. Greenhaus *et al.* (1990) argue that it often involves "access discrimination" in the recruitment and selection process and "treatment discrimination" which takes place after access to the occupation has been achieved. Such discrimination can have substantial effect upon performance in a current job, and thus upon future career development. Ethnic discrimination and prejudice can lead to talent wastage as some organizations might prefer not to hire the best candidates due to their ethnic background, discrimination becomes the active element aimed at denying members of particular ethnic groups equal access to societal rewards (Nyambegera, 2002).

I use the example of Britain, which has recently experienced a massive wave of immigration, driven in part by the need for organizations to address skills supply issues (see the discussion of MNC skills supply strategies by Ashton Brown and Lauder, this volume Chapter 16) to signal some of the issues. At this stage of the chapter, the review is on the implications of ethnicity for domestic HRM though it should be evident throughout the discussion that as IHRM functions have to cope with greater diversity, many of the issues discussed are generalizable.

Moreover, in the same way that the field of IHRM has slowly been "educated", and in turn tries to educate others, about the workings of culture, we now need to unravel what is implied by ethnicity and how people's thinking about it influences their behavior inside international organizations. What sorts of factors are invoked in the cognition of employees when the issue of ethnic identity comes into play? The following sections show that under the umbrella issue of "diversity", a wide range of HR policy comes under scrutiny and complex attitudes, mindset, and emotions are unleashed. I shall return to the specific issue as it relates to international management later.

Ethnicity research in British HRM

Britain today is irrevocably multiracial. With the influx of immigrants from the countries of the New Commonwealth in the 1950s and 1960s, a new dimension has been added to the tapestry of ethnic relations – that of racial visibility. No longer is Britain a "white" society. The arrival of the Polish, the Ukrainians, and the Jews during the Second World War presented its own ethnic dilemmas. But the advent of large numbers of Indians, Pakistanis, and Bangladeshis from the Indian sub-continent, and Afro-Caribbean from the West Indies has changed the color of life in Britain. Similarly, the USA is a nation of groups as well as individuals. More recently, Britain has experienced large influxes from EU accession countries, again bringing issues of ethnic identity to the fore. These groups vary along a number of dimensions, including size, wealth, education, race, culture, religion, and language (Healey, 2003). Over the past three decades, the number of immigrants arriving in the USA each year has increased from less than 300 000 to almost one million (US Bureau of the Census, 1999: 10).

For black and minority ethnic women, in Western democracies the complex intersection of gender and race creates further constraints on career development. The careers of ethnic minority workers were set against a national concern over racism in British society. This concern was highlighted in the Report on the Stephen Lawrence Inquiry (MacPherson, 1999). However the impact of the inquiry was far wider than this. It stated unequivocally "it is incumbent upon every institution to examine their policies, outcome of such policies and practices to guard against disadvantaging any section of our communities". Indeed the inquiry recognized the pervasiveness and complexity of racism by drawing attention to the discriminatory impact of institutional racism, defined as the collective failure of an organization to provide an appropriate and professional service to people because of their color, culture or ethnic origin which can be seen or detected in processes; attitudes and behavior which amount to discrimination through unwitting prejudice, ignorance, thoughtlessness; and racist stereotyping which disadvantages minority ethnic people (MacPherson, 1999: 6.34).

According to the Commission for Racial Equality (2006), Britain's ethnic minority population has been growing strongly due to high birth rates and net international migration. A study of ethnic minorities in Britain, for example, revealed that, while different ethnic minority groups are differently distributed across the labor market, all are under-represented among employers and managers of large establishments (Modood, 1997).

Research into discrimination both on the grounds of ethnic origin, and of other characteristics such as gender reveals the many forms such unequal treatment may take. In spite of this, it was reported that the white minority/ethnic minority gap in employment rates was reduced from 16.9 to 15.4 percentage points between spring 2003 and spring 2005 (Commission for Racial Equality, 2006). However, a study of Newham Community Health Service found that only two non-executive directors were from ethnic minorities and all the other five executive directors were white (Khan and Cunningham, 1997). A study by McNaught (1994) found out that this lack of appropriate staffing was a contributory factor to inequality of access to health care exemplifying institutional racism, and a demonstration of lack of efficient use of human resources.

Table 21.1 shows ethnic minority employment by region within England. Nearly half of all ethnic minority people in work lived in London in 2004. A further tenth lived in the South East, while West Midlands contained a tenth. The lowest ethnic

TABLE 21.1 Ethnic minority employment, by region 2004.

Country, or Government Office region within England	Regional share of ethnic minorities in work (% of UK)	Ethnic minority employment rate	Ethnic minority share of people in work
England	1.4	59.0	8.2
North East	1.3	59.7	2.3
North West	7.4	51.4	4.6
Yorkshire and Humberside	6.5	53.3	5.5
East Midlands	5.9	62.0	5.6
West Midlands	10.3	55.6	8.3
Eastern	6.0	66.8	4.5
London	46.0	58.4	27.3
South East	10.7	67.4	5.4
South West	2.9	71.8	2.5

Source: Data compiled from Labour Force for spring 2004 to winter 2004/5.

minority employment rate in Britain was found at North West of England (51.4%) and the highest in South West (71.8%).

A recent survey of equal opportunities in the private sector in Scotland found that almost twice as many ethnic minority men and women are "white" and considered that they might have been discriminated against during the recruitment process (Equal Opportunities Commission, 2006). Previously published research by the Commission shows that some minority ethnic groups face greater disadvantage in employment relative to the white majority. There is widespread concern about the impact of this for both individuals and the economy. Minority ethnic women face discrimination on the grounds of both their gender and ethnicity. The political, cultural, and demographic landscape of Scotland means that race and employment issues are significantly different to those of England and Wales. Research on minority ethnic people is limited and fragmented and there is almost no research on minority ethnic women in Scotland (Scottish Executive, 2000).

As noted earlier, a special report on race in the UK appearing in *The Guardian* indicated that research has found that men from ethnic minorities in managerial and professional jobs earn 25% less than their white colleagues (Andalo, 2007). Further, comparable pay scales revealed that black African and Bangladeshi men were likely to face the greatest pay discrimination. Researchers working on behalf of the Joseph Rowntree foundation found ethnic minority women graduates also found it hard to climb the career ladder and employment prospects differed between the ethnic groups. The same paper reported that Warwick University agreed to pay £35 000 in compensation to an Irish academic after a unanimous employment tribunal ruled that it discriminated against her on the grounds of her race (Dyer, 2007). Furthermore, a similar study found that ethnic minorities suffer from economic "apartheid" in Britain, revealing that two-thirds of Pakistani and Bangladeshi children are living in poverty.

The literature that is available on the role of ethnicity in British HRM, then, reveals the complexities involved in analyzing minority ethnic experience. It is clear that 'easy' and narrow cultural assumptions are frequently made about the employment position of minority ethnic women, and references to their social and family roles mask other factors such as workplace discrimination.

Ethnicity research in US HRM

Due to segregation and discrimination in the USA many black African Americans mirror the hostility of whites and as the goals of full racial equality and justice continue to seem remote, frustration and anger continue to run high (Healey, 2003). A nationwide research found that middle-class blacks lag far behind middle class whites in economic resources. Using white collar occupations as their indicator of middle class membership, Oliver and Shapiro (1995) found that the median income of middle class blacks was only about 70% of the median income of middle class whites. Not only is their economic position more marginal, middle-class blacks commonly report that they are unable to escape the narrow straitjacket of race. No matter what their levels of success, occupation or professional accomplishments, race continues to be seen as their primary defining characteristic in the eyes of the larger society (Cose, 1993). Without denying the advances of some, many analysts argue that the stigma of race continues to set sharp limits on the life chances of African Americans.

The story is not different for other minority groups in the USA. For example, Healey (2003) asserts that at the dawn of the 21st century, Native Americans remain among the most disadvantaged, poorest, and most isolated of minority groups. Their present status reflects the long, bitter competition with the dominant group, their colonized origins, and their lengthy exclusion from mainstream society. By the dawn of the 20th century, the situation of Mexican Americans resembled that of Native Americans in some ways. Both groups were small, numbering about one half of 1% of the total population (Cortes, 1980: 702). Both differed from the dominant group in culture and language, and both were impoverished, relatively powerless, and isolated in rural areas distant from the centers of industrialization and modernization. These are just but a few examples of the ethnic composition of the American minority groups because there are Puerto Ricans, Cuban Americans, Latinos, and Caribbean immigrants, and so forth.

Ethnicity research in African HRM

The literature on HRM in Africa tends to argue that ethnicity is a creation of colonization in most African countries and, as such, is tied to the forceful bringing together of various people by colonizers and defining them territorially (Kamoche, 2000; Nyambegera, 2002). This certainly is seen in the case of Kenya and Uganda. Colonizers placed various groups in a hierarchy of racial privileges, rights, and status in politics, economy, and social life. European settlers, for example, maintained a racial supremacy, racial advantages and privileges through a system of monopoly of high potential land, agricultural labor, government services, and most profitable crops (Leys, 1975). Africans at the opposite extreme in the racial divide lived under appalling conditions in poor and congested reserves, overcrowded urban centers, with poor or no government services, and were subjected to extremely poor working conditions, while Asians were mainly shopkeepers.

However, Nyambegera (2002) argues that it is possible that ethnic identities may be as a result of the different practices that are in people's values, concluding that it would be erroneous to assume that ethnic groups have similar cultural practices. Spalding (2000) explains that tension in Nigeria is due to incompatible values and ethnicity and shows why events or ideas may be acceptable or unacceptable. Similarly, in South Africa, black employees subscribed to different work values on the basis of their orientation to either "Western" or "traditional" cultural values bringing about differences in the various ethnic groups (Orpen, 1978).

Ethnicity therefore, manifests itself in many forms in most African countries and within their HRM practices. For example, Kamoche (2000) asserts that favoritism in recruitment and promotion is one such form. Nyambegera (2002) argues that managers cannot afford to overlook the diversity of their human resources and how this influences behavior, because this would affect the promises inherent in HRM if it is not well managed. There is therefore need for the managers to embrace the model of inclusion as opposed to exclusion in its workforce, regardless of their ethnic association to realize the organizational effectiveness.

Horowitz (1985) observed that the growing literature on ethnicity and development is silent on the relationship between foreign direct investment or foreign aid and ethnic interests. Analytical arguments are beginning to emerge that contend that ethnicity is an important factor leading to inadequate policies, wasted foreign aid resources and limited economic resources. For example a recent World Bank study argues that Africa's ethnic diversity tends to slow growth and reduce the likelihood of adopting good policies and that high diversity may lead to increased strife, political instability, and destructive competitions by ethnic factions (World Bank, 2006).

Oucho (2002) similarly contends that most countries are locked in ethnic conflicts. The challenge is even greater as many of the former British colonies in Africa, Asia and Pacific are each battling ethnic crises in which land is the core issue in relation to economic performance and the welfare of the people. Roosens (1989) and Kandeh (1992) also observe that ethnicity has to do with material goods, whether in a negative or positive way. This has been seen in the case of Sierra Leone, where state and class formation led to the development of ethno-political identities, making some ethnic groups feel superior as they were allowed to enjoy particular privileges such as employment.

Nyambegera (2002) argues that the colonizers theoretically treated all ethnic groups as equals however, the colonial patrimonial of the divide and rule approach to colonial governance and the emergence of the intermediary class to facilitate extraction and maintain order tended to give the advantage of the elite from the numerically dominated group. For Obi (2001) ethnic groupings in African organizations play a role in the exclusion of talented and capable people. Oucho (2002) asserts for example that the diversity of Kenya's ethnic structure has aroused feelings of "tribe" and race. The term "tribalism" has become so ingrained in the Kenyan society, whether in official discussions or in general statements, that, historically, it was by no means offensive and was part of the country's rich political complexity. Events in 2008 were to change this perception. This is a clear example of how ethnicity can be susceptible to political manipulation where those in positions of authority have done this to establish and maintain political power.

Oucho (2002) points out that those racial hierarchies and constitutional debates are often limited to demanding rights and privileges that the other race possesses, or to its corollary of removing constraints on lesser privileged racial groups. Indeed as the constitutional debates raged in Kenya in the 1950s, racial tensions were drawn into the conflicts around the constitution that pitched European settlers, African, Asians and Arabs, as racial groups in opposing and contentious positions with regard to their location in any constitutional agreement. The wave of democratic political change led to the identification of democracy in terms of multi-party politics. The drive toward Western liberal democracy engendered the polarization of particularistic groupings, as parties crystallized, mostly on the basis of ethnic and regional interests rather than common ideology or political principles.

According to Holmquist (2002) the historical roots of ethnic and racial divisions in Kenyan society were, in part, as a result of unequal patterns of historical capital accumulation. Kamoche (2000: 143) observed, before events were eventually to demonstrate, that managers in some organizations in Kenya acknowledged that ethnicity was a potential source of conflict. The inequalities between identity groups have a lot to do with the nature of business–government relations and the relative proximity of certain ethnic and racial categories to government power. These divisions within society and the business community are deep, despite arenas of cooperation and common interests among them. Historically uneven capital accumulation between ethnic, racial, and national communities, also means that each defines its interests differently *vis-à-vis* government policy.

According to Kamoche *et al.* (2004) an era of multi-party politics in Kenya was accompanied by wideranging economic reforms and liberalization. While this created a new sense of confidence and hope for a better future, free of the oppressive antics of the erstwhile one party state, in reality, the county remained under the control of an administration that was still steeped in the old ways characterized by lack of accountability, endemic corruption, and a token of knowledge of democracy. Holmquist (2002) asserts that the Kenyan African capital is far from homogeneous; one of the most striking recent comments about the trajectory of investment by the Kikuyu and Kalenjin was that there may be a trend toward pulling back into regional ethnic blocks, a kind of *majimbo* (regionalism-by-investment) pattern because of chronic state-sanctioned ethnic cleansing and a high level of ethnic tension.

The above analysis shows the complex institutional forces at play in an African context. Racial discrimination in organizations is institutionalized at key stages in the employment process (recruitment and selection, reward systems, working time, equal treatment, training, promotion, redundancy), such that personnel systems and procedures, as well as other structures and practices within organizations, embed barriers to the creation of equal opportunities (Healey, 2003).

At the center of this issue, the institutionalization of ethnicity is practiced. Politicians may use their ethnicity as a tool for political brinkmanship. All around the world, the talk among political leaders is about what any one of them can bring to the table, which is a subtle way of asking how many people they can marshal during elections. Many political decisions become based on ethnicity and not on ideology. Coalitions are formed and broken not on the account of what particular leaders stand for, but purely on the basis of the ethnic votes each can mobilize. What is emerging is a case of political domination of the minority communities by the majority groups. Most of the practices are brought about by the politicization of the public sector labor market, and the lack of respect for professionalism. This is manifested through the ethnicization of recruitment and promotions, as brought by the colonial administrative technique of divide and rule, which served as a tool for subduing and controlling indigenous populations. However, the practice has outlasted active colonial rule and now permeates the neo-colonial state in the form of ethnicity (tribalism) and/or nepotism (Mulinge and Munyae, 2000; Nyambegera, 2002).

Understanding the Impact of Ethnicity on Organization and Employee Management

The element of "difference" with regard to ethnicity has implications for the design and implementation of equality policies within human resource departments. Brewster *et al.* (2007) show how countries differ in terms of culture and institutional functioning, noting that a clear understanding of this is needed by international human resource managers. What does the above review of cross-national approaches to ethnicity show us?

Cross-national understandings of ethnicity

The discussion of African ethnicity above shows that it manifests itself through tribalism in recruitment, employment, and training by giving preference to kith and kin (e.g., Blunt, 1980). Ethnicity in Africa also manifests through the culture of exclusion – "the local versus foreigner mentality". In spite of this awareness, very little has been done to tackle the apparent problems brought about by ethnicity in African organizations, except in South Africa, where attempts at reconciliation prompted affirmative action in employment and other spheres of society. This phenomenon is brought about by the group orientation of most African states from where individuals derive their identity by belonging to communities, clans, and tribes, whose norms and values come first (see, for example, Nyambegera *et al.*, 2000). In most cases Africans in employment are expected to assist their kith and kin in securing jobs, which ends up with organizations being filled with people of particular ethnic groups (e.g., Nzelibe, 1986; Kamoche *et al.*, 2004). Authors on HRM in Africa recommend that Western management concepts should be relevant to this context by considering the constraints faced by organizations in these environments (e.g., Kamoche, 1997).

European traditions of negative ethnicity mean that it is experienced through discrimination in employment. Certain jobs cannot be given to certain ethnic groups. The Joseph Rowntree Foundation found that black Africans and Bangladeshis, in spite of good qualifications, are judged on the basis of their color in employment. Further, the foundation reported that ethnic minority groups are being overlooked for jobs and paid lower wages (Dodd, 2007). Ethnicity on religious grounds is experienced in certain areas of Europe, for example, Catholics versus Protestants (Northern Ireland) and Christians versus Muslims (former Yugoslavia). White supremacy organizations which discriminate people on the basis of the color of their skin are found in Russia, Germany, and France.

In the USA ethnicity is fostered through encouraging different wages for different races. Ethnicity in Asia is manifested through the caste system entrenched in the Hindu culture, where mankind is born into a social strata and remains there. In the Middle East, the slave mentality toward some races is still prevalent. However, in Japan, ethnic homogeneity is a major force for economic progress (Taplin, 1995). Similar arguments are empirically presented by Blunt (1980), i.e., that ethnic homogeneity in organizations does not have only negative consequences – in certain circumstances it can lead to organizational effectiveness.

Ethnic assimilation

What is known about the issue of ethnic – as opposed to cultural – assimilation? I use studies from America – ostensibly one of the cultural and ethnic melting pots of the world – as an example to show the different forces at play. These studies seem to indicate that minority ethnic groups have "almost" been assimilated, or are currently being acculturated. Healey (2003) points out that the extent of acculturation of Asian Americans is highly variable from group to group. Japanese Americans represent one extreme because they have been part of the American society for more than a century, and the current generations are highly acculturated. This, Healey argues is because immigration from Japan has been low throughout the century and has not revitalized the traditional culture or language. As a result, Japanese Americans are probably the most acculturated of the Asian American groups. Other extremes are groups such as Vietnamese Americans, who are still in the first generation and have scarcely had time to learn the American culture and the English language. In between are groups such as the Chinese Americans; some with roots in the US going back even farther than the Japanese Americans, and some are newcomers.

Healey (2003) argues that in such areas as jobs and income, success and equality of the Asian Americans as a single category is sustained. Studies indicate that both males and females are over-represented in the highest occupations of managerial and professional groups, which is a reflection of the high levels of educational attainment for the group. The Bureau of the Census (2003) shows that, in particular, Chinese, Japanese, and Indian Americans tend to be over-represented at the highest level of the workforce. However, a high percentage of some Asian groups are concentrated in low-paying jobs in the service sector and in the unskilled labor force. In terms of poverty, Asian Americans as a whole rank between non-Hispanic whites and the racial and colonized minority groups.

The economic situation of Hispanic Americans, however, is much more mixed. Many members of these groups, especially those who have been in the United States for several generations, are doing "just fine. They have, in ever-increasing numbers, accessed opportunities in education and employment and have carved out a niche of American prosperity for themselves, and their children" (Camarillo and Bonilla, 2001: 130-131). However, Healey (2003) notes that Mexican Americans, Puerto Ricans, and Cubans are under-represented in the highest status jobs and over-represented in unskilled jobs. Unemployment, low income, and poverty continue to be issues for all the three Hispanic groups. The unemployment rates for Hispanic Americans run about twice the rate for non-Hispanic whites, and the poverty rates for the groups as a whole are comparable to those of African Americans (Camarillo and Bonilla, 2001: 110-111).

Healey (2003: 255-256) describes the state of African Americans in very graphical detail. It is clear that at the dawn of the 20th century, African Americans were a southern rural peasantry, victimized by segregation *de jure*, enmeshed in the share-cropping system of agriculture, and blocked from the better-paying industrial and manufacturing jobs in urban areas. Segregation had disenfranchised them and stripped them of the legal and civil rights they briefly enjoyed during reconstruction. The huge majority of African Americans had limited access to quality education; few political rights; few occupational choices; and few vehicles for expressing their views, grievances, and concerns.

Today, at the beginning of the 21st century, African Americans are highly urbanized, dispersed throughout the United States, and represented in virtually every occupational grouping. Members of the group are visible at the highest levels of American society, from the Supreme Court to corporate boardrooms and in the most prestigious universities. African Americans have become an urban minority group, and the fate of the group is inextricably bound by the fate of America's cities. Automation and mechanization in the workplace have eliminated many of the manual labor jobs that sustained city dwellers in earlier decades and mainly African Americans (Kasarda, 1989). The manufacturing, or secondary segment of the labor force has declined in size, while the service sector has continued to expand. The desirable jobs in the service sector have increasingly demanding educational prerequisites affecting African Americans in terms of representation. The service sector jobs available to people with lower educational credentials often pay low wages and offer no benefits, no security, and no links to more rewarding occupations. This form of past-in-present institutional discrimination constitutes a powerful handicap for colonized groups and African Americans who have been excluded from educational opportunities for centuries. These are clear challenges for any international human resource manager operating in such circumstances.

IMPLICATIONS FOR IHRM AND THE FUTURE RESEARCH AGENDA

From the studies reviewed, it is clear that research has tended not to draw upon theory, or attempt to build theory. What then can be done that will help researchers to start using and developing theory? I argue that four things are important.

First, for HRM in general, as well as for the fields of IHRM and organizational psychology, developing useful theory around ethnicity is becoming an important challenge. This can only be done, however, by rejecting absolute notions or essentialism and recognizing the lack of basic divisions between humans on the basis of skin color and physiognomy (Richards, 1997). Through examining the roles and meanings that ethnicity plays within contemporary society and organizational life, we can begin to develop more specific ideas about how ethnicity might impact on the careers and workplace experiences of individuals.

Second, there is much potentially useful theory about understanding ethnicity outside the fields of employment, management, and organizational psychology that could usefully be adopted and in some cases adapted. What we can gain from such work is a more 'rounded' view of ethnicity – conceptualizing it as a phenomenon not only related potentially to the experience of discrimination, but also as a *subjective identity*. Ethnicity can be seen as potentially influential not only in terms of how the individual is perceived and treated within the organization, but also in terms of how and when the individual conceptualizes his or her 'ethnic self' and how that is subsequently relevant to experiences at work. The links to the research on culture (see Sackmann, this volume Chapter 4) by researchers such as Sackmann and Philips (2004) and Erez and Gati (2004) is clear here. In understanding identity fusion, we can look at how different dimensions have a bearing upon behavior. For example, by looking at ethnicity alongside gender (see also De Cieri, this volume Chapter 10) we can learn how the two identities combine to influence workplace experiences. Other elements of identity such as social class, age, nationality and so forth can also at times be usefully included in studies on ethnicity at work.

Third, extra-organizational processes (such as structural inequalities, the availability of social capital) and their potential impacts on what takes place within an organization (such as stereotyping, discrimination, and power relations) are also factors that should be included in theorizing about ethnicity in organizations. Ogbonna (1998) and Burchell (1992), for example, both make reference to the potential impact of external variables on the perceptions that individuals may hold of their chances of succeeding in the labor market. The relationships between events and processes in wider society, the organization, the small group and the individual, are all key to understanding the role played by ethnicity in organizations.

Fourth, in developing theory, there is a very specific and urgent need to gain a clearer understanding of the role played by discrimination in organizations. Organizations, as microcosms of society, are likely to reproduce practices that result in unfair outcomes for individuals from minority ethnic groups. Hence, understanding discrimination requires us to look beyond explaining differences in assessment scores, as discrimination is likely to play a major role in the experiences and actions of minority ethnic individuals.

Diversity has become an increasingly important factor in organizations as the workforce and general population has become more heterogeneous in ethnicity, age, gender and so forth. Indeed, within the field of IHRM exactly what is meant by diversity has become a central debate. It is about diversity of mindset. Organizations in Europe and the US have recognized diversity's impact and put in place polices that protect such diversity (Cassell, 1996; Dass and Parker, 1999; Lawrence,

2000). It is recognized that managing diversity as one approach that furthers equal opportunities could be a source of improving organizational effectiveness (Cassell and Biswas, 2000). Diversity presents particular challenges for future international human resource managers. Employees from a broad range of cultures and different backgrounds are present in the workforce owing to the waves of migration and have a significant influence on the cultural, economic, and social changes in communities and organizations.

A central point being made in this chapter is that by examining the "ethnicized order" in organizations, the importance of bringing ethnicity into our understanding of comparative and employment management – and now I would also argue for the field of IHRM – becomes clear. Literature on ethnicity indicates a rigidity of racist practices, which despite much rhetoric, organizations are failing to address. It is time for employers to acknowledge the ethnic factor in employment and the manner in which material conflicts can be articulated in identity terms. There are different types of multi-ethnic societies, ranging from plural post-colonial societies characterized by relatively independent, strong groups, to post-slavery societies. Therefore the state and the labor from these different types of societies should reflect the social formation in which they are part. Ethnic identity cannot be written off just as unauthentic perception a diversion to the analysis based on the labor process. Instead, ethnic identity has to be seen as part of the terrain of labor capital conflict and corporation, which can be used as a resource for boundary definition, that enables and disables political mobilization.

Clearly, more research is needed to understand the effects of ethnicity. The following are some of the gaps that are recommended to advance this cause. There is a strong need to conduct research within organizational settings which concerns itself with the effect of the organizational context on how minority ethnic employees experience their careers (such as that by Ross, 2004). Most of the work conducted to date has not focused on the role of organizational contexts in the experience of ethnicity.

Globalization is one such context. Understanding how an individual's beliefs about agency are brought to bear has become increasingly important for four reasons:

1. Global interconnectedness means that forces operating remotely now produce local effects in cultures.
2. Some transnational market forces may be perceived as eroding or undermining valued cultural aspects of life.
3. Technological developments, such as the internet, are changing the dynamics and opportunity for personal agency.
4. Mass transnational migrations of people seeking a better life are creating further intracultural diversity and new hybrid cultural forms.

Research should be directed at understanding the psychosocial determinants of cultural behavior, and the governing mechanisms that regulate these. Ethnicity plays a part in both. The question that needs to be answered is: How do humans function as individuals, despite the cultural embeddedness of their behavior?

In this context, issues relating to diversity and organizational climate and culture have not been fully covered (Hicks-Clarke and Iles, 2000; Wilson, 2000), and more strenuous efforts need to be made to seek out samples that include higher numbers of minority ethnic employees to make the results of such research more meaningful in relation to issues of ethnic diversity. Most of the research reviewed focuses either on non-professionals or on employees in general and does not sufficiently illuminate the role of qualification/skill level in the workplace experiences of minority ethnic employees. More evidence is required to understand the situation of minority ethnic professionals more generally. With the numbers of minority ethnic graduates increasing, this issue is likely to become more salient. There is also a need to research the experiences of minority ethnic professionals in order to understand the impact of societal factors on a group with high-level skills and qualifications. These individuals potentially straddle two worlds:

+ a privileged position within the labor market due to their skills and qualifications, and
+ a potentially less privileged position because of their ethnicity.

Developing an understanding of how such individuals experience and navigate an environment that may potentially provide them with these two conflicting experiences is of considerable value in terms of our gaining a greater understanding of how ethnicity might impact on the way organizations are experienced.

Research carried out so far also indicates that there is a distinct lack of qualitative studies of minority ethnic workers within an organizational context. It will not be possible to get a full understanding of how minority ethnic workers experience the workplace if such research is not conducted. The type of qualitative research that is needed is that which seeks to gain a better understanding of how the individual has experienced or is experiencing the workplace and what impact that might have on his or her perceptions and employment behavior. Methods such as life history, in-depth interviews and the critical incident technique might be useful for helping researchers to gain broader insights into the role and experience of ethnicity within organizations.

Minority people come from a range of different backgrounds, face different forms of stereotyping, and display differences in class and cultural backgrounds (Jenkins, 1986; Pang, 1996). These factors are likely to impact on the way different ethnic groups are treated within the labor market or workplace and may help to account for the differences in the levels of workplace discrimination perceived by different ethnic groups (Modood and Berthoud, 1997). On the whole, existing research fails to explore these potential differences. Therefore, as well as recognizing the diversity within ethnic groups, researchers should be conscious of the potential differences between ethnic groups in the way ethnicity is experienced within organizations.

The effect of ethnicity is not well documented, particularly as it impacts on employment relations, especially in Africa. Although some attention has been given to the ethnic impact on recruitment and selection in such countries as Kenya (e.g., Blunt, 1980), and a call for more research in Sub-Saharan Africa (e.g., Nyambegera,

2002), very little attention has been given to managing the diversity apparent in work organizations in Africa.

More research needs to be carried out in the area of effectiveness of diverse and homogeneous work groups, as demonstrated in the USA (see, for example, Cox, 1992). It is notable that most IHRM literature focuses on cultural homogenization which, in a sense, translates into support for ethnic homogeneity though contradictory to diversity interventions. Researchers have not given workable solutions to guide practitioners operating in the diversely ethnic countries like those in Africa and Asia.

There is also a strong need to conduct research within organizational settings and research which concerns itself with the effect of the organizational context on how minority ethnic employees experience their careers (see, for example, Ross, 2004). Most of the work done to date has not focused on the role of organizational contexts in the experience of ethnicity. US diversity researchers have indicated the importance of variables such as organizational climate (e.g., Dass and Parker, 1999) and the impact it can have on how organizations are experienced by minority ethnic employees and the extent to which they feel genuinely valued and accepted.

CONCLUSION

Ethnicity is a double-edged sword. On one hand, ethnic groups promote the forces of modernization; phrased more fashionably, they constitute a form of social capital. But this social capital may be extremely limited in its power and influence. For example, in the United States minorities are linked in a fictitious unity. They are part of the same structures but are separated by lines of color and culture; long histories of exploitation and unfairness. This society owes its prosperity and position of prominence in the world no less to the labor of minority groups than to that of the dominant group (Healey, 2003). By harnessing the labor and energy of these minority groups, the nation has grown prosperous and powerful, but the benefits have flowed disproportionately to the dominant group. There is a similar situation in the United Kingdom. Minority group progress has stalled well short of equality, however, and the patterns of poverty, discrimination, marginality, homelessness, and despair continues to limit the lives of millions. The recent debates about the new wave of immigrants and their role in the economic well-being of the country has also brought to the surface uncomfortable truths about the broader operation of the labor market and the role of ethnicity within it.

Managers therefore, need to recognize the impact of ethnicity, since it is clear that groups can be very brutal toward one another. On the one hand, they can promote urban migration and education, and ethnic groups may advance the private fortunes of their members. Furthermore, ethnic groups may organize politically and occasionally engage in acts of violence, destroying wealth and discouraging the formation of capital. Ethnic groups can thus both generate benefits and inflict costs on societies. There is therefore a need to move from exclusion of the most talented people to inclusion, which ultimately is the best approach as this will embrace diversity and increase organizational effectiveness.

Organizations have to base managing diverse groups on both a business case (Ross and Schneider, 1992) and deliberate HRM policies of inclusion (Wilson, 2000). The business case's emphasis is on proper utilization of the skills and potentials of all employees, regardless of race, ethnicity, age, and gender, which links issues of managing diversity to strategic HRM (Storey, 1995). Managers must learn to value difference and to manage such difference, as it is an essential element in an organization's culture and values. Organizations in diverse ethnic communities could attempt a recipe of both equal opportunities and the new concept of managing diversity to increase organizational effectiveness and edge out a strategic competitive advantage.

It is evident that ethnicity has not been given enough attention, and hence it would be helpful if researchers examined more fully its impact on employment relations. If organizations adopted the approaches of equal opportunity and, even better, managing diversity, this might help in dealing with issues embedded in their local context, consequently leading to organizational effectiveness and harmony. What is also clear is that after more than 50 years of published research concerning ethnicity, we are still a long way from having well-developed or comprehensive explanations of it, or data about how ethnicity impacts upon individuals within organizations. It is also not possible to measure and judge individuals who are different from each other unless we have a fuller understanding of what such differences mean in different contexts and how their differing positions within society affects how they experience the workplace. Ethnicity is too bound up within the experience of living in the wider society to be studied solely as a psychological phenomenon.

REFERENCES

Andalo, D. (2007). Ethnic minorities blocked from top jobs. *The Guardian.* http://www.guardian.co.uk/race/story/0,,2068948,00.html.

Banton, M. (2000). Ethnic conflict. *Sociology,* 34 (3), 481–498.

Blunt, P. (1980). Bureaucracy and ethnicity in Kenya: Some conjectures of the eighties. *Journal of Applied Behavioural Science,* 16 (3), 336–353.

Brewster, C., Sparrow, P.R., and Vernon, G (2007). *International Human Resource Management.* London: Chartered Institute of Personnel and Development.

Burchell, B. (1992). Towards a social psychology of the labour market: Or why we need to understand the labour market before we can understand unemployment. *Journal of Occupational and Organizational Psychology,* 65 (4), 345–354.

Bureau of the Census (2003). *We the American Asians.* Washington: US Department of Commerce.

Camarillo, A., and Bonilla, F. (2001). Hispanics in a multicultural society: A new American dilemma? In N. Smelser, W. Wilson, and F. Mitchell (eds), *American Becoming: Racial Trends and Their Consequences* (Vol. 2). Washington, DC: National Academy Press, pp. 103–134.

Cassell, C., and Biswas, R. (2000). Editorial: Managing diversity in the new millennium. *Personnel Review,* 29 (3), 268–73.

Cassell, C.M. (1996). A fatal attraction? Strategic HRM and the business case for women's progression at work. *Personnel Review,* 25 (5), 51–66.

Commission of Racial Equality (2006). *The reception and integration of new migrant communities.* London: CRE.

Cortes, C. (1980). Mexicans. In S. Thornstrom (ed.), *Harvard Encyclopedia of Ethnic Groups.* Cambridge, MA: Harvard University Press, pp. 697–719.

Cose, E. (1993). *The Rage of a Privileged Class.* New York: Harper Collins.

Coughlan, R., and Samarasinghe, S. (1991). *Economic Dimensions of Ethnic Conflict: International Perspectives.* London: Inter Publishers.

Cox, T. Jr (1992). The multi-cultural organization. *Academy of Management Executive,* 5 (2), 23–40.

Dass, P., and Parker, B. (1999) Strategies for managing human resource diversity: From resistance to learning. *The Academy of Management Executive,* 13 (2), 68–84.

Deng, F.M. (1997). Ethnicity: An African predicament. *Brookings Review,* 15 (3), 28–31.

Dodd, V. (2007). Report finds 'economic apartheid', *The Guardian.* http://www.guardian .co.uk/race/story/0,,2068553,00.html.

Dyer, C. (2007). University agrees to pay 35,000 pounds after losing discrimination case. *The Guardian.* http://www.guardian.co.uk/race/story/0,,2063308,00.html.

Equal Opportunities Commission (2006). *Facts about Women and Men in Scotland 2006.* Manchester: EOC.

Erez, M., and Gati, E. (2004). A dynamic, multi-level model of culture: From the micro level of the individual to the macro level of a global culture. *Applied Psychology: An International Review,* 53 (4), 583–598.

Erez, P., and Earley, R. (1997). *Culture, Self-Identity and Work.* New York: Harper-Collins Press.

Greenhaus, J., Parasuraman, S., and Wormley, W. (1990). Effects of race on organizational experience, job performance evaluation, and career outcomes. *Academy of Management Journal,* 33 (1), 64–86.

Hannon, J., Huang, I.-C., and Jaw, B.-S. (1995). International human resource management and its determinants: The case of subsidiaries in Taiwan. *Journal of International Business Studies,* 26 (3), 531–554.

Healey, F. (2003). *Race, Ethnicity, Gender, and Class: The Sociology of Group Conflict and Change* (3rd edn). Thousand Oaks, California: Pine Forge Press.

Hicks-Clarke, D., and Iles, P. (2000). Climate for diversity and the effects on career and organizational attitudes and perceptions. *Personnel Review,* 29 (3), 324–45.

Hofstede, G. (1980). *Culture's Consequences: International Differences in Work-Related Values.* Beverly Hills, CA: Sage.

Holmquist, F. (2002). *Business and politics in Kenya.* Occasional Paper – Center of African Studies. University of Copenhagen.

Horowitz, D.L. (1985). *The Ethnic Revival.* London: Cambridge University Press.

Jenkins, R. (1986). *Racism in Recruitment.* London: Cambridge University Press.

Kamoche, K.N. (1997). Managing human resources in Africa: Strategic, organizational and epistemological issues. *International Business Review,* 6, 537–558.

Kamoche, K.N. (2000). *Sociological Paradigms and Human Resource: An African Context.* Aldershot: Ashgate.

Kamoche, K.N., Nyambegera, S.M., and Munyae, M.M. (2004). HRM in Kenya. In K.N. Kamoche, Y. Debrah, F. Horwitz and G.K.I. Muuka (eds), *Managing Human Resources in Africa.* London: Routledge, pp. 87–101.

Kandeh, J.D. (1992). Politicization of ethnic identities in Sierra Leone. *African Studies Review,* 35 (1), 81–99.

Kasarda, J.D. (1989). Urban industrial transition and the underclass. *Annals of the American Academy,* 501, 26–47.

Khan, T., and Cunningham, C. (1997). A matter of interpretation. *Health Service.*

Kihlstrom, J.F., and Cantor, N. (1987). *Personality and Social Intelligence.* New York: Prentice Hall.

Lawrence, E. (2000). Equal opportunities officers and managing equality changes. *Personnel Review*, 29 (3), 381–401.

Leys, C. (1975). *Underdevelopment in Kenya: The Political Economy of Neo-Colonialism 1964–1971.* London: Heinemann.

MacPherson, W. (1999). *The Stephen Lawrence Inquiry.* London: The Stationery Office.

Marger, M.N. (1994). *Race and Ethnic Relations: American and Global Perspectives.* California: Wadsworth.

Mason, D. (2000). *Race and Ethnicity in Modern Britain.* Oxford: Oxford University Press.

Mayrhofer, W., Sparrow, P.R., and Zimmermann, A. (2008). Modern forms of international working. In M. Dickmann, C. Brewster and P.R. Sparrow (eds), *International Human Resource Management: A European Perspective.* London: Routledge, pp. 219–239.

McNaught, A. (1994). A discriminating service: The socio-economic and scientific roots of racial discrimination in /the National Health Service. *Journal of Professional Care*, 8 (2).

Modood, T. (1997). Employment. In T. Modood and R. Berthoud (eds), *Ethnic Minorities in Britain: Diversity and Disadvantage*, London: Policy Studies Institute.

Modood, T., and Berthoud, R. (1997). *Ethnic Minorities in Britain: Diversity and Disadvantage.* London: Policy Studies Institute.

Mulinge, M.M., and Munyae, M.M. (2000). The ethnicisation of the State and the crisis of African development: The Kenyan experience. *Journal of Cultural Studies*, 2 (1), 141–159.

Nyambegera, S.M. (2002). Ethnicity and human resource management practice in sub-Saharan Africa: The relevance of managing diversity discourse. *International Journal of Human Resource Management*, 13 (7), 1077–1090.

Nyambegera, S.M., Sparrow, P., and Daniels, K. (2000). The impact of cultural value orientations on individual HRM preferences in developing countries: Lessons form Kenyan organizations. *International Journal of Human Resource Management*, 11 (4), 639–663.

Nzelibe, L.O. (1986) The evolution of African management thought. *International Studies of Management and Organization*, 16 (2), 6–16.

Obi, C.I. (2001). *Changing Forms of Identity Politics in Nigeria.* Göteborg: Elanders Digitaltryck AB.

Ogbonna, E. (1998). British ethnic minorities and employment training: Redressing or extending disadvantage. *International Journal of Training and Development*, 2 (1), 28–41.

Oliver, M., and Shapiro, T. (1995). *Black Wealth, White Wealth.* New York: Routledge.

Orpen, C. (1978). The work values of western and tribal black employees. *Journal of Cross-cultural Psychology*, 9 (1), 99–112.

Osaghae, E. (1995). *Structural adjustment and ethnicity in Nigeria.* Research Report No. 98, Uppsala: The Nordic Africa Institute.

Oucho, J.O. (2002). *Undercurrents of Ethnic Conflict in Kenya.* Netherlands: Koninklijke Brill, NV.

Pang, M.Y.N. (1996). Barriers perceived by young Chinese adults to their employment in companies in the UK. *International Journal of Human Resource Management*, 7 (4), 891–904.

Perkins, A.G. (1993). Diversity. *Harvard Business Review*, 71 (5), 14.

Pilkington, A. (2003). *Racial Disadvantage and Ethnic Diversity in Britain.* Basingstoke: Palgrave Macmillan.

Richards, G. (1997). *Race and Racism in Psychology: Towards a Reflexive History.* London: Routledge.

Roosens, E.E. (1989). *Creating Ethnicity: The Process of Ethnogensis.* Newbury, CA: Sage.

Rosenzweig, P.M., and Nohria, N. (1994). Influences on human resource management practices in multinational corporations. *Journal of International Business Studies*, 25, 229–251.

Ross, C. (2004). Ethic minority personnel careers: Hindrances and hopes. *Personnel Review*, 33 (4), 468–484.

Ross, R., and Schneider, R. (1992). *From Diversity to Equality: A Business Case for Equal Opportunities*. London: Pitman.

Sackmann, S.A., and Phillips, M.E. (2004). Contextual influences on culture research: Shifting assumptions for new workplace realities. *International Journal of Cross Cultural Management*, 4 (3), 370–390.

Schneider, B. (1987). The people make the place. *Personnel Psychology*, 40, 437–56.

Scottish Executive (2000). *Equality Strategy: working together for equality*. Edinburgh: Scottish Executive.

Simpson, G., and Yinger, J.M. (1985). *Racial and Cultural Minorities: An Analysis of Prejudice and Discrimination* (5th edn). New York: Plenum Press.

Smith, A.D. (1981). *The Revival of Ethnicity in the Modern World*. London: Cambridge University Press.

Spalding, N. (2000). A cultural explanation of collapse into civil war: Escalation of tension in Nigeria'. *Culture and Psychology*, 6 (1), 51–87.

Sparrow, P.R (2006). International management: Key challenges for industrial and organizational psychology. In G. Hodginson and J.K. Ford (eds), *International Review of Industrial and Organizational Psychology*, Vol 21. Chichester: John Wiley & Sons, pp. 189–266.

Storey, J. (1995). *Human Resource Management: A Critical Text*. London: Thompson Business.

Taplin, R. (1995). *Decision Making in Japan*. Richmond, Surrey: Curzon Press.

US Bureau of the Census (1999). Historical Census Statistics on the Foreign-born Population of the United States: 1850–1990. Population Division Working Paper No. 29. Washington: US Department of Commerce.

Wilson, E. (2000). Inclusion, exclusion and ambiguity: The role of organizational culture. *Personnel Review*, 29 (3), 274–303.

World Bank (2006). World Development Report 2006. Washington: World Bank.

22

Shaping History: Global Leadership in the 21st Century

We have a responsibility in our time, as others have had in theirs, not to be prisoners of history, but to shape history. . .
                              —Former US Secretary of State Madeleine K. Albright (1997)

INTRODUCTION

Shaping history is the challenge of global leadership – creating a 21st century in which organizations enhance, rather than diminish, civilization. Cooperrider and Adler (2006) have produced the concept paper behind this describing the Global Forum on Business as an Agent of World Benefit: Management Knowledge Leading Positive Change co-sponsored by the Academy of Management and the United Nations Global Compact. For global leaders, economic viability is necessary, but is no longer sufficient for organizational, let alone societal, success. And success? None of us can claim that the 20th century left a legacy of worldwide success – a success defined by peace, prosperity, compassion, and sustainability. When reflecting on our children's inheritance from the 20th century, we may feel discouraged and shamed. Yes, we have advanced science and technology, but at the price of a world torn asunder by a polluted environment, cities infested with social chaos and physical decay, an increasingly skewed income distribution that condemns large portions of the population to poverty (including people living in the world's most affluent societies), and rampant physical violence that continues to kill people in ostensibly limited wars and seemingly random acts of aggression. No, society could not exit

*This chapter is a revised and updated version of a chapter originally published in Burke, R.J. and Cooper, C.L. (eds) (2002). *Leading in Turbulent Times*. Oxford: Blackwell Publishers, pp. 302–318.

Handbook of International Human Resource Management.   Edited by Paul R. Sparrow
© 2009 John Wiley & Sons, Ltd

the 20th century with pride. Unless we collectively learn to treat each other and our planet in a more civilized way, it may soon become blasphemy to even consider ourselves as a civilization (Rechtschaffen, 1996).

ENTERING THE 21ST CENTURY

As the 20th century has become history, have the events of the opening decade of the 21st century encouraged us? Unfortunately, no. If anything, many economic and societal trends appear to be heading in the wrong direction. We need look no further than the events of September 2001 to be humbled into silence, if not despair. Review just a few of the facts from that fateful month.

September 2001 opened with the UN-sponsored World Conference Against Racism in Durban, South Africa. The official title of the UN Conference was the United Nations' World Conference Against Racism, Racial Discrimination, Xenophobia and Related Intolerance. As the world watched with high expectations, the conference drowned in a cacophony of intolerance, expressed by official delegates from more than 160 countries as well as by thousands of representatives of non-governmental organizations. 'The meeting, which was intended to celebrate tolerance and diversity, became an international symbol of divisiveness...' (Swarms, 2001: A1). According to the world press, the results reflected 'less a new international unity than a collective exhaustion' (Slackman, 2001: A1).

One week later, on September 11, terrorists destroyed the World Trade Center and parts of the Pentagon, killing over 3000 people. In the immediate aftermath, while stock markets plummeted, public rhetoric and behavior became increasingly susceptible to simplistic definitions of good and evil and calls for large-scale military retaliation. The escalation of ignorance-based hatred attempting to pit the Western world against Islamic communities and nations became palpable. Perhaps the danger, absurdity, and pain can be best symbolized by the fate of a woman living far from both Durban and the World Trade Center. As the woman, a Montreal doctor, made her usual hospital rounds the week after the terrorist attacks, she was strangled. Why? Strictly because she is Muslim. Her status as a physician and good citizen, working daily to save the lives of her fellow human beings, was obliterated in the eyes of her attacker solely because she wore a headscarf that symbolizes a religion he failed to understand.

Hate and intolerance, optimism reduced to hopelessness, compassion eclipsed by anger, ignorance motivating senseless action: Is this the scenario that will define the 21st century; that will define our children's and our children's children's future? Possibly, but hopefully not. Hope for a better future rests largely with the quality of business, political, and societal leadership offered by women and men worldwide.

Although from the perspective of September 2001 it seems otherwise, the 21st century need not become just a time of terrorism, intolerance, fear, and deteriorating economic conditions. It also could herald an era of unprecedented worldwide prosperity, communication, and creativity; led in large part by global companies and organizations (Friedman, 2006).

The ability of global companies to work successfully across cultures, however, while better than the track record of participants at UN-sponsored racism conferences, remains problematic. Historically, three-quarters of all international joint ventures fail according to an A.T. Kearney study reported in Haebeck *et al.* (2000) and in Schuler and Jackson (2001). The same study, as cited by Schuler and Jackson, concludes that 'only 15 per cent of mergers and acquisitions in the US achieve their objectives, as measured by share value, return on investment and post-combination profitability' (for research on the instability of international joint ventures, see the review by Yan and Zeng, 1999). Although the definitions (complete termination versus significant change of ownership) and overall results vary, numerous studies have reported substantial international joint venture instability, including 55% termination reported by Harrigan (1988), 49% termination reported by Barkema and Vermeulen (1997), and 68% instability through termination or acquisition reported by Park and Russo (1996).

One wonders, at times, why societies choose to continue to become more globally interconnected and companies choose to continue to expand beyond their borders, when the track record of global cross-cultural relations remains so dismal. For a notable exception to this track record, see the description of the Norway-based global company, Norske Skog, in Adler (2003). Weaving the peoples of the world together, whether in companies or in society at large, is clearly not easy. Our current approaches beg for new – or perhaps ancient-but-forgotten – perspectives. Is it not possible to imagine a world defined by peace and prosperity in the 21st century (see Fort and Schipani, 2004)? Would not our wisest global leaders know how to guide us in creating such a world? Is this a naively idealistic assumption? Perhaps, but not historically. Such visionary leadership only appears naive from the parochial perspective of the last 9000 years.

As archaeologists and other scholars have observed, there have always been legends and writings about an earlier, more harmonious and peaceful age (Eisler, 1987)[1] . The Bible, for example, tells us of the Garden of Eden. But many people assume that these are only idyllic fantasies, expressing universal yearnings and seemingly exaggerated aspirations. Only now, thanks to new scientific dating methods and specific findings, are archaeologists exposing facts that support the supposed myths and fantasies of our distant past (Gimbutas, 1991).

New excavations reveal that these alleged legends derive not from idealistic fantasies, but from folk memories about real flesh and blood people who organized their societies along very different lines from our own. At Chatal Huyuk and Hajilar, for example, both located in modern-day Turkey, archaeologists date communities to 7000 BCE, 90 centuries ago. These peaceful communities were located in the middle of fertile plains, not in defensible positions against stone cliffs or atop mountains nor surrounded by moats, walls or other defense systems. Their art, moreover, shows no sign of either individual- or community-level violence. Excavations reveal only minimal indications of hierarchy.

---

[1]This section is excerpted and adapted from Riane Eisler's insightful 1987 book.

Just as Columbus's discovery that the world was not flat made it possible for our ancestors to 'find' a world that, in fact, had been here all along, the archaeologists' findings are allowing us to rediscover prosperous communities that interacted peacefully and cooperatively with their neighbors (Eisler, 1987). Their findings allow us to ground supposedly naive, unattainable idealism in the reality of history. Perhaps not coincidentally, women led most of these ancient communities.

IS SUCH AN IDYLLIC SOCIETY POSSIBLE AGAIN?

What would it take to remarry such idealism with contemporary global realities? First, we would need to again believe that prosperity and a civilized way of living together on this planet are possible; that 21st-century humanity is capable of success, broadly defined. The contemporary discussion on global corporate citizenship addresses the possibility, and the necessity for companies to simultaneously do good and do well (see, among others, Hawken *et al.*, 1999; Lovins *et al.*, 2000; McDonough and Brangart, 2002; Prahalad and Hammond, 2002; Prahalad and Hart, 2002; Laszlo, 2003; Hart, 2005; Prahalad, 2005). To that end, the archaeologists' findings are crucial. We know that we achieved such success at one time; the only question is whether we can achieve it again in this century. The logic of building future success based on past success is inherent in the appreciative inquiry strategies (see Cooperrider *et al.*, 2003) and other strength-based approaches (see Cameron *et al.*, 2003).

Second, we would need to believe that change is possible; that society is capable of moving from a world organized around war and violence, the extremes of poverty and wealth, and an overall mentality of scarcity to one organized around peace, prosperity, compassion, and abundance. The initial work on positive psychology (Seligman, 1998, 2003; Seligman and Csikszentmihalyi, 2000; Synder and Lopez, 2002), which then led to positive organizational scholarship (Cameron *et al.*, 2003) is relevant in this regard.

Third, we would need to move from discrete local perspectives to broadly encompassing global perspectives. We would need to move away from divisiveness and return to more unifying images and strategies. For humanity to embrace each of the beliefs needed to create a healthy, economically vibrant, and sustainable global society, we would need approaches to leadership that differ quite markedly from those offered by most leaders in recent history.

Where is society to find leaders to guide it toward beliefs that differ so markedly from those of the recent past? While most societal commentators continue to review historical patterns of men's leadership in search of models for 21st-century success, few have begun to recognize, let alone appreciate, the equivalent patterns of women's leadership and the potential future contributions that women leaders could make (see De Cieri, this volume Chapter 10, for an analysis of the issues associated with women in international management). What could the world's women bring to the role of leading society? Are we entering an era in which both male and female leaders – rather than just men alone – will literally and symbolically shape history?

Women Leading Countries and Companies: No Longer Men Alone

While rarely recognized or reported in the media, the trend toward women joining men in senior leadership positions began in the 20th century, and now, in the 21st century, it is accelerating. The pattern is easiest to see when observing leaders of countries. Whereas in the past almost all political leaders were men, the number of women selected to serve as president or prime minister of their country in the last half century has increased markedly, albeit from a negligible starting point. As highlighted in Figure ??, of the 78 women who have served as president or prime minister of her country, none came into office in the 1950s (or the 1940s), just three came into office in the 1960s, six in the 1970s, nine in the 1980s, 35 in the 1990s, and had reached 25 in the first six years of the 21st century. Just in the last full decade (the 1990s), there was an almost 300% increase in the number of women serving their country at the highest level of political leadership relative to the prior decade. As listed in Table 22.1, countries as dissimilar as France, India, and Rwanda have all selected women to lead them. Whereas the increase is impressive, the total is not. Given that there are more than 193 countries in the world, many with both a president and a prime minister, and each with multiple leaders over the past 50 years, a total of 78 women in a half century is neither a large nor an impressive number.

Are the increasing numbers a new trend? Yes. Of the 78 women leaders, 62 (almost 80%) were the first women that their respective countries had ever selected to lead them. Ruth Dreifuss, for example, became President of Switzerland in 1999 after a 700-year history of male-led democracy. Among the women who were not 'firsts' – in other words, those who followed another woman into office – 16 were the second woman selected by their countries, and two women were the third and fourth woman respectively that their country, the Netherlands-Antilles, had ever selected. As shown on Table 22.2, the countries that have selected many women to lead them represent a culturally, geographically, and economically very

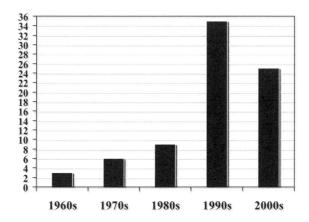

FIGURE 22.1 Number of women political leaders.

TABLE 22.1 Women political leaders: A chronology.

Country	Name	Office	Date
Sri Lanka	(Sirimavo Bandaranaike)	Prime Minister	1960–65, 1970–1977, 1994–2000
India	(Indira Gandhi)	Prime Minister	1966–1977, 1980–1984
Israel	(Golda Meir)	Prime Minister	1969–1975
Argentina	(Maria Estela [Isabel] Martínez de Perón)	President	1974–1976
Central African Rep.	Elizabeth Domitien	Prime Minister	1975–1976
Netherlands Antilles	Lucinda da Costa Gomez-Matheeuws	Prime Minister	1977
Portugal	Maria de Lourdes Pintasilgo	Prime Minister	1979 (5 mo.)
Bolivia	Lidia Gueiler Tejada	Interim President, Prime Minister	1979–1980
Great Britain	Margaret Thatcher	Prime Minister	1979–1990
Dominica	Mary Eugenia Charles	Prime Minister	1980–1995
Iceland	Vigdís Finnbógadottir	President	1980–1996
Norway	Gro Harlem Brundtland	Prime Minister	1981;1986–89;1990–1996
Yugoslavia	Milka Planinc	Prime Minister	1982–1986
Malta	Agatha Barbara	President	1982–1987
Guinea Bissau	Carmen Pereira	Acting President	1984 (3 days)
Netherlands Antilles	Maria Liberia-Peters	Prime Minister	1984–1986; 1989–1994
The Philippines	Corazon Aquino	President	1986–1992
Pakistan	Benazir Bhutto	Prime Minister	1988–1990; 1993–1996
Lithuania	Kazimiera-Danute Prunskiene	Prime Minister	1990–1991

Haiti	Ertha Pascal-Trouillot	President	1990–1991
Burma (Myanmar)	Aung San Suu Kyi	Elected President[b]	1990-[b]
German Democratic Republic	Sabine Bergmann-Pohl	Chairman of the Volksammer (Staatspräsident)	1990 (6 mo.)
Ireland	Mary Robinson	President	1990–1997
Nicaragua	Violeta Barrios de Chamorro	President	1990–1996
Bangladesh	Khaleda Zia[a]	Prime Minister	1991–1996; 2001-[a]
France	Edith Cresson	Prime Minister	1991–1992
Poland	Hanna Suchocka	Prime Minister	1992–1993
Canada	Kim Campbell	Prime Minister	1993
Burundi	Sylvia Kinigi	Prime Minister	1993–1994 (4 mo.)
Faeroe Islands	Marita Peterson	Prime Minister	1993–1994
Rwanda	(Agatha Uwilingiyimana)	Prime Minister	1993–1994
Turkey	Tansu Çiller	Prime Minister	1993–1996
Netherlands Antilles	Susanne Camelia-Romer	Prime Minister	1993; 1998–1999
Bulgaria	Reneta Indzhova	Interim Prime Minister	1994–1995 (3 mo.)
Sri Lanka	Chandrika Bandaranaike Kumaratunga	President and former Prime Minister	1994–2005
Haiti	Claudette Werleigh	Prime Minister	1995–1996
Bangladesh	Hasina Wajed	Prime Minister	1996–2001
Liberia	Ruth Perry	Chair, Ruling Council	1996–97

(Continued)

TABLE 22.1 (*Continued*)

Country	Name	Office	Date
Ecuador	Rosalia Arteaga	President	1997 (3 days)
Bermuda	Pamela Gordon	Premier	1997–1998
Bosnian Serb Republic	Biliana Plavsic	President	1997–1998
Ireland	Mary McAleese[a]	President	1997[a]
New Zealand	Jenny Shipley	Prime Minister	1997–1999
Guyana	Janet Jagan	Prime Minister, President	1997–1999
Norway	Anne Enger Lahnstein	Acting Prime Minister	Sept 1998 (24 days)
Bermuda	Jennifer Smith	Premier	1998–2003
Lithuania	Irene Degutienë	Acting Prime Minister	1999 (22 days)
Mongolia	Nyam-Osorily Tuyaa	Acting Prime Minister	July 1999 (9 days)
Switzerland	Ruth Dreifuss	President	1999
Latvia	Vaira Vike-Freiberga	President	1999–2003
Panama	Mireya Moscoso	Executive President	1999–2004
New Zealand	Helen Clark[a]	Prime Minister	1999[a]
Finland	Tarja Halonen	President[a]	2000[a]
Philippines	Gloria Macapagal-Arroyo[a]	Executive President	2001[a]
Senegal	Madior Boye	Prime Minister	2001–2002
Indonesia	Megawati Sukarnoputri	President	2001–2004
South Korea	Chang Sang	Acting Prime Minister	July 2002 (20 days)
Serbia	Natasa Micic	Acting President	Dec. 2002–Feb. 2004

Country	Name	Title	Dates
São Tomé and Principe	Maria das Neves de Souse	Prime Minister	2002–2004
Finland	Anneli Jäätteenmäki	Prime Minister	April-June 2003 (2 mo.)
Peru	Beatriz Merino	Prime Minister	2003 (6 mo.)
Netherlands Antilles	Mirna Louise-Godett	Prime Minister	2003–2004
Georgia	Nino Burdzhanadze	Acting President	2003–2004
Macedonia	Radmila Sekerinska	Acting Prime Minister	2004
Austria	Barbara Prammer	Acting Joint Head of State	July-August 2004
New Caledonia	Maria-Noëlle Thérmereau[a]	President	2004[a]
Mozambique	Luisa Dias Diogo[a]	Prime Minister	2004[a]
The Bahamas	Cynthia A Pratt	Acting Prime Minister	2005 ($3\frac{1}{2}$ months)
São Tomé & Principe	Maria do Carmo Silvera	Prime Minister	2005–2006
Ukraine	Yuliya Tymoshenko	Designate Prime Minister	2005
Germany	Angela Merkel[a]	Chancellor	2005-[a]
Liberia	Ellen Johnson-Sirleaf[a]	President	2005-[a]
Chile	Michelle Bachelet[a]	President	2006-[a]
Jamaica	Portia Simpson-Miller[a]	Prime Minister	2006-[a]
South Korea	Han Myung Sook[a]	Prime Minister	2006–2007
Switzerland	Micheline Calmy-Rey[a]	President of the Confederation	1/2007-[a]
Israel	Dalia Itzik[a]	Acting President	1/2007-[a]

( ) No longer living
[a] Currently in office
[b] Party won 1990 election but prevented by military from taking office; Nobel Prize laureate.
© Nancy J. Adler, March 2007

TABLE 22.2 Countries having selected more than one woman leader.

Bangladesh	Khaleda Zia	**Prime Minister**
	Hasina Wajid	**Prime Minister**
Bermuda	Pamela Gordon	**Premier**
	Jennifer Smith	**Premier**
Finland	Tarja Halonen	**President**
	Anneli Jäätteenmäki	**Prime Minister**
Haiti	Bertha Pascal-Trouillot	**President**
	Claudette Werleigh	**Prime Minister**
Israel	Golda Meir	**Prime Minister**
	Dalia Itzik	**Acting President**
Ireland	Mary Robinson	**President**
	Mary McAleese	**President**
Liberia	Ruth Perry	**Chair, Ruling Council**
	Ellen Johnson-Sirleaf	**President**
Lithuania	Kazimiera-Danute Prunskiene	**Prime Minister**
	Irene Degutienė	**Prime Minister**
Netherlands Antilles	Lucinda de Costa Gomez-Matheeuws	**Prime Minister**
	Maria Liberia-Peters	**Prime Minister**
	Suzanne Camelia-Romer	**Prime Minister**
	Mirna Louise-Godett	**Prime Minister**
New Zealand	Jenny Shipley	**Prime Minister**
	Helen Clark	**Prime Minister**
Norway	Gro Harlem Brundtland	**Prime Minister**
	Anne Enger Lahnstein	**Prime Minister**
Philippines	Corazon Aquino	**President**
	Gloria Arroyo	**President**
Sao Tome and Principe	Maria das Neves de Souse	**Prime Minister**
	Maria do Carmo Silvera	**Prime Minister**
South Korea	Chang Sang	**Acting President**
	Han Myung Sook	**Prime Minister**
Sri Lanka	Sirimavo Bandarnaike	**Prime Minister**
	Chandrika Kumaratunga	**President**
Switzerland	Ruth Dreifus	**President of Confederation**
	Micheline Calmy-Rey	**President of Confederation**

diverse group of nations, including Bangladesh, Bermuda, Finland, Haiti, Israel, Ireland, Liberia, Lithuania, Netherland-Antilles, New Zealand, Norway, Philippines, Sao Tomé and Principe, South Korea, Sri Lanka, and Switzerland.

Given these trends, there is no question that more women will be leading countries in the 21st century than have ever done so before. In the opening years of this century, 25 additional women had been selected to lead their countries.

WOMEN LEADING COMPANIES

Are there similar increases in the number of women leading major corporations (see, among others, Adler, 1997a, b, 1999b, 2002a, b, 2005, 2007; Adler and Izraeli, 1994)? Whereas the patterns among business leaders are not as clear as those among political leaders, surveys suggest that an increasing number of women are leading global companies. The initial numbers, however, are very small. Even including executives who held positions below the number one position in their companies, women still held less than 5% of the most senior management positions in the United States and less than 2% of all senior management positions in Europe at the end of the last century (United States statistics are based of the research of Catalyst as originally published by Wellington, 1996 and European statistics are reported in Dwyer *et al.*, 1996).

Moreover, not until the late 1990s did either the *Fortune* top 30 or the *Financial Times* (FT-SE) 100 include a woman among their lists of leading CEOs, and this with the appointment of Carly Fiorina, former CEO of Hewlett-Packard and Marjorie Scardino, CEO of Pearson Plc. In updating this chapter, even by 2007, the *Fortune 500* still included only 10 women CEOs, a mere 2%.

Contrary to popular belief, however, women's scarcity in leading major corporations does not reflect their absence as leaders of global companies. Unlike their male counterparts, most women chief executives either create their own entrepreneurial enterprises or assume the leadership of a family business (Adler, 1999a, c has discussed women who are global entrepreneurs).

WOMEN LEADING: A WORLDWIDE TREND, NOT A LOCAL PECULIARITY

As Table 22.3 highlights, similar to women-led countries, women-led businesses exist almost everywhere in the world. They are not clustered in just the few countries considered to be female-friendly – those countries providing women with equal property rights, equal access to education, healthcare, and employment, and equal protection under law. The women leaders come from the world's largest and smallest countries, the world's richest and poorest countries, and the world's most socially and economically advantaged and disadvantaged countries. They come, moreover, from every geographical region, represent all six of the world's major religions, and lead companies in a wide range of industries. The changing trend toward women's leadership is a broad-based, worldwide phenomenon, not a trend limited to a few particularly pro-women countries, industries or regions.

Moreover, most major corporations that select women as senior business leaders are not those that have implemented the most advanced female-friendly policies (such as day-care centers, flextime, and other equal employment opportunities). Among the 61 American *Fortune 500* companies employing women as chairmen, CEOs, board members, or one of the top five earners, for example, only three are companies that *Working Woman* identified as the most favorable for women employees.

TABLE 22.3 Global women business leaders.

Listed women lead or have led companies with revenues over US $1 billion, or banks with assets over US $1 billion.[a]

Ernestina Herrera de Noble, Argentina, $1.2 billion: President and editorial director of *Grupo Clarin*, the largest-circulation Spanish newspaper in the world.

Francine Wachsstock, Belgium, $2.25 billion: President of the board of administrators, La Poste, Belgium's state-owned post office and largest employer.

Beatriz Larragoiti, Brazil, $2.9 billion: Vice president (and owner) of Brazil's largest insurance company, Sul America S.A.

Maureen Kempston Darkes, Canada, $18.3 billion: President and General Manager of General Motors of Canada.

Ellen R. Schneider-Lenne, Germany, $458 billion in assets: Member of the Board of Managing Directors, Deutsch Bank AG, responsible for operations in the UK (deceased).

Nina Wang, Hong Kong, $1–2 billion in assets: Chairlady of Chinachem Group, property development.

Tarjani Vakil, India, $1.1 billion in assets: Chairperson and managing director, Export-Import Bank of India, highest ranking female banking official in Asia.

Margaret Heffernan, Ireland, $1.6 billion: Chairman, Dunnes Stores Holding Company, largest retailing company in Ireland.

Galia Maor, Israel, $35.6 billion in assets: CEO of Bank Leumi le-Israel.

Gloria Delores Knight, Jamaica, $1.86 billion in assets: President and managing director, The Jamaica Mutual Life Assurance Society, largest financial conglomerate in English-speaking Caribbean (deceased).

Sawako Noma, Japan, $2 billion: President of Kodansha Ltd, largest publishing house in Japan.

Harumi Sakamoto, Japan, $13 billion: Senior managing director, The Seiyu, Ltd, a supermarket and shopping center operator expanding throughout Asia.

Khatijah Ahmad, Malaysia, $5 billion: Chairman and managing director, KAF Group of Companies, financial services group.

Merce Sala i Schnorkowski, Spain, $1.1 billion: CEO of Renfe, Spain's national railway system, currently helping to privatize Colombian and Bolivian rail and selling trains to Germany.

Antonia Ax:son Johnson, Sweden, $6 billion: Chair, The Axel Johnson Group, retailing and distribution, more than 200 companies.

Elisabeth Salina Amorini, Switzerland, $2.8 billion: Chairman of the board, managing director, and chairman of the group executive board, Societe Generale de Surveillance Holding S.A., the world's largest inspection and quality control organization, testing imports and exports in more than 140 countries.

Emilia Roxas, Taiwan, $5 billion: CEO, Asiaworld Internationale Groupe, multinational conglomerate.

United States-based *Fortune 500* firms led by women CEOs as of 2007

Claire Babrowski, RadioShack, $5.1 billion: CEO of consumer electronics retailer.

TABLE 22.3 (*Continued*)

Brenda C. Barnes, Sara Lee, $19.7 billion: CEO of food consumer products firm.

Susan M. Ivey, Reynolds American, $8.3 billion: CEO of tobacco company.

Andrea Jung, Avon Products, $8.1 billion: CEO of personal and household products firm.

Anne Mulcahy, Xerox, $15.7 billion: CEO of office equipment company.

Paula G Rosput Reynolds, Safeco $6.3 billion: CEO of insurance company.

Patricia F. Russo, Lucent Technologies, $9.4: CEO of network and other communications company.

Mary F. Sammons, Rite Aid, $16.8 billion: CEO of food and drug store.

Marion O. Sandler, Golden West Financial, $6.7 billion ($124.5 billion in assets): CEO of savings institution.

Margaret C. Whitman, Ebay, $4.6 billion: CEO of internet services and retailing firm.

Examples of countries with women leading companies with revenues over a $250 million:

Donatella Zingone Dini, Costa Rica, $300 million: Zeta Group, fifth largest business in Central America, conglomerate.

Nawal Abdel Moneim El Tatawy, Egypt, $357 million in assets: Chairman, Arab Investment Bank.

Colette Lewiner, France, $800 million: Chairman and CEO, SGN-Eurisys Group, world's largest nuclear fuels reprocessing company.

Jannie Tay, Singapore, $289 million: Managing director, The Hour Glass Limited, high end retailer of watches.

Aida Geffen, South Africa, $355 million: Chairman and managing director, Aida Holdings Ltd, residential commercial real estate firm.

Ann Gloag, United Kingdom, $520 million: Stagecoach Holdings Plc; Europe's largest bus company.

Liz Chitiga, Zimbabwe, $400 million; General manager and CEO, Minerals Marketing Corporation of Zimbabwe; in foreign-currency terms, the biggest business in Zimbabwe.

[a]Based on Kelly (1996): CEOs of *Fortune 500* firms based on *Fortune 500* list as reported at http://money.cnn.com/magazines/fortune/fortune500/womenceos/

As can be seen, the trends among political and business leaders appear similar. More women are leading global firms than ever before, with the vast majority being the first woman whom their particular firm has ever selected to hold such a senior position. Based on these trends, we can easily predict that women's voices will become a more common, and therefore more important, addition to the world's global leadership dialogue in the 21st century. Change is not only possible, it has already begun to happen.

GLOBAL LEADERSHIP: NUMBERS ARE NOT ENOUGH

Increasing the number of women in senior leadership positions is certainly a necessary condition for equity, but it is not a sufficient condition for shaping history.
The fundamental challenge is not simply to select more women as senior leaders.
Rather, it is to provide a form of leadership in the world that will foster global society's survival and prosperity.

Based on research observing women managers, many people have predicted that
women leaders would exhibit a new sought-after 21st century leadership style, incorporating new, more inclusive, trustworthy, and humanistic approaches. They base
their predictions on research studies that have concluded that a disproportionate
number of women exhibit many, if not all, of the following qualities (see, among
others, summary of traits in Fondas, 1997: 260):

> empathy, helpfulness, caring, and nurturance; interpersonal sensitivity, atten-
> tiveness to and acceptance of others, responsiveness to their needs and mo-
> tivations; an orientation toward the collective interest and toward integra-
> tive goals such as group cohesiveness and stability; a preference for open,
> egalitarian, and cooperative relationships, rather than hierarchical ones; and
> an interest in actualizing values and relationships of great importance to
> community.

By contrast, the traits that have been culturally ascribed to men include (Fondas,
1997: 260):

> an ability to be impersonal, self-interested, efficient, hierarchical, tough
> minded, and assertive; an interest in taking charge, control, and domination;
> a capacity to ignore personal, emotional considerations in order to succeed; a
> proclivity to rely on standardized or 'objective' codes for judgment and eval-
> uation of others; and a heroic orientation toward task accomplishment and a
> continual effort to act on the world and become something new or [different].

To date, however, no research that has focused on senior leaders (rather than
employees or managers) exists to support or refute claims that women would make
more effective 21st century leaders than would men. Not surprisingly, similar to
men, women exhibit a wide range of leadership visions, approaches, and levels of effectiveness (Adler, 2002). One need look no further than the ouster on corruption
charges of Turkey's former prime minister, Tansu Ciller, or the demise of Sotheby's
former CEO Diana Brooks (indicted, along with Sotheby's former chairman, Alfred
Taubman, on criminal conspiracy and price fixing charges) to know that women
leaders, like their male counterparts, are neither perfect nor a universal solution
to the world's or any particular company's problems. Blumenthal and Vogel (2001)
have described the case against Sotheby's former chairman, A. Alfred Taubman, on
criminal conspiracy charges for a price-fixing scheme with archrival auction house,
Christie's (see also the business press in November–December 2001, including the
New York Times reporting).

Do some women exhibit exemplary styles of leadership? Yes; not all women, but certainly many give us reason for hope, especially those not mimicking the style of leadership of most 20th century male leaders. Ireland's first woman president, Mary Robinson, for example, brilliantly took her commitment to human rights into the presidency of Ireland, transforming the position from one of ceremony to one of substance. She then let go of the presidency – a typically feminine use of power, 'letting go' – in order to continue her human rights agenda on a broader, worldwide scale at the United Nations. Aung San Suu Kyi, the legally elected leader of Burma (Myanmar) has been incarcerated in her own home by the military for more than 10 years. While under house arrest, the military dictatorship even denied her the right to see her husband one last time before he died of cancer. Given her situation, does Suu Kyi advocate annihilating the military dictatorship that has imprisoned her and her people for so long? No, to this day, she fearlessly advocates dialogue – words, not guns – a unity strategy typically attributed to what many consider to be a more feminine approach to leadership.

Agatha Uwilingiyimana, the former prime minister of Rwanda, similarly exemplifies the courage it takes to break with traditional leadership approaches and use unifying strategies – strategies many attribute to a more feminine approach. By 1993, the level of violence in Rwanda had forced the Hutus and Tutsis to seriously consider signing a peace agreement. But who would have the courage to sign such a paper with a sworn enemy? No one relished the risk, as extremists on both sides considered those who would sign as traitors. At that crucial moment in Rwanda's history, no man would accept the risk of becoming a peace-making prime minister. In July 1993, it was Uwiligiyimana, in the name of peace and unity, who agreed to serve her country as prime minister. Less than a month later, the peace agreement was signed. Less than a year later, extremist Hutus began hunting down and killing Tutsis and moderate members of the Hutu government. Agatha Uwilingiyimana, a moderate Hutu, was one of the first to be murdered. Although reported as a Tutsi murder in the Western press, Agatha was killed by her own people, by extremist Hutus who rejected her attempts at unity and peace.

Is the situation in Rwanda so extreme that it would be inappropriate for the rest of the world to attempt to learn anything from Uwiligiyimana's story? The answer is a resounding no. Think for a moment of some of the other women leaders with whom we are perhaps more familiar. Former President of the Philippines, Corazon Aquino, like Uwiligiyiama, also believed in building coalitions with the opposition. She invited members of both her own and the opposition party to join her presidential cabinet. The world press, viewing her leadership through the obsolete lens of divisive 20th century perspectives, labeled her invitation to the opposition as the naive act of a housewife who doesn't know what it means to be president. In response, Aquino explained that she never again wanted political differences resolved by murder. She wanted to preclude the possibility that any person would to have to watch the political assassination of his or her spouse as she had been obliged to when her husband, Benigno Aquino, opposition leader at the time, was murdered on the tarmac upon his return to the Philippines. In her cabinet, animated discussion replaced murder as the accepted form of political discourse.

Aquino, similar to Robinson in Ireland, refused to run for a second term because she believed that democracy, not her longevity as president, was more important. Having lived through years of Marcos' dictatorship, she believed that Filipinos deserved to choose a new president after she had served her initial six-year term. Each of these leaders went outside the patterns of history and said 'Enough! There has to be a better way.'

Are the stories of more inclusive leadership all stories of political leaders? Of course not. Rebecca Mark, for example, as CEO of Enron Development Corporation, negotiated the first major commercial agreement among Arabs and Israelis following the Oslo Peace Accords. It should be noted that this was long before the demise in 2001 of Enron, under the leadership chairman Kenneth L. Lay. Among many other business articles covering Enron's downfall, see Oppel and Atlas (2001).

Rebecca Mark saw coalition building – including links across groups that the world had always viewed as enemies – as a smart business. Did people question her judgment? Of course they did. Did she do what hadn't been done before? Yes. As Rebecca Mark's decisions show, true leadership, by definition, is not the act of the usual. When Enron collapsed, Rebecca Mark was one of the few executives who was not indicted.

As both business and political leaders, women regularly challenge conventional wisdom in their approach to leadership. Britain's Anita Roddick, founder and former CEO of The Body Shop, for example, regularly challenged conventional practice in the beauty and healthcare industry. She challenged conventional product design, for example, by not allowing animal testing. The Body Shop challenged the conventional marketing strategies of its competitors by not promising women unattainable beauty. The company challenged convention in its organization design and strategic intent by tying societal commitments to product strategies, long before corporate social responsibility came into vogue. Sweden's Antonia Ax:son Johnson, CEO of a fourth-generation, 200-company family business, The Ax:son Johnson Group, eliminated all war- and violence-related toys from her company's department stores. Although the toys would have increased revenues, they were not consistent with Ax:son Johnson's concept of 'the good company'.

PEOPLE'S ASPIRATIONS: HOPE, CHANGE, AND UNITY

To understand the dynamics of the 21st century, we must go beyond strictly attempting to assess if, or how, women's approaches to leadership differ from those of their male counterparts. We know that they differ in some cases, but certainly not in all, or perhaps even most, cases. Given the absence of consistently substantiated differences and, at the same time, the rapid increase in the number of women leaders (especially in the last decade), we must ask why countries and companies worldwide – for the first time in modern history and after so many years of male-dominated leadership – are choosing women to lead them, often for the first time. It appears that people worldwide may want what all women symbolize, but what only some women leaders in fact exhibit.

Leadership symbolism: The possibility of change

Perhaps the most powerful and attractive symbolism of women leaders is the possibility of significant change. When a woman is chosen as the first woman to become president, prime minister, or CEO – when no other woman has ever held such an office in the particular country or company, and when few people thought that she could be selected – people begin to believe that other, more substantive and less symbolic changes are also possible. The combination of a woman being an outsider at senior leadership levels previously controlled by men, and of her beating the odds in attaining a top position, provides powerful public imagery supporting the possibility of broad-based societal and organizational change. The fact that most women in senior leadership positions, to date, are the first women to assume those positions, underscores the beginning not just of symbolic change, but of real change. Mary Robinson's presidential acceptance speech captures the unique event of Ireland electing its first woman president coupled with the possibility of national change:

> ...I was elected by men and women of all parties and none, by many with great moral courage who stepped out from the faded flags of Civil War and voted for a new Ireland. And above all by the women of Ireland...who instead of rocking the cradle rocked the system, and who came out massively to make their mark on the ballot paper, and on a new Ireland.
> —(From a speech in the RDS, Dublin, 9 November 1990 as reported in Finlay, 1990: 1)

The fact that women who become leaders are perceived to differ from their male counterparts (whether or not they actually do) fosters the sense that change is possible. In Kenya, for example, when Charity Ngilu became the first woman to run for president, many Kenyans saw her as representing 'a complete break with [the] divisive tribal politics of the past' (McKinley, 1997: section 1, p. 3). As one Kenyan observed, 'Charity is talking about unity, and this unity will unite both men and women... If we vote for a man, there will be no change. With a woman, there will have to be a big change' (McKinley, 1997: section 1, p. 3).

The symbolism supporting the possibility of change is almost identical in the business world, where most women CEOs are 'firsts'; not only the first woman, but also often the first outsider that the company has selected to lead them. The discussion of women who are firsts often being 'double strangers' and acting as the 'thin edge of the wedge' (Czarniawska and Sevon, 2005) is useful in this regard.

Notable examples include Marjorie Scardino, the first woman, first outsider, and first American to become CEO of Britain's Pearson Plc, as well as the first woman to lead a *Financial Times* (FT-SE) 100 firm; Carly Fiorina, the first woman and first outsider to lead Hewlett-Packard, a *Fortune* top-30 firm; and Charlotte Beers, the first woman and the first outsider whom Ogilvy and Mather Worldwide had ever brought in to lead their worldwide advertising business.

Leadership symbolism: The possibility of unity

In addition to the possibility of change, women also symbolize unity – and women leaders are no exception. Nicaragua's former president Violetta Chamorro, for example, became a symbol of national unity following her husband's assassination. Chamorro even claimed 'to have no ideology beyond national "reconciliation"' (Benn, 1995). Chamorro's ability to bring her four adult children (two of whom were prominent Sandanistas while the other two equally prominently opposed the Sandanistas) together every week for Sunday dinner achieved near legendary status in war-torn Nicaragua (Saint-Germain, 1993: 80). Chamorro gave symbolic hope to her nation that it too could find peace based on a unity that would bring all Nicaraguans together. That the behavior of a woman leader led to family unity becoming a symbol for national unity is neither surprising nor coincidental.

On the basis of similar dynamics, Pakistan's former prime minister Benazir Bhutto and the Philippines' former president Corazon Aquino each came to symbolize unity for their strife-torn countries. As the scope of governments' influence, and companies' operations, expand to encompass the world, the desire and need for unifying strategies increase. Currently, women symbolize the hope for unity within multinational constituencies and multicultural contexts.

The hope that women leaders will foster unity and inclusiveness is heightened by the ways in which women gain access to power. In contrast to many of their male counterparts, most women leaders develop and use broadly-based popular support, rather than relying primarily on traditional, hierarchical political party or corporate structural support. This broadly-based inclusiveness, often seen as a precursor of other hoped-for unifying strategies, has been particularly apparent among the aspiring women political leaders who often are not seriously considered as potential candidates by their country's main political parties. They are consequently forced to gain support directly from the people (which, of course, is a profoundly democratic process).

Mary Robinson, for example, campaigned in more small communities in Ireland than any previous presidential candidate before either her party or the opposition took her seriously. The opposition later admitted that they did not seriously consider Robinson's candidacy until it was too late to stop her (Finlay, 1990). Similarly, Corazon Aquino, whose campaign and victory were labeled the People's Revolution, held more than 1000 rallies during her campaign, while Ferdinand Marcos, the incumbent, held only 34 (Col, 1993). Likewise, Benazir Bhutto, who succeeded in becoming Pakistan's first woman and youngest prime minister, campaigned in more communities than any politician before her. Only later did her own party take her seriously (Anderson, 1993; Weisman, 1986).

In business, the disproportionate number of women who choose to start their own companies echoes the same pattern of broadly-based support. Rather than attempting to climb the corporate ladder and to break through the glass ceiling into senior leadership positions in established corporations, these entrepreneurial women build their success directly in the marketplace. The types of broadly-based support developed by women political leaders and entrepreneurs differ only in their source, with the former enjoying support directly from the electorate and the latter gaining support from the marketplace. In both cases, the base of support is outside the traditional power structure and hierarchy, and therefore more representative of new and more diverse opinions and ideas. Women leaders' sources of support, and therefore of power, more closely reflect the flattened network of emerging 21st century organizations and society than they do the more centralized and limited power hierarchies defining most 20th century organizations.

CONCLUSION

As Czech Republic President Vaclav Havel (1994: A27) described the world as 'going through a transitional period, when something is on the way out and something else is painfully being born,' it is not surprising that people worldwide are attracted to women leaders' symbolic message of bringing change, hope and the possibility of unity. The interplay of women's and men's styles of leadership will define the contours and potential success of 21st century society. The risk is in encapsulating leaders, both women and men, in approaches that worked well in the 20th century but foretell disaster for the 21st century. The challenge is in the urgency and complexity. However, as poet David Whyte (1994) enjoins us:

> *The journey begins right here, in the middle of the road, right beneath your feet.*
>   *This is the place.*
>   *There is no other place, there is no other time.*

REFERENCES

Adler, N.J. (1997a). Global Leaders: A Dialogue with Future History. *International Management*, 1 (2), 21–33.

Adler, N.J. (1997b). Global Leadership: Women Leaders. *Management International Review*, 37 (1), 171–196.

Adler, N.J. (1999a). Global Entrepreneurs: Women, Myths, and History. *Global Focus*, 11 (4), 125–134.

Adler, N.J. (1999b). Global Leaders: Women of Influence. In G. Powell (ed.), *Handbook of Gender and Work*. Thousand Oaks, CA: Sage, pp. 239–261.

Adler, N.J. (1999c). Twenty-First-Century Leadership: Reality Beyond the Myths. In A.M. Rugman and R. Wright (eds), *Research in Global Strategic Management, Volume 7*. Greenwich, CT: JAI Press, pp. 239–261.

Adler, N.J. (2002a). Global Managers: No Longer Men Alone. *International Journal of Human Resource Management*, 13 (5), 743–760.

Adler, N.J. (2002b). Women Joining Men as Global Leaders in the New Economy. In M. Gannon and K. Newman (eds), *Handbook of Cross-Cultural Management*. Oxford: Blackwell, pp. 236–249.

Adler, N.J. (2003). Global Strategy: Successfully Partnering with the World. In M. Goldsmith, J. Belasco, and L. Segil (eds), *The Leader As Partner*. New York: AMACOM, pp. 223–230.

Adler, N.J. (2005). Leading Beyond Boundaries: The Courage to Enrich the World. In L. Coughlin, E. Wingard and K. Hollihan (eds), *Enlightened Power: How Women Are Transforming the Practice of Leadership*. San Francisco: Jossey-Bass, pp. 350–366 and 505–507.

Adler, N.J. (2007). One World: Women Leading and Managing Worldwide. In D. Bilimoria and S.K. Piderit (eds), *Handbook on Women in Business and Management*. Cheltenham: Edward Elgar Publishing, pp. 330–355.

Adler, N.J., and Izraeli, D. (eds) (1994). *Competitive Frontiers: Women Managers in a Global Economy*. Cambridge, MA: Blackwell.

Adler, P.S., and Kwon, S.-W. (2002). Social capital: Prospects for a new concept. *Academy of Management Review*, 27 (1), 17–40.

Albright, M.K. (1997). Harvard Commencement Address as reported in the *New York Times*, June 6, p. A8.

Anderson, N.F. (1993). Benazir Bhutto and dynastic politics: Her father's daughter, her people's sister. In M.A. Genovese (ed.), *Women as National Leaders*. Newbury Park, CA: Sage, pp. 41–69.

Barkema, H., and Vermeulen, F. (1997). What Differences in the Cultural Backgrounds of Partners are Detrimental for International Joint Ventures? *Journal of International Business Studies*, 28 (4), 845–864.

Benn, M. (1995). Women who rule the world, *Cosmopolitan*, February.

Blumenthal, R., and Vogel, C. (2001). Trial Prosecutor Depicts Ex-Chief of Sotheby's as Price Fixer. *New York Times*, December 4, p. A20.

Cameron, K.S., Dutton, J.E., and Quinn, R.E. (eds) (2003). *Positive Organizational Scholarship*. San Francisco: Berrett-Kohler.

Col, J.-M. (1993). Managing softly in turbulent times: Corazon C. Aquino, President of the Philippines. In M.A. Genovese (ed.) *Women as National Leaders*. Newbury Park, CA: Sage, pp. 13-40.

Cooperrider, D.L., and Adler, N J. (2006). *The Global Forum on Business as an Agent of World Benefit: Management Knowledge Leading Positive Change, Concept paper*. Cleveland, OH: Case Western Reserve University, Weatherhead School of Business.

Cooperrider, D.L., Whitney, D., and Stavros, J.M. (2003). *Appreciative Inquiry Handbook*. Bedford Heights, OH: Lakeshore Publishers.

Czarniawska, B., and Sevon, G. (2005). *The Thin End of the Wedge: Foreign Women Professors as Double Strangers in Academia*. Sweden: Gothenburg Research Institute.

Dwyer, P., Johnston, M., and Lowry, L. (1996). Europe's Corporate Women. *Business Week*, April 15, pp. 40–42.

Eisler, R. (1987). *The Chalice and the Blade: Our History, Our Future*. San Francisco: Harper & Row.

Finlay, F. (1990). *Mary Robinson: A President with a Purpose*. Dublin, Ireland: The O'Brien Press, p. 1.

Fondas, N. (1997). The origins of feminization. *Academy of Management Review*, 22 (1), 257–282.

Fort, T.L., and Schipani, C.A. (2004). *The Role of Business in Fostering Peaceful Societies*. Cambridge: Cambridge University Press.

Friedman, T.L. (2006). *The World is Flat: A Brief History of the Twenty-First Century*. New York: Farrar, Straus and Giroux.

Gimbutas, M. (1991). *The Civilization of the Goddess: The World of Old Europe*. San Francisco: Harper San Francisco.

Haebeck, M.H., Kroger, F., and Trum, M.R. (2000). *After the Mergers: Seven Rules for Successful Post-Merger Integration*. New York: Prentice Hall/FT.

Harrigan, K.R. (1988). Strategic Alliances and Partner Asymmetries. In F. Contractor and P. Lorange (eds), *Cooperative Strategies in International Business*. Lexington, MA: Lexington Books, pp. 205–226.

Hart, S.L. (2005). *Capitalism at the Crossroads*. Upper Saddle River, NJ: Wharton School Publishing (Pearson Education).

Havel, V. (1994). The new measure of man, *New York Times*, July 8, p. A27.

Hawken, P., Lovins, A., and Lovins, L.H. (1999). *Natural Capitalism: Creating the Next Industrial Revolution*. Boston: Little Brown & Company.

Kelly, C. (1996). 50 World-Class Executives, *Worldbusiness*, 2 (2), 20–31

Laszlo, C. (2003). *The Sustainable Company: How to Create Lasting Value Through Social and Environmental Performance*. Washington DC: Island Press.

Lovins, A.B., Lovins, H., Hawken, P., Reinhardt, F., Shapiro, R., and Magretta, J. (2000). *Harvard Business Review on Business and the Environment*. Boston: Harvard Business School Publishing.

McDonough, W., and Braungart, M. (2002). *Cradle to Cradle*. New York: North Point Press.

McKinley, J.C. Jr. (1997). A Woman to Run Kenya? One says, "Why Not?" *The New York Times* (world late edition), August 3, Section 1, p. 3.

Oppel, R.A. Jr., and Atlas, R.D. (2001). Hobbled Enron Tries to Stay On Its Feet. *New York Times*, December 4, pp. C1 and C8.

Park, S.H., and Russo, M.V. (1996). When Competition Eclipses Cooperation: An Event History Analysis of Joint Venture Failure. *Management Science*, 42 (6), 875–890.

Prahalad, C.K. (2005). *The Fortune at the Bottom of the Pyramid: Eradicating Poverty Through Profits*. Upper Saddle River, NJ: Wharton School Publishing (Pearson Education).

Prahalad, C.K., and Hammond, A. (2002). Serving the World's Poor, Profitably. *Harvard Business Review*, 80 (9), 48–57.

Prahalad, C.K., and Hart, S.L. (2002). The Fortune at the Bottom of the Pyramid. *Strategy + Business*, 26 (1), 2–14.

Rechtschaffen, S. (1996). *Timeshifting*. New York: Bantam Doubleday Dell Audio Publishing.

Saint-Germain, M.A. (1993). Women in power in Nicaragua: Myth and reality. In M.A. Genovese (ed.), *Women as national leaders*. Newbury Park, CA: Sage, pp. 70–102.

Schuler, R.S., and Jackson, S.E. (2001). Seeking An Edge in Mergers and Acquisitions. *The Financial Times*, Special Section, Part Two: People Management, October 22.

Seligman, M.E.P. (1998). *Learned Optimism: How to Change Your Mind and Your Life*. 2nd edition. New York: Free Press.

Seligman, M.E.P. (2003). Positive Psychology: Fundamental Assumptions. *Psychologist*, 126–127.

Seligman, M.E.P., and Csikszentmihalyi, M. (2000). Positive psychology: An Introduction. *American Psychologist*, 55, 5–14.

Slackman, M. (2001). Divisive U.N. Race Talks End in Accord. *The Los Angeles Times*, September 9th, p. A1.

Snyder, C.R., and Lopez, S.J. (eds) (2002). *Handbook of Positive Psychology*. New York: Oxford University Press.

Swarns, R.L. (2001). Race Talks Finally Reach Accord On Slavery and Palestinian Plight. *The New York Times*, September 9th, p. A1.

Weisman, S.R. (1986). A Daughter returns to Pakistan to cry for victory. *The New York Times*, April 11, p. 12.

Wellington, S.W. (1996). *Women in Corporate Leadership: Progress and Prospects*. New York: Catalyst.

Whyte, D. (1994). *The Heart Aroused*. New York: Currency Doubleday, p. 27.

Yan, A., and Zeng, M. (1999). International Joint Venture Instability: A Critique of Previous Research, A Reconceptualization, and Directions for Future Research. *Journal of International Business Studies*, 30 (2), pp. 397–414.

Index